EL: Origin of the Blood
Part Two
by Fearless One

"We shall have World Government, whether you like it or not, by conquest or consent."
— Paul Warburg

Copyright © 2024 by Fearless One

ALL RIGHTS RESERVED. No part of this book may be reproduced or transmitted in any form by any means, electronic or mechanical, including photocopying and recording, or by any information storage and retrieval system, except as may be expressly permitted in writing from the author.

Chapters

Part Two	1
~Universal Deceit~	4
~Superiorly General~	56
~Beneath the Dirty Robes~	109
~Orsini~	158
~Medici~	200
~Aldobrandini~	240
~Rothschild~	277
~Li~	328
~Du Pont~	369
~Designer Diseases~	408
~Land of Confusion~	449
~Dying for Truth~	499

~Universal Deceit~

Welcome back dear reader, Let's pick up where we left off. The United Nations works hand in hand with the Vatican to carry out the agendas of the upper elite, dictated to them by the Jesuit Order. The New World Order, the final solution of the elite, is the Global Empire — a repeat of what they have had off and on throughout history but on a much larger scale! So, let's find out what the Order of the United Nations is.

The International Telecommunication Union was founded in 1865 as the International Telegraph Union, followed by the Universal Postal Union in 1874. These were the precursors, allowing the elite to control communication, worldwide, long before the internet, and from this exact moment on they have done so. Both are now United Nations specialized agencies. In 1899, the International Peace Conference was held in The Hague to elaborate instruments for settling crises peacefully, preventing wars, and codifying rules of warfare. The IPC adopted the Convention for the Pacific Settlement of International Disputes and established the Permanent Court of Arbitration, which began work in 1902. As you already know, select persons of elite bloodlines were involved in this.

In 1919 the League of Nations, an organization conceived during the first World War, was established under the Treaty of Versailles "to promote international cooperation and to achieve **peace** and **security**". Naturally, this was another renaming of a group already in place. The League was created and advertised to the world as an organization that would help the little, incompetent governments maintain peace, which is so hard to do. Today these types of groups (DAVOS, G Oders, Bilderberg, etc.) are called "think tanks", to keep you deceived as to their true purpose. The International Labour Organization was also created under the Treaty of Versailles as an affiliated agency of the League. In 1920 the League had formed a Covenant which was accepted by 42 nations. The League of Nations ceased its activities in 1939 after "failing to prevent the Second World War", or so the public was told. However, we know by now how the elite work and its "failure" was a ruse to create the true organization the elite had planned all along: the **United** Nations.

Arthur Balfour, a member of Horts Apostles, Westcott's Eranus, was President of the Society for Psychical Research, and Prime Minister of England. He was the instrument of the League of Nations and a devoted friend of the Rothschild's, who assisted the Rothschild's in forming the nation called Israel (a perversion and inversion of the true Israel which is every person who believes in the Living God...Israel ceased to be a physical entity over two thousand years ago, as the elite know full well). The nation established by the Rothschild's and Balfour holds the Rothschild's emblem of the 6-pointed star, but instead of it being red it is blue on a white background. Arthur Balfour not only held seances at his home, like most elite, but initiated a group called the Synthetic Society whose goal was to create a one world religion. He and fellow order member Frederic Myers created The Preamble of Religions, which includes many occult details such as the fact that departed spirits can communicate. This is nothing new, as it was written in Biblical texts as well as in Luciferian documents for thousands of years. Everyone worldwide acknowledges the fact that demons exist, every religion has their way of dealing with problematic demons and every elite has their own way of using them to influence agendas. We already know, or should know by now, that demons are able to be communicated with, used to attack people, and affect things, and that demons control their own armies of demons, being that many of them were leaders of their own tribes as discussed. Certain things such as Solomon's Ring and Crowley's bracelet, mirrors, screens, and more, have long been used to enable easier communication with the spirit world, for Luciferians. See, dear reader, THEY need something to help them communicate while those who have a relationship with the Living God need no idols, rituals, or jewels to communicate with Him.

The final meeting of the League of Nations took place in 1946. It was established after many leaders, including President Roosevelt, called for **Unity** and **Peace** and a governmental order that could maintain it since humans are incapable of simply not killing each other, because of their inferiority, governments had to be replaced with something even more "powerful". The public's approval of the elite's Peace and Unity, during a time of war which was planned and implemented for the purpose of establishing the order, was a solid step forward for the elite's plans. These plans had been written down by many, including most recently Albert Pike who described the 3 world wars as they would be orchestrated by the elite. As usual no one paid much attention. People don't really care about such things... Regardless, this is how it ALWAYS is done.

In 1947 the United Nations, now in full working order, held a general assembly to decide the fate of Palestine, and approved the creation of fake Israel. As is easy enough to find, the activities of the UN affected many countries thanks to their military order called "Peacekeepers" who invaded numerous regions such as the Congo in 1960 where the UN also dictated by force (jihad) how the country should be run. Next was Cyprus, and India, Pakistan, and so forth.

You will notice the ever-present keywords of Peace and Unity the elite will **always** use to manipulate the mindless. Meanwhile, those who maintain human intelligence understand the importance of separations: each should maintain his own, focus on the betterment of his own country and the non-interference of others (the natural law of No Trespass). Each should respect and love the other, making the differences in our communities and countries something to be celebrated and something beautiful, leading to the strengthening of us all. This has been equated with intolerance and racism by the elite in order to divide and conquer. We are all equal, equally wonderful because of our individual, unique histories. The elite do not want independence in any form, they want control over **all** therefore you must be forced upon each other so that the tensions created by this, and the resentment created by this will cause them to label you racist, form wars around it and more. Of course, their keywords sound nice, dear reader. That is how deception works. The reality of it is unsustainable, as we have seen, but prophecy **will** be fulfilled. It is the elite who are the only ones propagating racism. Without their beliefs, humans would grow up human, and racism wouldn't exist, as they themselves have confirmed.

"Race is not a biological reality, but a myth." — UNESCO 1950

"Man is truly the manifested deity in both its aspects -- good and evil. Since mankind is god, it follows that mankind will become freed from its false gods and find itself finally -Self-Redeemed. Or rather, **some** of mankind is "god-informed" and capable of self-redemption - namely, the Aryan and other civilized nations. Others, such human specimens as the Bushmen, the Veddhas of Ceylon, and some African tribes are **lower** human creatures, **inferior races** that are now happily...dying out. Verily mankind is 'of one blood,' but not of the same **essence**." — Helena Blavatsky

During World War I, a trial organization called Collective Security Through World Government was brought forth, promoted by President Woodrow Wilson. He proposed globally enforced peace. While this order was established to fail, which it did, the Council of Foreign Relations was born and succeeded in its place, as intended. Meanwhile the public is led to believe that there was a natural progression, a trial and error...this is never the case, dear reader. On December 29, 1941, President Roosevelt, Prime Minister Churchill, and Roosevelt's aide Harry Hopkins drafted the "Declaration by United Nations". The term "Four Policemen" was coined, referencing the 4 major countries involved in the United Nations implementation, the United States, the United Kingdom, the Soviet Union, and the Republic of China. If you ever thought there was a difference or conflict between any of these nations, think again. They are all on the same team, always have been, always will be. Aren't they good at propaganda? The Informal Agenda Group, a group of CFR members, formed the United Nations in 1945.

"The name "United Nations", coined by United States President Franklin D. Roosevelt, was first used in the "Declaration by United Nations" of 1 January 1942, during the Second World War, when representatives of 26 nations pledged their Governments to continue fighting together against the Axis Powers. In 1945, representatives of **50 countries** met in San Francisco at the United Nations Conference on International Organization to draw up the United Nations Charter. Those delegates deliberated on the basis of proposals worked out by the representatives of China, the Soviet Union, the United Kingdom and the United States at Dumbarton Oaks, United States in August-October **1944**. The Charter was signed on 26 June 1945 by the representatives of the 50 countries. Poland, which was not represented at the Conference, signed it later and became one of the original 51 Member States. The United Nations officially came into existence on 24 October 1945, when the Charter had been ratified by China, France, the Soviet Union, the United Kingdom, the United States and by a majority of other signatories. United Nations Day is celebrated on 24 October each year." — UN website (one of many deleted pages)

51, another significant number to the elite, is often seen in their politics. One of many reasons the US says it has 51 states, even though there are more... The United Nations was built on land donated by 33rd degree Freemason and Chairman of CFR John D. Rockefeller, who financed the Order. The UN is represented by a logo/flag which is a recreation of the Hittite symbol of the sun god (Lucifer) depicting the flat earth encompassed by Lucifer's web, dividing it into 33 sections, surrounded by the laurel wreath of the gods. The elite use colors, symbols, and numbers to signify who they are in all they do. They hide under the guise of peace. The color of the flag of the UN is white and blue. Blue is the supreme color of masonry; the ancient high priests and druids wore blue robes. Babylonians clothed their idols in blue, and numerous civilizations used blue to signify their deities, as discussed before. Blue, the color of the water of the flood, the symbol of perfection to Hebrews, the symbol of truth to the Druids, to the Chinese the symbol of deity, and to medieval Christians the symbol of immortality. An interesting and unrelated side note: Japanese arborists and gardeners wear cotton uniforms, dyed blue from a plant which serves as a natural insect repellant. Blue is revered by the elite orders as the color of enlightenment. The other color is white. White symbolizes purity and righteousness. These colors are used for the top orders, and top elite controlled countries and platforms. It is the color scheme used for Facebook, Twitter, Israel, NATO, Greece, Finland, CERN, CFR, League of Nations, and more. Take a moment to realize the logos and symbols used by organizations you engage with. While there is much I could write about the United Nations, there's simply no point. The elite themselves detail their movements and agendas and desires. That is why so many quotes are included in this document: why restate what's already been said? So, let's see what the United Nations is really all about.

"Alger Hiss became the acting Secretary General after the establishment of the UN. The April 16, 1945 issue of Time magazine called him "one of the

State Department's brighter young men". It was Hiss and Joseph E. Johnsons (who later became Secretary of the Bilderbergers) who wrote much of the UN Charter, patterning it after the Constitution of Russia, and the Communist Manifesto." – David Allen Rivera, Final Warning

"The Constitution of the USSR is almost identical to the Constitution of the UN." – Des Griffin

"We deplore the division of mankind on Nationalistic grounds. We have reached a turning point in human history where the best option to Transcend the limits of National Sovereignty and to move toward the building of a world community in which all sectors of the human family can participate." - Paul Kurtz, Humanist Manifesto II

"The creation of an authoritative world order is the ultimate aim toward which we must strive." – Winston Churchill

"Nations must unite in a world government or perish." – Charles de Gualle

As with every government, the pope crowned the ruler of the United Nations and blessed the Order.

"Pope Paul VI wrote a Papal Encyclical that called on the nations to abandon sovereignty to form a world government." – William T. James

"I agree that National Sovereignty is the Root of the Evil." – Philip Jessup CFR and World Court Justice

The United Nations, now established and built, had an overseer, like all other Orders – a level of hierarchy which controlled all actions and the direction the Order would take. This was called the Lucifer Publishing Company, now called Lucis Trust Company, located at 666 United Nations Plaza. Inside UN headquarters is a meditation room which is 33 feet long, 18 feet wide (18=6+6+6) and in the shape of a pyramid. This temple is complete with a black stone altar which is magnetic. The foundation of this goes deep into the bedrock underneath, tapping into "frequencies" which allow the rock to form an altered state of consciousness to those in close proximity. Remember what lies beneath? Understand what they are truly tapping into. There is so much more, in every detail of this building, that praises and acknowledges their master, such as the murals covering the walls of the building that houses those who decide the fate of nations. Luciferians are all about the symbols... Today the elite don't have to be as secretive as they once did, using special handshakes and pins and metals and art.

"Founded by Juliet Hollister in 1960, the Temple of Understanding has as one of its goals, the creation of 'a spiritual United Nations'. In its work to promote understanding between religions on the basis of the oneness of the human family, the Temple has numbered amongst its members and supporters such influential world servers as U Thant, Eleanor Roosevelt, Thomas Merton, Jawaharlal Nehru, Anwar el Safat, S. Radhakrishnan. In Addition to the main center in New York, where it is based as the Cathedral of St. John the Divine, the Temple has active chapters in India and the UK and representatives in Africa, Latin America, Asia, and the Middle East." — World Goodwill Newsletter 1994

The World Goodwill Order, another organization within the UN, was established by Luciferians Foster and Alice Bailey, who inherited Helena Blavatsky's Theosophy after Annie Besant. Both she and her husband were members of multiple Luciferian Orders including Freemasonry. They stated the aim of this order was to cooperate in the world of preparation for the reappearance of christ. Remember, dear reader, to Luciferians, Lucifer himself is their christ, the inversion of Truth, who will physically rule the world from Jerusalem in a physical global government establishment wherein the elite themselves will be the second in command. This is what they believe, which is why they say "christ" and "lord" and use terms of the Living God. This also fulfills prophecy given long ago. One must understand Luciferians and how they work...Always ask yourself, which christ do they talk about? Understand your reality and the prophecies regarding your future and it is all very clear. Don't take my word for it, **listen** to what they have already told you!

High Priestess Alice Bailey's world prayer is filled with Luciferian terminology, as those who are aware will see clearly. Lucifer=light=christ=god. Masters=elite. Titled the Great Invocation (invoking Lucifer) this chant is as follows:

> From the point of **Light** within the Mind of God
> Let **light** stream forth into the minds of men.
> Let **Light** descend on Earth.
>
> From the point of Love within the Heart of God
> Let love stream forth into the hearts of men.
> May Christ return to Earth.
>
> From the centre where the Will of God is known
> Let purpose guide the **little wills** of men -
> The purpose which the **Masters** know and serve.
>
> From the centre which we call the race of men
> Let the Plan of Love and Light work out

And may it seal the door where evil dwells.

Let Light and Love and Power
restore the Plan on Earth.

This derogative and arrogant chant is the perfect description of the Luciferian's use of light=darkness and darkness=light.

"Lucifer represents Life, Thought, Progress, Civilization, Liberty, Independence. Lucifer is the Logos, the serpent, the savior." — Helena Petrovna Blavatsky, the Secret Doctrine.

"It is Satan who is the god of our planet and the Only god." — Helena Blavatsky

"The **Celestial Virgin** which thus becomes the mother of gods and devils at one and the same time; for she is ever-loving beneficent deity. But in antiquity and reality **Lucifer** or Lucifer or Luciferius is the name. Lucifer is divine and terrestial light, 'the Holy Ghost' and 'Satan' **at one and the same time**." — Helena Blavatsky

As you see, I hope, the elite themselves describe their own beliefs clearly. It is a belief of confusion wherein everything male or female or animal or mineral are all Lucifer, and everything is inverted and corrupted to establish this as fact. You will see when reading their writings that they also create their own made-up words and terms. 'If *you* don't know what it means, then *you* must be of lesser intelligence'...typical kindergarten mentality. There is nothing I state in this document which is not stated by the elite, and others before me. Nothing I need substantiate or defend, for it is all Truth. Truth, unlike lies, is not able to be twisted to suit one's own opinion or purpose. There is right and wrong, as each of us is born understanding and feeling throughout life. Luciferians equate everything as the same, as one. If this were true then they would have no issue with those who believe otherwise, because it's all equalized but they have major issues with those who do not follow them-proving the point and fact that Lucifer is not all and everything as they state. Unlike the elite, I hope you understand it...I hope that Light is the true and real light of Truth, the light that dissolves all confusion, and not the other way around as Luciferians aim.

"No one will enter the New World Order unless he or she will make a pledge to worship Lucifer. No one will enter the New Age unless he or she will take a Luciferian Initiation." David Spangler, Director of Planetary Initiative, UN

"Evidence of the growth of the human intellect, along the needed receptive lines (for the preparation of the New Age) can be seen in the "planning" of various nations and in the efforts of the United Nations to formulate a world plan. From the very start of this unfoldment, three occult factors have governed the development of all these plans. Within the United Nations is the germ and seed of a great international and meditating, reflective group — a group of thinking and informed men and women in whose hands lies the destiny of humanity. This is largely under the control of many Fourth Ray Disciples, if you could but realize it, and their point of meditative focus is the intuitional or **buddhic plane** — the plane upon which **all hierarchical activity** is today to be found." — Alice Baley, Discipleship in the New Age

"One could tell several moving stories of the spiritual transformation the UN has caused to the point that this little speck on earth is becoming a holy ground. For example, the rational, intellectual economist Dag Hammarskjold found god at the United Nations and inspiration for his work as a world servant in the mystics of the Middle Ages. Towards the end, his Markings overflow with spirituality and mysticism." - Robert Muller

"The underlying philosophy upon which the Robert Muller School [named Lucifer Publishing Company] is based will be found in the teaching set forth in the books of Alice A. Bailey. The school is now certified as a United Nations Associated School providing education for international cooperation and peace." — Robert Muller, World Core Curriculum

"A World Core Curriculum may seem utopian today. By the end of the year 2000 it will be a down-to-earth daily reality in all the schools of the world." — Robert Muller

And so, it came to be. Today the education systems of every country are dictated by the United Nations, which is in turn dictated by the plans and constitutions laid out by the Luciferians who developed it. The plan established by Alice Bailey, and carried out by the UN, regarding education and the mind of children is summarized by 10 steps, which have already been fulfilled. They were:
1. Take the Living God Out of the Public.
    a. "Change curriculum to ensure that children are freed from the **bondage** of Christian culture. Why? Because children go to school to be equipped to face life, they are willing to trust, and they are willing to value what is being given to them. If you take God out of education, they will unconsciously form a resolve that God is not necessary to face life. They will focus on those things the school counts them worthy to be passed on and they will

look at God as an additional, if one can afford the additional." – A. Bailey

2. Take Parental Rights and Responsibility Away.
    a. "Break the communication between parent and child. Why? So that parents do not pass on their Christian traditions to their children, liberate children from the **bondage** of their parent traditions." – A. Bailey
3. Destroy Traditional Family Entity
    a. "It is **oppressive** and that the family is the core of the nation. If you break the family, you break the nation. Liberate the people from the confines of this structure." – A. Bailey
4. Make Sex Free and Murder Legal
    a. "Build clinics for abortion – "Health" clinics in schools. If people are going to enjoy the joy of sexual relationships, they need to be free of unnecessary fears, in other words they should not be hampered with unwanted pregnancies." – A. Bailey
5. Make Divorce Easy
    a. "In these days of the shattering of the old form and the building of the new, adaptability is needed." - A. Bailey
6. Normalize Homosexuality
    a. "The development of homosexual habits warp the life of many intelligent people." "Homosexuality is what you call a "left-over" from the sexual excesses of Lemurian times, an inherited taint, if you like. Egos who individualized and incarnated in that vast period of time are the ones who today demonstrate homosexual tendencies." See more detailed explanation in A. Bailey's Laws and Rules Enumerated and Applied
7. Debase Traditional Art
    a. As true Art requires talent and beauty, new artforms were promoted by Bailey and others, aimed to corrupt, and defile the imagination of people because art is the language of the spirit, that which is inside. Art has now been destroyed, having once been things of beauty, uplifting the viewer, now are perversion that corrupt.
8. Use Media to Change Minds
    a. "The greatest channel you need to use to change human attitude is media." – A. Bailey
9. Create Interfaith Movement
    a. "Promote other faiths to be at par with Christianity and break

this thing about Christianity as being the only way to heaven, by that Christianity will be pulled down and other faiths promoted. Promote the importance of man in determining his own future and destiny. [Humanism] Tell man he has the right to choose what he wants to be, and he can make it happen, he has the right to determine his cause." — A. Bailey
10. Have Governments Make These Laws and the Church to Endorse it
    a. "...That the church must change its doctrine and accommodate the people by accepting these things and put them into its structures and systems." — A. Bailey

As you can see from the statements and agenda listed above, Luciferians desire to corrupt all that the Living God ordained: family, intimacy, and most importantly the developing mind. Your mind is easily manipulated through subliminal messaging and more, as we found out in the last chapters. You are capable of controlling it yourself, but have most likely never been raised properly to have the necessary skills... This means that it will be harder and take more practice for you to undo the damage done to you throughout your childhood years. Your mind can control your body and your soul unless it has been protected and shielded by the Living God. When a parent gives up their own rights of responsibility over their own child which they chose to bring into this world by their own decision to have intercourse, that child is no longer theirs. That child is then owned by the institutions of the elite: trash. This is an unforgivable act for parents to make. Parents are the ONLY ones who have a right and responsibility over their child. No one else has any right to influence the child in any way! Not relatives, not friends, and not strangers. It is the parents' duty to protect what they choose to create not throw it away, as so many do - easily proving their own corruption. The elite have succeeded in this plan so thoroughly that people today view their own children as a burden or a disruption to their self-centered pathetic lives. Don't forget...Everyone gets what they deserve, in the end. Everyone. Take comfort from this, dear reader. This mental deficiency will be discussed in more detail in later chapters, so let's keep going forward, dear one.

"We have meditations at the United Nations a couple of times a week. The meditation leader is Sri Chin, and this is what he said about this situation: The United Nations is the chosen instrument of God; to be a chosen instrument means to be a divine messenger carrying the banner of God's inner vision and outer manifestation. One day, the world will treasure and cherish the soul of the United Nations as its very own with pride, for this soul is all-loving, all-nourishing, and all-fulfilling." — Donald Keys, president of Planetary Citizens and author of Earth At Omega

Today every single media outlet is owned and operated by only a handful, worldwide, who are owned by several elite families. Whatever country you are in, your media is controlled by the same elite who control the media of the countries surrounding yours. These are all owned by the same Jesuit-run and controlled organizations. This means all TV, all movies, all radio, all newspapers are all under the same ownership and agenda for propaganda. The Music and Movie industries were created and slowly evolved from being focused on a good story or talented musicians and turned for the purpose of becoming what it is today: sex and violence. Thanks to the indoctrination of romance, over the centuries, sex has become equated to love, and in the mind of a child this leads to acceptance of pedophilic relationships and the erroneous mentality of love being only physical. No longer is the person what matters, but the body alone, and as the mature know, what we are born looking like doesn't matter at all. Subliminal messaging, as mentioned in previous chapters, is a main tool of mind control and carried out by the sub-orders of the Jesuits. Everything is done in the world to make it easier for Luciferians (pedophiles) to prey on the innocent, destroying their bodies and minds forever and tainting their souls. It is a World Wide Web. Lucifer, the highest ranking of the cherubim, was the guardian of the throne of God. He was the Angel of Music, which is why Luciferians always mention frequency, vibes, and use the tool of worship to the Living God (music) against Him — and you.

"Music is made one of Satan's most attractive agencies to ensnare souls; but, when turned to a good account, it is a blessing. When abused, it leads the unconsecrated to pride, vanity, and folly." - Ellen G. White

"Through music you hypnotize people and when you get them at their weakest point you can preach into their subconscious what we want to say." — Jimmy Hendrix

"I wanted to marry Lucifer. I feel his presence in my music." - Tori Amos

Never fear, dear reader. The Living God, Jesus, is capable of changing minds and hearts at Will. There's nothing **anyone** can do to control that.

"I think that everything I had been through up to that point in my life led me up to where I finally made the commitment and accepted [Jesus] as my Lord and my Savior, instead of just a part time, "get me out of trouble" God. I think that's where the difference lies." — Lou Gramm

"Religion is when people try to act good because they're afraid to go to hell. A relationship with Jesus Christ is for people like me who have already been to hell... Didn't Jesus leave all his perfection and beauty from his spiritual paradise at home as a King on his throne to come to the earth to hang out with us dirty, lying, cheating, messed-up, selfish humans? Are any of us better than the fans at Korn concerts? No! Every single human being on the planet is just as in need of God's love as the next. We all need Jesus, and my mind has been thoroughly blown away by the fact that I was chosen for this extremely unique call into the metal scene." - Brian "Head" Welch

"Jesus put his hand on me; it was a physical thing. I felt it. I felt it all over me. I felt my whole body tremble. The glory of the Lord knocked me down and picked me up." — Bob Dylan

The best thing any human alive today can do is turn it all off, unplug every electronic technological internet-active device you have and stop listening to the elite!! It is insane that this must be stated...but unfortunately, dear reader, the population of the world has become as ignorant and lifeless as the elite have long believed and have worked diligently for decades to create. This, unlike what they believe, is not your natural state so stop being "woke" and wake up and be human again!

"Do not worry if not all religions will join the United religions organization. Many nations did not join the UN at its beginning, but later regretted it and made every effort to join. It was the same with the European community and it will be the case with the world's religions because whoever stays out or aloof will sooner or later regret it." — Robert Muller at the Parliament of World Religions

"The world will not change and find **peace** if there is not a New Education." — U Thant

"The United Nations is the way, the way to oneness, that leads to the Supreme Oneness. It is like a river flowing toward the source, the Ultimate Source." - Sri Chinmoy, UN Chaplain

"In the sphere of international relations, a sense of greater or shared responsibility is particularly needed. Today, when the world is becoming increasingly interdependent, the dangers of irresponsible behavior have dramatically increased. Unless we realize that now we are part of one big, human family, we cannot hope to bring about **peace** and happiness." - Dalai Lama

"To achieve world government, it is necessary to remove from the minds of men their individualism." — Christian World Report

"The true light of Lucifer cannot be seen through sorrow, through darkness, through rejection. The true light of this great being can only be recognized when one's own eyes can see with the light of the christ, the light of the **inner SUN**. Lucifer works within each of us to bring us wholeness, and as we move into a New Age, which is the age of man's wholeness, each of us in some way is brought to that point which I term the **Luciferic Initiation**, the particular doorway through which the individual must pass if he is to come 'fully' into the presence of his light and his wholeness...Lucifer comes to give us the final gift of wholeness.

Lucifer prepares man in all ways for the experience of christhood and the christ prepares man for the experience of god. But the light that reveals to us the presence of the christ, the light that reveals to us the path to the christ comes from Lucifer. He is the light giver. He is aptly named the **Morning Star** because it is his light that heralds for man the dawn of a greater consciousness. He is present when that dawn is realized. He stands no longer as a tester to the tempter but as the great **initiator**, the one who hands the soul over to the christ and from the christ on into ever greater realms." — David Spangler, Reflections on the Christ

"Abolition of the family! Do you charge us with wanting to stop the exploitation of children by their parents? To this crime we plead guilty." - Karl Marx, The Communist Manifesto

"The people who have taught us to believe whatever they were told by their parents, or their teachers are the people who are the menace to the world." - Dr. G. Brock Chisholm, Director General of the UN's World Health Organization, on September 11, 1954

"If we want to talk about equality of opportunity for children, then the fact that children are raised in families means there's no equality. In order to raise children with equality, we must **take them** away from families and communally raise them." - Dr. Mary Jo Bane, U.S. Department of Health, and Human Services

The motto of the United Nations Children's Fund (UNICEF) is "Every child is our child". This is what pedophiles believe. This is what Luciferians believe. The Rockefeller and Ford Foundations financed the reprinting and distribution of UN textbooks into schools, immediately implementing the new system of education, decades ago. At the same time, elite controlled indoctrinators were put in place in colleges and schools to make sure the new programming was enforced, and music, radio and TV shows became scripted to target children and further indoctrinate the elite's ideals. Many countries had a "hippie" movement of free love and liberty, which proved to the elite that their indoctrination in those countries was solidified. This is the moment when "entertainment" became something to do, something to pay attention to, and something to spend time and money on. Everyone was expected to have a TV, go to the movies and concerts. Instead of furthering development, relationships, and life, time was wasted and thrown away.

Nikita Khrushchev of the USSR remembered:

"I suppose you could say my political education began during my boyhood in the little village of Kalinovka where I was born. My schoolteacher there was a woman named Lydia Shchevchenko. She was a revolutionary. She was also an atheist. She instilled in me my first political consciousness and began to counteract the effects of my strict religious upbringing. My mother was very religious, likewise her father - my grandfather....

When I think back to my childhood, I can remember vividly the saints on the icons against the wall of our wooden hut, their faces darkened by fumes from the oil lamps. I remember being taught to kneel and pray in front of the icons with the grown-ups in church. When we were taught to read, we read the scriptures. But Lydia Shchevchenko set me on a path which took me away from all that."

"Comrades, Hitler gained control of the Youth in Germany before he was able to wage a successful Nazi Revolution in Germany. We Communists gained control of the Youth in Russia before we were able to wage a successful Communist Revolution in Russia, and Comrades, we must gain control of the Youth in the United States if we are to wage a successful Communist Revolution in that nation. For this purpose, we are ordering our Comrades to set up a new Communist Youth group in the United States." — Joseph Stalin, 1948

"In the struggle to establish an adequate world government, the teacher has many parts to play. He must begin with his own attitude and knowledge and purpose. He can do much to prepare the hearts and minds of children for global understanding and cooperation...At the very top of all the agencies which will assure the coming of world government must stand the **school**, the **teacher**, and the **organized** profession." — Joy Elmer Morgan of the National Education Association, 1946

"At UNESCO, EI is one of 16 organizations worldwide holding the coveted status of NGO in formal associate relations." — Education International (EI)

"The underlying philosophy upon which the School is based will be found in the teaching set forth in the books of Alice A. Bailey by the Tibetan teacher Djwhal Khul." — Robert Muller, World Core Curriculum Manual

Another Humanist (term meaning Luciferian) who has been vital to the formation of the Baileys' agendas, was Julian Huxley, the director of UNESCO (United Nations Educational, Scientific, and Cultural Organization). Julian was a member of the Communistic Colonial Bureau of British Fabian Society and signer of the Humanist Manifesto II. In 1947 he announced that psychoanalysis and "deep" psychology would be applied to education (mind control). In order for this to be effective, he explained that education would have to be extended all the way back to the nursery and continue to death. The UNESCO Constitution was written by many Freemasons, including Archibald MacLeish of the Skull and Bones Order. Reinhold Nieburh was a co-founder of UNESCO and signed the UN's Sex Education Curriculum called SIECUS. This was another elite move, stripping the rights of parents away and indoctrinating children for sex when that is not a function anyone who isn't prepared to have and raise children has any business knowing about. It's completely unnecessary, unless you're a pedophile, desiring children who are easier to groom and rape.

"It is the position of SIEVUS that contraceptive services should be available to all — including MINORS who should enjoy the SAME rights of free and independent access to contraceptive care as do others. It is the position of SIECUS that the use of explicit sexual materials can serve a variety of important needs in the lives of countless individuals." — New York Times SIECUS ad released October 1969

"Education will be **universal** and **lifelong** and will nurture a sense of world citizenship." - Millennium Forum Declaration of May 2000

"In 1989, the UN General Assembly adopted the United Nations *Convention on the Rights of the Child* (**CROC**), which, shorn of its pretended concerns for the welfare of children, is a blatant statist attack on the family and parental authority and responsibility. It proposes a massive intrusion of government into family matters. Implementation of the CROC would radically alter the parent-child relationship, interjecting government-appointed "child advocates" between parents and children. Ultimately, it aims at stripping parents of their traditionally recognized rights to control the upbringing and education of their children and to pass on to their children their religious values and beliefs. If the people of the United States allow the conspirators in our government to subject us to the supposed authority of the CROC, we will soon see UN-approved government child "experts" assuming complete control over our children and parental rights completely destroyed." - William F. Jasper, The United Nations Exposed

Naturally, Luciferians desire to corrupt as many as possible, at as young of an age as possible and back in the 1960's the process of corrupting and perverting, stunting the bodies and minds of the youth, had begun in full force, once again. The developing mind cannot comprehend these things, which is proven by numerous studies on the disorders established in the young who are exposed to sex before the mind is fully developed. It is well-known and documented as being eternally damaging. Since Pedophiles rule the world, this distortion and trauma-based form of mind control is preferred and today, it has been achieved, accepted, and accommodated.

"If UNESCO is attacked on the grounds that it is helping to prepare the world's people for world government, then it is an error to burst forth with apologetic statements and denials. Let us face it: the job of UNESCO is to help create and promote the elements of world citizenship. When faced with such a "charge", let us by all means affirm it from the housetops." — Julian Huxley

"In the classroom with children under 13 years of age, before the child enters school his mind has already been profoundly marked and often Injuriously, by earlier influences — first gained, however dimly, in the Home." - John Dewey (included in UNESCO's educational guidebook Volume V, compiled by Huxley)

"The kindergarten or infant school has a **significant** part to play in a child's education. Not only can it correct many of the errors of home training, but it can prepare the child for **membership** ... in the world society.... As long as the child breathes the poisoned air of nationalism, education in world-mindedness can produce only rather precarious results. As we have pointed out, it is frequently the family that **infects** the child with extreme nationalism. The school should therefore use the means described earlier to combat family attitudes that favor **jingoism**." — United Nations Educational, Social, and Cultural Organization (UNESCO), 1949

"Child rape crimes are being inadvertently funded in part by United Kingdom tax-payer," — Professor Andrew Macleod ex UN

Andrew McLeod attempted to blow the whistle in 2017 on the UN's pedophilic activities, but no one really cared. His report revealed 3,300 active pedophiles on the UN's payroll, that he knew of, at that time, who have been paid to rape over 60,000 children across the world. The UN works just like the Red Cross and the Muslim and Catholic Churches in this regard. Numerous coverups have been exposed and ignored, as the elite continue what they do without consequence.

Among the dozens who have risked and given their lives to whistle blow about the elite is former UN Executive and President of the Club of Rome for Europe, Calin

Georgescu, who reported in May 2023 that more than 8 million children per year disappear. The entire population of Switzerland or Jordan or Sierra Leone every single year is taken by the pedo elite for Satanic rituals, and no one does one thing about it. YOU, dear reader, have done NOTHING about it.

The total number of personnel serving currently in so called "peace keeping" operations is 107,622. The United Nations Peacekeepers work with DynCorp, the Clinton Foundation, the Heritage Foundation, and many more, to funnel children into the United States and Canada and Europe for the elite to feed on. India is one of the largest contingents of Peacekeeper troops with 8,102 Peacekeepers in uniform. Another of the largest contributors is Pakistan which has more than 8,750 in United Nations operations while Bangladesh tops them all with over 9,000 personnel.

United Nations Peacekeepers use candy and food to lure children to them, in order to rape them. The children cannot say no to food because they are starving and are typically in refugee camps, due to poverty, violence, and disease. War is created by the elites to carry out these acts, without anyone looking. While the world watches Russia or ISIS or whatever lies are propagated by the elite, worrying about the immigration crisis formed and carried out by the CIA, the same people get away with kidnapping and raping children, murdering families who speak out or try to fight, murdering researchers who go to find these trafficking rings to bring them to an end. Those who fight for freedom, those who fight for truth, are silenced. The United Nations Peacekeepers have stated their excuses for their actions. They have said:
>"That is what happens in war."

That is not what happens in war. People do not do these acts simply because they have a weapon in their hands. The negative frequency that comes of doing the acts these people do go against our natural frequency. Raping, murdering, and kidnapping and selling children are NOT human acts. This is NOT a product of war. It is a product of the individual DECISION to perform these acts thanks to the level of their corruption. An individual CHOICE. They decide to rape children. They choose to sell them, to murder their families, to keep everyone silent.

One 14-year-old girl's testimony is as follows: This perfect, beautiful, child was raped by 11 Peacekeepers, sent from the United Nations to "help" the struggling and dying people. This starving, innocent, child was violated by soldiers (grown men) every day in exchange for money, in exchange for cookies, and in exchange for juice. Do you have something to drink right now, or do you have to be gang-raped first? Are you free to earn money by getting a job or do you have to be raped by older men? It goes without saying that all of these things: pedophilia, rape, are acts which are dominated by men, just like transgenderism and homosexuality.

"I did not even have breasts," said a girl who was forced to have sex with an **estimated 50 Peacekeepers**, over a period of 3 years when she was 12-15 years old. One of these disgusting men paid her 75 cents.

Another boy was 15 the first time he was sexually violated by UN Peacekeepers. Over the next 3 years he was raped by over 100 Sri Lankan Peacekeepers on average 4 times per day. Think about that. Imagine what it must be like. THAT is real. It's happening at this moment. It isn't something happening to a foreigner either. Statistics prove that 1 in 3 girls are raped by the time they are 6 years old, and 1 in 4 boys is raped by the time they reach the same age. I personally only knew one person who had not been raped by the time they were 10 years old. That is how prevalent pedophilia is today. Stop ignoring reality.

Another boy confessed to being raped by more than 20 Sri Lankan Peacekeepers. Most would remove their name tags before taking him to United Nations military trucks where he was forced to put his mouth over the adults' genitals or be sodomized by them. This is the same of the White Helmets of Syria, the child trafficking unit deployed to that region during the last war-the purpose of the war. 114 UN Peacekeepers from Port-au-Prince, Haiti, were known to be involved in child trafficking, many are involved with the Clinton and Obama sex rings. These pedophiles were from Bangladesh, Brazil, Jordan, Nigeria, Pakistan, Uruguay, and Sri Lanka, according to UN data and interviews, no one was imprisoned. UN Peacekeepers are also documented as involved in the sexual abuse and exploitation of Haitians working with the Clinton Foundation.

An 11-year-old boy was gang-raped by a group of Uruguayan UN Peacekeepers. They filmed their actions on a cell phone. The video ended up going viral but despite this important piece of evidence **NONE** of the rapists went to trial in Haiti and only 4 of the 5 were convicted of private violence in Uruguay, a minor charge. Officials stated the video "was a prank gone wrong". Sure...

The UN is also involved with child sexual abuse and rape in the Central African Republic and the list goes on and on. The numbers given in statistics, by WHO and UN and any organization can only be taken as SMALL estimations, at best, since no one listens to children and children rarely report these things. Victims have been killed off by being given deadly cholera strains while being sexually abused. One specific strain has been linked to Napoli's Peacekeepers, who killed approximately 10,000.

"Let us declare in one voice, we will not tolerate anyone committing or conning sexual exploitation and abuse. We will not let anyone cover up these crimes with the UN flag." - United Nations Chief Antonio Guterres

"Children as young as 9 are forced to trade oral sex for food from UN peacekeepers in warzones while officials looked the other way. Memos about the sexual abuse in the Central African Republic were "passed from desk to desk, inbox to inbox, across multiple UN offices, with no one willing to take responsibility", the report found. It added: "The welfare of the victims and the accountability of the perpetrators appeared to be an afterthought, if considered at all." – Johnathan Bucks of Express

Of course, there is only one voice in the United Nations saying this, and it is his own, because he is a poster child. 100 girls in the Central African Republic were sexually assaulted by international Peacekeepers. At least 3 of them were tied up, undressed, and forced to have sex with a dog, by a French military commander in 2014. Malida Joseph, who was raped by one Peacekeeper and narrowly escaped being gang-raped, in Cite-Soleil said,

"I would like to see my attacker face to face and tell him how he destroyed my life."

Like others, she never reported the crime.

"They will look at this as one big joke," she said, "as far as the UN goes, they came here to protect us, but all they have brought is destruction."

Madeline Reece the former top UN Human Rights official in Bosnia, states:

"There is no mechanism to call Peacekeepers to account, to the code."

In an article on UN Peacekeeper Criminal Conduct, she has state:

"without an enforceable code of conduct, immunity often means impunity."

There is no way to enforce what the elite do, because they write the laws and do not write the laws specifically to serve their own purposes. This is why they always give the same excuses of ignorance and incompetence. This is exactly how they always get away with their activities. The victims exposed in the Bosnian Peacekeepers human trafficking in the 1990's and 2000's, is much like that of the Central African Republic. Whistleblower Katherine Kovacs, who worked for DynCorp did much research and raising awareness on this issue before. In one of the reports, she states:

"Covert and now overt attempts to remove, terminate and discredit those who blow the whistle on their deeds. The terms "cover-up" and "whistleblower" are common within the walls of the United Nations and Peace keeping missions. I became aware of the sexual abuse in CAR last year, while doing some consulting with international experts related to "Code Blue Campaign", to consider the best way to expose and disrupt the continued practice of the UN.

What used to be complicity by the UN by turning a blind eye has grown into a one-eyed monster, blatantly impeding proper investigations and prosecution of crimes committed by peacekeepers. The smoke screen still lies with blaming the member states and claiming the UN has no control over disciplinary measures or prosecutions of peacekeepers from contributing states. To some extent this is true.

There were many cases, but they were never prosecuted: Young girls from Romania, Ukraine, Moldova, and other Eastern European countries being brought in to service the UN and military bases as sex-slaves. The cases involved the officers from many foreign countries, including the USA, Pakistan, Germany, Romania, Ukraine, government contractors, and local organized criminals. The human rights investigators were never allowed to fully investigate, the suspects were immediately removed from the mission or transferred to other missions. The young women were simply sent back to their home countries."

In July 1999, the Kosovo Protection Force entered Kosovo, the war-torn province of Serbia, in order to force some protection on the ethnic Albanians. More than 20,000 United Nations troops were on the ground, within days of the passage of the authorizing UN Security Council resolution. Within months, the human rights community drew attention to the establishment and intensification of human sex trafficking into Kosovo. In August 2004, Amnesty International (also exposed for trafficking) reported that young women from Eastern Europe were being abducted, drugged, sold into human trafficking rings in Kosovo. Those who get paid get paid because they do their job.

Ted Gunderson uncovered years' worth of information on high-level pedophilic satanic rituals performed by the elite. This case became known as the Franklin Files and also exposed the American Child Protection Services' involvement, and their extensive child trafficking business. Former US Representative Cynthia McKinney knew about the government's involvement in human trafficking (as everyone in any leading position does) and in 2005, she grilled Donald Rumsfeld on DynCorp's trafficking business of selling women and children. The most recent exposure came from WikiLeaks' release of tens of thousands of emails from the former White House chief of staff, under Bill Clinton, John Podesta, who also served as Hillary Clinton's campaign manager. These emails, which are always released in a massive flood of documents, so that no one really looks, showed John Podesta was a vital part of these child trafficking rings, satanic rituals, and much more. Alan Dershowitz, Kevin Spacey, Chris Tucker, Donald Trump, Naomi Campbell, Lawrence Krauss, Bill Gates, Stephen Pinker, Sarah Kellen, Prince Andrew, Ghislaine Maxwell, Virginia Giuffre, Jean-Luc Brunel, Les Wexner (founder of L Brands, which owns Victoria's Secret), Ehud Barak (former Prime Minister of Israel), Courtney Love, Peter Marino, Tom Pritzker, Steven Mnuchin (former U.S. Secretary of the Treasury), Jeffrey Epstein, and many, many, more are involved in the child sex trafficking ring called the Lolita Express. The ring was named after the Epstein's plane which was used to transport children to rape parties. Pizzagate, which is the name given to the child trafficking ring exposed from the POTUS' emails, is a large operation but hardly the only one, and definitely not the first. While this was quickly spun into propaganda about a pizza shop, to be controlled and dismissed as it was, the real pedo ring was hidden from the public, lost in confusion, and the pedo's continued without hinderance.

"In a blow to victims of human trafficking worldwide, a massive child sex ring was exposed in Haiti - involving international 'peacekeepers' with the United Nations as well as other high-level officials from around the world - and no one went to jail." — Matt Agorist of Free Thought Project

"Ages of consent exist because minors are rightly considered incapable of giving informed consent. Particularly if they are vulnerable or have been groomed." — Jack Montgomery of The National Pulse

"The United Nations is an organization created to ennoble mankind actually **enables chaos and global discord**. As disturbing as the picture painted by U.N. Me may be, Horowitz manages to keep us laughing throughout the film. And just when you're left shaking your head at one outrage or another exposed in U.N. Me, Horowitz reliably enters with comic relief." — Israel Video Network

"The totalitarian threat to the family posed by UNESCO, NEA, EI, NTL, ASCD, Carnegie, et al., is real and presents itself in three significant ways:

1. **The Rule of Law.** The militant shock troops first lobby for ratification of UN treaties, such as the Convention on the Rights of the Child. Once ratified (or even before ratification), they fraudulently assign these treaties the exalted status of "international law," which, they assert, overrides all federal, state, and local authority. In order to show our respect for the "rule of law," they and their prostitute "legal scholars" say, we must "harmonize" our laws and policies with those of the "international community." They know that most local officials, school board members, state legislators, and congressmen are unfamiliar with, and unable to muster an effective defense against, the supposed authority of "international law". Thus, the UN treaties provide the homegrown revolutionaries with the weapons to undermine our laws and transform our government and institutions into subservient instruments

of the UN to enforce global political correctness.

2. **The Global School Board.** Through UNESCO, NEA, EI, and hundreds of other organizations and think tanks, the global structure bureaucracy is already being established for a worldwide socialist system that is intended to provide school teachers with indoctrination and certification, schools with accreditation, and students with the subversive materials and programs they "need" for graduation.

3. **The New Faith.** In our "interdependent" world, the UN provides the new focal point to teach children about our global "oneness." Loyalty will be transferred from the family to the state and from the nation to the UN. Children will be (or are already being) taught to be "citizens of the world." They are being programmed to reject "narrow," "divisive," "bigoted," "dogmatic" Christianity and to adopt pagan and occult beliefs." — William F. Jasper, The United Nations Exposed

"How many of you Senators know what the UN is doing to change the teaching of the children in your own hometown? The UN is at work there, every day and night, changing the teachers, changing the teaching materials, changing the very words and tones - changing all the essential ideas which we imagine our schools are teaching to our young folks. How in the name of Heaven are we to sit here, approve these programs, appropriate our own people's money - for such outrageous "orientation" of our own children, and of the men and women who teach our children, in this nation's schools?" — Senator William Jenner, 1953

The United Nations is after your children, your home, your country, your laws, your freedom, your money, your mind, and your soul.

"A new report from the Joint United Nations Programme on HIV and AIDS (UNAIDS), in conjunction with the International Commission of Jurists and the Office of the High Commissioner for Human Rights (OHCHR), states that criminal law all around the world needs to be adjusted to allow for minors to legally consent to sex with adults or whomever.... If the UN gets its way, it will also become illegal for anyone to try to change a person's "sexual orientation, gender identity or gender expression," meaning children who become successfully indoctrinated into such things cannot be urged, even by their own parents, to turn away from such perversions. This Proves That Transgender Mutilation of Children Is Directly Tied to Pedophilia." — Ethan Huff of Freedom First Network

The UN and UN Sub-Order WHO both declare that their pedophiles do not touch children. I can tell you from personal experience, this is simply not how pedos work. As the months go by more and more labels are made for pedophiles to make them more accepted by YOU, to legalize the destruction of the future and the annihilate innocence and purity. This is the true purpose of the programming you have undergone for the past 60 years. This is the reason divorce was normalized in movies and TV shows, why tradition and virginity were made a joke and something to be avoided in movies and TV shows, why teenagers having sex was normalized and sex equated to love has all been programmed into you over these decades. This is the entire point of it all: to get you so corrupted and perverted that you allow and "tolerate" pedophiles ripping children to shreds mentally and physically, throwing them away like worthless trash. Luciferians cannot abide anything pure or true. Luciferians MUST drag you and everyone down to their pathetic level of degeneracy.

While I could easily go on and on with UN sources about pedophilia and Luciferianism, I hope the point has been made and that you understand fully what the elite are. I hope, dear reader, that you finally get what the families I have and will discuss in this book do and believe in. Without exception.

In 1972 a treaty granted the United Nations control over historical landmarks by their World Heritage Organization. Today the world is freckled with World Heritage sites, UN controlled land. What they do at these sites, you already know. This was done according to plan, as David Rockefeller Jr. had (decades earlier) begun the process when he financed the restoration of the Cathedral of Reims, Versailles, and Fontainebleau in 1924. In 2012 the UN published this excerpt on their website, which was then removed. Note that this is how they work. You are given all of the information you are supposed to have to use your own free will to allow or disallow their activities, but they do not have to leave information out in the open for any length of time. Their website once contained document #sgsm14498 titled Secretary-General, Marking Historic Donation to League of Nations Library, Hails Rockefeller Foundation's 'Global Philanthropy' which states:

"Following are UN Secretary-General Ban Ki-moon's remarks on the eighty-fifth anniversary of the donation by John D. Rockefeller to endow the League of Nations Library, in Geneva, 10 September:

I am honoured to be here on this eighty-fifth anniversary of the historic donation of John D. Rockefeller Jr. to the League of Nations Library. At the time, Mr. Rockefeller said he made the gift based on the conviction that "peace must finally be built on the foundation of well-informed public opinion." This powerful statement rings true today.

It is fitting that we are naming this room after him. I thank the family for donating the portrait of John D. Rockefeller that was displayed at the Rockefeller Foundation for 65 years. In offering this generous gift, David Rockefeller said he hoped it would serve as a reminder of his father's generosity — but more importantly his conviction that strong international organizations can help create a just, equitable and **peaceful** world.

The Rockefeller family has lived up to this conviction, providing immense support for the League of Nations and the United Nations over the years. The original donation to this library was particularly significant. Even today, the interest provides approximately $150,000 every biennium to this wonderful library. That makes it possible to care for its many priceless historical treasures, including a signed copy of the Treaty of Versailles and the Covenant of the League of Nations.

This Library is also the home of the original letter from Alfred Nobel announcing his intention to create the Nobel Prize and the Official Transfer of the League of Nations to the United Nations. This collection is so important that it is inscribed in UNESCO's Memory of the World Register.
This Library also safeguards more recent history, including the <u>Universal Declaration of Human Rights</u>, with original letters from Eleanor Roosevelt and René Cassin. I applaud the mission of this library to serve international understanding. I am deeply grateful to all the staff. You make an enormous contribution through your help for researchers and citizens who are interested in the United Nations' history and work. <u>I personally want to thank the Rockefeller family for my own office</u> — and the entire United Nations campus on the East Side of Manhattan.

When Rockefeller's donation of the land was announced in the General Assembly in 1945, the Hall was <u>filled with loud applause</u>. The United States Ambassador cheered Mr. Rockefeller's "magnificent benevolence". I am deeply grateful to the esteemed members of the Rockefeller family and the Rockefeller Foundation for continuing the <u>noble tradition</u> of supporting international organizations devoted to **peace**. As recently as this past June, at the Rio+20 summit on sustainable development, the Rockefeller Foundation and the United Nations Global Compact launched a new framework for action to help meet social and environmental needs.

The Rockefeller Foundation is a shining example of global philanthropy. In a few minutes, we will open an exhibition which shows the importance of philanthropic contributions in history and connects them to today's success stories. I have seen these successes in my travels around the world. In Africa and Asia, contributions to health initiatives are saving lives. In the developed world, philanthropists are mobilizing action to protect the environment. And globally, many help sustain United Nations initiatives for peace, human rights, and development. My action agenda for my second term as the Secretary-General places great emphasis on just these kinds of partnerships and platforms. I hope they will be the wave of the future.

This library traces its lineage from the past century — but it is also moving forward into the future. As a modern centre of excellence, this library contributes to the Foundation's goal of informing citizens who can make a difference in our world. Let us carry forward this mission for another 85 years and beyond."

Now, remember another one of their goals is to dissolve the economy of every nation which will force them under the New World Order umbrella. This order was further promoted and established through the Gorbechev Foundation whose conference documents speak of a new world civilization.

"We affirm that the economy of all nations is a seamless web, and that no one nation can any longer effectively maintain its processes of production and monetary systems without recognizing the necessity of collaborative regulation by international authorities. We call upon all nations to strengthen the United Nations and other institutions of World Order." — A. Ralph Epperson

"A socialized and cooperative economic order must be established." — Paul Kurtz, Humanist Manifesto I

"The UN, through its international conferences and special sessions, has called the world's attention to the need for a New International Economic Order. The work of the UN goes forward, steadily building the foundation for a New World Order." — World Goodwill Commentary

"We the members of the United Nations solemnly proclaim our united determination to work urgently for the establishment of a New Economic International Order." — UN Monthly Chronicle 1981

"A complete change in the world's financial and economic order is imperative." — Benjamin Crème, the Reappearance of the Christ, and the Masters of Wisdom

The United Nations has been involved in countless scams and hoaxes to bring about their agendas. The horrors they have been allowed to get away with in poverty-stricken countries are beyond nauseating. One such scam is Oil for Food Operation. Given that the main financier is Rockefeller, father of the Oil industry, it is not so strange that the UN would use this strategy.

"From its inception, the Oil-for-Food program was riddled with flaws and loopholes, opening the door for the grievous abuses that followed. One of the major flaws was that Saddam Hussein was given the right to 1) select the parties who would buy the Iraqi oil, and 2) select the suppliers of the humanitarian aid. Hussein was also allowed to set the price at which Iraqi oil would be sold. All the seeds for a giant scandal were put into place. Hussein had the ability to determine with whom to deal and set the official price of Iraqi oil. Furthermore, the rules did not force Hussein to deal directly with the end-users; instead, he was allowed to sell oil through middlemen. For political purposes, Hussein would sell the oil at a discount to the middlemen and they, in turn, sold it to the end-users at market prices. Nice work if you can get it!

Another flaw in the program was that all deals were confidential between Hussein and the UN. Under this arrangement, the UN was not to examine the contracts for Iraqi oil except between the Iraqi Oil Ministry and the first purchaser. The story is that the UN had no idea the middlemen were adding surcharges to the contracts awarded them by Saddam, and therefore they went totally unnoticed by the UN. In one alleged example, UN Oil-For-Food administrator Benon Sevan was granted an allocation of 7.3 million barrels of Iraqi oil, on which he could expect to make a $3.5 million profit. Not a bad take for an international bureaucrat! For a graphic representation of how the scam worked, click here." — Gary D. Halbert

"Strategically placed across the country from Elmondorf, Alaska to Avon Park, Florida, three of these "detention centers" are now operational in a slightly different guise, two others are on a stand-by basis, and the rest are ready and available with a minimum of preparation-and all that's needed to fill these camps with thousands of Americans is for somebody to launch "Operation Dragnet". It will be swift and legal. The law is already on the books. They represent every shade of political and social opinion from Right to Left and include a big span of middle-of-the-road citizens who have never committed an offense more heinous than having subscribed to an unapproved periodical." — Sergei Monast

According to the United Nations website (on a page which was, naturally, taken down) Agenda 2030, which is a renamed Agenda 21, called Roadmap for Creating the New World Order, is still possible, but

"only if there is a fundamental, and urgent, change in the relationship between people and nature, and a significant reduction in social and gender inequalities. These urgent changes which must occur, were "discovered" by an "independent" group of UN scientists who launched their report at the 2019 SDG Summit, which was made available on the key date of the 11th of September, 2019. The scientists concluded that an optimistic future is still attainable, but only by drastically changing development policies, incentives, and actions. The world has already been drastically changed by the elite in just the last couple of years. The growing number of international migrants has now reached 272 million, outpacing the growth rate of the world's population. Europe naturally hosts the largest number of international migrants, at 82 million, followed by North America, at 59 million. North Africa and Western Asia host around 49 million migrants, and even sub-Saharan Africa has experienced a significant influx in foreign populations." — UN Global Sustainable Development Report 2019

All of this man-made instability is naturally producing a breakdown of cultures and societies worldwide: Change and Unity…as planned. This helps push the instability of countries, and being overwhelmed by the influx of people, currencies, education, and healthcare is plummeting. This of course was the plan so a World Health Care system and Global Currency will be easy to put in place. It is all working out well for the elite. United Nations Secretary-General António Guterres launched the United Nations Plan of Action to Safeguard Religious Sites.

"When people are attacked because of their religion or beliefs, all of society is diminished," the Secretary-General said during the briefing. "Houses of worship around the world must be safe havens for reflection and **peace**, not sites of bloodshed and terror."

A mapping of what the United Nations recognizes as "religious sites" across the world has been developed in full cooperation with governments and other relevant stakeholders to produce an online interactive tool.

Detailed in Agenda 21 and Agenda 2020, the UN has published all of its plans, which most have ignored. The numerous orders created by the UN have long since implemented hundreds of "smart" cities across the world. Smart Cities, also called Strong Cities, (notice the keywords that manipulate your thinking) are completely controlled by the UNs Global Police Force. Why? Because the UN had purposely populated these cities with an influx of immigrants who destabilize and raise the crime rates in these areas. This facilitates the elite's "problem" that you are not safe, and you need them to secure you. Your "reaction" is just as they plan it to be, and you allow them to move in with their "solution": Control. These dense cities, controlled by Smart-grid technology and predictive policing, will control your resource consumption, movement, length of life and also manage your death for you. When they are activated, these cities will be under Martial Law, as detailed in their reports, which are easy to find, because they must be, because you have free will.

How will all of this control be accomplished? Technology! Technology has only been created and distributed for this purpose, as many who are aware have known since the radio.

"The GDPR is just the latest example of Europe's caution on privacy rights... In 1930s Germany, census workers went door to door filling out punch cards that indicated residents' nationalities, native language, religion, and profession. The cards were counted by the early data processors known as Hollerith machines, manufactured by IBM's German subsidiary at the time, Deutsche Hollerith Maschinen GmbH (Dehomag)." - Olivia Waxman of Times

After the War, when Germany was divided between Russia and US, its state surveillance remained intact as the secret police force known as the Ustashe. They were free to screen mail, search people's apartments, bug bedrooms and bathrooms, and torture citizens of whom they were suspicious just as the US and numerous other countries do today. They kept files on everything from people's friends to their sexual habits. We all (should) know how they ended up using this information. This is what we call SMART.

Using technology, officials are able to gather city "intelligence" (data about you). This intelligence when integrated with operations, makes the cities **smarter** and **safer**. This is how it is sold to you. Communication is **essential** for this system to operate. There must be data. Sensors are a crucial component as is Geospatial technology (GPS), which provides the necessary framework for collecting data, which is secured by Blockchain. This massive amount of data is used to feed (is sorted and organized by) supercomputers and Artificial Intelligence. In 2015 Rosalind Peterson, the president of Agriculture Defence Coalition, addressed the United Nations on chemtrails, geoengineering, and weather modification (HAARP) which is used to control the climate of the world today. In this way, thanks to this technology, which is all over the world, the elite can decide how to control the weather of any region. Is there a region that has a higher number of a specific enemy? Implement tornados, earthquakes or floods and wipe them out. Clean and simple.

Kakogawa City, Japan used an increase of violence (in 2015) to bring about their Smart City. Local Authorities implemented spyware with which "residents can monitor their children and elderly relatives through an App". Convenient. In 2017 and 2018, the city installed 1,500 networked cameras and 2,000 sensors both in fixed locations (generally in school areas) and on 265 government vehicles and 176 Japan Post motorcycles. You have witnessed the same in your country. Look away from your hand-held elite-filled screen and notice the world around you. The system is able to detect residents carrying Bluetooth Low Energy tags to confirm their location. Representatives from Kakogawa City joined the G20 Global Smart Cities Alliance Launch Event, in Yokohama in October 2019, under the aegis of the Cabinet Office of the Government of Japan and the World Economic Forum Centre for the Fourth Industrial Revolution Japan (C4IR Japan). The Local Authorities will be used in many cases to implement illegal, human rights violating, "Smart" systems. US, Scandinavia, Asia, and Europe have already implemented facial recognition, through Local Authorities, among many other things which were perfected with the help of Covid. Every region is pushing the Smart City Agenda. Know what your Local Authorities have been doing to advance it! Let's take a look at what they did to expand this project in recent decades.

As stated, technology must be in place before Smart Cities can be fully initiated. This is the purpose for India being brought into the mix, as the tech trial region. To the elite, India is the perfect platform, as the entire country is disposable. In 2006 UN's Davos initiated 'India Everywhere'. Infosys had been working to "brand" India and gave $150,000 that year to India Brand Equity Foundation to finance India Everywhere. Commerce Minister Kamal Nath explained to the world about the "10 paradigm shifts taking place simultaneously in India. We now want people to see India as a manufacturing base, as the youngest nation with fortunate future demographics."

Over 2000 global leaders congregated with prominent Indian business leaders such as YC Deveshwar, Chairman of ITC and President of CII; Mukesh Ambani, Chairman of Reliance Industries, and co-chair of the WEF Annual Meeting; Nandan Nilekani, CEO, President, and Managing Director of Infosys Technologies. Other CEO's from India included Rahul Bajaj, Bajaj Auto; Hari Bhartia, Jubilant Organosys; Ramond Bickson, Taj Hotels; Gunit Chadha, Deutsche Bank; Tarun Das, Chief Mentor, CII; J N Godrej, Godrej & Boyce Manufacturing Co; Naresh Goyal, Jet Airways; Ajit Gulabchand, Hindustan Construction Company; Ratan Jindal, Jindal Stainless Limited; Baba N Kalyani, Bharat Forge; K V Kamath, ICICI Bank; Nand Khemka, Sun Group; N Srinivasan, Director General, CII; Vijay Mallya, UB Group; Nikhil Meswani, Reliance Industries; Sunil Bharti Mittal, Bharti Enterprises; Lakshmi N Mittal, Mittal Steel; Dhruv M Sawhney, Triveni Engineering & Industries; Malvinder Singh, Ranbaxy and Ajay Khanna, CEO, India Brand Equity Foundation. The India Brand Equity Foundation (IBEF) and Ministry of Tourism spearheaded a focused communication campaign to enhance the Brand India.

On Jan. 26, 2006, Finance Minister P. Chidambaram hosted 8 Japanese businessmen, including the chairmen of Toshiba, Nomura Securities, Sumitomo, the chief of Japan's external trade organization and a young member of the Japanese parliament. Soon after, Japan was suddenly interested in being involved in the new rail-freight corridor connecting Bombay, Delhi, and Calcutta.

"We will build our infrastructure with Japanese help," - P. Chidambaram

Dell began building a large PC manufacturing facility in India. The 'India Everywhere' campaign is built on three pillars: India's vibrant democracy, growing market, and its promise of assured returns for global investors.

"Any identity system by a government is centralized, which is the source of corruption, inequality, injustice, misery and poverty in a massive scale." - Andreas M. Antonopoulos

The biometric authentication system is fragile, therefore unstable, and insecure. However, if you have privacy (freedom), they cannot control you, and that is what they live for. So, it is always sold to you the same way: as a benefit and safety. Judges on the Indian Court's bench said,
"Aadhar gives dignity to the marginalized. Dignity to the marginalized outweighs privacy."

"The loss in information due to limitations of the capture setup or physical conditions of the body, and due (to) the feature representation, there is a non-zero probability that two finger prints or IRIS prints coming from different individuals can be called a match." - Dr. Justice B.S. Chauhan and Justice J. Chelameswar's Supreme Court Order passed in 2014

"In order to further enhance security of overall authentication system and make it more inclusive, it is hereby directed that TSPs (these are your SIM card providers along with others) shall implement two factor authentication in their systems using face authentication. In case the resident provides the Aadhar number then the authentication shall be performed using two factors of (i) fingerprint or iris and (ii) face." - UIDAI Bangalore, run by Indian engineers with backgrounds at Google and Intel.

Naturally, this shaky system had to be perfected, and what better way than to have a worldwide ability to test it out, with enough time to update and solidify the program. This was the purpose of the Covid event. However, several years before the event was initiated, the World Bank began pushing for a Biometric ID and the United Kingdom implemented one, but then withdrew it given the extreme instability of the system. Countries like Estonia and Belgium have advanced national identity schemes that do not collect biometrics. The Philippines National ID system, Phil-ID created ripples, but all countries soon turned their focus to the Aadhaar system, as directed. The National Database and Registration Authority (NADRA), based in Islamabad, developed solutions based on Biometrics and RFID technology and has the largest IT infrastructure in Pakistan with highly qualified technical and managerial resources enabling **NADRA** to provide customized solutions to any country. President Trump's "Real I.D." was minted in his REAL ID Act during Covid, like most countries. The announcement of a unified passport for all African nations was one more visible sign of the move toward a world government. 44 countries gathered to sign the African Continental Free Trade Area treaty. South African President Cyril Ramaphosa made the suggestion of a single currency for Africa. The idea was first floated in 1991, eight years before the Euro was introduced to the European Union. Meanwhile, the CIA deployed tools provided by its technology firm Cross Match Technologies for spying that compromised India's vast Aadhaar data bank. The CIA's 'Express Lane' program steals biometric data of its partner agencies. While IDs are important, digital currency allows for this to be implemented seamlessly. Both bases are covered, as one should expect.

"Do it quickly, do it quietly, and build a coalition of powerful interests who will overpower any opposition." - Aadhar creator Nandan Nilekani

Cryptos are proving to be just as unstable as Biometric IDs. But don't worry, dear reader, it's easy to correct with the right amount of money and thanks to AI running Cryptos, it's all automatic! The European Central Bank announced its inspectors had found shortcomings and miscalculations worth more than 10 billion euros. This hasn't slowed the advancement of AI down. It just needs more data. In 2019 Davos' theme was 'Identity in a digital world'. German Chancellor Angela Merkel, Swiss President Ueli Maurer, Japan's Shinzo Abe, Italy's Giuseppe Conte, and Israel's Benjamin Netanyahu among the more than 3,000 participants, including heads of state/government, CEOs of global corporations, central bankers, economists, civil society leaders, media heads, celebrities, and heads of international organizations like IMF, WTO, OECD, and World Bank. The political leaders from India attending the event include Madhya Pradesh Chief Minister Kamal Nath and Union Commerce and Industry Minister Suresh Prabhu. Also in attendance was Gautam Adani, Mukesh Ambani, Sajjan Jindal, Anand Mahindra, Nandan Nilekani, film producer and director Karan Johar, former RBI Governor Raghuram Rajan, New Development Bank President KV Kamath, IMF Chief Economist Gita Gopinath, and Microsoft's Indian-origin CEO Satya Nadella. The theme of the event was 'Globalization 4.0: Shaping a Global Architecture in the Age of the Fourth Industrial Revolution'. Things have progressed exponentially since then and the elite's goals are within reach at last.

"I think it is no exaggeration to say we are on the cusp of the further perfection of extreme evil, an evil whose possibility spreads well beyond that which weapons of mass destruction bequeathed to the nation-states, on to a surprising and terrible empowerment of extreme individuals." - Bill Joy

"Artificial Intelligence is a tool to massively amplify OUR ability to Control the World." — Bilderberg 2015 report

"So the enabler for AI is machine learning. AI has become so pervasive in our lives we don't come to recognize that it's powering a lot of things. You probably use it dozens of times a day without knowing it." - Intel's Nidhi Chappell

"It's been almost two decades since Peter Shor came up with a breakthrough algorithm for finding the prime factors of a number with a quantum computer, sparking great interest in quantum computing. But commercial adoption has been pretty much nonexistent. On Thursday, though, Google came forward with news that it's launching a Quantum Artificial Intelligence Lab that will include a quantum computer, apparently making it the second company to pay for a quantum computer. The development suggests that quantum computing could finally be taking off." - Jordan Novet May 16, 2013.

"Quantum Computation will be the first technology that allows useful tasks to be performed in Collaboration between parallel universes [where the Fallen live]." - David Deutsche, Physicist at the Centre for Quantum Computation, Oxford University

Smart cities will collect so much of your data that not only your physical activities will be known and easily manipulated, as they already are, but your neural functions as well!

In 2013 President Obama disclosed the US governments' $100 million brain-mapping research project called...BRAIN... This was matched by a $1.3 billion commitment from the European Union. Leaked documents reveal that DARPA researchers were on the verge of being able to change people's moral beliefs, stop political dissonance through remote control of people's brains, and more. Smart Dust Scientists at the University of California Berkely revealed they had found a new way to interact with the brain and to allow human brains to interact with machines. By inhaling electronic sensors, the size of dust particles (added in Chemtrails called Neural Dust), which attach themselves to the cortex, humans are easily remotely controlled through ultrasound. This will also make it possible for them to take that neural-netted system that has your brain imprint on it and transfer it to a robotic clone or double, which is the elite's tech goal for themselves: immortality through technology. In Beijing on January 22, 2015, Ray Kurzweil stated that Google's co-founder, Larry Page, hired him to build a synthetic neo-cortex, to link everyone's brain to the Cloud. Google co-founder Larry Page is a leading promoter of immortality through technology, as one would expect. But I digress, let's continue with the technology the elite wish to use on you in their New World Order. Keep in mind, dear reader, that they will never be able to control your free will unless you give it to them willingly, whether that is because of your own ignorance or not.

The ability for Worldwide V2k exploitation, The Hive Mind, is possible and will come in time. Suzanne Maher in her article titled The Human Target – Directed Energy Weapons and Electronic Warfare, discusses a Military Intelligence Program which uses these "smart grid" frequencies to target individuals. The smart cities brought to us by the United Nations Agendas are being put in place to facilitate these and many other programs. We all have been sprayed with microprocessors, micro sensors, nano bots, smart dust, etc., from the chemical engineering of our skies and the manipulation of our weather. A nanometer is a billionth of a meter and this tech is so small it can fit inside a blood vessel. Our bodies and brains have no protection against this nano technology which is one of many things contained inside of vaccines. The purpose of Covid vaccinations was to implement this aside from altering RNA in another soft kill method of attack and depopulation. It is simply a matter of activating the program that has been implanted in our bodies with the use of frequencies through CERN or D.E.W's.

> "If we understand the mechanism and motives of the group mind, it is now possible to control and regiment the masses according to our will without them knowing it." – Edward Bernays

The fact that 5G is the foundation of the Smart Society should terrify everyone to the point of action...but people today are so braindead, no one can think enough to act. The 5G systems will increase the level of harm to a level where illness and death from them can no longer be denied. France passed a law in 2015 "banning Wi-Fi from all nursery schools". In fact, the law states that Wi-Fi must be turned off in all elementary schools when it's not in use. Ridiculous...since Wifi is still there and active. Too little, too late. They know this, which is the purpose for them passing these laws to placate the complacent masses. It works every time. 5G uses a higher and faster range of the Radio Frequency spectrum than its predecessors. Since the frequency waves are smaller, they dissipate quicker, so the problem upon implementation was 5G coverage. The solution for this is MORE antennas.

Thanks to Elon Musk who is a vital instrument for the elite in this agenda, space was filled with 5G satellites which surround the earth in unnatural frequency! The technocracies of the world have eagerly anticipated the launching of 20,000+ commercial 5G satellites to create the Smart Grid. SpaceX launched a further 60 Starlink satellites as of February 2020, bringing the future broadband service's satellite count to 300 since the first entered orbit in May 2019. There are no legal limits on exposure to Electro Magnetic Radiation. There are no legal limits to the number of satellites allowed to float over our heads. When 5G rolled out in Vienna, immediately reports began to expose the classic symptoms of EMR poisoning:

nosebleeds, headaches, eye pains, chest pains, nausea, fatigue, vomiting, tinnitus, dizziness, flu-like symptoms, cancers, sterilization, and cardiac pain. People exposed to this also report a tight band around the head, pressure on the top of the head, short, stabbing pains around the body, and buzzing internal organs. For those who can't understand their own body's signals: This means there is something wrong. But this is something you cannot get away from unless you DO something about it. Those who don't think they experience these symptoms are merely too used to it and unaware to listen or understand their body.

When you have never been healthy, you can't see how sick you are.

Also included in Agenda 21 is the elite's detailed plan to eliminate more than half of the population of the world, through vaccines. Bill Gates, being the main man in vaccine development for depopulation, owning $23 million Monsanto shares, he calls his agenda the Solution for the World. Bill is a firm and outspoken supporter of Death Panels which he works to implement in the world, to determine who should be euthanized and who should be allowed to live. I will go into this subject further when we discuss the diseases the elite, including Bill, have made for you. Thanks to the trial run (covid) the elite know that the world is already prepared to accept one government, to follow one stream, and to abandon their rights. The covid run solidified the world on one platform-the internet, as intended. Little is able to be done now without being connected to it. The global event implemented the necessary laws and structures for the global government to be set up at a moment's notice, **without question** from the public. Thanks to this, the world is willing and ready to accept what is to come.

"The unelected officials of the Globalist regime known as the United Nations have unveiled their plans to inject millions of children with the COVID-19 inoculations. According to UN and World Health Organization (WHO) white papers, the child doesn't need to give informed consent at all." - Conservative Zone

The United Nations stands with the Vatican as the organizations who will establish this and fulfill the ancient prophecy. Although the elite in their pride, believe they are acting to fulfill Lucifer's goals to rule the world, which they are, they are also fulfilling the prophecies that the Living God dictated long ago. As I've stated before, it all begins with the war between Muslims and Jews which is taking place **right now**. When Jerusalem falls, the elite's agenda will be complete.

"I know not with what weapons World War III will be fought, but World War IV will be fought with sticks and stones." — Albert Einstein

Unfortunately, he got it wrong again. It is the Palestinians who have sticks and stones and are at war right now. In the 2009 United Nations Millennium Development Goals Report, the 10 regional districts of the world were published once again. Every government has its citizenry divided into districts, states, or countries, to control them more easily. So, it was done on a global scale, for the purpose of forming a global government. Dear reader, the elite are more than ready to have a global government. All they needed was **your** approval and acceptance and you gave it freely during their **first drill** called covid. Now the war has begun, fulfilling prophecy, and after that we will see the rise of the global leader — one man who calls for **peace** and economic stability!

"The common enemy of humanity is man. In searching for a new enemy to unite us, we came up with the idea that pollution, the threat of global warming, water shortages, famine and the like would fit the bill. The real enemy then is humanity itself." — Aurelio Peccei

That's right, dear reader, it's **ALL** a game. A Hoax. This is all the elite can create: lies. Climate Change and Global Warming are now terms everyone is familiar with, though most have no clue what it really is...because it does **NOT** naturally exist. NASA and the UN are the leading organizations that propagate hoaxes to the world. Propaganda continues on and you live your life in fear, obeying whatever the elite tell you. This is not to say that the elite are not using their technologies to facilitate this, but it is not natural and is easily fixed if the humans living on this earth would stop **allowing** the elite to destroy it.

"The United Nations can offer new life. These institutions play a crucial role in our quest for a New World Order." — President George Bush Sr.

"We must move forward together, as one, in a renewed spirit of Fraternity and Solidarity." — Pope Francis

Before I can discuss Greta, and the agenda she is used for, you must know the basics about the geoengineering agenda the elite have been working on, thanks to technology. For more than a century the elite have been using technologies to control the weather and terraform the earth for their final goal, which is to bring the Fallen back to rule, physically.

Geo-engineering not only involves mining, to eliminate Earth's life, but altering the atmosphere, water, and most importantly your DNA. This calls for a lot of technology to create this otherwise nonexistent, UN-Natural threat. Weather Modification techniques include Chemtrails. As the public have been given devices and screens to look down at, the elite have invaded the skies. Go figure. Those who have seen the sky are able to notice Chemtrails. Unlike <u>Con</u>trails, which follow very shortly behind a plane, forming a trail of <u>con</u>densation which dissipates in no time,

Chemtrails are large, long and do not disappear. You can look up, wherever you are in the world, and see them. They are not difficult to spot because they are not natural. They place a film between you and the real sky. Operation Cloverleaf, which is Chemtrails, provides a layer in the sky between the earth causing us to not only be bombarded by Wi-Fi radiation from our phones and cell towers, but those waves are bounced back and forth and back again, engulfing us in DNA damaging frequencies with maximum potency.

"I don't think there's anybody that has looked at the sky with a bit of brains, and thought in fairness, that could argue that something isn't happening that wasn't happening before. Contrails were something that followed the trail.... from an airplane, that were narrow and dissipated very quickly. Chemtrails go from horizon to horizon, and they spread, and they criss-cross and they go next to one another and pretty soon the whole sky is cloudy." - Former Premier of British Columbia Bill Vander Zalm

On December 9, 1948, the Australian Chronicle published an article about the plane vapors in the sky above Adelaide stating:
"South Australians were seeing something that became so commonplace in England during the war that people scarcely bothered to look."

As with all elite agendas, this has been going on for a very long time and the patents are easy to find, if you'd only look. The patent for Rain-Maker technology was filed on August 6, 1913 (No. 1,103,490). Patent 1,338,343 for Process And Apparatus For The Production of Intense Artificial Clouds, Fogs, or Mists was filed in 1920 followed by the Process of Producing Smoke Clouds From Moving Aircraft in 1927. The following year the Process of Producing Artificial Fogs was patented. Meanwhile the bankers and select families were raking in their wealth while propaganda was controlled. In the 1930's some of the patents for the Geoengineering agenda were for atomizing attachments, electrical systems, and spray equipment for airplanes. In the 1940's the patent office filled with files for smoke and fog technologies. On October 24, 1950, a Method of Crystal Formation and Precipitation was patented (No. 2,527,230). It was the updated version of No. 725,156, which was filed in 1947. This method is commonly called Cloud Seeding and (at the time) used silver iodide. There have been thousands of patents produced for Weather Modification, surveillance and weaponization. The following year the patent for the Process for Controlling Weather was made. So, what exactly is in Chemtrails?

Chemtrails contain these toxins: nano particles of Aluminum, Barium, Strontium (a radioactive tracer used in beacons of all shapes and sizes), Ethylene Dibromide, often called Dibromoethane, Arsenic, Bacilli, Cadmium, Chromium, Desiccated Human Red Blood Cells, Enterobacter Cloacal, Enterobacteriaceae, Human white

Blood Cells-A (restrictor enzyme used in research labs to snip and combine DNA), Lead, Mercury, Methyl Aluminum, Mold Spores, Mycoplasma, Nano-Aluminum-Coated Fiberglass, Nitrogen Trifluoride (Known as CHAFF), Nickel, Polymer Fibers, Pseudomonas Aeruginosa, Pseudomonas Florescens, Radioactive Cesium, Radio Active Thorium, Selenium, Serratia Marcscens, Sharp Titanium Shards, Silver, Streptomyces, Sub-Micron Particles (Containing Live Biological Matter), Morgellons, Unidentified Bacteria, Uranium, and Yellow Fungal Mycotoxins.

In the 1970's the Club of Rome began to implement the plan presented in The Report from Iron Mountain. In 1963 the book had been published, after 2 years of deliberations and planning. It detailed the philosophy that a country in peace will die. It goes on in the elite's shark-like thinking, to state that a country should be at constant war in order to have a stable economy. The book also gives various alternatives such as reporting on alien life-forms, and using technology as slavery, and the most promising idea: the threat of overwhelming pollution.

"The common enemy of humanity is man [meaning You, not them]. In searching for a new enemy to unite us, we came up with the idea that pollution, the threat of global warming, water shortages, famine and the like would fit the bill. But in designating them as the enemy, we fall into the trap of mistaking symptoms for causes. All these dangers are caused by human intervention, and it is only through changed attitudes and behavior that they can be overcome. The real enemy, then, is humanity itself." - The Club of Rome in The First Global Revolution, 1991

While they were spraying toxins on you, they were filling the media with Climate Change nonsense. In the 1970's the propaganda claimed that we were all going to freeze. In 1971 Leonard Nimoy (Spock) was used by the media to create many advertisements warning people of an impending ice age. Everyone believed it and lived in fear. Guess what, dear reader, IT WAS A HOAX! The Hoax was put into action in Germany and Sweden in 1972. Europe, especially Scandinavia and northern EU, is and has always been the elite's stronghold. The population of this region, like so many others, has little awareness or understanding of freedoms or rights of any kind, as they have not had them. The entire Climate Change agenda is focused on eugenics. The media is filled with a constant attack on life, blaming the fake problem on your very existence, degrading you! The main keywords for the propaganda in this agenda are "fossil fuels", "carbon emissions", "greenhouse gases", "solar radiation management", "carbon taxes", "carbon credits", "sustainability", "sustainable development", and "smart growth".

"Think tanks and other strategists script the scenario of debate, create and define the terms and generate most of the talking points and barbs that get exchanged back and forth in the financial, political, academic and scientific theaters and the controlled media, as well as in blog comments." — Jon David Miller, M.A.

The United Nation's Agenda 21 (1992) and Agenda 2030 (2015) both detail the plan for Sustainable Development and explain the steps the elite have been taking to achieve it. The Problem is you, as they have said.

The Reaction to this "Problem" is "divesting" and the extreme energy shifts, transportation shifts and more. The Solution is to maintain the population at a minimum, within technologically controlled cities worldwide. The creation of Smart Cities has been underway for over a decade. This was the purpose for 5G implementation even though by the time it was rolled out everyone was aware of the severe and deadly health risks involved. In 1997 Dr. Arnold A Barnes Jr, addressed the US Army Air Force about advanced weapons and technologies and discussed the process of "owning the weather in 2025". His Weather Modification presentation goes over the issues at that time, including the UN's convention prohibiting the military of hostile use of environmental modification. As he discussed, the US has been active in this since the 50's when they were capable of clearing and creating fog and doing a variety of other things by helicopter. The US was responsible for Ho Chi Minh Trail flooding (Operation Popeye) as well as contrail suppression. By the time of the presentation the US, and many other governments, were capable of fog and cloud creation and dispersal, changing precipitation, ionosphere modification and hole boring. Dr. Arnold also states that the energy requirements for major storms were still too large to maintain. Technology has advanced wildly since then. Elon Musk is another elite agent, who has promoted the mindset of fear and the elite's lies stating:

"We're running the most dangerous experiment in history right now, which is to see how much carbon dioxide the atmosphere can handle before there is an environmental catastrophe."

Carbon Dioxide is what you exhale. Carbon Dioxide is a natural element, and thanks to our wonderful atmosphere, which is self-sustainable, it is naturally filtered. Unfortunately, we live in an UN Natural world today, a world where so many metals and toxins have been purposely sprayed into our atmosphere so that it is clogged. However, dear reader, if the elite simply stopped these activities, the natural atmosphere would cleanse itself as it does, and all would be natural again. But you have to live in fear, and you have to be made to believe that you are the problem. Ever since 1990 drinking water in US and EU have shown high levels of contaminants including Arsenic, Aluminum, Barium, Strontium, and more. Since then, everyone else has experienced the same contamination from Australia to Spain, Mexico, Japan, Russia, and more (excluding China). Almost every government is using Chemtrails, showering you with toxic metals and killing you cell by cell. Dr. Leonard Horowitz has spoken out about Chemtrails and the mystery flus and illnesses that have been increasing since the 1990's. He has worked to expose the Medical Agenda behind this.

"Look at the mental state of people. Look at all the different drugs that we are using just to maintain our minds. One thing to add is this: Water samples on top of Mount Shasta, California have aluminum levels that are high enough to kill small rodents. The levels are off the chart with the highest being at 4,800 times the maximum contaminate level for drinking water. In a recent snow sample, the level was 100 times the level for aluminum in snow." - Robert Lee, Your Daily Journal

Your natural body uses the lymph system to filter toxins and keep you healthy. Unfortunately, the elite have been loading every product you use with poisons. For example, deodorants and anti-perspirants add aluminum, which soaks into your skin and goes directly into your lymph nodes. Processed food is filled with chemicals and preservatives and is usually stored in Metal. Several decades ago, the PBS published a report stating that the UN planned to depopulate the world by 3 billion through food malnutrition with their agenda called Codex Alimentarius. Masters of the "soft kill", starving the populations of undesirable countries and continents is an easy, risk-free solution to the elite's issue of You. In July of 2022 another report was published by PBS stating that world hunger had risen to the point where now 2.3 billion people are severely or moderately starving! Meanwhile food is imported and exported, people are not allowed to have land of their own to grow their own food, and the food that is imported and exported to every country in the world ends up as waste, piled up and composted.

You brush your teeth with the poison called Fluoride which is also added to city water supplies along with Chlorine. Fluoride is well-known for causing brain damage, among many other things. Meanwhile Baking Soda, which eliminates plaque and builds enamel, is only used by the aware to keep their mouth (the most receptive and absorbent environment on your body) clean! Health begins in your mouth. Your Lymph nodes aren't able to filter out the toxicity of your environment, so you get acne, rashes, bumps, a multitude of "things" which we now have. You buy medicine from your "doctor" to fix it, supporting the system and furthering the poisoning. Aluminum alone can cause brain degeneration, which is seen in most people today. It causes your natural body to be unable to digest harmful toxins in order to evacuate them from your system.

Man-made disorders, UN-Natural Illnesses!

These toxins line your lungs and saturate your blood, causing your body to be unable to fight infection or illness. What does the body do with toxins? It wraps them in fat, which can turn into tumors depending on the substance, in an attempt to store it as far from yourself as possible. While your own body automatically acts and reacts appropriately for your protection, people think that whatever they can stuff into their mouths must be ok for them. Ignorance. The elite love the slow-burn so they use toxins that won't immediately kill you. They use toxins that will build up, pass onto your children, and cause numerous medical problems for your entire life, and your children for their lives.

They make more money off of you if you're not completely dead. But think about this dear reader: Do you know anyone who has had cancer or Alzheimer's or autism? How do you feel knowing that these didn't exist before the elite began their chemical war on you? How do you feel now understanding that the people that you know who have suffered and continue suffering from these diseases never would have had them in the first place, if you and your parents and their parents at any time had simply deleted the elite and stopped them from continuing to do these things to you? How do you feel knowing (as you should) that wrapping the cancerous or infected region with Caster Oil and using the proper Natural methods completely eliminates these things without the use of barbaric butchery or pharmacology! Does that Fact change anything?

Nassim Nicholas Taleb of Black Swan has made the case for applying the Precautionary Principle when it comes to GMOs, another tool used by the elite to poison and kill you slowly. His argument is that allowing genetically modified organisms in our eco and food systems carries **unknown risks** that we have no way of overseeing, and that these risks may cause **irreversible damage** to the very systems mankind relies on for survival. No big secret there. This is the reason for the massive die-offs seen today, including birds, bees, fish, and other creatures we need to survive. Since the fall of the Berlin Wall in 1989, the number of flying insects on nature reserves in Germany had dropped by at least 76% more than three-quarters.

"The fact that the number of flying insects is decreasing at such a high rate in such a large area is an alarming discovery." - Hans de Kroon lead researcher

"Insects make up about two-thirds of all life on Earth but there has been some kind of horrific decline." - Professor Dave Goulson researcher.

These men state in their studies that:
"We appear to be making vast tracts of land inhospitable to most forms of life, and are currently on course for ecological Armageddon, if we lose the insects then everything is going to collapse."

Bird populations across the French countryside have fallen by a third over the last decade and a half. The primary culprit, researchers state, is the intensive use of pesticides on vast tracts of mono-culture crops, especially wheat and corn. What do you know, wheat and corn. The first two and most used GMO products. The problem is not that birds and animals are being poisoned, but that the insects on which they depend for food have disappeared, estimating that flying insects have declined by 80%. Bird populations have dropped by more than 400 million in 30 years. 400 million. Thank you Chemtrails and GMOs! Let's continue our discussion on the elite's slow-kill technologies.

Autism, like Alzheimers, is related to aluminum poisoning, which has been concluded and exposed by numerous scientists and doctors. One study from the University of British Columbia details that children are poisoned by the aluminum, which is in vaccines, which many children are forced to receive at very, very, young ages (when they are most vulnerable and in need of responsible Adult care). In 2000 the CDC published that 1 in 150 children had the increasing disorder of Autism. By 2008 it was 1 in 88.

"Ingestion of certain forms of barium (e.g., barium carbonate or barium fluoride) in toxic amounts can lead to gastrointestinal signs and symptoms (e.g., vomiting, abdominal pain, and watery diarrhea). Within 1—4 hours of ingestion, profound hypokalemia and generalized muscle weakness can develop which may progress to paralysis of the limbs and respiratory muscles. Severe hypokalemia induced by barium toxicity can cause ventricular dysrhythmias." - CDC

"Microscopic motes (nanoparticles) are able to infiltrate the tiniest compartments in the lungs and pass readily into the bloodstream...are most strongly tied to illness and early death, particularly in people who are already susceptible to respiratory problems." — New York Times, 2006

"The Welsbach Patent calls for megatons of 10 micron-size aluminum oxide particles to be spread in the atmosphere. The EPA calls particles this small "an extreme human health hazard" leading to 5% increased death rate within 24 hrs." — William Thomas, Chemtrails Confirmed

In 1996 the report titled Weather as a Force Multiplier: Owning the Weather in 2025 was published by the US Air Force. It states:
"In the United States, weather-modification will likely become a part of national security policy with both domestic and international applications... While most weather-modification efforts rely on the existence of certain preexisting conditions, it may be possible to produce some weather effects artificially, regardless of preexisting conditions...Nanotechnology also offers

possibilities for creating simulated weather. A cloud, or several clouds, of microscopic computer particles, all communicating with each other and with a larger control system could provide tremendous capability. Interconnected, atmospherically buoyant, and having navigation capability in three dimensions, such clouds could be designed to have a wide range of properties. They might exclusively block optical sensors or could adjust to become impermeable to other surveillance methods. They could also provide an atmospheric electrical potential difference, which otherwise might not exist, to achieve precisely aimed and timed lightning strikes. Even if power levels achieved were insufficient to be an effective strike weapon, the potential for psychological operations in many situations could be fantastic."

In the early 2000's, when the elite's geoengineering agenda began to increase, and the public started noticing, the distraction (cover story) was immediately spun through the propaganda channels, giving you Climate Change caused by Carbon Emissions! Geoengineering has been going on in every country in the world for decades under many names, including Operation Cloverleaf. Scientific reports, kept from the public, detail how greenhouse gases cannot absorb enough heat to cause "global warming".

"Carbon dioxide absorbs less than 16% of all the frequencies making up the heat." – Dr. Peter L. Ward

The maximum length of time that CO2 could cause heat of any kind for is 20 Milli-Seconds. It is impossible for "fossil fuels" to be an issue. The Earth naturally goes through seasons and stages of warming and cooling as it always has, just as the shorelines and arctics' ice plates shift, shrink, and grow. In 2014 a ship full of elite Climate Changers were sent to "Antarctica" to see how the melting process was coming along. Their huge ship was trapped in the thick ice, that formed as they attempted to travel through. The rescue ship also became trapped in the ice. However, this Hoax (not false flag because it's not real) has caused hundreds of laws to be changed in many countries, forcing people into public transportation, higher taxes, energy "shortages", and more. The elite, having planned this for some time, immediately transferred their companies "divesting" in fossil fuels, making everyone else go bankrupt if they couldn't immediately change all of their equipment to support the new fad. The elite have made billions on this fraud, once again.

In 2001 US document HR-2977 defined Chemtrails as an "exotic weapon". In the same year Al Gore became the new face of the agenda, spreading the fear of climate change and global warming this time. He had a different script: You are the problem. People have swallowed it up, believing what the elite believe: that your life should end, because you are the problem. This manipulation causes doubt, confusion, and fear.

"The promotion of the overpopulation myth is also used to justify the depopulation and infertility protocols of public poisons, including the push for toxic vaccinations. as well as a high volume of routine abortions... Researchers have uncovered the patents, plans, programs, methods, and make-up of weather warfare, including the ubiquitous geo-engineering toxic metals spayed in the air and radio frequencies bounced off of them that are used to effectively control weather systems and other events such as earthquakes and fires." – Jon David Miller, M.A.

In 2007 Australia granted $10 million to Matt Handbury, Rupert Murdoch's nephew, to test Russian rain technology. In 2009 Australia purchased rain-making technology from Thailand. In 2010 and 2011 Victoria, Australia was flooded. Do you think a flood you have experienced in your area or country is natural? Think again. How many people died? How many homes were destroyed?

"Environment Minister Malcolm Turnbull bet $10 million taxpayers' dollars, plus $1 million GST so that he could make it rain, even when there are no clouds. He did so by bankrolling research into a mysterious ionization technology promoted by the Australian Rain Corporation. Electrification of the ionosphere to create clouds out of thin air. Certainly, sounds a lot like the secret Australian rain device - no photographs allowed - that so excited the Minister and those who will share his six-month $10 million research funding." - Greg Hoy

Over the past decades California has endured many attacks from elite technology which caused numerous, precise, and controlled, deadly fires. The population is destroyed and waits for their destroyers to save them. This is nothing new. In Vietnam the US used weather modifiers to flood regions and commit genocide on the population. The Frequencies of HAARP and other technologies are used to target and activate weather change. Volcanoes have been erupting, earthquakes have been forged and hurricanes as well. The majority of the weather we experience today is manufactured. Man-Made. UN Natural.

"Climate change is an engineering problem, and it has engineering solutions." -Former Secretary of State and Exxon Mobil CEO Rex Tillerson

In 2010 a report was composed by scientists and aerospace engineers titled: Case Orange. This report discussed Chemtrails and gave conclusive evidence of organized covert stratospheric modification using technology. The report was funded by the Belfort Group and presented at their Chemtrail Symposium.

"The US has developed a type of weapon called High Frequency Active Auroral Research Program. HAARP strikes the upper atmosphere with a focused and steerable electromagnetic beam." - Environment Minister Anil Madhav Dave

There are many hundreds of HAARP locations in the world, but the most famous one is Alaska's. These are used in cooperation with Chemtrails, which the frequencies of HAARP activate, and militarize. Thus, the quadrillion nano particles flying around and in your body at all times are programmable and controllable. This is another piece of mastery shown to the public in plain view, by the elite who control these things through the Rand Corporation, Council of Foreign Relations, Trilateral Commission, and other organizations. You ever wonder what your leaders do behind closed doors? They plan to destroy you, their enemy, while they perform their ritual child sacrifices. This is Not new, and it will Not go away just because you choose to deny it and act as though these people are the same as you and me. Because of their beliefs, they are not.

A 7.2 magnitude earthquake hit Mexico causing heavy damages to a hospital in Jamiltepec, where over 30 patients, including newborns, have been evacuated and are now being treated outside. Taiwan was hit by a 6.1 earthquake followed by a 5.5 aftershock. In Iran a 7.3 magnitude quake hit a few months ago. Capetown is on alert as a three-year-long drought has left millions in desperate need of water. 8.4 million people are on the verge of starvation in Yemen and more in other war centered areas. The point is to keep them destabilized and dying. Weather modification and Chemtrails are conveyed to the public as seeding clouds for rain and creating storms to help develop areas, though scientists have debunked this. Meanwhile the reality is the Chemtrails help kill everything under them and the storms they manufacture are made to devastate the already devastated. In January Paris flooded severely. A drought-breaking downfall caused massive flooding in North Queensland Australia. More than 40 people have been rescued from floodwaters from ex-cyclone Nora. Water levels were peaking at 14.7 meters. More than 800 people have been killed and 24 million affected following widespread floods across south Asia. Severe flooding has devastated communities and destroyed crops in India, Nepal, and Bangladesh. Disease and starvation always follow. At least 115 people have died and more than 5.7 million are affected. Keep in mind this has all happened in one year, 2018.

Are these people just numbers to you? Do you think their pain and agony does not affect everything around them? Rippling to yourself. One day sooner than you expect, you will be included in these numbers. It will be you, dear reader. No one will help you.

Naturally the United nations has immediately stepped in as UNICEF is trying to collect information on children affected by the floods. UNICEF, one of the exposed United Nations child trafficking rings. Because of economic and social collapses, food scarcity and more devastations, children in countries like Venezuela have formed gangs, using machetes to fight each other for "quality garbage", so they have something to eat. You think about that for a moment. That is the future the elite want for you.

"Global <u>dimming</u> is another term people aren't familiar with, 20% of the Sun's rays are not hitting the Earth. That means there's a lot of metal up there." - Dane Wigington, of Bechtel Power Corp

Ken Calderia is an atmospheric scientist at the Carnegie Institution for Science's Department of Global Ecology. Although he is an advocate for global warming, he was forced to admit that global warming doesn't exist when confronted by Journalist Paul Adams at a Geoengineering debate in Berkeley in 2013. He stated that development was focused on "putting pathogens in a cloud" to "rain down on your enemy and do chemical and germ warfare". That's how things are spread nowadays.

The plans they have details and decided in Agenda's 21 and 2030 are enforced by the UN's International Council for Local Environmental Initiatives. Find the location in your region. They are the ones forcing the elite's control and poison on you. They, your government, your government's military, your media outlets, and more. Multiple agendas (or operations) are woven into one giant integrated system of surveillance, propaganda, command, profit, and control. The best weapon is one your enemy accepts freely without question. Mark Carney, the Governor of the Bank of England, stated at the UN Climate Action Summit on September 23, 2019, that 130 top banks were channeling all investments (totaling $47 Trillion) into speculative "green" sophism while supporting the Paris Accord demand of shutting down a multitude of coal-fired power plants dooming millions. The UN's IPCC plan calls for population reduction and states that economic growth shouldn't exceed 1%.

Professor Ole Wæver of the University of Copenhagen was interviewed about the upcoming COP25 in 2019 and stated:
"If there was something that was decided internationally by some more centralized procedure and every country was told 'this is your emission target, it's not negotiable, we can actually take military measures if you don't fulfil it', then you would basically have to get that down the throat of your population, whether they like it or not. A bit like what we saw in southern Europe with countries like Greece and the debt crisis and so on. There were decisions that were made for them and then they just had to have a more or less technocratic government and get it through."

As with everything the elite do, there are always people watching. The elite are working towards a goal, and if you don't know what that is and do not pay attention to the things they do, how would you ever know what's going on in the world? Kristen Meghan, US Air Force Bio Environmental Engineer blew the whistle on this but has been ignored, to no one's surprise. She exposed that copious quantities of unmarked chemicals were being transported onto planes. When she revealed her information, she was threatened with forced institutionalization and told that her daughter would be taken from her. This is a standard elite scare tactic. Thankfully she has put out a ton of information on her website TheChemtrailDiary.

On August 14, 2015, a conference was organized to expose climate engineering programs. This was held in North Carolina and only 1000 people attended. The list of attendees who spoke and exposed the worldwide governmental plot included Rosalind Peterson who worked for the US Department of Agriculture, Francis Mangels a former US Forest Service biologist, Mario Ramirez, US Navy, Dr. Hamid Rabiee, Mark McCandlish of the defense industry, as well as Kristen Meghan. The conference was recorded and has been publicly accessible since it took place.

The Earth is capable of completely healing itself because natural things ARE naturally self-sustainable. In order to heal, <u>all abuse must be stopped</u>. The same is true of your own body. You cannot simply take some vitamins and expect the years of abuse to be cleaned away so that your natural body will finally be able to heal itself and restore itself properly. That requires action from you, and an ounce of responsibility, which is why nothing will ever be done.

"In searching for a new enemy to unite us, we came up with the idea that pollution, the THREAT of global warming, water shortages, famine and the like would fit the bill. All these dangers are caused by human intervention, and it is only through changed attitudes and behaviour that they can be overcome. The real enemy then, is humanity itself. Democracy is not a panacea. It cannot organise everything and it is unaware of its own limits. These facts must be faced squarely. Sacrilegious though this may sound, democracy is no longer well suited for the tasks ahead." - Club of Rome.

Now, dear reader, I regret to inform you that we have come to the next and latest face of Climate Change: Greta Thunberg. Like so many before her she is the elite's blond-haired blue-eyed puppet. Let's discuss the devils who pull her strings.

As the story goes: Greta Thunberg "became" famous after skipping school at 15 years of age, to strike at the Swedish Parliament on August 20, 2018. Ingmar Rentzhog, founder of the social media platform We Have No Time, just happened to be passing by at that same time and posted a photo of her on his Facebook page. In November, more than 17,000 students in 24 countries took part in skipping school strikes. By December, Greta gave a speech at the United Nations Climate Change

COP24 Conference. The public was programmed for her through the Simpsons, as is the point of those types of shows. In 2007, the movie The Simpsons' plotline was based on "Pollution and Violations of the Environment Protection Act". Greta has become the instant leader of the worldwide youth environmental movement called Fridays for Future (a sub-branch of a larger elite foundation). Pope Francis has met with her, and she has received many awards.

"I want you to **panic**. I want you to feel the **fear** I feel **every day**." — Greta Thunberg, Davos 2019

While that statement alone should have made the world ignore her immediately, for decades the world has been indoctrinated by the elite and believe everything they are told...incapable of independent thought. Protests directly inspired by Greta, occurred in more than 30 countries, from Sweden to Brazil, India, and the United States. In March of 2019 Greta was nominated for a Nobel Peace Prize. She has been named one of the world's most influential people, Modern Day Che Guevara, Crusader, Joan of Arc of Climate Change, Pippi Longstocking of Climate Change, Jesus' Successor, Guru of the Apocalypse, and most accurately: Patron Saint Of The Age Of Stupidity.

In August of 2019, Greta sailed from Plymouth, UK to New York City, US, in a €4 million, zero-carbon, yacht. The yacht was owned and piloted by the Rothschild's Pierre Casiraghi, grandson of Prince Ranier and actor Grace Kelly. Greta made the pilgrimage without a toilet or shower because she never protested hygiene or health, just elder abuse. It seems using the ocean for waste management is acceptable, or did she recycle and reuse?

In occult areas, the boat traveling by sea is symbolic of making the journey across life. Water (blue) symbolizes emotion (emotions are fluid in the immature and unintelligent, always changing, and difficult to navigate without the proper vessel). Aquarius (one of the many symbols used in the "New Age" movement) is symbolized by the water bearer. Cancer, Pisces, and Scorpio are attributed to water as well. During this same time the media was filled with stories of the "floods" of migrants crossing the sea to invade other continents. Greta constantly uses the elite symbols and hand gestures including Lucifer's Eye and 666. All elite's use the 666 symbols and hand gestures so often, let's take a moment to dissect it and unravel the deception. In the published Bible only the number 666 and not the **symbol** nor the full meaning behind it exists. When looking at original texts, in their original language, we find that The Mark of the Beast is not a physical thing and could never be. The Mark of the Beast is the worship of the entity who is the embodiment of 666. 666 is the number of MAN, as in humans. Worshiping Man. The one called the Antichrist or the Beast, who will be elected by the world as a Global Leader, will be this 666. The man will be killed, and prophecy details the way he will be killed and the wounds he will have. As prophesied, Lucifer will then inhabit his body and a false resurrection will take place, which the world will believe and thereby call for him to become the world's leader and bring peace and stability. Believing in him, Lucifer, will mark those who do. THIS is the mark of the beast. It is a mark on your soul — a mark of the elite promise you must have.

"It's tragic. The cases [of devil worship in Kenya] are rising so fast and the devil worshipers say they have a mission of converting 90 per cent of youth to the occult by 2015." - Pastor JJ Gitahi

So, dear reader, every time the elite use this gesture in music, movies, speeches etc., know that they are elevating Lucifer, giving him acknowledgement and at the same time indoctrinating you to accept the mark. This is exactly what the elite and all of their agendas and programs are aimed towards bringing to fruition.

Greta's lack of understanding of what she is talking about is obvious in her interviews. Having grown up under ritual abuse and mind control, she was raised to activate the chaos the elite need. Mindless Militarism. The Agenda is not to add knowledge to children so they will grow up to be aware, responsible adults, but to simply have less education and more training in rioting and violence. World-wide Mind Control of Children. Global Child Abuse via Crusade Radicalism. The elite have made children the "wise ones", smarter and more responsible than their parents which fulfills their indoctrination schemes of the past decades. This same philosophy is perpetrated in movies and music today, as one would expect.

Greta is involved with lobbyists, PR hustlers, paid-for eco-academics, and a think-tank founded by an ex-minister in Sweden's Social Democratic government with links to the country's energy companies. These companies are preparing for the biggest rise of government contracts in history: Sustainable Smart Cities of the United Nations 2030 Plan.

On September 23, 2019, she wagged her finger, shaming adults at the United Nations Climate Action Summit. By this time the number of climate strikers that she had gathered had reached 3.6 million children in 169 countries. Greta has been addressing and meeting with world leaders, who are all controlled puppets themselves, carrying out the agendas the elite give to them. The public actually believe these meetings have value and significance! Lawsuits have been filed against Argentina, Brazil, France, Germany, and Turkey for their pollution. In October of 2019, President Putin commented that we (adults) should be keeping children and teenagers out of extreme situations. As usual, he is the voice of logic. Adults have a moral obligation to BE adults, in relation to children, and not be carried away by emotions, icons, selfies, images of mass protests, messiah complexes or revolutionary delusions.

The UN has used child-puppets for a long time. In 1990 the UN used the 15-year-old child Nayirah, whose "emotional" speech was the green light for President Bush to advance into the illegal war against Iraq. It didn't matter one bit that her testimony was FALSE. The same thing in 1992, 12-year-old Severn Cullis-Suzuki, daughter of Canadian environmentalist, David Suzuki, talking to the UN about the environment. The elite have been working to indoctrinate you into the belief that children are now smarter than adults, by blaming the destruction the elite have caused on you and forming propaganda and actors to support the idea. The trend can be seen not only in the language they use in meetings such as these but also on TV shows and movies which now promote child rule and the lie that a developing mind is more intelligent than a well-educated, wise, and mature mind. Sadly, not many adults can fit this description today, but you are capable of change. The mind doesn't fully develop until one 24-31 years of age, depending on the gender. Learning only stops when you choose. Let us not forget our history.

The Children's Crusade of 1212 was led by Nicholas, an eloquent shepherd from Germany. The young boy gave public speeches, gathering up a large following which he led through Europe to Genoa. This was supposed to lead them to Jerusalem. Many left the march, and 2 out of every 3 died on the way. When the remaining 7,000 finally made it to Genoa, Nicholas met with Pope Innocent III who told the children to return home. Nicholas did not survive the second crossing of the Alps and his father was arrested and hanged by angry families whose relatives and children had perished while following the child.

The second Children's Crusade movement of that same year, during the same time, was led by a 12-year-old French shepherd boy named Stephen. Stephen came to fame after claiming to have a letter for the king from Jesus. Over 30,000 juveniles and children had been amassed, Stephen led them through France on their way to Jerusalem. They survived by begging for food, however, before they left France most of them had returned to their families. History always repeats itself because the elite are always working on the same agenda.

Who owns Greta Tintin Eleonora Ernman Thunberg? Let's find out. The man who posted the first picture of Greta in 2018, Ingmar Rentzhog, of We Have No Time, was trained by Al Gore's Climate Reality Project. He is on a mailing list of climate activist Bo Thoren, leader of the Fossil Free Dalsland group. Bo sent out an email a week before the planned strike which is why Ingmar "happened to be passing by". Ingmar was a long-time family friend and fit the PR role well. Sara Malena Ernman, Greta's mother, grew up to become a European celebrity opera soprano and author. Greta's strike on the Parliament just so happened to coincide with the publication of Scenes from the Heart, Svante and Malena's memoir which details how "saving the planet had saved their family". Timing is everything.

Greta's father, Svante Fritz Vilhelm Ernman Thunberg, is a talent agent and managing director of the media company Ermahn Produktion AB. Svante Arrhenius, one of Greta's relatives, was the author of the Global Warming scam. He was given the Nobel Prize for Chemistry in 1903, becoming the first Swedish Nobel laureate. He was colleague of Alfred Nobel (a Russian Rockefeller) and became the Director of the Nobel Institute. He was a board member for the Swedish Society for Racial Hygiene and a Eugenicist. His children and grandchildren went on to expand the Sustainable Development planning and practice, as you can see in Greta. The Thunberg's are a long-standing Swedish Freemason Cult family and are named in the old Bavarian Illuminati book. At that time members of the family were philosophers (social engineers) from Uppsala and acquainted with founder Adam Weisshaupt.

Greta's elite circle goes further than that. Ingmar Rentzhog and his CEO David Olsson have backgrounds in finance, not environmental activism. David is the founder of Svenska Bostadsfonden, one of Sweden's biggest real estate funds. Ingmar's investors included Gustav Stenbeck, whose family controls Kinnevik, one of Sweden's largest investment corporations. Ingmar is also the founder of Laika, an investment relations company, and on the board of heir Kristina Persson's Global Utmaning (Global Challenge). She financially backs politician Olof Palme, was deputy governor of Sweden's central bank, and is a New Ager who openly discusses her reincarnations and communication with the dead. The other board members are Petter Skogar, president of Sweden's largest employer association, Johan Lindholm, chairman of the Union of Construction Workers and member of the Social Democrats' executive board, Anders Wijkman, president of the Club of Rome, chair of the Environmental Objectives Council, and a recipient of Bo Thorén's call for youth mobilization. Catherina Nystedt Ringborg, former CEO of Swedish Water, adviser at the International Energy Agency, and former vice-president at Swedish-Swiss energy giant ABB is also a member. Many of Greta's speeches mirror Anders Wijkman's Club of Rome speeches. Another one of Greta's speech writers is climate change professor Kevin Anderson.

Greta was raised in a drug-induced, ritual abuse pedophilic environment. She is completely mind-controlled, as is evident in her interviews and pictures. Whoever Greta was, hasn't existed in some time. Greta is almost always accompanied by her George Soros provided handler, Luisa-Marie Neubauer who guides and shields her from journalists who ask the 'wrong' questions. Luisa-Marie Neubauer works for One Foundation which is funded by the Bank of America, Coca Cola, SAP, Google. The ONE Foundation was created in the early 2000's by George Soros, Bill Gates, and Bono, "to better inform Americans about extreme poverty around the world". The parent company was an anti-poverty advocacy organization called DATA which used celebrities to bend the focus of world leaders. Luisa-Marie was personally recruited to be part of ONE and a member of the Greens, receiving a stipend from the Heinrich-Böll Foundation.

"Swedish authorities showed up at Greta's parents' house and have launched a child abuse investigation." — Jim Stone

Greta's parents, who have enjoyed a lot of time in the spotlight because of their exploited child, have told reporters that Greta can see carbon dioxide, a colorless, naturally occurring trace gas already in the atmosphere... Of course, she has not been challenged to prove her superhuman cyborg vision, nor her fake medical diagnoses, because she is untouchable. She has an army of social media monitors who censor all negative posts and comments about her and like every elite puppet: the narrative is scripted and controlled in every single way. Another thread of the elite's agenda to indoctrinate violence in children is ANTIFA.

"Greta has been pictured wearing pro-ANTIFA clothing and raising money for ANTIFA causes in Europe," Charlie Kirk stated when discussing photos of the entire family wearing their matching Antifa shirts. Greta was also pictured in the same shirt as she recorded a song with the band The 1975. All revenue from the recording will go to the environmental extremist organization, Extinction Rebellion. The Swedish section of Extinction Rebellion is led by Antifa-Hero Jonathan Pye who was sentenced to four years in prison for his involvement in the Gothenburg riots of 2001.

"If I commit acts of violence, it is like a game of chess. Then I think coldly and tactically." — Jonathan Pye

The United Nations promotes child exploitation, human trafficking, mind control, in order to continue the agenda. They want you to believe that you, not the elite's technology and agendas, have created the malfunctions we face today. Greta is an ignorant puppet who needs to be put in time out. While there are so many more agendas the UN has carried out, I will discuss them in other chapters. The topic of the UN could easily take several books all on its own to cover everything the corrupt global government has perpetrated on the ignorant and complacent masses.

"No human force will ever be able to destroy the United Nations, for the United Nations is not a mere building or a mere idea; it is not a manmade creation. The United Nations is the vision-light of the Absolute Supreme, which is slowly, steadily, and unerringly illuminating the ignorance, the night of our human life. The divine success and supreme progress of the United Nations is bound to become a reality. At his choice hour, the Absolute Supreme will ring his own victory bell here on Earth through the loving and serving heart of the United Nations." — Robert Muller

In 2023 the UN has finally officially announced war on Christians, their only true enemy. They have waited many centuries to do this and must be so exceptionally relieved. It is no longer the aware who claim this, but the elite themselves! Fulfilling another prophecy and promise given to us by the Living God who told us that Christians will be most persecuted in the final age and will be few in number by the end. Hope is renewed by the UN's proclamation of war as Christians have long expected and waited, watching for this moment to arrive. It is here, dear reader! Welcome to the beginning!

"The United Nations has warned Christians that if they do not **fully embrace** the legalization of **pedophilia**, they will be **excluded from participating in society**. UN chief Victor Madrigal-Borloz says religious freedom can only be tolerated if religious people fully embrace the globalist agenda." — Baxter Dimitri

~Superiorly General~

So now that you know more about some of the Orders of the upper elite which were established to oversee the world, let's discuss one that controls all of them, upper and lower: The Jesuits.

There are two distinct levels of the elite, and in those levels many families exist within a much more detailed hierarchy. Today, we see some of them merging. The upper elite, or Papal Bloodlines, are called such because these bloodlines WERE the Popes of the Papal States and established the first Vatican. They were the Pharaohs of Egypt, the Caesars of the Roman Empire, and the Sultans and Emperors of ancient societies including Maya, Sumeria, Persia et al. The upper families control the Company of Jesus as the High Grey Council of Ten, pulling the strings of the Jesuit Superior General who is called The Black Pope. The Black Pope is the controller of the White Pope who works hand in hand with the United Nations and every governmental ruler of the world. Here in Part II, you will notice when we get into the family chapters, once again, that several of the families included in the upper elite were not Papal bloodlines. This is because the Vatican holds little of the power it once did and with this lessening of power, other families have been able to emerge and grow, expanding into the role of an upper elite family. The Rothschild's have elevated themselves to upper elite in recent generations along with the Li family and Duponts because of their global influence and control. Unlike the families mentioned before, who only affected a handful of countries or a single region, these 3 have been added to the upper elite list because of their impact on the world as a whole, which is the defining factor of the upper elite. Don't worry, dear reader, I will also detail several Papal bloodlines as they have remained in power.

Many say that the Jesuits were created by Ignatius Loyola in the 1500's, but we know after what we have covered in Part I, that this was simply another switch of terms, with another puppet posterchild. Before this they were known under numerous other Orders, including the oldest known as Magi (Magicians, Sorcerers). Inigo Lopez de Recalde, born in the castle Loyola in 1491, was commissioned by Alessandro Farnese to be the face of the new order under the name Ignatius Loyola. His youth was rattled with crime and, as one police report states, he was "treacherous, brutal, and vindictive". He was the perfect pawn, given his lack of education and explosive, highly emotional nature, which only increased after his nervous breakdown which took place after he broke his leg. The description of his character, which mirrors all elite's puppets is described by his biographer.

"He put the books to one side and day-dreamed. A clear case of the wakeful dream, this was a continuation into the adult years of the imaginary game of the child... if we let it invade the psychic realm, the result is neurosis and surrender of the will; that which is real takes second place! The weak mind indulging in mysticism is on dangerous ground, but the intelligent mystic presents a far greater danger, as his intellect works in a wider and deeper way... When the myth takes over from the reality in an active intelligence, it becomes mere fanaticism; an infection of the will which suffers from a partial enlargement or distortion." — Jesuit Robert Rouquette, author of the biography Saint Ignace de Loyola

"Putting aside all private judgement we should always be ready to accept this principle: *I will believe that the white I see is black, if the hierarchical Church so defines it.*" — Ignatius Loyola

Inigo was a Spanish knight from the Basque family who did some jail time in Tivoli, outside of Rome. However, already having connections with the elite, in 1539 Pope Paul III had the Governor of Rome publish a statement of innocence of Ignatius and he was freed of all heresy. Francis Borgia and Francis Xavier were two of his disciples. As mentioned in Part I, the Society was founded in 1534 on the traditional feast day of Lucifer (traditional since 70 AD and still celebrated by the Vatican today) in a secret ceremony in the crypt of the Chapel of St. Denis. Those who were present and given credit for creating this renamed Priory of Sion cult, are Ignatius of Loyola, Francisco Xavier, Alfonso Salmeron, Diego Laínez, and Nicolás Bobadilla all from Spain, Peter Faber from Savoy in France, and Simão Rodrigues from Portugal. The Society of Jesus (Jesuits) was supported by the Venetian Doge, Andrea Gritti, and Alessandro Farnese as Pope Paul III, Francis Borja, Duke of Grandia, grandson of Pope Alexander VI and the patron of Ignatius of Loyola. Francis Borja was the main financier and architect in the formation of the Jesuits into the first dedicated military order of monks of the Catholic Church. Since I will discuss the families involved in the appropriate family chapters, let's jump right in and see the oath they swear to and live by. The following initiation ceremony and oath is taken from the testimony of Dr. Alberto Rivera ex-Jesuit who described this ceremony, which was also detailed in the book Subterranean Rome by Carlos Didier which was published in the 1800's after being translated from an earlier French publication. It is also preserved by the National Library of Australia, the US Congressional Records and more. It is an important oath for the elite.

The ceremony begins with the initiate, a minor ranking Jesuit priest, being taken to the Chapel of the Covenant of the Order. The Superior Priest stands in front of the altar and beside him stand 2 monks. One monk holds a flag of the gold and white papal colors, and the other holds the Jesuit Order black flag which contains a dagger and red cross over skull and crossbones. On the Jesuit flag is the acronym INRI, which stands for Iustum, Necar, Reges, Impious, meaning 'It is just to exterminate or annihilate impious or heretical Kings, Governments, or Rulers'. The initiate kneels on the floor over a red cross and is handed a black crucifix (the Roman idol of the celebration of the death of Jesus). He is then handed a dagger which the Superior continues to hold through the ceremony, with the tip of the dagger held at the initiate's heart. It is recorded that the Superior (Black Pope) states:

"My son, heretofore you have been taught to act the **dissembler**: among Roman Catholics to be a Roman Catholic, and to be a spy even among your own brethren; to believe no man, to trust no man. Among the Reformers, to be a reformer; among the Huguenots, to be a Huguenot; among the Calvinists, to be a Calvinist; among other Protestants, generally to be a Protestant, and obtaining their confidence, to seek even to preach from their pulpits, and to denounce with all the vehemence in your nature our Holy Religion and the Pope; and even to descend so low as to become a Jew among Jews, that you might be enabled to gather together all information for the benefit of your Order as a faithful soldier of the Pope.

You have been taught to insidiously plant the seeds of jealousy and hatred between communities, provinces, states that were at peace, and incite them to deeds of blood, involving them in war with each other, and to create revolutions and civil wars in countries that were **independent** and **prosperous**, cultivating the arts and the sciences and enjoying the blessings of peace. To take sides with the combatants and to act **secretly** with your brother Jesuit, who might be engaged on the other side, but openly opposed to that with which you might be connected, only that the Church might be the gainer in the end, in the conditions fixed in the treaties for peace and that the end justifies the means.

You have been taught your duty as a spy, to gather all statistics, facts and information in your power from every source; to ingratiate yourself into the confidence of the family circle of Protestants and heretics of every class and character, as well as that of the merchant, the banker, the lawyer, among the schools and universities, in parliaments and legislatures, and the judiciaries and councils of state, and to be all things to all men, for the Pope's sake, whose servants we are unto death.

You have received all your instructions heretofore as a novice, a neophyte, and have served as co-adjurer, confessor, and priest, but you have not yet been invested with all that is necessary to command in the Army of Loyola in the service of the Pope. You must serve the proper time as the instrument and executioner as directed by your superiors; for none can command here who has not consecrated his labors with the **blood of the heretic**; for "without the shedding of blood no man can be saved". Therefore, to fit yourself for your work and make your own salvation sure, you will, in addition to your former oath of obedience to your order and allegiance to the Pope, repeat after me..."

And the oath is sworn:

"I, _ now, in the presence of Almighty God, the Blessed Virgin Mary, the blessed Michael the Archangel, the blessed St. John the Baptist, the holy Apostles St. Peter and St. Paul and all the saints and sacred hosts of heaven, and to you, my ghostly father, the Superior General of the Society of Jesus, founded by St. Ignatius Loyola in the Pontificate of Paul the Third, and continued to the present, do by the womb of the virgin, the matrix of God, and the rod of Jesus Christ, declare and swear, that his holiness the Pope is Christ's Vice-regent and is the true and only head of the Catholic or **Universal Church** throughout the earth; and that by virtue of the keys of binding and loosing, given to his Holiness by my Savior, Jesus Christ, he hath power to depose heretical kings, princes, states, commonwealths and governments, all being illegal without his sacred confirmation and that they may safely be destroyed.

Therefore, to the utmost of my power I shall and will defend this doctrine of his Holiness' right and custom against all usurpers of the heretical or Protestant authority whatever, especially the Lutheran of Germany, Holland, Denmark, Sweden, Norway, and the now pretended authority and churches of England and Scotland, and branches of the same now established in Ireland and on the Continent of America and elsewhere; and all adherents in regard that they be usurped and heretical, opposing the sacred Mother Church of Rome.

I do now renounce and disown any allegiance as due to any heretical king, prince or state named Protestants or Liberals, or obedience to any of the laws, magistrates, or officers. I do further declare that the doctrine of the churches of England and Scotland, of the Calvinists, Huguenots and others of the name Protestants or Liberals to be damnable and they themselves damned who will not forsake the same.
I do further declare, that I will help, assist, and advise all or any of his Holiness' agents in any place wherever I shall be, in Switzerland, Germany, Holland, Denmark, Sweden, Norway, England, Ireland or America, or in any other Kingdom or territory I shall come to, and do my uttermost to extirpate the heretical Protestants or Liberals' doctrines and to destroy all their pretended powers, regal or otherwise.

I do further promise and declare, that notwithstanding I am dispensed with, to assume my religion heretical, for the propaganda of the Mother Church's interest, to keep **secret and private** all her agents' counsels from time to time, as they may entrust me and not to divulge, directly or indirectly, by word, writing or circumstance whatever; but to execute all that shall be proposed, given in charge or discovered unto me, by you, my ghostly father, or any of this sacred covenant. I do further promise and declare, that I will have no opinion or will of my own, or any mental reservation whatever, even as a corpse or cadaver (perinde ac cadaver) but will unhesitatingly obey each and every command that I may receive from my superiors in the Militia of the Pope and of Jesus Christ. That I may go to any part of the world withersoever I may be sent, to the frozen regions of the North, the burning sands of the desert of Africa, or the jungles of India, to the centers of civilization of Europe, or to the wild haunts of the barbarous savages of America, without murmuring or repining, and will be submissive in all things whatsoever communicated to me.

I furthermore promise and declare that I will, when opportunity present, make and wage relentless war, secretly or openly, against all heretics, Protestants and Liberals, as I am directed to do, to **extirpate and exterminate them from the face of the whole earth**; and that I will spare neither age, sex or condition; and that I will hang, waste, boil, flay, strangle and bury alive these infamous heretics, rip up the stomachs and wombs of their women and crush their infants' heads against the walls, in order to annihilate forever their execrable race. That when the same cannot be done openly, I will secretly use the poisoned cup, the strangulating cord, the steel of the poniard or the leaden bullet, regardless of the honor, rank, dignity, or authority of the person or persons, whatever may be their condition in life, either public or private, as I at any time may be directed so to do by any agent of the Pope or Superior of the Brotherhood of the Holy Faith, of the Society of Jesus.

In confirmation of which, I hereby dedicate my life, my soul and all my corporal powers, and with this dagger which I now receive, I will subscribe my name written in my own blood, in testimony thereof; and should I prove false or weaken in my determination, may my brethren and fellow soldiers of the Militia of the Pope cut off my hands and my feet, and my throat from ear to ear, my belly opened and sulphur burned therein, with all the punishment that can be inflicted upon me on earth and my soul be tortured by demons in an eternal hell forever!

All of which, I, _, do swear by the Blessed Trinity and blessed Sacraments, which I am now to receive, to perform and on my part to keep inviolable; and do call all the heavenly and glorious host of heaven to witness the blessed Sacrament of the Eucharist, and witness the same further with my name written and with the point of this dagger dipped in my own blood and sealed in the face of this holy covenant."

Upon receiving the wafer cracker from the Superior, he dips it into his own blood and eats it. This is called the eucharist and is a ritual performed by Catholics during mass, as well as the cross worship which I will discuss in the next chapter. You will notice how many of these secret deeds have come about, such as abortion, murder of whistleblowers and rulers, coups, revolutions and more. For those still not connecting the dots, as discussed before, the UN's plan to control education was implemented by Jesuits who control every major college and university. If you want to control the world, you must control the minds of those who inhabit it. Clubs and Orders in these universities and colleges are where the fresh blood pools to be picked up by Jesuits and Freemasons, to continue the agenda of eliminating Christians and controlling all others. The Jesuit Order controls the movements of the CIA, who control all other countries' secret services. But I digress...the ceremony continues after the cannibalistic ritual, as the Superior gives a brief Q&A, stating:

"You will now rise to your feet, and I will instruct you in the Catechism necessary to make yourself known to any member of the Society of Jesus belonging to this rank. In the first place, you, as a Brother Jesuit, will with another mutually make the ordinary sign of the cross as any ordinary Roman Catholic would; then one cross his wrists, the palms of his hands open, and the other in answer crosses his feet, one above the other; the first points with forefinger of the right hand to the center of the palm of the left, the other with the forefinger of the left hand points to the center of the palm of the right; the first then with his right hand makes a circle around his head, touching it; the other then with the forefinger of his left hand touches the left side of his body just below his heart; the first then with his right hand draws it across the throat of the other, and the latter then with a dagger down the stomach and abdomen of the first.

The first then says Iustum; and the other answers Necar; the first Reges; the other answers Impious. The first will then present a small piece of paper folded in a peculiar manner, four times, which the other will cut longitudinally and on opening the name Jesu will be found written upon the head and arms of a cross **three** times. You will then give and receive with him the following questions and answers:

From whither do you come? The Holy faith.

Whom do you serve? The Holy Father at Rome, the Pope, and the Roman Catholic Church Universal throughout the world.

Who commands you? The Successor of St. Ignatius Loyola, the founder of the Society of Jesus or the Soldiers of Jesus Christ.

Who received you? A venerable man in white hair.

How? With a naked dagger, I kneeling **upon** the cross beneath the banners of the Pope and of our sacred order.

Did you take an oath? I did, to <u>destroy heretics and their governments</u> and rulers, and to spare neither age, sex nor condition. To be as a corpse <u>without any opinion or will of my own</u>, but to implicitly obey my Superiors in all things without hesitation of murmuring.

Will you do that? I will.

How do you travel? In the bark of Peter the fisherman.

Whither do you travel? To the <u>four quarters of the globe</u>.

For what purpose? To obey the orders of my general and Superiors and execute the will of the Pope and <u>faithfully fulfill the conditions of my oaths</u>.

Go ye, then, into all the world and <u>take possession of all lands</u> in the name of the Pope. He who will not accept him as the Vicar of Jesus and his Vice-regent on earth, let him be accursed and exterminated."

The Catholic cross is an inverted cross, a ritual that followers do frequently to execrate Jesus Christ. After doing the hokey pokey of pointing the wounds of Jesus, it is corrupted by the symbolic slitting of the throat and dagger stab down the abdomen. Hopefully you can understand what those who hold "authority" over you believe. This is how every religion not already under strict control of Rome came to be infiltrated and corrupted as seen today. So many billions of people are indoctrinated and completely oblivious to the reality of what they are involved in.

"The higher I went in the Jesuit Order, the more corruption I saw within the institution. I was invited to attend a secret black mass by high-ranking Jesuits, including Superior General Pedro Arrupe, in a monastery in the northern part of Spain. When I knelt to kiss the ring of a high official, I saw a symbol on that ring that made my blood run cold. It was a Masonic symbol [the compass and the square]! A thing I hated, and I had been told to fight against it. I found out the Jesuit General was also a Mason and member of the Communist Party in Spain." - Alberto Rivera, Ex-Jesuit Priest

"Military obedience is not the equivalent of Jesuitic obedience; the latter is more extensive as it gets hold of the whole man and is not satisfied like the other, with an exterior act, but requires the sacrifice of the will and laying aside of one's own judgment." – J. Huber, author of Les Jesuites

This is the definition of Liberty and Freedom, as defined by the elite. To refresh your memory, when the Christian faith began to rise, after the resurrection of Jesus, the Roman Empire slaughtered as many as they could. As the Roman Empire began to crumble and fall, it resurrected itself as the Vatican led by the same Caesars of Rome now renamed Pontifex Maximus, the White Pope. Without pause, they have tirelessly worked to control and divide Christianity in numerous ways.

Christian is an overly broad term now, thanks to the misuse of it by the Catholics who, in the current semi-centennial, equate themselves with Christians. Publicly, this is the distorted understanding. A blatant lie.

Through Roman Catholic Canon Law, the Vatican believes (publicly) that the Pope has been vested with 2 powers: Spiritual and Temporal, and is the deity called Holy Father. Yet again the Luciferian terminology signifies the Holy Father as not being the Living God, who is called Our Father, but of a man, the Pope, who is called Holy Father by all who serve him. It is a Luciferian perversion of the true term, as we have seen countless times before. One must be wise. The Pope lost his temporal power of ruling countries in 1517, because of the Protestant Reformation. Thus, the Jesuits were born to reinforce their power in 1534. Since the beginning the Pope has been selected by the culmination of the upper elite families, who at this time unified their control. Today, the White Pope is no longer of a bloodline, and has no real power, rather, he is the best formed minion for the upper elite's plans. The Black Pope was created and placed in authority over the White and is directed by the Grey Pope who IS of one of the upper bloodlines.

"The Roman Inquisition had been administered since 1542 by the Jesuits." — Tupper Saussy, Rulers of Evil

"Created by Loyola and Sanctioned by Paul III, in seeking to destroy the protestant reformation and restore the dark ages with the White Pope exercising his Temporal Power as the Universal Monarch of the world, authored the 25 Sessions of the Council of Trent and Established themselves as the Confessors and Advisors of the monarchs of Europe, promoting absolute monarchial despotisms through which they ignited monstrous wars, characterized by pitiless massacres of Protestants and Innocents such as:
The Dutch Revolution 1568-1648
The Thiry Years' War 1618-1648
The Puritan Revolution 1644-1653
The Seven Years' War (French Indian War) 1754-1763
While oppressing and weakening the peoples of the nations and the semitic Hebrew/Jewish race with the Holy Office of Inquisition, aided by the Knights of Malta and later, Scottish Rite Freemasonry from 1540-1773." — Eric John Phelps

The Council of Trent was then convened by Pope Paul III (Alessandro Farnese) **three** separate times from 1545 — 1563. It declared a formal curse on Protestants, with the intent to return the world to the "Dark Ages" under the dictatorship of the Pope. The Jesuits began infiltrating missions and churches, as well as gaining powerful positions as confessors to kings as they had done in previous times, under different names. They used their confessions as blackmail to aristocracy, and this is how they continue to maintain power over leaders. Leaders typically arise from the lower bloodlines, which is how the hierarchy works. Since its formation the only confessors of the Pope (considered god on earth) is a Jesuit priest.

"The Pope's confessor, an ordinary priest, MUST be a Jesuit. He MUST visit the Vatican once a week at a fixed time, and he alone may absolve the Pope of his sins." — Nino Lo Bello, The Vatican Empire

The Spanish Catholic forces took possession of the royal baton, after they extinguished the Protestant revolt headed by William of Orange at the Battle of Mookerheide in 1574. In 2017 Black Pope Arturo Sosa Abascal, presented the wooden baton to King Willem-Alexander and Queen Maxima, during a ceremony following their meeting with Pope Francis. Since its formation, ALL Orders and cults have been established based on the Jesuit philosophies and rituals.

Pope Clement XIV (Giovanni Vincenzo Antonio Ganganelli) signed a decree in 1773 and banished the Jesuits, taking and/or destroying all their assets. He understood the outright malevolence of the Jesuit Order and sought to control it by eliminating them. The recordings of what happened next were preserved by Richard W. Thompson in his book The Footprints of the Jesuits, published in 1894, which details:

"A peasant woman was persuaded, by means of a disguise, to procure entrance into the Vatican, and offer to the Pope a fig in which poison was concealed. Clement XIV was exceedingly fond of this fruit and ate it without hesitation. The same day the first symptoms of severe illness were observed, and to these, rapidly succeeding violent inflammation of the bowels. He soon became convinced that he was poisoned and remarked: 'Alas! I knew they would poison me; but I did not expect to die in so slow and cruel a manner.' His terrible sufferings continued for several months, when he died 'the poor victim,' said Cormenin, 'of the execrable Jesuits to which Bishop of Pistoia, Scipio di' Ricci, the nephew and heir of Jesuit General Ricci, fully agreed.'"

"Weishaupt and his fellow Jesuits cut off the income to the Vatican by launching and leading the French Revolution; by directing Napoleon's conquest of Catholic Europe…by eventually having Napoleon throw Pope Pius VII in jail at Avignon until he agreed, as the price for his release, to reestablish the Jesuit Order. This Jesuit war on the Vatican was terminated by the Congress of Vienna and by the secret, 1822 Treaty of Verona." — Emanuel M. Josephson

While the Jesuits had control over all rulers, philosophers, educators, and so forth, it is hardly meaningful that so many were in public support of the Order. However, some of those who spoke out in their support of the Jesuits, as they were forced to include Alexandre Jean-Baptiste de Boyer, Marquis d'Éguilles who served during the Jesuits' Jacobine Revolution of 1745. He highlighted how their persecution could weaken the monarchy. Abbe Proyart publicly praised the Jesuits during his time and protested that their suppression harmed education and morality. Voltaire, whose birth name is Francois-Marie Arouet, was used by the elite in many ways. As a member of the elite circles and clubs, his influence was used to claim the Jesuits' innocence regarding regicide and predicted the decline of religious influence in favor of philosophy, as he was tasked to do.

"As Criton Zoakos' report proves, Jesuit organizing of Jacobin mobs "at the base" is always coupled with controls "at the top" of the local social pyramids, affording the top executives of the Jesuit order a virtually unparalleled capability for large-scale social manipulations. It is this character of Jesuit deployment which creates for the outsider the optical illusion that the Societas Jesu is split into "left" and "right" tendencies. But individual Jesuit operatives, including those who publicly "switch" from "left" to "right" and vice versa, are able to maintain their self-consistency, and their effectiveness, because to them, their principal strategic perspective, for which they undergo life-long training, is the destruction of technology-oriented "industrial capitalist" formations throughout the world." -Vin Berg of Executive Intelligence Review

Charles-Louis de Secondat, Baron de La Brède et de Montesquieu (1689-1755) was also used by the Jesuits to praise and condone their actions, as all aristocracy were. Nothing has changed in all of history, dear reader. Montesquieu highlighted the Jesuits' positive influence in Paraguay and their ambition to govern "for the betterment of society". At this time, Paraguay was part of the Spanish colonial empire, and it experienced European diseases, exploitation of Indigenous populations, and conflicts with Indigenous groups. These things are exploited and expanded upon, if not completely formed, by Jesuit involvement. The Jesuits established a network of missions, known as the Jesuit Reductions or Reductiones, in various parts of Paraguay inhabited by indigenous Guarani people. Under the guise of conversion, the Jesuits forced their education on them, and uniquely organized the natives' economic and social structures. The Guarani residents now lived in communal settlements and worked collectively on farms and workshops, similar to how the slaves were organized in the US later on.

The Jesuit missions in Paraguay often clashed with authorities and settlers who sought to exploit indigenous labor and resources without their approval. The best slave is a slave who doesn't know he is a slave. In 1767, King Charles III of Spain issued a royal decree expelling the Jesuits from all Spanish territories, including Paraguay. After such a long time of peace, with the Jesuits happily controlling the region, now that they were to leave, suddenly, a war broke out. The Guarani War took place from 1756 to 1757 between the Jesuit missions and Portuguese and Spanish colonial authorities over control of the region. While exact numbers cannot be determined, given the differences in various historical accounts, an estimated 1,511 Guaraní were killed and 152 taken prisoner, while only 4 Spanish and Portuguese were killed. In 1776, the region became part of the Viceroyalty of the Río de la Plata, which included present-day Argentina, Bolivia, Uruguay, and parts of Brazil. These regions are still controlled by the Jesuits today. In 1811 Paraguay, referred to by elites as a barbarous nation, received its independence.

"Their perseverance in this field of zeal was universally admired; it **secured success** during more than two centuries; and the latest missionary expeditions of their society proved, that the original spirit was not decayed. Whoever had caught it from the institute of Ignatius was a scholar without pride; a man disengaged from his own conveniences; indifferent to his employment, to country, to climate; submissive to guidance; capable of living alone, and of edifying in public; happy in solitude, content in tumult; never misplaced. These men planted Christian faith in the extremities of the East, in Japan, in the Molucca islands; they announced it in China, in the hither and further India, in Ethiopia and Caffraria. Others, in the opposite hemisphere, appeared on the snowy wastes of North America; and, presently, Hurons were civilized, Canada ceased to be peopled only by barbarians. Others, almost in our own days, nothing degenerate, succeeded to humanize new hard-featured tribes, even to assemble them in Christian churches, in the ungrateful soil of California, to which angry Nature seems to have denied almost every necessary for the subsistence of the human species.

They were but a **detachment from the body** of their brethren, who, at the same time, were advancing, with rapid progress, through Cinaloa, among the unknown hordes of savages, who rove through the immense tracts to the north of Mexico, which have not yet been trodden by the steps of any evangelical herald. Others, again, in **greater numbers**, from the school of Ignatius, with the most inflexible perseverance, amidst every species of opposition, continued to **gather new nations** into the church, to form new colonies of civilized cannibals, for the kings of Spain and Portugal, in the horrid wilds of Brazil, Maragnon, and Paraguay...The new settlements, called Reductions, of Brazil and Paraguay, were real fruits of the zeal of the Jesuits. Solipsian empires, and gold mines **to enrich the society**, existed only in libels.

The Jesuits were advancing, **with gigantic strides**, to the very centre of South America, they were actually civilizing the Abiponian barbarians, when their glorious course was interrupted by the wretched policy of Lisbon and Madrid. <u>The missionaries of South America were all seized like felons</u>, and shipped off, as so many convicts, to the ports of old Spain, to be still farther transported to Corsica, and, finally, to the coasts of the pope's states." -

Bartholomew Yates Rycroft Charles Dallas, Esq., Chapter 3 of his book The New Conspiracy Against the Jesuits Detected and Briefly Exposed

In 1776 Adam Weishaupt, Jesuit Priest, was used to found of the Illuminati. He wrote:

"The degree of power to which the representatives of the Society of Jesus had been able to attain in Bavaria was <u>all but absolute</u>. Members of the order were the **confessors** and **preceptors** of the electors; hence they had a direct influence upon the policies of government. The <u>censorship of religion</u> had fallen into their eager hands, to the extent that some of the parishes were even compelled to recognize their authority and power. **To exterminate all Protestant influence and to render the Catholic establishment complete**, they had taken possession of the instruments of <u>public education</u>. It was by Jesuits that the majority of the Bavarian <u>colleges were founded</u>, and by them they were <u>controlled</u>. By them also the <u>secondary schools</u> of the country were conducted."

That's how it is worldwide today. Every country adopted this except for Russia, where Orthodox Christianity opposed the Vatican's jurisdiction for a short time before it was infiltrated. The Jesuits continued to meet in Russia and had the Pope poisoned for his banishing them. The Jesuit Order instigated the French Revolution, the Napoleonic Wars, just as we see them doing today. Pope Pius VII (Barnaba Niccolò Maria Luigi Chiaramonti) reinstated the Jesuit Order in 1814.

"This war [American Civil War 1860-1865] would never have been possible without the sinister influence of the Jesuits. We owe it to Popery that we now see our land reddened with the blood of her noblest sons. Though there were great differences of opinion between the South and North, on the question of slavery, neither Jeff Davis nor any one of the leading men of the Confederacy would have dared to attack the North, had they not relied on the promise of the Jesuits...The protestants of both the North and South would surely unite to exterminate the priests and the Jesuits, if they could learn how the priests, nuns, and monks, which daily land on our shores, under the pretext of preaching their religion are nothing else but he emissaries of the Pope, of Napoleon III, and the other despots of Europe, to undermine our institutions, alienate the hearts of our people from our constitution and our laws, destroy our schools, and prepare a reign of anarchy here as they have done in Ireland, Mexico, Spain and wherever there are any people who want to be free." – Charles Chiniquy

"So hurtful was the Jesuit Order found to be, that up to 1860, it was expelled **no fewer than 70 times** from countries which had suffered from its machinations. In spite of Continental warnings, England [under Queen Victoria who opened up communication with the Vatican in 1877 and enabled the Order to carry out its second Irish massacre], has become a Jesuit dumping ground. Those whom other countries have found from sad experience to be enemies, Britain allows to land on her shores, and to carry on unmolested their work of iniquity. We are carrying **toleration to excess** and unless there is a change of policy, this nation will one day pay a heavy penalty." - Hector Macpherson

"The Jesuits are a MILITARY organization, not a religious order. Their chief is a general of an army, not the mere father abbot of a monastery. And the aim of this organization is power - power in its most despotic exercise - absolute power, universal power, power to control the world by the volition of a single man. Jesuitism is the most absolute of despotisms - and at the same time the greatest and most enormous of abuses." - Emperor Napoleon Bonaparte

The elite Jesuits have been kicked out of countries throughout history, until recently as everyone now accepts them. The original, uncensored, personal writings of the founding fathers of the US described them in detail and many more have continued to expose them.

"My history of the Jesuits is not eloquently written, but it is supported by unquestionable authorities, is very particular and very horrible. Their restoration is indeed a step towards darkness, cruelty, perfidy, despotism, death...I do not like the appearance of the Jesuits...Shall we not have regular swarms of them here, in as many disguises as only a king of the gypsies can assume, dressed as painters, publishers, writers, and schoolmasters? If ever there was a body of men who merited eternal damnation on earth and in hell, it is this Society of Loyola's... We are compelled by our system to offer them asylum." - John Adams, 2nd President of the US, 1816, in a letter to Thomas Jefferson, 3rd President

"It is my opinion that if the liberties of this country — the United States of America — are destroyed, it will be by the subtlety of the Roman Catholic Jesuit priests, for they are the most crafty, dangerous enemies to civil and religious liberty. They have instigated MOST of the wars of Europe." - Marquiss and General Lafeyette

"The war [the American Civil War] would never have been possible without the sinister influence of the Jesuits." - Abraham Lincoln, one of seven US Presidents to be killed by the Jesuits

"And do Americans need to be told what Jesuits are? They are a secret society, a sort of Masonic order, with superadded features of revolting odiousness, and a thousand times more dangerous. They are not merely priests, or of one religious creed; they are merchants, and lawyers, and editors, and men of any profession, having no outward badge by which to be recognized; they are about in all your society...They can assume any character, that of angels of light, or ministers of darkness, to accomplish their one great end, the service upon which they are sent, whatever that service may be. They are all educated men, prepared, and sworn to start at any moment, and in any direction, and for any service, commanded by the general of their order, bound to no family, community, or country, by the ordinary ties which bind men; and sold for life to the cause of the Roman Pontiff." - Samuel Morse, recorded by J. Wayne Laurens, The Crisis

"The religion of Masonry is a system of absolute despotism, and like that of Rome, demands a blind unquestioning obedience to all its laws, rules, and edicts, whether 'right or wrong'. What a singular commentary on the indifference, the subserviency, or the cowardice of society, that an institution, professedly organized by such cunning knaves (the Jesuits), and for such base purposes, and which has been sustained by fraud, falsehood, and deception, from the commencement of its career to the present time, should be permitted today to dictate to, if not virtually to rule the nation and to create such a dread in communities that even some of the ministers of Christian denominations who detest its vile philosophy, and who would like to see it swept from the face of the earth, are absolutely afraid to mention its name, either in the pulpit, prayer meeting, or the Sabbath school, lest its secret vendetta vengeance might in some concealed manner be wreaked upon them." - Edmund Ronayne, ex-Freemason of Keystone Lodge author of The Master's Carpet; Masonry and Baal-Worship Identical

When people stand up and recognize them publicly, their house of cards crumbles. The ONLY power they have is fear. The current American President Joe Biden has two honorary degrees from Jesuit colleges and is a ruthless pedophile, known war criminal, and top authority within the political faction of the Jesuits inside the United States....just like many of his predecessors.

"It is my opinion that if the liberties of this country - the United States of America - are destroyed, it will be by the subtlety of the Roman Catholic Jesuit priests, for they are the most crafty, dangerous enemies to civil and religious liberty. They have instigated most of the wars of Europe." - George Washington

"The Jesuits, by their very calling, by the very essence of their institution, are bound to seek, by every means, right or wrong, the destruction of Protestantism. This is the condition of their existence, the duty they must fulfill, or cease to be Jesuits." - G.B. Nicolini, 1854

"They are a public plague, and the plague of the world...From the Jesuit colleges there never is sent a pupil obedient to his father, devoted to his country, loyal to his prince." — Mary Frances Cusak, The Black Pope: A History of the Jesuits

"Nor will it contribute a little to our advantage, if, with caution and secrecy, we foment and heighten the animosities that arise among princes and great men, even to such a degree that they may weaken each other. But if there appear any likelihood of reconciliation, then as soon as possible, let us endeavor to be the mediators, lest others prevent us...

Let proper methods be used to get knowledge of the animosities that arise among great men that we may have a finger in reconciling their differences; for by this means we shall gradually become acquainted with their friends and secret affairs, and of necessity engage one of the parties in our interests...

Immediately upon the death of any person of post, let them take timely care to get some friend of our Society preferred in his room; but this must be cloaked with such cunning and management as to avoid giving the least suspicion of our intending to usurp the prince's authority...

Princes and persons of distinction everywhere must, by all means, be so managed that we may have their ear and that will easily secure their hearts: by which way of processing, all persons will become our creatures, and no one will dare to give the Society the least disquiet or opposition...

Finally, the society must endeavor to effect this at least, that having gotten the favor and authority of princes, those who do not love them at least fear them." — W.C. Brownlee, Secret Instructions of the Jesuits 1857

So, the Jesuits continued controlling history and the movements of all government leaders. Charles Chiniquy writes:

"'You see that your friends, the Jesuits have not yet killed me. But they would have surely done it when I passed through their most devoted city, Baltimore, had I not defeated their plans by passing incognito a few hours before they expected me.' New projects of assassination are detected almost every day, accompanied with such savage circumstances, that they bring to my memory the massacre of St. Bartholomew and the Gunpowder Plot. We feel, at their investigation, that they come from the same masters in the art of murder: the Jesuits. So many plots have already been made against my life, that it is a real miracle that they have all failed, when we consider that the great majority of them were in the hands of the skillful Roman Catholic murderers evidently trained by the Jesuits.' I know that Jesuits never forget nor forsake. But man must no care how and where he dies, provided he dies at the post of honour and duty."

You can easily tell which orders and cults have been created by the Jesuits based on that fact alone: they always state they never forgive and never forget. The only people commanded to forgive are Christians, no other group holds to this.

"Anyone can be Anonymous. We will never forgive. We will never forget." — Anonymous HQ

"The members of the Society are divided into four classes — the Professed, Coadjutors, Scholars, and Novices. There is also a secret fifth class, known only to the general and a few faithful Jesuits, which, perhaps more than any other, contributes to the dreaded and mysterious power of the order. It is composed of laymen of all ranks, from the minister to the humble shoe-boy...These are affiliated to the Society, but not bound by any vows. They are persons who will make themselves useful. They act as the spies of the order and serve, often unwittingly, as the tools and accomplices in dark and mysterious crimes. 'The ends justify the means,' is his favorite maxim; and as his only end, as we have shewn, is the order, at its bidding the Jesuit is ready to commit any crime whatsoever." - G.B. Nicolini of Rome, History of the Jesuits

"Let whoever desires to fight under the sacred banner of the Cross, and to serve only God and the Roman Pontiff, His vicar on earth, after a solemn vow of perpetual chastity, let him keep in mind that he is part of a society. . . Let all members know, and let it be not only at the beginning of their profession but let them think over it daily as long as they live, that the society as a whole, and each of them, owes obedience to our most holy lord, the pope, and the other Roman pontiffs, his successors." — an excerpt from the Jesuit Constitution of 1540

Continuing onto the Jesuit's world wars, everything went according to plan. After the Jesuits' activities in Poland and Parliaments of Europe, the region was prepared for the Vatican's Adolf Hitler. In 1941, Adolf Hitler and Benito Mussolini invaded Yoguslavia, and the elite's Independent State of Croatia was formed. Ante Pavelitch who had headed the Nazi Ustase, was made dictator of the faux state. In May he gave the crown to the Duke of Spoleto, Prince Aimone Roberto Margherita Maria Guiseppe Torino of the Savoy Dynasty, who assumed the name "Tomislav II". Simultaneously, Pope Pius XII (Eugenio Maria Giuseppe Giovanni Pacelli) gave a private audience to Ante Pavelitch, Cardinal Salis-Sewis, vicar-general to Cardinal Stepinac and several others. These meetings are done to confirm plans previously made, as everything the elite do is done behind closed doors and confirmed by the shaking of hands in public. In Cardinal Stepinac's diocese 280,000 Orthodox Christians were murdered.

"So, the Holy See did not fear shaking hands with a certified murderer, sentenced to death by default for the murder of King Alexander the First and Louis Barthou, a chief of terrorists having the most horrible crimes on his conscience! In fact, on the 18th of May 1941, when Pius XII gladly welcomed Pavelitch and his gang of killers, the massacre of Orthodox Croats was at its height, concurrently with forced conversions to Catholicism." - Herve Lauriere

By July 1941, the Jesuit and Vatican's planned exterminations of Protestant, Gospel believing Christians was initiated its Liberation with the deportation of 300,000 Serbians and the slaughter of more than 500,000. That's just in one small area of the Jesuit's focus during that decade. It is important to understand the Vatican's involvement in these events, especially since the Hitler was named the Son of the Catholic Church, by the Pope. Jesuit Frans Von Papen was Adolf Hitler's mentor, chancellor of Germany, and first vice-chancellor of the Third Reich. He noted in his book how well Hitler carried out the Vatican's plans for death camps. The Catholic youth groups were renamed Hitler Youth thanks to Frans. Journalist J.A. Voigt wrote:

"Croatian politics consisted of massacres, deportations or conversions. The number of those who were massacred reaches hundreds of thousands. The massacres were accompanied by the most bestial tortures. The "Oustachis" put out their victims' eyes and made garlands with them, which they wore, or presented as mementos. In Croatia, the Jesuits implanted political clericalism."

"I learned much from the Order of the Jesuits. Until now, there has never been anything more grandiose, on the earth, than the hierarchical organisation of the Catholic Church. I transferred much of this organisation into my own party... In my "Burgs" of the Order, we will raise up a youth which will make the world tremble... Hitler then stopped, saying that he couldn't say any more." — Adolf Hitler

"The SS had been organized by Himmler according to the principles of the Jesuit Order. The rules of service and spiritual exercises prescribed by Ignatius Loyola constituted a model which Himmler strover carefully to copy. Absolute obedience was the supreme rule; every order had to be executed without comment." - Walter Friedrich Schellenberg, SS

"The Third Reich is the first world power which not only acknowledges but also puts into practice the high principles of the papacy." — Franz von Papen, chamberlain to the Pope

"The Fuhrer had come to power, thanks to the votes of the Catholic Zentrum [overseen by Jesuit Ludwig Kaas], only 5 years before, but most of the objectives cynically revealed in Mein Kampf were already realized; this book was written by the Jesuit Father Bernhardt Stempfle and signed by Hitler. For it was the Society of Jesus which perfected the famous Pan-German programme as laid out in this book, and the Fuhrer endorsed it." — Edmond Paris, The Secret History of the Jesuits

"Hitler, Goebbels, Himmler, and most members of the party's "old guard" were Catholics. It was not by accident that, because of its chiefs' religion, the National-socialist government was <u>the most Catholic Germany ever had</u>... This kinship between National-socialism and Catholicism is most striking if we study closely the propaganda methods and the interior organisation of the party. On that subject, nothing is more instructive than Joseph Goebbel's works. He had been brought up in a Jesuit college and was a seminarist before devoting himself to literature and politics... Every page, every line of his writings recalls the teaching of his masters; so he stresses **obedience**... the **contempt for truth**... "Some lies are as useful as bread!" he proclaimed by virtue of a moral relativism extracted from Ignatius of Loyola's writings." - M. Frederic Hoffet

"Joseph Ratzinger [Hitler Youth] is an expert at making people disappear, having run the papal Inquisition — renamed the Congregation for the Doctrine of the Faith — for many years. But the very absoluteness of his power as Grand Inquisitor made Ratzinger many enemies, and the latter are gathering nowadays to help expose their adversary." — Kevin Annett

In this same time, from 1941 to 1945, the Roman Catholic Ustashi of Croatia slaughtered around one million Serbian Orthodox Christians. The death squads were led by Monks, Priests, and Friars, just as they always have been. The same was going on in South American countries including Venezuela and Argentina. Meanwhile you were distracted with propaganda about the Jews and its only they who deserve all attention given to any genocide in history. This does not mean that their past is less impactful than anyone else's, but it does mean that no ONE group of people deserves any more notice regarding their past than another, for we all have a past. While there were almost 6 million Jews murdered by the elite, 2 million of these were children and not all were Jewish! On the other hand, 14 million Chinese were wiped out in the war as well as 7.4 million Russian civilians. 20 percent of Poland was killed off, totaling 5.8 million, while 1.9 million Japanese were killed, along with 4.2 million Germans, not counting the 3 million who died of starvation in POW camps that 11 million Germans were put in by the Allied Forces. Meanwhile 50 million Christians had been wiped out in the 20th century. This is met with silence or ignored entirely. Most alive today have never been affected directly by the persecutions perpetrated on our ancestors, still many attempt to be treated as though they have, which is pitiful and dumb. It's time to wake up and stop the self-pity and narcissism and start standing up.

"In the 20th Century the Jesuits have conducted their Inquisition under the names of Nazism, Fascism, Communism, and Islamic Terrorism with their Inquisitors, Adolf Hitler, Francisco Franco, Josef Stalin, and Osama bin Laden. Today the Black Pope orders his Holy Office of the Inquisitions, renamed in 1965 'The Sacred Congregation for the Doctrine of the Faith', through his International Intelligence Community headed by Papal Knights, including Skull and Bonesman George W. Bush. To the abhorrent Jesuit doctrine of Regicide, we must now direct our attention that we may understand an established policy calculated to obtain or maintain the mastery of all nations following well-planned assassinations.

In the past, the Order's assassins were either Jesuits, like Jacques Clement, or killers easily connected to the influence of the Company, men like John Wilkes Booth. Today these professional terminators are cleverly distanced from their Masonic master, the Black Pope, and given deceptive titles by the Pope's internationally controlled Press corps, jurists, and historians; such titles as 'Anarchists", "Nihilists", "Rogue Agents" within intelligence agencies, or just "Lone Nut Assassins". Sometimes these individuals, in fact, do the killing, consciously and unconsciously. They sacrifice themselves, die in the act, or are punished for their crimes..." — Eric John Phelps

Today, as we saw in the previous chapter, the Jesuits have succeeded in their agenda to control ALL education, and ALL economies of the world. If you were not homeschooled, you have been programmed by Jesuits which is why you so easily accept corruption and perversion as normal and acceptable. As we have seen throughout the family chapters thus far, and those to come, the Jesuits control all things in the world today.

"The Jesuits are among the most important owners of the four greatest aircraft manufacturing companies in the US: Boeing, Lockheed, Douglas, and Curtis-Wright." — Avro Manhattan

The Economic Consultative Committee holds the monthly G-10 meeting on a Sunday at 7 pm. The 18 members are from all areas of the world and discuss, plan, and carry out the Global Economy Agenda.

"Like many of those working for the UN or the IMF, some of the staff of the BIS, especially senior management, are driven by a sense of mission, that they are working for a higher, even **celestial** purpose and so are **immune from normal considerations of accountability** and transparency." — Geopolitics.co

The Vatican Treasury holds the imperial wealth of Rome and is owned by the Rothschilds. Imperial wealth grows in proportion to its victories in war, as the Jesuit empowerment Regimini militantis ecclesiae implies, the Church-at-War is more necessary than the Church-at-Peace. Let's discuss some Jesuits more personally, and the False Flags they were a part of!

On August 6, 1945, Black Pope Pedro Arrupe was with a small group of Jesuits in Japan. Ever since the formal expulsion of the Jesuits from Japan in 1614, the elite wanted it back. This was the simple purpose for the Atom Bomb Hoax and the Pearl Harbor False Flag and subsequent war. Nuclear Terror, like the War on Terror, is a blanket keyword used to keep you in fear and make the elite look like benefactors, containing this horrible weapon. Pedro and his novices were residing in the Novitiate of the Society of Jesus in Nagatsuke 2 kilometers from Hiroshima while some others were staying at the Parish House, which was less than 1 mile from ground zero. According to the media, the Jesuits, with minor injuries, were called miracle survivors and praise was given to the goddess Mary.

"Father Cieslik wrote in his diary that they only sustained minor injuries from the broken windows - but nothing resulting from the atomic energy that was unleashed... No disorders ever developed, and in 1976 Father Schiffer attended the Eucharistic Congress in Philadelphia and told his story. He confirmed that the other Jesuits were still alive and without any ailments." – Catholic News Agency

"I was in my room with another priest at 8:15 when suddenly we saw a blinding light, like a flash of **magnesium**. Naturally we were surprised and jumped up to see what was happening. As I opened the door which faced the city, we heard a formidable explosion similar to the blast of a hurricane." – Pedro Arrupe

Media propaganda was spread wildly, and the Japanese caved to Jesuit control, persecuting Protestants while blessing Catholic Missionaries. At the time, the Jesuits needed America to be their military superpower. Shock and Awe instills fear which allows easy control. The public once again believed in something that was not real, a production of the elite. As with every false flag, the keywords and mental control agenda are the same: unity and peace. This false flag event worked to bring more Japanese under the control of the Catholic Church, since they had always been against the Jesuits and the elite's banking system. Meanwhile Japanese researchers and whistleblowers have come forward to relay how the US was blamed for these attacks when in fact it was the Japanese government. Since both are controlled by the Jesuits, they are both culpable and were aware of the true agenda. $25 Billion was spent on the Manhattan (A-bomb) Project.

"If atomic bombs are to be added as new weapons to the arsenals of a warring world, or to the arsenals of nations preparing for war, then the time will come when mankind will curse the names of Los Alamos and Hiroshima. The people must unite, or they will perish... It did not take atomic weapons to make man want peace. But the atomic bomb was the turn of the screw." - J. Robert Oppenheimer

"Peace through superior violence inevitably leads to the atom bomb and all that it stands for." — Mahatma Gandhi

We are told that over 10,000 atomic bombs have been "dropped" by mistake, mishandled, and thrown around various countries; however, there is no evidence. Apparently all one need do when a nuclear bomb falls is to crawl under a desk or some such place and cover your head with your arms. **Magnesium** coated napalm bombs were used to create the bright flash of the explosion. The cities of Hiroshima and Nagasaki looked exactly like Rotterdam in 1940 after the blitz. There were no deaf and blind survivors which would have been most, if not all, had it been nuclear. All injuries and deaths were the result of napalm fire and mustard gas, according to the unaltered medical records and eyewitness testimonies at that time. According to the media propaganda the killer was radiation!

Like the Moon landing and every other false flag event, every picture, every video of the bombs was created by the Jesuits in Hollywood and the public was told that this is what nuclear was. As experts have proven, the videos and pictures of the "Atom bomb" were not taken anywhere near Hiroshima or Nagasaki. The aftermath photos that were taken of Japan showed the people living in their homes, which were still standing, and going about their lives as normal. Buildings, bridges, and cars were all intact and in working order. The radiation stories were spread to create fear, just as radiation was physically spread in the area, many days after the bombing, as the truth that none existed became too well known. Unfortunately, radiation only lasts for a brief time.

All the while photographs of naked uninjured children were spread around newspapers worldwide, celebrating pedophilia by forcing it on you, forcing it into your mind. The photographers who set up the shots of the naked children running down the street have long since exposed their days work of shooting and reshooting until the children ran perfectly for the right image, as can be seen when looking at all photos of the shoot which show the naked children being smeared with dirt, standing in the road waiting for instructions, and more. When you are aware, you will notice that children are always used in images of False Flags and usually the same child is used for many different false flags. One easy way to tell is to remember the images you see, and the actors used in them... You can see in all the footage of so-called nuclear bombs the clouds don't even disperse, which is impossible. That footage or the photographs of the children prove the lie, the hoax of the A-Bomb and the False Flag of the war on Japan. It's all photoshopped, and not even well, if you look with your eyes.

"It wasn't dropping nuclear bombs - and Edwin Corley does a pretty good job in his The Jesus Factor, in trying to tell you what else it was." - Len Horowitz

"Both the war (2022) in Ukraine and the nuclear threat (1945) are fake and always have been. The nuclear fake is now being used to cover up the vaccine genocide (2019) and to try to protect Pfizer and other parties from a lynching." — Miles Mathis

The firebomb debris, which left no crater, no EMP effect, also left buildings still standing which were cleaned up with no problem. As stated before, cars, phones, and everything else were still in working order and unaffected, the electric train was even working as soon as the rails were cleared of debris. None of this is possible with nuclear bombs even if it was possible for them to explode in the first place. Explosive Fission is a hoax. It is impossible. Mustard gas is oily and lingers, which the strange smelling toxin did in Hiroshima. The testimonies of many specifically mentioned the gas. We are told that the effects of nuclear radiation include cancer, leukemia, and more. However, these are the effects of Mustard Gas, which is proven as well with the fact that people who went into the area up to one month after the bombing were affected by the gas. This cannot happen with radiation!

"At Hiroshima, we merely find a tiny bit of what looks like a mixture of reactor waste and reactor fuel. At Nagasaki, we find plutonium in considerable amounts. It can be shown, however, that this plutonium was not dispersed in 1945, but only some two years later." — Henry Makow

So, the Jesuits were able to create more money upon the expansion of the "nuclear" scheme while gaining control over Japan and more followers of the Catholic Church worldwide, among other things. While I could go into detail on the physics theories of nuclear crap, I will summarize with a quote. There's no point in wasting my own time writing something out when someone else has already said it!

"When fission occurs the strong forces keeping the protons and neutrons of atom A together disappear producing heat E and radiation R, while the two new, free neutrons N have problems finding other atoms A to continue fission. There is no explosion!
If a free neutron N is not absorbed by another atom A, it dies after ten

minutes or becomes a proton and an electron and a meson. There is no explosion!

The free neutrons n may produce more fission, but only due to moderation (slowing down!) inside a peaceful nuclear power plant/reactor (or a laboratory). The heat E warms the water, and the radiation R is damped by the water and the enclosure of the power plant. Easy to show at any nuclear power plant. There is no explosion!

This fission has since been studied in laboratories for years and is described in peer reviewed papers. It takes place in nano-scale - the atoms A cores are very, very small and the neutrons n are even smaller and are very, very fast - fission takes a nano-second - and can be done by moderation in nuclear power plants and laboratories. There is no explosion!" — Anders Bjorkman

Theories and lies are all that the modern scientific community pursues which is why most of their comments begin with the word "if". Theories are just theories, and the educational system is based on them. None have been or ever will be proven because they are nonsensical imaginings of a bored mind pretending to be more intelligent than you in order to achieve the goal: confusion and complacent acceptance. Physics is there to keep the Nuclear Bomb hoax alive, and keep you controlled — spending your life studying nonsense and making up theories to comfort yourself.

The Soviet Japanese Neutrality Agreement of 1941 is understood when you know the chain of events leading to this outrage. In the same year the US had built another secret base called Lookout Mountain Air Force Station in Laurel Canyon, California. This station was used to "create government films" (propaganda). The physicists who had been formulating and expanding on the theories of fission and atoms had been taken to the US to work on the nuclear project, to militarize their theories. These physicists, like Neils Bohr and others, worked together to fulfill the US hoax, knowingly. In 1947 when the CIA was officially formed, thousands of propaganda films were created there.

"Lookout Mountain is thanked in the credits to Return of the Jedi in 1983, so it must have still been open then. They want you to think it was closed in 1968, so that you can't connect it to the Tate/Manson event in 1969. But the Wikipedia page has actually been rewritten in the past year to change the date of closing to 1968. When I was writing my Tate paper, I saved a copy of the Wiki page, and at that time the date of closing was listed as 1969, not 1968. So they have rewritten the Wiki page in response to my Tate paper. It is not the first time a Wiki page has been rewritten or scrubbed in response to my papers." — Miles Mathis

For those who do look into the short sources list included at the end of this book, you will notice most are deleted, which is why I didn't bother to save all sources (which would have been impossible anyway since each sentence written here is verified by 4 or more sources before it's written). I can confirm the altering of websites and news articles and other facts online as I experienced the same as Mathis explains above. Many pages were altered WHILE I was reading them, the internet is NOT for you. I hope you look into Mathis' writings on this topic, as he includes pictures which are needed to destroy the illusion completely. You will see Robert Oppenheimer standing at ground zero of the "Trinity" test, in his suit, directly after the bomb had exploded. Common sense and logic, if you have any, will prove the hilarity of this. But I digress, that fact you should be well aware of given the length of time the internet has been in use. Mathis also details some numerology involved in this Event, stating:

"Why 108 long tons, rather than 100, 109, 110, or any other number? Because this number is another numerology marker. It has come up in several of my papers, both on my science site and on my art site. In accelerators, the proton has a mass increase limit of 108 times. I am the first to have shown why. When I discovered that, my partner at the time - who was studying Eastern religions - said to me "Oh, that is weird. That number is very important in Hinduism". Shiva has 108 names. There are 108 Mukhya Shivaganas. Buddhist rosaries have 108 beads. The number is also important in Judaism, which may be more to the point here. The number 18 is associated with Chai, and 108 is a low multiple of that, being 6 x 18. 108 is also important in martial arts. It is a tetranacci number. It is the hyperfactorial of 3. Since Oppenheimer was Jewish and involved in studying or at least quoting Eastern religions, I take it that the number 108 was not an accident. Right after the alleged blast, he quoted from the Bhagavad Gita: If the radiance of a thousand suns were to burst at once into the sky, that would be like the splendor of the mighty one. The number 108 is also aces and eights, dead man's hand. It is also Chai."

While many appreciate pointing out the Jewishness of every False Flag, I see no point. That deception was begun by the Jesuits themselves in the late 1700's and, knowing this, I refuse to entertain it. The families are behind them all as I have proven, the Jesuits are the ones responsible for carrying out and creating these agendas. The Jews are nothing more than their favorite puppets and have been throughout all of history as we have seen.

In 1955 the Space Hoax began, as Hollywood filmmakers including Stanly Kubrick, who exposed the hoax of the moon landing which he produced in Hollywood, were perfecting the art of manipulation. In 1957 the International Atomic Energy Agency was partnered with the United Nations and depicts a flag of blue and white. While they give no information on how they have maintained peace and stopped further nuclear war, they claim to do so. Billions have been able to be made in the name of peace and war, encompassing nuclear lies. In 2020, nine countries spent more than $72 billion on 'nukes'. The US projects that it will spend $634 billion from 2021-2030. The reason for this is "technological advances". The reality is that there isn't a country in the world that has nuclear bombs of any kind. They will confirm this by their silence on the entire subject. Meanwhile leaders of the world sign treaties, sanction countries, and go to war using the grand excuse of Nuclear Terror. In 2020 Northrop Grumman received $31.7 Billion from the US government. General Dynamics received $10.8 Billion, Lockheed Martin $2.1 Billion, and Boeing $105 Million. Remember who owns these companies? The Jesuits!

"Northrop Grumman and Boeing and Lockheed and General Dynamics make a lot of money out of preparing for such a war. The congressmen get campaign contributions, they get votes in their district and almost every state for preparing for that." — Whistleblower Daniel Ellsberg

In 2021 the UN wrote a treaty to ban all nuclear weapons. On and on it goes. The fact remains: Nuclear bombs are not capable of exploding on impact or at all! If they did, all pilots and their planes would be destroyed every time they were dropped. They would not be able to get away fast enough. The pilot, Paul Tibbits, who "dropped the A-bomb" with his crew of 14, died in 2007 at the ripe old age of 92. He ran the National Crisis Center at the Pentagon. The other pilot who dropped the other bomb also survived the bomb and died at age 88 in 2009. Both were in good health and lived long. After killing hundreds of thousands of people in a staged war, America still calls them heroes, as every person who murders others is called. Depravity is astounding.

"In Hiroshima I was prepared for radically different sights. But, to my surprise, Hiroshima looked **exactly** like all the other burned-out cities in Japan. There was a familiar pink blot, about two miles in diameter. It was dotted with charred trees and telephone poles. Only one of the city's twenty bridges was down. Hiroshima's clusters of modern buildings in the downtown section stood upright. It was obvious that the blast could not have been so powerful as we had been led to believe. It was extensive blast rather than intensive.

I had heard of buildings instantly consumed by unprecedented heat. Yet here I saw the buildings structurally intact, and what is more, topped by undamaged flag poles, lightning rods, painted railings, air raid precaution signs and other comparatively fragile objects. At the T-bridge, the aiming point for the atomic bomb, I looked for the "bald spot" where everything presumably had been vaporized in the twinkling of an eye. It wasn't there or anywhere else.
<u>**I could find no traces of unusual phenomena.**</u>
What I did see was in substance a replica of Yokohama or Osaka, or the Tokyo suburbs — the familiar residue of an area of wood and brick houses razed

by uncontrollable fire. Everywhere I saw the trunks of charred and leafless trees, burned and unburned chunks of wood. The fire had been intense enough to bend and twist steel girders and to melt glass until it ran like lava — just as in other Japanese cities. The concrete buildings nearest to the center of explosion, some only a few blocks from the heart of the atom blast, showed no structural damage.

Even cornices, canopies and delicate exterior decorations were intact. Window glass was shattered, of course, but single-panel frames held firm; only window frames of two or more panels were bent and buckled. The blast impact therefore could not have been unusual." -Major Alexander Seversky

Nuclear plant leaks like Fukushima and Chernobyl have created more damage than Napalm. Nuclear energy is a clean source of energy produced and used for AI, as we have discussed. It's always been and always will be all about advancing technology to the point where the Fallen can be released from the Deep. Nuclear chemical damage does **not** pass from generation to generation, and while you are shown horrible pictures of deformed children, these deformities are not from radiation. All forms of life come back to normal once the nuclear vapor has cleared. It also does not last long, and it is not a permanent contaminant — nothing is. It has been proven that hemp plants absorb and clean it out of the ground, air, and water. If nuclear contaminated sites were planted with hemp, all contamination would be cleared by **the first crop**. Since this is practically free to do, the governments censor the research and the doctors and scientists who speak out.

While radiation (heat) is real and can be dangerous, which is why so little of it can get past our atmosphere, the veil, alive, it has been exaggerated to a point that is outrageous. Gustave Le Bon made a piece of tinfoil more radioactive than uranium with ultraviolet light. I guess it's time to take off our hats and use our brains. His books were banned in the US, like a great many others.

"The masses have never thirsted after truth. Whoever can supply them with illusions is easily their master; whoever attempts to destroy their illusions is always their victim." — Gustave Le Bon

Galen Winsor, a plutonium physicist, is well known for his demonstrations wherein he licked a pile of highly radioactive uranium off of his hand. He is also videoed igniting a chunk of plutonium (on his hand) into a spray of flaming dust in his public talks to make people understand their irrational fears. He drank reactor cooling water and filled his swimming pool with it and swam every day. He coated his basement floor, in his home, with enough radioactive material to send any Geiger counter reading off the scale. He died healthy and peacefully in 2008, aged 88. He believed nuclear waste was recyclable and could be stored safely above ground. Let's continue.

The elite do not want you to know many truths, because truth sets you free, and they must keep you controlled. Instead, they spread decades of propaganda and fear to drain money from you. Controlling you through your emotions which are always changeable and predictable. Now that we are all so convinced the earth is contaminated with so much radiation and nuclear waste that we will all die, they can take more of your money and create "green" and "energy saving" programs to create technology to counter-act the "global warming" farce! Trillions of dollars are spent on these programs **and** their opposing programs.

"I found almost all the wealth and all the treasures of the Province of America in the hands of the Jesuits...All this property and all these considerable revenues which might make a sovereign powerful, serve no other purpose than to maintain ten [Jesuit] colleges... To this may be added the extraordinary skill with which they make use of and increase their super-abundant wealth. They maintain public warehouses, cattle fairs, butcher-stalls, and shops. They lend out their money for usury, and thus cause the greatest loss and injury to others." - Bishop Palafox, 1647

The previous Superior General was Adolfo Nicolás Pachón, born in Spain on April 29, 1936, the same year as Jorge Bergoglio. Adolfo joined the Jesuits in 1953 and was made a priest on March 17, 1967. He was made Black Pope on January 19, 2008. Like the former Spanish Black Pope, Pedro Arrupe, Adolfo is fluent in several languages and has lived most of his life in Japan, working with the poor in Asia. He strongly supports the liberation theology and praises the poor for being poor, whereas the White Pope is violently against it. Adolfo graduated from Sophia University in Japan, a Jesuit stronghold, where he became a professor and worked in its underground laboratories. He founded the St. Ignatius Church which was built across from Sophia University. As the lead Jesuit in Japan, he worked to maintain the Jesuits control over the leaders of the region, who were educated in Jesuit schools including Sophia, and members of their clubs. Adolfo would also have been in charge of controlling the orders of that country including the White Dragon Society, and other such mafia groups which are all founded by Jesuits for Jesuit purposes. Adolfo Pachon was known to have a part in planning and implementing the False Flag of Fukushima in 2011 which killed over 15 thousand people. Naturally, he wasn't taken to court for this. However, he was finally forced to resign after he became too publicized during his trial for genocide, child trafficking and other abuses, and was replaced at the General Congregation Jesuit meeting in 2016 by Arturo Sosa. Adolfo died on May 20, 2020, a perfect day for Jesuit numerology.

"Asia has a lot yet to offer the Church, to the whole Church, but we haven't done it yet. Maybe we have not been courageous enough, or we haven't taken the risks we should." — Adolfo Pachon

Superior General Arturo Sosa Abascal, the current Black Pope, was selected October 15, 2016. One year later he "baptized himself" as a Buddhist. He is the Jesuits' first non-European leader in the congregation's nearly 500-year-long history and the first Superior General to be elected under a Jesuit Pope. Both are from Latin America, home of the Nazis post WWII. Arturo is a part of the Arcana Arcanorum controlled by the upper Bloodlines within the I-Mori (these are the Farnese, Orsini, Aldobrandini, Somaglia, and Breakspear families). Their command center is within the Borgo Santo Spirito, which is <u>missile protected</u>. Arturo Sosa Abascal is from a prominent family in Caracas. His father, Arturo Sr. was a professor of Economic Theory at the Central University of Venezuela, President of the Finalven Financial Company, and Vice President of the National Banking Council. He became a member of the Social Christian Government Board that formed after the fall of the dictatorship of General Marcos Pérez Jiménez in 1958. He also worked as the Minister of Finance between 1982 and 1984, during the administration of President Luis Herrera Campins, and in charge of refinancing its $9.6 billion short-term foreign debt.

The Black Pope holds the power over the banking system, controls Maritime Laws, Space Laws, and every international intelligence community in the world, CIA, FBI, NSA, SIS, MI6, Scotland Yard, Mossad, CSIS, DGSE, FSB. As the White Pope has his castle on Vatican Hill, so the Black Pope has his on Aventin Hill, one of the seven hills in Rome. This is the palace of the Knights of Malta who are under direction of the General alone. President Herrera Campins is widely criticized for having increased the Government bureaucracy by 50%. Carlos Andres Perez was then made President and launched a program with IMF loans just as George Soros did in Ukraine. Riots, martial law, and general strike followed, leaving hundreds killed in street violence. In 1992, Colonel Hugo Chavez and supporters made two coup attempts. Around 120 people were murdered in suppression of coups, and Hugo was jailed for two years before being pardoned and becoming the next leader. Interesting, no? So orchestrated...

Superior General Arturo Sosa, before he became superior, was Chair of Contemporary **Political Theory** and the Chair of **Social Change** in Venezuela at the School of Social Sciences. In 1966, Arturo joined the Jesuits after receiving his degree in political science from Universidad Central de Venezuela, and a doctorate in philosophy from the Universidad Católica Andrés Bello, where he was a member of the founding council. In 1975, he met Superior General (Black Pope) Pedro Arrupe. In 1977, he was ordained by the Pontifical Gregorian University in Rome and soon he became a professor at the Andrés Bello Catholic University, where he lectured at the seminar on History of Political Ideas in Venezuela. Pope Paul VI died in the beginning of August 1978; his successor John Paul I ran the church for only 33 days before being assassinated by the Jesuits, and on October 16, John Paul II took over the government. This completed the trinity of Popes for that year.

From 1979 to 1996, Arturo was the Director of the SIC Magazine, Director of the Gumilla Center, Research Coordinator of the Rómulo Betancourt Foundation and a full-time researcher at the Institute of Political Studies of the Faculty of Political Science of the Central University of Venezuela for two years. He participated in the 33rd General Congregation of the Society (1983) where he was the youngest delegate. This is where he began his close relationship with Jorge Bergoglio (Pope Francis). Both are Marxists and humanists who believe in dictatorships and have both supported them in their own countries (among a great many other things). Marxists (extreme Communists) refer to socialism as the first, necessary phase on the way from capitalism to communism, which is the elite's preferred governmental structure.

In an interview, Jorge Bergoglio was asked:
"So, you yearn for a society where equality dominates. This, as you know, is the program of Marxist socialism and then of communism. Are you therefore thinking of a Marxist type of society?"
He replied:
"It has been said many times and my response has always been that, if anything, it is the communists who think like Christians."

The Pope uses the keyword Christian to hide himself, like many others use the term Jew. The elite have always been Dictatorial and Tyrannical in their beliefs and hierarchical structures, which are in opposition to Christian doctrine. Dictators are kept in power by the elite. In 1989, Arturo Sosa signed a letter welcoming Cuban President Fidel Castro to Venezuela. He was involved with many Castro followers as he was one himself. Over the following years, Arturo worked tirelessly building "comunidades cristianas de base" (Basic "Christian" Communities) which were committed to building Socialist societies in Latin America and especially in Venezuela. For those who haven't kept up with your history, South America has been used by the elite for thousands of years as a testing ground of persecution. In 1962 the Mexican village of Yerba Buena became one of many cult centers as two brothers, Santos and Cayetano Hernandez, convinced villagers that they were prophets sent by Inca gods. They introduced 18-year-old prostitute, Magdalena Solis, as the reincarnation of an Aztec goddess Coatlicue. The cult engaged in drug-fueled orgies, ritualistic murders, and demanded human sacrifice. Magdalena forced followers into various forms of depravity, including incest and raping children. In 1963, she performed a ritual sacrifice of at least 4 people, ripping their hearts out and drinking their blood. The cult was exposed when a 14-year-old boy happened upon the cave during a ritual sacrifice. The terrified child ran 15 miles to report the cult. This is hardly the only cult utilized in this region. Others include the Matamoros cult. It is a hive of CIA black operations which can run rampant and unrestricted, among other Jesuit activities. Every quarter of the world is used for a specific purpose. Africa, for another example, is primarily used for mining exploitation while the populations are experimented on, kept uneducated and depopulated, like the middle east. These 2 continents in particular are kept from advancing as Europe and Eastern Asia have.

Just as Karl Marx taught that praxis was the birthplace of theory, and theory was built in order to guide practice, so disciple Arturo Sosa was dedicated to rewriting the Catholic Magisterium. This is what the Jesuits do. He is a firm believer in the Marxist Liberation theology, which proposes a political salvation, adopts materialism and atheism. The results of this structure can be seen in the US, Venezuela, Europe, Scandinavia, as well as Argentina and other countries. While working for the SIC Magazine Arturo put out a great many articles pushing the theories he believes in and pushes today: re-interpreting Christianity from a Marxist viewpoint to Divide and Conquer those who would seek Truth. Marxism cancels out Christianity, like every other elite system, so both cannot exist together. One cannot be both.

"Sosa was an active promoter and defender of the 1992 coup d'état. Without losing his independence, he was linked to various groups on the far left. He did grassroots work in neighborhoods, wrote pamphlets, and strongly opposed the economic reform that Social Democrat President Carlos Andrés Pérez promoted." — a former Democratic Action Party Senator

"Both Sosa and José Virtuoso —current rector of the UCAB- are political scientists and were close in the postgraduate courses of the UCV and the Universidad Simón Bolívar (USB) to circles affected by insurrectional movements, who were interrogated and detained in 1989 and 1992 by the Disip (former political police) and the DIM (Directorate of Military Intelligence)." - Aveledo Coll

Arturo dedicated himself to working the blurry line between the coup military on behalf of the Venezuelan Catholic Church, as a Jesuit, and being in charge of "ensuring respect for Human Rights". From 1982 to 1996 Arturo was a professor at the School of Political and Administrative Studies at the Chair of History of Political Ideas of Venezuela, at the Central University of Venezuela. Arturo attended the 34th General Congregation in 1995, where he was befriended by Superior General Adolfo Nicolás Pachon. Together they practiced child sacrifice and rape rituals, with other Jesuits, as is required.

From 1985 to 1994, he served as a teacher and held the chair of Analysis Socio-Political of Venezuela on the command and general staff in the Superior School of the Air Force. Until 1996, he was the coordinator for the social apostolate of the Jesuits in Venezuela and director of the Centro Gumilla (a school for research and social engagement of the Jesuits). In 1996, he was made the Superior of the Society and Vice Chancellor-President of the Foundation Council. Since 1998 he has been a member of the General Preparatory Council of the Society of Jesus. In 1999, he was quoted by the school's magazine stating:

> "The personal leadership that Hugo Chávez Frías has exercised in recent months, has served as a retaining wall for the strong and growing currents driving anomie and anarchy in Venezuelan society."

On April 11, 2002, while a coup d'état was in progress, Hugo Chavez revealed that the first call he made was to Arturo Sosa! He stated in a TV interview:

> "First I invoke God, I was saying on the phone to Father Arturo Sosa, to God and to all the saints, father let's send the blessing and all the saints, so that nothing serious is going to happen here."

Arturo was in fact incarcerated in 1989 and 1992 by Venezuela's military intelligence agency because of his involvement with the military coup of Hugo. In 2004, he became a professor at Jesuit Georgetown University in Washington, DC and was made rector of the Jesuit University in Táchira. In 2006, he was the Professor of the Chair of Venezuelan Political Thought at the Catholic University of Táchira. In 2013, Arturo, who was now president of the Catholic University in Tachira, Venezuela, presented a lecture called Political Implications of a Humanizing Globalization. In 2014 he became a member of the Curia of the Society of Jesus and worked with the International Houses for Jesuits, in Rome. He worked between multiple colleges, as has every Superior before him, including the Pontifical Gregorian University, the Pontifical Biblical Institute, the Pontifical Istituto Orientale and the Vatican Observatory intimately with Superior General Adolfo Nicolas. Only then did he begin to publicly distance himself from the Chavez group.

> "Fifteen years of Chavista government have failed to establish the foundations of a new political legitimacy...I refer to this regime as a system of domination, not as a legitimate system." - Arturo Sosa in Medellin, Colombia, August 2014

Upon hearing this, the Provincial Secretary of the Society of Jesus in Venezuela, Francisco Javier Dupla, exclaimed his hopes that Arturo would bring to the entire congregation the "style of government" that he displayed in his homeland: Military Dictatorship. At the 36th General Congregation of the Society of Jesus, Arturo Sosa was finally made Superior General of the Jesuits. The title of the First Plenary Assembly under General Sosa was "Rowing into the Deep". Remembering what Deep/Dark mean and their symbolism, this is not encouraging. During his first Mass as Superior General, the next day, he reflected on seeking to do not only the improbable but the impossible, stating:

> "Nothing is impossible TO God."

His statement equated himself to God, by which he means nothing is impossible for Arturo, inverting the biblical text that says All things are possible THROUGH Christ. He went on to say:

"To **seek** the impossible is a Christian mission and a way of expressing one's faith."

This is just another warped deception. Words have meaning, and if you don't understand where Luciferians definitions come from, you will be deceived by their lies. It is just like attempting to converse with someone from a different culture. Although you may speak the same words and know the meaning of each individual word, the entire context and understanding is twisted, based on the vastly diverse cultural indoctrinations of the speaker and listener. This is exactly why understanding the history and culture of the time is so important for Christians when reading the books of the Bible which were written in different time periods and regions. Knowing the terminology used at the time the particular book was written, and understanding the author of each book in the Bible is critical to understanding the deeper points. It's about history. Arturo Sosa Abascal made statements in an interview with Giuseppe Rusconi published February 18, 2017, on the blog Rossoporpora. In this interview he directs comments at Jesus' words on marriage as quoted in Matthew 19:5-6 and 8 which says:

"For this reason, shall a man leave father and mother, and shall cleave to his wife: and the two shall be one flesh. Therefore they are no more two, but one flesh. What God has joined together, let no man put asunder. It was because of your hardness of heart that Moses permitted you to divorce your wives; but it was not this way from the beginning."

Arturo commented:

"What is known is that the words of Jesus must be contextualized. This attests that the word is relative, the Gospel is written by human beings. Discernment leads to a decision: one must not only evaluate but decide. The Church has always reiterated the priority of personal conscience. Doctrine does not replace discernment, nor does the Holy Spirit."

Translation: Your opinion is the only thing that matters. Whatever you want the words of Jesus to mean, that's what they mean. There is no right and wrong. Doctrine doesn't have meaning. The Holy Spirit God promises to all who believe, as a guide and protector of the soul, has no value.

His words merely spread doubt, as intended. The elite have been working for many decades bringing the New Age (New Aeon) philosophy into mainstream mentalities and it is permeating the Christian culture today at a rapid rate. Luciferianism must be normalized, as previously discussed. Free will is what allows us to choose love, wisdom, or ignorance. That is why the Living God gave it to you. He didn't want drones, insects of the Hive Mind, as the Fallen do. He wanted you to *want* to love. He wanted you to choose. As Paul said to the Christ Followers of Ephesia:

"You must no longer live as the Gentiles do, in the futility of their thinking. They are **darkened** in their understanding and **separated** from the life of God because of the **ignorance** that is in them due to the hardening of their hearts. Having lost all sensitivity, they have given themselves over to sensuality so as to indulge in every kind of impurity, and they are full of greed. That, however, is not the way of life you learned when you heard about Christ and were taught in him in accordance with the truth that is in Jesus. You were taught, with regard to your former way of life, to put off your old self, which is being corrupted by its deceitful desires; to be made new in the attitude of your minds; and to put on the new self, created to be like God in true righteousness and holiness. Therefore, each of you must put off falsehood and **speak truthfully** to your neighbor, for **we are all members of one body**."

Continuing to work to unite religions under the One Religion of the New World Order: Luciferianism, Arturo spoke with Buddhist monks in Cambodia in July 2017. He visited the oldest Buddhist temple in Siem Reap, Cambodia and meditated with the monks in front of the huge idol of Buddha. In his speech he did not mention God or the Bible as is customary for a Jesuit speech to contain, but rather continued to degrade them with his usual relativism, indifference, and agnosticism. His speech had nothing to do with the soul but only to do with the flesh. The 2010's were used to unify the religions of the world, warping Buddhism and Catholicism. In the past, until this time period, a trained Catholic priest would politely but firmly, reject any invitation to attend a "religious ceremony" of a non-Catholic nature. Even if one was operating on the pretext of attempting to convert people to the Catholic faith, one would NOT attend these ceremonies and would absolutely not be pictured participating in a ritual. See Canon 1325 § 3, Canon 1258 and Canon 731, § 2. However, the Jesuits are infiltrators and no longer hide that fact. They are all two-faced as their oath demands. Today it is all out in the open and people are readily accepting it.

The New World Order can hold only one religion. So, all of the divisions the elite have created and controlled over the centuries must now be brought together, no matter how completely opposite they are and ridiculous it is. Indifference is the best way to nullify a belief. You can clearly see today how much progress they have made on this front, dear reader. Today many Muslims believe they hold the same beliefs as Christians, Christians believe they are the same as New Agers and everyone believes in "god". Remember, dear one, Lucifer is the god of this world...for a time. Once again Arturo himself states the purpose of the Jesuits.

"We need to **assimilate** the entire preferences in all its complexity. Each preference includes at least three complementary dimensions...We are not working for the poor. We are working with them in their style of life and we work for "social justice", for change. We (Jesuits) need to change **economical, political,** and **social** policies AND causes." - Arturo Sosa

After the Jesuit-backed migrant invasion of Europe back in 2017, the Black Pope immediately spoke out to shame European countries into accepting floods of militant Islamic migrants, consequently destroying the nations.

"No country has the right to turn away migrants! The goods of the land are for everyone." - Arturo Sosa

Translation: No country is an independent authority for its own preservation. No country's citizens, economy or culture is worth sustaining. It must all be destroyed. It has all gone as planned and sovereignty and independence has died. Those who do not remember Jesuit Albert Pike's letter to Giuseppe Mazzini, here is a relevant excerpt, taken from Gregory Garrett's book titled The Scientism Delusion Techno Mysticism And Techno Spiritual Warfare:

"The Third World War must be fomented by taking advantage of the differences caused by the "agentur" of the "Illuminati" between the political Zionists and the leaders of Islamic World. The war must be conducted in such a way that Islam (the Moslem Arabic World) and political Zionism (the State of Israel) mutually destroy each other.

Meanwhile the other nations, once more divided on this issue, will be constrained to fight to the point of complete physical, moral, spiritual and economical exhaustion...We shall unleash the Nihilists and the atheists, and we shall provoke a formidable social cataclysm which in all its horror will show clearly to the nations the effect of absolute atheism, origin of savagery and of the most bloody turmoil.

Then everywhere, the citizens, obliged to defend themselves against the world minority of revolutionaries, will exterminate those destroyers of civilization, and the multitude, disillusioned with Christianity, whose deistic spirits will from that moment be without compass or direction, anxious for an ideal, but without knowing where to render its adoration, will receive the true light through the **universal manifestation** of the **pure doctrine of Lucifer**, brought finally out in the public view. This manifestation will result from the general reactionary movement which will follow the **destruction of Christianity** and atheism, both conquered and exterminated at the same time."

"The future of Europe depends heavily on the workforce that comes from other countries. For this, a common strategy must be planned. Migrants are a source of wealth: to escape from wars and famines are men and women who have the desire to work." — Arturo Sosa

The migrant flood included Jesuit Islamic State fighters, as well as jihadis from Boko Haram, al Qaeda, the Muslim Brotherhood and so forth. As planned, every country's economy has taken a huge hit from this event alone, not to mention the violence the terrorists and extremists have brought with them. They are not workers... Germany now has 75% of immigrants on long-term unemployment and life on benefits, in Switzerland over 80% of Somali migrants are on welfare. Rape and violent crimes which were practically nonexistent in Scandinavia have escalated, perpetrated by migrants. There was already a job shortage problem in Europe before this, but such was the design. Once Europe was infiltrated and began its decline, the Americas were targeted. When Covid was implemented, even with the numerous documentation and testimonies of its falsity, the US government held firm in its task to destroy the economy of the nation by forbidding people to work and forcing vaccinations on the public. These diseases, economic collapses, militaristic lockdowns will continue and only increase GLOBALLY until the agenda is complete, as they have already stated.

In 2018, Arturo Sosa Abascal became the new president of the Union of Superiors General. On July 8, 2019, the Pope appointed him as a member of the Congregation for the Institutes of Consecrated Life and for the Societies of Apostolic Life. Pope Francis had a special meeting with Arturo which concluded with The Universal Apostolic Preferences. These rules, called preferences, are to give "a horizon, a point of reference to the whole Society of Jesus. They capture our imaginations and awaken our desires. They unite us in our mission. The new Preferences are four areas vital for our world today. **The Society of Jesus will pay special attention to them in the next ten years**."

In August 2019, Arturo once again stated that the devil is not real, and this time he went even further to claim that the devil cannot possess a human vessel:

"The devil exists as the personification of evil in different structures, but NOT in persons, because he is not a person, he is a way of ACTING evil. Symbols are part of reality, and the devil exists as a symbolic reality, not as a personal reality."

So, Arturo Sosa is the devil since he ACTS like it? There is no evil, only action. This is what the elite would like you to believe. Pedophilia is sold to us today as being an uncontrollable action, nothing more, so it's not a big deal. Pedos just can't help destroying people's lives, bodies, and minds. Assumed consent.... not self-control...right? Self-control and willpower have been demonized words in recent decades as humanity has declined. They are the qualities that make us human but have been long ignored as people today are made to be weak in every way. According to the Roman Catholic Church, what he stated is heresy and carries with it an automatic excommunication (see Canon 2314). In any other decade he would have been, but the point is to create **doubt** and **diminish belief** and further deaden the soul of the individual and the whole of humanity. The International Association of Exorcists responded stating:

"In the face of these serious and confusing statements, which have already been expressed in the past by Father Sosa Abascal at the supplement of El Mundo, some doctrinal clarification in the light of the magisterium, even of the current Pontiff, is necessary... The real existence of the devil, as a personal subject who thinks and acts and has made the choice of rebellion against God, is a truth of faith that has always been part of Christian doctrine. This truth is confirmed by a document of the Congregation of the faith, published by "L'Osservatore Romano" on June 26, 1975. The text examines in a detailed way the declaration of the Lateran Council IV."

They continue on to discuss Pope Francis' Apostolic Exhortation Gaudete et exultate written in March 19, 2018 which states:

"We therefore do not think that it (the devil) is a myth, a representation, a symbol, a figure, or an idea. **This deception leads us to drop our guard, to neglect us and to remain more exposed**. If this truth is denied, one easily falls under the devil's clutches, who "like a roaring lion goes around looking for someone to devour". As an International Exorcist Association, we like to end by reporting what was stated by the Italian Episcopal Conference at n.5 of the Presentation of the Italian version of the new Rite of Exorcisms, promulgated by the Holy See on 22 November 1998 (De exorcismis et supplicationibus quibusdam):

The disciple of Christ, in the light of the Gospel and of the teaching of the Church, believes that the Evil One and the demons exist and act in the personal and community history of men. Indeed, the Gospel describes the work of Jesus as a struggle against Satan (see Mark 1: 23-28; 32-34; 39; 3, 22-30 and passim). Even the life of his disciples entails a battle that "is not against creatures made of flesh and blood, but against the **Principalities and Powers**, against the **rulers of this world of darkness**, against the **spirits of evil** (Ephesians 6:12).

The Catechism of the Catholics [of which Arturo Sosa is a trained representative of the highest position] states that Angels are spiritual, non-corporeal beings and "Satan was at first a good angel, made by God: 'The devil and the other demons were indeed created naturally good by God, but they became evil by their own doing.'"

In September of that same year, Arturo commented on the political battle within the Vatican:

"Francis is fighting against clericalism and this exercise of power and proposes a synodal church. It is essential that this path continues, according to the will of the Church expressed clearly in the Second Vatican Council, of which Pope Francis is a legitimate and direct son."

Arturo believes the synodal process introduced by Pope Francis "creates unity", and that the church shows "true reform" the "closer it comes to the design of the Second Vatican Council." This is true, as was the purpose of the Second Vatican. What is synodality you may wonder? Basically, it is where all of the Catholic Church's hierarchy and rules are <u>up for interpretation</u> as anyone sees fit, this eliminates authority and responsibility and accountability. Do What Thou Wilt.

In December of 2019, Arturo decided to attempt to patch up his remarks about the devil. During an interview regarding 6 Jesuits and 2 employees who were killed in November 1989 by Salvadoran soldiers at the University of Central America in San Salvador, he stated:
"The power of the devil obviously still exists as a force that tries to ruin our efforts."

The elite are never so eloquent when they attempt to justify themselves. Progressive, Secular, New Age = Elite Belief System. It's not hard to see the trends and see through the deception...if your pride will allow you to and if you know your history! Later that same year, Arturo stated that Christians, the mortal enemy of Catholics, have "**formed** symbolic figures such as the devil to **express** evil".

"It is hard to imagine a more convenient ideology for anyone who prefers to "go with the flow" rather than swim against the currents of this world. But as G. K. Chesterton pointed out, it is only the dead who do nothing but drift downstream...The truths that God revealed to us through His Words **do not vary**, and neither does God Himself." - Dr. Jeff Mirus

Those who do not understand the occult will fall for the "New Age" deception as so many have already. As the elite follow Lucifer, and therefore promote the new world religion of "New" Age occultism, we will see increasingly that they will speak out to convince you that the devil is not real. Is it all starting to make sense? Why are they so scared of their enemies the Christians? That should be obvious... The moral structure that makes us human beings has already been so totally watered down to mean nothing in Society. This will only increase exponentially as the finishing touches are established for the New World Order. Everyone who will remain in the completed New World Order WILL BE Luciferian, as the elite have stated. It is not a debate. That is what ALL of their agendas, and everything that they have done for thousands of years has been focused on. Because we are already in such a degraded state, the leaders will not only use the keywords of unity, peace, and global government but the "New Age" even more than they have already.

"For the first time in the history of the Jesuit order, **the process of discernment** involves not only the Jesuits but also the women and men who are engaged with them, including non-Christians and the followers of other religions." — Arturo Sosa

Translation: The Jesuit Order is expanding, harvesting as many as possible, especially non-Christians who are the easiest to sway as they are unprotected. You are currently living in the alternate reality.

Arturo Sosa stresses the crucially important educational role Jesuits are playing and will continue to play through schools and universities, and he envisaged greater networking in order to have "a global impact". Speaking of education, which has been mentioned multiple times now, let's take a quick look further back in history and see the effects of the Jesuits on education and religion in the past when they had a different name. In the later BC era, Judaism was the only belief system which spoke out against the elite and exposed their corruption. Religious doctrines were changed, books were re-written, and they quickly had no resemblance to their former contents. In this time, around 200 BC there were many orders, but I will look at 2 which are important for our genealogy at this time: Sadducee's (meaning Just) and Pharisees (meaning Separated). The Sadducee's were a small group in charge of the Temple and keeping the teachings of the Torah. The Judaeans were controlled by the Pharisees, who were sages and priests of the Babylonian Talmud. The Sadducee's had tried to maintain control over the Pharisees by giving them no power in their system. The Sadducee's protected the Torah, making sure it wasn't altered and remained pure. The modern-day Jesuits were the ones called Pharisees (also Habarim, and the Synagogue of Satan) and they changed Judaism forever.

The Pharisees made themselves the only ones allowed to write the law, or any such thing. They were persistent in their desire to change the Torah and emphatically preached tolerance and acceptance, much like they do today, eliminating right or wrong, good, or bad. I can't count how many times I have read, in the multitude of ancient texts, historical accounts, journals, and other documents, warnings about lawyers and especially warnings against putting them in positions with ANY power. All lawyers are trained to do is manipulate and deceive. True to the original term hypocrite meaning two-faced, actor, they interpret words to mean <u>whatever they need them to</u> at any given time. Interpretation leaves too much room for manipulation. The truth speaks clear enough, to those who are capable of not interpreting. This is why most people cannot understand the Biblical texts. Most will interpret based on their limited understanding when the Bible must be read and understood as it interprets itself, this takes study and an <u>open mind</u>.

The Sadducees' untouched, original biblical texts cover the Jesuits of their day extensively, as did the Christian documents before they were edited in the 1500's published Bible, specifically calling them the Synagogue of Satan, pious men, and men in robes, especially pointing out purple robes as well as warning about their "dwelling on the seven hills" which is Rome! This is why the Bible of the Reformation time period, the Geneva Bible, was banned – because it specifically documented, in its footnotes, that the Pope is the Antichrist. This was the purpose for the Jesuits Gunpowder Plot of 1605, which was carried out to eliminate the publication of the King James Bible through the murder of the king. In the mid 1600's the Vatican took it upon itself to alter the Bible even more, eliminating several books from it. As you have already discovered, you cannot delete Truth. It remains…So let's continue.

Out of Judaism, Christianity was born — the continuing story and fulfilment of prophecies documented in Judaic texts. The reason these two groups are targeted is to erase their beliefs, that is all. The Synagogue of Satan is the name of the order before they became known as the Society of Jesus… Rather obvious if you understand the occult. Catholicism was created by the Synagogue of Satan, to control the masses and keep them from the truth.

The Pharisees wrote the Talmud, destroying all they could of the original Judaic documents and replacing them with their own personal opinions and philosophies. The Babylonian Talmud, which is used today, was not created until 600 AD. However, the Pharisaic "Talmud" is what it was based off of and was used before 600 AD, by the civilizations of Mesopotamia, Samaria, and Assyria. The goddess of the Talmud is Lilith. She is called Kali, by the Hindus and in Greece she was named Hecate. She is the goddess of sexual liberation and perversion. She is Lady Liberty. Her rituals involve the drinking of blood and cannibalism. Perhaps these details seem unimportant to you, but to the web of lies and the truth, they are necessary. The Talmud of that time, just like the Talmud we know today, gave them all the loopholes needed to rape, murder, and practice all sorts of other satanic rites, even stating that raping children under three years old is not a sexual act or bad at all (Ketubot 11b). It claims that if you rape a child under three years of age, boy or girl, once the act is done, they become virgins again.

This is how the elite work, they infiltrate not destroying by erasing but by infecting, tainting, taking away all proclamations of truth and rewriting their own lies.

Around 50 BC King Herod, friend of the Pharisees, was threatened by the Sadducees. He had attempted to conquer the land of Canaan, just as they are doing today. The Sadducees threatened his life because of his warmongering in Galilee and when Herod was king, 10 years later, he had 45 of the 71 Sadducee's executed along with those who had their support. Over his reigning years, the Sadducee's were killed off until only two Sadducee families remained. Those who survived sewed the remaining documents in their clothing and lived in hiding to keep them safe. With the Sadducee's out of the way, the elite were free to control the rest of the monarchs through their order the Council of Elders (which advised and influenced the monarchs) unchallenged. They used the synagogues, stolen from the corpses of the Sadducees, as their media outlet, just as they use the Vatican today. Pharisees, described as sons of Satan who is the master of lies and deception, were the ones exposed by Jesus. This is the reason the elite had Him killed, without evidence, as a political dissident, which only fulfilled prophecy as usual. Whenever the elite believe they have won a victory, it is the moment they have truly lost. Jesus physically destroyed their profit-making marketplaces and spoke out against them to the public and to their faces, saying:

"You [Pharisees] travel over sea and land to win one convert, and when you have won him, you make him twice as fit for hell as you are yourselves."

The Pharisees were pious indeed, claiming they were superior beings, not human. So, these Pharisees were known, at that time, for exactly what they are. How then, could they regain their cover? You have seen their oath which the Jesuits use today. They decided to create a new face for themselves. They would become controllers of education. They taught from the Hebrew temples and synagogues and educated all new Hebrew scholars, priests and other "holy men". They lied, passing themselves off as educators, carers of the poor and sick, and **tolerant** of the Law. Very slowly, as we see today, they changed their tune until everyone accepted the "new and improved" Pharisees. Of course, as always, this is a very simplified summary so you can see the bigger picture.

The same tactics have been vigorously used by Pope Francis and Arturo Sosa! Both urge the world to be tolerant and accept everything they put out. So, we are to accept and tolerate their torture, rape, trafficking, and murder of children in Venezuela, Argentina, the Vatican, and the world? We are to tolerate the Jesuits human sacrifices and blood lust? We are to accept our own slavery and murder? Dear reader, I hope you are intolerant for only then are you capable of being free.

This is how the elite infect all of us, religiously and educationally, which leads to total domination.
In 2020 the Jesuits pushed the new key-phrase "One World: Together At Home" under the guise of supporting healthcare workers in the fight against the Corona plandemic. Who were the highlighted "stars"? Lady Gaga: the "hermaphrodite" poster child of Baphomet who has helped in a major way, like Beyonce, Kanye West, Sia, and many more to induce the mental disorders needed for the bright new world order. The list of Jesuit puppets and pawns used for this agenda produced by WHO and Global Citizen include Jimmy Fallon, Jimmy Kimmel, Stephen Colbert, Friends from Sesame Street, Andrea Bocelli, Billie Eilish, Chris

Martin, David Beckham, Eddie Vedder, Elton John, FINNEAS, John Legend, Kacey Musgraves, Keith Urban, Kerry Washington, Lang Lang, Lizzo, Maluma, Paul McCartney, Priyanka Chopra Jonas, Shah Rukh Khan, and Stevie Wonder.

"**The United Nations system is fully mobilized**: supporting country responses, placing our supply chains at the world's disposal, and advocating for a global cease-fire. We are proud to join forces with 'One World: Together At Home' to help **suppress** the transmission of the virus, **minimize** social-economic impacts on the global community and **work together** now to advance **Global Goals for the future**. There is no greater case for collective action than our joint response to COVID-19 - we are in this together and we will get through this together." - António Guterres, Secretary-General of the United Nations

"We Jesuits are people of hope; we believe **another world** is possible." — Arturo Sosa

$128 million was donated to the cause. In 2020 Jesuit priest Marko Ivan Rupnik was excommunicated due to too much publicity from his victims. He was charged with numerous sexual, psychological, and spiritual abuses dating back 30 years. As usual, nothing happened, and he was welcomed in his homeland of Slovenia where his abuses took place. Victims are never protected. The excommunication was lifted from Marko, shortly thereafter.

One of the women abused, who had her body ripped apart, stated in an interview:
"Erotic games that were always worse in his workshop at the Collegio del Gesù in Rome, while he was painting or after the celebration of the Eucharist or after confession. He became more aggressive: I remember a very violent masturbation that I couldn't stop and during which I lost my virginity. Father Marko asked me to have three-way relationships with another sister in the community because sexuality should be, according to him, free of possession, in the image of the Trinity where, he said, 'the third took up the relationship between two, the last step in this descent into hell was to move from theological justification to an exclusively pornographic relationship. The Church and the Jesuit order knew the facts since 1994, when I personally took my request for resignation from the vows to the Archbishop of Ljubljana, in which I denounced the abuses of Father Rupnik."

"The case of Fr. Marko Rupnik, which became public last week, is a good example of how much we still have to learn, especially about people's suffering. This case, like others, causes us shock and sorrow; it forces us to understand and empathize with the suffering of <u>all those involved</u> in one form or another. It confronts us with the challenge of <u>respecting this pain</u> at the same time as we scrupulously initiate the procedures demanded by civil or canonical laws... After the Dicastery had studied the file and reported that the complaints received were legally prescribed, we sought to move from the level of legal proceedings to the task of taking care of the suffering caused and trying to heal the open wounds. Maintaining the restrictive measures on Fr. Rupnik's ministry constitutes one element of a complex process, which we know <u>takes time</u> and for which there are <u>no predefined formulas</u>. It is part of the apprenticeship we are doing, <u>trying not to get it wrong</u>." — Arturo Sosa

Whenever the elite are exposed, they do their best to appear incompetent due to ignorance. Sorry, but we are just too uncaring to help correctly... Repugnant. Thousands of years of documentation on healing from sexual abuse are nowhere to be found when it comes to the elite's actions. Predators are never corrected, and victims are simply ignored.

In another part of the world, Nome, Alaska, Father James Poole was known for setting up a Catholic mission radio station. This station relayed his Jesuit messages alongside modern pop tunes, earning him the title "Western Alaska's Hippest DJ" in a 1978 People magazine feature. Like most, if not all, Jesuit Priests, he was a notorious sexual offender. As per court filings, he victimized at least 20 indigenous females, as young as 6. One indigenous Alaskan woman reported that she was impregnated by the man at age 16. She was then forced by him to have an abortion and falsely accused her father of the crime which led to the imprisonment of her guardian, her own parent. Elsie Boudreau, an indigenous Alaskan, volunteered at the radio station founded by James Poole. From the age of 10 to 16, she was molested and raped by the man. Like all priests' activities, his pedophilia was not unknown to the Church. Historical letters from the 1960s between Jesuit leaders hinted at James' questionable behavior. Despite such alarming revelations, his predatory acts continued unchecked for decades. One Jesuit leader highlighted his unhealthy obsession with sex. James Poole spent his retirement at Gonzaga University in Spokane, Washington. Recent investigations by the Northwest News Network and Reveal from The Center for Investigative Reporting unveiled that for over 30 years, Gonzaga's Cardinal Bea House sheltered at least 20 Jesuit priests accused of sexual misdeeds, in remote Alaskan native villages and Northwest Indian reservations. Go figure. THIS is what they do! Indigenous people are the ones used, enslaved, and raped by these men throughout history.

In 1986 Bishop Michael Kaniecki of Fairbanks wrote to Archbishop Francis Thomas Hurley of Anchorage:
    "Hopefully, my letter will nip this mess in the bud. Tried to cover all bases, and yet not admit anything."

Despite accusations and exposures of their heinous crimes, when priests reach retirement, they are moved to places like Cardinal Bea House on Gonzaga's grounds without the knowledge of the university or its student population. This is also what happens to priests who are exposed and not retired, but simply moved to another parish to continue their "good work". Why, you may still wonder? The reason for this is that they ARE carrying out their true purposes and roles, as ordered by the Church and the Jesuit Order. They are doing nothing wrong, according to the Orders. It's only the public who doesn't understand this.

Father John Whitney believed that if James Poole had resided elsewhere, he might have continued his predatory behavior... Meanwhile, James was known to visit the campus library and engage with students, continuing his work. The Cardinal Bea House, within Gonzaga University's campus, is owned by the Jesuit order and not the university. Father James Jacobson was another who was relocated to Cardinal Bea House, after sexually violating individuals in the Alaska Native community of Nelson Island. He confessed during a deposition to having consensual relations with seven indigenous women, fathering four children, and using church resources to solicit prostitutes in Anchorage and Fairbanks while he was the head of a Jesuit boarding school in Glennallen. Another priest, Henry Hargreaves, preferred to molest young boys. Upon being exposed for his pedophilia and homosexuality he was relocated to Cardinal Bea House by 2003. After a short time, he was permitted to conduct prayer services in multiple Native American communities across two reservations in Washington state. This is what reservations and other Jesuit communes are there for. As of 2010 it was known that 50,000 indigenous Canadian children had been tortured to death by these groups, while they had been imprisoned in boarding schools run by Jesuits. Most indigenous societies were once peaceful, crime-free, and just in their governmental structures. Thanks to the Jesuits and their orders, they were indoctrinated, corrupted, used and killed when it suited the elite. Do not be surprised that it continues today because you have done nothing to stop it!

"I went to residential school in Muscowequan from 1944 to 1949, and I had a rough life. I was mistreated in every way. There was a young girl, and she was pregnant from a priest there. And what they did, she had her baby, and they took the baby, and wrapped it up in a nice pink outfit, and they took it downstairs where I was cooking dinner with the nun. And they took the baby into the furnace room, and they threw that little baby in there and burned it alive. All you could hear was this little cry, like "Uuh!", and that was it. You could smell that flesh cooking." — Irene Favel

Since the 1600's the Jesuits have worked to cull the indigenous nations of Canada. First, war was declared against them in a conspiracy to gain control of the fur trade in the region. By 1640 the Jesuits set out to eliminate all Algonquins, imposing diseases, weapons, and alcohol on them. In 1749 laws were passed in Canada to reward those who scalped any male Indians, whereupon the local magistrate would pay £10 each. Half of the amount was paid to those who brought in the scalp of a woman or child. While the American Colonies were shipping in African slaves, Canada used its indigenous tribes. By the 1800's the tribes were infected repeatedly with deadly diseases, followed by the implementation of a law that dissolved their rights to land. By the end of the 18050's the Jesuits had established missions in British Columbia and Okanagan and from then on worked diligently to eradicate the Indian Chiefs, replacing them with Catholic puppets. The indigenous were again attacked with diseases and their lands were stolen by the Church. By the 1880's Jesuit controlled "schools" were established and indigenous children were forced into them, ripped away from their families and lives to be tortured and killed. Over the next century children were abducted en mass and funneled into these genocidal facilities.

"The eradication of foreign people is a good and lawful thing, meritorious, and divinely honorable." – Sir Francis Bacon

The Oregon Province's record of sexual misconduct among Jesuits records 92 Jesuits who were accused of sexual misconduct. Most are not reported. 80% of these took place in indigenous territories within the Oregon Province. Jesuits established institutions such as schools and orphanages around the world, in areas like the Alaska Native community. 2 guesses why this is.

"There are no longer any known abusive priests at Cardinal Bea House. In the past couple of years, they have been relocated south to the Sacred Heart Jesuit Center in Los Gatos, California.
Sacred Heart is a former training school, where some of the abusive priests began their preparation for Jesuit life decades ago. The facility is hidden behind a hilltop winery, which also used to be owned by the Jesuits and was used to produce Communion wine. The order stopped its wine production in 1986 and the winery is now operated by a secular company." - Emily Schwing of NW News Network

On and on it goes, nothing at all changes. Already dozens more have been exposed for their crimes of pedophilia in the new locations, as more follow suit in the former.

"To invade, search out, capture, vanquish, and subdue all Saracens and pagans whatsoever, and other enemies of Christ wheresoever placed and to reduce their persons to perpetual slavery." - Papal Bull Romanus Pontifex, 1455

On February 3, 2023 (2-3-23), the Jesuit's interactive world map was launched. The map features 13 filters, providing information and geolocation data on each Jesuit social center.

"Father Sosa applauded the publication of the interactive map on the <u>eve of the Third International Day of Human Fraternity</u>, a day in which the UN recognizes the gesture of Pope Francis and the Grand Imam of Al-Azhar in signing the important <u>joint document on Human Fraternity</u>." - sjesjesuits.global

Remember what Fraternity really means? This, and the joining of Catholicism with Islam is one of the final moves in the agenda, as I will discuss in the next chapter. The Jesuit Conference of South Asia accounts for close to 25 percent of the whole Society and the majority of the 4,027 Jesuits were from India. Arturo Sosa spent 11 days visiting his Jesuit conferences and companions in Delhi, Jabalpur, Ambikapur and Raipur. His views are predictable. In interviews he never answers a question with any depth of thought or value but remains vague like a good elite. He is a Jesuit and has no free will of his own, no free thought. While openly claiming the devil does not exist and that archaeologically discovered and authenticated historical documents are unable to be proven real, his allegiance is clear. To sum up NovusOrdoWatch.org stated it best when they said:

"We have bad news for Mr. Sosa: We do know what Christ really said, and we also know what Sosa really said - lame excuses about "context" notwithstanding."

I will add another excerpt from Eric John Phelps' book wherein he exposes the Jesuits and writes a list of personal duties we each have. While he focuses on Americans alone, many of the points he makes apply to everyone, regardless of the country we live in. The Jesuits are everywhere and infecting everything, so I have condensed the principles laid out by him to give you the following call to Christians and non-Christians alike:

"We as God's people, having received the Lord Jesus Christ as our personal Savior according to His blessed Gospel, must repent of our personal and national sins. Then we must forsake them. Some of those sins are:
1. Permitting the army of the Black Pope, the Company of the Society of Jesus, to exist, mightily prosper and absolutely control the government of the US, through its Council on Foreign Relations, within our borders.
2. Believing the Jesuit-controlled American Press which has continually lied and deceived us throughout the 20th Century.
3. Permitting the Jesuits' Federal Reserve Banking System and United Nations to exist within our borders, as these two bodies have successfully destroyed popular liberty and the national sovereignty of every nation in the world pursuant to the purposes of the Jesuits' 'Holy Alliance'.
4. Waiving our 4th and 5th Amendment rights (secured by the Bill of

Rights at the insistence of the Baptists of Virginia and so dearly paid for with torrents of blood by our Protestant forefathers) through filing our confessions every April 14th, paying the heavy and progressive Communist income tax, thereby financing a multitude of sins.

5. Permitting the drafting, vaccinating, and sending of our sons abroad to fight the Pope's foreign wars, [such as the war in Vietnam, Serbia, Iraq, Afghanistan, Germany, Japan, et al.] resulting in the further destruction of American "liberals" and foreign "heretics" s condemned by Jesuits' Council of Trent.

6. Permitting the Jesuits in control of the government of the American Empire, to use our military and financial might to enthrone dictators around the world whose first allegiance is to Rome, thereby restoring the Temporal Power of the Jesuits' "infallible" Pope, returning the world to the Dark Ages.

7. Consenting to the Jesuits' Supreme Court decisions in removing the Protestant Bible and prayer from the bulwark of American liberty so hated by the Jesuits — the Public School System.

8. Consenting to the immigration of millions of Roman Catholics and pagan persons whose loyalty to the Pope or their own race, religion and nationality is greater than their loyalty to our Protestant Constitution and Republican form of government, thereby creating a multitude of agitations justifying more centralization of power in Washington DC.

9. Consenting to the Jesuits' Supreme Court's several decisions of forced integration resulting in the destruction of BOTH the white and black communities through amalgamation, as the exchange of viruses, bacteria, and parasites, unique to each, creates powerful combinations in the offspring producing a non-resistant, weak, and sterile population within 5 generations.

10. Consenting to the Jesuits' Supreme Court's decision of legalized abortion, resulting in the mass murder of unborn babies, polluting the land with innocent blood, ultimately collapsing the Ponzi Scheme called "the Social Security System" justifying mass murder of the elderly by the coming fascist dictator, "provoking the Lord against us, to consume us, until there be no remnant nor escaping in the land" by means of a massive military invasion composed of a coalition of nations, cleansing the land with the blood of unrepentant and unforgiven American murderers.

11. Consenting to the cattle brand of the Jesuits' Social Security Number as a means of identification to be used by their International Intelligence Community, begun by Hitler's SS at Dachau.

Remember, the Cult of Inanna (Semiramis) was quite large back in the Mesopotamian day spreading as Isis to the Egyptian Empire and continuing under many different names through history? To no one's surprise, androgynous and hermaphroditic men were heavily involved in the cult. The male priests took female names and lived as homosexuals. It has always been men who have pretended to be women, as they do today. It's just another way to disrespect and abuse females. Rituals to worship Inanna/Ishtar involved men dressing as women, dancing war dances, child sacrifice and rape, and practicing homosexual orgies. Inanna was the changer of Men to Women. We see her influence wide-spread and growing today. Sadly, we will bite the big gay bullet in chapters to come. Sex rituals took place between kings and priestesses. The symbols of Inanna include an eight-pointed star shown alongside the crescent moon, which was the symbol of Sin in Sumeria. The symbols of this cult have been used by the family who created it ever since: the Aldobrandini's. The same symbols are seen embroidered in gold, on the garments of the Pope and the rituals continue in all elite orders, at the highest levels if not lower.

Criton Zoakos of the Executive Intelligence Review published an article on November 27, 1979, called Jesuit Role Exposed in Third World Affairs. While it is very difficult to place only an excerpt of this, I will hope that you read the article in its entirety on your own. He states:

"That political faction is the ancient core of the European nobility, the Pallavicinis, the Sursoks, the Colonnas, the Hapsburgs, the Cecils, and others- who trace their family lineage to the gens Julia of Julius Caesar, to Aeneas of defeated Troy, or to the archpriests of the Isis cult in ancient Egypt. That political faction maintains power over a major part of the world's international financial institutions, a powerful grip over key raw materials holdings, and strategic control over numerous governments, such as the Belgian and Dutch thrones, the Grand Duchy of Luxembourg, key institutions of the Swiss government, most institutions of the British government, and international institutions, including the International Monetary Fund, the Bank for International Settlements, the United Nations Educational, Scientific, and Cultural Organization (UNESCO), the United Nations Institute for Training and Research (UNITAR), United Nations Committee on Trade and Development (UNCTAD), and the· World Council of Churches...

Only a few decades after its founding, the Societas Jesu succeeded in launching two basic types of social-control' techniques which defined European politics and history in the 17th and 18th centuries and, in renewed form, in the 19th and 20th centuries in a different way. These two basic techniques are: "intellectual projection movements" and left-wing "Jacobinism." The relative effectiveness of the "intellectual projection movement" technique of the Jesuits can best be viewed by examining the truth behind the so-called Enlightenment period of European history. The entirety of the Enlightenment was a Jesuit creation from beginning to end. Locke. Hobbes. Montesquieu. Rousseau. atheist Voltaire and even Rene Descartes were trained and launched by the Jesuits! Descartes was most likely assassinated by the Jesuits, as Voltaire insinuates, because he had broken out of their control despite the campaign of intimidation launched by his "friend," the Jesuit agent Mersenne...

The third major project of the Society, the launching of the Enlightenment, was a carbon copy of two historical precedents with which Jesuit insiders have always identified with great nostalgia: the Apollo cult's "sophist" movement in "golden age" Athens, launched as a counteroperation against the Ionian philosophic-scientific movement; and the earlier so-called Akhenaton (Amenhotep II) revolution in Egypt, which launched a fraudulent "sun-worship," "monotheistic" cult in order to smash the scientific technological revolution led by the priesthood of Amon.

The second principal Jesuit technique, "left-wing" Jacobinism, was also developed as a carbon copy· of earlier social-control precedents, such as Athenian democracy, which executed Socrates, and the Phrygian Orphic cults which were deployed against the Ionian city-states. As the Marquis de Lafayette informed George Washington, the Jacobin movement of the French Revolution was the controlled creation of the Societas Jesu. Father Pierre Teilhard de Chardin, SJ., probably the most "projected" Jesuit intellectual of the current century (after Karl Rahner, the friend of Avery Dulles, the Jesuit brother of the former CIA chief Allen Dulles) is more responsible than anyone else for a mass brainwashing form known as the "cult of the United Nations"."

Today the Aldobrandini family heads a branch of the Jesuits inner cult known as the Ninth Circle. Let's talk about this Jesuit cult for a moment, and the activities they practice. The Ninth Circle cult is a group most known for ritual human sacrifices, pedophilia, and cannibalism. Human trafficking supplies Elite rituals which demand human sacrifice and child rape. In every civilization throughout history there have been ritual human sacrifices. The Aztec priests sacrificed children regularly, as well as other victims, atop their pyramids which were crowned with altars. Armed with obsidian blades they would make an incision in the thin space between two vertebrae in the neck, decapitating the body. Next, the head was defleshed and the skull was used as decoration in their ossuaries. Such human skeleton decorations have been preserved in the Vatican Catacombs, French Catacombs, and thousands of others speckled across the world. As I have said...nothing changes. In Egypt child sacrifice of infants was also carried out and in Canaan children were boiled alive in the belly furnace of Moloch, the golden bull. This continued through the middle ages, and today. In 2020 a statue of Moloch was places in front of the Colosseum of Rome, a site of the human sacrifice of Christians. Carthaginians also sacrificed their own infants as offerings of thanks... In Mesopotamia (current days Turkey, Iraq, Kuwait, Syria, and Saudi Arabia) the same religious practices took place. Mass graves of sacrificed children have also been uncovered in Mayan Peru. These children had all had their hearts cut out of them in a ritual that took place in 1450. Today, in the US, Mormon groups have been exposed for their child ritual abuse and sacrifice. Ritual sacrifice is also seen to be on the rise in Uganda and in India children are sacrificed to Kali. On and on it goes as innocents is destroyed.

On April 7, 2014 Superior General Adolfo Pachon was charged, with many others, by the International Common Law Court of Justice in Brussels for participating in child rape and sacrifice rituals connected to the Jesuit Ninth Circle Satanic Cult. Over 48 witnesses came forward, to no avail. Pope Jorge Bergoglio and Archbishop of Canterbury Justin Welby are among those who have been charged many years ago for their activities including child trafficking, rape, and murder, as members of the Ninth Circle. Naturally, nothing has happened because of this, and neither experienced any discomfort. Dead and mutilated children were found in cold room containers by International Tribunal into Crimes of Church and State (ITCCS) teams and local police, after they disrupted Ninth Circle child sacrifice rites at Catholic facilities in Zwolle Holland, Dijon France, and Lucerne, Switzerland. There were 8 children rescued, all under age 6, and 19 cult members were arrested. One document obtained during the investigation was called The Magisterial Privilege (which has been removed even though it was filed into the ICLCJ Court record...) states that prior to taking office each new Pope participated in killing infants and drinking their blood.

"Forensic remains, evidence and records of murdered children evidently were ordered destroyed by Archbishop of Canterbury Justin Welby," - Kevin Annett of the ITCCS.

"The authorities are ignoring or colluding in a massive global child trafficking and killing network, so it now falls on every man and woman to protect the children of their communities. This arrest warrant allows common law peace officers and citizens the power to halt and detain anyone they know or even suspect has harmed or may harm children. The police are obligated to either assist the warrant holder or stand back and not interfere with the arrest. We have a list of known perpetrators in five countries, and they will be arrested."
— ITCCS official

As mentioned, the Ninth Circle Cult has been taken to court by many witnesses, but nothing happens. Children are sacrificed by Cardinals, Bishops, Princes, and Queens. They are sacrificed in Cathedrals, orphanages, and catacombs. This is the elite we have discussed. This is what they do in their spare time, dear reader. This is who runs your country and your religion. Let's get into it.

In 2008 a mass grave site containing child human remains was uncovered at the Mohawk School.

"According to the two witnesses all nine Ninth Circle Satanic Cult participants repeatedly raped, then murdered, disemboweled and dismembered the child, consumed her blood, burned the corpse and buried her remains directly west of the Mohawk School building." - Kevin Annett

On February 28, 2013, six international Common Law Court judges of the Brussels International Court found Queen Elizabeth, Prince Philip, Catholic Pope Joseph Ratzinger, and 37 other elites to be guilty of kidnapping and murdering 50,000 indigenous children in Canada. Other documented members of the Order are John Paul II, High Court Justice Judge Fulford, Prince Alfrink Bernhard, King Hendrick, Queen Beatrix and her father, Prince Johan Friso and his wife Mabel Wisse Smit, the top man of the Dutch army force and the present undersecretary of the Raad van State; officials of the Canadian, Australian, UK and US military and governments including the CIA, plus prominent government ministers, judges, politicians and businessmen of the US, Belgium, Holland, Canada, Australia, France, Ireland and UK.

"Cannibalism is a radical but realistic solution to the problem of overpopulation." — Prince Philip

Going back even further it is known that on Oct. 10, 1964, the Canadian Kamloops Indian Residential School children attended a picnic with Queen Elizabeth and Prince Philip who were seen leaving with 10 children of the school. The children, like so many others, were never seen again and were soon forgotten. 3 additional eyewitnesses confirmed child murders carried out during 1996 and 2000 in Oudergem, Belgium and Zwolle, Holland. In 2004 a witness described "a Catholic prelate" was the murderer of 3 juveniles in Holland, also stating:
"A criminal syndicate called 'The Octopus' provides the children by taking them from juvenile detention centers."

"I was there, I saw the whole thing. I was told they were kids from the juvenile detention centres in Brussels. They were let loose naked in the forest and hunted down and shot. The killers included Prince Friso of Holland and his wife's friend, the billionaire George Soros, Dutch Prime Minister Mark Rutte, and Prince Albert of Belgium. After they shot down the young ones they cut off the boys' penises and held them up like trophies, cheering and applauding." — Dutch Lawyer called Josephine to protect her identity

Regarding the mass grave of over 800 decapitated children uncovered at a Catholic orphanage in Tuam Ireland, Ireland's police force, Garda, testified before the ICLCJ Court stating:
"The forensic people have told us that the configuration of the remains and evidence of continual decapitation and dismemberment resemble the usual signs of ritualistic murder."

Catholic orphanages have a long and well documented history of poisoning children, or killing them off in other ways, giving various excuses. In 2014, five Judges of the International Common Law Court of Justice in Brussels judged evidence on over thousands of missing Canadian, US, Argentine and European children who were victims of an international child sacrificial cult referred to by the court as the Ninth Circle. Lakefield College School in Canada also has reports of pedophilia perpetrated by Catholic priest Keith Gleed. Over 34 child mass grave sites were identified in Ireland, Spain, and Canada and all have been refused excavation by the Canadian Government, Crown of England, and Roman Catholic Church. The elite make laws that keep you trapped and them free. One investigation of an Irish Catholic nunnery (like all monasteries and convents the inhabitants are encouraged into pedophilia and homosexuality — which is the purpose of them) revealed 796 children's bodies who had been sacrificed. These babies had been decapitated and dismembered by people in robes.

The prosecutor stated to the jury:
"The plan was born of a **twisted** notion to derive **spiritual power from the lifeblood** of the innocent, thereby assuring political stability of the Papacy in Rome. These acts are not only genocidal but **systemic** and **institutionalized** in nature. Since at least 1773, they appear to have been performed by the **Roman Catholic Church, Jesuits, and every Pope**."

"During some renovations to a room annexed to the Apostolic Nunciature in Italy, situated in Rome, Via Po n.27, some human bone fragments were found." - Press Office of the Holy See 2018

It is not uncommon for children to go missing in Rome, especially. The citizens know who takes them and what happens to them, so little is said or done about it anymore and people do not stand and fight but roll over and choose to become complacent. Children go missing all the time, right? In the US they sure do. 750,000 children go missing in the US alone, every year. And you thought when I mentioned 80 million disappeared children per year it was a stretch, didn't you. Babies "die" after or during birth in hospitals, right? Wonder why?! I worked in a hospital for many years, which was considered to have the highest "successful birth" rate in the state. The big success was that **only 1 out of every 3** babies born there "didn't make it". I was the one in charge of taking bodies to the morgue and in my years there, I only took one dead baby to the freezer. This alone should outrage enough mothers around the world to create a revolution of such magnitude that it could never be stopped. But mothers have been indoctrinated into child murder for decades, abortion is no longer shocking. The other babies were taken for purposes mentioned above. Hospitals are the most unsafe place to have a child, among other things.

If you still don't understand the magnitude of this, all you need to do is look up how many children go missing each year in Italy or in any country or state. Keep in mind in the US and other places they purposely do not list them in one place, you must look through county, state, district listings to total numbers. The witnesses have proven who they themselves saw at these sacrifices, drinking the blood of dead babies after torturing and mutilating them which involves but is in no way limited to peeling the skin off one layer at a time over the entire body, until everything underneath can be seen. This method was expertly depicted in the French horror film Martyr should any of you wish to see what it is like.

Peter Alexander Chernoff confessed to the Police he had kidnapped Kevin Collins, aged 10, to be sacrificed by the cult of the Bohemian Grove. He testified that the Satanic ritual involved 9 participants and 9 knives. Kevin Collins was snatched off the streets of San Francisco and sacrificed as he lay, strapped down, on the table. As Kevin lay there, feeling utterly neglected and unloved, the 9 blades were pushed up through him. The murderers were: Willy Brown, Arlin Spector, Barney Frank, Roger Mahoney (LA cardinal), Pope Ratzinger, Robert Bird, George Bush Senior, Warren Buffett and the Master of Ceremonies, Michael Aquino. Another Order founded by Jesuit Victor Drevon and baron Alexis de Sarachaga, is called Hiéron du Val d'Or (meaning "Sanctuary of the Golden Valley"). Formed in 1873, the cult still practices mystic, esoteric, Islamic, and New Age ideologies. One leader, Paul Le Cour, became a precursor to the New Age movement, with his 1937 writing, The Age of Aquarius.

The elite push to make their corruption normal and accepted by an open society again. We have seen exponentially increased Luciferian activity over the past 10 years alone. In Tokyo, Japan a restaurant named: The Resoto ototo no shoku ryohin, which means "Edible Brother", promotes cannibalism, and serves human flesh. Remember the diseases caused by cannibalism? One solid example, for those who don't know what to look for, can be seen in photos of the original Hillary Clinton, who can be seen with holes in her tongue. The British company

"HumanLeather.co.uk" boasts about their "exclusive real human leather products" online stating:

"All products are carefully hand-crafted by experienced master craftsmen, with YEARS of experience in handling the finest leather known - human leather."

We see it more and more in movies and TV shows, programming you to feel Cannibalism is normal and acceptable, just like Pedophilia and homosexuality. Both are defined as sexual perversions and mental disorders meaning they are unnatural — not normal and able to be cured. While mental disorders can be easily resolved, as they all stem from hormonal imbalances, the sick are not cared for and healed but rather exalted while their disorders are spread to others through indoctrination.

Every country has experienced the same degradation provided by the Jesuits who practice these rituals frequently. Every person alive today is responsible for this, just as those who ignored them and remained complacent in the past are also accountable. What are you going to do to change it, dear reader? Will you continue to allow your fellow man, your brothers and sisters, your children, your parents, and friends, to be deceived, controlled, poisoned, killed, raped, and ritualized to satisfy the never-filled lusts of the elite? The decision is yours. The choices you make each day in every action are yours. This brings us to the next order under control of the Jesuits: The Vatican.

"He who thinks he knows the Jesuits by having read all the books that were written in the past centure to unmask them, would be grossly deceived. The Jesuitism of that day was an **open war against the Gospel and society**; the Jesuitism of the present is a slow but contagious and deadly disease, which secretly insinuates itself; it is a poison taken under the name of medicine." — Luigi Desanctis 1808-1986

~Beneath the Dirty Robes~

The White Pope is the puppet ruler of the Vatican, one of the palaces on the 7 hills. In Latin Vatican is Vaticano meaning Warning. The Etruscan's, who inhabited and controlled the region of the Roman Empire before the Romans were named, worshipped Vatika, goddess of the underworld. As evidenced in the symbolism used by the Vatican, they are sun worshippers. To recap, the White Pope controls the people of the world through its rulers and religion but is controlled himself by the Black Pope who in turn is controlled by the Grey Pope. The Grey Pope must be of the Upper Elite bloodlines and is selected by the leading five families and their master. The Greys elect two popes: a black and a white in a ceremony called the Arcana Arcanorum Rite of Atlantis. Both of the popes we see today are part of the Synagogue of Satan currently named the Society of Jesus. The bloodlines exposed in Part II are all involved in these groups. Last chapter closed with a brief discussion about the Ninth Circle, a cult of which Pope Francis is a member. Let's begin this chapter with a look under the dirty robes of the Great White Pope.

Jorge Mario Bergoglio was allowed to enter this world on December 17, 1936. He's brought with him corruption, evil and death. As the mainstream story goes, he was on his way to propose to his girlfriend, when he stopped in the church for confession and had an "epiphany", commonly known as a tap on the shoulder by men in black dresses. He decided that day to become a priest and in 1958 Jorge became an official Jesuit.

In the 1970's Jorge was a Superior of the Society of Jesus of Argentina. He has murdered, raped, and tortured children, women, and men. This is reminiscent of every pope's personal background. Pope Francis assisted the government structure that trafficked over 30,000 children during the Dirty War. We know of two survivors. So, who did he work with?

In January 1945 Grand Master Joseph Mengele and a few others left Germany while Adolf Hitler escaped Berlin using a suicide cover story. Admiral Doenitz took command upon the announcement of his death. Submarines U-530, U-977 and others began a secret journey from Norway soon after. Two months later, the submarines were surrendered in Mar del Plata, Argentina, after allegedly being lost from the submarine convoy enroute to Antarctica. General Gehlen, head of Nazi Intelligence was captured by US Army and flown to Washington; other Nazi and British agents were imported to the US, along with Werner Von Braun and other developers of the V-2 rockets. As soon as the Nazis had been transferred to Argentina, they began more false flags, spread by the media, to create division and uprising from the citizens just like those seen in recent years called Black Lives Matter (more). During this time the Propaganda machines worked overtime to not only insist that 6 million Jews were murdered, but ignite the A-bomb scare, as previously discussed. Remember from 1941 to 1945, the Roman Catholic Ustashi in Croatia, butchered Serbian Orthodox Christians in a genocide overseen by Jesuits Aloysius Stepinac and Ivan Saric while just a short time later Jesuit Jorge Bergoglio led the death squads in Argentina, while at the same time Arturo Sosa did the same in Venezuela.

After the Pope's Second Thirty Years' War from 1914-1945 NATO was founded, uniting the European and western world. NATO is run exclusively by the US, like the UN and CIA, who controls every SS of the world. Every country involved and occupied by NATO are subjects to the Pope. To expand on NATO for a brief moment, in 1949, Asia was brought under the same control, after a series of planned protests and propaganda smears. CFR's George C. Marshall and Dean Acheson facilitated the successful communist revolution in 1949 while US President Harry Truman issued the Second Emergency War Powers edict in 1950, which is still in effect with President FDR's edict of 1933. The Korean War, which was America's first war without a congressional declaration of war, was launched and has changed since. Thales-Raytheon Systems provides NATO with Integrated Air and Missile Command and Control Systems, which cover NATO's territorial space, including 15 European countries. As of 2021 there are around 750 NATO bases in at least 80 countries. But back to the Nazi's.

In Chile, another Nazi who had been relocated to South America was notorious pedophile Paul Shaeffer. He opened a commune in 1961 called Colonia Dignidad where he was able to rape all the children he wanted to. He also conspired with military dictator Augusto Pinochet who used his secluded commune as a torture base. In 2005, after fleeing to Argentina, he was arrested for his violations and died in prison.

> "Even later, when Colonia Dignidad was dissolved and the people were no longer subjected to the daily torture, the service lacked the determination and transparency to identify its responsibilities and to draw lessons from it." -Foreign Minister Frank-Walter Steinmeier

Draw lessons from it...like, don't torture others? Lessons, as the elite call them, are never learned and change nothing. Just another pacification technique.

Walter Schreiber arrived in Argentina in 1952 after being extracted with 9,000 other Nazis in the Jesuit's Operation Paperclip. ID changes for all 9,000 were supplied by the Vatican. Walter met up with all his old friends, including Fritz Hollmann, Peter Hochbichler (CIA), George Hunter White (known as Mr. White),

Sid Gottlieb, Dr. Joseph Mengele (known as Mr. Black, Dr. Green, Father Joseph, Vaterchen, and others) and made new friends, including Jorge Mario Bergoglio who was playing with his chemistry set at the time. Jorge lived in the same town as these men. CIA agents frequented them as well as MOSSAD agents Isser Harel, Shimon Ben Aharon and others who had resided in Argentina since April 1960. Adolf Eichmann (known in Argentina as Ricardo Klement) was in Buenos Aires, being kept "safe" by CIA. Joseph Mengele was the doctor who took care of many elite sterilizations, including the sterilization of Stanley Ann Dunham who was the poster mom for Barry Obama. In 1956 until 1958 CIA agent Stanley Ann Dunham, daughter of CIA agent Stanley Dunham, moved to Buenos Aires to have tests done on her by Mengele, to be prepped for "service", as documents state. She was then put in place at the Hawaii University to pick up her next assignment, her adoptive son who is said to have been born Barry Mohammed Soebarkah on March 7, 1960.

President Juan Peron was murdered in 1974 so his wife could take over and begin mass slaughter. Henry Kissinger was America's Secretary of State at this time and urged the Argentinian regime "to act" before Congress resumed session. He reassured the regime that Washington would not cause it "unnecessary difficulties".

Rita Arditti describes, in her book Searching for Life, the abuses of power of the leaders of the Argentine Catholic Church. She also details the set patterns for the disappearances, tortures, and murders, including vivid descriptions of the tortures, such as the torturing of children in front of their parents, torturing of unborn children inside of pregnant women, and inciting guard dogs to attack them. Jorge Mario Bergoglio was a torturer and like all Jesuits was publicly the protector of the people, while he used his influence and position to funnel them to the Nazis and participate in their senseless tortures. The disappearances of Argentina during this time were nothing more than sadistic fun for the elite. These people were kidnapped and tortured for no reason whatsoever. Just for the fun of it.

In his spare time, when he wasn't preaching a sermon to the public or advertising peace in a political speech, or kidnapping and raping the multitudes, he was trafficking them. The Jesuits keep extremely detailed records and lists of **all** of the people they kidnap, torture and murder. They always have. Data has always been one of the primary focuses of the elite. They like to watch. The records from the camps in Germany were not recovered because, like all of their lists and notes on everyone in the world, they were locked in the Vatican archives and select Jesuit strongholds like the one in Buenos Aires. In 2005 a human rights lawyer accused Jorge of kidnapping and torturing two priests, Orlando Yorio and Francisco Jalics, in 1976. A lawyer filed a suit against him regarding this issue. They were kidnapped and tortured because their consciences couldn't handle the strain of their crimes. The pair had left their churches and went to live with the population in the poor towns, which are called Villas Miserias! (Miserandos) Meaning: Misery Towns.

Remember this keyword and its importance to Jorge as we continue. The priests were tortured, but found alive five months later, drugged, and semi-naked. Yorio accused Jorge Bergoglio of effectively handing them over to the death squads by declining to tell the regime that he endorsed their work.

Deputy Education Minister Emilio Mignone spoke out regarding Jorge Bergoglio's involvement in the disappearance of his daughter Monica. She worked in the ghettos of Buenos Aires and was kidnapped in 1976, the same week that Priests Orlando and Francisco were taken. Jorge Bergoglio had spread rumors that Orlando Yorio and Francisco Jalics were communists and subversives. While the priests were being tortured Jorge made feeble attempts to have them treated less harsh, which were obviously to save face. At the same time, he continued spreading rumors about them which he knew would lead to their deaths. Apart from the testimonies of so many who witnessed Jorge's involvement, it is also documented and confirmed by multiple documents including one written by Jorge Bergoglio himself, on Society of Jesus stationary, dated 1979. Yorio who died in 2000, said in a 1999 interview that he believed that Jorge did nothing "to free us, in fact just the opposite". Francisco Jalics moved to a monastery in Germany and refused to discuss it after being threatened into silence. Naturally, Jorge denied the claim, ignoring the multitude of charges for his war crimes. The reason the charges came up was because the priests were the only ones who survived the hands of Jorge Bergoglio.

Argentinian Navy Captain, Adolfo Scilingo, testified to how dissidents were killed, as recorded in The Flight, by author Horacio Verbitsky:
"...by being thrown into the sea while still alive. Scilingo said this method had been approved by the Church hierarchy because they considered it a Christian form of death."

Documents also prove that Jorge Bergoglio was involved in the abduction of 500 newborns. The children of pregnant women, born in the torture chambers, were delivered to loyal supporters and aristocrats of the Junta, to be raised as their own. Many still have no idea of their true parentage. Many still protest this as those who survived and knew about the babies to be born, wish for their return just as strongly as they wish for justice to be served on the Nuns and Priests who live openly without facing any consequences for their actions.

Estela de la Cuadra is one such protester. Her pregnant sister, Elena, was taken in early 1977 and gave birth during her imprisonment to a daughter, Ana. She lost a total of 5 family members during the military dictatorship and has asked for records so she may find out what happened to them. Pope Francis has ignored her requests and "in the 2011 court hearing into the cases of missing children, he was asked if the Church had ever held or was, at the time, currently holding, a commission of enquiry

into these matters."
He responded with indifference, feigning ignorance as the elite always do:

"I don't know if the hierarchy had such a body during the military dictatorship. It's possible that a lay group of the faithful of a religious congregation set something like that up or is currently doing it. I don't know."

As the leader of the largest diocese in Argentina, Buenos Aires, he didn't know what the structure was at that time and had never heard of any abuse? Not even slightly believable.

One of the survivors' family members stated in an interview about Jorge which was obviously set up to show "solidarity": (The question was about if they thought he would do well in the Vatican.)

"Because Bergoglio thrives on power, I really doubt that the Roman Curia can step all over him like they did to Pope Benedict XVI. In that regard, the former pope proved to have no skill whatsoever to handle power, no executive skills. So, I think Bergoglio is going to handle the power much better, and to the eyes of society and the Christian community he may also show a more humble and austere side of the Church...he has attitudes close to the poor, but I don't think it's a "liberate them" attitude."

Surely, he was paid enough for that response to pay his next months' rent. In 1992 Jorge Bergoglio was named auxiliary bishop of Buenos Aires to prepare him for the launch to the Vatican. By 2001 he was made Cardinal. Jorge played a decisive role in Argentina's most famous abuse case by commissioning a four-volume, 2,000-plus page forensic study against a convicted priest that concluded he was innocent and that his rape victims were lying and that the case should have never gone to trial. Despite the study, Argentina's Supreme Court, in 2017, upheld the conviction and 15-year prison sentence for the Rev. Giulio Grassi, a celebrity priest who ran homes for street children across Argentina now works at Don Basco School in Solis and Moreno, after being relocated there once he was found out to be a violent pedophile. The Argentine Network of Survivors of Ecclesiastical Sexual Abuses contains more than a hundred victims whose abusers have been protected diligently by Jorge Bergoglio. He has protected pedophiles across the world, stating clearly to the world that these "untouchable" pedophile priests, are doing their master's work. Also in 2017, Argentinian Bishop Gustavo Zanchetta was charged with inappropriate behavior with seminarians and having homosexual pornography on his cellphone. As one would expect, he remained in place as bishop of the northern Argentine diocese of Oran until 2017, when he resigned suddenly, only to be given a top job at the Vatican by Jorge, his confessor. In the same year, Luigi Capozzi, the secretary for Cardinal Francesco Coccopalmerio, was arrested in his Vatican apartment for cocaine abuse and homosexual orgies.

Because Luciferianism is about inverting the law of the Living God, homosexuality and pedophilia are acceptable sexual acts while natural intercourse as created by the Living God to produce life, is rejected, violently. One example of this is the monastery situation which actively nurtures the homosexual lifestyle and environment of pedophilia for male and female sects. Another example of this is seen in the 1600's, when the Vatican banned women from singing in church choirs. The man-centric, woman-hating cult used this as an excuse to castrate prepubescent children (always boys, of course) so they would retain the high-pitched voices that Catholic boys' choirs are notorious for. The children suffered the horrendous, life-long health effects of losing one's hormones, like any hormone imbalance, including bone, muscle, and mental problems. Once they reached a certain age they were thrown out of their famous lifestyles as Church puppets, and spent their lives in poverty, and sickness.

During Jorge's time as a leader of the Buenos Aires diocese, more than 100 priests there were reported for pedophilia among other things, as is documented by the Courts and the Church and stored in Vatican records. The Pope is well known for ignoring the requests of the abused, as the website Bishop-accountability records:

"In addition to Bergoglio's failure to respond to victims, the public record contains no evidence that he released any information about abusers. In fact, he denied that the problem existed in his archdiocese."

"We have examined news and court archives to identify nearly 100 clergy in Argentina publicly accused of sexually abusing minors and vulnerable adults. Most of these cases involve alleged abuse that occurred in the last 20 years; the online public record contains very little information about clergy sexual abuse in Argentina before 1995." — Bishop-Accountability.org

Angel Tarcisio Acosta was sentenced in 1986 for the corruption and abuse of children at his place of work, the Salesian Institute, Instituto Religioso Pío XI. In this rare instance, he spent 18 years in prison. Ricardo Giménez was also imprisoned in 1996 for child molestation but was released the following year. He is known to have molested up to 20 children. Again, these numbers are always far lower than the reality as children do not come forward and when they finally do, they are ignored. Children don't come forward for many reasons, the main being that children are hardwired to trust the adults in their life to protect them. When that is so severely and violently betrayed the mind, due to trauma, splits. This split is such a shock, it causes the system to shut down completely. It's as if the white static fuzz one can find on TV stations or hear on the radio at times, consumes the entire body: the brain is unable to process, think or react, the body freezes and can't respond to what the mind wants it to do, and the child is left entirely helpless and struck with this feeling and reaction for life. This is trauma. This is how Mind Control is performed and perfected. Pedophiles know this, and use it, knowing that whatever they do the likelihood of the child saying anything about it is so low it's not worth worrying about. In addition, victims like those of priest Fernando Enrique Picciochi, are paid for their silence. Fernando, who was under the direction of Jorge Bergoglio like the rest at this time, was relocated to the US to continue his good work.

Among the priests who raped and abused small children is Daniel Omar Acevedo, Jose Carlos Aguilera, Luis Anguita, Nestor Aramayo who raped the children he was a confessor to, Francisco Jose Armendariz who became known for his pedophilia upon the birth of his daughter, whose mother was still a child herself. Walter Eduardo Avanzini was caught on camera paying children for sex but was transferred from his position in the Instituto Parroquial to work for the Ministry of Education. Ricardo Giménez, Isaac Gómez, Humberto González, Cristian Gramlich, Julio César Grassi, Juan De Dios Gutiérrez, Alfredo Nicola, Moisés Pachado, Alicia Pacheco Sr., Miguel Ángel Santurio, Mario Napoleón Sasso, Jorge Scaramellini Guerrero, Luis Eduardo Sierra, Bishop Abelardo Silva, Juan José Urrutia, Aníbal Valenzuela, and Gustavo Óscar Zanchetta are just a handful of the hundreds of Argentinian priests and bishops who have been exposed for the pedophiles they are. The number of Catholic rapists and pedophiles grows considerably when looking at them on a global scale. It's difficult to find those who are not corrupted and perverted in this way. The exposure of their deeds doesn't stop them in their work, they are merely transferred and allowed to continue.

"Daniel Pittet was 8 years old in 1968 when the priest abused him, and it took him four years before he could find the courage to tell anyone. The priest was then moved from Switzerland to France, where he abused other children. Now 57 and married with six children, Mr. Pittet met his abuser last year, and he recalls that the priest 'was frightened, and looked at him but never asked forgiveness. He didn't seem to repent of the evil he had done.'" — Gerard O'Connell of American Magazine

"'A single case of abuse is intolerable,' said the bishops, while rejecting estimates of as many as 440,000 victims of clerical sexual abuse in Spain." — Bishop-Accountability.org

In 2007 the Archdiocese of Los Angeles released Personnel Files of priests who were exposed and taken to court for their rape of children. This only contained 124 files of redacted names and positions, while the Church claimed transparency.

In 2010, Argentina legalized gay marriage and Bergoglio described the new law and gay adoption as:
"a scheme to destroy God's plan...a real and dire anthropological throwback... a move by the father of lies to confuse and deceive the children of

God."

On March 13, 2013, Jorge was elected by the Jesuits as the new White Pope. As soon as he was made Pope, his scripted tune of tolerance and acceptance of all was parroted to the people. He dismissed his past thoughts and statements by saying:
"Who am I to judge?"

Funny, according to the Church, he is god on earth and the only one allowed and expected to judge. His "motto" is "Miserando atque Eligendo". This is the middle of a sentence in the Bible which directly translates to "pity and choosing" coming from a story where Jesus had pity (compassion) on a man, choosing him to be a disciple. Miserando means miserable or pitiful. Jorge related to the public that this meant "lowly but chosen" and states it represents himself, the ever humble and lowly superior being, crowned in gold taken from the murdered and clothed in white to cover his blood-soaked soul.

The Motu Propria, which means "of his own accord", is an official law written and signed by the White Pope without council or advice or co-signatures or approval. The law is instantly implemented and can be created anytime the pope himself "deems sufficient". This law is above ALL laws on Earth. It carries more power than anything issued by the United Nations, Inner Temple, Middle Temple, the Crown of Great Britain, any Monarch, and any head of state. The Motu Propria issued by Pope Francis on July 11, 2013 just 3 months after his rise to Pope, states:
"In our times, the common good is increasingly threatened by <u>transnational organized crime</u>, the improper use of the markets and of the **economy**, as well as by <u>terrorism</u>. It is therefore necessary for the international community [One World Order] to adopt adequate legal instruments to prevent and counter criminal activities, by promoting international judicial cooperation [Global One World Police] on criminal matters. In ratifying numerous international conventions in these areas, and acting also on behalf of Vatican City State, the Holy See has constantly maintained that such agreements are effective means to prevent criminal activities that threaten human dignity, the common good and peace."

Notice in the second sentence, after stating the problem, he gives a commanded solution and how to carry out that solution. Don't get distracted by fancy and lovely sounding words. He has just declared martial law on the world. Since Jorge imposed Vatican martial law in 2013, the entire world has been legally and publicly known to be governed by the Vatican as a police state. All independent (sovereign) countries' policies and agreements on criminal justice were dissolved with this law, giving the Pope the right to crucify any heretic he wishes.

Remember, in the 1900's the Jesuits succeeded in their control over all the world with the implementation of personal numbers, barcodes and data assigned to each human born, making them a product of the Vatican.

"The Vatican created a world trust using the birth certificate to capture the value of each individual's future productive energy. Each state, province, and country in the fiat monetary system, contributes their people's value to this world trust identified by the SS, SIN or EIN numbers (for example) maintained in the Vatican registry. Corporations worldwide (individuals became corporate fictions through their birth certificate) are connected to the Vatican through law (Vatican to Crown to BAR to laws to judge to people) and through money (Vatican birth accounts value to IMF to Treasury (Federal Reserve) to banks to people (loans) to judges (administration) and sheriffs (confiscation)." — Gold Shield Alliance

Thanks to Google and social media spy machines, they have even more: your thoughts. They have owned you all since birth and now they can throw you away just as easily as an old shoe. In October 2011 the Vatican suggested one bank, run by a global entity. This has been in existence since the Roman Empire switched to the Vatican, but the public has been kept oblivious, and must be brought to light now that the time is right. In this declaration the Vatican called for all countries to cede their sovereign powers. This is one of the agendas discussed in the UN chapter, as they were instrumental in this plan. The Vatican has large investments with the Rothschilds who have become the Vatican's Treasury holders. Other large investments from the Vatican include those with the Hambros bank, Credit Suisse, Morgan, Chase, First International, Banker's Trust Co, and many more. In 2012 Sicilian Godfather Mateo Messina Denaro and Father Ninni Treppiedi were named as 2 of the men involved in the Vatican Bank's laundering of mafia money totaling millions of Euros since 2007. The Vatican has shares in Gulf Oil, Shell, General Motors, Bethlehem Steel, General Electric, International Business machines, TWA, to name a very few. It is the largest shareholder of the Beretta Arms Company.

During the crusades, which will be discussed in the next chapters, the Vatican grew and captured most of the gold in circulation. Being as their main goal is to destroy the world slowly, they desire and work towards a world of poverty. If the same amount of money was in circulation, there would be no level of poverty. Now do you understand why the elite claim to love the poor? The poor who only exist because of them? The elite are masters at taking money out of your hands through "economy collapse" and "war". The puppets and slaves of the Vatican: People, Kings, Queens, Presidents, all give tithes and extravagant gifts to the Vatican regularly. Rare works of art, jewels, gold, and more are given to the Vatican and locked away. Saved for the elite alone. In 2018 President Erdogan gave Pope Francis a medallion of an angel upon his visit. The Palestinian leader once gave Pope Francis a set of pearl white Stations of the Cross. The pontiff had them installed in the Chapel of the Vatican Hall where the Synod of Bishops meets.

Jorge Bergoglio's sister, Maria describes him by saying:

"Personally, he's got a strong character, and he's also got a deep belief in his convictions that's unbreakable. Nobody is going to be able to force him to compromise on what he believes in."

In one of her interviews, she goes on to answer why she wanted Cardinal Odilo Pedro Scherer to be chosen:

"I've always liked him. He's for the poor. It wasn't based on any really deep analysis, but it always seemed to me that in his pastoral work he chose the poor."

Meanwhile Jorge was sold to the public as being concerned about the poor…like every other pope. When he was Archbishop of Buenos Aires, he did not live in the palatial Archbishop's residence but instead lived in a Spartan apartment, which hails his Spartan bloodline.

March 2, 2013, an anonymous cardinal (anonymous in order to stay alive) commented on Jorge as Pope saying:

"Four years of Bergoglio would be enough to **change** things."

The Popes coat of arms depicts gold and silver keys and various Jesuit symbols including the sun, 3 nails, the triangular papal crown, a 6-pointed star, iron crosses, and what looks like the bud of a marijuana plant but is said to be a spikenard flower, which is used in wine, as an anointing oil, and more. It represents the saint of the Universal Church. Upon his selection to become the public leader of the Catholic Church in March 2013, he had to choose a new name, like all others before him. Unlike others he decided to become the first Francis, taking the name of Francis of Assisi. Remember him? Jorge told reporters he did so because St. Francis is:

"the man of **poverty**, the man of **peace**, the man who loves and protects creation. How I would like a church that is **poor** and that is for the **poor**!"

This is conflicting with another statement he made claiming that he chose the name upon remembering something Cardinal Cláudio Hummes said to him when he was elected:

"Don't forget the **poor**."

Needing constant reminder to do so, he chose the name of Francis. The last "vision" of St. Francis of Assisi has been labeled a prophecy by the Church. As you know full well by now, the elites have written down many of their agendas. St. Francis was born Giovanni di Bernardone in 1181. His last words were another rewording of ancient prophecy of the End Times:

"The time is fast approaching in which there will be great trials and afflictions; perplexities and dissensions, both spiritual and temporal, will abound; the charity of many will grow cold, and the malice of the wicked will increase. The <u>devils will have unusual power, the immaculate purity of our Order</u>, and of others will be so much obscured that there will be <u>very few Christians who will obey the true Sovereign Pontiff and the Roman Church</u> with loyal hearts and perfect charity.

At the time of this tribulation <u>a man, not canonically elected, will be raised to the Pontificate</u>, who, by his cunning, will endeavor to draw many into error and death. Then scandals will be multiplied, <u>our Order will be divided</u>, and many others will be entirely destroyed, because they will consent to error instead of opposing it. There will be such diversity of opinions and schisms among the people, the religious and the clergy, that, except those days were shortened, according to the words of the Gospel, even the elect would be led into error, were they not specially guided, amid such great confusion, by the immense mercy of God.

Then <u>our Rule and manner of life will be violently opposed</u> by some, and terrible trials will come upon us. Those who are found faithful will receive the crown of life; but woe to those who, trusting solely in their Order, shall fall into tepidity, for they will not be able to support the temptations permitted for the proving of the elect. <u>Those who preserve in their fervour and adhere to virtue with love and zeal for the truth, will suffer injuries and, persecutions</u> as rebels and schismatics; for <u>their persecutors, urged on by the evil spirits, will say they are rendering a great service to God</u> by destroying such pestilent men from the face of the earth. But the Lord will be the refuge of the afflicted and will save all who trust in Him.

And in order to be like their Head, these, the elect, will act with confidence, and <u>by their death</u> will purchase for themselves eternal life; choosing to obey God rather than man, they will fear nothing, and they will prefer to perish rather than consent to falsehood and perfidy. Some preachers will keep silent about the truth, and others will trample it under foot and deny it. <u>Sanctity of life will be held in derision</u> even by those who outwardly profess it, for in those days Jesus Christ will send them not a true pastor, but a destroyer."

As always, this sentiment has been repeated by the elite throughout history. They know the truth and the prophecies better than most who study them. However, they are deceived by their own pride into believing they will be the ones who win and rule the physical world in the end. Remember back to 1922 and the Bailey's? According to Alice A. Bailey, Lord Sanat Kumara (a demon) conducts business in an enormous room in his palace (the Vatican) called The Council Chamber of the Lord of the World. The Lord of the World is another title for Satan. The Lord of the World is also the book Pope Francis has recommended everyone read. The book opens with two priests, the elderly Father Percy Franklin and the younger Father John Francis. The book "predicts" the last pope will have a short papacy, and no real belief in God, just as Jorge has often claimed. Francis turns into the anti-christ, an exact mirror of St. Francis' words. The two popes coexist, which is only possible when a true Pope resigns but remains a pope ad sempiternam, meaning: by all means, at all times, in all places, eternal, and an uncanonically elected cardinal is chosen by a papal conclave. Pope Francis in today's time has "predicted" his papacy will be short and has told us many times. Does that mean he is to be the pope ad sempiternam?

January 26, 2016, the White Pope, and top political and economic international leaders met in a meeting of the Knights of Malta. Jorge delivered his speech on the New World Order and addressed healing the planet by dissolving the world economy. The Laudato Si he has given was implemented and the Vatican called for the dissolution of the United States, United Nations, Federal Reserve, and much more through a constant spray of letters written by Vatican's spokesman, Joseph Ray Sundarsson. One such note of Joseph's states:

"The purpose of this letter is to initiate the peaceful dissolution of the corporate 'United States', a judicial entity that has no life force of its own, modeled on the Islamic Sultan, and its replacement with living men and women who are masters of their destiny, servants of all people and become beloved of YHVH, Our Father, the blessed One who has Mercy with His world."

The Global Settlement Foundation has a cryptographically "secured" electronic currency in place. One world currency waiting on the nod from the White Pope. The last attempt to stop this was carried out in 1933 by whistle blower Major General Smedley Butler, USMC. Congress at the time had enough power to put a halt to the entire process. Today, it has no power at all. March 4, 1939, President Roosevelt states in a secret committee:

"I am making no concessions to business, or for relief. I have a military machine sufficient to stop any organized revolt. I am putting MY PEOPLE ahead of all instruments. I'll have had a full understanding with Chamberlain, and we will destroy this unemployed condition with a WAR, and a WAR only. To Hell with the American people, as far as a Democracy is concerned. It does not exist. It never did, and we will never let it happen that way. I am going to crush business, infest America with all the aliens possible, and in the last analysis, declare Martial Law, and confiscate everything I need for a true and forceful Dictatorship. My New Deal is a failure, and I know it, but no one else will tell me that I must discontinue my present activities, and program."

The instruments mentioned are All American Citizens. By 'Infest America with

Aliens', he means weaponized immigration, which was planned for over a century and finally carried out in the last decade. President Roosevelt and Churchill, puppets of the elite Jesuits, carried out a planned war after they bombed themselves at Pearl Harbor, put hundreds of thousands of Asians in America into FEMA concentration camps and had every intention of creating a mass immigration to destabilize and destroy every economy in Europe and America, leading to the One World Order. Because there was still enough power in Congress, because people stood up for what was right, the plan was destroyed. As always, the Jesuits laid low, erased history, and started again. The perfectly groomed dictator Barack Obama successfully carried out the plan. He released his first statement accusing the CIA's militant Islamic group called ISIS of committing genocide against religious minorities. In the detailed list of groups recognized as victims, Christians were not included. Father Behnam Benoka, an Iraqi priest, sent a detailed letter to Pope Francis regarding the horrors Mideast Christians were experiencing.

"He [Pope Francis] called me. He told me certainly, sure I am with you, I won't forget you... I will make all possible to help you." — Behnam Benoka

However, that September, Pope Francis stood before the world at the United Nations where his energy was, once again, spent on defending the environment. In his speech which lasted nearly 50 minutes, only once did Francis make reference to persecuted Christians - and even then, they did not receive special attention but, in the same breath, their sufferings were merged with the "equal sufferings of members of the majority religion" that is, Sunni Muslims (the only group not to be attacked by ISIS, a Sunni organization). But I digress. Let's get back to the timeline.

After accusations whistleblower Natacha Jaitt made in early 2018 that dozens of high-profile sports, entertainment personalities, journalists, and other elite, in Argentina were involved in child prostitution, including Gustavo Vera, a close friend of Jorge Bergoglio. Natacha tweeted in October 2018 that Vera was Pope Francis' "accomplice." She wrote:

"Justo Gustavo Vera is a pimp, sex-trafficker, and accomplice of the Pope and, as I predicted, was tried for misappropriation of funds at Alameda and other illegal acts. God will do what is just, someday. Amen."

Let's take a moment for this whistleblower who died for truth. Natacha Jaitt was a well-known media personality who previously worked as a model, actress, escort, before becoming a TV and radio presenter in Argentina and Spain. She was hired to investigate and gather information on Gustavo Vera's child trafficking ring, which has extensive connections to Argentinian TV shows. This is how it works. TV shows are businesses, used as covers by the elite so they can easily carry out their true desires and works. Game Shows and other TV shows including Date shows and Big

Brother Big Sister, entire industries such as Hollywood, Disney, Bollywood, and the rest are all fronts to profit from your support of their deeds: pedophilia and child trafficking.

Natacha had been working on this for many years and exposed this ring often through twitter and radio. She exposed several Argentinian football teams' sexual abuse of children, among other things. Rare as it is, several children had come forward, exposing these people. Many more came to Natacha personally to help her expose the ring and all the people in it. She was able to follow the people involved and record their pedophilic activities with a lot of proof. Between 2004 and 2011, players from the club's academy were abused by a transgender person known as "La Lore," who was HIV positive. The tactic of using a main child to attract others is one commonly used in the pedo world and has been for centuries. Children are trusting of other children and not always trusting of the mentally ill. Natacha uncovered this international ring in Spain as well, while posing as a contestant in Big Brother. In Spain Natacha Jaitt was stabbed in the throat, in 2016, and charged with extortion in 2017, as she allegedly blackmailed sports journalist and football player Diego Latorre who is involved in the pedophile ring, as exposed by one of the children. Natacha had a seemingly brief, sexual relationship with Latorre as she knew he was involved in the ring and used her body as a way to gain information. This is the easiest way to get information from a man, as all women are aware. After exposing him, the media was forbidden from mentioning Latorre. Natacha's father died that same year.

In 2018, there was finally an investigation about sexual abuse of minors at the Club Atlético Independiente. A few people were brought to court including Martín Bustos, a referee. He was the first to be detained as a result of the investigation, for paying children to have sexual relations with adults. Tomás Beldi, Bustos' attorney, was charged with aggravated cover up after he destroyed a device which had vital evidence on it. Another man involved in the pedophile ring is Juan Manuel Díaz Ballone, who manages football players, mostly operating in the southern region of the Buenos Aires Province. Alejandro Carlos Dal Cin was detained for abusing a minor and "taking advantage of his sexual immaturity". Wording is always so important...wouldn't want to call it what it is. RAPE. Silvio Fleyta, a 24-year-old, was responsible for approaching the young children and convincing them to engage in sexual activities. Leo Cohen Arazi worked in Public Relations and has been accused of abusing several minors. He was also accused by several of the victims of serving as the nexus with other adults who engaged in sexual activities with them. The allegations were further confirmed by former 'Big Brother' contestant, Marian Farjat.

Natacha Jaitt said on La Noche de Mirtha, that the phone numbers which had been used to set up sexual events with children, exposed in the investigation, belonged to not just the Football members but journalists, actors, politicians, and other high-profile Argentine personalities. She testified to the prosecutor of the Office of Avellaneda, which led to 7 people being detained. That same year she became very ill and was hospitalized, as one would expect given the people she was exposing. After accusations made in early 2018 that dozens of high-profile sports, entertainment personalities, journalists, and other elite, in Argentina were involved in child prostitution, including second in command of the ring Gustavo Vera, and leader Jorge Bergoglio, Natacha tweeted what many whistleblowers do:

"WARNING: I am not going to commit suicide, I am not going to take too much cocaine and drown in a bath, or shoot myself. So if this happens, it wasn't me. Save this Tweet."

For those who have been whistleblowers and those who watch them, this message is always sent out when one knows their life will be taken for what they have done. Natacha explicitly stated in her exposing interview, that Gustavo Vera is a pedophile and runs a trafficking network using his charity organization La Alameda to shut down his competition. She recounted how Jorge Bergoglio saved pedophile priest Grassi from facing punishment, after he was exposed, by relocating him to a new area where he had access to vulnerable children.

Pope Francis, of course, is well known for covering up and creating and expanding child trafficking and prostitution rings from Italy to Argentina. It was one of his main jobs in collaboration with commanders Jorge Videla and Emilio Massera during the Dirty War. Artem Reshetnyak also came forward about Gustavo and is engaged to one of Gustavos prostitutes. He wrote an article explaining how the media lies and discussed how homosexual and pedophilic sex slavery is more common than adult female sex trafficking. After Artem exposed Gustavo on his blog, an official came to his home (where he lived with girlfriend and escort, Lucilla) and gave a warning: his girlfriend had to stop promoting herself (as a prostitute) as per Gustavo's orders, and if he didn't stop talking about Gustavo online, they would kill him. He confirmed Natacha Jaitt's work and proofs with his own about Gustavo and his child trafficking front company, La Alameda. One reporter explains:

"Children often live in closed circuits in the club, far from their relatives, in the hope that professional football will be the break they need to save them from poverty. One youth player exposed that he had been abused, that he had had sex with men in exchange for money and that players were recruited to the prostitution ring by another club member. He exposed that he knew of 19 other students who were victims of this pedophile ring."

La Almeda promises to help victims working in **poor** conditions in illegal sweatshops, but instead takes advantage of them. La Almeda is one of Jorge Bergoglio's Argentinian child sex fronts, which is headed by his friend Gustavo Vera. Another organization that works with them is the Stolen Childhood Network, and another is

The Solidarity Network which pretends to look for missing children but kidnaps them instead. Gustavo sees the Pope every other month and chats on the phone weekly.

In Argentina, like many countries, many children live in poverty. It is popular for those children to be sent to clubs (in this case football clubs and tv shows) with the hope that they will become famous. These children are then given promises by men or children who pretend to be their friends (baiters), to bring them into groups and organizations or charities used to traffic. They are in the total care of the organizers (handlers), who arrange the sex trafficking by telling the child if they come to a party, or if they come meet these people (customers), they will be paid, given gifts, etc. Since these children are considered disposable property, they are raped, sold, and murdered without remorse by an endless river of pedophiles. Children are the product the elite will always want. In order to take your children from you openly they create "protective services" and "police" to do it by force. To keep the police and other low-level grunts in line with the agenda, they are watched by the ever-continuing hierarchy the elites have formed: government, then military, then secret ops etc. etc. etc.

"During most of the 14 years that Bergoglio served as archbishop of Buenos Aires, rights advocates say, he did not take decisive action to protect children or act swiftly when molestation charges surfaced; nor did he extend apologies to the victims of abusive priests after their misconduct came to light." - Washington Post

Lucia Perez is another child murdered in the ongoing South American plague called "femicides", carried out by Gustavos mafia. 895 femicides were registered in Argentina between July 2015 and 2019. Lucia, a 16-year-old girl was murdered on October 8, 2016, by Matías Farías and Juan Pablo Offidani. Alejandro Maciel was charged with aggravated cover up, there is always a patsy. Drugged, suffocated, raped, beaten, and murdered, they cleaned her up, changed her clothes, and took her dead body to a health center to make it look like she overdosed. Just as the CPS trafficking ring in the US, and UN international rings, children are targeted in South America because they have no resources, no power, the judicial system is not concerned with maintaining their safety or upholding the law for them. The headquarters of the human trafficking operation is the in the Northern part of Argentina, but the network has an international reach: Brazil, Paraguay, Uruguay, Chile, Peru, Spain, Italy, and Rome. Natacha Jaitt said in 2019 that director Pablo Yotich and Maximiliano Giusto drugged and raped her, a punishment for her work.

"We have to look after Natacha Jaitt because (former Intelligence chief Jaime) Stiuso could get rid of her like he did former special prosecutor Alberto Nisman after he was done with him." - Gustavo Vera

Natacha Jaitt was found dead on 23 February 2019, naked, in a bed at Xanadú. A few days before, she was with Mirtha Legrand, who worked with her on the cases. Raúl Velaztiqui led Natacha Jaitt to the Xanadú events facility in Tigre, Argentina and was arrested shortly after Natacha was found dead. Authorities stated that he gave "false testimony".

"There were some noticeable contradictions in the declarations he made yesterday and those made on the weekend." - Buenos Aires province's Attorney General Julio Conte Grand

Raúl claimed that he had found Natacha's mobile phone in his car, when in fact security footage showed him taking the item from the room and storing it in his backpack. He told authorities that he had not touched or modified anything in the possible crime scene when, according to security cameras, he removed a towel which he then used to cover Natacha's phone. The Jaitt family lawyer Alejandro Cipolla agreed that she was most likely murdered and insisted that investigators not rule out the possibility that her producer and friend Raúl Velaztiqui was involved in the murder. The police found a fanny pack filled with drugs discarded in a sewer, as though someone had run away from the place and thrown it there. They also found a motorcycle and a cell phone. It was discovered that at least three more people were with Natacha, who were captured by security cameras while fleeing the place, before police arrived. In the video recording you can see them throwing a package into the ditch. Two people who were in the hotel made a call to 911 and said that there was another woman there, who had vanished on a motorcycle with the friend of the owner, Bartolín. She was an escort who worked for Gustavo Vera.

"I continue to believe that this was a homicide and a plot to end Natacha's life. It was poorly managed, and they left her there. My sister was with three people who consumed cocaine. Imagine the environment she was in." — Natacha's brother, Ulises Jaitt

Natacha's closest friends, brother, and attorney have adamantly insisted she would never have used cocaine because of a medical condition she suffered. There are multiple reports over some time in the media, following her hospitalization for health issues. Being a drug user makes murder easily written off by the masses and is frequently used by agents to discredit those they fear. The official blood test results from Natacha Jaitt's body do not indicate that she consumed cocaine prior to her death. The autopsy report claimed the cause of death was "Heart and respiratory failure (multi-organ failure) that led to pulmonary edema." Pulmonary Edema, meaning fluid in the lungs...internal drowning, is a method commonly seen in silent murders. It is easy for anyone present to have mixed a drink made with any one of the elite's beloved poisons, such as fentanyl or the combination of thiopental and pentoxifylline, or midazolam which show as pulmonary edema. Acute pulmonary edema can also occur after a single oral dose of acetazolamide. Hydrochloric acid inhalation has a delayed onset of 2-12 hours before it ends with pulmonary edema.

The outstanding feature of Phosgene poisoning is massive pulmonary edema. With exposure to high concentrations, death may occur within several hours; in most fatal cases, pulmonary edema reaches a maximum in 12 hours followed by death in 24-48 hours. Some patients show little sign of early respiratory irritation and still develop fatal pulmonary edema, passing it off as a cold or flu. There is also a time during which abnormal chest signs are absent and the patient may be symptom-free. This interval commonly lasts 2 to 24 hours but may be shorter. It is terminated by the signs and symptoms of pulmonary edema. PFIB is another asphyxiating weapon commonly used by elite agents, which causes pulmonary edema in even low concentrations. The autopsy also revealed traces of cocaine in her nasal passages and No where else. Lawyer Cipolla has stated that it was not determined that cocaine which was found in her nostrils is the same that was found inside the place where she died. Police have interrogated the owner of Xanadú Guillermo Gonzalo Rigoni, his friend Gaspar Esteba Fonolla, producer of shows Raúl Velaztiqui Duarte, an electrician Gustavo Andrés Bartolín, and a 19-year-old woman, Luana Micaela Monsalvo.

"The consumption of human trafficking and pedophilia is very big in the worlds of media and politics. If I unfortunately die trying, I want to let you know that few are innocent and, just in case, I left a USB drive, not at home, but in the hands of an anonymous person, so everything will come to light!" - Natacha Jaitt

Pope Francis' Argentinian-based international pedophile child trafficking ring exposed by Natacha included, but is not limited to:

- Gustavo Vera and his La Alameda Foundation is the main ringleader and Popes Right hand man.
- Enrique Pinti is a famous comedian, close friend of Gustavo and customer.
- Matías Farías, Juan Pablo Offidani, and Alejandro Maciel who killed Lucia Perez.
- Pablo Yotich and Maximiliano Giusto drugged and raped Natacha Jaitt.
- Luana Micaela Monsalvo and Raúl Velaztiqui Duarte who were present at Natacha Jaitt's murder. Luana is a high-end escort and girlfriend of Gustavo. Raul is a producer.
- Vera and Brian Lanzelotta, Big Brother contestants and international child traffickers.

- Diego Latorre, a Football player, and journalist.
- Leo Cohen Arazi, a homosexual and HIV positive sexual partner of Delgado. Together they baited children into the ring. Leo is a public relations manager and owns a bar used for transactions.
- Club Atlético Independiente is a front organization which kidnaps and traffics children.
- Liliana Parodi is exposed in Natachas interview, wherein she explains how Gustavo Vera obtained children for Big Brother for her personally.
- Juan Cruz, another panelist for Big Brother.
- Juan Carr who runs The Solidarity Network, another front company used to traffic children.
- "Father" Grassi works at Don Basco School in Solis and Moreno, to acquire and rape children.
- Stolen Childhood Network is another front organization used to funnel in children.
- Martín Bustos, a football referee.
- Alejandro Carlos Dal Cin, managed various building consortia in La Plata used by the ring, also a player. representative, arrested for raping a child.
- Silvio Fleyta, a football player who helped attain children for the ring.
- Juan Manuel Díaz Vallone tournament organizer, mostly operates in the southern region of Buenos Aires but has a long reach as football player and contestant in Inseparables Amor al Límite TV show.

Former youth players reported a child prostitution ring, and others, went to Natacha Jaitt for help which is how she got started in exposing this ring. An estimated 152 million children around the world are forced to work due to poverty. There were 19 players investigated regarding abuse who mentioned football (soccer) players, all males. Contacts with minors were made through social networks including Whatsapp, which Natacha used to track the ring. Even though these children didn't have money for anything, they had a phone. One WhatsApp group where the contacts of the abusers, were associated under the name of "los topus".

Red Infacia Robada, which is the Stolen Childhood Network was founded by Catholic Nun Marta Pelloni, a friend of Pope Francis. She is the daughter of an Argentine Army officer of the veterinary service. The same year she became rector of the

Colegio del Carmen and San José, in Catamarca, one of her students, María Soledad Morales, was murdered by people who have close ties with the mafia exposed by Natacha Jaitt. Immediately after the murder, Marta began protesting and organizing groups to stand up against the elite powers that prevailed. She has since participated in the Anti-Mafia Congress and is very outspoken about the organized crime that we call government and leadership. In 2013, Marta Pelloni was awarded the international Prizes of Navarra Prince of Viana. She has accused obstetrician Dante Binner, brother of the national deputy and former governor Hermes Binner, who kidnapped Liliana Montenegro's twins, of "being part of the mafia group selling babies".

"At the heart of the Vatican in the 16th century Casina Pio IV, home to the Pontifical Academy of Sciences, the Voices of Faith's first edition on 8 March 2014 was held. Sister Marta Pelloni told the audience how they fight against domestic violence, the trafficking of women and children, and organized corruption." — Vatican Radio

"The Latin American antitrata meeting organized in Buenos Aires by the Santa Marta (GSM) group, brings together bishops, religious, laity, experts, and police chiefs from around the world. It was created Jorge Bergoglio in 2014 for "Finding solutions to the serious criminal problem" which raises human trafficking. Participants included: the bishop of San Juan, Jorge Lozano; Sisters Valmí Bohn (Brazil), Lidia Cruz (Guatemala), Conchi Burgos (Peru) and Rosita Milesi (Brazil); Néstor Roncaglia, Chief of the Argentine Federal Police; Alicia Peresutti, from the NGO Vínculos en Red, and Martha Pelloni, from Red Infacia Robada." — Ambito

"The owner of Red Infacia Robada, Sister Marta Pelloni and Gustavo Vera of the La Alameda Foundation, arrived in Río Gallegos to seek the adhesion of institutions to the National Anti-Mafia Network. They met with the former federal judge of Río Gallegos, Ana Cecilia Alvarez, While still a Buenos Aires archbishop, Pope Francis participated in the organization of the anti-Mafia congress and provided names for the inter-religious table. From this experience emerged the National Anti-Mafia Network. The National Anti-Mafia Network is claimed to fight in common against the mafias of trafficking, labor slave, drug trafficking, corruption, and money laundering." - Fundacionalameda

Juan Carr owns Red Solidaria and is a friend of Pope Francis, having grown up and worked with the Catholic Church his entire life. In 1997 he was elected Social Innovator by the Ashoka Entrepreneurs Association of Washington, USA. What is Ashoka? Beginning in India in 1981, Ashoka started identifying and supporting the world's leading social entrepreneurs who have ideas for far-reaching "social change". Ashoka became official in 1987, inspired by the Sanskrit word Ashoka that means the "active absence of sorrow," and by the Indian Emperor Ashoka, one of the world's earliest entrepreneurs. After unifying India in the 3rd Century BC, Emperor Ashoka renounced violence and became one of history's most tolerant, global-minded, and creative leaders, pioneering innovations in economic development and social welfare.

The Red Solidaria movement has 800 volunteers and 38 offices up and down the country. His education is in veterinary services. When he was 33, Red Solidaria was created by 3 of his friends and his wife. Jorge Bergoglio has always been a major supporter both of devout Catholic, Juan Carr, and of the concern for the poor he espouses with Red Solidaria. In 2011 Juan also created Mundo Invisible with his 3 friends. He was nominated by UNESCO for the Nobel Peace Prize in 2012 and two years later, declared an Illustrious Citizen of the city of Buenos Aires.

"Bergoglio has been the one who brought these two dimensions of the faith together — the spiritual and the social. I'm from the diocese of San Isidro, not Buenos Aires, but even from a distance I knew that Bergoglio was important, not just for his social commitment but also in the political arena. The most important for me was when I was invited to present the biography of Bergoglio, titled El Jesuita, here in Buenos Aires. That night, I said that I was honored to present Jorge Bergoglio to the audience, someone I believe will one day be a saint. The next day, Bergoglio called me to thank me for what I said about him. I told him I'd like to trade in the speech to get him to help me achieve zero hunger in Latin America, because that's really my obsession. He agreed immediately: "Of course," he said. A couple of months later he becomes the pope! My main goal now is to "Bergoglioize" Latin America! We need to turn the message of this Jesuit, his ideas and his work, into a broad Latin American message." — Juan Carr

Pedophilia has always been and always will be the way of life for the elite. In 2016 Pope Francis paid almost $4 Billion to combat pedo lawsuits. In 2019 the Vatican told its clerics that reporting child abuse by priests is "not necessarily" their duty. The same lack of responsibility can be seen in Italy as the poor people have suffered the Vatican kidnapping their own children for sex and murder and dumping their bones in the catacombs and sewers.

Among the Untouchables protected by the Pope is the Antonio Provolo Institute for the Deaf. One of the worst cases yet among the global abuse scandals plaguing the Catholic Church: a place of silent torment where prosecutors say pedophiles preyed on the most isolated and submissive children. Court and church documents, private letters, and dozens of interviews in Argentina and Italy, expose that church officials up to and including Pope Francis were warned repeatedly and directly about a group of predators that was led by Rev. Nicola Corradi. Dozens of pedophiles had full access to the helpless children in their care. Even with the mountain of evidence, nothing was done.

Argentinian Bishop Gustavo Zanchetta was found to have inappropriate behavior with seminarians and had homosexual, pedophilic, pornography on his cellphone, and yet was allowed to stay on as bishop of the northern Argentine diocese of Oran until 2017, when he resigned suddenly, only to be given a top job at the Vatican by Pope Francis, his confessor.

The Network of Survivors of Ecclesiastical Abuse of Argentina denounced Pope Francis' historic Vatican summit against pedophilia in the Catholic Church, describing it as an "act of simulation and hypocrisy."

Bishop Robert Cunningham of the diocese of Syracuse, NY stated that priests have been wrongly accused of sexual abuse against young boys for centuries. He states:
"at 7-years-old, children know what they're doing, so it isn't rape."

In court he claimed that a child between 14 and 15 years old gives consent for rape, and that the child is to blame for the pedophilic violation of men who cannot control themselves. This is the lie that all pedophiles proclaim, to convince themselves that they are not doing anything wrong. Meanwhile truth dictates that the developing mind is not completely developed until the age of 25-30 depending on the immaturity of the individual. So, until this age, we are all children without the ability to fully consent to anything because of our mental and emotional and physical states. Tell a lie often enough, regardless of the documented proof to the contrary, and demons are excused.

Charles Bailey, a survivor of a priest's abuse, asked then-Bishop James Moynihan whether the church held child victims partly responsible for sexual abuse by priests.

"Moynihan said that right to my face — 'The age of reason is 7, so if you're at least 7 you're culpable for your actions.' That kind of floored me," said Bailey.

"During the ceremony they sacrificed a little boy. After that the man dressed in scarlet went to the side of the room and I had to kneel before him and kiss his ring and swear my undying loyalty to the New World Order." — Svali, a whistleblower of Vatican cults and author of Breaking the Chain

As mentioned before, Pope Francis is a member of the Ninth Circle, among other Luciferian Orders. In an interview, Kevin Annett of the International Tribunal into Crimes of Church, and State in the Brussels Common Law Court of Justice, revealed that 2 adolescents claimed that Pope Francis raped them while participating in child sacrifices. 8 eyewitnesses confirmed this in court. Jorge Bergoglio has also been exposed as a perpetrator in satanic child sacrifice rites during his time as a priest and bishop in Argentina, according to records obtained from the Vatican archives. Witnesses have also documented in court that he helped traffic children of missing political prisoners into an international child exploitation ring run by an office at the Vatican.

The Jesuit Order's document "Magisterial Privilege", presented in court, dated Dec. 25, 1967, details how every pope is required to participate in Ninth Circle Satanic ritual sacrifices of newborn children, including drinking their blood. This is what leaders of the world are involved in, in order to get where they are. If you don't understand this by now, then this document will never open your eyes. One eyewitness described seeing the Queen of England:

"...sacrifice people and eat their flesh and drink their blood. One time she got so excited with blood-lust that she didn't cut the victim's throat from the left to the right in the normal ritual but tore the flesh off the body with her bare hands. There is a lot of rivalry between them for who gets to eat what part of the body and who gets to absorb the victim's last breath and steal their soul."

In 2014 NewsInsideOut.com journalist Juan Lankamp investigated elite pedophile clubs. In his investigation he was able to produce evidence of the interconnection of MK programs and elite clubs which ritualistically and regularly practice child abuse, including rape and cannibalism, human hunting, trafficking among other things. Those who are members of these clubs are members of the Vatican, DEA, Wackenhut, the Bilderbergers, Intelligence agencies including the CIA, Military, Corporations, Schools, civic organizations, and more as we already know. His work also proves how the US is used by the elite as the elites technological and infrastructure base for their global pedophile, child sacrifice and child-trafficking networks. Among those named by Juan is Pope John Paul II, who according to an ex-Jesuit Jose Luciano, participated in child sacrifice in one of the elites' bunkers, near the Vatican.

In order to be selected for any position of authority, in any country or religion, one is a member of orders and practitioner of rituals such as this. As documented in the court, the Canadian government and Privy Council Office in London granted all members of the Ninth Circle exception from all criminal, civil, and military jurisdiction.

"Documents from Vatican secret archives presented to court <u>clearly indicate that for centuries</u> the Jesuits had a <u>premeditated plan to ritually murder kidnapped newborn babies</u> and then <u>consume their blood</u>. The plan was born of a twisted notion to derive spiritual power from the lifeblood of the innocent, thereby assuring political stability of the Papacy in Rome. These acts are not only genocidal but systemic and institutionalized in nature. <u>Since at least 1773, they appear to have been performed by the Roman Catholic Church, Jesuits, and every Pope.</u> Survivors of these rituals describe newborn babies being chopped to pieces on stone altars and their remains consumed by participants. During the 1960's the survivor-witnesses were forced to rape and mutilate other children and then cut their throats with ceremonial daggers. " - Kevin Annett

Why, you may wonder? THIS is Catholicism! This is what it truly is and denying this fact as countries have done only in the current century, doesn't negate this fact. As Caeli Francisco explains:

"The frequency of the energy vibration of someone who is demonically possessed is synchronized by his/her DNA, which is demonic DNA. The DNA coding of such a person represents a desire to control, cold-blooded attitudes, an obsession with ritualistic behavior, an obsession with sex and the need for a kind of consciousness that will gratify the physical senses at the suppression of all else.

During either the act of child abuse or a ritual sacrifice, demons absorb the deeply negative energy generated by such horrors. The vibration frequency of the combined negative emotions, like fear and terror of the victim, animal lust and cold-bloodedness of the perpetrator, resonates in the domain or dimension where Satan and his demons dwell, generating energy for them to manifest in the third dimension.

During such acts, magnetic links are created that draws the consciousness of the victim through the abuser into the demonic entity. And thus by the spilling of blood - the physical expression of the life force - and the adrenaline that enters the bloodstream at times of extreme terror as well as heightened excitement, the energy of both the sufferer as the sacrificer is absorbed by the demon."

It always comes around to the DNA. I will discuss DNA in greater detail in chapters to come, but know this, dear reader: **everything** affects your DNA unless you have been protected with the blood of Jesus (which is not a physical thing but a spiritual one). Just as studies have proven that DNA is altered when in a meditative (Luciferian) state, it is altered in a vastly different way when engaged in true prayer to Jesus.

Let's talk about the Cult of Catholicism in more detail. Remember, dear reader, in our first chapters I discussed heavily the first cults formed after the flood. These cults have never changed, apart from their names, and the practices and rituals remain today just as they were then. One such ritual which I mentioned in the previous chapter is the Eucharist, one of many rituals practiced by the religion of Osiris which Semiramis founded. Catholicism is this religion. The practice of the cannibalistic ritual of the Eucharist should be apparent to all, but I will go into it, nevertheless. Today members of orders including the Ninth Circle practice true cannibalism, while the Eucharist is presented to the public as an acceptable substitute. For many decades Christians who refused to practice this Luciferian ritual were murdered.

"The Year of the Eucharist has its source in the amazement with which the Church contemplates this great **Mystery**. He also spoke of rekindling the amazement of the Eucharist, calling the Catholic Mary 'Mother of the Eucharist." – Pope John Paul II

The Monstrance, typically depicted as a star or sun with a glass center, is used by the Church, and houses the Eucharist Host. This is a Luciferian tool for magic which, as videos and recordings expose, transforms the material placed within it into skin and blood. As seen in videos and pictures, the Eucharist, a wafer disc which represents the sun, is covered in blood, and ingested by Catholic cult members. The literal consumption of death. This is what the Church calls transubstantiation, the transformation of bread into human flesh. This is one of the more obvious perversions of what Jesus taught, as previously detailed. During His time here, Jesus used the terms understood by the people at that time in history. This is why circumcision was implemented since it was a common ritual among priests and prominent levels of society to signify their specialness. It was a sign of elevation, and easily understood by the people of Abrahams time. It was chosen for this reason just as Abraham was commanded to sacrifice his son, as the elite religions of that day did frequently, so that the Living God could send an angel to stop it, showing Abraham that the Living God would never ask one to go through with that ritual, being a God of Life and Mercy. The cannibalism which was in all religions at the time of Jesus and before, is the reason Jesus used the bread and wine as symbols of his body and blood to make it easily understood to the people of that time that Jesus, the Living God, was all that one needed to accept to have salvation and all other rituals were irrelevant. But I digress, once again explaining the obvious. Let's continue.

Among the numerous idols Catholicism worships is the Monstrance, the sun. So, let's discuss the symbolism of the cross/sun before we go further. The cross has always been one of the more prominent Luciferian symbols used by the elite. Recently it has become equated with Christianity, thanks to the Church's indoctrination. Every true Christ Follower knows this is far from truth. The cross symbolizes protection from negative forces, spiritual connection to energy, connection to god and more. It is a celebration of the death of Jesus, a victory for the Fallen Ones who were well aware of Jesus long before he was brought to Earth.

Knowing this should give you a good idea of what it means to Luciferians. The Dictionary of Mysticism and the Occult, defines the cross as the uniting of the male phallus (vertical bar) and the female vagina (horizontal bar). This is what all symbols come down to. Sex magic is the only magic of Lucifer. It all has to do with distorting and corrupting what the Living God has made. The cross has been used in sun worshipping cults as well as by leaders such as the Egyptian and Assyrian kings. It is a symbol of Apollo's scepter, the pairing of the 8 rays of the sun creates the cross. The point where the bars of the cross meet is called the Axis Mundi or World Axis - the joining of heaven and earth.

"By bearing the cross of **incarnation**, like the **Cosmic Christ** [Lucifer] before us, we can know the light of our inner spiritual cross of **Illumination**, Resurrection and Salvation. By acknowledging, accepting, invoking, and applying **Cosmic Wisdom**, **Universal Love** and connecting the two through the power of the **Holy Creative Spirit**, we can personally know the Christ Within. When this happens, we partake of the true spiritual communion or Holy Mass [mass=death], in which all are joined in the Mystical Body of Christ. It is here, that all true and sincere believers are united in the Invisible Church. It is necessary, my dear brothers in the Lord [of Cosmic Consciousness], to give you a clear idea of the interior Church; that of the illuminated community of God, which is scattered throughout the world but which governs by one truth and is united in one spirit." - Bishop Theodotus

Remember the concepts of incarnation, illumination and cosmic universalism are Luciferian philosophies. As previously discussed, the UN and other sacred elite places contain walls and ceilings covered in murals depicting Luciferian symbols and icons. Underneath the Vatican, the original temple is maintained. Hypnos and Isis statues and Medusa depicted on vases, are among the many gods of the elite. Various mausoleums within the Vatican are used for an array of rituals including the worship of the dead. The Audience Hall of the Pope is shaped like the head of a serpent, complete with fangs, containing a monstrous sculpture of fanged creatures with reptilian skin in a place of torment and damnation which looms on the stage. Under the Basilica is the temple of Lucifer in the necropolis named Mausoleum U, containing a depiction of Lucifer, the Morning Star, as well as a depiction of Vesper, the evening star. This room is dedicated to the true god of the Vatican.

"Yes, it's true. Lucifer is enthroned in the Catholic Church. Anybody who is acquainted with the state of affairs in the Vatican in the last 35 years is well aware that the prince of darkness has and still has his surrogates in the court of St. Peter in Rome." - Dr. Malachi Martin, former Jesuit

If one pays attention to the Latin chanted in Catholic masses, or understands the language at all, it's evident that the one worshipped is Lucifer. The reason Latin is used by the Catholic Church is the same as the reason for the Quran being preached in Arabic, because it is the ancient language used in the time of Jesus, and one used for Luciferian incantations (chants) which is what Masses are. Chants bypass the conscious, implanting ideologies into the subconscious mind. Just like Music, chanting is a mind control technique. A recording of the Vatican's Easter Mass, an Osiris Cult Holiday, makes translation easy. Pope Francis' chant translates to:

"Flaming Lucifer finds Mankind, I say: Oh Lucifer who will never be defeated, Christ is your son. Who came back from hell, shed his peaceful light and is alive and reigns in the world without end."

As the elite have told us time and time again, their god and the god of this world, and the god you are commanded by them to worship is Lucifer. I have already discussed the necromancy of the Catholic religion: naming saints, praying to saints, and such, but will also be detailing much of the Papacy in the next family chapters since they were the Papal Bloodlines, so let's continue.

"One of his main ruses is to use so-called Christianity and religion with a carefully planned process of mind-control working through church liturgy and rituals by which the unwary churchgoer is mesmerized and lured into the magic he sees played out around him and by which he becomes so transfixed that he unfailingly believes every word spoken and every act performed, that this is the only way in which to worship God in order to achieve salvation." – Caeli Francisco of Humans Are Free

"This is my attitude and the attitude of the Holy See today. And those who meddle are not obeying the Holy See." - Pope Francis regarding the internal affairs of the Russian Orthodox Church

Taking a look at the Orthodox Church of Russia and Ukraine, and their relationship with the Vatican, and collaboration to bring the NWO. Greetings world. About 4 months after the split of the Ukranians from the Russian Orthodox Church, Pope Francis met with Grand Imam of al-Azhar Sheikh Ahmed al-Tayeb. Together they signed a "One World Religion" agreement. While this seems minor, every minor, little step the elite take is a small victory on their way to achieving the real agenda. For example, the MH flight shot down over Ukraine was one of the Jesuits False Flags to start the current war against Russia. Russia wanting to keep Crimea, lots of fighting on Ukrainian borders, were scripted and planned to lead the public to believe a war when it broke out between Ukraine and Russia. The puppet ruler was put in place thanks to the Rothschilds and funded by George Soros through the IMF for this purpose alone. With war comes elite control.

In 2016, Pope Francis and Patriarch Kirill embraced and kissed one another **three**

times before they signed a joint declaration.
> "We are brothers," Francis said embracing Kirill.
> "Now things are easier," Kirill agreed.
> "This is the will of god," replied the Pope.

Roman Catholic and Russian Orthodox churches hadn't spoken since the Great Schism of 1054 when Orthodox broke away from the Vatican control. What had been impossible for Rome to regain was made possible through centuries of hard and dedicated work. This is how the elite do things! While you live day to day, they live century to century which is why they accomplish so much. Religion is all about politics, demographics, money, and power.

> "One people, one church and one culture." - President Vladimir Putin

Ukraine was the birthplace of Russian Orthodoxy, in the 10th century (not to be confused with the original Eastern Orthodoxy which is in every other country besides the US). The religious sector of the Rothschild created USSR consisted of the Russian Orthodox and Eastern Orthodox Churches, which continued even after the dissolution of the empire. Supervision over Ukraine has been granted to the Moscow Patriarchate (the Kirill) since 1686. After Byzantium fell to the Ottomans, the Moscow (Russian) Church became the de facto great power in world of Orthodoxy. The Byzantine Patriarch, known as the Patriarch of Constantinople (leader of the Orthodox Religion) is now called the Ecumenical Patriarch. Though there is much more to the history, as always, the split meant that Orthodox leaders in every country had to decide whether they would follow the Kirill of Russia who is under the Pope, or the historical leader of Orthodox: the Ecumenical Patriarch (of Istanbul) who is also under direction of the Pope. Once again, the elite's unity won and another step towards the publicly recognized One Religion was taken.

> "The Patriarch of Constantinople will no longer have any right to be styled as he is now, the leader of the 300 million Orthodox population of the planet." - Metropolitan Hilarion of Volokolamsk, head of external relations for the Russian church

Since 1965 the Vatican has openly worked to bring their "separated brothers" back to "holy mother church". In the 1995 encyclical Et Unum Sint, Pope John Paul II said he intended:
> "to encourage the efforts of all who work for the cause of **unity**."

The Vatican's 'ecumenical movement' was started by Pope John Paul II as well. He was one of the puppets who catapulted the agenda forward. Under the advertisement of "bringing **unity** of all professing Christians", the real strategy was to bring all religions under the power and influence of the papacy. In June 1999, Archbishop of Canterbury urged all Christians to recognize the Pope as the supreme authority of a new global church live on **CRN News**. In 2016, Jorge met with the Lutherans (a Catholic controlled sect) in Sweden in order to further develop the One Religion, as is his purpose, and stated:

"Now, in the context of the commemoration of the Reformation of 1517 we have a new opportunity to accept <u>a common path</u>, one that has taken shape over the past 50 years in the ecumenical dialogue between the Lutheran World Federation and the Catholic church."

The Reformation was the revolution against the Vatican. Remember, Martin Luther was a whistleblower, who nailed his document to the door of the church which exposed the Vatican's lies and control over the Christian world, and how the Christian texts and beliefs had been adulterated into a religion: mind control for profit. This ripped Followers of Christ out from under the control of the Vatican. This did not last long as the movement was infiltrated and on and on it went. A group divides to get away from elite mentality and control, and eventually gets infected again, then divide again and so on. Because it gets so twisted, making truth so difficult to unravel from the web of lies, many people discredit the whole topic and all related topics in their frustration. Automatic Shut Down. The elite have taught you all so well. Those who won't look will never see and those controlled by their own pride will never understand.

The level of Luciferian control of the world as a whole has been evidenced in the exponential rise of demonic possession recorded in the last decade alone. For example, in 2018 Sicilian Friar Beningo Palilla told Vatican Radio that there are roughly 500,000 cases requiring exorcism in Italy **each year**. He called for an across-the-board improvement in training, as <u>training of exorcists has plummeted since Pope Francis took office</u>.

"It is Satan who has been introduced into the bosom of the Church and within a very short time will come to rule a false Church." — Padre Pio, Francesco Forgione, Capuchin friar, priest, and mystic

"Today Satan rules the world. The masses no longer believe in God. And, yes, Satan is in the Vatican." - exorcist of Rome, Gabriele Amorth

In February 2019 Pope Francis signed a peace declaration on 'Human Fraternity' with Ahmed el-Tayeb, Grand Imam of al-Azhar, during an inter-religious meeting in Abu Dhabi. Remember, Unity and Fraternity are synonyms in the Jesuit/Masonic doctrine. The Grand Imam is the religious head of Sunni Islam, which represents 90% of Muslims. He is the pope of Islam and leads the world's largest religious denomination, followed by Catholicism. Pope Francis met leaders of non-Catholic

Christian religions such as Orthodox, Anglicans, Lutherans and Methodists, and others including Jews, Muslims, Buddhists, and Hindus while seated in a chair and not the usual elaborate throne used in the ornate hall for audiences. While he said 'history has shown that any attempt to eliminate God produced much violence,' he reached out to those who seek truth, goodness and beauty without belonging to any religion. He stated that people who belong to no religion were "precious **allies**". Goodness and Beauty have nothing to do with anything, especially religion, since no one is "good", and "beauty" is worthless.

By mentioning the elimination of god, Francis showed that it was a legitimate consideration of the Vatican to create One Religion! This declaration states:
   "God wills the diversity of religions."

The declaration also says that humanity will live together. What have we been doing for the last 7 thousand years? Regardless, by documenting it, making it law, it is a baited switch. Peace and unity of all religions means deleting essence of those beliefs and cultures. By default, this declaration having been signed, means all religion is now one religion, under the same Vatican umbrella. A Dominican theologian remarked on the declaration saying:

   "In its <u>obvious sense is false</u>, and in fact heretical. The various religions say incompatible things about who God is and how He wants to be worshiped. Therefore, <u>they cannot all be true</u>. Therefore God, who is truth, cannot will all religions."

It doesn't take a theologian of any kind to see this. It is logical. Why this concerns everyone: There is a total of 5.85 billion people involved in an organized religion, out of the 7.7 billion estimated in the world today. Asian "new age" Buddhist religions include over 535 million people who believe "You are God" as the "Eternal Self". Hindu (about 1.12 billion people) believe in 33 gods, some say many more, in female and male interchangeable forms. In addition to multiple gods they also believe in the Eternal Self like all Roman-Egyptian religions. Islam (about 1.9 billion people) believe Allah is God who is Muhammad the Prophet. Out of the 15.2 million Jews, only 26% believe in the Living God in part, denying His human form Jesus and his spiritual form, The Word. The rest are Zionist or Kabbalist Jews who believe in Lucifer outright. General Christianity (around 1.08 billion people) believe in the Living God who is 3 persons, The Creator, His Son, and the Spirit of God. Unfortunately, the vast majority of them are in denominations under strict Catholic control. Roman Catholics (about 1.2 billion people) believe in multiple gods, including the Pope.

Torah Jews shun, hate and are actively violent against those who are not Jewish, which is determined by blood alone and does not include the Ashkenazi (Babylonian) bloodlines. Muslims are commanded to hate and violently destroy all those who oppose Islam. Those who disobey, especially women, are beaten, tortured, and killed. The men in the Islamic religion believe that pouring acid on a family member is acceptable, just as they believe that forcing their women to blow themselves up, killing others in the process, will benefit them. Hindus, Islamists, and others believe that when a man rapes a woman, it is the woman's fault when in reality it is the fault of he who is filled with corruption and evil. Islamism, Hinduism, Judaism and Catholicism are kept in religio-political governing institutions and controlled entirely by the elite. Modern Judaism and Islamism commands followers to hate and kill and destroy by their religion. Buddhists are given the gift of complacency because they get another try next time. Nothing ever has true meaning or value, not even you, because it's about the self. Catholics, like Muslims, Buddhists, Hindus, Wiccans, and Jews are kept bound to ritual and regulations: blasphemy and idolatry. Each one is incompatible with the other apart from the fact that all but Torah Jews and Christians acknowledge that their god is Lucifer in their texts and services. This is what Unity means when the elite use the term. The final goal of this Unity is for the elite to rule from Rome as well as Jerusalem.

"The fact that people are forced to adhere to a certain religion or culture must be rejected, as too the imposition of a cultural way of life that others do not accept. This is outrageous as every person has a different cultural background, which is part of that person. Furthermore, and even more obviously, all of humanity cannot agree on a great many things." - Grand Sheikh of al-Azhar, Ahmed el-Tayeb

This is as it should be. But now, you MUST accept, tolerate someone else's way of life (which we all know by now means to put on a pedestal of privilege above the rest). Just as the Jews, Gypsies and others were supposed to tolerate and accept the Nazis slaughter of them, so this next elite sponsored wave of slaughter **"must be tolerated"**. Just as in recent days you have tolerated government forced inoculations, just as the Nazis carried out. While it was seen as abhorrent in those days, today it is accepted by all. However, for Islamists their commandment is clear.

"Whoever changed his Islamic religion, then kill him." - Bukhari 9.84.57

Let's take a peek into the history behind this Fraternity...the agenda of the 3rd World War: the war on Jerusalem.

"As far back as the eighth century AD, emissaries were sent to Jerusalem by Emperor Charlemagne to negotiate an agreement with the Muslim Caliph Haroun al-Raschid. The result was that Jerusalem became a protectorate of the Holy Roman Empire." — Ron Fraser of The Trumpet

As discussed, the UN is the political order, controlled by the Jesuits, as the Vatican is the religious order. Both hold true to the same agendas and achieve them in various ways, all the while working hand in hand. In 1947 the UN's General Assembly resolution 181 began working to demilitarize Jerusalem as a separate entity in the United Nations Trusteeship Council, which would draft a statute for Jerusalem and appoint a Governor. This wasn't able to take place due to the fact that Jerusalem at that time was divided between Israel and Jordan. The next year it was brought up again, but this time the Arab nations rejected Israel as a nation, voiding the UN's ability to implement their agenda. Therefore, in 1950 Israel declared Jerusalem it's capital, making the city whole again. At this point, the Rothschild's created Zionist Israel began to ooze into other countries, claiming the territories for itself, illegally, and against the will of the UN. While Israel has expanded its territory, no one has intervened. Why? Because it's all going according to plan. The 3rd war must take place, and it must take place over Jerusalem. So, over the next decades Israel persecutes Palestine openly, to bring the world to attention, dividing it between those who support the side of Israel and those who support the side of the persecuted and occupied Palestinians. In 1951 Herbert Armstrong, wrote a detailed article published in The Plain Truth which I have included here, in part, as it explains the history and prophecy well.

"Here is the published present plan, in the event of a Russian invasion of western Europe leading to occupation of Rome: 1st, Pius XII, fearing martyrdom, would abdicate his throne, Then, shorn of his authority, he would remain in the Vatican, perhaps a prisoner of the Reds. 2nd, those Cardinals who head Vatican departments would flee from Rome to the new location of the Vatican, in Catholic Quebec, in Canada. 3rd, there, a conclave of cardinals would be called to choose a new Pope and reestablish the Vatican in the Western Hemisphere. The new Pope might very probably not be an Italian. Only Italians have been Popes since 1523. But the new Pope, for political reasons, probably would not be an American, Frenchman or German, and most likely is not even as yet a cardinal. The present Pontiff is 75 years old. Therefore, he probably will not be the Pope to figure in the prophesied closing events of this age. 19 of the cardinals are past 75-too old to be made Pope. Pius XI1 is expected shortly to create and announce several new cardinals, and the Pope to figure in the closing events of Bible prophecy may well be one of them...

Former Catholic-dominated eastern Europe is now Soviet-dominated. By enforced propaganda, by prohibitions and restrictions, by prison bars and death, ruthless Communism has all but extinguished the authority and voice of Rome in these important countries. Further, Catholic missions now face extinction in Asia...

If Germany and Nazi-Fascism is the Fatherland, Roman Catholicism is portrayed as the Mother. And the world in general little realizes how politically active the woman has been carrying on while her paramour has been forced into inactivity above ground...

Roman Catholicism is much more than a religion! The Vatican is CHURCH and STATE, combined! And every Roman Catholic is bound by allegiance to the Pope, who is Civil Ruler as well as Church Head, above any other allegiance, religious, political, or otherwise. When Roman Catholicism dominated Europe, through the middle-ages, it ruled Europe! If it could dominate the world today it would rule the world! And it is time the American people realized that the real GOAL of Roman Catholicism is to DOMINATE AND RULE THE ENTIRE EARTH! Every real Catholic, far enough into Catholicism to realize its ultimate aims, fully expects to see America and the world ruled by the Vatican from Rome! The Roman hierarchy does not require people to be "born again"-actually converted, their entire lives changed by the Spirit of God-in order to become members.

One is not "converted" in order to become a Catholic. One merely "embraces" Catholicism-that is, accepts its tenets, its authority, and joins the Church as one would join a secret lodge. They employ elaborate pomp and ceremony, psychological eye-appeal, beautiful music, mysticism, and superstition, to make membership attractive and appealing to the senses. It is a form of religion designed to attract and gain masses and multitudes, not repentant individuals. "Catholic" means universal. Their goal is to become the universal-the only Church-ruling the world politically!

The world seems unable to see the hidden real purpose when a Dictator is bent on world domination and rule whether it be the Pope, Stalin, or a Hitler. Satan is not a visible red devil with tail, horns, and a pitchfork. <u>The real Satan is invisible.</u> The world doesn't see him or recognize his works.

How many have realized these staggering FACTS: The oldest political Dictatorship on earth is the Vatican! The Roman Catholic Church is far more than a religion. It is also politically a WORLD POWER. And, until the sudden rise of the Soviet Union at and following the end of World War II, Roman political Catholicism was the greatest World Power! It ruled directly over 350,000,000 people! And the power of its influence spread to additional hundreds of millions! And how many people know that the real objective of Catholic political power is precisely the same as the goals of Communism and Fascism-to gain dominance, control, and rule over the whole world!

Until World War II the Roman Catholic Empire ruled 350,000,000 people about one-sixth of the earth's population. It even had 4,000,000 members in Russia. In Poland it had 20,000,000 members, and in Hungary and Czechoslovakia another 15,000,000. Up to World War II only the 4 million Russians were lost to Rome. But during and after World War II the Soviet power swept westward. The Russian boot was firmly planted in eastern Europe from Finland down through Latvia, Estonia, Lithuania, Poland, East Germany, Czechoslovakia, Hungary, Rumania, Yugoslavia, Bulgaria. Catholic power had been retained in these nations by deals with friendly governments. That is the way Catholicism works thru alliances and secret agreements with national governments. But now for the first time the Papacy saw a total Power rise up against it, surge over its domain, and employ its total resources to destroy Romanism. We in the United States heard little and observed less about the mortal struggle that ensued as the Soviet forces occupied these countries...

How did the Communists wage this war on Rome? First, they legislated against Catholic schools and marriage. Catholic leaders were stripped of special privilege, Catholic property was confiscated, including vast landed estates owned by religious orders and churches, schools, and hospitals. Monasteries were closed. The Catholic Press was suppressed, controlled, or abolished. Catholic political action groups were disbanded. When priests protested or rebelled, they were quickly found guilty of treason or disloyalty...

The Bible, in Ephesians 5, and II Cor. 11, interprets the symbol, "woman," as a church. In Revelation 12 God's true church is described under this symbol. But the Church of God is pictured as a pure woman, clothed in glory, keeping the Commandments of God, having the true Word of Jesus Christ, persecuted, and martyred by Satan. The Apostle Paul calls the New Testament Church of God a "chaste virgin," to be presented, as the affianced Bride, to Christ. In Ephesians 5 she is described as cleansed from sin, a glorious Church, "holy and without blemish," "not having spot or wrinkle" in her character.

But in Revelation 17 we stand aghast as we behold a great, powerful, unmarried but fornicating Mother Whore (v.1), having fornicating relations with the kings of this world, arrayed in the colors of harlotry and royalty, gaudily and expensively bejeweled, full of filthiness and drunken with the blood of the saints whom she has caused to be martyred! She is pictured as a politically ruling Church, reigning over kings of civil nations (V.18). In chapter 18 she is described, under title "Babylon," as the home and depository of demons, and everything foul and loathsome! (v.2), who has **deceived all nations** (v.3), entered political alliances with worldly civil rulers, and with the captains of industry and commerce. The stench of her sins has reached clear to high heaven (v.5).

Thus, her political, economic, religious, and social aspects are clearly described. In Revelation 17:3 and 8 is pictured the symbolic "BEAST" upon which she sits, and over which she rules. And even the Roman Catholic Douay Bible footnotes have described this "Beast" accurately as the Roman Empire-tho recent revised editions have altered this identification. What Church united with the Roman civil government all thru the Middle Ages, for considerably more than a thousand years, actually ruling over the kings of Europe, martyring real Christians who believed in and lived by the Bible? It was the Roman Catholic Church-state! The Pope wears a triple crown, designating civil and political, as well as religious authority...

The prophecy of Revelation 13 foretold the fall of the Roman Empire in 476 A.D.-the "deadly wound" suffered by the beast (v.3)-but it was only one of its "heads," which was killed, and the BEAST lived on, for its "deadly wound was healed," (v.3). Any history or encyclopaedia will tell you the Roman Empire was restored in 554 A.D., when Justinian, emperor of the Empire in the east, came with his armies to re-establish the Empire at Rome, at the behest of the Pope. Prior to this, Justinian had acknowledged the supremacy of the Pope, not only as ecclesiastical, but as political world-ruler. And the restoration of the Empire was accomplished under one of these "deals" between Justinian and the Pope!...

Finally, notice why, when, and where, the Pope will move the Vatican. Some phases of these same End-time events are foretold in Daniel 8, and 10-12. Chapters 10, 11, and 12 together form one long prophecy-the longest in all the Bible. Chapter 10 is the introduction; the 12th chapter is the close. The main prophecy is in chapter 11. It would require two long articles to explain this prophecy in detail. It begins with the end of the reign of the Persians, and the invasion of Alexander the Great (v.3) followed by the four divisions of the Empire in the hands of his four generals (v.4). Thereafter the King of the south refers to ancient Egypt and its successors, while the King of the North refers to the Kings of Syria, and the powers who succeeded in that territory.

In other words, the kings north and south of Palestine. The theme is the various happenings to Palestine. The prophecy proceeds in elaborate detail to foretell events which actually occurred, down to Antiochus Epiphanes, 168, B.C. This vile and despicable ruler is pictured in verses 21-31. He is the one who originally placed the "abomination of desolation" (v.31; Mat. 24:15) in the Holy Place in Jerusalem...

The TRUE Gospel-the very Gospel Jesus brought and taught-the same Gospel believed and preached by the original true Church in apostolic days has not been proclaimed to the world for 1800 years! It is now going forth in this great work, in dynamic power! Jesus Himself said, "This Gospel of the KINGDOM (today's organized Churches don't preach it!) shall be preached in all the world for a witness unto all nations: and then shall the END (of the age) come." (Mat. 24: 14.) That is our call and commission. For that purpose, this great work of God has been raised up by Gods power!"

While there is much more to his lengthy article, I will leave the rest for you to find and study on your own, dear one. It is included in the sources list found at the end of this letter. Let's continue with a bit of our own timeline.

Since 1964 the Vatican has been a permanent observer in the UN, with a mission in New York. The same year Giovanni Battista Enrico Antonio Maria Montini, called Pope Paul VI, visited Jerusalem, making a point not to stay overnight as well as to refuse Israel's statehood. However, in 1980, after successfully indoctrinating the public to see Israel as a Christian state, rather than the reality of it: a Zionist dictatorship, the Vatican acknowledged its legality, appeasing the masses. In 1983 Pope John made a big show of publicly attending the synagogue of Rome and claiming that Judaism was the "big brother" of Catholicism. In 1993 the Vatican, under Pope John Paul II, Karol Józef Wojtyla, signed an agreement, acknowledging Israel as a legal State, allowing the Vatican property rights and tax exemptions, along with the ability to tax Israel accordingly. What this means is that the Vatican now owned Israel.

Later in that decade, the pope declared the Vatican's desire to rule from Rome and Jerusalem, fulfilling prophecy. In 1996 Secretary General of the Vatican, Serge Sebastian, announced that Rome recognized Palestinian sovereignty over East Jerusalem. In 1999, after working diligently to expand the Vatican's control over Muslim nations, Pope John and the Palestinian Authority, Yasir Arafat, signed an agreement which recognized the Palestinian's "freedom of conscience". This meant that he legally documented his acknowledgement of his right to convert to another religion. This is monumental, as it is a public statement of the Vatican's control, once again, over another religious order. In the 1st the Kaiser attempted to seize control of Jerusalem for the Vatican, with the support of the Sultan Abdul Hamid who also helped establish German Templer colonies in Palestine. In the 2nd World War, Adolf Hitler met with Grand Mufti of Jerusalem, Haj Amin al-Husseini, discussing the expulsion of the Jews with the help of the Arabs who wished to begin a war in the middle east. The record of their meeting details their relationship in full.

"In this struggle, the Arabs were striving for the independence and unity of Palestine, Syria, and Iraq. They had the fullest confidence in the Fuhrer and looked to his hand for the balm on their wounds, which had been inflicted upon them by the enemies of Germany." – Toi Staff of The Times of Israel

The Muslim nations, as discussed before, have always been used by the elite as a military order, to serve their purposes. Adolf told Haj to hold off on his war in the region of Jerusalem because warring on Jerusalem at that time would be premature, according to the elite's detailed plans which dictated that the war of Jerusalem would be in the 3rd, not 2nd war. Since we have discussed how the Muslims are used by the CIA order to spread death, let's discuss for a moment why Muslims are so easily used by the elite, and have been throughout all of history. It's because they believe in the same thing.

Hilal bin Sahar is Lucifer, translating to **god of the dawn.** The symbols of Islam are the **crescent moon,** called the Hilal and the **star,** called Sahar. Just as the Catholics, Jesuits, and all Luciferians worship the Sun, so do Muslims for they are the same. Allah is described (in texts) as the greatest Deceiver of ALL the Deceivers. You already know who the greatest of the Fallen is. The Word Miim-Kaf-Ra is used when referring to Allah. Miim-Kaf-Ra means:

"To practice deceit or guile or circumvention, practice evasion or illusion, to plot, to exercise art or craft or cunning, act with policy, practice stratagem."

"ومكروا ومكر الله والله خير الماكرين" which translates: And they cheated/deceived, and God cheated/deceived, and God (is) the best (of) the cheaters/deceivers." – Quran 3:54

"افامنوا مكر الله فلايامن مكر الله الا القوم الخاسرون" which translates: Did they secure God's scheme/deceit ? So **no(one) trusts God's scheme/deceit except the nation the losers.**" - Qur'an 7:99

"وقد مكر الذين من قبلهم فلله المكر جميعا يعلم ماتكسب كل نفس وسيعلم الكفار لمن عقبى الدار" which translates: And those from before them had cheated/deceived/schemed, so to God (is) all the cheatery/deceit/scheme. He knows what every self gains/acquires , and the disbelievers will know to whom (is) the house's/home's end/turn (result)." - Qur'an 13:42

Deception is always sad. **Willful ignorance** is worse.

The Quran is preached in ancient Arabic, just as the Catholics preach in Latin, to keep people from being able to access information and also to enable to frequency shift obtained in chanting, without the knowledge of participants. Unacceptable ta'wil (meaning interpretation) is where one "transfers" the apparent meaning of a verse to a **different** meaning by means of a **proof**. If there is proof of fallacy, it is to be ignored. If any proof goes against what Muhammad's followers wrote in the

Quran decades after he died, it is to be ignored. This is opposite of both Biblical and Judaic texts, which are glad to provide proof of Truth, and encourage everyone to verify it. This is what makes something Truth: Irrefutable Proof, otherwise called Fact. Every Christ Follower knows that above all is <u>Love for all, equally, without judgment,</u> making divisions impossible in the true believer. This is the basis of what we today call a civilized, or 1st world, society construct.

Followers of the Quran are forbidden from interpreting the content themselves but must rely on the commentary texts written by Islamic leaders-exactly as the Talmud is for the Jews. Although the burqa and niwab are not mandatory according to the Quran and have nothing to do with religion at all. They are merely fanatics symbols of women's enslavement. While Islamic symbols are not illegal in any country, Kuwait and Iran have banned Buddhist and Hindu symbols. Ashkenazi Jewish symbols aren't illegal in any country and even the ancient practice of circumcision is enforced in non-Jewish countries. Meanwhile, over 58 countries have made Christian symbols illegal. If you show them you will be tortured, jailed and in the majority of countries, killed.

The ritual of pilgrimage and circling idols, done in Mecca around the Black Cube, is also the exact same as it was in 600 AD. Muslims kiss the black stone today, the same stone used in the UN's Temple. Just as the Jewish community today kisses and bows down to a wall. Catholics kiss rings and statues. Buddhists, Hindus, Muslims, and Catholics stroke beads ritualistically. They are all stone worshipers. Other rituals seen in all elite constructed religions include homosexual pedophilia. Bacha bazi is a slang term in Afghanistan for a wide variety of activities involving sexual relations between older men and younger adolescent boys, typically bought, and sold as sex slaves. These children are more likely to be kidnapped and used in this way, than girls. Even at wedding parties, the boys are the ones dressed as women and forced to dance for the men. Islamic nations are male-dominated cultures. A documentary called *The Dancing Boys of Afghanistan* stated:

"young Afghan boys are sold to warlords and powerful businessmen to be trained as dancers who perform for male audiences in women's clothing and are then used and traded for sex."

Rape of defenseless children, irreparably damaging the mind, was common practice among the Samurai, who referred to this as "Shudō," or, "The Way of the Young." The pedophilia of elite Orders has been systematically implemented in all Jesuit controlled religions, which is all of them, today. In 2018 Tommy Robinson of the English Defense League was arrested and jailed for 13 months, for exposing a pedophile ring of 29 Muslim men who preyed on children as young as 15 months.

"British authorities knew of a massive child sex trafficking ring for decades but did nothing about it... because police feared if they arrested the

Muslim perpetrators, the media would call them racist." — Frank Holmes

Islamophobia has become the new elite term to take over antisemitism, keeping you from seeing and speaking truth. This is far from the only Muslim pedophile ring known to the world. Between 1997 and 2013, in Rotherham, a Pakistani child sex ring abused 1,400 children. One girl was doused with gasoline and told she'd be set on fire if she told anyone. In 2013 there were 57 gang-grooming cases in Britain. In 2016, 1,153 people reported pedophilic abuse to the child sexual exploitation team in Bradford, following the forced immigration of Islamic militants into the country. In Rochdale, one ring was exposed for having trafficked 47 girls. In Calderale, 20 men were arrested for trafficking girls. On and on it goes. People prefer to stay silent as defending the innocent requires action and thought.

Meanwhile, Minister Louis Farrakhan, the leader of the Nation of Islam, stated in 2019 that certain people call themselves Jews to hide their identity as members of the Synagogue of Satan. Aside from the typical elite rantings, he stated that pedophilia, sexual perversion, rape culture, casting couches, gay marriage, abortion, sex trafficking, prostitution, anal sex, and certain sexual practices are due to the influence of the Talmudic Jews. In 2020 Moroccan activist Najia Adib spoke out about the rampant pedophilia in Muslim culture. She calls for the death penalty to be applied to those who destroy children, siting the torture, rape, and murder of kidnapped 11-year-old Adnane Bouchouf.

"Sexual abuse is more prevalent in Arab and Muslim countries than others. In these societies, the child is deprived of will and does not have any value within the family, and we always call him young and ignorant." — Najia Adib

While Muslims live with their rituals, pedophilia, violence, and hate, worshipping the god of deception, with uncertainty about their salvation, as well they should... They live with constant questions: "Have I fasted enough to earn salvation?" "Have I gained the highest status in this world to be worthy?" Christians are positive and assured of their salvation as it can never be earned.

"I tell you the truth, those who listen to my message and believe in God who sent me have eternal life. They will never be condemned for their sins, but they have already passed from death into life." — John 5:24

By now you can easily see why Muslims have been used by the elite throughout history, they are the war dogs, the jihadists who can be loosed on the earth at any time of the elite's choosing. This band of men is only useful to the elite until they have acquired Jerusalem. Therein lies the purpose of the Human Fraternity and the public unification of the Imam, Sheik, and Pope, who have always been on the same team in the background. To go deeper, ex-Jesuit Priest turned Christian Alberto Rivera exposed the Pope's control over the creation of Islam before he was poisoned for this truth. He revealed:

"What I'm going to tell you is what I learned in secret briefings in the Vatican when I was a Jesuit priest, under oath and induction. A Jesuit cardinal named Augustine Bea showed us how desperately the Roman Catholics wanted Jerusalem at the end of the third century...

Early Christians went everywhere with the gospel setting up small churches, but they met heavy opposition. Both the Jews and the Roman government persecuted the believers in Christ to stop their spread. But the Jews rebelled against Rome, and in 70 AD, Roman armies under General Titus smashed Jerusalem and destroyed the great Jewish temple which was the heart of Jewish worship...

On this holy placed today where the temple once stood, the Dome of the Rock Mosque stands as Islam's second most holy place... In a tribal contention over a well (Zamzam) the treasure of the Kaaba and the offerings that pilgrims had given were dumped down the well and it was filled with sand - it disappeared. Many years later Adb Al-Muttalib was given visions telling him where to find the well and its treasure. He became the hero of Mecca, and he was destined to become the grandfather of Muhammad. Before this time, Augustine became the bishop of North Africa and was effective in winning Arabs to Roman Catholicism, including whole tribes. It was among these Arab converts to Catholicism that the concept of looking for an Arab prophet developed...

After his mother and grandfather also died, Muhammad was with his uncle when a Roman Catholic monk learned of his identity and said, "Take your brother's son back to his country and guard him against the Jews, for by god, if they see him and know of him that which I know, they will construe evil against him. Great things are in store for this brother's son of yours."

The Roman Catholic monk had fanned the flames for future Jewish persecutions at the hands of the followers of Muhammad. The Vatican desperately wanted Jerusalem because of its religious significance but was blocked by the Jews. The Vatican wanted to create a messiah for the Arabs, someone they could raise up as a great leader, a man with charisma whom they could train, and eventually unite all the non-Catholic Arabs behind him, creating a mighty army that would ultimately capture Jerusalem for the pope. In the Vatican briefing, Cardinal Bea told us this story:

'The mistress of the pope, Khadijah had a cousin named Waraquah, who was also a very faithful Roman Catholic and the Vatican placed him in a critical role as Muhammad's advisor. He had tremendous influence on Muhammad. While Muhammad was being prepared, he was told that his enemies were the Jews and that the only true Christians were Roman Catholic. He was taught that others calling themselves Christians were actually wicked impostors and should be destroyed. Many Muslims believe this.

Muhammad began receiving "divine revelations" and his wife's Catholic cousin Waraquah helped interpret them. From this came the Koran. In the fifth year of Muhammad's mission, persecution came against his followers because they refused to worship the idols in the Kaaba. Muhammad later conquered Mecca and the Kaaba was cleared of idols. History proves that before Islam came into existence, the Sabeans in Arabia worshiped the moon-god who was married to the sun-god. They gave birth to three goddesses who were worshipped throughout the Arab world as "Daughters of Allah" An idol excavated at Hazor in Palestine in 1950's shows Allah sitting on a throne with the crescent moon on his chest.'

In their "holy" book, the Koran, Christ is regarded as only a prophet. If the pope was His representative on earth, then he also must be a prophet of God. This caused the followers of Muhammad to fear and respect the pope as another "holy man." The pope moved quickly and issued bulls granting the Arab generals permission to invade and conquer the nations of North Africa. The Vatican helped to finance the building of these massive Islamic armies in exchange for three favors:

    1. Eliminate the Jews and Christians (true believers, which they called infidels).
    2. Protect the Augustinian Monks and Roman Catholics.
    3. Conquer Jerusalem for "His Holiness" in the Vatican.

Under Waraquah's direction, Muhammad wrote that Abraham offered Ishmael as a sacrifice. The Bible says that Isaac was the sacrifice, but Muhammad removed Isaac's name and inserted Ishmael's name. As a result of this and Muhammad's vision, the faithful Muslims built a mosque, the Dome of the Rock, in Ishmael's honor on the site of the Jewish temple that was destroyed in 70 AD. This made Jerusalem the 2nd most holy place in the Islam faith. How could they give such a sacred shrine to the pope without causing a revolt?

The Muslim generals were determined to conquer the world for Allah and now they turned toward Europe. Islamic ambassadors approached the pope and asked for papal bulls to give them permission to invade European countries. The Vatican was outraged; war was inevitable. Temporal power and control of the world was considered the basic right of the pope. He wouldn't think of sharing it with those whom he considered heathens.

The pope raised up his armies and called them crusades to hold back the children of Ishmael from grabbing Catholic Europe. The crusades lasted centuries and Jerusalem slipped out of the pope's hands. Turkey fell and Spain and Portugal were invaded by Islamic forces. In Portugal, they called a mountain village "Fatima" in honor of Muhammad's daughter, never dreaming it would become world famous. Years later when the Muslim armies were poised on the islands of Sardinia and Corsica, to invade Italy, there was a serious problem. The Islamic generals realized they were too far extended. It was time for peace talks. One of the negotiators was Francis of Assisi.

A light control was kept on Muslims from the Ayatollah down through the Islamic priests, nuns, and monks. The Vatican also engineers a campaign of hatred between the Muslim Arabs and the Jews. Before this, they had co-existed peacefully.

The next plan was to control Islam. In 1910, Portugal was going Socialistic. Red flags were appearing and the Catholic Church was facing a major problem. Increasing numbers were against the church. The Jesuits wanted Russia involved, and the location of this vision at Fatima could play a key part in pulling Islam to the Mother Church. As a result of the vision of Fatima, Pope Pius XII ordered his Nazi army to crush Russia and the Orthodox religion and make Russia Roman Catholic." A few years after he lost World war II, Pope Pius XII startled the world with his phoney dancing sun vision to keep Fatima in the news. It was great religious show biz and the world swallowed it."

You have seen this same script followed with every Jesuit created religious order discussed thus far. The Muslims who travelled to Egypt in the 600s were called Magaritai and were well documented just as they were documented by every country they invaded during this time of expansion. Following the death of Mohammed, as previously mentioned, his followers, called Moslems, continued to expand their empire in the shape of the crescent. Rashidin Caliph Abu Baker Al Saddik who now led the people sent his military leader, Khaled bin al Walid to take over more territory, stating:

"By God, I will distract the Christians from the whispers of Satan with Khaled bin al Walid."

Khaled is noted for his military skills and involvement in suppressing the rebellion of the Muslims against the Rashidun Caliphate when they took power after the death of Mohammad. In August 636, a battle against the Byzantines lasted 6 days. On the 6th day, after days of continuous attacks by the Byzantines, the Muslims decided to attack and managed to gain the upper hand. Khaled's strategies led the Muslims defeat of the Byzantine army. Arabs, having grown for generations as warring tribes with never-ending conflicts of ever kind, had more talent for warfare than the spoiled Byzantines. With this addition, their region now reached from Spain to north Africa to Constantinople and the inhabitants were forced to practice the moon and star religion. As their constant wars continued against the Mediterranean region, eventually Constantinople, the Balkans, Persia, and part of India fell under the banner of Islam. From this time until the middle ages, the Moslem world became a leader in medicine, astrology, and more. Seeing the power the Papal religion had obtained, the Papal States decided to keep the Muslims impoverished, uneducated, divided amongst themselves and more violently against all outsiders. They have been programmed like this for generations. The same is found in the Zionist Societies. Both were activated with the help of the Bush and Obama administrations who carried out their purposes to place puppets in middle eastern countries while the CIA set up a multitude of violent groups. As this history will be covered in upcoming chapters, let's continue with the Vatican's relationship with the UN in their goal to control Jerusalem.

In a resolution given in 2000, the UN decided that Israel's laws, jurisdiction, and administration on Jerusalem was illegal and null and void. "Peace in the Middle East" became the motto of the day. In 2005 German Josef Ratzinger became Pope Benedict XVI and the following year he visited Auschwitz as well as a synagogue in Cologne, where he made a point of repeating the Vatican concept that Judaism and Catholicism were brothers, a fraternity. As a child, Joseph was a member of the Hitler Youth and a well-known Nazi by the time he entered the Vatican as he worked as an S.S. Chaplain's assistant at the German Ravensbruck Concentration Camp. It has been documented by the Vatican records and witnesses that in 1962 Joseph Ratzinger participated in child sacrifices as a member of the Knights of Darkness, an order created by the S.S. in 1933. Almost every single pope has the same background, as required.

In 2008 Joseph ordered changes to the Catholic prayer used on Good Friday so that it would include Jews. Jews naturally disliked this as it forced them to recognize Jesus Christ which they do not. Soon thereafter the Vatican stated that Gaza was like a concentration camp, accusing Israel of being a second Germany. Back and forth it goes, as the Vatican wiggles its way into Israel, while supporting the Muslims. Both are pawns of the Jesuits. The elite always play both sides.

In 2014 Pope Francis made his journey to Jerusalem, after spending several days in Jordan and Palestine. He made certain to have a massive photo-op at the Israeli security wall in Palestine's Bethlehem, which helped display the Vatican's dislike of Israel and support of the Palestinian persecution. Pope Francis also made a point of stating that Palestinian leader Mahmoud Abbas was a man of peace. During this time, and the days of his visit, many false flags were carried out against Jewish persons, throughout Europe, in the elite's agenda to expand "antisemitism" in order to fulfill their purposes. Just like racial violence doesn't exist without elite involvement, the same goes for antisemitism, antimuslimism, and the rest. Non elites are unconcerned with such nonsense, and rather live their lives in peace. This default of peace is unacceptable to the elite who must have war. Francis had told Israeli President Shimon Peres and Palestinian leader Abu Mazen during a "peace" meeting at the Vatican that:

"all of this takes courage; it takes strength and tenacity."

In 2019 when Pope Francis had a private meeting with United Nations Secretary-General Antonio Guterres, the relationship of the two orders became known to the world. Not only had the current pope been the first to unite all religions under the Vatican but was now openly involved in politics including climate change and the UN's Sustainable Development Goals (SDGs). Welcome to the New World Order. The following year the Pontifical Academy of Social Sciences held a conference on "fraternal inclusion" with Jeffrey Sachs, the SDGs' chief architect and population-control advocate as keynote speaker.

In February 2022 on the 2nd anniversary of the Day of Human Fraternity, which the United Nations General Assembly approved in 2020 to be celebrated, Pope Francis, the Grand Imam of Al-Azhar and President Joseph Biden issued statements emphasizing the need for the mindless masses to realize that we are all people...called to live together in peace. Like the declaration of Human Fraternity, their speeches were filled with belittling and demeaning terminology.

"Together, we have a real opportunity to build a better world that upholds universal human rights, lifts every human being, and advances peace and security for all." — Catholic President Joseph Biden

"We see this in the **little** wars, in **this third world war now** being fought piecemeal, as peoples are destroyed, as children go hungry, as their opportunities for education decline... It is destruction. Either we are brothers and sisters, or everything falls apart." — Pope Francis

Let's take a moment to look at Jerusalem. Going back just a bit, several years ago, President Trump celebrated in Jerusalem with Zionist Benjamin Netanyahu (who has vowed to destroy the US), on the "historical day of triumph for peace". The Trump administration, while beneficial to the American people, helped solidify and expand the Vatican's agenda. Jared Kushner, son-in-law, was made senior adviser leading the Israeli-Palestinian peace effort. While they preached peace IDFs killed dozens and injured hundreds while Israeli murder of Palestinians in Golan Heights was rampant and unchecked. Thousands of Palestinian demonstrators have been killed and injured. While you're distracted with elections, protests, and peace talks, the elite are happily working on their agendas.

The real game is played for Gold, Oil, Drugs, Organs and, as we already know, Children. When one of the elite's small weeknight parties requires over 1,000 children, they have to be able to feed the demand. On the organ side of things, Dr. Hussein Nofal of the Medical Forensics department in Damascus estimated that at least 18,000 Syrians have had organs removed during the war on Syria, since 2012. 6.5 million people have been displaced within Syria and another 4.8 million have become refugees forced to flee to other countries. With another 386,000 estimated dead, that's 11.7 out of 22 million humans in Syria who have violently lost their lives or homes. Israel is number one when it comes to organ trafficking, as it is legal and encouraged. Israeli healthcare system subsidizes transplant holidays up to $80,000 in reimbursement for organ recipients traveling abroad for transplants plus Insurance carriers pay 100% of the bill. While it is bombing and shooting civilians in Syria, Palestine and along the Gaza strip, Israel who is an illegal occupier, has been funneling oil from that area, with the help of several lower elite families including the Cheney's, Murdochs, and Rothschilds. As the Vatican works to gain control of Jerusalem, in order to rule the world from there, the Israelis have been working to build the temple itself, complete with all necessary artifacts. It's all ready, just waiting for the opportune moment. Let's discuss the elite's temple which will enthrone the Antichrist, as they have stated, and as prophecy has declared.

Rabbi Berger stated that the non-Jewish President Trump was the representative of the descendants of Edom who would build the Temple and placed his face on top of Persian King Cyrus' face on a coin minted for the new temple. This was all for your benefit, to condition you to the building of the temple. The face matters little. It's about the agenda and indoctrinating you to the point where you don't pay attention. Know your history.

King Cyrus built the second Temple in Jerusalem in the 3rd year of his reign. The temple was opened on the 3rd day in the month of Ader, which is around the month of March in the Gregorian calendar. In those days the Judeans had been slaves, and King Cyrus freed them and called them from all the surrounding lands, where they had been dispersed, to come back to their land. He also gave them all the gold and silver and more from Solomons Temple, the first Temple, in order for them to build a second Temple. The tribe of Levi were the priests in charge of the temple and all duties associated with it. In order for the temple to be built, for it to be legitimate, the priests and so forth had to come from their associated bloodlines and they must be pure. In the time of Cyrus, they scouted to find the priests and others who would work there. A great problem arose when they realized then that the bloodlines had all been diluted and intermixed, thanks to their displacement from their countries. Thus, prophecy was fulfilled again, as there was no way to build a physical temple. Remember, the temple is you, dear reader. Since the time of Jesus, our physical bodies are the temples which house the Holy Spirit of the Living God. But the deceived and proud do not listen and with this limitation, corruption takes place to make physical the things that are not.

Solomon had built his temple on the threshing floor which David bought but this is not where the Jews have focused on building their temples. The Dome of the Rock is the highest point of the temple mount and threshing floors were never built on hills, but in curved valleys. Under the Dome of the Rock, was the Roman Fortress of Antonia. In 135 AD, Hadrian filled in about 50 feet of earth over top of where the temple stood and enlarged the temple mount and built a Roman temple of Jupiter where the Dome of the Rock is today.

In 325 AD Constantine tore down the temple of Jupiter and built an octagon church on the same site. In 700 AD the Muslims found the foundations of Constanine's octagon church and built the Dome of the Rock. However, the foundation walls of the traditional Temple Mount would not, in all likelihood, be included in the manifest of destroyed edifices because it was Roman owned at that time and considered separate from Jerusalem. So, the Roman elites who destroyed the original temple and buried it also hid it further by building their own temples in the same area. Flavius Josephus wrote that the entirety of the temple was indeed in total ruin and destruction after 70 AD. He went on to say that if he had not personally been in Jerusalem during the war and witnessed the demolition of the temple by Titus that he wouldn't have believed it ever existed. Other historians from that time agree in the fulfillment of the prophecy that the temple was utterly destroyed. Archaeology and eye-witness evidence suggests that the temple was destroyed so severely that what was left of it was dust. So, the wall the Jews pray to is a Roman Fortress symbolizing their past slavery and worshipping the control of Rome who works to regain the territory. Ironic.

Jumping ahead in history, in the 1300's the Equestrian Order of the Holy Sepulcher of Jerusalem, a sect much like the Templar Knights, was formed. This Vatican, or Holy See owned group has had one purpose: to help advance the Vatican's control in the Holy Land. The Order focuses primarily on education, being involved in schools, seminaries, and centers that provide health and social services. It also has a collaboration in place with the Congregation for the Oriental Churches to support larger projects throughout the Middle Eastern area. Simon Kassas, chargé d'affaires of the Vatican's mission to the United Nations, said the Vatican believes Jerusalem needs an "internationally guaranteed" special status, in order to ensure freedom of religion for the city's inhabitants, "as well as secure, free and unhindered access to the holy places by the faithful of all religions and nationalities."

In 2018, American envoy to Israel David Friedman posed next to a poster of Jerusalem's skyline with a computer-generated rendition of the Third Jewish Temple placed over Al-Aqsa mosque, Islam's third holiest site. As this was all taking place on one side, the other side was taking its necessary steps to forward the agenda. The Arab League consists of 22 nations in the Middle East and North Africa which are: Algeria, Bahrain, the Comoros Islands, Djibouti, Egypt, Iraq, Jordan, Kuwait, Lebanon, Libya, Morocco, Mauritania, Oman, Palestine, Qatar, Saudi Arabia, Somalia, Sudan, Syria, Tunisia, the United Arab Emirates, and Yemen. In 2018 Palestinian diplomats called on Arab nations to cut ties with countries that moved their embassies in Israel to Jerusalem. As the Palestinians and many others have loudly stated, moving the embassy to Jerusalem is an act of war.

"The U.S. embassy move to Jerusalem represents a step of war and provokes feelings of Arabs and Muslims everywhere." - Iraqi Foreign Minister Ibrahim al-Jaafari

"The US leadership has punished the Palestinians, whereas Israel, which violates international law, has been rewarded. We will not allow today to be the day the Muslim world loses Jerusalem." - President Recep Erdogan

On the day the US embassy was moved to Jerusalem (in 2018), Gaza was attacked and 58 people were murdered. The Pope in his typical eloquence, said:
"War is called war, violence is called violence."

In this historic year, Cardinal Pietro Parolin, Vatican Secretary of State, took part in the 66th Bilderberg Conference as the first high-ranking Vatican official to physically attend the order. Archbishop Ivan Jurkovic, the Vatican's observer at UN agencies in Geneva, urged people on both sides to let "wisdom and prudence prevail." He then quoted the pope stating:
"All those involved in the recent deplorable actions must recall, well beyond the question of borders, the 'unique identity of Jerusalem, which is sacred to Jews, Christians and Muslims, in which the holy places are venerated by the respective religions, and which has a special vocation for peace."

In this year of firsts, President Erdogan's visit to Pope Francis was the first visit of head of state from Ankara to the Vatican for 59 years. Remember the tribute he made to Francis upon his visit? The last Turkish leader to visit the pope was Celal Bayar, received by John XXII, who had been nuncio to Turkey between 1934 and 1943. The public statement from them about the meeting is that they agree the situation in the Middle East and the need to:
"promote **peace** and stability in the region through dialogue and negotiation, with respect for human rights and international law."

Once again, they show they believe war is peace. The war has been initiated and all we need do now is wait for the Pope to take Jerusalem. Let's close this chapter with a brief look at the programs used by the Vatican to track and communicate with the Fallen, whose leader will be placed on the throne in the temple at Jerusalem.

A priest, a rabbi and an imam walk into a space program... That's right, dear reader. If you hadn't connected the dots by now, these 3 work together with NASA and other space orders in their communications with Lucifer and the fallen. Extraterrestrial is simply the keyword used by the elite for Lucifer and the Fallen Ones they worship, to keep the mindless deceived. Remember, that the US government has a treaty with a group of the fallen calling themselves Etherians and communicates with them regularly through SIGMA while the Vatican and other institutions do the same which is the reason many such orders were formed such as the NSA, CIA etc.

Secret space program whistleblower, Corey Goode revealed:
"the call to world **unity** is a prelude to disclosure of extraterrestrial life."

For many years it has been well known that the Vatican has been actively seeking it's "Cosmic Christ", the alien god of the Catholic Church. Not only do Vatican documents detail this fact, but whistleblowers and the Church itself have openly exposed this. Over the years many Jesuits and Catholic priests, Cardinals, Archbishops et al. have exposed these facts and more, after leaving the Church and becoming Christians.

"Alien life not only exists in the universe and is "our brother" but will, when manifested, confirm the true faith of [Roman Catholic] Christianity and the dominion of Rome." — Jesuit Priest Jose Funes

Jose Gabriel Funes is a Jesuit priest and former head of the Vatican Observatory which was founded by Pope Leo XIII in 1891. The Vatican owns the space programs of the world, including many telescopes, one of which is called the Lucifer Project. Lucifer is the Vatican's acronym for their Large binocular telescope near-infrared Utility with Camera and Integral Field unit for Extragalactic Research. Yes, even with such a lengthy name they decided to call it Lucifer.

Genrikh Mavrikiyevich Ludvig had been given access to the Vatican archives in the 1920's. There, he read many manuscripts and ancient texts regarding UFOs and extraterrestrials, dating back to 3200 BC. In these texts he discovered that aliens influenced various ancient civilizations including the Egyptians, the Mayans, and the Mesopotamians. He discussed in lectures, how the pyramids in Egypt, under certain ritual manipulations, generate an energy-informational exchange with the "cosmic mind". Remember that the use of the terms Universal and Cosmic are attributed to Lucifer and the Fallen. That is what these terms mean. In 1938, Genrikh was named a Vatican counterintelligence agent by the Soviet Union and placed in a concentration camp. As always, the things he discovered have been known by those who follow the Living God for thousands of years. Nevertheless, the elite want to control the narrative you see regarding aliens, so the topic is controlled, and the reality is hidden from you.

In 2021 the Vatican Observatory and NASA teamed up to produce a masterclass to discuss the future of humanity, the economy, and current world crises. Naturally a space program should be invested in economics, a focus of the UN. Jeffrey Sachs was among the speakers, along with NASA engineer Artur Chmielewski, Vatican Observatory's Guy Consolmagno, and cosmologist Michal Heller. In 2014 NASA received over $1 million for a program the hold at Princeton University's Centre of Theological Inquiry for which they hired 24 scholars in order to address "global concerns".

As stated in 1868 and remains true today:
"The papal church Supreme in Europe was based on ignorance and could only be maintained while ignorance continued. The whole efforts of the clergy, therefore, have been and are directed to this one end: To keep the world in their leading strings by crushing out the mind of the world."

Just as I will discuss the Jesuits throughout every chapter, as I have thus far, so the Vatican and the Popes will be discussed in greater detail, in the coming chapters, so let's move on and look at some Papal Bloodlines!

~Orsini~

The first on our upper family list is the Orsini family. This bloodline of popes, dukes, counts and knights are intermarried with several other elite bloodlines, all of whom would be considered the "upper" bloodlines, those who have had control over the rest throughout history. Their motto is: Senza Rimproveri, which means 'Without Reproach'. The family crest is a white-silver shield with a "Tudor" red rose and 3 diagonal red stripes. The rose is properly called The Tudor Rose or Union Rose and is a secret symbol of the mystics and cultists. The symbol has a twofold meaning. A double rose, (a white rose inside a red one) represents the 2 orders. The white rose is in the shape of a pentagram and represents the Silver Star (SS) outer order, the red rose, which is the shape of an upside-down pentagram, represents the Inner Order of the Knights Companions of the Order of the Garter, the Knights of Rhodes and Malta: The Companions of 300 Knights of the Order of the Round Table.

They are descendants of the Julio-Claudian family of ancient Rome. This family, like many others, was torn apart because of their greed, generation after generation. Nephews were named heirs instead of sons, who couldn't be trusted. I'll take the timeline back through the family's history as we go along, so let's begin with the first Orsini.

Around 499 AD, Caio Orso Flavio Orsini, a member of the Roman Synod, began using the Orsini surname. Cajo, Kaius, Cajus, are all forms of the Roman name Gaius (Gaio), which was used by the family as well. This fits very well with the family's claim to be of the Julio-Claudian line, which used the Gaius name as one of their 5 praenomen. Caio Orso Flavio excelled in his military career as a General of Constantius' army. He inherited his fathers' titles, becoming the next Praetor of Spoleti and Rector of the Province of Umbria. His many grand successes made several other Generals angry and jealous, causing him to retire. Nevertheless, his fame spread throughout Rome and Emperor Theodosius II gave the family the hereditary title of Prince. Caio's children were Primiano, Tarquinio, Orso, Quintiliano, and Sestino. In 431 the Orsini family became the Prefects of Umbria. The family's first hereditary lands and castles were in Umbria and soon Lazio as well. His sons constructed castles, fortresses, and towers, and the Orsini family gained even more lands and wealth over the following few generations. Primiano (also spelled Firmiano) became a lieutenant for King Theodoric, of the Ostrogothic Kingdom of Italy. Grandson Celius became a vicar for Imperial Rome and great grandson Ariberto, was the earliest documented family member in the Knights of Malta, a hereditary position.

Ariberto's son, Costanzo was the father of Pope Paul I, who became the ruler of the newly forming Papal States, and Pope Stephen II. Paul and Stephen worked together as allies with King Pepin of France. Stephen, who had become pope in 752, entered the position as the kingdom was falling. Eastern Rome had been invaded by the Abbasid Caliphate and Constantinople would send no troops. Pepin had recently defeated the Muslim invasion of Gaul and the brothers were hopeful of their success. In 754 Stephen consecrated Pepin as king and the Frankish army was set loose on Italy. Along with fighting off the Muslims, the Lombards had been taking over Papal territory. Pepin assured Stephen in a letter, that he would regain the lands of the Lombards and give them back to Rome. Upon Pepin's victory, Stephen crowned him king of France. In 756 the victory was complete, and the Papal States were secured. While big brother Stephen was handling affairs of state, Paul was useful in his role as Deacon until 757 when Stephen died, and he took the throne until his own death in June of 767. The following generations of Costanzo's offspring held the name Bobone before switching to Orsini.

Orso's great-to- the-8th grandson, named Orso de Orsini, was born around 938. Orso's grandson was named Bobone. Bobone had 5 children. Like all nobility of the time, they were occupied by the military and the Catholic Church. Bobone's son Pietro had worked in the Church and signed papal bulls until he died around 1073. Bobone's other sons, Senator Giovanni and Orso became the fathers of Cardinals Gaetano, Bobone and others.

In 1106 Pietro's son Giacinto Boboni was born and the name Boboni was used off and on as was Orsini. Giacinto was the leader of 2 mission to Spain in the 1150's before becoming Cardinal Deacon of St. Maria in Cosmedin. He was named Pope Celestine III in 1191 and died 6 years later. Serving as the 175th Pope, he crowned Roman Emperor Henry VI and soon after excommunicated him for holding King Richard in prison. He then excommunicated Alfonso IX of Leon because he didn't approve of his marriage to Teresa. Before he died, he confirmed the Teutonic Knights as a military Order of the Church. Giacinto's brother, Pietro was a Cardinal. While he was pope, Giacinto made his nephews cardinals, and the fiefs of his family grew. At this time, only the Pope could allow buying and selling, and as the families shuffled the position from cousin to cousin, they gained money, land, and titles for generations. One of the family's monstrosities, Palazzo Orsini, in Rome, was put up for sale in 2012, for $36 million and bought by Giorgio Armani SpA. It was built in 13 BC and is what the Colosseum was fashioned after. The painting 'The Battle of Anghiari' by Leonardo Da Vinci includes two knights: Lodovico Trevisan and Giovanni Orsini. Like most paintings, they include the real people of the time.

By the 1100's a branch of the family was using the name Orsini, meaning "bear", and inhabiting the region of Orsini in the Viterbo Province. Another line of the family lived in the neighboring territory of the same province, called Farnese. Family members of the old ruling class of the Roman Empire gave titles to their relations and grew up in the ranks of Cardinals, condottieri, and knights. In the Farnese region of Viterbo Province, cousin Count Marquis Prudentio de Farneto was born in 1154, to Petro Prudenzio. He became a Consul of Orvieto and defeated refugees who tried to flee to Rome. It was Prudentio's son Pietro who was first named Farnese. Up until this time the family owned the castles of Ischia and Farnese, as their territory focused on Lake Bolsena.

The family is still inhabiting the same region where their ancestors' Fanum Voltumnae (shrine of Voltumnus, the god of death) remains. The twelve Etruscan city-states would renew their bond with ritual sacrifices each year in the cults "sacred grove" of Fanum Voltumnae. During this ritual, the games, called ludi, were held along with religious festivals. The Romans later copied these rituals and beliefs in their Coliseum, making the cult a public affair. In the Viscus Tuscus a shrine to Voltumna stood, named Vertumnus by the Romans.

Meanwhile, each family was upgrading their castles and palaces expanding their wealth and status for years to come. The Farnese family had Castrum Farneti (which translates to Castle of Fame), which they built in the early 900's AD, on top of the Temple of Priapos. The castle's main hall (shaped like a pentagon) is decorated with paintings of Hercules, who "created the volcanic lake" near the site. The stairway had been constructed so that it was easy for horses and mules to climb, so that Farnese men didn't have to dismount to go through the home. To say the palace is elaborate would be an understatement. The elite's symbols and religious rituals are depicted in color, on their walls and ceilings, everywhere you look. Priapos is the reportedly cursed and deformed son of Aphrodite, who represents masculinity and fertility. He is a mirror of the tri-deities Tykhon, Konisalos, and Orthanes who were depicted much the same way. As in all of these cults, ritual sex and sacrifice of male donkeys were practiced. Naturally, he is depicted with an oversized phallus, a Phrygian (Mysian) hat, and bees. A passage about him in Ovid Fasti, which is reminiscent of the story of Ham, states:

"It was night. Wine induced slumber and prone bodies lay everywhere, conquered by sleep. Lotis rested furthest away, tired from partying, in the grass beneath some maple branches. Her lover rises and, holding his breath, tracks secretly and silently on tiptoe. When he had reached the snow-white Nympha's secluded bed, he took care his breathing was soundless. And now he was poised on the grass right next to her, and still she was filled with a mighty sleep. His joy soars: he draws the cover from her feet and starts the happy road to his desires. Then look, the donkey, Silenus' mount, brays loudly, and emits untimely blasts from its throat. The terrified Nympha leaps up, fends Priapus off, and awakens the whole grove with her flight. And the god, whose obscene part was far too ready, was ridiculed by all in the moon's light. The author of the clamour [the donkey] was punished with death. He's a victim dear to Hellespont's god."

The cult first began in Lampsakos, Greece. The city of Priapos, named after their god, became a member of the Attica-Delos Naval Union in 478 BC. Diodorus Siculus' Library of History records:

"The Aigyptians [Egyptians] in their myths about Priapos say that in ancient times the Titans formed a conspiracy against Osiris [Dionysos Sabazios] and slew him, and then, taking his body and dividing it into equal parts among themselves, the slipped them secretly out of the house, but this organ alone they threw into the river, since no one of them was willing to take it with him. But Isis tracked down the murder of her husband, and after slaying the Titans and fashioning the several pieces of his body into the shape of a human figure, she gave them to the priests with orders that they pay Osiris the honors of a god, but since the only member she was unable to recover was the organ of sex she commanded them to pay to it the honors of a god and set it up in their temples in an erect position. Now this is the myth about the birth of Priapos [who the author identifies with the Egyptian god Min] and the honors paid to him, as it is given by the ancient Aigyptians."

In 1450's the Orsini branch of the family built the Palazzo Orsini Pio Righetti. This was erected atop the Temple of Venus Victrix. Venus Victrix was the founding goddess of the Julian line. The temple became known as the Temple of Pompey since he had built it as part of his theatre complex. A bronze statue of Hercules stands in the courtyard. Hercules is another ancestor the Orsini and Farnese families have in common. The families' heirlooms are held in museums, their storehouses. They display the marble statues called Hercules Farnese, Farnese Bull, and Apollo Farnese as well as Prince Filippo Orsini's statue, Apollo Crowning Himself. Like all statues from this time, Hercules and Apollo are depictions of specific historical people: the elite's family members. Museums are elite family memorabilia and collected relics and you're not allowed to see most of it, but you should understand what and who is shown there, such as an ancient oracle bone, called the Liver of Piacenza, which is a bronze, life-size replica of a sheep's liver. This was used in ritual animal sacrifices by a haruspex, a witch who has studied divination and "reading" of entrails of sheep and birds, particularly the livers. It is covered with inscriptions in Etruscan, which was the language used before Latin, in 100 BC, and is preserved by the Farnese family. The Orsini name is derived from the Latin name Ursa which in Etruscan is Arz. The term can then be traced through the elite bloodline of the Urartian Assyrians who ruled Babylon.

Let's take a closer look.

Caio's ancestor, Flavius Ursus, had been a politician and soldier of Rome, serving Emperor Constantine I as a Consul of Egypt in 338. We can find the Ursus name in the same positions, as one would expect, going all the way back to Flavius Ursus in the 80's AD. Described as being very bright and educated, he was part of the Emperor's inner circle as all relatives are. When Emperor Domitian was plotting to kill his own wife, Domitia Longina, Flavius was the one who talked him out of it. Domitian disliked him for this, but spared his life and made him a Consul. His brother or cousin, Lucius Julius Ursus was a Consul under Domitian as well as Trajan. Lucius' brother was Tiberius Julius Lupus III (named for his father) and like his brother, he was a prefect of Egypt. Generation after generation the family maintained the Roman Empire's Egyptian territory. During the First Jewish-Roman War, the population of Alexandria had formed groups and fought amongst themselves. The chaos continued until Tiberius was ordered by Emperor Vespasian (Titus Flavius Vespasianus) to close the Jewish temple. The historian Josephus wrote:

"Why, comrades, this thirst for our own blood? Why set asunder such fond companions as soul and body? One says that I am changed: well, the Romans know the truth about that. Another says, It is honourable to die in war: yes, but according to the law of war, that is to say 'by the hand of the conqueror.' Were I now flinching from the sword, I should assuredly deserve to perish by my own sword and my own hand; but if they are moved to spare an enemy, how much stronger reason have we to spare ourselves? It would surely be folly to inflict on ourselves treatment which we seek to avoid by our quarrel with them.

It is honourable to die for liberty, says another: I concur, but on condition that one dies fighting, by the hands of those who would rob us of it. But now they are neither coming to fight us nor to take our lives. It is equally cowardly not to wish to die when one ought to do so, and to wish to die when one ought not: What is it we fear that prevents us from surrendering to the Romans? Is it not death? And shall we then inflict upon ourselves certain death, to avoid an uncertain death, which we fear, at the hands of our foes? No, it is slavery we fear, I shall be told. Much liberty we enjoy at present! It is noble to destroy oneself, another will say. Not so, I retort, but most ignoble.

In my opinion there could be no more arrant coward than the pilot who, for fear of a tempest,
deliberately sinks his ship before the storm. No; suicide is alike repugnant to that nature which all creatures share, and an act of impiety towards God who created us. Among the animals there is not one that deliberately seeks death or kills itself; so firmly rooted in all is nature's law-the will to live. That is why we

account as enemies those who would openly take our lives and punish as assassins those who clandestinely attempt to do so."

Bravery means finding something more important than fear, dear reader. In 73, Tiberius Julius died and by 79 Mount Vesuvius had erupted, destroying Pompeii and Herculaneum. The Emperor tried to maintain morale and built the Colosseum (Arena of Death). In the following year Rome was flooded by fires and plagues. In 83 Lucius took over the family's Egyptian post, after having served in various positions in Rome, such as praetorian prefect. In 90 AD Lucius added the name Servianus to his name, in honor of the family who had adopted him.

Tiberius' daughter Julia was married to Praetorian Guard Marcus Arrecinus Clemens and had several children including Arrecina Tertulla who was married to Emperor Titus Flavius Caesar Vespasianus. Emperor Titus later married Princess of Judaea and Queen of Chalcis, Julia Bernice who was the daughter of Marcus Julius Agrippa, who is more commonly known as Herod, King of the Jews, and Agrippa the Great. The rest of Tiberius' bloodline carried on in the Clemens family. If we continue going back, we find the name Titus Flavius Sabinius many times in the tree, as well as Domitian and Vespasius in various forms. The Flavian Dynasty took over the Roman Empire after Nero and the ruling dynasty of the Julio-Claudian bloodline had ended. The Ursus name is a cognomen of the Julian bloodline, which explains their persistent positions of authority and wealth. The name is also used by the cousin branch of the family, the Cornelia line. Following the family trees of the Flavians, the brothers Lucius Julius Ursus and Tiberius Julius Lupus, who note that they are Julian, all family members, including the Emperors Vespasian, Domitian, and Titus, are all related and descendants of Titus Flavius Petronius from the Sabine region of Italy, where the family had been for several generations. In 48 BC Titus had been a centurion of Emperor Pompey and a tax collector, which his son Titus Flavius Sabinus continued.

Let's quickly discuss the history of this region, and where the people who inhabited it came from with a quick recap of the family's genealogy as discussed in the first few chapters.

The very first ruler of the Egyptian/Nubian region soon became known as Pharoah. His descendants quickly became the rulers of the Middle East up through Turkey, the rulers of Asia from Babylon to Russia, and the rulers of Africa. Their genealogy is easy to follow from the records of the Old Kingdom in Egypt, Zanakht in 2649 BC, to Netjerkare Siptah in 2152 BC. We know that by 2250 BC the Tower of Babel had been built and cursed. The Babylonian Empire and many others had been established for a hundred years. Nebuchadnezzar II had taken rule of Babylon, destroyed the First Temple in Jerusalem, stole the Ark of the Covenant, and deported the Hebrew Jews to Babylon, successfully corrupting the Hebrew genealogy, and using them as cover for the rest of history.

By 1776 BC Hammurabi, known for his "eye for an eye" philosophy which the elite have passed down, was yet another deified ruler. Following the bloodline leads straight through the New Kingdom (aptly called...) run by the same families. Meanwhile, the Etruscans and Sabines had broken away from the neighboring empire of Lydia. The mighty and powerful Kingdom of Lydia had stood since 1200 BC, and included King Croesus, who made gold and silver coinage which made him famous because of his **extreme** wealth and power. His son was named Atys, a name seen in the family who settled in Sabine.

Historians documented that a break-away group of Lydians (descendants of Lud, son of Shem of Noah, like all Anatolian tribes) sailed to Greece and Italy, and were called Etruscans or Tusci, by the small Roman tribes who inhabited the region. They were called Tyrrhenoi by the Greeks. The word means "people who build towers". The Etruscans became the dominant culture in the region whose extreme differences were documented by historians. They were respected as ancient founders of Greece and Rome, who noted their lineage to **Hercules**, just as King Croesus did. Their religious and political practices continued through Rome's history and remain unaltered, today. The architectural styling, which is most recognized as Roman, the rounded arches, columns, statues of Apollo, Zeus, and other gods all come from this society. The people made their wealth through salt and wood trade with the Celts. After a while, a group split and formed the Sabines. As Rome's power grew, the 2 groups stood against them and waged war against Romulus. A side note: by 396 BC the Romans invaded Vei.

"Veii had been the capital of Etruria, not inferior to Rome, either in number of arms or multitude of soldiers, so that relying on her wealth and luxury, and priding herself upon her refinement and sumptuousness, she had engaged in many honourable contests with the Romans for glory and empire...as the city was furnished with all sorts of weapons, offensive and defensive, likewise with corn and all manner of provisions, they cheerfully endured a siege." — Plutarch

Roman Emperor Claudius, a known member of the Claudio Sabine bloodline, in 10 BC, was the last documented person to know the Etruscan language. But let's get back to the timeline, for I'm sure you're wondering by now when the link to the Julio-Claudian line comes in.

<u>The Claudian gens is one of the elite families of Sabine aristocracy!</u>

Around 750 BC the Sabine women were abducted by Romans during a festival, and raped, which caused the inevitable conflict between the two kingdoms. Soon

thereafter the Sabines' king Titus Tatius waged war on Rome and came to an agreement to jointly rule with Romulus, until he was murdered 5 years later. Titus' daughter Tatia had been married to Numa Pompilius, the next ruler of Rome. In the 6th year that Rome had been a Republic, (504 BC) Attius Clausus moved from the Sabine region of Regillum, to Rome where he changed his name to the Latin version Appius Claudius Sabinius Inregillensis. Attius (a form of Tatius), was the son of Gaius and brought to Rome his wealth and power. Because of this he quickly became a member of the Roman Senate. From this point on, the common names of the family members were Gaius, Appius, and Publicus. As time went on the family branched and some used the last name Pulcher, Nero, Crassus, Marcellus, and others.

During Attius' time in Senate, the last King of Rome had fled, and the Republic had been established by the aristocracy which he had been sure to capitalize on. There had been many battles and wars from the various areas of Italy as the tribal way of life was becoming obsolete in the region. The Latins, exhausted from endless war, decided to betray their allies, the Volsci, and informed Rome of their plans for invasion. To thank them, the Senate released 6,000 Latin prisoners. Unfortunately, while this was going on, the people of the kingdom had amassed great debts from the constant wars. The economy was suffering, and the prisons were overcrowded. Men who had fought for their country (which was too broke to pay their salaries) were rounded up and chained because of their debts. The people were enraged, and riots broke out. Attius ordered that everyone be arrested, while others hoped to establish order and peace. Senator Publius Servilius, spoke to the angry masses, telling them that no one who would volunteer to fight the Volsci would be charged with debts and the creditors were forbidden from harassing them or their families. Those who had been chained were freed in order to fight the incoming enemy. Publius led the army against the Volsci and had a great victory, with the help of the Sabines.

Meanwhile, in Rome, Attius had 300 Volscians publicly beaten and beheaded. Before this, his arrogance and viciousness were well known. Upon Publius' victorious return to Rome, Attius was incensed. The men who fought had been allowed to keep their spoils, instead of giving them to Rome. While the people rejoiced and creditors were paid, Attius had discovered a new enemy: Publius. Attius ordered the people who had been arrested for debt before the battle, be arrested again along with others who had any debts. When the people called on Publius to save them again, he was unable to go up against Attius' power, and the people who the day before had sung his praises now hated him just as much as they hated Attius. When the next Sabine invasion took place, Attius had no way of forcing the people to fight. Time went on and the Senate of Rome was in panic, trying all they could to regain the hearts of the people. Attius refused to give any leniency and ordered more arrests. Disgusted by the peoples' disregard for the law, and the Consuls' inability to maintain it, he stated:

> "I urge you, therefore, to appoint a dictator, from whom there is no right of appeal. Do that, and you will quickly enough throw water on the blaze. I should like to see anyone use force against a lictor then, when he knows that the power to scourge or kill him is wholly in the hands of the man whose majesty he has dared to offend!"

This idea was considered by the Senate and, much to Attius' dismay, Publius' brother Manius Valerius Maximus was made dictator of Rome in **494 BC**. Manius remained in the position for one year, having been able to raise an army that would serve and secure Rome. Even though he was an elected dictator, the Senate was in control (as always), and refused to address the ever-growing issue of debt. Not wishing to have a role he could not fulfill, Manius resigned. The Senate tried to lead the military once again, but the soldiers mutinied. Although Attius opposed the Senate's decision to establish a tribune for the people and discharge their debts, the people agreed to the terms and the soldiers returned to Rome. When the people were poor, Attius called them animals, unable to control themselves, and when Rome suffered a famine, he stated to the Senate that the people were lazy and incapable of farming. Throughout his life, up to his death, Attius worked diligently to keep the power of Rome in the hands of the aristocracy. Anyone who desired otherwise was arrested and/or killed.

This brings us to 2 of Attius' sons Gaius Claudius Sabinus Regillensis, and Appius Claudius Crassus Inregillensis Sabinus. In **471 BC** Appius was made Consul of Rome and commanded an army against the Volsci. Appius and his brother Gaius were known to share their father's temperament and belief that anyone not of an aristocratic bloodline was sub-human. When his army was defeated in battle, Appius inflicted the harshest punishments. When they refused to attack, causing them to lose equipment and more, officers who left their posts were beheaded and every 10th man in the army was executed. For his actions he was taken to trial when he returned to Rome. Appius was backed by the Senate and the historian Livy noted his actions in court stating:

> "Never before had anyone been brought to trial before the people whom the plebs so thoroughly detested, both on his own and his father's account... There was the same expression, the same defiant look, the same proud tones of speech, so that a large number of the plebeians were no less afraid of Appius on his trial than they had been when he was consul. He only spoke in his defence once, but in the same aggressive tone that he always adopted and his firmness so dumbfounded the tribunes and the plebs' that they adjourned the case of their own accord, and then allowed it to drag on."

In the meantime, he had been elected decemvir, a new order which he had helped create. The consuls had decided to select 10 men, all who were members of the consul already, to be in charge of writing the Roman law. During this time, Appius was able to give the appearance of being a fair-minded person based on the laws he made. The other decemvirs, knowing Appius' personality well, agreed that they should all retire from the position at the end of the year, and select a new team to continue the work the following year. Much to their dismay, Appius selected 9 others to be decemvirs including his brother Gaius, and the 10th place he gave to himself, establishing total control over the order. This time around, Appius' personality came through loud and clear. Lictors (bodyguards) who had previously been unable to carry their axes in the city of Rome, were assigned to the decemvirs and armed. The new symbol of the Roman Law was established, and the decemvirs were able to act as individual dictators, with authority over the life and death of anyone who disagreed with them. Over the next several months the violence and abuse continued and grew, and the people began to rebel. This resulted in his trial, which was soon put on hold. Appius became sick and died before the trial resumed.

Coming forward in the genealogy to 300's BC we find the beginning of another branch of the family, a new dynasty. Appius Claudius Caecus was the son of Dictator Gaius Claudius Crassus and grew up to become the same. He was a censor in 312 BC and passed laws to allow the sons of freed slaves to serve in the Senate and gave voting privileges to rural tribes. This Appius was better at being likeable in the eyes of the people and decided to construct the Appian Way and Aqua Appia, the 1st aqueduct in Rome. He had other interests than those of his fathers and uncles and decided to publish the legal procedures and calendar which had previously been kept from the public and only allowed to be seen by the priests. In addition to this, he wrote several books. In 285 BC he was elected the Dictator of Rome. Several years later, he went blind, leaving his children to carry on the line. His son, Gaius Claudius Centho became Dictator after him. Son Publius Claudius Pulcher began the Pulcher branch, through his children. Likewise, another son Tiberius Claudius Nero founded the Nero Dynasty through his. Their children became the next generation of Senators, Praetors, and Consuls of Rome and a long line of Tiberius' and Appius' continued.

The following generations bring us directly to 42 BC when Tiberius Claudius Nero. He had been a commander of Caesar's fleet in Egypt and was made priest due to his victory. Tiberius was then sent to build colonies in Gaul. After becoming praetor, he married his cousin Livia and soon their son Tiberius was born. During this time, he supported Marcus Antony and fought against Octavian Augustus to protect Julius Caesar from his assassins. Caesar and Augustus are titles, not names. The family fled Rome for some time and lived in Greece until peace was established and they could return. Upon their return, Octavian Augustus decided he was in love with his mortal enemy's wife, Livia, even though she was pregnant with their second child. Octavian divorced his wife and forced Tiberius to divorce Livia, and even ordered Tiberius to give her away in her wedding to Octavian.

Son Tiberius and newborn son Nero Claudius Drusus were sent to be raised by their father. Tiberius educated his sons well and cared for them but died when the children were still young. The boys were reluctantly adopted by the first Roman Emperor, Augustus. Their mother Livia had a statue made of son Tiberius, as Cupid, which was placed in the temple of Capitoline Venus. A replica was also placed in Augustus' bedroom. Though Octavian and Livia tried to have an heir, all they conceived died. Tiberius grew up in the palace, with all privileges and experiences, but was disliked by Augustus. He was married to Vipsania Agrippina and though they lived happily, they had only one son, Nero Claudius Drusus, known as Drusus II, and Drusus Julius Caesar. Because Tiberius' son was not from Claudian or Julian bloodlines, his right to be heir was removed by Augustus. Augustus forced Tiberius to divorce his wife and marry newly widowed Julia Caesaris, which caused Vipsania to miscarry their next child. Vipsania was sent away, and Tiberius was forbidden to see her ever again. Augustus' daughter Julia was married to Tiberius and the only child they managed to conceive died just after it was born. Tiberius was then forced to adopt Germanicus, Augustus' grandson-in-law. Soon Julia's promiscuous lifestyle began to bring "bad press" to Emperor Augustus. So, she was arrested and exiled where she went mad and starved to death.

"You know what my needs are. Let us see to it that no one possess anything." — Nero Claudius

By 14 AD Octavian Augustus had died without a blood heir, and Tiberius became Emperor of Rome. Tiberius had come to be known as a ruthless military leader, cruel and perverted, as often happens when a child develops in an unfit environment. He abolished Egyptian and Jewish religious groups in Rome, and banished astrologers. He consolidated the Praetorians for efficiency, crushed city riots, and banned the right of sanctuary. While Tiberius had no respect for, nor much attraction to, women, he was ready to hop on men and boys from any given angle. During a ceremony he rushed one man out, along with his brother and a flute player in the temple and raped them all. When they complained about it, their legs were broken like many before and after them. His sexual corruption even led a noble woman to kill herself.

"How grossly he [Tiberius] was in the habit of abusing women even of high birth is very clearly shown by the death of a certain Mallonia. When she was brought to his bed and refused most vigorously to submit to his lust, he turned her over to the informers, and even when she was on trial he did not cease to call out and ask her "whether she was sorry"; so that finally she left the court and went home, where she stabbed herself, openly upbraiding the ugly old man for his obscenity. Hence a stigma put upon him at the next plays in an Atellan farce was received with great applause and became current, that "the old goat was licking the does." — Suetonius

In the 18th year of Tiberius' reign, Jesus was crucified in Judea. Shortly after his death, the Roman Governor at that time, Pontius Pilate, wrote to Tiberius an account of the crucifixion, resurrection and miracles which were performed by Jesus for the 3 weeks he remained in Jerusalem after his resurrection. The letter was taken from the Library at Rome, translated by Drs. McIntosh and Twyman and verified by the copy of the original preserved by the British Museum, in November 1935. Upon receiving this letter Tiberius made a report to the senate, desiring that Christ might be added to the gods of the Romans. The senate refused.

Tiberius' son, Drusus, was given many accommodations and positions in military and politics and married his cousin Little Livia. Tiberius' adopted son Germanicus had always been loved by Augustus and became a much-loved military leader just like his father. The people praised him as though he were a god. Syria, Judea, and many other districts of the Roman Empire were all on Germanicus' side, should he ever think of challenging Tiberius. Now that Augustus was dead Germanicus was not a favorite to anyone in power, every victory he had in battle, every celebration the public threw for him, only made Tiberius hate him more. When the people first heard Germanicus was ill, the entire country was in shock and sadness. Upon hearing the news of his recovery, there was a stampede to the Capitol to pay their vows. Tiberius was woken from his sleep by the crowds rejoicing in united song, singing:
"Safe is Rome, safe too our country, for Germanicus is safe."

During this time, Livia, Drusus' wife, was in a relationship with Tiberius' right-hand man, Sejanus. Sejanus was one of Tiberius' many lovers and in charge of removing threats to Tiberius. Tiberius sent Cneius Piso to govern Syria, to oppose Germanicus and excite hatred of him without raising suspicion. A false flag was carried out to form a movement that would benefit the ruling elite. Piso attacked Germanicus in every way he could, but Germanicus remained unaffected. This only put fuel on the fire. Eventually Tiberius had enough, and dark spots appeared all over Germanicus' body, a side effect of poisoning. Germanicus died foaming at the mouth. We have seen this in several whistle-blower deaths called suicides, it is one favorite method for the elite. The public grief could be calmed neither by any consolation nor edict, and it continued even during Rome's festal days of the month of December. Piso was framed for the murder and killed himself. Drusus was then taken under Tiberius' wing and often spoke for Tiberius in public affairs while Tiberius retreated to his orgies.

Tiberius changed laws as he saw fit. One law was in place at that time which defined treason as any injurious attempt against the emperor. Tiberius used this to mean whatever he wished. This control and fear grew until society grew suspicious of each other and trust and friendship were only in dreams. Drusus was poisoned to death a few years later, by Sejanus. In the Roman region of Israel, the Jews began to revolt under Pontius Pilate. An amphitheater fell, killing 50,000 people and the empire was a disaster, but this was of no concern to Tiberius. He spent most of his time at his palace in Capri, to be left to his twisted practices. His fascinations included mind control, pedophilia and more. He had little boys and girls stand in what were called Nooks of Venery, made up as Pans and nymphs, in outside bowers and grottoes. These children were there only as sexual props for anyone in the garden. People openly called this the old goat's garden. He had an entire library of pedophilic paraphernalia. Today people are shocked about the Lolita Express, Boys Town, Epstein Island, the Clinton/Obama child-trafficking of Haiti, or the Franklin Files, but pedophilia and ruling have gone hand in hand through all of history.

Tiberius trained little boys, called tiddlers, to crawl between his thighs when he went swimming and tease him with licks and nibbles. Unweaned babies would be put to his organ as if to the breast. This causes extreme trauma to the mind of an infant, which splits the mind throughout life. Forced and undesired sexual acts are not always damaging physically but they are **always** damaging mentally, regardless of age. People are quick to find any excuse to make their wickedness acceptable; to make you tolerate it, as if they were "born that way". Everyone believes they are good, but it's beyond clear that no one is.

Sejanus, still intent on killing off the rest of the bloodline, declared Germanicus' sons Nero and Drusus, enemies to the state. They starved to death in prison, while Agrippina, their mother, was banished. In this time many people were put to death and imprisoned. Sejanus was constantly working to make himself Emperor of Rome while Tiberius was preoccupied on his pedophile island. Just when the senate thought it was too much, Tiberius ordered Sejanus to be imprisoned and the senate executed him, his entire family and extended family. Anyone with connection or friendship with Sejanus was killed, regardless of wealth or station. Tiberius, covered in ulcers, bald and bent from age at 67 years old, grew tired of the justice system and ordered that anyone accused of a crime should be put to death without further examination. He left the ruling to his Lieutenants and Mesia was seized by the Dacians and Sarmatians, Gaul by the Germans, and Armenia by Parthians. As Tiberius aged, Germanicus' son, Gaius Caligula, had grown in his reputation. It was said he was a serpent that would sting the empire, and a Phaeton that would set the world on fire. Caligula was adopted by Uncle Tiberius and raised as heir to Rome. He grew to be even more corrupt than Tiberius.

Everyone was relieved to be rid of Tiberius when he died and though his grandson Gemellus was rightful blood heir, Caligula was nominated and declared Emperor by the senate. The joy the people felt for this election was not confined to the Roman Empire, and victims without number were sacrificed upon the occasion. Caligula knew how to play the crowd and threw a huge illustrious funeral for Tiberius. After that he ran to the islands of Pandataria and Pontia, to remove the ashes of his mother and brothers, exposing himself to the danger of tempestuous weather, just to give a luster to his piety. Upon his return, he ordered funerals for the ashes and ordered the month of September to be called Germanicus, in memory of his father. When Caligula fell sick, a multitude crowded all night long around his palace, and some even devoted themselves to death, in case he recovered.

Pontius Pilate was banished to Gaul and the knights were strictly inspected. Many people were banished and killed, as must happen when one side takes over, the other side must be erased. As jealousy increased, Caligula called in the death vows and many more people, including Tiberius' grandson Gemellus, were murdered. He ordered the heads of all statues of Jupiter to be removed and replaced with his head. He would sit in temples of the gods, be they male or female, taking their place and forcing all to worship him. Caligula then built a temple for himself, wherein he **was** the god, and soon after made himself a priest of his own temple. He often courted the moon, inviting it to come to bed with him, and embrace. He frequently had whispered conversations with the statues of Jupiter.

"I have existed from the morning of the world and I shall exist until the last star falls from the night. Although I have taken the form of Gaius Caligula, I am all men as I am no man, and therefore I am a god." - Caligula

Following in his ancestors' footsteps, Caligula committed incest with his 3 sisters, prostituting Livia, and Agrippina to his companions. Afterwards, he banished them as adulteresses and conspirators against his person. His 3rd sister, Drusilla, was taken from her husband Longinus, and kept as Caligula's wife. She was appointed heiress of the empire and after she died, she was deified, and all were forced to worship her. After attending a wedding, Caligula commanded the bride be brought to him, as his wife. After a few days he became bored. When the woman went back to her husband, Caligula banished her. This happened to several women. Milonia, being neither young nor beautiful, held his attention more than others, due to her sexual perversions.

People were killed by Caligula for wearing a color that attracted more attention than his, or for having nice hair, or for being too tall. Caligula was ruled by his jealousy, vanity, and envy. His horse stables were made of marble and ivory and his favorite horse was made a senator. He had jewels that would dissolve in his food and served pure gold to his guests instead of food. His ships were just as extravagant as the rest of his things, but his crowning engineering feat was the floating bridge at Puteoli. When this bridge was built, 3 miles long, he then had houses built on it to accommodate him and his guests, equipped with pipes running fresh water to them. During the large celebration upon the building of the bridge, Caligula road chariots up and down it. After the next day, the feasting and drinking continued and Caligula ordered many of his attendants to be thrown into the sea, and one of the ships, filled with spectators, to be sunk. The people who tried to climb back onto the bridge were forced back into the water to drown.

After these few years of obscenity, Caligula had spent all the money the Roman Empire had. Taxes were raised and the few who had named Caligula their heir were poisoned so he could collect their wealth. He killed knights and other noblemen for their money. He ordered most of the senate to be murdered and appear as suicides. Those who he owed money to often found themselves becoming food for Caligula's wild animals. His fascination with torture grew. He directed every movement of torture, made jokes, and rated the performances of the victims as and after they died. His corruption was so unbearable that before his 4th year as Emperor, he was stabbed to death by a group of conspirators, one of whom shouted:
"Think on this."

Caligula's wife was then also stabbed to death and his daughters head was smashed against the wall until her brain spilled out. The bloody history of Rome is well documented, leading to Nero who burned it to the ground so he could blame it on the Christians. He died in 68 AD, but the many uncles, cousins, and aunts continued the bloodline, although the ruling dynasty had been killed off. It is one of the women in this family who is said to be the progenitor of the Claudio blood in the Orsini family.

I think by now you have a good idea of the types of people the Claudio line produced, and it is easy to find plenty of biographies about the Caesars of Rome. The personality traits and characteristics don't change throughout the family, which was left to start from the aristocracy and work their way back into ruling power once the next governmental system had been established once again. This is where Constantine, an ancestor of the Medici family comes in! The name is also used by the Orsini family, because they are all related and have been intermarrying for generations. Constantine is a member of the Medici family, however, the changes he made in the Empire are important to understand as we go through the timeline, in this chapter. Therefore, I will go into Constantine and his sons' brief bios here before we carry on with more Orsini's. Remember, I already mention several of the Orsini's who held hereditary, family, positions in Constantine & Sons royal court and military.

Emperor Constantine further corrupted the Followers of Christ in 320 AD. Among his military generals is one named Ursus. Looking at the military leaders of Rome at this time, the Ursus name comes up from time to time including Roman soldier Urus, a member of the royal court, who killed Emperor Petronius Maximus, descendent of Nero. Because of the swift expansion of the belief in the Living God, and the freedom it gives, the Elite's power immediately fell in the minds of the public, by the time Jesus had risen from the dead and lived in Jerusalem for the next month. When there is any position of power or rule over others, corruption immediately takes root. After a few hundred years of slaughtering Christians throughout the Empire, the numbers kept growing. By 283, Pope Eutychian had buried 324 murdered Christians with his own hands.

In 311 Emperor Galerius had made Christianity legal, because they could no longer maintain control over it. Constantine began a corporate takeover of the Imperial Roman Empire and renamed it the Holy Roman Catholic Church, solidifying the elite's control. Up until this point, because of the division and constant changes in the Empire, the Papacy had only been able to function with the permission of the Emperor. Now, the aristocratic bloodlines which had only gotten into the Papacy until this time, through a true election, were able to infiltrate at last. He forced the implementation of worship on Sundays, the traditional pagan holy day. All of Rome's ancient rituals and feat days they used to celebrate their many gods: Easter, Christmas, etc. were also forced into the Christian body. Thankfully, Jesus told his followers that regardless of the day, the Living God can be celebrated. There are no rituals outside of religion: there are no rituals in Christianity. The Catholic Church also incorporates other pagan rituals such as Communion, Transubstantiation, Confession, Confirmation, Holy Orders and more.

"Ah, Constantine, how much evil was born, not from your conversion, but from that donation
that the first wealthy Pope received from you!" – Dante Alighieri

By the time Emperor Constantine had taken control and done all of this, the newly named Holy Roman Church began corrupting the terminology of Christ followers. The Church, like Saints, is a term used by Jesus Christ, meaning all believers. Before His time, these terms did not exist because everyone worshipped in a building called a Temple. The elite took over and corrupted the churches that the apostles had been sent out to form, several of them are mentioned in the Book of Revelations, turning the church into an organization for profit and mass deception, which was exposed by the Living God. People rarely pay attention... What more did Constantine "the Great" do for the elite, you may wonder?

"O' miserable followers of Simon the Magician, you who take the things of God that should be wedded to righteousness and use them as prostitutes to earn you money. The trumpet will sound for you because you are in the third ditch." – Dante Alighieri

The Roman Emperor, called Caesar, was renamed Roman Pope; the Roman Senators were changed to Cardinals, causing the Roman College of Senators to be renamed the College of Cardinals while the Magistrate of College of Senators was renamed the Dean of College of Cardinals. Pontifex Maximus was changed to Supreme Pontiff of College of Cardinals. Roman Calendar and Holy Days of the gods was renamed the Calendar Holidays of the Saints. The Apotheosis of the Gods was renamed the Canonization of the Saints. The term Catholic, meaning Universal, was used for the names of the temples. The Vestal Virgins were then named Nuns, likewise with monks...another obvious Luciferian practice (to those who can see). Pontifex Maximus was the high priest of College of Senators Pontiff. High Priest is another elite term used before Babylon for the pagan religious orders. Who we call Cardinals and Popes are priests of Zues, Apollo, Diana, Mars, Jupiter, Baal, Dionysys, Pythia and so on. Roman Governors were renamed Archbishops; the Imperial Chair of Jupiter where Caesar sat, was renamed, and is still called the Throne of St. Peter. A total perversion. Peter was a disciple of Jesus and named a heretic, like Jesus was, by the Jewish leaders who had demanded it of the Roman Empire.

Because of their belief in the Living God, Peter was crucified, and Paul was beheaded. Andrew had gone through Asia Minor and was crucified there. Thomas had been sent to the region of India and Syria and was speared to death by soldiers. Philip went to North Africa as well as Asia Minor and was arrested and killed. Matthew went to Persia and Ethiopia where he was stabbed to death. James was stoned and clubbed to death, Simon went to Persia and was killed after refusing to sacrifice to their sun god and Matthias was burned to death. Bartholomew was murdered for what he believed, and John was exiled by Emperor Domitian of the Orsini family but died of old age. Rome attempted to hold back this uprising by crucifying any who claimed to follow Christ. The Romans labeled them Christians, using them for human sacrifices in the Olympic Games. Unfortunately, the message spread, bringing even more upheaval within the Roman Empire, especially the more it perverted Christ's doctrines. Since this time period every person who walks into a Church on Sunday is breaking the command of the Living God while simultaneously claiming they are Followers of Him. This has led to the grand deception of today.

By 337 AD, Constantine finalized the elites' agenda for his rule, securing the Roman Empire and now all rulers would be crowned by the Bishop of Rome (Pope), who allows their rule. Catholic missionaries (Roman Knights) were the military front in the Roman crusades, taking back land and gold for Rome. Those who stood against the Catholic Empire were destroyed. When Constantine died, his son Constantine II became emperor jointly with his brothers Constantius II and Constans. The Empire was divided between them and their cousins, Dalmatius and Hannibalianus. Needless to say, peace was not something that existed at this time, as the family slaughtered itself for greed. Constantine received Gaul (France), Britannia (Britain), Mauretania (Algeria) and Hispania (Spain). Constantius received the eastern provinces, including Constantinople, Thrace, Asia Minor (which are Italy,

Greece, Albania, Macedonia, Bulgaria, Turkey), Syria, Egypt, Israel, Lebanon, and Cyrenaica (Libya). Constans, initially (under the supervision of Constantine II) received Italy, Africa, Illyricum (Albania), Pannonia (Hungary, Slovakia, Austria, Croatia, Serbia, Slovenia, Bosnia and Herzegovina), Macedonia (South East Europe), and Achaea (Greece).

Constans desired to rule freely without being supervised by his brothers, because they knew the corruption which grew in his blood. Constans ambushed Constantine, killing him in 340 AD near Aquileia, and became ruler of two thirds of the empire. 10 years later, Constans was assassinated by usurper Magnentius. The last remaining son of Constantine the Great, Constantius II, gathered the loyalty of many other rulers, and placed his cousin as ruler of the eastern empire. Constantius then marched against Magnentius in one of the largest and bloodiest battles ever between two Roman armies called the Battle of Mursa Major. A series of wars occurred between them across the empire, until finally Magnentius killed himself in 353. By 361 Constantius had become so ill, he knew he would die. Before dying of fever, he named Julian his successor. During this time, around 398, Pope Siricius began to be called Holy Father. The last man to hold the title of Emperor of Rome bore the same name as the first, Romulus. Romulus' father served in Attila the Huns' court and hailed from Pannonia. He abdicated the throne in 476 leaving behind no monuments or changes. He ensured that the power of the Papacy was strengthened so it could survive, and the elite bloodlines could become rulers once again.

By the time Caio Orso Flavio was born the Western Roman Empire (France, Spain, Italy, parts of Britain, Germany, Austria, Africa and more), had disintegrated, and the aristocracy (relatives of the past Emperors) were the rulers of their states. The variations of Farnese, Orsini and others were being made, along with their hereditary positions and lands. They allied with each other and warred against each other and the remaining political power: the Papal States. Meanwhile, the Eastern Roman Empire was commonly called the Byzantine Empire and contained the lands around the rest of the Mediterranean and Black Seas. Western Rome had been under constant attacks from northern tribes. The elite who always ruled, changed their titles, and became Popes and Bishops, simply dropped to the background to rule. Today they simply use their controlling Orders and use the Pope like a puppet.

By the 1200's the family had spread out and was so large that they distinguished themselves as Orsini of the Campo de Fiori, if they lived in Pompey's Theatre (one of their oldest owned territories), and Orsini de Ponte who lived in their castle Sant'Angelo, and so on.

Riccardo Maio I "the Apostolic" Orsini was born around 1160, in Bari, Italy. He married Margaritone, the daughter of the Grand Admiral of Sicily, Margaritus

Brindisi, of the elite Brindisi family. Together they had 2 sons, Maio II Orsini d'Epiro and Benedictus Orsini. Thanks to his marriage, Riccardo became Count of Kefalonia and Zakynthos. In 1194 Emperor Henry VI made him Baron of Rome and gave him the Abbey of Materdomini di Nocera. When he died, his son Maio inherited the titles and lands of his father while second born, Benedictus served the Church as the 1st Bishop of Kefalonia. Maio II married and had several children of his own while being made vassal of Epirus and Achaia by 1236. His heir, Riccardo, inherited his titles and land in 1260, before he was 18 years old.

By 1270 the region had become a vassal of the Kingdom of Naples. Riccardo became Captain General of Corgu and Butrint in 1286. He was one of a group of 100 knights who fought for Despot (similar to Duke) Nicephorus I of Epirus against the invasion of the Byzantine Empire. The king had sent his daughter Maria to be a hostage of Cephalonia, meaning she was under the protection of Riccardo Orsini until the battle was won, as a show of good faith. Unfortunately, Riccardo had other plans and married her to son and heir, John I Orsini (Ioannes), without King Nicephorus' knowledge. The king was quite enraged when his daughter returned to court, with her husband! All went according to plan and soon grandson Nicholas took over the rule of Epirus. When the Prince of Achaea died, Riccardo was made the next ruler until 1300. 3 years later, Riccardo was killed by one of his knights, Lion.

Son John I Orsini had inherited the lands of Cephalonia and Zakynthos and moved into his father-in-law's court. Thankfully, they were able to become friends and John was given the island of Leucas as well. The wealthy Nicholas III of St. Omer had been married to sister Giullerme and the marriage proved to be most unhappy. After informing her brother of how Nicholas treated her, keeping her confined and ignored in the castle, John had his cousin William Orsini bring her back home. When King Charles II ordered an attack on Epirus, John was only too eager. Hoping to take over the rule of the "Duchy" himself, John went to war. The invasion failed, and Charles was determined to try again the following year. That didn't go according to plan either and another attempt was made in 1307. By this time, John was anxious to add the land of Epirus to his own and jumped at the chance to try again. It was simply not meant to be for poor John. The Latin soldiers had an outbreak of a disease which rendered them unable to fight as planned. In 1317, after a life of battles and family drama, John died, leaving son Nicholas to inherit.

Nicholas not only inherited his father's titles and lands, but his mentality and spirit as well. Immediately, he ambushed and murdered his uncle Thomas I, the Despot of Epirus and gained the territory his father, like his grandfather before, had worked to take his whole life. Nicholas then married his aunt, the widow of Thomas, Anna Palaiologina, who was the daughter of the Byzantine co-emperor Michael IX Palaiologos. He refused to pay tributes to the Prince of Achaea, as he had promised, and the power went straight to his head. The Angevins had a rightful claim to Epirus, and the way Nicholas took over the region upset many others. In 1319 he was officially recognized by Emperor Andronikos as the Despot of Epirus. Now Nicholas was enjoying life. He sent ambassadors to Venice to form an alliance and offered many bribes.

The Venician Republic refused because Nicholas was part of the Byzantine Empire, and by 1320 he had begun to harass the Byzantines of Epirus. Soon a civil war broke out in the Byzantine Empire and Nicholas tried to profit from this by taking more lands in the region. His greed had grown too large, and he was pushed back by the Byzantine armies. In 1323 he was murdered by his brother, John II. The following year John of Gravina, who was the owner of the lands John ruled, deposed John as Count of Cephalonia and the family's long-standing post was gone. John now only had Epirus and was forced to acknowledge Emperor Andronikos II Palaiologos' rule. John married his cousin Anna Palaiologina and joined the Orthodox Church for which he was given the title of Despot. In 1335 John died. It is said he was poisoned by his wife.

His son and heir Nikephorus II Orsini took over Epirus while Anna served as regent. Daughter Thomais Orsini was married to Emperor Simeon Uros Palaiologos of Serbia and Greece. Their daughter Maria became the ruler of Epirus after her husband died. On the bloodline goes.

In another part of Italy, the brothers and sisters of Riccardo had continued to live. Giacinto Orsini's brother Pietro had several sons. Cardinal Niccolo and Cardinal Uguccione had their lives laid out for them, controlling, and expanding the Empire. Oddone and Bobone were in military service, overseeing the family territory. Son Orso became the father of Senator Matteo, Napoleone, Rinaldo, Gentile, Giacomo, and Giovanni, also called Giangaetano. Giovanni married Stefania Rossi and had become the Lord of Vicovaro, Licenza, Roccagiovine, Bardella, Ampollione, Cantalupo, Porcile and Nettuno before long, and bought the Castle of Civitella in 1215. He named his sons after his brothers. Son Matteo Rosso Orsini was made Lord of Vicovaro. In 1241 Matteo became the Senator of Rome and defeated Emperor Frederick II in 1243.

As the Lord of the Eternal City (Rome), Matteo was intimately involved with Giovanni di Pietro, who was used by the Church as the face of a new movement and subsequent Orders. Giovanni was given the name Francis of Assisi by the Church. Matteo ensured the spread of Francis' cult and profited from the orders he created throughout the kingdom, along with his sons Cardinal-Deacon Uguccione and Cardinal Gentile. He added "the Great" to his name and by the time he died he was Lord of Vicovaro, Licenza, Bardella, Cantalupo, Roccagiovine, Galera, Fornello, Castel Sant'Angelo di Tivoli, Nettuno, Civitella, Bomarzo, San Polo, Castelfoglia, Nerola, Mugnano, Santangelo and Monterotondo. The populations of these districts put their taxes into Orsini pockets and the family grew.

Giovanni's son Napoleone was made Captain of Orvieto, as well as Gonfaloniere of the Church before becoming a Senator of Rome like his ancestors. His sons were named Matteo and Orso. Napoleone's sister Mabilia was married to Senator Oddone Colonna, of the Colonna elite family. Together they had 6 children including Margherita Colonna "the Blessed", a nun, Cardinal Giacomo Colonna, and several Counts, Dukes, and Senators.

Matteo married Perna Caetani, Giovanna dell'Aquila and Gemma Monticelli. His many offspring included sons Gentile Orsini, Lord of Mugnano, Penna, Neptune and Pitigliano, Giovanni Gaetano, Rinaldo, Lord of Monterotondo and Marino, Napoleone, Lord of Vicovaro, and Cardinal Giordano. Giovanni became a cardinal in May of 1244 and soon became a canon. When Pope Innocent IV fled to Genoa because his people had made him feel unsafe, if he continued to live in the Eternal City, Giovanni went with him. They disguised themselves to hide from those who knew them and went to France before heading to Sutri and Genoa. Giovanni signed a complaint against the government of Viterbo and spoke out against the maltreatment of cardinals and the Curia. In 1276 the papal throne changed seats 4 times.

The following year, Giovanni became Pope Nicholas III. He became a priest one month later, to fulfil the requirements of the position. During his time as pope, he decided who was crowned ruler of their own countries, and who wasn't. He forced the surrounding kingdoms to swear oaths to the Papacy and, like all other popes, ensured the bloodlines' control. He entitled 3 of his nephews with cardinalship, and the rest were elevated as well. As a life-long friend of the newly called Saint Francis, he regularly visited the Franciscan Orders and was deeply involved in its growth. Almost 200 of his bulls were directed on behalf of the Franciscan Order. He spent a great amount of money to restore the 2 papal palaces: Lateran and Vatican, before spending more to build himself a country house which sits atop the hill of Soriano nel Cimino in Viterbo. Unfortunately, this is where he died, from a heart attack or stroke, so suddenly he didn't have the chance to confess to a priest, which is important in Roman cults. Dante Algieri, who exposed much of the history of his time, mentioned Nicholas III, who was now in the 8th circle of hell because he sold positions in the Vatican for profit.

Rinaldi's son Napoleone Orsini Frangipani had been made cardinal by Uncle Giovanni. He became Cardinal Deacon in 1288 and spent his extensive career in service to the Vatican's wishes, mainly bringing territories under the control of the Holy See. In 1301 he oversaw retaking the city of Gubbio and succeeded. He became close to the Colonna family, who had been involved in a long feud. Soon he was made Canon and Prebend of Suthcave in the Church of York. In 1305 Napoleone became

Archpriest of St. Peter's Basilica in Rome. After the death of Napoleone's good friend and beneficiary Pope Clement V (Raymond Bertrand de Got), the cardinals went into an extensive conclave to decide on the next ruler of Rome. They finally decided to elect Cardinal Jacques Duèse to become Pope John XXII. Before he was even coronated, Napoleone had control of the new Pope whom he persuaded to give cousins Peter and Paul de Comite, their own Canonries and Prebends. During this time Napoleone also wrote a book called Testament at Avignon. When the Pope died, another was to be selected and Napoleone was involved in another conclave. During his lifetime he participated in 6 conclaves. Cardinal Jacques Fournier was named Pope Benedict XII and on January the 8th 1335, he was crowned by Napoleone in Avignon.

After 57 years as a soldier of Rome, having elected 7 popes and crowned 3, Napoleone died in 1342, at the age of 79, just one month before Pope Benedict XII. His sister Agnese was soon married to Senator Giovanni Colonna, the Count of Ancona. Together they had 10 children who carried on the Colonna name, now containing Orsini blood. They grew up to become cardinals and counts, like their ancestors. The elite families not only owned all the land, and the people who lived on them but through the Vatican, they also controlled who owned lands outside of Rome, and who ruled them. Rinaldi's grandson Francesco refused the position of Royal Vicar of Rome and remained a politician, marrying his daughter to Canon Juan Colonna.

In 1262, another nephew of Giovanni, son of Gentile, was Matteo Rosso Orsini. He was made Cardinal and soon fought against Peter de Vico, who had invaded the Papal States. Cardinal Matteo was a member of many conclaves by the time he was 13. After his uncle became Pope Nicholas III, Matteo was made Archpriest of the Vatican Basilica, Rector of the great Hospital of the Holy Ghost, and Cardinal Protector of the Franciscan Order. In 1281, Matteo and his uncle, Cardinal Giordano, were attacked and taken prisoner by a French party who had been dismissed by the Orsinis. Once the party had placed Pope Martin IV they were released. In 1305 Matteo died and was buried in Orsini Chapel in St. Peter's Basilica.

Now you have seen one line for a few generations, let's look at another branch of the Orsini family. Romano Orsini, Lord of Pitigliano, and Vicar of Rome was born to Gentile II Orsini, in 1270. He married Anastasia de Montfort; the Countess of Nola and they had 7 children. Sueva del Balzo married Romano's grandson, Count Roberto Orsini, in 1330. Their children began the Orsini del Balzo branch of the family. Roberto's son, Count Raimondo Orsini del Balzo became the Prince of Taranto and spent his career as a Teutonic Knight and went to Prussia for war. Upon his return to Rome in 1381, and in 1385 he helped free Pope Urban VI (Bartolomeo Prignano). Because he helped the pope, the Count was given license to build a Convent, Hospital, and a Church. Raimondo married the Countess Maria of Enghien, which expanded the family's wealth and land, making him the most powerful Count in Southern Italy. During this time, because of his position and power, the kings he supported thrived while those he opposed were dethroned. Raimondo's brother, Niccolo had become a cardinal, which only helped the family. The rulers of the Roman Empire were determined by his involvement, which was continued through his son. He died in a siege in on January 17, 1406, and was buried in Santa Caterina d'Alessandria which he had built with his son.

By the time he died, Raimondo had been given the titles of Prince of Taranto, Count of Soleto, Baron of Acerra, Altamura, Lavello, Locorotondo, Minervino, Trevico, and Tricase. He was Duke of Baria, Dominus of Lecce and Veglie, Gonfalonier of the Church, Captain General of Terra di Otranto, Chamberlain of the King of Naples, and member of the Order of the Ship. Most are hereditary. His son, Giovanni Antonio Orsini del Balzo married the daughter of Oddone Colonna (Pope Martino V), Anna. In 1414 he became Prince of Taranto and more, due to his inheritance. Giovanni was now the proud owner of more than 300 castles, and their territories which included 30 bishoprics and 7 archbishoprics. He led a rebellion against King Ferrante of Aragon but was defeated time and time again. In 1463, while staying at Altamura Castle, waiting to meet and reconcile with Ferrante, he was strangled by one of the kings' men, Paolo Tricarico. All he owned was returned to the Vatican, but the del Balzo Orsini line continued on. Today, Francesco Del Balso, an Italian mafioso, operates in Canada.

It is at this time that the Rosenberg dynasty of Austria (who control the Rosicrucian Orders and more) began using the Orsini name. As you can see by their coat of arms, the Orsini bears are on either side of the red rose. This branch was also involved in alchemy, concocting potions. Their work accomplished the poisoning of Italy's water with what came to be known as the Black Plague. Today the family is involved with Bayer, Evonik, Merck and other elite-controlled corporations. Before we continue with Raimondo's family, let's take a look at this branch.

Wolfgang Andreas Orsini Rosenberg was one in a long line of Austrian Grafs and Princes. His 6 children spread the family down to grandson Vinzenz in 1722. Vinzenz was made Imperial Chamberlan in 1742 and was deeply involved in politics and military. He financed the construction of the Klagenfurt General Hospital, the Maria Theresian orphanage, and other facilities. Maria Theresia was married to a Medici and was the celebrated Queen of Austria, Hungary, Croatia, Bohemia, Transylvania, Mantua, Milan, and more. When his father died in 1765, Vinzenz inherited all his titles and properties including the Rosenberg Palace. Now he was the ruler of Sonnegg, Greifenburg, Grafenstein, Keutschach, Welzenegg, and Maria Loretto. In 1790 he was appointed Imperial Prince with others from his family. His fortune was split between his 10 children. Vinzenz's cousin Franz Xaver was born a year after him and was a diplomat in London, Milan, Copenhagen, and Madrid before becoming the Grand Duke of Tuscany. In 1766 he became the Chancellor of the Grand Ducal State, War, and Finance. Like his family, he was close to Maria Theresia and Peter Leopold as well. He built the Rosegg Castle and was a Knight in the Golden Fleece Order, the same Order all Orsini's are in. Franz died in 1796 and was buried in his castle. The Rosenberg family of Austrian nobility is quite evident so let's get back to Raimondo Orsini in Italy.

Raimondo had a brother, Niccolo Orsini, (also called Niccolo Ursins) who was the Count of Nola and died in 1399. Ursins is the name of another one of their founded territories located in France. The Ursini branch of the Orsini family had a lengthy feud with the Colonna families and others, until a Papal Bull passed, ordering peace. This is why around this time, names and spellings were changed in many families, including the Farnese, an Orsini branch. Later on, when the House of Bourbon had taken the throne of Naples, many mafias were formed by several families, or lower branches of the families. The Ursino line has since produced mafia men Luciano Ursino, Giuseppe Ursino, and Luigi Ursino. As you already know, the Mafia (all groups) are involved in murder, trafficking, kidnapping, torture, and more, worldwide.

Gian Gaetano Orsini became a Cardinal in 1316 and was sent to regain control of papal lands. In 1327 he returned to Rome with the army of King Robert of Naples and confirmed the people's submission to the pope. Meanwhile his cousin, Matteo Orsini was a member of the Dominican Order and taught theology in Paris, Florence, and Rome. In 1326 he was named Bishop of Girgenti followed by Cardinal-Priest of Saint Giovanni e Paolo. Apart from funding the Convent of St. Dominic in Bologna he promoted the Order until his death.

Cousin Giordano Orsini became Archbishop of Naples in 1400. In 1405 he became a member of the College of Cardinals and received several titles. Later, he became the dean of the college. In 1412 he was made Cardinal-Bishop of Albano, followed by Sabina. In 1408 he abandoned his obedience to Rome and attended the Council of Pisa and elected Pope Alexander X as well as John XXII, and Martin V. In 1417 he was sent by the pope to England and France to establish peace between them. After his success, a decade later, he was sent to eliminate heresy in Bohemia and surrounding regions. As the need for power grew, Rome sent Giordano to destroy "usurpers of ecclesiastical possessions". In 1419 he became a member of the Grand Penitentiary. Yes, dear reader, that's the word the Holy See uses. Penitentiary. In the following year he was named Abbot Commendatory of the Imperial Abbey of Farfa. Apart from being a patron of literature and art, he founded the Augustinian monastery in the family's territory of Bracciano as well as a chapel in St. Peter's Basilica, where he was buried. In 1434 he received his final promotion and became Archpriest of the patriarchal Vatican Basilica. Upon his death his library of 244 manuscripts were confiscated by the Vatican Library.

Latino Orsini, son of Count Carlo of Bracciano, was a member of the Church at a young age. By 1438 he had become a subdeacon and was sent to the Episcopal See in Conza. The following year he was sent to the See of Trani as Archbishop. He inherited enormous wealth from his father and had a son named Paul. In 1454 Latino became Archbishop of Bari, leaving the See of Trani to his brother, Abbot of Farfa, John Orsini. He worked to get his friend Francesco della Rovere elected as pope and in 1471 when Francesco was crowned Pope Sixtus IV, he was rewarded with the position of Camerlengo of the College of Cardinals. He benefitted greatly from his friendship with the pope who made him Archdiocese of Taranto and placed him in positions at the top of the government of the Papal States. After becoming Commander-in-Chief of the papal fleet, he was sent to war against the Turks. When he returned, he took over some of the responsibilities of the pope including crowning Ferdinand as King of Naples. He built the monastery of St. Salvatore in Lauro, where he established the canons regular. Upon his death, his son Paul inherited his wealth and titles. Centuries later, an island in Antarctica was named Orsini Rock in his honor.

Count Carlo's son Napoleone had several wives including cousins and had 8 surviving children. While his brother became Archbishop, Napoleone had more interest in the military and was a member of the Army of the Papal State, the Florentine Army as well as the Neapolitan Army. In 1452 he sieged the town of Foiano della Chiana, followed by Castellina. 3 years later he rounded up an army of 3,000 to disrupt the coronation of the next pope and demand fiefs. His brother Latino convinced him to let it go and Napoleone instead joined the family feud with the Colonna's and Borgia's which Pope Pius II (Enea Silvio Bartolomeo Piccolomini) ended. Quickly their friendship grew, and Napoleone had become a handler of the Pope within years. During this time, he had taken 13 fortresses of Everso, of the Anguillara family. In 1461 he was sent to defeat Sigismondo Malatesta, who was attempting to replace King Ferdinand I with one of his friends. Napoleone was victorious and entered the Kingdom of Naples in the following year. He was made Papal Captain General for his services and was now head of the Papal Army for Pope Pius II. The Pope immediately pointed his finger at Lord Roberto Malatesta, and Napoleone went to battle. Unfortunately, in 1469 he was wounded in battle and his son Gentile Virginio was captured. Gentile had grown up with his father's military desires and had been a mercenary for King Ferdinand. In 1470 Napoleone began renovating the fortress of Bracciano into an extravagant castle, fit for the Orsini family. Meanwhile, his children had been married off to other elite families. Of his daughters, Gustina was married to Lord Stefano Colonna, Bridget married Cousin Camillo Orsini, Lord of Lamentana, and Eleanora married Lord Nicolo Caetani. In October of 1480, Napoleone died, leaving his lands to his son Gentile.

After the death of his father, the new Lord of Bracciano, Gentile, attempted to continue the feuds he had begun with the Colonna, but because of his defeat, he was forced to give up several counties. In 1484 he joined Girolamo Riario in an attack against Lorenzo Colonna. They kidnapped him and burned his home. In 1486 he had a great victory in the Battle of Montorio and his military career continued. Gentile was married several times, like his father, and had 4 known children. In 1494 he fought with his cousin Niccolo Orsini, and many others against King Charles VIII but was captured. By the next battle he had managed to escape. After another year of feuding with the Colonna's over territory, Gentile was imprisoned for refusing to surrender the family's state of Bracciano. While imprisoned he was poisoned and died, leaving his son Gian Giordano as heir to the Orsini's lands and wealth.

Orso di Rinaldo Orsini, Signor of Monterotondo, died in 1424. He and his wife, Lucrezia d'Aldobrandino Conti, had a son Giacomo Orsini, Signor of Monterotondo. Giacomo married his cousin, Maddalena Orsini and had a daughter Clarice. She was married to Lorenzo de' Medici, who ruled the Florentine Republic. 3 of their 10 children died but one son became Pope Leo X. There was a plot to have the family killed and Clarice and the children were sent away. While fleeing the city, one of her sons was murdered. Lorenzo stayed apart from her most of the time, even before the escape. He was in love with someone else before they were married and had many affairs. Lorenzo was not with Clarice when she was dying, nor did he attend her funeral. Most of the lives of the elite are tragic. Instead of breaking from the family she allowed herself, like so many others, to be used as a breeding vessel, lived a life of solitude and, because of her tolerance and acceptance, allowed the bloodline to continue. Because of her dedication she was hunted and abandoned and left to die alone.

One of her children, Giuliano di Lorenzo de' Medici, was Duke of Nemours (which became Florence). Daughter Lucrezia Maria Romola de' Medici married Jacopo Salviati in 1486 and had 10 children including Cardinal Giovanni Salviati, Cardinal Bernardo Salviati, Maria Salviati (mother of Cosimo I de' Medici, Grand Duke of Tuscany), and Francesca Salviati (mother of Pope Leo XI). Another daughter of Clarice Orsini, Countess Antonia Romola de' Medici, married Piero Ridolfi in 1494 and had 5 children, including Cardinal Niccolò Ridolfi.

Cardinal Niccolo Ridolfi was made archbishop of Florence on January 11, 1524, by Giulio de'Medici, called Pope Clement VII. Niccolo was archbishop until 1532, as well as administrator of Vicenza, Forli, Viterbo, Salerno, and Imola. He was a hostage of Hugo of Moncada with other cardinals during the Sack of Rome in 1527. He was also on the conclave and a deacon of Santa Maria in Via Lata as he became Cardinal Protodeacon. Loyal to the core, as Medici's are, he was member of a special commission of 11 cardinals for reform of the Roman Curia (basically a board of directors for the pope). On January 8, 1543, he was named Archbishop of Florence for the 2nd time. He died in 1550. As you can see, the Medici, Colonna, Orsini lines are all quite impressive as far as titles and wealth goes. However, I will talk about the Medici family in their own chapter, so let's see what this line is up to now by looking at the Farnese branch.

In 1468 Alessandro Farnese was born to Pier Luigi Farnese and Giovanella Caetani. He grew up, like most of the aristocracy at that time, in the Church. Alessandro had several brothers and sisters including Giulia Farnese, called Giulia la Bella, had married Orsino Orsini when she was 15. Orsino's brother Cosma became a cardinal and Orsino carried on the family titles and lands. Orsino and Giulia were married young and, unfortunately, Orsino was awkward and odd. The unequal match made life difficult for both of them, and the young and very beautiful Giulia allowed herself to wander. Orsino was one of the grandchildren of Carlo Orsini, Lord of Bracciano, whose daughter Elena married Gentile Migliorati, beginning the Orsini Migliorati branch with son and heir Ludovico Orsini Migliorati.

Pope Leo IX donated the estate of Monte Giordano and the title of Baron to Lodovico Orsini, when he was young. The Golden Rose which was the symbol for sovereign princes, was used by the Popes, and Lodovico began using it in the Orsini Coat of Arms, along with 2 bears. An inscription below the coat of arms states "Haec Rosa magnanimi defenditur unguibus Ursi Nam genus Ursinum Roma vetu sta trahit." Which translates to: "This magnanimous Rose is defended by the claws of the Bear. For the race of the Bears has been drawn from ancient Rome." Ludovico married Adriana Mila, a cousin of the Borja family, and together that had one child, Orsino Orsini who married Giulia Farnese. From the time Lucrezia Borja was 3, until she was 13, her education and upbringing were taken care of by her cousin Adriana.

Rodrigo de Borja had become Pope Alexander VI and had a mistress, Vanozza Giovanna Cattanei, and 4 children by her, all of whom were given titles and money fitting children of aristocracy. Once Rodrigo rose in the papacy, Vanozza was dismissed and replaced by Giulia, who became his mistress. She was called the "pope's whore" by the public but was one of the richest women of the time. The Farnese family had obtained many fiefdoms (towns and cities who paid tax to the family, causing their wealth) by this time, and being the mistress of the Pope only expanded her fame. She lived on an estate close to Rodrigo with her husband, Orsino, who tried to keep her out of Rome. However, Adriana de Mila was fully supportive of Giulia's affair and urged it to continue. Orsino was forced to return his wife to her lover, where she stayed until she became too old and was dismissed. While in service to Rodrigo, Giulia gave birth to a daughter, Laura. Orsino was forced to accept her as his own, and she became his heir. For his service, Orsino was made mayor of Carbognano. Giulia became the governor of Carbognano, after Orsino died at the age of 27. The golden-haired blue-eyed Giulia is in many paintings from that time, typically titled: The Virgin and The Unicorn, the unicorn being an elite religious symbol of the horse with a phallus on his head. Her images have been sculpted and painted and placed throughout the Vatican as the Virgin Mary just as the Medici family used one of their members as the image of Jesus. Both are still used by the Church today, to be worshipped by commoners as gods.

It's impossible to mention Orsini genealogy without going into Farnese as you have noticed by now, so let's take a look back in the Farnese/Orsini bloodline. Pier Luigi Farnese Sr. and Giovanella Caetani, had 6 children including Alessandro Farnese. Pier had inherited lands and wealth from his family and became Lord of Valentano, Capodimonte, Musignano, Gradoli, Piansano, Canino and more. He was a famous and powerful man, who had amassed a great amount of real estate and wealth through taxation and war, and his children were taught his philosophy of secret administration and enforcement of good relations through marriage. Of Pier Sr.'s siblings, Gabriele Francesco, was married to Isabella Orsini and became Lord of Cellere, Canino, Gradoli, Marta, and more. Ranuccio's daughter Lella, was married to Giulio Orsini. Pier's sister Lucrezia married Francesco Anguillara and gave birth to Battistina and Vannola Orsini who married Bruno Conti.

Pier was made the papal vicar of Canino. His children were married to other aristocratic families and spent their lives devoted to the Church, the Holy Roman Empire. Daughter Giulia, whom we just discussed, became the mistress of Pope Alexander VI, Rodrigo Bogia, and wife of Orsino Orsini. The Farnese family has always married into the Orsini, Monaldeschi, and Conti lines. This is not something done randomly, but purposely. It also gives us an idea of what families were part of the early family's tribe. Pier Sr.'s son Angelo became the condottiero of the Papal States: the territories owned by the Holy See of Rome (the Eye). Angelo Farnese married Angela Orsini and had one daughter, Bernardina, who married Cousin Ulisse Orsini. Bernardina's daughter Giulia married Cousin Roberto Orsini.

In the meantime, his son Alessandro Farnese was sent to study at the University of Pisa and was part of the court of Lorenzo de' Medici. Up until this point it was the Medici family who dictated who would be Pope. By 1491 he had become a member of the Roman Curia. The Roman Curia is an Order, created by Odo of Chatillon, Pope Urban II. Basically, this order is the hereditary parliament of the Pope. Until the 1960's the bloodlines inherited membership to this order, just as the lower elite were hereditary members of Masonic orders. Same, same. They live in hierarchy because it keeps "one hand from knowing what the other hand is doing". This tactic is used in everything the elite control.

In 1493 Alessandro was made Cardinal Deacon after being financed by his sister, Giulia. During this time, he expanded the family's temple in Valentano and built the Palazzo Farnese, a castle on top of the Caprarola hills. He developed much of the

Farnese territory which reached from the Tyrrhenian Sea to Lake Bolsena. By 1500 Alessandro had a mistress; Silvia Crispo, the wife of Giovanni Battista Crispo. Silvia had 3 children with her husband and 4 with Alessandro. Alessandro's daughter Costanza was his favorite and his incestuous pedophilic relationship with her was well known. Many severe taxes and restrictive laws were enforced by him. This caused cities, like Perugia, to want to renounce membership of the system. Because of their desire for freedom, they were invaded and overpowered by Alessandro's sons.

By 1513 the previous Popes Julius, and Leo, had legitimized the children of Alessandro, who was named Bishop of Parma even though he was not an ordained priest. In 1517 Martin Luther physically nailed a document detailing 95 theses to the door of the church in Wittenberg. As mentioned before, repeatedly throughout history believers of the Living God have studied the Biblical texts enough to understand them and have subsequently tried to free themselves from the Luciferian tarpit which is Rome. In the 1520's Alessandro became the Dean of the College of Cardinals. His mother and niece were to inherit large sums of money, which he needed if he wanted to buy his way into the Pope position. Alessandro killed them both and in 1534 he was crowned Pope Paul III.

"There is no redemption from Hell." — Pope Paul III

Magicians or Priests had been carrying out the same practices, since the flood, but as the world grew and control was more difficult to maintain, a very specific, militant Order was formed which we have discussed in previous chapters. The elite families, together with Alessandro Farnese, founded the Society of Jesus, the Jesuit Order, in 1536. Interestingly, in Gematria, the words Orsini and Jesuit share the same numbers. Other Orders Alessandro formed while Pope to serve this purpose include the Theatines and Barnabites. By the time Martin Luther's actions had turned into a movement, Alessandro had established the Orders to contain and control Christians who would stand up. Through the Councils, Christians were banned from becoming Bishops, selling certain products, establishing certain facilities and businesses, and had to meet requirements before being approved for marriage. Soon Alessandro Farnese was rewarded with the position of Grand Master of the Supreme Order of Christ, another military order. With several other sub-elite family members, Ignatius Loyola was used as the ace of the Jesuit Order in 1540.

"Here I stand, I can do no other." — Martin Luther

The Jesuit Order works with the Council of Ten, established earlier in 1310, but evolved into a council that headed State Inquisitors by 1539. They had total authority to convict anyone they chose. Thanks to the success of the Jesuit Order,

Asia was now able to be overthrown, which the elite had long attempted. Through deception and manipulation, the Jesuit Order spread Catholicism, and the religion and cultures of Asian countries were inverted to Rome's Will. At the same time, other families were invading the region with banks, wars, and opium, dissolving individuality, and freedom on all fronts and replacing leaders with more accommodating puppets. This side of history will be discussed in upcoming family chapters. This is exactly why Asian countries, in particular, hate the western world. They hate the elite and the Vatican, but it has been lumped into one thing: Westerners. Just as the elite have lumped Catholicism into Christianity.

The Jesuits, who control the CIA, MOSSAD, and other elite orders, work to bring about the New World Order, which will be a religious-political government, with one man as the Holy Emperor, a deified man the entire population of the world will be forced to worship. They have continuously worked to make history repeat. The elite's final empire requires ALL countries in the world to accept and demand one government in order to achieve "peace" and "unity". However, dear reader, if you want to know what the New World Order will look like, look at Nebuchadnezzar II of Babylon, or any Egyptian or Roman Empire. Know your history.

Nicolaus Copernicus dedicated De Revolutionibus Orbium Coelestium (On the Revolutions of the Celestial Spheres) to Alessandro Farnese. As Pope, he hired Michelangelo to paint the Last Judgement in the Sistine Temple as well as the Crucifixion of Saint Paul. The focus Catholicism has on the destruction of Christ and His followers is overwhelming. Like every aristocratic family they patroned many artists, philosophers, and the like, in order to control their work as they do today. Today start-ups are bought out and taken over if they are the best or geniuses or if they can be used to serve the elite's purposes. Michelangelo, for example, had no option to say no to painting a high ceiling without the proper materials or supports, forced to lay on wooden planks on his back for hours on end until the work was complete, because he depended on the money, he was given by the elite who supported his life. If he didn't follow their demands, he would have never been heard of. Same with Galileo, and so many others.

In 1542 Alessandro published his Decree License ab Initio, which founded the Congregation for the Doctrine of the Faith, another order which focused on controlling Christians through censorship and persecution. The council burned people to death by the hundreds and rounded up Jews, throwing them into Spanish jails. He then built the Piazza del Gesu, also called Tempio Farnesiano, for the Jesuit Order. One of the famous statues made for the cult and displayed in the temple is called Religion Crushes Heresy. It is a statue of a woman, wielding a cross (the Roman instrument of death), stepping on 2 men who are falling back in fear. Other statues are of the Farnese poster child, Spanish Knight Ignatius Loyola, who was now named a Saint by the Church. In the center of the temple stands a large golden sun, surrounded by altars. The headquarters of the Jesuits was changed in 1925 to Villa Barberini. Alessandro then cut Britain's King Henry VIII out of the Church and welcomed those from the Levant region to relocate to Ancona and be part of the Papal States.

Alessandro Farnese Jr., now called Gran Cardinale, was given many lands and positions because of his grandfather Pope Paul III. He was made Vice-Chancellor of the Holy Roman Church, Governor of Tivoli, Archpriest of St. Mary Major Basilica, Archpriest of St. Peter's Basilica, and if that wasn't enough, he was Administrator of Jaen, Vizeu, Würzburg, and Avignon. By 1536 he was Bishop of Monreale where he founded a Jesuit college in 1552. In 1538 he was made Bishop of Massa and Cahors, followed by Archbishop of Tours and Benevento and Cardinal-Bishop of Ostia and Velletri. Being the heir, he inherited his father's estates upon his death. He continued restoring the family's buildings including the Church of the Gesu, the Villa Farnese, and the monastery Tre Fontane. During these years, he served as Papal Legate between King Charles of the Holy Roman Empire and King Francis of France. In 1550 he acquired the northern portion of Palatine Hill in Rome and converted the ruins of Tiberius' palace into his summer home where the gardens became famous as one of the first botanical gardens of Europe. In March of 1589 Jr. died and was buried in his Church of Gesu, in front of the altar. Let's get back to his cousins, the Orsini's.

Pierfrancesco Vicino Orsini was born in 1523 to Gian Corrado Orsini and Clarice, whose father was Cardinal Franciotto Orsini. Pierfrancesco grew up under the care of Uncle Girolamo after his father died when he was 3. When Girolamo died, he and his brother were sent to the Abbot of Farfa. In 1535 he became Prince of Bomarzo, Collepiccolo, Castelvecchio, Montenero, and Mompeo, after marrying Giulia Farnese, the daughter of Galeazzo, cousin of Alessandro. In 1545 cousin-in-law Alessandro, now Pope Paul III, had Pierfrancesco and his military to reinforce Emperor Charles V's army and fight the Protestants. After being held prisoner for several years, he was set free in 1547 and built a garden for his wife, who had worked for his release. To thank her, he built her a Middle-Ages Disney land, a garden called Villa delle Meraviglie, more commonly known as the Sacred Wood or Park of Monsters. Out of the volcanic rock surrounding the region, huge monsters and gods were carved. Alchemical symbolism is seen throughout the garden. The entryway to the park presents 2 sphinxes, who guard the Wood. Proteus is the next large statue seen. Coming out of the side of a hill, the immense face, with an open mouth, balances a large stone globe, on top of his head. On the globe (on top of the world) is a castle covered in Orsini symbols. An Etruscan tomb was recreated in the park, as well as a temple wherein Giulia Farnese is likely buried. The Fountain of Pegasus, Venus On a Shell, a leaning house, nymphs, dragons, and more adorn the Sacred Wood. There is even an Ogre, whose mouth you can walk through. Long before it was completed, Pierfrancesco was called to Hesdin to fight the French with Orazio Farnese. Orazio was killed and Pierfrancesco was taken prisoner again.

In 1556 Pierfrancesco took part in the War of Italy, in opposition of Spanish viceroyalty of Naples. 100 of his infantrymen were ambushed and killed by townspeople who assisted the Colonna and Spanish side. Giulio Orsini and his calvary were ordered to destroy the village and execute all the inhabitants. Due to this viciousness, Pierfrancesco retired from the military in 1557. The following year he helped arrange the marriage of Cousin Paolo Giordano Orsini to Isabella de'Medici. His sister Marebale had a son Fulvio but by the time he was 9 they had both been abandoned by her husband. Fulvio, the descendant of Ursus de Paro, from the Mugnano line of Orsini, then grew up in the Church and studied ancient languages. He soon became noticed by Pope Paul III, Alessandro Farnese, and was made his personal antique dealer and librarian. He handled the ordering and development of all of the Farnese collections. Because of his work researching and collecting, he wrote many studies on antiquities and was able to build his own collection of paintings, gems and more. He published many documents including a new edition of Arnobius and translated the Septuagint. Over the years he gathered hundreds of manuscripts and books, which were later taken by the Vatican Library. Fulvio became a patron of El Greco, a painter. His personal collection of paintings, including 7 paintings by El Greco, over 400 gems, marbles, and antiques, was absorbed by the Farnese family when he died.

Giovanni Battista Orsini, also called Jean-Baptiste des Ursins, was the son of Lorenzo and Clarice Orsini, sister of Cardinal Latino Orsini. He grew up like most others in his family, in the education and service of the Church. In 1467 he became the 39th Grand Master of the Order of the Knights Hospitaller and auditor of the Roman Sacra Rota. Soon thereafter he was made Canon of a chapter of the Lateran Basilica. In 1477, uncle Latino Orsini retired as Abbot of the Benedictine Monastery of San Salvadore Maggiore and Giovanni was put in his place. After participating in the conclaves of 1484, Pope Innocent VIII (Giovanni Battista Cybo) was elected, and Giovanni became his papal legate. In this position he worked to secure the region from the Ottomans who were constantly invading. In 1490 he took on another of his uncle's positions as apostolic administrator for the Archdiocese of Taranto and soon accumulated the post of administrator of Romagna and Bologna as well. Rodrigo Borgia was his favored candidate to become the next pope, and in 1492, Giovanni participated in the conclave again, and Rodrigo was made Pope Alexander VI. Giovanni was repaid with a Roman palace, Castle Soriano, and Castle Monticelli. Giovanni Orsini's shield can be seen on the walls of the Castle of Rhodes (another property of his), next to the emblem of the Order of the Hospital of Saint John of Jerusalem.

On January 21, 1495, Giovanni had been elected as Camerlengo of the Sacred College of Cardinals. 2 years later he became Archpriest of the Basilica of Santa

Maria Maggiore. In 1500, his nephew Aldobrandini di Pitigliano had come of age and was in need of a position in government. Giovanni gave him the monastery of San Lorenzo. After meeting other family members including Duke Francesco Orsini and his brothers Giolio and Paolo, near Lake Trasimeno, a plan to kill the Pope's son, Cesare Borgia, was laid out. Unfortunately, the badly established plot resulted in his arrest and imprisonment. On January 3, 1503, he was sent to the Castel Sant'Angelo, where less than one month later, he was poisoned to death. Pope Alexander VI ordered the doctors to write false documents stating that Giovanni's death was natural.

The birth of Paolo Giordano Orsini, 1st Duke of Bracciano took place in 1541. His grandparents were Gian Giordano Orsini who married Felice della Rovere, one of the illegitimate daughters of Pope Julius II (Giuliano della Rovere), and the Count Bosio Sforza who married Costanza Farnese, an illegitimate daughter of Pope Paul III (Alessandro Farnese). Paintings of Costanza can be found in many places, depicting her red curls, typically braided, and pulled up, and rosy cheeks and elegant clothing and jewels. You can easily see the family resemblance in her portraits and those of Clelia, Alessandro Farnese Jr.'s daughter. Costanza's husband, Bosio, was from the longstanding aristocratic Sforza-Orsini branch. Their grandson Federico carried on the titles and bloodline through his children with Beatrice Orsini. But back to Paolo!

Gian Giordano Orsini had several children including Girolamo Orsini who married Pope Paul III's daughter Francesca and had 2 children, Felice Orsini, who married Marco Colonna II and Paolo Giordano Orsini. Girolamo was convicted of murdering his brother Napoleon over property. Thanks to his father-in-law the Pope, he was pardoned, and the crime was set on his brother Abbot Francesco. Francesco Orsini was convicted of murder and extortion and his lands and monies were taken and given to his nephew Paolo. Girolamo died just before Paolo was born, 3 days after being hit on the head while in Rome. Son Paolo grew up as a wealthy, spoiled boy, and married Isabella de' Medici, whom he didn't like and never lived with. Instead, he furthered his military career as a General of the Spanish infantry in 1572. On July 16, 1576, Isabella was on a hunting trip at the Medici Villa of Cerreto Guidi. Her brother, Grand Duke Francesco I de' Medici reported:

"While she was washing her hair in the morning ... She was found by Signor Paolo Giordano on her knees, having immediately fallen dead."

However, it was not believed as witnesses soon testified that Paulo strangled her to death in front of the servants, around noon. Paolo carried on his life-long affair with his cousin, Troilo Orsini, much easier after that. Isabella's sister had also had an "accident" just days before. It is extremely common that most of the women drop like flies, either because of murder or because of giving birth every year of their lives. Soon Paolo had another mistress, Vittoria Accoramboni who was married to Francesco Peretti. Within days, Francesco was assassinated, and Paolo married Vittoria, just 8 months before he died in November 1585. One month later, Vittoria was killed by Ludovico Orsini, in order to keep Paolo's assets in the family. They were given to Paolo and Isabella's son, Virginio Orsini.

Virginio Orsini had been born in 1572 and became the 2nd Duke of Bracciano with not only the weight of the Orsini blood but the Medici as well. As an Orsini family member, he was a knight of the Order of the Golden Fleece, the Orsini family order. He married Flavia Peretti and had 11 children, including another Paolo Giordano who became a prince of the Holy Roman Empire after marrying Princess Isabella Appiani but had no children. Another son, Alessandro Orsini, was a Cardinal and a patron of Galileo and the Jesuit Order. Shakespeare's play, Twelfth Night, opens with the character of Duke Orsino saying:
"If music be the food of love, play on."

The play was performed in Virginio's honor at the Court of England in 1600. During his life, Virginio was surrounded by the most famous artists and composers of his time, including Cristiano Malvezzi and Emilio de'Cavalieri who composed the first opera of Florence and Rome, where he died in 1615. Although son Paulo had no children, son Ferdinando Orsini III, Duke of Bracciano had sons Virginio and Flavio Orsini IV. Flavio became the 5th Duke of Bracciano, Prince of Nerola and Scandriglia, Imperial Prince and Cardinal. He spent his life going to war for the pope and benefitting from the titles and wealth he received. Virginio became a Knight of Malta and went to war against the Turks. In 1641 he was made Cardinal and Protector of the Polish and Portuguese Orient. In 1675 he was made Cardinal Bishop of Frascati where he died one year later.

Meanwhile, Pope Paul III's son Pier Luigi Farnese Jr. had become the Duke of Parma and Piacenza, in the Province of Viterbo. Parma was now the capital of the Curia. Pier's life was shadowed with public humiliation and bullying for being an illegitimate child of the pope. By the age of 17 he had been married to Girolama (Gerolama) Orsini, the daughter of Ludovico Orsini. Pier and his brother Ranuccio had become notorious mercenaries who fought in the sacking of Rome in 1527, on opposite sides. While Pier was off fighting, Girolama stayed in the Papal Court and raised the family. Her brother Gianfrancesco Orsini had become Knight of the Order of Saint Michel and Lord of Sorano, Manciano, Fiano, Morlupo, Saturnia, Monte della Guardia and Montemerano. Pier's first son was Alessandro Farnese Jr. As the ruler of his small kingdom, he taxed his people mercilessly and a culture of darkness and murder thrived.

By 1537 Pier had been named the Duke of Castro, and all his lands and titles were tied to the blood of his children. Pier soon built a citadel, palace, and mint to secure his kingdom as an independent state, using the money taken from the population.

His people knew him as a ruthless, homosexual, cruel man who lived in the luxury formed from his abuse of his own people. He was charged with the rape of bishop Cosimo Gheri in 1537, but Cosimo was found dead before the case went through court. After a decade of rampant homosexuality and murder from their ruler, counts Francesco Anguissola, Agostino Landi and marquises Giovan Luigi Confalonieri and Girolamo and Alessandro Pallavicini decided that Pier must go.

On September 10, 1547, Pier was stabbed multiple times by the 4 men, until he died. His body was then hung from a window of his palace in Piacenza. After showing it to the people, the body of Pier was dumped into a pit. After 81 years of extravagance and violence, Alessandro Farnese died in 1549 from a catarrh. He was entombed in bronze and is worshiped in St. Peter's Basilica. Pier's son Ottavio had been married to Princess Margaret, daughter of King Charles V of Spain by the time he was 13. Altogether Girolama and Pier had 5 children, including twins. One of the twins died while in infancy. After retiring to the Palazzo Farnese, Girolama died in 1590 and was buried at the Farnese family crypt at the Sanctuary of Santa Maria della Steccata.

By now the Orsini family is quite large, like the others. Now we see the 8th and 11th Counts and Dukes of Orsini and dozens with papal titles.

The following generations bring us to the children of Niccolo Orsini of Pitigliano. Of his 9 children, daughter Elena Marie was married to Prince Cem, the son of Mehmed II the Conqueror and younger brother of Sultan Bayezid II who lived under the protection of the Knights Hospitaller. He had attempted to overthrow his brother and become Sultan himself, but this didn't go as planned and Cem was forced to escape. Sultan Bayezid paid Pope Innocent VIII (Giovanni Cybo) to keep him away from the Ottoman Empire. This cost him 120,000 crowns, the Holy Lance (which had pierced the side of Jesus as he hung on the cross), 100 slaves, and an annual fee of 45,000 ducats. Now trapped in a foreign land, Cem made the best of it by marrying into the Orsini family. Elena and Cem had 4 children, Pierre Mohammed Sayd, Sehzade Abdullah, Oghuz-Khan, and Sah Ayse. Elena's siblings were married into other elite families, but the following generation was married within the Orsini family.

Pietro Orsini, the Count of Muro Lucano, was made Prince of Solofra in 1623. His son Ferdinando III, Duke of Gravina, was father of Pietro Francesco Orsini, who was crowned Pope Benedict XIII. He became the Bishop of Manfredonia, Bishop of Cesena and then Archbishop of Benevento. His life-long friend was mystic Serafina di dio, whose real name was Prudentia Pisa. She was canonized after she died. Pietro was a member of the Dominican Order, an elite Order which was created for one purpose, to defeat heretics. This order named him Vincenzo Maria in 1671. He enjoyed making huge displays during masses, which created a disturbance. During his time as pope, he canonized and sainted a multitude of people. He expanded the church by elevating 29 cardinals and consecrated over 100 bishops. He passed a papal bull which encouraged all in the Dominican Order to gather members and train them. There have been several denied attempts to turn him into a saint since his death in 1730. The name Domenico was often used by the family for many generations, since the 1300's, because of their affiliation to the Order.

One of the nephews of Pietro was Ferdinando Bernualdo Filippo Orsini. Born in Solofra, Ferdinando was the son of a prince and grew up as royalty, inheriting his father's titles and lands upon his death. He married Princess Giovanna Caracciolo in 1711, who unfortunately died 4 years later. So, Ferdinando then married Princess Giancinta Ruspoli Marescotti and became a Knight of the Golden Stole. Unhappy in her marriage, after producing 4 children, she left him for Rome. The family had been entangled for the past generation in feuds which caused increasing debts. Cousin Flavio Orsini attempted to use his wife, Marie-Anne "Princess of the Ursins" to gain a foothold for the family in Spain, by sending her to be Queen Elizabeth Farnese's maid but still the debtors grew in number as the war against the Colonna family continued. Ferdinando's uncle, Pope Benedict XIII, forced the two to reconcile and rectified the family's situation by merging Gravina and Bracciano into one, making the title Prince of the Sacred Soglio. He also gave Ferdinando the title Prince of Roccagorga. His wife stayed in Rome, and he went to Naples, as they could not get along. He later bought a palace in Monte Savello and made it the new "capitol" for the family. Time and time again he attempted to enter politics but was shut down by the other families. He was even turned away by the Golden Fleece Order and died alone, in 1734.

Let's take a moment to talk about Queen Elizabeth. Born in 1692, Elizabeth (also called Isabel de Farnesi, Elisabetta, Isabella) became the Queen of Spain as the 2nd wife of King Philip V, arranged by Cardinal Alberoni. She became the mother of Charles III. Having control over her weak husband, Elizabeth ruled Spain and through many wars, succeeded in expanding her reach to Italy so her children could rule there. One of her sons Carlos (Charles III) became King of Naples, Sicily and Spain which were passed down to his son Charles IV. Among her 6 children is Maria Antonietta who became Queen of Sardinia after marrying King Victor Amadeus III. Charles III had 19 children, most of whom died in infancy and more who died while young. One son, Gabriel Antonio Francisco, married Maria Ana Vitoria Josefa and had 4 children. He died November 23, 1788, in Madrid. His brother, Ferdinando I Antonio Pascual Juan Nepomuceno Serafin Genaro Benedicto, King of the Two Sicily's, had 20 children total with his two wives, Maria Karolina von Habsburg-Lothringen and Lucia Migliaccio, Duchess of Floridia. His children include Princess Luisa of Naples and Sicily and Grand Duchess of Tuscany, Prince Alberto di Borbone, and Princess of Asturias Maria Antonia as well as Charles IV, king of Spain, Sicily, and Naples. Meanwhile, back in the Orsini line...

Ferdinando Orsini's sons were Domenico and Raimondillo. Born in 1719, Domenico was the heir to his father's fortune and became Duke of Gravina, Prince of Solofra, Vallata, Roccagorga, Count of Muro Lucano, Patrician of Naples, Genoa, Ancona, and Venice and more, upon his death. By the time he was 18 he had been assigned the position of ambassador of Queen Maria Amalia as assistant of Pope Clement XIII. When he was 19, he married Princess Anna Paola Flaminia Odescalchi and had 4 children. In 4 short years, Anna died, and Domenico turned to the papacy for comfort. The next year, 1743, he was made Cardinal Deacon. Over the next few years his comfort came from the many titles and fortunes he collected. In the late 1760's he became the ambassador of King Ferdinand IV for the Holy See. Knight of the Insigne and Royal Order of San Gennaro, Domenico died in 1789 and was buried in the basilica of San Giovanni. Meanwhile, his brother Raimondillo became the friar for the Congregation of the Oratory by the age of 20. Knowing from birth that he would not be burdened with the family properties, as second born, his station was in service to Rome. In 1724 he was made Bishop of Melfi and Rapolla. Before too long he became Archbishop of Capua and Corinth. After serving as Chancellor of the Order of San Gennaro in 1738, he went on to become the titular Patriarch of Constantinople before his death in 1750. There are many dozens of bishops in the Orsini family, including Archbishop Bertoldo Orsini who served from 1323-1325, Poncello Orsini, Bishop of Aversa, and Bishop Tommaso who served in Strongoli in 1566 before becoming Bishop of Foligno in 1568.

Francois Marie Orsini was born in 1638 in Corsica, France. His great grandson, Xavier Orsini had 14 children with his wives Magdeleine Benigni and Angele Catherine Mattei. Born in 1773 Xavier was a sea man until he died. His children bore the name Orsini Benigni, the name of 1st wife, Magdeleine Benigni. His children and grandchildren stayed in France. 1819 brings a bit of good old family fun into the spotlight, once again with Felice Orsini. Felice Orsini had 2 sisters, Filippa Maria, and Irena. Filippa Maria Orsini married Francesco Giovannucci and had 9 children, several who were in the military. She died in Massachusetts in 1920. Irena Orsini married Gaetano Presutti and they had 3 children. She died one year after her sister, also in Massachusetts. Massachusetts, like most New England states, is under very strict control of the elite blood lines. Whether British Bankers or Roman Catholic soldiers many families moved to those areas. But back to Felice.

Felice Orsini was a member of the Carbonari revolutionary sect. Friend of Giuseppe Mazzini, he joined the Giovane Italia group as well. While part of this international espionage group, he was assigned secret missions by Giuseppe and after escaping a prison in Mantua, he rested in Britain in 1856, with some British elite friends. In the same year he published his autobiography: The Memoirs and Adventures of Felice Orsini. The next year he published a book called The Austrian Dungeons, detailing his heroic escape. After this became public, Guiseppe told him they were no longer friends, and Felice decided that French ruler, Louis Napoleon, was in the way of Italy's freedom. On January 14, 1858, he knew the Emperor and his wife were on their way to see the new opera, William Tell. Felice planned the attack and gathered some friends to help him. They tossed a total of 3 bombs at the dictator's carriage. 8 people were killed, and 142 more were wounded, including Felice. The Emperor and his wife were unharmed, and Felice was arrested the next day at his home. Accomplice Gomez was sentenced to hard labor, for life and Di Rusio escaped his death sentence and ended up being sent to an island for punishment. From there he escaped and made it to the US where he became an officer in the Battle of Little Big Horn in 1876. On March 13, 1858, Felice was executed by guillotine. Abraham Lincoln had this to say about him:

"an enthusiast [who] broods over the oppression of a people till he fancies himself commissioned by Heaven to liberate them. He ventures the attempt, which ends in little else than his own execution."

Around this time, we see the Jesuits gain full control in America, after trying for 95 years. Though they founded it, Thomas Jefferson, a Freemason who was cautious of the elite Jesuits, copied much of the Declaration of Independence from the Mechlenburg Declaration, which kept them on a leash. Americans really were as free and independent as they could be, for a moment. In 1871, the original Constitution FOR the United States of America was changed to the Constitution OF the United States of America, which was written by a Jesuit Roman Catholic Pope, after a financial deal to help the struggling economy. This is also when the Vatican created their 3rd city-state: Washington DC.

Today it's easy to find the Orsini name in many of the politicians and leaders in America. The Italian, main strain of the bloodline attempts to continue to hide in the shadows of the Vatican.

Duke Filippo Orsini married Francesca Romana Bonacossi and together they had sons Domenico and Benedetto. Domenico was the heir and became the 22nd Duke of Gravina. He decided to get into finance and after spending time gaining experience in Milan, he took a position in Paris. While working at Generali France, where other family members continue the legacy, he met his wife, and they were married. He enjoyed an active life in International Tennis Tournaments. He began an initiative called Progetto Italia which encouraged citizen journalism.

Ron, also called Roy Orsini was murdered by his wife Mary Lee Hatcher in 1982. She also conspired in a very detailed plan to murder someone else. The US media went crazy over the news, and it became one of the most sensational murders of Arkansas history. Mary Lee confessed weeks before she died of a heart attack in 2003.

Alessandro Orsini was born April 14, 1975, and became the director of the Observatory on International Security at the University LUISS "Guido Carli" of Rome, working with Nicoletta and John Orsini. He taught Sociology of Terrorism for the Department of Political Science and has lectured at the places one would expect, such as Harvard, MIT, Johns Hopkins, Boston College, Brookings Institution, Trinity College, and other Jesuit schools. Over in the US, Brad Orsini is the director of Jewish community security under Jewish Federation of Greater Pittsburgh. He is an ex-FBI agent.

In September 2001 Special Agent Bradley Orsini was demoted and received a 30-day suspension without pay for a series of policy violations that occurred from 1993 through 2000. These included but are not limited to having an inappropriate relationship with a subordinate, making improper vulgar and sexual comments, forging names and initials on chain-of-custody forms, evidence labels and interview forms. He threatened a subordinate with violence and improperly documented the seizure of a weapon and ammunition from a search. This is a small list. Regardless of this or because of it, he was awarded the Western Pennsylvania Law Enforcement Agency Directors Award for leading the FBI response to several false flag events including the Franklin Regional High School stabbing and the Monroeville Mall shooting which, as we know, were carried out by the Jesuits of which he is a member.

The Orsinis are also involved in the movie, fashion, and other entertainment (mind control) industries. One Italian Roman Catholic actress, Isabella Orsini, married to Belgian Prince Eduardo de Ligne. They have 2 children, Princess Althea Orsini de Ligne and Princess Athenais de Ligne. Isabella is daughter of Lolita Rossi and member of the order and Jesuit Mario Orsini. A few of the other actresses are Kate Orsini, Valerie Orsini, and Marina Orsini who was married to Canadian actor Serge Postigo for some time. In recent years, the Jesuit position of Grey Pope was handled by Pepe Orso Orsini, who went by Maximus, succeeded by Henry Breakspear.

Ciro Orsini was born in the 1940's, in Italy. In 1978 he founded Ciro's Pomodoro, a pizzeria, in London, which soon became a franchise with locations in Kiev, Riga, Bahrain, Lahore, Beijing, New Delhi, and elsewhere. Ciro's Pizza Pomodoro Ltd of London has a revenue of $6 million. His first restaurant in Los Angeles was managed by his good friend, mafia man Franco Nicoletti, and became home to many mafia members. In the 1990's his partner of the London restaurant was murdered. The murder was never solved. The restaurant's website, which is promoted by Ukrainian mail order bride, trafficking companies, states:

"If we tell you that twelve Orsini men married twelve daughters of kings and emperors, you might slightly begin to understand the man."

In Ciro's social circle are many actors and Hollywood personalities including Hal Stone, Al Pacino, Pamela Anderson, Silvester Stalone, Sacha Stone (who calls himself the messiah), Ozzy Osbourne, Steven Seagal, Bob Van Ronkel, Armand Assante, and Stevie Wonder. His girlfriend, model, and actress Jill Weatherwax, was murdered shortly after he began to show disinterest in her. Jill was 27 years old when she was found dead, having been brutally and viciously beaten in her face and head, and stabbed 29 times from her skull to her hips. A typical crime of passion, but naturally, the case remains unsolved. He, like most in his family, view women as nothing more than a vessel to pump sperm into. Many of his friends' girlfriends have exposed in interviews that he tried to pimp them out to his other elite friends.

Ciro is also friends and coworkers of Serghei Skobeltin (who lived on the same street as Ciro in Miami), Sorin Sapunarescu, and Rodion Sokroviciuc of Russia and Romanian mob boss Nicu Gheara. In Romanian documents Ciro is exposed as being part of the long-standing trafficking ring which expands from the ex-Soviet countries to the US. The documents Ciro is mentioned many times in, detail the activities of the group which are drug trafficking, money laundering, extortion, prostitution, and human trafficking. Like many of his friends and family, he is highly interested in children and has founded a charity called Ciro Orsini and Armand Assante Children's Fund which is partnered with Homeless Worldwide. Next, he founded Help Children Now, for children displaced by war and the International Tribunal of Natural Justice (a faux court for victims of ritual abuse).

"Everyone gets the truth, **no one goes to jail**." Robert David Steele, Chief Council of ITNJ

This company, like many others, is merely a honeypot used to gather up those who have decided to speak out about their ritual abuse, or mind control programming. Over a decade ago it was exposed, once again, how the elite of every country, use their foundations and charities as front companies to launder their money through as well as their products: children and drugs. Naïve people assume that those who establish such organizations would only do it for righteous reasons... why? People don't understand the elite, nor do they want to. They don't understand the mind and desires of Luciferians.

"The public as a mass does not think, will not defend what it believes, and will not analyze the propaganda which is constantly in circulation against any public man who refuses to play along with the gang." — Manly P. Hall, Freemason and Mystic

With friend Chris Reynolds Gordon and a few others, the elite sex club Heaven Circle was born, followed by several others including Nights of St. Francis. The clubs mirror the ancient and modern clubs of the elite involving drugs, alcohol, orgies, bondage, and other perversions. These clubs are used for not only Luciferian rituals, but human trafficking and Mind Control Trauma Programming. The clubs share the same logo, the All-Seeing Eye icon, and call themselves The Masons. Thanks to technological advances the videos and after-hours events are able to also bring in revenue, being sold online. The Nights of St. Francis and Heaven Circle conglomerate claim to be a reincarnation or an upgraded renamed version of the Hellfire Club, which was exposed for its abhorrent activities. The president of the club was called the Devil. This is the club Ciro Orsini couldn't wait to revive, keeping true to his bloodline's beliefs and activities. The club's website states:

"We are one of the four secret societies."

In recent years, he has dabbled in movie acting and producing and has been involved with the Number One Girl, Finding Soraya, A Song to Kill For and more, accumulating a net worth of $17 million. He has been used for numerous publicity stunts, promoting whatever current agenda is taking place. Ciro was in the news in 2022 for his heroic travel to the Polish border, to bake pizza for the people fleeing the country. In following chapters, the lifestyles of the people discussed in the family chapters will be more extensively dissected. If I were to add to every other family member's bio, the same orders, the same pedophilia, and the same rituals, it would be all too repetitive, so I have discussed those things in their appropriate section. These Luciferian activities, which are a deep part of each elite's life are, to many people, inconceivable. So, I will spare the fragile and ignorant brains reading this book, and not discuss it endlessly in each and every chapter.

Ida Elizabeth Orsini came into the spotlight in 1980, when she won the Pulitzer Prize for her investigative reporting on the Church of Scientology. She worked as a reporter for the St. Petersburg Times, Arkansas Democrat-Gazette and Richmond News Leader on top of being involved in marathon waterskiing. She was the wife of Andrew Angelo Orsini. Andrew's father, Serafino Orsini brought the family to Indiana, US, from Italy.

In the 1980's the Orsini family became even more deeply involved in alchemy. Orsini Specialty Pharmacy was founded by Tony Orsini and Michael Fieri, in the hopes of expanding technology. This privately owned, independent company focuses on rare diseases and gene therapies. The company accumulates $405 million annually. At the same address are Orsini Healthcare, with an annual revenue of at least $300 million, and Orsini Pharmaceutical Services Inc., which has an annual revenue of $50 million. Having become the largest independent biotech pharmacology company in the US, in 2019 Consonance Capital Partners invested. In 2022, the Carlyle Group acquired a stake in the Orsini Specialty Pharmacy as well. Other rich, current-day Orsini's include Franc Orsini, who owns thousands of stocks in Lear Corporation. On top of making over $4 million a year as Executive Vice President of Lear, his stock is worth much more.

Remember Queen Elizabeth Farnese? Several generations of her children brought about Juan Carlos Alfonso Víctor María who married Princess Sofía of Greece and Denmark. In 2014 he abdicated his throne to their son, Felipe VI, following a long line of scandals. Knight of Malta and Jesuit, Juan Carlos murdered his younger brother Alfonso with one bullet through his forehead. Of course, this has been completely covered up by multiple fantastic stories such as: Alfonso was playing with the gun while he was cleaning it and shot himself accidentally. How does one clean a loaded gun? The next story was that Juan was holding the gun and Alfonso came into the room, bumping Juan's arm with the door which caused him to pull the trigger. The bullet then bounced off the wall, leaving no marks on it, and lodged itself directly into the center of Alfonso's forehead. Still another version is that Juan did not know the gun was loaded and pointed and fired it at Alfonso. One more is that Alfonso didn't know the gun was loaded and he pointed it at himself, directly in the forehead, and pulled the trigger. When a gun is loaded, it is easy to tell. Other abuses of his power include spending exorbitant amounts of money on personal hunting trips. He brags about his elephant and bear kills and was considered for the Black Pope position. Once the country had had enough of his irresponsibility, and started standing up, he stated he had been considering abdicating for quite some time, passing it to his son. When they are realized, when people start not taking their nonsense any longer, they walk away.

Now that we are caught up on the history of the location and one of the upper elite families, let's continue with the infamous Medici line.

~Medici~

The Medici family claims to descend from either Charlemagne, or Captain Averardo Medici, whose name is seen throughout the family. Most likely Captain Averardo was related to Charlemagne in some way, as all higher positions were given to relatives in these times, as we have seen through numerous families. Medici was the original title given by the Roman Empire to Legionnaires who were trained in the treatment of wounds, at the time called Medici, today it's called Medicine. Averardo was a knight of Emperor Charlemagne who defeated a giant named Mugello in Florence. The coat of arms the Medici family uses, which was permitted by Charlemagne, depicts 6 red circles (called pills) which are said to symbolize the points of the giant's iron mace that Averardo caught with his shield. After his victory the coat of arms was made for his family who then inhabited the place, calling the city Mugello. Later, the emblems of their coat of arms which decorate Florence contained 5 red "pills", in a V shape, with a blue sphere in the top center which included 3 gold fleur-de-lys. The golden Fleur-de-lys on a blue background is the symbol of the family before this time, which many branches continued to use in their evolving coat of arms as branches split and grew. Using coat of arms symbolism, it's easy to see many branches of the same family and how they spread.

This is the upper elite. They have long-standing control over many regions of the world. They were the kings, emperors, princesses, and the aristocracy of Europe and beyond. They formed the countries we know today and the systems with which they are governed. The public was made to believe that they had lost that power, through causes the families protected, while they passed laws and secured their wealth and power as they rule from the background. It was by this time in history that the elite had learned that hiding themselves from the public while controlling the economy, laws, and media, was the best way to ensure their continuous rule.

From Averardo Medici, no one used the title as their name until Boson Medici d'Arles, in 885. His mother, Bertha, was the daughter of King Lothair II, the great grandson of Emperor Charlemagne. His father was Theobald "the Rich", Count of Arles of the Bosonid Dynasty. His firstborn son was named Hugh (Ugo) and became King of Italy as his blood dictated. Second came Boso, also called Bosone VI of Provence, who became the Marquis of Tuscany and the founder of the Frank Dynasty, as Charlemagne was for the Italian Dynasty. Because of the marriage into the Charlemagne line, the Medici's claim to be related to Emperor Charlemagne is valid. Because I already discussed Charlemagne's history in the Orsini chapter, to maintain the understanding of the time period, let's continue. The blood of Charlemagne was united with the blood of the Carolingian Dynasty. Hugh inherited his father's lands and positions. By this time, Boso had married Willa of the House of Welf. Her father was King of Burgundy, and her brother was Emperor Louis "the Blind". In 905 the Emperor Louis had been captured, blinded, and deposed. Hugh immediately became his chief advisor and regent. A few years later Louis made him Duke of Provence and Marquis of Vienne.

Meanwhile, Boso had taken several counties and been given positions by his brother the king. The family had its share of drama, especially since their mother was an illegitimate child, as were a couple of their brothers.

> "Boso for his part, being King Hugh's brother by the same father, was very anxious himself to become marquess of Tuscany, and was lying in wait, ready to entrap Lambert. Accordingly, on Boso's advice King Hugh sent a threatening message to Lambert, warning him not to call himself his brother any longer. To that Lambert, who was of a proud and undisciplined temper, instead of replying modestly, as he should have done, returned the following violent answer:
> 'The king cannot possibly deny that I am his brother and that we both came to life by the same passage and from the same body. This truth I desire to prove by the ordeal of single combat in the sight of all men.'" — Antapodosis by Liudprand of Cremona

This upset Hugh and after Lambert won a duel with a servant of Hugh's, he was arrested and blinded. This is how Boso was rewarded with his half-brother's land of Tuscany. Over the next decade, Hugh was at war with King Rudolph of Burgundy, his uncle, hoping to add the kingdom of East France to the kingdom of Italy. In 933 he succeeded. To maintain peace in the family, Uncle Rudolph gave his daughter Adelaide to Hugh's son Lothair. Hugh's daughter Alda was married off to Alberic II, who had been another rival for the empire. Boso was ever supportive of his brother and gave up his post in Tuscany when Hugh wanted his illegitimate son Hubert to have it instead. Meanwhile, the Duke of Saxony, Henry "the Fowler" had come from Germany and was made King of East France. Not liking this at all, Hugh, and his brother Boso decided to depose him and place Hugh's son on the throne.

In 912 Willa died, leaving Boso with a handful of children. Upon her death, Willa's mother, Queen Willa of Burgundy, married Hugh, Boso's brother. If you think this is dizzying, Queen Willa's father was Boson, King of Provence, grandson of Boson "the Elder". Boson "the Elder", the founder of the Bosonid Dynasty, is the great grandfather of Hugh and Boso as well. This is how 90% of the marriages are in these families, besides that they use the same names so often it makes the family tree difficult to untangle at times, but never impossible. In 931 Boso served as a mediator between the Holy See of Northern Italy, the Patriarchate of Aquileia and due to his successes, he was given the position of Margrave the following year. In

940 Count Boso patroned the family's St. Barnard d'Romans monastery. Like most of the men in his family, Hugh had many mistresses and wives, and a number of children. Hugh remained King of Italy until his death in 947, however, his son Lothair had been crowned King-to-be in 931, after the arguments with Lambert.

Lothair married the daughter of his great-uncle, Adelaide, and had one known daughter. When Lothair died, Adelaide, who had become the widow of a king for the 3rd time in her life, attempted to claim the kingdom for her daughter, Emma. Unfortunately, jealousy ran through this family and the daughter of Boso, Willa, had been married to margrave Berengar. While he was from a royal family, filled with kings and dukes, Willa wanted the title of Queen, as her mother had. She had been raised in mysticism and sorcery and cast spells on people. Liudprand of Cremona documented her adultery as well, describing one of her lovers as "soot-colored, hairy, and short with a tail-like appendage".

Berengar had been at war with Hugh, for the kingdom of Italy and it's said that he poisoned Lothair, which led to his death in 950. During this time Lothair's wife Adelaide had been kidnapped and tortured by Willa. Because of this she was made a Saint. Finally, Berengar became King of Italy, by naming his son Adalbert as co-ruler. After Lothair died, Berengar forced his son Adalbert to marry widow Adelaide. In 960 he invaded the Papal States, attacking Pope John XII. Hugh's daughter Alda, who married Alberic II, Duke of Rome, had a son, Count Ioannes of Albon, the brother of Octavian, who became Pope John XII. Alberic II was called Prince and Senator of all the Romans. Unfortunately, by 961 Berengar's army had abandoned him, and his kingdom was taken. He lived the next 3 years hiding and running, until he surrendered and was put in prison where he died in 966. Willa and Berengar had many children, whom I will discuss along with Emma. While I have only discussed a few of the daughters and sons of Boso and Hugh, let's pick up with the next generation after we take it back.

Theobald, King Hugh's father, was the grandson of Boson "the Elder", Count of Arles, Valois, Burgundy, Sieur d'Antibes, and Turin. Boson is called the founder of the Bosonid Dynasty, a branch of the Carolingians. His children were Boson d'Arles II, heir of the family's titles and wealth, Hubert, also called Hucbert who was the father of Theobald, Theutberga, one of many wives of King Lothair II, great grandson of Emperor Charlemagne, and Richilde who was married to Abbot Bouin of Vienne. When Boson died in 855 his daughter Theutberga was still very young. She was taken in by her brother, Hucbert who had become the lay abbot of Saint Maurice, and Count of Transjurane Burgundy. Boson's daughter Richilde had many children including Boson d'Autun, Count of Vienne and Duke of Provence, Margrave and Duke of Burgundy, Richard II "the Justicer", Buvina who married Count Thierry II, and Richilde who married Emperor Charles II "the Bald". When we come forward in the timeline, I will discuss this family more.

So, Boson "the Elder" was descended from the Carolingian Dynasty, and knowing that they hail from Lothair and Charlemagne, the family tree is set before us. Charlemagne, called Carloman Magnus, was the King of the Franks, King of Italy, and the Holy Roman Emperor until 814. Remember I discussed him in the Orsini chapter. His 9 sons created what is known as the Carolingian Dynasty. The sons split up and became kings of their own nations, forming the 5 branches of the Dynasty. The Lombard branch descended from Pepin and his sons and daughters, and their children were the nobility of the region. The son of Louis "the Pious", who was also named Pepin, became the founder of the branch of Aquitain. The 2nd son of Louis founded the German branch while the 3rd son founded the French. Charlemagne's other son, Lothair, formed the Lotharingian branch which the Medici's descend from.

Lothair's sons ruled Italy, Lotharingia, and Lower Burgundy but because their children were all female, the family titles were dissolved, the daughters married their cousins of highest rank, and the family warred amongst themselves to retake the kingdom piece by piece. However, by this time, thanks to their great grandfather Emperor Charlemagne, the Church was now the throne. This brings us to Boson Medici d'Arles.

The line of Charlemagne leads us straight back to great-great grandfather Ansegisel de Metz, born in 610 in France. In 639 Ansegisel married Beggue, who was made a Saint like her mother and mothers before. As we saw in other lines, during this time and before, rulers were made into deities and worshipped. Ansegisel had travelled to Germany and Belgium and had become the Count of Metz, Duke of Brabant, and Dux of King Sigbert III of Austrasia, meaning he had 2 legions under his command. He had many children including Pepin II, named for Beggue's father. In 662 he was murdered in a feud with his enemy and fellow nobleman Gundewin. Upon his death, Beggue, a Belgian royal, built Saint Begga's Collegiate Church in Andenne, Belgium, where Ansegisel was buried. Building temples and convents is a common practice of families. Convents allowed for a publicly accepted place to imprison their children who weren't useful for breeding and more.

> "If the populace knew with what idiocy they were ruled, they would revolt." - Charlemagne

At this time, it was common for the firstborn to be the heir- Charlemagne and titles of their parents, while second born children and lower, were expected to serve the temple or be married off for governmental purposes. For example, daughter Clotilda was married to King Theuderic III of Neustria and named a Saint. Upon the death of her husband, she became Queen Regent of Neustria and Bourgogne. Her sons were Childebert III "the Just", King of the Franks, and Clovis IV, also King of the Franks. Her brother Pepin II of Heristal became the Mayor of the Palace of Austrasia and became known as Pepin "the Fat". Being the heir, he inherited the titles and lands of the Duke of Austrasia. In 679 he went to battle against his rival, King Theuderic III and defeated him in the Battle of Tertry, almost 10 years later. In Paris they signed a treaty and Pepin was made Mayor of Austrasia, Neustria, and Burgundy. Pepin, rejuvenated with his successful war, called himself Prince of the Franks. During his life, he had many children with his wives and mistresses, to whom he gave positions and lands, ensuring the empire he had gained control over would remain in the family.

One brother of Ansegisel was Chlodulf, called Saint Cloud, who took his father's position as the next Bishop of Metz in 657. He spent his life using his family's wealth to make the cathedral of St. Stephen luxurious. His sons became the Bishop of Trier and Duke of Austrasia. Meanwhile, another brother, Walechise, became Count of Verdun. One son's family became the line of the governing elite, the other the line of the religious elite and the last was given the scraps. Ansegisel and his brothers were children of Saints. Their father, Saint Arnulf was the Bishop of Metz, of the Frank Dynasty, and their mother was Saint Dode. Arnulf (Arnold) was the advisor of the Merovingian court, and a member of the family. He was descended from a long line of nobleman and inherited the lands (between rivers Moselle and Meuse) and wealth of his father. He was raised in the court of King Theudebert II and was well educated. Soon he was put in charge of 6 districts and married to Abbess Doda. In 611 he was offered the position as Bishop of Metz, and because his wife had recently become a nun of Treves, he took the position. In 613 the grandmother of Theudebert had taken over the kingdom, and Arnulf joined in the revolt against her. She was tortured and killed and Chlothachar II was put on the throne. In 628, with the kingdom secured, Arnulf retired and became a monk in the Remiremont Abbey in Vosges, which he had built many years before.

After moving to Habendum, he died around 643 and made a Saint. Following his genealogy back we find his great grandfather, great-great grandfather and so on, were Praetorian Prefects of Gaul (France). The Prefect of Gaul was formed by Constantine I in 337, to maintain the kingdom under his sons' rule. Prefects held the position of chief aide, meaning they oversaw their section of the Roman Empire, under the command of the Emperor, and handled all administrative and judicial responsibilities. They were the highest ranked commanders of the Roman elite soldiers called the Praetorian Guard. Another member of the family is Theodorus I who became the Archbishop of Milan until 490. This genealogy takes us back to Bishop Gaius Sollius Modestus Apollinaris Sidonius, son-in-law of Emperor Avitus and son of the Prefect of Gaul. Knowing how names are given, in the appropriate time period, and what that means, we know that Gaius was a member of the Sollia family. The Sollia's were potters, monument makers and consuls of the Roman

Empire dating back to BC times. Sollia and Sollius lived in Auvergne-Rhone-Alpes in France, where a monument was built for Sollius upon his death. Sollia was the heir to her husbands' lands. Marcus Sollius, possibly their son, was named during the reign of Caligula in Pinna, Italy. Marcus Sollius Atticus dedicated a monument in Picenum to his brother who was an officer of the military of the treasury of Imperial Rome, legate of the Legio VII Gemina, and consul of Rome, which led to the family's titles and wealth for generations. However, the region the family inhabited was called Gallia Celtica because of the Celtic tribes who had migrated into the area hundreds of years before. The tribes who lived in the same area the Sollia's did included several federations: the Aquitani, Belgae, and Galli, who were also called Celtae.

In Part I the tribes were detailed so we already know how the Celtic tribes are traced back to Japheth, Noah's son. Arnulf's mother was the daughter of Chlothar I, King of the Franks. This line can be traced back to the Merovingian Dynasty, started by the sons of King Clodio (also spelled Chlodio, Clodius, Cloio), of the Sicambri in 270 BC, who had been Salics before, from the Illyrian kingdom, in the Baltic region, established by King Boemus and his wife Pannonia in 2000 BC. It wasn't called Pannonia until Rome took it over. King Boemus and other rulers of the surrounding tribes were descended from the sons of Japheth, son of Noah. From this line we come to Falius Eutropius several hundred years later, born in Sabine territory, who married Claudia Crispina and fathered Emperor Constantius I Chlorus and others. Constantius leads directly to his descendant Caesar Gaius Flavius Valerius Constantius Chlorus, father of Constantine the Great. We have already come full circle, since I have discussed this family line extensively, in Part I, which runs through many including the Rockefellers.

Let's come forward in time to the Bosonid Dynasty where we left off. The children of Rochilde, daughter of Boson "the Elder", included Empress Rochilde who was married to Charles "the Bald", Emperor of the Western Empire and grandson of Charlemagne. Rochilde's son Boson d'Autun became King of Provence and Count of Vienne. He married Ermengardis, the daughter of Louis II, Emperor of Italy, and had many children including Queen Willa of Burgundy, who was mentioned before for her ruthlessness. Another son of Rochilde, was Richard "the Justicer", Margrave and Duke of Bourgogne France. Let's talk more about the next generation, the great grandchildren of Boson "the Elder".

Richard "the Justicer" had 9 children. Son Rudolph inherited many of his father's titles and lands, and in 923 he became King of Western Francia. He was crowned by the Archbishop of Sens and gave the family's Dukedom to his brother Hugh "the Black". Upon becoming king, Rudolph went to war against King Henry "the Fowler", of East Francia. There were still infighting and land grabs taking place between the families and that didn't stop because men who were once Dukes were now Kings.

When Rudolph was made king, Henry had already made an alliance with King Robert, who had been King of West Francia for one year before Rudolph was crowned. Henry took this opportunity of change to secure the land of Lorraine. Although Rudolph fought against him, Henry's army was larger. Rudolph had little support from other nobles because all of the nobles wanted to be King. The Vikings began raiding West France, spreading Rudolph's army across the kingdom. By 925 Henry had obtained the territory and the Vikings had been pushed out. The upheaval allowed the Normans to begin pillaging and plundering for themselves, further destabilizing the region. During a battle with them Rudolph was injured.

Meanwhile, Henry had the support of the other nobles, and had an army strong enough to defend the region. While Rudolph spoke with his cousin Louis "the Blind", the Holy Roman Emperor, about the newest invaders, the Magyars (Hungarians), Henry was defeating them. For the past decade Louis had been at war with the Magyars who continuously invaded Italy, making it difficult for him to gain support as the Emperor. In 905 Louis had heard the complaints of the nobleman of Italy and invaded. Berengar, ruler of the Magyars, was pushed back to Pavia, in Northern Italy. The victory was short-lived because of the lack of support of the people. Quickly the news of Louis' small army reached Berengar who came back with even more men and captured Louis who was hiding in the Catholic Church of St. Peter. In July of 905 Louis' eyes were taken along with his crown and titles. Rudolph and Louis had much in common, and no doubt Rudolph didn't want to end up like his cousin. While Rudolph was buying time, as often as possible, Henry kidnapped the Hungarian prince and achieved a 10-year treaty with them. Unfortunately, he had no intention of upholding his end of the deal and spent the next few years fortifying his land and invading the Slavic territory. When they invaded again the Hungarians were destroyed.

By 935 Rudolph had become infested with lice, crabs, and other creatures who live on filthy things. He died the following year and was buried in the abbey of Sainte-Colombe. He had previously passed his titles and wealth to his brother Hugh, while sister Richilde married Count Lietaud I of Macon. Richild's great-great grandson was Knight Templar, Count d'Anjou, Tours, and Maine, and King of Jerusalem, Fulk V. His son inherited the kingdom and passed it down as the family grew. Sister Adelaide married Count Reginar II of Hainaut. After having several children, she became a Saint and Queen of Italy, as well as Regent of the Holy Roman Empire. Cousin Valperto had become Archbishop of Milan, like his great grandfather before, and the family grew in influence and wealth.

So, dear reader, by now the Medici's were Kings of Jerusalem, France, and Italy!

Boson d'Autun had 4 children that we know of. His son, Louis "the Blind", and daughter Queen Willa of Burgundy I have already discussed. Willa's children include

Willa of Burgundy, King Louis II of Provence, and King Rudolph II of Upper Burgundy and Italy. After much infighting, Rudolph was married to Bertha in order to maintain peace in Burgundy. During this time Emperor Berengar was creating his trouble for the other side of the family, and Rudolph II led their armies to Italy along with his cousin Rudolph who was now King of Western Francia. In 924 they had victory and Berengar was dead. Although Rudolph II wanted to be made Emperor, after his victory in Italy, his uncle Hugh was chosen for the position. The Kingdom of Burgundy was passed to his son Conrad who was given the nickname "the Peaceful". Conrad was brought into the court of Germania at a young age and when he was old enough, he was crowned King of Burgundy and married his cousin Mathilde. His political and military life were spent working with Otto, another cousin, to ensure the kingdoms of Burgundy and Italy didn't unite. Having a good handle on politics, Conrad was well liked and had great influence over the Church and the people. Thus, he was made King of Provence and ruled Burgundy from his new capital of Vienne. With his several wives, he had many children including King Rudolph III, Queen Berthe of the Franks, and Burchard who became the archbishop of Lyon. Upon Rudolph's death the kingdom was incorporated into the Holy Roman Empire, alongside of Germany and Italy. The Two Burgundy's of the Medici family were no more.

Conrad's sister Adelaide had married King Lothair II (son of King Hugh and great-great-grandson of Boson "the Elder"). They had one daughter, Emma, before Lothair was poisoned to death. Remember, Adelaide had attempted to keep the throne of the Holy Roman Empire until her daughter Emma had grown. Unfortunately, rivals (Cousin Willa) had kidnapped and tortured her. She was able to escape only to be forced to marry Otto I, who was made Emperor. The 4 children who followed were not brought into the world by the wishes of their mother, but by force. Adelaide was made a Saint. This is the life of most women; everything is done to them by force while men do what they will. Nothing changes. Emma was married to Lothair IV, King of France, and had several children. Daughter Mathilde became an Abbess, which is expected of many young girls, and son Otto II became the next Holy Roman Emperor. Carrying on his father's work and vision, he expanded the empire through Germany and Italy. The kingdom was secured with his marriage to Princess Theophanu of the Byzantine Empire and together they had 4 children including Abbesses Adelheid and Sophie. Because of her brother's constant invasion, Emma's marriage was difficult. Not only was her brother invading her husband's territory, but her husband's brother was regularly attacking her with claims of infidelity!

Even after being exonerated by the Synod of Sainte-Macre, Emma had to fight for her children to be recognized by their father. When Emma's son Louis became king, he banished Emma and the Bishop she had an affair with out of court, claiming they had poisoned his father. Louis who had been named "the Sluggard", died without an heir, one year later while Emma spent the rest of her days in a convent, like so many other women, shut away from the world. While Otto II was in the middle of a war against the Muslims, Danes, Saxons, and Slavs, he suddenly died, leaving his 3-year-old son Otto the disheveled Empire in 983.

On the other side of the family, King Hugh's children, the 4th generation of Boson "the Elder" had grown up! Hugh's son Prince Boso became the Bishop of Piacenza and was also the Imperial Chancellor. Hugh's daughter Berthe Evdokia became the wife of Byzantine Emperor Romanos II, but died before they had any children. Hugh's son Uberto (Hubert) was made Marquis of Tuscany in 937. Soon thereafter he became Duke and Marquis of Spoleto and Camerino as well. In 945 he joined Pope John XII against Berengario d'Ivrea who was trying to gain more land. Uberto was expelled from Tuscany for some time. His wife Willa founded the Badia Fiorentina abbey in Florence after his death.

King Hugh's brother, Boson d'Arles who had become the Margrave of Tuscany, had several daughters, as discussed before. Daughter Willa married Berengar d'Ivrea who became King of Italy, kidnapped her cousin Adelaide, and used her witchcraft and manipulation to take the crown she desired. Before her death she had many children. Daughter Gisla was married to Count Rambaldo I and Gilberga was married to Marquis Aleram, son of Guglielmo "the Pagan", of Montferrat. Sons Guido and Conrad took on their roles as Dukes and Margraves, attempting to take more land for themselves and preserve the territories they inherited. Daughter Rozala was married to Count Arnulf II. Arnulf is from a long line of Flanders nobility. They were married in 976 and had several children before Arnulf died in 987. Their son Baldwin IV inherited the titles and lands, which were ruled by Rozala for some time, since the children were so young. When she remarried, she lost the regency, which was given to her mother-in-law.

Rozala married Robert II, of the Capetian dynasty. He became King of the Franks because of his bloodline and was expected to marry the daughter of a king, as soon as possible. Although Rozala was much older than him, she was deemed the proper fit because of the land and wealth she would bring with her, which the men would then take. Rozala changed her name to Susanna after their marriage and Robert felt she was too old to have children. Bitterness grew between them. 4 years after they were married Robert demanded an annulment, due to their lack of children. Rozala returned to her family and her son Baldwin remained a principal advisor for Robert who went on to marry the daughter of Conrad "the Peaceful", Bertha. Because they were so closely related, the marriage was voided, and he married once again before having many children. In the meantime, Rozala had lost all she ever had, land, wealth, titles which all belonged to Robert, even though the contract had been dissolved. Her son Baldwin and his son Baldwin V, continued to pass down the nobility of Flanders for many more generations.

In 950 Willa's son, grandson of Boson d'Arles, Adalbert, took the Kingdom of Italy, with his father Berengar, after King Lothair II died and Adelaine had refused to marry him, fleeing her imprisonment. Adalbert discovered she was being kept safe in the Castle of Canossa and attacked. In 957 Duke Luidolf invaded Lombardy, and Adalbert went to war. He was soon defeated, but that didn't deter him. In 960 he joined his father in the attack on Pope John XII. This led to him being defeated by Otto who was then crowned Emperor of the Holy Empire. After fleeing to Corsica, Adalbert died in Autun. His son Otto William I became Count of Burgundy and Macon and had many children.

In 1125 a war began in Italy between those who supported the Papal States and those who supported the Holy Roman Emperor. The dynasty who supported the Pope was the House of Welf, a branch of the House of Este, both of which are frequently married into the Medici line. They are commonly known as Guelphs. Those who opposed were their cousins, the House of Hohenstaugen, called Ghibellines. This war was just a family feud. Henry, of the House of Welf, had been the heir of Uncle Lothair II, Emperor of the Holy Empire. Unfortunately, Lothair favored his cousin Conrad III, of the House of Hohenstaugen. Because of his support, Conrad won the election. Conrad then dissolved Henry's ownership of lands and titles, which the family spent the next generations taking back in a crown-grab. The Ghibellines used the Holy Roman Empire's flag, a white cross on a red field, like Denmark and Malta use. The Guelphs used a white flag with a red cross on it, like England used until 1606. In 1289 the Ghibellines had been defeated, causing the Guelphs to divide, becoming the Whites (opposed the Pope) and the Blacks (supported the Pope). On and on it goes, but let's not get ahead of ourselves. The Medici family were allies of the Guelphs and fought for their Papal States. The Papal States, formed by the upper elite lines to replace the Roman Empire, had by now withstood invasions and civil wars.

Giambuono Medici was born in 1131 to Bernardo di Potrone, the grandson of the Physician and Governor Medicus of Potrone, and Bartolomea Machiavelli. Giambuono was given the last name Medici and passed it onto his sons Chiarissimo and Bonaguinta. Like all families, the first born would carry out the political works of the family while the second would go into service of the Temple. He became involved in politics at a young age, an interest carried on by his son Chiarissimo who inherited several of the family's towers and houses after Giambuono's death in 1192. Together Chiarissimo and Bonaguinta financed the construction of the Camaldoli monastery in 1240. Chiarissimo became a member of the Council of the City of Florence, where the family had lived for centuries. His sons were Chiarissimo II, Filippo, Ranieri and Averardo. Meanwhile, his brother Bonaguinta had become a member of the Communal Council and had 2 sons, Galgano and Ugo. As a long-standing wealthy family of the region, even Count Guido Guerra was financially backed by Bonaguinta's sons. Banking is the family business, and the business of the families they married with, but their wealth and influence went back much further.

Chiarissimo's grandson Averardo II was born in 1270 to son Averardo and Benricevuta de' Sizi. When prior Averardo was 29 years old, he became the Gonfaloniere di Giustizia (magistrate of justice) which made him a leader for the Florence militia and the College of Priors. His father had spent his life involved in real estate, acquiring territories in Mugello, just north of Florence. Averardo Jr. continued this work and divided the properties between his sons, in 1320. He was chosen by the General of the Guelph party, Count Peter, to wage war against Lord Uguccione Faggiola, of the Ghibellines. Jr. succeeded in 1311 when his in-law Teghia de' Sizi surrendered, giving him patronage of a church. Averardo Jr. had 6 children with his wife, Mandina Arrigucci, including Sir Jacopo, Salvestro Chiarissimo who sired the Cafaggiolo and Popolano lines of the family, and Heifer, who sounded the Medici di Ottajano and Medici Toraquinci lines. The banking company Filii Averardi was founded by his sons. While the Medici family was never the largest or one of the largest banking or medical empires of the time, nor the most powerful, their businesses and interests helped to solidify and develop laws and tactics that ensured the continued control and rule of many other families. In 1321 Jacopo, another son of Averardo, was contracted by Ravenna to be responsible for their mint. The family expanded Filii Averardi to Ancona and Treviso and built an inn for travelling merchants. Brother Francesco was made the treasurer of the church of Liège, where the family had built another inn.

By 1291 Bonaguinta's great-grandson Ardingo had become the Signoria (ruler) of Florence and together with his brothers founded the Mercato Vecchio (meaning The Old Market), an investment and loan company. In 1301 Ardingo's cousin, Bernardino was made Signoria. He was a member of the financial guild called Arte del Cambio. As we already discussed, guild memberships are inherited, as they are a hereditary Order. Ardingo Medici had become a prior and a member of the Signory in 1291. Soon he married Gemma de' Bardi and was immediately advanced to the position of Gonfaloniere of Justice for the Papal State of Florence. Ardingo had an interest in industry and, after seeing the influence of his family's banks and other companies, focused on commerce. His son, Francesco di Ardingo de' Medici became one of 7 members of the Great Council of Venice's new government. The Great Council had been established by the elite of Venice in 1172. Through this Council they controlled what laws were written and passed, as well as judicial functions. The Council appointed all public officials and formed the Senate which had 200-300 members. It was the Senate, which was used to appoint the Council of Ten, created in 1310, as the ultimate power of authority. The Council of Ten were handpicked elite family members who worked together to solidify control of the nation, internationally and internally. Does this sort of organization sound familiar to you, dear reader?

Cousin Alamanno became a Knight of Florence in 1314, helping to fight for the cause. Other cousins at this time were involved in the military and politics, or the military and the church, or the family tradition of alchemy (medicine). By this generation, many members of the family had already created merchant guilds and banks, and business was good for the ruling class. Alamanno, the grandson of Chiarissimo Sr., had 3 sons and a daughter with his wife Margherita Palagi. Son Andrea Medici grew up to become mayor of Florence and had several children who carried on with family business. Another son, Salvestro, was born in 1331 to the patrician class of Florence. By this time, he and his brothers had lived through another Black Death event, one of many. In 1338, Florence had 4,000 citizens on welfare and about 17,000 beggars in the streets out of the total population of 80,000. After the plague hit in 1349, and so many people died, there were lands and businesses to purchase and trade, which expanded the wealth of the elite.

"In subsequent plague outbreaks, which occurred every 20 years or so, movement began to be restricted through curfews, travel bans, and quarantines. This was part of a general concentration of state power." — Eleanor Russell

We have seen it happen time and time again, the planned biowarfare events which are just one of the many ways the elite profit from your suffering, fear, and death. There should be no need to go into detail on the False Flag events of the Bubonic plague, so let's continue. Roughly 25,000 people in Florence were workers for the wool industry, called Ciompi. Being the lowest class, these people were not able to get skilled jobs, be part of a guild, or have any say in politics. As Salvestro grew, the Guelphs began to exclude those they didn't like from being able to have guilds (a sort of union/club), mainly the Ciompi. Salvestro decided to get into politics and curb the appetites of the Guelphs and help the "little people". In 1370 he became Gonfaloniere and revived laws which reduced the power of nobility and helped create the utopia the Ciompi demanded. This caused quite a stir and several families protested the changes and the Ciompi couldn't live up to their desires. Threats were given, homes were burned down, and other violence grew until July 1378, when Salvestro was made a knight and began acquiring income from businesses in the town. He was vital to the controlling and expansion of guilds over the following years as he implemented changes and enforced laws without compassion. For this he was banished in 1382, leaving his 3 sons behind. Meanwhile, another branch of the family was growing. The great-great grandson of Chiarissimo II Medici had been born, Nicolo. He and his brother Michele carried out the typical lives, keeping up the lands their family had inherited, bought, and taken, passing them onto their sons.

Filippo's other son Cambio had spent his years in politics, on behalf of the Guelphs. In 1374 his son Vieri followed in his footsteps, becoming the next Captain of Pistoia and Prior of Pistoia, a mystic Vallombrosian Order. Vieri was married twice and had many children. As part of the Medici family, he was educated in the family's Arte del Cambio, one of the top banking guilds. The shipping company, Viere di Cambio de Medici and Company was one of many he founded. Vieri partnered with other upper families involved in banking and trade, including Medici Bank founder and cousin, Francesco di Bicci de' Medici. Francesco had inherited not only the family's banks but manufacturing companies as well. The cousins' company opened branches throughout Venice, Genoa, Rome, and various cities of Europe. Many members of the family at this time were considered unethical moneylenders. Keeping their independent and private loan practices, Vieri and others practiced usury. He was often consulted by the local government. When all but one of the banks of Vieri were dissolved the family maintained their private businesses on the side and accumulated real estate. Real estate that was used many times to repay debts. After Vieri retired from banking, he became involved in politics, leaving his son Giovanni to take over his positions and titles. Unlike his cousin Salvestro, Vieri was an ally to the Albizzi who had been behind the Ciompi Revolt. All of Vieri's children were married more than once, like many cousins and uncles in the family. Sons Niccola and Cambio founded a bank and carried on the family's profession. Unfortunately, like their father, they were not bank-minded people and ended up selling much of the family's real estate to cover debts.

Francesco di Bicci de Medici and his brother Giovanni were the grandsons of Salvestro Chiarissimo Medici and Lisa Donati. A line of Cosimo's came from Giovanni, all raised and bred for banking. When he was 3, his father Averardo died, leaving his inheritance to be divided between his 4 sons. While this didn't leave young Giovanni with much, his uncle Vieri had become a famous banker and brought him into the family business. Because of his loyal work, Vieri left his banks to Giovanni upon his death. Unlike his uncle and cousins, Giovanni had the brain for numbers and instantly the banking empire grew. Gaining notoriety quickly, because of his name and increased wealth, the Papal States declared him Chief Papal Banker, also called "God's Banker". Apart from banking he owned several factories and was a member of 2 guilds, the family's Arte del Cambio and Arte della Lana. Giovanni funded artists and sculptors and constructed and updated many buildings. In 1397 Giovanni moved the company to Florence between Via Porta Rossa and Via dell'Arte della Lana. In 1402 he was elected Prior of the banker's guild and Podesta (administrator/judge) of Pistoia before becoming Gonfalionere of Justice for Florence.

In 1414 Giovanni "predicted" the Pope would be ruler, permanently. This was put into action 3 short years later, go figure. Because of his support, having financed Baldassare Cossa so he could become cardinal and quickly thereafter pope, he was rewarded greatly with positions and more. Unfortunately for Giovanni, he was placed in political positions including Signoria of Florence, Gonfaloniere and governor of Pistoia. He had no interest in politics, having learned much from his uncle on how to really control the country through banking, and often wrote letters to his sons reminding them not to get involved in politics, unless they were assigned a position, which they should then carry out without incident. He instilled the focus on banking into his sons, which is why the family, like many other elite families, was successful. Still, as Signoria he replaced the tax system with another which focused on properties. When he died in 1429, he was the second richest man in Florence. His 2 surviving sons, Cosimo and Lorenzo took over the family businesses and joined the ranks of the wealthiest families in Europe.

This brings us to Cosimo Medici, known as the First Medici, who had been indoctrinated in the family's philosophy of Backstage Management. He and his twin brother, who died in infancy, were named after the Arabic physicians, and saints, Cosmas, and Damian. His surviving brother, Lorenzo was also called "the Elder", like Cosimo and educated in humanism, which the family had been involved with for the past generation. Cosimo was the heir to the Medici Bank which had branches in Venice, Naples, Geneva, and Rome. The position of God's Banker was passed down through the generations, for as long as the bank stood. Cosimo expanded the bank to London, Bruges, Milan, and Pisa. The bank worked on behalf of the Papal States, funding bishoprics, papal licenses and more. He controlled the votes with his wealth, and through that he controlled the entire government of Florence. This tactic is seen in every country today, all elections are controlled by bankers, from the beginning of the Order.

> "The man he [Cosimo] chooses holds office. He is who decides peace and war. He is king in all but name." — Pope Pius II

Meanwhile, Cosimo came across to the adoring public as intended: uninterested in politics. This was because he financed orators, poets, philosophers, and artists. Cosimo purchased and inherited most of the lands surrounding Florence and made a point to ally himself with new immigrants to the city. He hired the best architects and sculptors to construct his many ideas such as the Palazzo Medici, which houses the Magi Chapel which includes portraits of the family disguised as "the 3 Wise Men". The Chapel is decorated with mosaics and marble, showing off the extravagance and wealth of the family. The Palazzo Medici was used to hold a dinner for Benito Mussolini and Adolf Hitler in 1938. Being overly friendly with his slaves, Cosimo had an illegitimate son, Carlo, who was forced to be a canon. During his life he became the Papal tax collector of Tuscany, the dean of Prato, and Abbot of San Salvatore. He was included in the painting which stands in Prato Cathedral called Funeral of St. Stephen, standing behind the Pope.

> "Man will never be free until the last king is strangled with the entrails of the last priest." — Denis Diderot

The Strozzi and Albizzi families once again decided they didn't like the Medici's and in 1433 they imprisoned Cosimo in the Palazzo Vecchio. Lorenzo raised a small army and attempted to free his brother but ended up being arrested. Some demanded his execution but instead he was exiled from Florence. He took his bank to Venice and set up shop again. His brother Lorenzo soon followed, and they built the first public library of Florence. Donatello di Niccolo di Betto Bardi, a sculptor, was commissioned by the Medici's to create the statue of David to symbolize the Medici's victory over the Albizzi "Goliath". The statue also helped the Medicis achieve the love of the people of Florence who viewed David as their patron saint, whose figure now represented the divinity of the Medici family. An avid book lover, he hired people to travel to Syria, Egypt and elsewhere to copy books and add to his collection. When Niccolo de Nicoli died, his beneficiary Cosimo bought his collection of 800 manuscripts.

In 1440 Lorenzo died in his house called Careggi and buried in the Basilica of San Lorenzo. His 10-year-old son Pierfrancesco was adopted by his uncle Cosimo and raised to carry on his father's affairs. Lorenzo is the ancestor of 7 kings of France. While in exile, Cosimo's hate for his enemies grew. He used his influence to place trusted allies and mercenaries in government positions, such as Francesco Sforza who was sent to maintain Milan as Duke. Orchestrating the Lombardy wars, Cosimo had established a balance of power and profit. In 1439 Pope Eugene IV moved the Council of Ferrara to Florence, at Cosimo's request. In 1445 Cosimo founded a Platonic Academy, supporting the family's humanist beliefs. In 1460 the Hermetic Corpus, a collection of texts about astral magic and the ancient Greek god Hermes, which had been written in the 100-300's AD. A monk brought it to Cosimo as a gift, and he had Marsilio Ficino translate it, as he had translated many other documents collected over time.

Marsilio's philosophical focus was to establish a theory that would unite all people. As such, he was excited to be the first to translate and dissect the Hermetic Corpus, since Hermes Trismegistos was said to be a contemporary of Moses. The document provided the model of reality wherein the things that happen on earth affect the things in the heavens and vice versa. This is known commonly today as: "as above, so below". Because of the expansion of many different philosophies during this time, all holding the common thread of magic, gemstone cutting became a suddenly booming industry, as gemstones are believed by those who believe in occult religions to contain magic. The elite families jumped on the opportunity to mine, trade, and sell carved stones.

Cosimo and Marsilio's collection included the Hygromanteia, another mystic text known today as the Key of Solomon, which the Freemason and many other such groups use. However, the book becomes wrongly entangled with King Solomon because of this title. It was written by an unknown author in the 300's AD, and King Solomon died in 931 BC. The book contains spells and rituals used to invoke gods and their related planetary bodies. In case you don't know by now, dear reader, the planets are not what they seem and not what NASA tells you. As numerous historical documents have already exposed, including the Bible, the heavenly bodies are alive. Just as Earth is alive. Where do you think aliens (Angels and the Fallen Ones) live, who are not locked in the Abyss? Why do you think planets contain pyramids, and frequency signals unique to themselves, among many other things? This is the real world. Those who practice Satanism, called mysticism, contact demons (the souls of the giants) and devils (the angels who followed Lucifer in the revolt and were exiled from heaven) and believe they control them with stones, mirrors, and potions. This is why the symbol of the star is often used to signify Luciferianism and why it is the symbol the elite use so frequently.

"For fifty years, I have done nothing else but earn money and spend money; and it became clear that spending money gives me greater pleasure than earning it." – Cosimo de Medici

Cosimo's son Giovanni had become the director of the Ferrara branch of the Medici Bank and in 1454 he was elected Prior of Florence. One year later he was given the position of General Manager of the Medici Bank. He was irritated by this because he preferred to surround himself with art instead. He enjoyed collecting things from jewels to instruments and coins. He built the Villa Medici in Fiesole and patroned his father's friends including Michelozzo Michelozzi who built most of the family's homes, and Filippo Lippi, who painted most of the family's portraits. Although Giovanni had been the heir of his father's empire, he died in 1463. His son Cosimo, also called Cosimino, inherited his properties. In 1464 Cosimo died at Careggi, passing his estates, palaces, and businesses to his son Piero, who was married to Lucrezia Tornabuoni and had several children. After his death, Cosimo was given the title Pater Patriae, meaning Father of the Fatherland. The last person to receive this title was Emperor Julian in 361. Piero was given the nickname "the Gouty" because he was always ill, which kept him from being named as his father's heir. Instead, he became Gonfaloniere. Because he was so perpetually sick his bedroom became his office, making the Palazzo Medici the seat of the Florentine government. In 1465 King Louis XI gave Piero a new coat of arms, containing 6 balls surrounding a ball containing the arms of France, the Fleur-des-Lys I mentioned before. Although he wasn't a business-minded man, he kept the family bank running smoothly.

By the age of 28, adopted brother and cousin Pierfrancesco had been made ambassador of Florence and Prior of the guilds. He married Laudomia di Agnolo Acciaioli of the elite Acciaioli family, and they had 2 sons, Lorenzo, and Giovanni. In 1466 he participated in a coup with Luca Pitti, who had planned to overthrow Piero, his brother. They were backed by the d'Este family. Fortunately, Piero was warned and escaped. After this bout of freedom, Pierfrancesco made peace with his brother and was forgiven. He continued his life focused on the family business. When his son Giovanni was 9 years old, Pierfrancesco died, leaving his sons to be adopted by his cousin Lorenzo "the Magnificent". Piero had continued the family's collections of books and art, having Plato and other classics translated to add to his library, including the book Necromancy, which remains in the Medici Library and has been translated by Brian Johnson. The book had, until recently, been hoarded and preserved in the Florentine Laurentian Library. The newly translated book gives the public yet another book of negativity, including invisibility cloaking spells, demonic invocations, and a list of 66 of the family's demons. What an educational contribution to humanity. In 1469 after a lifetime of gout and lung diseases, he died. Altogether he had 6 children who survived, including an illegitimate son.

Let's get into the next generation, the grandchildren of Cosimo. Maria's son Luigi became a Cardinal whose portrait stands in the Uffizi Gallery. Her sister, Lucrezia, called Nannina, had several children with her husband Bernardo Rucellai, including Giovanni. Giovanni di Bernardo Rucellai became a poet and dramatist. His grandmother, Lucrezia Tornabuoni, had been a sonnet writer whose social circle included the philosophers and artists who attended and supported the Medici Academy. The portrait called Madonna of the Magnificat is a family portrait of Lucrezia and her children. In 1505 Lorenzo was an ambassador to Venice and spent much of his time travelling for his work. His uncle Lorenzo Medici made him Master of the Hunt and administrator of the Arte della Lana, the family's wool guild. As ambassador and advisor, he accompanied Pope Leo, his cousin, on negotiations.

Uncle Lorenzo was the brother of Maria and Lucrezia, and grew up in the Medici world of philanthropy and art. He was educated by the best diplomats and philosophers of the time. Like many in that time period, he was taught Greek. As a young man, Lorenzo was quite enthusiastic about jousting and tournaments of skill, which the Medici family sponsored. In 1459 Lorenzo's sister Bianca had 16 children with husband Guglielmo de'Pazzi who had grown up as a close friend of the family. She was a musician and gave organ concerts regularly. As the family had done for generations, Lorenzo, nicknamed "the Magnificent", continued the rule of Florence, through puppets and pawns. This caused many people to resent the Medici's, especially the Pazzi family. In 1469 Lorenzo married Clarice Orsini and together they had 10 children.

In 1478 Francesco Pazzi and a couple of his friends attempted to seize control of Florence. Backed by Pope Sixtus IV, the archbishop of Piza, a friend of Francesco Pazzi, supported the murder of Lorenzo's brother and co-heir, Giuliano. In April, Giuliano and Lorenzo were at Mass, in the Duomo. Suddenly their enemies appeared, and Giuliano was struck in the head with a sword. On the floor of the cathedral, he was stabbed 19 times while Lorenzo had been hurried out by a friend and rushed to Medici Palace. Lorenzo narrowly escaped only to find out his brother had been murdered. Enraged, he ordered all male members of the Pazzi family killed, as well as all conspirators to the assassination including the archbishop. Only his brother-in-law Guglielmo's life was spared, but he was exiled for the next 15 years. The Pazzi women were forbidden to marry Florentines, but because Guglielmo's daughters had Medici blood, they were exempt.

Pope Sixtus then took all of the Medici assets he could get his hands on, and excommunicated the government of Florence, including Lorenzo who by that time didn't care. Realizing this had no effect on the Medici's whatsoever, the pope rounded up an army and invaded Florence. That is what the elite typically do when they don't get their way: attack. Knowing that war wouldn't solve anything, Lorenzo travelled to Naples to turn himself in for imprisonment. While in prison he was able to reestablish the Florentine government and refine the constitution, securing the Medici rule. He worked to keep the Holy See and other states, out of Italy and allied himself with the Ottoman Empire. Soon he became interested in the mining and trade of alum, which had previously been controlled by the Ottomans until it was discovered in Genoa. The Medici Bank and Roman Curia funded the mining operations since 1462. Slowly tension rose among the people of the mining communities, and riots broke out. Lorenzo hired mercenaries to handle the crowds and several people were killed when they decided to destroy the city. This is reminiscent of the Rockefeller mining communities' revolts.

Lorenzo supported many artists and philosophers, including Marsilio Ficino, Poliziano, and Giovanni Pico who worked to merge Plato and Christianity...

In 1488 Lorenzo hired Mariano des Buono to create a book of art which included Catholic devotionals called a book of hours. The Medici Hours were made for each of Lorenzo's 3 daughters as a wedding gift. The 1st went to Lucrezia upon her marriage to Jacopo Salviati, the next was given to Luisa and Giovanni di Pierfrancesco, and the 3rd was for Magdalena who married to Franceschetto Cybo, son of Pope Innocent III. Today Magdalena's book of hours is part of the Rothschild family's private collection at Waddesdon Manor. Lorenzo built a sculpture garden at San Marco, funded painters to do murals in the Sistine Chapel, and spent an estimated $460 million on buildings and charities. The family had built many churches throughout the kingdom, to ensure religious control over the population. Each church was covered with Medici family members depicted in biblical scenes, and the altars contained the Medici family crest of each side, so no one could pass the altar without acknowledging their god Medici. The most popular or famous paintings include the painting of John the Baptist, who is Giovanni Medici and Saint Francis who is Piero Medici.

"The beast is swifter, always keeps the lead, while he, who's eaten by longing, raves." – Lorenzo de Medici

After his brother had been murdered, Lorenzo adopted Giuliano's son Giulio who grew up to become Pope Clement VII. Michelangelo had attended the Medici's school, which had been created for them to pool the best talent under their control. Once he was discovered as a teenager at school, he was taken to live with Lorenzo for 2 years. Michelangelo's work from that point on was done at the command of the Medici's. In April 1492 Lorenzo was at the villa in Careggi when his friend, Dominican Friar Girolamo Savonarola, from the Ferrara bloodline, came to visit. During the night, Lorenzo died and was buried with his brother in San Lorenzo. They were entombed in red granite sarcophagi which had been designed by Piero Medici. 50 years later the brothers were moved to the New Sacristy, the Medici Chapel, beneath a Madonna statue carved by Michelangelo.

"What I have dreamed in an hour is worth more than what you have done in four." – Lorenzo di Piero de'Medici

Lorenzo Medici and Clarice Orsini's sons Piero and Giovanni had by this time grown up. Piero was raised to take over the family's government of Florence, but his character made him unsuitable. He was always in fights with other family members because of his greed and it was thought that he poisoned his teacher in 1494. In 1486 he was married to Alfonsina Orsini but didn't attend the wedding or meet his wife until 2 years later. Somehow, they had 3 children. Piero was given the nickname "the Unfortunate" and his life as ruler of Florence was unsuccessful and unfortunate indeed. He didn't have the support or affection of his citizens, or his family members. His brothers allied with King Charles who had been trying to take land in Naples for some time. Eventually Piero decided to give in to Charles' demands and gave him several towns and fortresses in Tuscany. After his time at the negotiation table, he returned home to a very unhappy citizenry. His palace was looted, and the Medici's were exiled until 1512 when Giovanni forced them to surrender and accept Medici rule. Piero spent the rest of his life in Venice selling Medici jewels. In 1503 Piero drowned while fleeing the Battle of Gargliano.

Giovanni had been made Pope Leo X in 1512. Giovanni had hired artists to build arches for the celebration which showed the image of his father, Lorenzo, with the message "This is my beloved son", mocking Jesus' baptism by stating to the public that he was Christ, and his father was God. The elite have always used twisted symbolism and scriptures given and used by the Living God, to achieve their goals. Luciferianism relies on manipulation and deception, both of which are best served with a thin, corrupt line of truth.

"Rome, that sink of all iniquity." — Lorenzo de Medici

Giovanni's time in office was one of war and extravagance. In 1516 the war against the Cambrai had finally ended. This peace aroused the land-lust of Francesco Maria I della Rovere, who decided to retake the lands of Urbino. The year before he had been kicked out by the Papal military so in 1517, he set off to round up an army. By the end of January, he made it to Urbino with 5,000 infantry men and 1,000 cavalries. After easily defeating the government of the city, the people welcomed Francesco. Giovanni was unhappy about this and quickly hired 10,000 soldiers for his nephew Lorenzo whom he had given many titles to. Lorenzo was shot and wounded, forced to retreat, and be replaced by Cardinal Bibbiena who had no military experience and couldn't lead the army. Thankfully, Francesco ran out of money and with that, his army was gone. Giovanni gave the land of Urbino to Lorenzo, making him Duke. Unfortunately for Giovanni, his troubles had just begun.

The Papal States had now become stretched too thin, the many senseless wars and battles were too expensive to maintain. Giovanni had become a target for the cardinals and discovered they had planned to poison him. He took this opportunity to execute and imprison several of them and used this as an excuse to alter Cardinals College. In July of 1517 he wrote up a list of new cardinals whom he handpicked. Although this had never been done before, rumors fizzled out in time. Hundreds of new positions in the Vatican were created wherein he placed only people he could trust. This gave him a much-needed financial infusion. Soon thereafter he reinstated something called Papal Indulgences, which was a piece of paper that the people could buy to have freedom from hell, which the Catholics have used to control people through fear for centuries. The elite understand that while love is more powerful, fear is easy and long lasting, if carried out properly.

Giovanni wanted a new crusade for the Church and decided to go up against Sultan Selim I, who had been invading areas of eastern Europe. He planned a mighty and glorious show. He envisioned England, Spain, and Portugal building a mighty fleet so they could attack Constantinople. Meanwhile the Emperor and King of France would lead the army and the victory would be awe-inspiring. Unfortunately, this unrealistic plan was not meant to be. Europe was at odds with itself, and everyone had their own wars and battles going on. Cardinal Wolsey was supposed to explain the plan that the pope would be the lead guy between France and the Empire, but instead he told England that they were. The money he collected for the crusade was spent on other things. Cardinal Wolsey was not a reliable accountant. So, the crusade didn't happen and several years later a new sultan invaded Hungary. Giovanni sent money to the state to support the war effort and on and on it goes.

During this time the Church had become almost bankrupt from the constant wars and failed war attempts and at the same time Christians were rebelling against the forced Catholic religion. Giovanni threw extravagant banquets frequently, including one which was described by an attending ambassador as having had 65 courses. He is remembered for his statement in a letter written to his brother:

"God has given us the papacy, let us enjoy it."

Martin Luther had become famous overnight, when he posted his theses on the doors of All Saints Church and others in Wittenberg, Germany. His theses challenged the Catholic Church for its corruption of the scripture and the perversion of the Christian belief. In his 95 Theses Martin stated:

"The pope neither desires nor is able to remit any penalties except those imposed by his own authority or that of the canons.

Those who believe that they can be certain of their salvation because they have indulgence letters will be eternally damned, together with their teachers.

Because love grows by works of love, man thereby becomes better. Man does not, however, become better by means of indulgences but is merely freed from penalties.

Why does not the pope, whose wealth is today greater than the wealth of the richest Crassus, build this one basilica of St. Peter with his own money rather than with the money of poor believers?

Since the pope seeks the salvation of souls rather than money by his indulgences, why does he suspend the indulgences and pardons previously granted when they have equal efficacy?"

Ever since the flood, as you have seen here, the few who have a relationship with the Living God have been attacked by the rest. Every tactic has been used, and most have succeeded at one time or another. The most common attack and corruption is the use of individual Bible verses, taken out of context, to support an agenda.

"It has served us well, this myth of Christ." — Pope Leo X, Giovanni Medici

Giovanni, enraged by Martin's condemnatory statements, wrote the Papal Bull Exsurge Domine in 1520. This law censored 41 of the 95 theses, all the ones which opposed the Catholic Church, and several months later Martin burned his copy of the Bull, which Giovanni had sent him. This caused him to be excommunicated publicly when Giovanni wrote the Bull Decet Romanum Pontificem.

"Since they have burned my books, I burn theirs. The canon law was included because it makes the pope a god on earth. So far I have merely fooled with this business of the pope. All my articles condemned by Antichrist are Christian. Seldom has the pope overcome anyone with Scripture and with reason." — Martin Luther

Giovanni died of pneumonia in 1521, at the age of 45. His legacy is one of overspending and helping to fuel the Reformation, rather than keeping it under the Church's control. During his time as Pope Leo X, he established a close friendship with King Manuel who gave him a large embassy in Portugal. He allowed the Jewish community to have a Hebrew printing press in Rome, which printed the Talmud. This is the Babylonian religion that has stayed with the Jews since they were exiled to Babylon ages before, as discussed in Part I. After his death historians, journalists and Martin Luther wrote about Giovanni's homosexuality, which has always been rampant in politics and power.

"No person shall preach without the permission of his Superior. All preachers shall explain the Gospel according to the Fathers. They shall not explain futurity or the times of Antichrist!" – Giovanni, Pope Leo X

In 1523 Cousin Giulio Medici, who inherited the good looks of his grandfather, became Pope Clement VII after being the advisor to his Pope Leo X and Pope Adrian VI. He commissioned many murals that survive today on walls in Rome. He attempted to make peace with many of the Christian leaders while Italy was at war on all sides. Soon after, King Henry VIII broke England away from the Church's grasp, forming another variety and gathering all biblical texts and publishing them in one document, so all could read and know.

In 1527 Giulio was imprisoned during the Sack of Rome. Rome had been a city of pilgrimage, filled with people from all regions ever since the disciple of Jesus, Peter, who was sent to preach in Rome, had died. When Luther protested the Church, it caused a revolution and a split. Now those from the German region of the empire were against the papacy, having seen the abuse and lies it had created. As armies of angry Lutherans descended on Rome, Giulio was trapped and held prisoner in the Castel Sant'Angelo while the people stole, raped, and murdered. Around 8,000 people were slaughtered in Rome that first day alone. The city which had housed 55,000 just 8 months before, now contained 10,000 people. Giulio had been able to escape, which only deepened the rage felt by the people. Friends and family of Medici's were attacked and forced into hiding and terror. Soon Giulio had gathered an army and moved to invade Florence. Michelangelo, who was trapped in San Lorenzo church remarked:

"I hid in a tiny cell, entombed like the dead Medici above, though hiding from a live one."

Unfortunately for Giulio, his 11-year-old niece Catherine Medici had also been trapped in the city. The people threatened to pass the child around to the soldiers, forcing Giulio to retreat. In 1533 he married Catherine to King Henry II and the Medici blood took over the kingdoms of Europe. After returning to Rome from the wedding, he developed a fever and flu symptoms. Over the next few months, he aged significantly, lost sight, and his skin turned yellow. Days before he died, he commissioned Michelangelo to paint The Last Judgement in the Sistine Chapel. He was remembered as being intelligent and amiable, and skilled in accounting and science.

Pierfrancesco "the Elder", born in 1430, had been raised by Cosimo for a life of politics. He had been an ambassador and Prior of guilds, as previously discussed. His sons were Lorenzo and Giovanni who were raised by Cousin Lorenzo "the Magnificent" when their father died in 1476. By this time there are roughly 5 living Giovanni's in the Medici family and even more Lorenzo's. It makes it difficult to discuss everyone without getting confused, but I hope, dear reader, that you can keep up or easily find the names mentioned before and remember. Pierfrancesco's sons were educated by the same philosophers and scholars who taught their cousins, Marsilio Ficino and Angelo Poliziano whom Cousin Piero possibly poisoned to death. The boys were denied their inheritance which was squandered by their uncle and exiled by Cousin Piero "the Unfortunate" who feared they would attempt to take it from him.

In 1494 the brothers returned to Florence when Piero had been booted out. They were given the nickname "Poplano" meaning commoner and liked by the people enough to live in peace. Giovanni married Caterina Sforza and had a son, Ludovico before Giovanni died. Ludovico was renamed Giovanni in his honor. Older brother Lorenzo had met Amerigo Vespucci in school, and they remained friends through life. Amerigo is who the American continents are named after. In 1503 Amerigo wrote a letter to Lorenzo calling the Americas the New World. The term has been used by many to mean many things ever since, but North America in particular has been the New Rome ever since, continuing the Holy Roman Crusades in the name of peace, worldwide. Lorenzo had a love of the arts and was a patron to many. He commissioned Botticelli to create the Allegory of Spring as well as the Birth of Venus which are both well known to this day. He inherited the villas Trebbio and Castello and in 1483 he became ambassador to Paris. After many years of legal and physical battles over inheritance Lorenzo and Giovanni were given the family's Villa Cafaggiolo. While Lorenzo was well liked by the people and urged to take a political office, once his uncle had died, he refused, and preferred to spend his life surrounded by the artists he patroned.

"The Medici made me and the Medici destroyed me." – Leonardo da Vinci

In 1484 a direct descendant of Captain Averardo Medici was born to Lorenzo and Caterina. He was named Ottaviano and became the 1st Prince of Ottajano. By 1530 he held the title Gonfaloniere of Justice and soon became Senator. His marriages produced several children including heir Giuseppe and Alessandro who became Pope Leo XI. His children and their descendants became known as the Princes of Ottajano, and they maintained their branch of the Medici Dynasty around Naples. Ottaviano's son Berardetto, General of the Papal States, was married to his cousin Giulia Romola, the daughter of Alessandro "the Moor" Medici.

Let's take a look at the children of those previously discussed. Clarice, daughter of Piero and Alfonsina, had 10 children with Filippo Strozzi. The Strozzi/Medici banking empire was passed to son Piero who was the Marshal of France. Son Roberto was married to cousin Maddalena Medici, daughter of Pierfrancesco II. Among the other children are Leone who was a Knight of Malta, Lorenzo who became an abbot and cardinal, and Luigia who married Senator Luigi Capponi. After an exhausting life as a baby mill, Clarice died during childbirth or from a miscarriage before she was 30 years old.

Lorenzo was the Duke of Urbino and ruler of Florence, discussed before, had 2 children before he died, Catherine and Alessandro. Alessandro received the nickname "the Moor" because of his dark hair and eyes. Cousin Pope Clement VII, Giulio, made him Duke of the Florentine Republic which he maintained until 1537. Alessandro was married to Emperor Charles V's daughter Margaret. His children Giulio and Giulia were not the offspring of his wife, but of his long-time mistress Taddea Malaspina. Cousin Lorenzino moved to Rome in 1530 and began to make trouble. Giuliano di Lorenzo de'Medici, called Cardinal Ippolito, was one of his few friends in the family. When Lorenzino destroyed the heads of statues on the Arch of Constantine Giulio di Giuliano de'Medici, who was now Pope Clement VII, vowed to kill whoever had done it. Cardinal Ippolito saved Lorenzino's life, but Lorenzino was expelled from Rome. This brought him to Cousin Alessandro in Florence. Together they partied and had the adventures of wealthy, immoral children until January 1537. Alessandro was invited to Lorenzino's for a standard evening of debauchery. When Alessandro showed up, he dismissed his men and fell asleep waiting for Lorenzino to arrive with women. Unfortunately for him, women did not show up but rather men did. Lorenzino and his servant Piero stabbed Alessandro with swords and daggers, killing him. A few days later Lorenzino apologized for the assassination, claiming that he did it for the people of Florence. The pair fled on horseback to Silvestro Aldobrandini in Bologna. Unfortunately, the lawyer didn't believe Lorenzino's innocence, so they travelled to Venice to visit a banker and relative Filippo Strozzi. When Filippo was tortured and killed in 1538, Lorenzino went to France where he had many friends and became a diplomat for King Francis I.

In 1544 Lorenzino moved back to Venice, calling himself Marco, and altering his appearance. Because he was now more famous than Brutus, many men attempted to assassinate him. 4 years later most of the Florentines moved to France, leaving Venice void of allies for Lorenzino. By February 1548 he was murdered by Captain

Francesco da Bibbona who left a detailed, handwritten testimony about the event which can be found and read today. Francesco Vinta of Volterra had hired friend Bebo to kill Lorenzino now that he was back in Venice. Bebo brought his friend Captain Francesco into the deal, and they went to stay in Lorenzino's home with some friends who knew Lorenzino. Francesco stayed for months, watching and planning until one day Lorenzino and his friend Alessandro Soderini went to church. When they exited the building and were walking home, Francesco and Bebo jumped on them, expecting Alessandro to run away. Alessandro fought back valiantly, until Francesco cut off his hand and chopped his head open. Francesco then went to assist Bebo who had fled after knocking Lorenzino to the ground. Francesco then chopped Lorenzino's head in two and went about the rest of his day.

Alessandro's sister Catherine was married to the King of France. Catherine was a devout Catholic, like her family had been for generations. Also, like her family for generations, she was deeply invested in Luciferianism. She had been married to Henry II, King of France when she read the writings of Michel de Nostradame, more commonly known as Nostradamus, a clairvoyant and astrologer. After calling him to court, and making him her son's personal physician, he was tasked with writing the children's horoscopes and composing prophecies. A room was constructed at her villa, Chaumont-sur-Loire, with the specific purpose of housing an enchanted mirror, a fountain of purification, and an altar. In this room she also had many potions, amulets, and pots, as well as a divining rod. All of the equipment needed for practicing Luciferian rituals. Meanwhile her many children had been growing up. Catherine did nothing without consulting her team of magicians which included Cosme Ruggieri. Due to a prediction, moved away from Saint Germain L'Auxerrois to her Chateau de Blois. The letters she wrote in her time, which have survived, detail her requests to friends for favors and black magic. To ensure her safety, she formed the Flying Squadron. The Flying Squadron was a group of 300 spies who watched the court and executed Queen Catherine's demands. Needless to say, people Catherine didn't like didn't last long. It's said she poisoned her daughter's mother-in-law, and Jeanne d'Albret died after accepting a pair of gloves from her, which she had poisoned. Poisonous apples were sent to Prince de Conde but failed to reach his mouth because his doctor suspected something was wrong and fed them to the dogs, who died suddenly.

"The first lesson I ever learned was never to wait for a man's rescue." — Catherine de Medici

In 1548 her firstborn, 4-year-old Francis was betrothed to 5-year-old Queen Mary Stuart, the daughter of King James of Scotland. Mary had been made Queen when she was 9 months old and after she was betrothed, she was moved to France. In 1558 they were married but their marriage was never consummated. Francis suffered from undescended testicles and as a result they had no children. When

Francis was 15, he was made king, due to the death of his father. Because Francis was ill and weak, and the kingdom was on the verge of bankruptcy following the wars of his father, he split the rule between the 2 of his wife's uncles. Duke Francis Guise headed the army while his brother Charles became the administrator of finance, justice, and diplomacy. He made many more sudden changes in the administration and membership of the court, which caused an uproar among the aristocracy of France.

Francis' father Henry had been very hard on the Huguenots of France. They were protestants who followed John Calvin's teachings as well as Martin Luther's. During these few hundred years, more and more splits began to take place among those who wished for freedom from Rome. The more they split, the more places Rome had to infiltrate and control which caused another split and so on. By the time King Henry died and his child took the throne, the country had been involved in the Italian Wars for almost a decade, and many officials had not been paid for a long time because of the financial crisis of the kingdom. The uncles decided to cut costs and enforce Catholicism to repair France. This only caused more outrage among the Huguenots who decided to take matters into their own hands. After months of planning and work, several leaders of the Huguenots had raised and gathered money to buy soldiers to carry out the assassinations of the Guise uncles and force Francis to change the policies. Unfortunately, the uncles were not new to the life of nobility and quickly heard about the conspiracy that would take place in Amboise.

In March 1560, the uncles sent out soldiers to round up everyone suspected to be involved. People were rounded up by the dozens and taken to the castle in Amboise for questioning. Most of them were released when it was discovered they were only involved in order to be paid. Several days later, 200 Huguenot horsemen rode into Amboise and attacked the guards there which only resulted in the deaths of more of the Huguenot leaders including Jean du Barry who co-organized the plan with Prince Louis Conde (of the Conti bloodline). Jean's body was displayed on the gates of Amboise and dozens more were arrested throughout the region. Over the next few days those who wished to surrender and go about their lives had 24 hours to disband, those who remained to fight for the Huguenots would be deemed rebels and anyone had legal right to kill them. In the days that followed the disbandment, hundreds were drowned and hung in public executions, regardless of titles or blood. In September of 1560, as searches and arrests continued through France, a stockpile of weapons were found in the home of Protestant Pierre Menard in Lyon. He confirmed that the conspiracy they had discovered in Amboise was a small part of a much larger goal which was supported and led by many, including John Calvin, a friend of Pierre. By December Francis' illnesses had overcome him and with his death came the end of the Guise uncles' power. After a short 17-month reign, Francis' crown was passed to his brother Charles, who was 10.

Following the path of his ancestors, Charles was made a Knight of the Order of the Garter in 1564 with fellow elites Francis Russell and Henry Sidney. In that same year Charles made an edict decreeing that January 1 would be the 1st day of the year. Up until that time every place used a different calendar and had a different day for the new year. This was adopted by the Catholic Church in 1582 and the new system was implemented throughout the world. Anglican Britain did not accept this until 1752. Charles, like his brother Francis before him, was in charge in title only and the kingdom was run by Mother Catherine. In 1562 the first of the French Wars on Religion began between the noble Houses of Bourbon and Guise. This continued off and on until 1570.

Charles was married to Elizabeth Habsburg, the daughter of Emperor Maximilian II, of the Holy Roman Empire and together they had one child, Marie-Elizabeth. Charles' mistress, Marie Touchet gave birth to his son, Charles de Valois who was given titles and lands. Due to the stress of life and his genetic makeup, he was weak and ill much of the time and soon, his mother did something he wouldn't be able to live with.

In 1572 Catherine orchestrated the False Flag called Saint Barthelemy Massacre, which started with the ringing of the bells of Saint Germain L'Aucerrois de Paris. The city of Paris was swarming with Huguenots who had come to witness the marriage of Protestant King Henry III and Catherine's daughter Margaret. The marriage was designed to create peace between the kingdoms, which no one really wanted. The bells tolled on an August evening, 2 days after Admiral Gaspard de Coligny had experienced an assassination attempt. Charles had ordered his assassination, along with many leaders of the Protestant Huguenots. The assassinations went on for weeks, spreading from the city through France. The Roman Catholics claimed 2,000 died while the Huguenot eyewitness, Maximilien says 70,000 were murdered. Regardless, the bodies were floating in the rivers of Paris for months and a reported that in one week 1,100 bodies were swept down the river, washing up on shore. Drinking water was poisoned. While the French celebrated the victory over the enemies of the Pope, the ruthless violence instilled those who remained with radicalized beliefs. This is what always happens when anything is backed into a corner and forced to protect itself against others who are violating them. The same principle is as true of animals as people, and has always been well-known, which is why these events are done **ON PURPOSE**, for a purpose.

> "Who but you is the cause of all of this? God's blood, you are the cause of it all!" - Charles IX to his mother during the massacre

The 2 years that followed the massacre tortured Charles, who had become bedridden. He died, unable to get over the repulsiveness of his mother, stating:
> "What evil council I have followed! O my God, forgive me...I am lost! I

am lost!"

In keeping with Luciferian practices, Catherine constructed wax figures of her enemies which were tortured while she wore protection talismans. Catherine's youngest son Francois used a talisman made for him by Cosme, to curse his brother Charles. When Cosme asked about his health, revealing to Catherine that he was involved, she performed rituals in an attempt to heal him which included child sacrifice. This is common in most (if not all) elite families and is most likely the reason so many of her children died before they were 1 year old (as seen in every other family). Infants and newborns are required for many Luciferian rituals. In 1575, one year after her son's death, Catherine gave Cosme the Abbey of St. Mahé and built a tower, called the Medici Column, for him at the Bourse de commerce. The tower's 147 spiraling steps led to a glass-covered platform where the 4 corners were made to match the 4 points of a compass. Together Cosme, Nostradamus, Luca Gaurico and the rest of her team predicted the reign and deaths of her husband and sons. She spent her life running from an early prediction that she would die near Saint Germain, and after fleeing on her deathbed her attending physician was named Julien de Saint Germain.

In 1573, during Henry's assault on the Huguenot occupied city of La Rochelle, Henry was elected King of Poland and peace was made. Henry was required to sign an agreement for religious tolerance in Poland and created the Order of the Holy Spirit. When his brother died in 1574, Henry III took the crown. He was Catherine's favorite and was the healthiest one in the bunch. Growing up as spoiled as he was, his personality was not unlike the rest in the family. He burned his siters books while taunting her and broke the nose off of a statue of Saint Paul. He enjoyed the life of an aristocrat, taking walks in the city, entertaining his many mistresses (though the rumors in court were more focused on his homosexual relationships), riding his horses, or reading the day away. Many ventures that were brought to him, he ignored or showed no interest in but he remained true to his mother and fought in the Wars of Religion.

Meanwhile brother Francois had been made Duke of Anjou, Touraine, and Berry in 1576 and became heir to the throne. Discontent with his position in life, Francois focused on military glory. After lengthy battles to win the Duchy's for himself, he met his fate in Antwerp where most of his army was slaughtered. His mother had no trouble writing letters to him, describing her disappointment and regrets that he hadn't died young. He contracted malaria and died in February of 1548. Henry was unable to produce any children with his wife, Louise, and after his brother, the last sibling heir had died, the crown was given to the next of his father's brothers. In August of 1589, Henry III was approached by Dominican Friar Jacques Clement, who claimed to have a message for him. When Henry waved his guards to back up, Jacques stabbed him in the stomach. The next day, Henry died, and the House of

Bourbon took the kingdom. His other siblings had married and produced many children of their own, who became the next generation of princes, abbesses, cardinals, and dukes. In 1589 Catherine died of pleurisy.

Well, now that you see where this branch of the Medici family wound up, let's take a look at another! Back in Florence, the son of Ludovico de'Medici had been born in 1519 and grew to become the Grand Duke of Tuscany, Cosimo I. He acquired the title and land when his cousin Alessandro de'Medici was assassinated in 1537. When exiles of Florence heard of Alessandro's death they quickly marched on Tuscany. Cosimo quickly gathered his army and sent them out to engage. The victory was swift, Cousin Filippo Strozzi who had orchestrated the revolt was killed and the prisoners were beheaded. By the end of the year, Cosimo had become an ally of France, and went to war with Italy. Soon he married Eleanora of Toledo. Unfortunately, Eleanora didn't like his daughter Bia, born of one of his mistresses, and Bia was sent to live in Villa di Castello with her grandmother. She died when she was 7. Out of Eleanora and Cosimo's 11 children, 8 survived to adulthood. One son, Giovanni was Archbishop of Pisa by the time he was 16, when he was made Cardinal. Cosimo was left with one contender to his title, and that was Lorenzino whom I discussed before. Cosimo hired the mercenary who assassinated him. As a patron of the arts, he taxed his people heavily to support expanding the family's collection. Naturally, he supported the family's long-standing schools, guilds, artists, extravagant parties, and more.

In 1565 Cosimo hired chef Bernardo Buontalenti to organize a banquet for the Spanish deputation. For this feast, Bernardo created a special invention. For dessert something never seen before was presented, consisting of eggnog, milk, and fruit. Called Buontalenti, it has become known as gelato. Cosimo used his wealth to update and finish some estates, including Pitti Palace which Eleanora had bought in 1549. Cosimo had the place enlarged and hired Giorgio Vasari to build the 760-meter-long corridor connecting the residence to Palazzo Signoria, now called Palazzo Vecchio where the government of Florence was held. The Vasari Corridor also included a 505-meter-long section connecting the Palazzo Pitti to the Uffizi. This way the Medici's didn't have to walk on the street or among the commoners but above them.

Cosimo contracted others to landscape extensive gardens and grottos. The palace was filled with portraits and scenes which were given Roman and Catholic religious titles, most containing Medici faces. Cosimo was a devout alchemist, and followed the religion his grandmother gave him, passing it onto his children as well. Don Giovanni was one of his illegitimate sons. He became a commander, architect, and diplomat. In 1615 he formed a close relationship with Kabbalist Benedetto Blanis. Their many letters are preserved by the Archivio di Stato of Florence. Giovanni had maintained the family's alchemy workshop and brought Benedetto to his court to study astrology, alchemy, demonology, and Kabbalah. It quickly spread through the nobles and elite of the region and Benedetto even taught Grand Duchess Christine dee Lorraine magical arts.

During this time, Alessandro Farnese had just created the Jesuit Order and Cosimo gave his financial support. In 1562 Eleanora and 2 of the children caught malaria and died. So, Cosimo married Camilla Martelli in 1570 and had one daughter before he died in 1574 at the family estate in Careggi. Francesco was the firstborn son and heir to Tuscany, with his brother Ferdinando as the runner up. Isabella had been married to Paolo Giordano Orsini when she was 16 years old. After several miscarriages they had a daughter, Francesca, whom they married to Cousin Alessandro Sforza. In 1576 she was killed by Paolo because of rumors that she was having an affair with his cousin, as discussed in the Orsini chapter. If you remember, she was the one who "drown while washing her hair". Cosimo's son Giovanni became the Bishop of Pisa and Pietro who married his cousin Eleanora in 1571. Several years later he accused her of adultery, and, using a dog leash, strangled her to death. The next year he went to live in the Spanish court and soon gained a reputation for his reckless and extravagant nature. By 1584 he was writing to his brothers for financial help to pay off his number of debts. The family brought him home to Italy and tried to arrange a marriage for Pietro because his reputation and living habits were bad for business, but he returned to Spain. In 1593 he married Dona Beatriz de Lara but continued seeing his mistresses Maria, who bore one of his children and Antonia, with whom he had 5 children. After his death in 1596, his children were adopted into the Medici family and brought to Italy. Cosimo's illegitimate child to survive to adulthood was Giovanni who became a military commander, a painter and architect as well as a diplomat. He died of smallpox in 1621 leaving behind one surviving son, Gianfrancesco Maria.

Francesco had inherited the titles and command of Tuscany and married Joanna, daughter of Emperor Ferdinand I. Joanna spent her short life in depression as Francesco went around with many other women. After bearing him 7 children, she died falling down the stairs while pregnant with the 8th. In 1578, a few months after Joanna died, Francesco married his mistress, Bianca. Francesco built the Medici Theater and Accademia della Crusca, carrying on the legacy of arts and education. In 1584 he contracted family friend Bernardo Buontalenti to build the Tribune Uffizi for his astrological and alchemical studies. Today the octagonal room holds the Medici's collection of paintings for tourists to view. Francesco built a secret room, Lo Studiolo, inside Palazzo Vecchio. Inside its hidden closets were piles of exotic potions, drugs including opium, and magical objects from all over the world.

The family had, for many generations, believed that people born with dwarfism held special powers and were kept close to the family and included in many portraits. In October, while Francesco and Bianca were at the Medici Villa, they were found dead from malaria. It was suspected they had been poisoned by brother Ferdinando, but although traces of arsenic were found on Bianca, malaria was discovered during forensic research. All but 2 children survived to adulthood. Daughter Marie was married to King Henry IV of the House of Bourbon, who were the blood relatives of King Henry II of France whom Catherine Medici married. Henry IV took over the throne of France when Catherine's children had died out. Never worry, dear reader…the elite always stay in the same places. Marie had become Queen of France and ruled it from 1610 until 1617 when her son Louis XIII was old enough to take over. Before we go back to France, Francesco's brother Ferdinando had become the Grand Duke of Tuscany upon his death.

Unlike Francesco, Cardinal Ferdinando was generous and mild natured. He had a mind for business and the family's banking empire thrived in every major city of Europe. He passed edicts of tolerance for Jews, persecuted foreigners, and heretics. His business savvy knew no bounds, as everything he touched flourished. In architecture and engineering, he upgraded his father's harbor, building a canal called Naviglio, and carried out an irrigation project in Val di Chiana. At Maria's wedding, Ferdinando sponsored a grand opera to be performed. In 1589 Ferdinando retired as Cardinal and married Christina Lorraine who had a very large dowry. After his cousin, King Henry III had been killed, Ferdinando supported Henry IV and his fight in the Wars of Religion. To the protestants dismay, Henry IV soon converted to Catholicism after receiving money and advice from Ferdinando Medici who was able to get his friend Ippolito Aldobrandini, Pope Clement VIII, to accept it. Taxes were raised, the Tuscan fleet was strengthened, and the military was sent to support the King of Spain and the Emperor of Rome in their battles. In 1608 he organized the Thornton Expedition and sent them to Brazil to form a colony. He had hoped to develop his own lands, independent of all the kingdoms that surrounded him but unfortunately, he died the following year. His children include Cosimo II whom I will discuss soon, along with Maria. Around this time, the family's net worth has been estimated to have been $129 billion.

Throughout the Renaissance, the Medici and a few other families controlled the movement, the artists, the philosophers, and the indoctrination that took place at that time. Today we praise the Renaissance movements as being some form of high evolution for us, when it was a time of jihad and total control, orchestrated and carried out by the elite. The Middle Ages/Renaissance era enabled the elite to strengthen the footholds they had created, mainly the Holy Roman Church.

Marie had become the Queen of France, mainly due to King Henry IV's enormous debt which he couldn't repay to Francesco Medici. She brought 2,000 of her friends to France and in 1601 she gave birth to their 1st son Louis XIII. Unhappy with her husband's many mistresses, one of whom he promised to marry, Marie was jealous and aggressive. Her life in court was a mirror image of Catherine's before her, shipped off to a man to breed and be abused. 5 children later, in 1610, Marie was finally given her coronation ceremony and crowned Queen of France. The next day King Henry was assassinated. Marie took her place as Queen Regent while Louis grew up. She kept Henry's religious tolerance laws in place, mostly because the people thought of her as a foreigner and didn't like her much. She had been a ballet dancer and decided to focus on bringing the arts to France. In an attempt to further ensure her political survival, she arranged the marriages of 2 of her children to the 2 children of King Philip III of Spain. This upset the people of France as well, but before the matter could go through the extensive and lengthy court system, Louis had come of age and was now King of France. Marie became his Regal Counsel, meaning nothing had really changed. Prince Henry II of Conde had been on Marie's heels since she was crowned Queen because he was of the House of Bourbon, a branch of Medici who had long run France, and expected to be on the throne. While tension in court rose, Louis' awareness of his mother's control grew. In April 1617 he decided to organize a coup which resulted in Marie's exile and the assassination of Concino Concini, one of Marie's closest friends. 2 years later, Marie escaped from the Chateau de Blois where she had been sent and gathered an army to wage war on her son. After she made a big fuss about the first war against her son, she waged another.

In 1620 her coalition had been defeated and Louis forgave her. She returned to court, bought, and reconstructed the Luxembourg Palace for herself, in Paris. As a patron of the arts, her many palaces and apartments were covered in murals and portraits of Roman gods and goddesses and the family. One of the painters commissioned by her was Peter Paul Rubens. He was hired to paint a 21-piece series of her glorious life. Henry IV is depicted as Jupiter and Marie as Juno. The decorating and constructing of the palace was a most expensive task, but it was only the people who paid for it, so Marie gave it no thought. During this time, while she busied herself with sculptors and painters, her friend Cardinal Richelieu had been working hard as well. He had worked to negotiate peace between her and her son and was able to get her back on the Royal Council. Now, however, she discovered that he had been advancing his own power too. This started a drama between the two which ended with Marie leaving the court in 1630. Louis told his mother that she was too interested in creating drama and told her to retire to Chateau de Compiegne. When she noticed the guards move away from the palace, she escaped, as Louis had expected her to do. When she left, it allowed Louis to make her a refugee and take her pension. Marie spent many years travelling from court to court before settling in Peter Rubens' house in Cologne.

In 1638 Louis dedicated France to the Virgin Mary. Because of Louis' homosexuality, it took he and his wife Anne of Austria (daughter of the King of Spain) 23 years to conceive a living heir, Louis XIV. 4 others were still born. After the successful birth Anne founded the Benedictine Abbey in Val-de-Grace in his honor. In 1640 their final child, Philippe, was born. In 1642 Queen Marie died of pleurisy. Her burial was without ceremony, one year later, when her body had been sent to France. Her heart was removed and shipped to La Fleche to be reunited with the heart of Henry IV, who demanded it. 2 months later, Louis XIII died after being sick for many months with inflamed intestines, tuberculosis and more. Among the last influences of King Louis is the fashion trend of men's wigs, which he had introduced. His son Louis became the longest ruling sovereign of France and was called the Sun King.

Of Marie's 5 children, she only lost 1 before he reached maturity. The premature death of children in these families is common, and one of the most common causes for young death in the Medici line is water buildup on the brain. This is how 4-year-old Nicholas died. Marie's daughter Henrietta Maria had become the Queen of England, Scotland, and Ireland. Henrietta had been given the same education as her brothers and sisters and had become a dancer and singer. Her artistic nature made her a frequent participant in the courts plays and religiously she enjoyed the Order of the Brothers of the Blessed Virgin Mary of Mount Carmel, more commonly referred to as Carmelites. She and King Charles I were married when Henrietta was 15 years old. Her portrait shows one of the courts dwarves, Jeffrey Hudson, and a monkey, often symbolic of an advisor to fools. Shortly after they were married, Charles became aware of Henrietta's ability to squander money. She had a large menagerie and collected excessive amounts of jewels, books, paintings, and more. Henrietta was always in the presence of her large entourage, which included 12 priests.

Finally, the King had had enough and ejected many of her "friends" including the Bishop of Mendes. Henrietta was assigned an expense manager, but that didn't slow her down. Although their arranged marriage was difficult at the beginning, it's said that they grew to love each other over time. The birth of Charles' first live heir Charles II, in 1630, was a time of celebration. Daughter Mary arrived one year later, followed by James, Elizabeth, Anne, Catherine, Henry, and Henrietta. In 1631 the ship Henrietta Maria was sent out on an expedition to the New World. The party explored around the Hudson Bay area of New York and travelled south, naming Maryland after Henrietta. During Henrietta's life as Queen, England was involved in several civil wars, which left her poor and plain. In 1660 she returned to her residence at Somerset House and was described as looking like any ordinary woman. Around this time her son James got courtier Anne Hyde pregnant and despite Henrietta's disapproval, they were married. At the age of 20, son Henry died of smallpox. That same year, by Christmas, daughter Mary was also dead of the same. In 1661 Daughter Henrietta was married to her cousin Philippe I and peace between England and France was solidified. In 1665 the Queen went back to Paris to live, due to the increasing decline in her health being in the damp British climate. After taking a large quantity of opiates, Henrietta died.

Meanwhile her sister Elisabeth had been married to King Philip IV of Spain and Portugal. As a child, growing up in court, she had been given the nickname Madame Royale. Even though her husband had numerous mistresses, and having had 3 miscarriages, Elisabeth managed to give birth to 7 children, 5 of whom died in infancy. In 1640 her husband was off fighting in the Catalan Revolt with his favorite official, Gaspar de Guzman, who had been the king's prime minister. Elisabeth disliked Gaspar because he had assisted Philip with his many affairs and had spread rumors about her to the king. In 1643 Philip realized that Elisabeth should be trusted to run the kingdom in his absence, and when he went to war again later that year, she was noted for her intelligence and ability to rule well. She used her own jewelry to secure loans from the banks for the military and would have done more in her lifetime, had she not died the following year. 2 of her children survived.

Over on the Italian side of the family, Cosimo II de' Medici had been born to Ferdinando I and Christine de Lorraine, in 1590 and inherited the kingdom of Tuscany and the title of Grand Duke in 1609. One year before he had been married to Maria Maddalena, daughter of Archduke Charles of the House of Habsburg. Together they had 8 children. Cosimo was tutored by Galileo Galilei who wrote to him asking for patronage, stating he would name the newly discovered moons of Jupiter after him. They were named the Medicean Stars and Galileo became the court mathematician and astronomer in 1610. Cosimo left most of the administration of his country to his ministers and spent his time enjoying the arts. Cosimo's reign was cut short when he died in 1621 of tuberculosis. His son Ferdinando II became the next Grand Duke. His sons Leopoldo and Giovan spent their lives in service to the Church, as Cardinals. Dozens of Medici were Cardinals though only several of them became Popes. The Pope is just a public face, the real work gets done behind the scenes, as always. Son Giancarlo joined the Sovereign Military Order of Malta when he was 9 years old. By 1638 in addition to being Grand Prior of Pisa, he was made General of the Mediterranean Sea. In 1644 he was made Cardinal-Deacon which cost him his General title.

Ferdinando II was made Grand Duke at the age of 11. His brothers were put in charge of their own area of government. Giancarlo became the finance manager and continued his interest in the arts, financing the construction of the Theater in Pergola and more. In 1630 the land was hit by a plague which killed 10% of the population of Florence. Ferdinando and his brothers travelled through Florence on foot to give help to the sick and Ferdinando made laws regarding public health. In 1633 his friend Galileo was taken to court by the Roman Inquisition but was allowed to live in Tuscany until his death. Ferdinando was fond of technology and worked on several kinds of measurement instruments such as the thermoscope, hygrometer, barometer and more. Together, Galileo and Ferdinando added a greenhouse to the Boboli Gardens and experimented with humidity to grow citrus there. Vittoria della

Rovere became his wife in 1633 and even though Ferdinando was a notorious homosexual, the pair fulfilled their duty and produced an heir, Cosimo, in 1642. After catching Ferdinando having an affair with Count Bruto, Vittoria left the court for many years. In 1643, having been at war with Pope Urban VIII, the treasury of Tuscany was empty, and the economy was destroyed. In the 1650's Ferdinando and Galileo worked to solidify Galileo's idea of interpreting phenomena according to geometric and mathematic laws by implementing it in the Accademia del Cimento, a scientific society. Unfortunately, it led to the dissolution of the club.

In 1660 another heir was born, Francesco Maria. In 1663 brother Giancarlo died of a stroke, leaving behind an unknown number of illegitimate children. In 1667 his brother Leopoldo was made Cardinal. Ferdinando died of a stroke, in 1670, leaving Cosimo III as the Grand Duke of Tuscany. In 1709, after an unsuccessful marriage, Francesco Maria was married to Eleanora. Because of his sexual promiscuity, Eleanora was disgusted by him and refused to produce an heir. She eventually went mad, leaving Francesco childless.

Ferdinando's sister Margherita had been married to Duke Odoardo Farnese, of Parma and had 8 children. Because of the plague, and the wars Odoardo insisted on being involved in, the people of the Duchy of Parma had become heavily taxed. However, the marriage of Margherita and Odoardo was one of loyalty and genuine love. Son Ranuccio II Farnese was married 3 times, twice to members of the d'Este family. Alessandro Farnese became the Governor of Habsburg Netherlands and Caterina became a nun.

Cosimo III married cousin Marguerite Louise, granddaughter of Queen Marie Medici and King Henry IV. Cosimo had grown up an avid sportsman and hunter who enjoyed being outdoors and active. His wife had grown up attending balls and theaters and before they were officially married, Cosimo discovered that she had been going out in public with Prince Charles, her cousin, without an escort. Soon their affair was uncovered, and the pair were quite unhappy. Marguerite began smuggling jewels out of Tuscany, for herself. At this time Tuscany, almost bankrupt, couldn't afford her expensive tastes, and her violent outbursts were getting tiresome. She was constantly doing things to enrage Cosimo or humiliate him, flirting with people in front of him, threatening him, and more. They were somehow able to conceive 3 children and continue the line. As often as he could, Cosimo travelled throughout Europe. While in England, visiting Oxford and Cambridge Universities, he met Isaac Newton, Robert Boyle, and other scientists. In 1672 Marguerite had become entangled in a deep depression which lasted several years, until finally, Cosimo allowed her to return home to France, after paying a sum equivalent to $98,740 today. She was confined to the Abbey of Saint Peter but went out to see multiple men. She caused trouble at the abbey because of her dramatic lifestyle, and her violent outbursts. After threatening to kill the Abbess, Cosimo allowed her to be moved to another convent and her pension was withdrawn.

In 1677 Cosimo finally had some peace in his kingdom and decided to pass some laws. One of them was the banning of intercourse between Jews and Christians, as well as the employing of Christians by Jews. In the 1500's another Cosimo Medici had been in charge of Tuscany and allowed the Jews to live there after being expelled from a region of Spain. Jews from that region were called Sephardic (Hispanic) Jews and were expelled from Spain and Portugal in the end of the 1400's. The Jews then went to settle in areas of Africa, Asia, and Europe, including Tuscany, where they had been invited to settle. Soon many more Jews came from Italy to settle in Florence, causing too large of an influx of migrants to the kingdom. Laws were passed to restrict the Jews, and a ghetto was created in Florence in 1571, to house those who chose to live in it. Back to our current Cosimo III, after passing several laws, and attempting to maintain segregation, he fell ill from the stress Marguerite caused him. The rest of his time was spent trying to produce heirs, and his children were disinclined to appease him. He attempted to marry his sons well, and form branches of the family abroad, to no avail. Finally in 1700 he went on a pilgrimage to Rome. After meeting with Pope Innocent XII, Cosimo was made a Canon of Saint John. Only a Canon of Saint John is able to see the cloth the Church says Christ wore before his crucifixion. Cosimo returned home with a section of Saint Francis Xavier's bowel.

By 1705 Ferdinando had become sick with syphilis and was growing senile. Because there was no apparent heir for the Medici's rule to continue, Emperor Joseph prepared to move in. The Emperor died before he could, and the matter of inheritance went to court. In 1712 Marguerite had apoplexy, which left her arm paralyzed. After hearing of the death of her favorite son, Prince Ferdinando, she had another which affected her speech. In 1717 Cosimo decided that the House of Este should succeed but instead Don Carlos, son of Queen Elisabeth Farnese and King Philip V of Spain, was chosen. In September 1723, Cosimo had some sort of seizure and died the following month. Cosimo's son Gian Gastone became the next Grand Duke, though he had no children, and repealed the laws regarding Jews and Christians. Upon his death the titles and lands were given to the House of Lorraine and the Medici's continued elsewhere.

Over in France the Medici line continued through Louis XIV, the Sun King of France, who had over 15 children with his wives and mistresses, he ruled so long he outlived many of them and left great-grandson Louis in charge when he died. In Tuscany the Medici's of Ottajano continued the dynastic rule with Giuseppe, 5th Prince of Ottajano. In 1737 he went to the Imperial Court to plead his inheritance as Prince and Grand Duke of Tuscany but was refused. He died suddenly in 1743, leaving his 4 children their titles and lands. His brother Luigi had become a lawyer in Naples and was surrounded by the most notable philosophers of the kingdom. Like most of his friends, he was a Freemason. Soon he became Chancellor, which gave him authority over the Urbana Police and Criminal Court of Naples. During this time, Naples had been involved in a war with France, who invaded in 1796.

In 1789 the Club Brenton, which had been formed in Versailles, went through several name changes and, after the political club relocated to Paris, the name changed to Society of the Friends of the Constitution. Their claimed purpose was to manage revolutions taking place at that time and protect assets from being taken by the nobility. Soon another name change took place, and the group became known as the Jacobins. In 1791 Maximilien Robespierre became the leader of the Jacobin Club and shaped the course of the French Revolution. By 1793 there were at least 500,000 members in France and, fear of the radical group spread as quickly as their oppression. In 1795 Luigi was arrested and imprisoned by the Jacobins for the next 3 years. Several months after he was freed, they arrested him again. In 1803 Luigi was made President of the Royal Finance Council, followed by Director of the Secretary of State. But by 1806 the French invaded, causing the Medici's and Bourbons, who ruled the region, to flee to Sicily. After tensions between him and the Sicilian Parliament grew, Luigi went to London in 1811. In 1815 the Bourbons returned to rule their land and Luigi was returned to his rightful place as Minister of Finance and became Knight of the Distinguished and Royal Order of St. Gennaro and Knight of Grand Cross of the Royal Order of St. Ferdinand and Merit.

Because of Luigi's work in the courts at this time, the Kingdom of Two Sicilies was formed, which started a new cycle of revolutions and riots. Nevertheless, he became Knight of the Illustrious and Royal Order of San Gennaro and Knight of the Order of the Elephant and worked to establish and regulate the shaky government and the people. As soon as the Two Sicilies were formed, Calmann (Carl) Mayer Rothschild came to Naples. Because of Carl's connection to Austria, the Austrian army was sent to Naples, to support King Ferdinand I. In the 1820's, Luigi served as Minister of Foreign Affairs, President of the Council of Ministers, and Minister of Finance and was Prime Minister until his death in 1830. During this time Carl had established CM de Rothschild and Figli, a satellite office for the bank, as well as a close working relationship with Luigi. In 1822 the Rothschild's were given the hereditary title of Baron by the Austrian Emperor Francis I who had previously been the Holy Roman Emperor Francis II. Soon the Rothschild bank was the main bank of Naples, the Duchy of Parma, and the Grand Duchy of Tuscany while also being the main source of loans to the Papal States. This is how the Rothschild family surpassed the upper elite families in the banking and government arenas and won their position in Part II. During this time many of the officially powerful positions were no longer held in plain sight but taken behind the curtain. Today the orders set up by the elite are what they work through to govern and those in government positions are merely puppets.

The next generation of Princes of Ottajano had grown and inherited their birthrights. Luigi's nephew Alessandro Medici was given a fief in Macerata for his service as Field Marshal in the Neapolitan army. His descendants became the bearers of the title Marquis of Acquaviva and Fornelli, while Cousin Giuseppe Medici became the 10th Prince of Ottajano and Duke of Sarno. Alessandro's nephew Edoardo Medici lived in Piedmont, at the Castle of Monale d'Asti. He had a son Paolo, who, like him, had a career in the Royal Army until 1918. Paolo moved to Milan and started an industrial company in 1923, which was managed by his son Cosimo. Cosimo married Francesca Sella, the daughter of banker Venanzio Sella and together they had 3 sons. So, the line continues, as do the family's businesses and titles.

Ottaniano Medici was born in 1957, in Milan. In 1974 his 5th cousin Giuliano de' Medici di Ottajano was born and grew to become the 15th Prince of Ottajano. Together they founded the International Medici Association. In 2015 the family began a movement called Save Florence, with Ottaviano as the man who will save Florence. Remember, when presented with a problem, there is always a solution waiting to be given to you. They have published manifestos explaining Medici Humanism, and the New Medici Humanism and calls for a New Renaissance. You, the people, can help by donating money to the Mediceo Arte e Ambiente fund.

Meanwhile, many generations ago, another Medici branch had settled in Croatia where the Villa Medici in Zadar County still stands. The names given to each generation by the family are the same: Giovanni, Antonio, Averardo, Cosmo, Bortolo, etc. The family leads us through Doctor Lorenzo Antonio Giovanni Battista Giulio, son of Cosimo Antonio Sebastiano Giovanni de Medici and relative of Louis, son of Gregorius Matheus Medici. Born in the part of the Austrian Empire known as Croatia in 1850, Louis (called Luka) became a mechanical engineer for Railways of the East. After the Balkan War, in 1912, the family moved to Constantinople. Louis and his wife Eugenie Marie Laget had 5 children. In 1951 their son, Eugene joined the RAF and became a Wing Commander during World War II. After the war he went to Nairobi as an accountant until he retired, moving back to London. Meanwhile several of his siblings had spent their lives in France, while others remained in Greece and Turkey.

In Italy, the Medici branch of Tornaquinci continued to thrive. Aldobrando Medici Tornaquinci was born in 1909 and became a member of the Italian Liberal Party, followed by the Republican Party. He earned the Silver Medal for Military Valor as Undersecretary of State. In 1945 Aldobrando was made President of the Central Commission which had been created to investigate crimes committed by Germans during that time. He had 7 daughters before he died in 1947, after contracting typhus.

Going back just a bit, in the late 1800's Rafael Medici, son of Francisco Medici and Mariana Paladim, was born in Sicily. Rafael married Maria Castrattaro and moved to Uruguay where they had 4 children. While the children were still young the family moved again, to Rio Grande do Sul, Brazil where Emilio was born. Emilio Grastattaro Medici had 5 children including his namesake Emilio Garrastazu Medici. In 1920 Emilio attended Porto Alegre and joined the army in time for the Brazilian Revolution. During this time Brazil's government was in a state of flux as many coups and changes took place. Certain foreign organizations were gaining control of the country at this time, and the Brazilian Army was used to depose President Getulio Vargas in 1945. By 1951 he had become President again, to the delight of US President Harry Truman.

By the 1950's Emilio had been made General, during the time of continued governmental unrest. After Getulio Vargas committed suicide, and more coups took place, General Artur da Costa e Silva, who was in the army with Emilio, was appointed President, after his military overthrew the current ruler. Everything went according to the plans Artur had laid out and soon Emilio was made Artur's Chief of Staff in 1967 as well as Director of the National Intelligence Service. 2 years later, Emilio had been chosen by the military to be President and in 1969 they overthrew Artur and Emilio Medici became President of Brazil for the next 5 years. By the time he got into office, the government had written and rewritten the Constitution which gave authoritarian power to the government. Censorship and violations of Human Rights were as rampant then as they are today, and Emilio was no exception. He enjoyed his ability to torture at will and kept the press under extreme censorship, so the public was kept in the dark just as the people elsewhere are kept in the dark and ignorant of the activities their governments carried out. Your ignorance allows them to destroy anything they want to, at will. Why do you assume they should tell you everything they do? Emilio's opponents were disappeared, and the people were segregated into or out of new zones called Indigenous Territories. The people were flooded with propaganda made to push nationalism.

Emilio was true to his genes and the economy of Brazil saw the largest growth in history. In 1970 Brazil even won the Football World Cup. Emilio began many construction projects including the Trans-Amazonian Highway. While the people of Brazil celebrated the continuous advancements, Emilio had bugs put into peoples' bodies, shocked them with electricity, crucified them, and more, without trial or charge. In 1971 Emilio became involved with President Richard Nixon. Together they planned to overthrow Salvador Allende of Chile. President Nixon's support was noted in a meeting on December 9, 1971, where he stated:
    "The President said that it was very important that Brazil and the United States work closely in this field. We could not take direction but if the Brazilians felt that there was something we could do to be helpful in this area, he would like President Médici to let him know. If money were required or other

discreet aid, we might be able to make it available. This should be held in the greatest confidence."

President Nixon worked through Henry Kissinger who was in contact with Finance Minister Delfim Netto, used by President Emilio. This is how politicians and elite always work, through a layer of encryption. The US government used Brazil to control the rest of the South American continent. A CIA weekly report put out on March 5, 1971, exposes the torture and execution of people in Brazil which the US government was aware of at the time it took place. Emilio was a member of the Military Order of Saint James of the Sword and the Order of the Tower and Sword. Before he could be overthrown, Emilio chose General Ernesto Geisel, one of his closest friends to become President of Brazil in 1974. 9 years later, Emilio died of kidney failure, leaving behind his 2 sons and wife.

Today, Calvin Cordozar Broadus Jr., more commonly known as Snoop Dogg, is now calling himself Cozomo de Medici as he expands his empire into crypto currencies. Snoop's Project Nothing earned 64.6 Ethereum, which was then put into other cryptos, and another project called Medici Emerging, which works to promote emerging artists. Fellow artist Sia uses the alias Bianca de Medici for the project. How is this making money? He is selling Non-Fungible Tokens (NFT), a block-chain based authentication for products that only exist digitally, meaning not in the real world. This is how the next generation will live: with possessions, friends, and skills that don't have meaning or even exist in the real world. The wallet associated with Snoop's Cozomo account has around $17 million in holdings.

Amongst the living descendants of the Medici are many princes. Prince William, Duke of Cambridge, and his brother Prince Harry, Duke of Sussex, are Medici's in part, through their ancestors King Charles II and King James II who were grandchildren of Queen Marie de Medici of France. Another prince is Lorenzo de Medici. Born in Catanzaro, Italy, he has become known for his philanthropic interests and carrying on the love and expansion of art, as his ancestors before him. In his project called Renaissance Pop, he has remade Medici family portraits in a contemporary style. Prince Lorenzo is a Knight of the Martirano Order, General Prior of St. Martin of Beatitudes Order, and Director of San Silvestro al Quirinale Church. His patronage goes to AIDS awareness and research including Cold Spring Harbor Laboratory, where James Watson assists in programs for cancer, plant biology, genomics and more. Aside from designing luxury cars, producing wines and oils, and his many real estate ventures, in 2020, Lorenzo partnered with American Express and Fidor Bank, founding the digital Medici Bank.

The Medici family has come full circle and is nowhere near non-existent. Let's continue now with the Aldobrandini family, the last of the papal elite genealogies I will go into.

~Aldobrandini~

As we have learned with each family history, not every elite bloodline is directly descended from the line of Cain, which was passed through Ham's children, as elite-sponsored theorists would have you believe. Nevertheless, we have also learned and seen how these 3 brothers' descendants have moved around, populated areas, set up kingdoms, built amazing monuments, temples, towers, and statues, and done very destructive and horrible things. Once more, the point is made that race doesn't exist but in the minds of the ignorant.

Today the Aldobrandini name has been merged with the Rothschild's, whom we will discuss next. Princess Olimpia Anna Liliana Aldobrandini, descendant of Napoleon Bonaparte, was married in 1974 to Baron David Rene James de Rothschild, the head of the French Rothschild branch. Their son, Alexandre Guy Francesco de Rothschild, has taken the helm at NM Rothschild and Sons, as of 2018. He states:

> "Rothschild & Co has grown into a global firm with three recognized and established businesses. I am delighted and honoured to lead the talented team which makes up this group. I look forward with great enthusiasm to working with this team to continue the firm's development in the direction so clearly established by my father."

Olimpia is the daughter of Prince Francesco Aldobrandini and Countess Anne-Marie Lacloche. Anne-Marie was the daughter of Jeweler Jacques Leopold Lacloche, and Nathalie Lacloche, whose first husband had been the infamous aristocrat, Count Giuseppe Volpi, one of Benito Mussolini's ministers.

Upon Olimpia's marriage to the Guardians of the Papal Treasure (the Rothschilds) her dowry included a collection of paintings consisting of those commissioned by the Duke of Ferrara, Borso d'Este. Together they have 4 children and as of 2022, David's net worth was $614.6 million. The Rothschild's have, since the 1800's, crossed over into the upper elite circle and the marriage to the Aldobrandini family acknowledges that fact. David was a member of the boards for Compagnie Financière Saint-Honore, De Beers Group, Groupe Casino, and more. He is also the president of the World Jewish Congress and the French Entente Cordiale Scholarship trust, among others. Since I will discuss the Rothschild's history in the next chapter, let's continue with the Aldobrandini side.

Prince Francesco Aldobrandini's siblings include Camillo Giovanni Giuseppe, Giovanni Ferdinando Amerigo, and Livia Maria Immacolata Luisa. Francesco wasn't only the

Prince of Rossano, but also inherited his father's titles and lands as the Duke of Sarsina. While Francesco's mother was a Contessa of the elite Saluzzo family, the mother of his siblings, hailed from Germany. Their mother was Princess Louise Rosario Trinidad Bernardette, the daughter of Graf Johannes Bernhard von Welczeck, another longstanding aristocratic line. Johannes was influential to Adolf Hitler and in the 1930's had established a project in Spain to monitor and infiltrate communist groups in Spain. In the Kennedy chapter I mentioned briefly how the same was done in the US as well. The elite decide you need control through fear, and death. They instigate, create, and expand groups that meet their current agenda. In this instance, as it had been so many times before and since, Rothschild's communism was used. When illegitimate Rothschild son, Adolf Hitler was put into power, and invaded Austria, Louis Nathaniel de Rothschild was taken prisoner. He had been heading the family's Austrian branch of their banking empire. In the 1930's he was worth over $10 billion (in today's value). After 14 months, the family paid his ransom of $400 million (today's value) and sold their mining and iron corporation Witkowitz. So, the Nazi's welcomed Graf Johannes von Welczeck and the Order secretly infiltrated foreign groups to control the narrative. As you can see by this brief look, these families are far from strangers. This is the world the Aldobrandini's were raised in.

Brother Giovanni Ferdinando Amerigo Aldobrandini looks identical to his ancestor, Cardinal Giovanni Aldobrandini who lived in the 1500's. Camillo Giovanni Giuseppe who inherited the titles of Prince of Meldola and Duke of Carpineto and Sarsina, became the father of Marchesa Cinzia Giovanna Lavinia Luisa Stefanina Capodilista who died in 2012. Camillo and Stephania Gallarati Scotti's other daughter is Paola Aldobrandini. She was named one of the most beautiful princesses in Europe by the Paris Match in 1995. Beauty is important to the elite. In 2002 she married Knight of Grace and Devotion of the Sovereign Military Order of Malta and Knight of the Sacred Military Constantinian Order of St. George, Angelo Federico Alessio Mario Gabriele Arcelli. Together they had 2 children who will inherit the same titles, orders, and establishments their parents have. In 2008 the Council of the Delegation for the Grand Duchy of Luxembourg named Paola as the council's Lady of Justice, partnered with Flavio Borghese who is the Knight of Justice. The council is a sect of the Sacred Military Constantinian Order of St. George with a newsletter called In Hoc Signo Vinces, which translates to "In this sign you will conquer".

This family is not an Aldobrandini paternal lineage but a Borghese. In the 1700's the Borghese, like other families including the Pamphili and Farnese, were merged with the Aldobrandini and the Borghese were given the titles and name Princes of Aldobrandini. Francesco Borghese, already a prince, decided to make a plea for the Aldobrandini princedom as well due to the fact that his ancestor was Olimpia Aldobrandini, who merged the families. So, let's see how this merger began.

Princess Olimpia Aldobrandini was born on the 20th of April 1623, the daughter of Prince Giorgio Aldobrandini and Ippolita Ludovisi who was the niece of Pope Gregory XV. Married to Prince Paolo Borghese of the elite Borghese family they had 5 children: Giovani Giorgio, Camillo, Francesco, Giovanni Battista, and Maria Virginia. Because she was the last remaining Aldobrandini, as her father had brought forth no male heirs, he requested that the Aldobrandini name be passed through the female line of the family, so it could live on. Fulfilling her duty to produce more Aldobrandini's, Olimpia's husband died. The following year, she was married into another elite family. New husband Camillo Pamphili was the nephew of Pope Innocent X. While Camillo was on his way to becoming a Cardinal, he became a husband instead so the two upper elite bloodlines could merge and expand. Olimpia's dowry included a collection of paintings which had been removed from the Duke of Ferrara's "Camerino d'Alabastro" as well as the family's estates in Montemagnanapoli, Frascati, Romagna in Rome and the Palazzo Aldobrandini, which remain in the Pamphili family today. Today Prince Jonathan Doria Pamphili and his family live in the 1,000-room estate of the Palazzo Doria Pamphili. Since the place was inherited by the family in the dowry of Olimpia, the family has merged it with the neighboring buildings forming one, multigenerational conglomerate of extravagance. Since the family only occupies 10 rooms of this palace, the rest is used by artists, writers, and organizations. The family keeps their name in the newspapers today with a steady stream of drama and pettiness. Olimpia had 5 more children with Camillo Pamphili: another Giovan Battista, Cardinal Benedetto, Flaminia, Teresa, and Anna.

Daughter Maria was married to Agostino Chigi della Rovere, 1st Prince of Farnese, brother of Pope Alexander VII and nephew of Pope Paul V. They had 17 Chigi children. As you see, the Chigi's are yet another upper elite family. Giovanni Battista Borghese became the 2nd Prince of Sulmona, and married Eleonora Boncompagni. Due to his father's early death in 1666, Giovanni became heir to his grandfather's fortunes. Because he was just a boy when this took place, he was placed under the guidance of Grandmother Camilla Orsini. As a teenager he was made a member of the Order of Calatrava and upon reaching adulthood he became the owner of extensive estates in the Kingdom of Naples as well as the Papal States. His marriage into the Boncampagni family only added to the lineage's elitism, wealth, and power. Together they had 4 children. After being made ambassador extraordinary to Pope Clement XI, he became a member of the Orsini family's Order of the Golden Fleece. Among his friends was mystic Miguel de Molinos and King Philip V of Spain who was a great benefit to him for many years, until the new Emperor of Naples, Charles VI took over.

Among the Pamphili children of Olimpia Aldobrandini is the other Giovanni Battista (John the Baptist). When he came of age, he inherited his father's wealth and titles including Prince of San Martino al Cimino, 2nd Prince of Valmontone, 4th Prince of Meldola and Sarsina. After he bought the town of Carpineto Romano, he became 4th Duke of Carpineto and Belvedere, as well. He was a great patron of the arts including artist Giovan Battista Gaulli and restorer of Churches. His marriage to Violante Facchinetti only added to his art collection and wealth. Together they had 4 children, 2 of whom married into the Colonna and Conti families. His sister Flaminia was married to Bernardino Savelli, followed by Niccolo Saverio Pallavicini and served her purpose. Sister Anna was married to Prince Giovanni Andrea Doria, of Melfi and gave him an heir. Sister Teresa married into the Cybo line, a branch of Medici.

It was the son of Francesco (of the Borghese children) and Adele la Rochefoucauld, who took the name Aldobrandini and became the ancestor of the Aldobrandini line we know about today. His name was Prince Camillo Francesco Giovanni Battista Melchiorre Aldobrandini Borghese. Camillo's siblings used the Borghese name and 2 of them were married to the la Rochefoucauld family. Camillo married Maria Kethely, followed by Marie d'Arenberg, and lastly, Louise d'Arenberg, Marie's sister. Altogether Camillo fathered 3 named children. Camillo's son Prince Pietro used the Borghese name but passed the Aldobrandini name onto the 6 children he had with Francoise la Rochefoucauld.

As with all of the siblings, his children married strategically well. 2 were married to Hungarian and Austrian Grafs and another married Grand Master of the Sovereign Order of Malta, Ludovico Chigi Albani della Rovere, of the elite Chigi and Rovere families. Camillo's daughter Princess Anna Elisabetta Borghese-Aldobrandini married Prince Filippo Massimiliano Massimo and had 7 Princes of Lancellotti. Lastly, Camillo's son Prince Giuseppe Camillo Francesco Pietro Aldobrandini was born in 1865. He was married to Maria Antinori, the Duchess of Brindisi and had 2 children, Clemente and Ferdinando, Duke of Brindisi. In an interview, one of the men who worked on the Aldobrandini estate during WW2, remembered the kindness of Clemente Aldobrandini and the protection he gave the people of his lands when the Germans invaded. Clemente became the father of Francesco, Camillo, Livia, and Giovanni whom we previously discussed, which brings us up to date on this line.

The lineage of the Borghese leads back to Tiezzo, a wealthy wool merchant who moved from France to Siena after buying the town of Monticiano, whom I will discuss later on, along with more Borghese family members. Let's continue with the Aldobrandini line who had come to the same province of Siena at the same time, like many who migrated with their wealth to the Papal States to expand it.

The family crest of the Aldobrandini's is a blue shield with 6 yellow suns and a yellow track splitting the suns, 3 above and 3 below, more commonly called Stars and Stripes. The Aldobrandini's have a palace on top of one of the 7 hills of Rome,

Quirinalis Hill. The story goes that it was on this hill the "holy shields" landed when they fell from heaven. The palace is complete with Pillars of Hercules, Atlas holding a sphere on his shoulders, and even what is called a forest giant. In the side of the hill behind the house, an area of the rock face is revealed and carved into it an angry face with the mouth as an entrance leading into the hill. Looking at satellite images of the entrance you can see a large opening on the other side of the hill as well as one directly across the ravine from it, leading into the next. The oak forest surrounding the villa is stunning, large old oaks looming high overhead giving wonderful shade to the dirt paths around the gardens and waterfalls. As one would expect of any palace, which costs an exorbitant amount of money, it is breathtaking. Even in its current state of disrepair, it is covered in custom paintings and statues of their ancestors.

One of the most famous paintings of this family is the Aldobrandini Madonna, painted in 1509 by Raphael. Showing the trinity: Madonna goddess Isis, a child on her lap handing a flower to a child with a coat of fur (symbolizing Pan/Lucifer) at her side. Each has the iconic incomplete halo which represents the incomplete ring of Saturn that they worship. Colors, positioning, facial expressions, hand signals, and more have great meaning to Luciferians. Stanley Kubrick has detailed in his interviews that he has been present to the sex parties of the Rothschild's and Aldobrandini's, which is where he got the inspiration for Eyes Wide Shut. There is a portrait of Kubrick inside the main hall with his autograph giving thanks to the Aldobrandini family for supporting his films. Another artist used and funded by the family is Picasso, a fellow Luciferian. He based his Taurus paintings from the orgies held at the Aldobrandini's castles and lodges. The Taurus represents the pope, who is always present. Another of the Aldobrandini family portraits is held in the Bibliothèque Nationale de France with the label of Prior of the City of Hierofolymites. This family of wealthy merchant nobility is also listed in the records of nobles of France.

As we learn from the origin of their name, the Aldobrandini's came from Germany. Before their name was latinized, as every migrating family did in the 12-1300's, it was Aldobrandeschi. Ildobrando Aldobrandeschi was the first in the family to change his name to the Latin version (Aldobrando Aldobrandini), beginning the line we know today as the Aldobrandini. On September 4, 1260, the Battle of Montaperti took place. The conflict between the Ghibellines and Guelphs whom we have discussed before, intensified as the Florentines, along with Tuscan allies, marched towards Siena in 1260. The Ghibellines, led by Farinata degli Uberti, had reinforcements but still faced a numerical disadvantage. The Ghibellines decided to execute a risky plan of ambushing at Monselvoli-Costaberci Ridge, east of Siena. Count Aldobrandino Aldobrandeschi, commanding the main Ghibelline force, played a crucial role. The Ghibellines employed strategic tactics, including a staged march and night raids, sowing caution among the Florentine commanders. The battle began around 10:00, with the Ghibellines gaining an initial advantage. However, the Florentines eventually gained the upper hand until late in the day when the cry of "San Giorgio" initiated a Ghibelline counterattack. Count Arras, leading German knights, ambushed and killed the Florentine commander, leading to a rout of the Florentine-Guelph forces. The Florentine cavalry suffered heavy losses, and their camp was sacked, resulting in significant casualties and captures. After the battle, the German soldiers in the Sienese army founded the Church of San Giorgio in via Pantaneto, dedicated to Saint George, their battle-cry during the fight.

Ildobrando was the great-grandson of Brunetto, a wealthy merchant who had 6 children by the late 1150's: Nero, Caruccio, Gemma, Donato, Tilla, and Rupa. His brother Jacopo had joined him in his migration to Siena. They were also relatives to Peter (Pietro) Igneo Aldobrandini, Cardinal Bishop of Albano in 1000. On the 4th of September 1270, Jacopo Aldobrandino was given notice to pay 101 silver marks to the Roman Curia or be excommunicated. Brunetto's son Caruccio was married and had one son Benci Aldobrandini. Benci, born in 1220, was married to Madonna Giovanna Altoviti. The Altoviti family are another aristocratic line, from which have come 11 gonfaloniers, 107 priors and more. Benci and Giovanna had many children including Giorgio who was married to Filippa Strozzi. A popular merchant of that time, Benci dedicated the square of Campo Corbolini to Giovanna, naming it Piazza Madonna degli Aldobrandini of Florence. The family inhabited this area, and Uncle Nero lived at the Palazzo Aldobrandini del Papa. The couple spent much of their time actively participating in various charities and were missed by the people when they died. Their sons Jacopo and Aldobrandino continued the family businesses and lineage. Annibaldo, was made Gonfaloniere of Company (Commander of the People's Militia) in 1366, Prior of the Arts (Patent Law), and Dodici Buonomini.

Benci's son Napoleon was a Prior of Liberty, member of the Dodici Buonomini, and Gonfaloniere of Company. Giorgio was a Gonfaloniere of Company in 1342 and Prior of Liberty by 1350. He was soon made a member of the club Dodici Buonomini (12 Good Men), and by 1365 he was Gonfaloniere of Justice of the Republic of Florence. In 1374 he was made Podesta and Captain of Pistoia. His cousin Benci, son of Giovanni Aldobrandini, was a Dominican monk in Santa Maria Novella and Canon of Siena. Nero, the heir of his father's mercantile wealth, had a son Jacopo, who had 3 known sons, Donato, Niccolo, and Aldobrandino. Donato expanded the family business into France and became very wealthy there. Jacopo had donated a large sum to the chapel in San Lorenzo and dedicated it to the memory of Brunetto di Aldobrandino. Unfortunately, we can't be sure if this Jacopo was Nero's son or one of the many children in the family who were named Jacopo, just like many were named Aldobrandino and Giorgio. Son Jacopo had 3 sons. Donato became Prior, Niccolo became a Prior of Liberty and Aldobrandino followed in his father's footsteps.

In 1204 an adventurer named Aldobrandini, from Tuscany, owned the port in Attalia, Turkey. He was a knight for the Byzantine Empire and assisted in the Siege of Antalya. During this time, many adventurers (knights between crusades, bored with non-violent life) and mercenaries began to grow throughout Italy. Venice was interested in expanding, as many areas were. Knights were sent out to establish territories, which formed a few decades of active piracy. Antalya was left to the Templar Knights, led by Aldobrandini, after the 4th Roman Crusade. The port was advantageous for trade and more, which is why the knights had controlled it in the first place. Unfortunately, the Byzantine Empire was dwindling as the Papal powers rose. Aldobrandini took control of this city until it was conquered by the Seljuks (Turkish Sunni Muslim Dynasty).

In the early spring of 1207, the coastal city of Attalia, in south-western Asia Minor, became the focal point of the Turks. The Seljuk Turks, led by the Sultan Kaykhusraw I, successfully captured of this strategic port, which was a gateway to the Mediterranean and used by the Knights for trade. Aldobrandini's rule over the port was noted by his mistreatment, particularly towards Egyptian merchants who sought refuge. Frustration and discontent brewed among the inhabitants, prompting them to send out a desperate plea for assistance. These cries soon reached Gautier de Montbeliard, the regent of Cyprus, who responded by occupying the town. However, he could do nothing against the relentless advance of the Turks, who proceeded to ravage the surrounding countryside. In March 1207, the siege reached its climax as the Sultan stormed the city with determination. The Sultan appointed Lieutenant Mubariz al-Din Ertokush ibn 'Abd Allah, as the city's governor. The fall of Antalya marked a significant chapter in the Seljuk Turks' expansion, granting them another key route into the vast Mediterranean. Despite this triumph, it took another century before the Turks set their sights on serious maritime endeavors. Meanwhile, the Papal Crusades continued, focusing mostly on trade and business.

While it is not possible to verify that Count Aldobrandino de Toscane (born in 1149, Tuscany), was the father of our Knight Aldobrandini, the dates and locations make it impossible for them not to be related. The Counts daughter Countess Elisa Marie Aldobrandini was married to Marquis Alberto Azzo d'Este, uniting the elite and wealthy families. Their son Aldobrandino d'Este founded the Aldobrandini-d'Este dynasty. His children included Queen Beatrice of Hungary and Saint Contardo. Contardo was the crown prince of Ferrara. After leaving his positions and inheritance he traveled to Santiago de Compostela but fell to his death in Lombardy. His body was later taken to St. Peter parish in Broni to be worshipped. In 1609 Pope Paul V approved of the cult of Contardo. Meanwhile Beatrice had become the 3rd wife of the elderly King Andrew II of Hungary. The marriage, conditioned on renouncing dowry and inheritance claims, lasted only one year due to the death of King Andrew. After this, tensions rose with her stepson, King Béla IV, who sought to banish Beatrice from Hungary. Accused of adultery when she claimed to be pregnant, Beatrice escaped with the help of ambassadors from Frederick II, Holy Roman Emperor. In Rome, she gave birth to a son, Stephen, whose legitimacy was not acknowledged by his brothers. Denied support from her uncle's court, Beatrice wandered Italy, never relinquishing her son's claims to ducal revenues from Hungary. Pope Innocent IV eventually granted her revenues from 35 Italian monasteries. Before we get too far ahead in this family's timeline, let's take it back to find their origins!

Brunetto and his offspring mentioned above used the names Aldobrandeschi as well as Aldobrandini, given their business as merchants took them through Germany, France, and the Papal States. The family members were the Counts of Soana and Santa Fiora and Lords of Maremma (the region between Tuscany and Lazio). Looking back at Brunetto, we can easily follow the Dynasty of Counts of Soana back through his father Ildobrandino (Hildebrand) IX Aldobrandeschi, the 1st conte di Pitigliano. As you can tell, he was from a long line of Ildobrandino's. This was a very poplar name in the family. Ildobrandino had 6 siblings including Giovanna who was married to Senator Luca Savelli, Lord of Palombara, Albano and Rignano. In 1234 Luca was involved in the sacking of the Basilica of St. John Lateran after siding with Emperor Frederick II against Pope Honorius III's successor, Gregory. This added to the family's wealth and lands which now included the region of Sabina. Giovanna became the mother of Giacomo Savelli who was made Pope Honorius IV. When he was made Pope, it was during the aftermath of the Sicilian Vespers, a rebellion against Angevin rule in Sicily wherein 13,000 French men and women were massacred in just 6 weeks. This caused his term to be entangled in the diplomacy with the Kings of France and Aragon and others. Pope Martin IV, his predecessor, had imposed ecclesiastical punishments and supporting Charles of Valois in his attempts to reclaim Sicily. Despite French and Papal forces' attacks, the Sicilians resisted and even captured Charles of Salerno, the Angevin heir. Upon Charles of Anjou's death in 1285, Honorius, more inclined towards peace than his predecessor, maintained Church support for the House of Anjou but did not revoke the penalties on Sicily. He enacted legislation in 1285 to protect Sicilians against unjust rule. After the death of Peter III, Sicily was divided between his sons and Pope Honorus refused to acknowledge them, excommunicating one in 1286. The battle between alliances continued until after Pope Honorius' death.

Many of Giovanna's offspring followed their father into politics and her daughters were married into elite families like Marsilia who was married to Napoleone Orsini. Giovanna designed Luca's tomb within the Basilica of St. Mary in a place called Madonna dell'Altare Celeste (Our Lady of the Celestial Altar). Later she was entombed there along with her son Pandolfo. The line produced several popes, condottiero, and senators and was merged with Orsini, Pamphili, and Borghese bloodlines.

Ildobrandino had been the heir and namesake of the family. However, when he died earlier than expected brothers Guglielmo and Boniface attempted to lead the family. They split the titles and lands between themselves, Boniface becoming count of Santa Fiora and Guglielmo becoming the Count of Pitigliano and Sovana, which used to be Soana. Boniface named his first son Hilebrandino X (Ildobrandino) after his late brother and father. Because Boniface didn't implement a battle against the Counts of Morrano, Guglielmo imprisoned him. Guglielmo was military-minded, which was needed as his lands were under constant attack. His main enemy was the Sienese. In 1224, after several years of battles, a treaty was signed with the Sienese to avoid destruction. However, the growing hostilities on both sides enabled the violence to resume by 1227. The two brothers joined the crusade of Frederick II with their in-laws, the Savelli. At that time, the Pope wanted the lands of Maremma for the Papal States. Although the Pope promised "great peace" between Siena and Florence in 1235, by the following year the guerilla warfare between Siena and the Aldobrandeschi family resumed. Back and forth it went for several decades. Guglielmo was praised by Dante Algieri who called him "the Great Tosco". Guglielmo's son Omberto was Lord of Campagnitaco and in 1259 he was suffocated in bed by men of Siena disguised as friars. Also mentioned in Dante's Purgatorio, Omberto is summarized with this statement:

> "The ancient blood and graceful deeds of my elders made me so arrogant, that, not thinking
> of our common mother, I had every man in contempt..."

Pride is often seen in the members of elite families, due to their upbringing, status, and wealth. It is a difficult weed to get rid of. The son of Guglielmo, Ildebrandino XI "il Rosso" (the red), Count of Sovana and Pitigliano had a daughter named Margherita. Born around 1255, she was about 15 years old when she was married off to Guy de Montfort and had 2 children. During the battle of Gulf of Naples, Guy was captured by the Aragonese, and died a prisoner. While her husband was away, she had a romantic relationship with Nello de' Pannocchieschi, signore di Pietra, and it was rumored that they were secretly married. Like all men of that time, Nello was pulled away to war and in 1292, the Countess met with in-law Napoleone Orsini and arranged a marriage for herself with his brother, Orsello (Orso) Orsini. This marriage would maintain peace in the region which was engulfed in constant battles. Together they had 2 daughers, Angela, who was married to cousin Petruccio Savelli and Maria who married Nicola Annibaldeschi. Margherita's daughter from her previous marriage, Tommasia de Montfort, was married to Prefect of Rome, Pietro de Vico and her remaining daughter, Anastasia de Montfort became Contessa di Nola, Dame de Chailly, Dame de Longjumeau after being married to Romano Orsini. Because of this marriage, after the death of Margherita the lands and wealth of this Aldobrandeschi branch were passed to the Orsini's who became the next dynasty of Counts of Soana. The next few years were a time of peace treaties and other such agreements, which only lasted until Orsello died. Upon his death, Nello attempted to become Margherita's husband once more. Unfortunately, Pope Boniface VIII, rejected the proposal and married Margherita to his grand-nephew, Loffredo Caetani in 1296.

The Pope had had his eye on the Aldobrandeschi lands for some time and assuming the weakness of women, he decided to persecute Margherita. Cardinal Gerardo Bianchi was sent to investigate her previous marriages which the Church declared bigamous. Pope Boniface annulled Margherita's marriage to his nephew. Knowing the scheme of the corrupted Pope, Margherita quickly married her cousin, son of Boniface, Guido Aldobrandeschi, which united the two branches and lands of the family. This began yet another war between the Aldobrandeschi's and the Papal States. All went as the Pope planned for a short time, until the Sienese discovered his plan to acquire the lands for himself. The rulers of Siena then signed a contract with Guido who sued the Pope for peace in 1302. Once again, the family could relax, but as usual this was short-lived.

Guido died shortly after the treaty was implemented leaving Margherita alone once more. At this time the Pope was too busy with another of his wars, with the Vespers, and Margherita was able to retire for a time. After Nello sold land to an abbey, the Pope allowed him to marry Margherita and they had one son, Binduccio de' Pannocchieschi. When Pope Boniface VIII died Margherita separated from Nello, who had decided to side with the Orvieto, who were enemies of the Aldobrandeschi's for several generations. He was forced to live in a castle chosen by the Orvietani, but soon left. Meanwhile, Margherita appealed to the senators of Rome for help against Orvieto but was betrayed. Her county was assigned permanently to the Pope's nephew Benedetto Caetani. Shortly thereafter she died. Let's continue back.

Ildebrandino, Guglielmo and Bonifazio were the sons of Count Ildebrandino VIII Aldobrandeschi and Countess Adelasia. Ildebrandino (VIII) was born around 1186 to Ildebrando Novello di Sovana, the 1st Count Palatine (Count of the Palace). In 1195, he received confirmation from Henry VI of the rights and possessions previously granted to his father by Frederick I. Despite this, he joined the Guelph League in 1197, opposing the Empire. In 1199, Ildebrandino became the captain of the people and podestà of Viterbo, successfully defeating papal troops in Cava di Gorga. However, in 1202, facing threats from Siena and Orvieto, he returned to the Church and made pacts with both cities in 1203. He was deeply involved in the military, as one would expect of a servant of the Church. In 1209, Ildebrandino followed the imperial legate Wolfcherio, patriarch of Aquileia, working on the restitution of taken lands to the empire. In 1210 and 1211, he was with Emperor Otto IV, who granted him benefits, including the possession of lands. In 1208, Ildebrandino made his will in favor of his son Ildebrandino "Maggiore" and three other sons. By 1212, he had passed away, and Ildebrandino was confirmed in Orvieto with the pacts signed by his father in 1203. As we have seen, the tensions between Siena, Orvieto, and the lands of the Aldobrandeschi, rose to war.

Father Ildebrando (Hildebrandin) "Novello" (meaning, the younger) succeeded his father Ugo as Count of Sovana at a young age. His mother Gemma ruled in his stead with stability and prosperity. Ildebrando allied himself with Emperor Frederick I and was given the title of Count Palatine in 1160. Frederick Barbarossa had grown up to become Duke of Swabia (Germany) before being made Emperor of Rome in 1155 by Pope Adrian IV. In 1160 he was excommunicated by Pope Alexander III due to his military involvement against the Papal States and Lombardy. During his reign he attempted to form a centralized power under the Holy Roman Empire, which was quickly dying and being absorbed by the Papal States, as planned. In 1160 Ildebrando formed an alliance with the city of Pisa in the hopes of clearing his name of charges of piracy against Pisan ships. During his visit to Pisa, he was given the title of standard-bearer and in turn he gave Pisa lordship over the Maremma coasts. The city of Pisa and the County of Aldobrandeschi fought together against Lucca and Genoa among others. In 1162, Ildebrando accompanied Archbishop and Chancellor Rainald of Dassel to Tuscany. On August 10, 1164, he received imperial protection from Frederick I and was given the ability of minting coins. During another siege, Ildebrando was taken prisoner by the Sienese, and forced to sign several pacts in their favor. After his death, Henry VI of Hohenstaufen, son of Emperor Frederick, transferred the imperial privileges to son Ildebrandino VIII in 1195, as previously discussed.

Ildobrando's father Ugo II, (Hugo, Uguccione) was the son of Malagagla Aldobrandeschi, Count of Soana, Lord of Arcidosso, and his wife Contessa Lupa. During this time the family lived in their castrum munitissimum, a military fortress, called Rocco Aldobrandescha, in their land of Grosseto. In 1137 the fortress was besieged after Ugo refused to pay tribute to Henry X of Bavaria. When Malagagla died, in 1120, Lupa and his brother Ildebrandino VI sold a portion of land owned by the family to the monastery of St. Salvatore. Other donations to the Church were given to the Holy Trinity Convent in Selva. Meanwhile brother Ildobrandino had married Maximilla, the daughter of Count of Sicily, Roger I "Bosso" and Queen consort of Jerusalem Adelaide del Vasto. Ildebrandino and Malagagla were the sons of Ranieri Malabranca Aldobrandeschi, Count of Soana and Marquis of Roselle until 1077. His father, Ildebrandino V was brother to Enrico and Raniero and grandson of Count Rudolf II and Willa, daughter of Prince Landolf "the Red' di Capua.

Rudolfo died when his son Ildebrandino IV was still a child, and the government of the county was ruled by Willa. Even as a child, he was involved in political activities alongside his mother, as documented during that time. While he turned a blind eye to Sigefredo and Gottifredo da Buggiano's venture to acquire the castle of

Verruca, he was active in the battles between Arduin and Henry II in Tuscia and formed several alliances between 1004 and 1007. In 1007 he was threatened by Pope John XVIII to be excommunicated. Bishop Pier Damian wrote about Ildebrandino IV stating:

"Hildeprandus comes Tusciae, qui dicebatur de Capuana, in tantum dives erat ac praepotens ut gloriaretur se plures habere cortesatque castella quam dies sint, qui numerantur in anno." Which translates to: "Hildeprand, Count of Tuscia, who was said to be from Capua, was so wealthy and powerful that he boasted of having more courtyards and castles than there are days counted in a year."

Rudolfo (Rodolfo) II was the namesake and heir of his father. Grandfather Gerardo I Aldobrandeschi was yet another Count of Soana and Marquis of Roselle, in this long dynasty. Born around 839, he was the brother of Lamberto and Rottilde. Gerardo was made Count of southern Tuscia and Count Palatino (Sacred Palace) by King Berengar II. This position was one of the most illustrious of the age and made Gerardo the overseer of the kingdom in the king's absence as well as the administrator of high justice. With this he had the power to create notaries, judges, and controlled lawyers in the land. The wife of his brother and himself are unlisted but his sister Rottilde was married to Count Rodolfo of Pisa. Gerardo had 2 known sons, Ildebrando and Rodolfo. While Rodolfo carried on the line we have discussed, Ildebrando became the founder of the family's line of Counts of Suvereto and had many children. Gerardo's father was Ildebrando III (Hildebrand) who was Count and Marquis of the March Obertenga after Oberto I was exiled. The family was close to King Berengar II, which is evidenced by their titles and lands at this time. Ildebrando's father whom he was named after was the founder of Aldobrandeschi counts. He was brother of Bishop Geremia of Lucca, Eriprando II and Ademari. The sons were Imperial Vassals like their father Eriprando.

Eriprando's brother Ilprando went into the Church but died in 800, before his father, leaving Eriprando to take over the titles and lands of the family. He was educated in the royal court and had a good mind for business. He increased the family's wealth due to his exchanges with Bishop Berengarius who was given a share of the family's Church of St. Benedict in Septimus. Among the family's inherited churches were the church of San Pietro a Vico and the church of San Giorgio in Grosseto. He was a signiferi (standard-bearer) for the legion of the Marquis of Tuscia (the Medici's) and helped defend Rome from an invasion by the Saracens. He died of old age, after retiring to court.

Eriprando's grandfather Ilprando I was the abbot of San Pietro Somaldi in Lucca until 770. As you can see by now the family centered in Lucca, Tuscany for many generations. Meanwhile cousin Ilprando (Ildeprando, Ildebrand) inherited the position of King of the Lombards and Italy. He was also known as "the Useless," and ruled along with his uncle Liutprand, until he died of a long illness. The same arrangement had been made for Liutprand as his father was also fatally ill during his reign. Before becoming king, Ilprando, the son of Duke Sigiprand, was a Duke as well. In 734, he was instrumental in the successful siege of Byzantine Ravenna. By 735, a diplomatic alliance was formed by Pope Gregory II who brought together the Byzantine exarch Eutychius, Duke Ursus of Venetia (the Orsini family), and Patriarch Antoninus of Grado. With a large Venetian fleet, they reclaimed Ravenna and captured Ilprando and the Duke Peredeo of Vicenza. In 739, as Liutprand campaigned against the church in the Duchy of Rome and Ilprando ravaged ecclesiastical lands around Ravenna. After Liutprand's death in 744, Ilprando succeeded unopposed but was quickly overthrown by a revolt led by his cousin Ratchis. This rebellion resulted in peace with Pope Zachary.

Following the family back through their position as Dukes of Asti, grandfather Ansprand was born in 655. Before his death, at the age of 57, he defeated usurper Aripert II and was made king of Lombard because of it. After several battles, wherein Aripert's son had been taken prisoner by Ansprand, Aripert fled the area, only to return to battle in Pavia where Ansprand's sons regent was defeated. Ansprand fled to the Duke of Bavaria Theodebert and while he was gone, Aripert imprisoned and mutilated his wife Theodorada, and his children Aurona, Imberga, and Sigiprando. Theodorada and her daughters had their ears and noses cut off and Sigiprando had his eyes ripped out. Only the youngest son Liuprand survived to rejoin his father. After raising an army in Bavaria, the men returned to battle with Aripert who would have easily won, had it not been for his pride. Believing the battle would be won, Aripert left his army. Because he left the battlefield, his army decided to quit and Aripert was killed. The people named Ansprand king of Lombard, and he placed his son, Liuprand, on the throne. Sadly, he wasn't able to enjoy his only surviving sons' victory as he died 3 months later. Ansprand was buried next to the Lombard necropolis in the Church of Sant Maria alle Pertiche in Pavia. Upon Liuprand's death, and according to his will, they were both placed in the Basillica or San Pietro in Ciel d'Oro.

Ansprand had been the tutor of King Cunincpert's son, Liupert and was a son of Raginpert (Raghinpert, Reginbert). Raginpert was a Duke of Turin and King of the Lombards for a short time. Son of Godepert and grandson of Aripert I, he usurped the throne from his nephew Liutpert, and replaced him with his son Aripert II. Upon the death of his granduncle, the son of Aripert I, King Cunnincpert I in 700, he took his army against Ansprnad, the guardian of King Luitpert and defeated Ansprand and his allies, winning the crown. He died 3 months later, leaving Ansprand and Aripert to battle it out. Meanwhile, Raginpert's other son, Gumbert had fled to France with his children to avoid the family squabble. There, his sons Reginbert became Comte de Orleans, Manfred became the founder of the Manfredingi dynasty who were the Counts of Toule, Metz, Orleans, and Verdun in France, and later Sicily and Malta.

Gumbert's great grandson Manfred III, Comte de Orleans, returned to Italy in 834 at the request of his nephew, King Lothaire I, who became the Emperor of Rome.

Gumbert and Raginpert's father, Godebert I was joint King of Lombards in Italy with his brother Perctarit. As we know, this never works out well and explains the infighting of this family for the generations to come. He was assassinated by his brother-in-law Grimwald, after asking him for help against his brother Perctarit. Godebert got more than he bargained for by relying on a friend and Grimwald chased Perctarit out of Italy and took the throne for himself from 662 until 673. Perctarit returned once he had amassed an army and defeated Grimwald. Godebert's only son, Reginbert, had a natural and legal right to the throne, as the kingdom was shared, but he was denied this, which is why he worked so hard to ensure his son would have his rightful place.

Father Aripert I had been elected King of Lombardy in 656, after his cousin Gundeberba's husband, King Rodoald had been assassinated. He was the first Catholic to be made king in Lombardia and was famous for building many churches. Aripert was one of the sons of Gundoald (Gundwald), who was the 1st Duke of Asti. Born around 565, he was a member of a long line of Bavarian aristocracy. His father Duke of Lower Bavaria, Prince Garibald I, had married Princess Waldrade, daughter of the King of Lombardy Waccho I. This was her 3rd marriage after being wife to King Theudebald I, of Austrasia, and King Clothair I of all Frank. She had no children by these marriages. After daughter Theodelinda was married to King Autari of Lombardy followed by a marriage to King Agilulf of Lombardy, son Gundoald received the duchy of Asti, and son Tassilo became Duke of Bavaria. Soon after, he married King Waccho I's granddaughter and had two sons Gundpert and Aripert. Unfortunately, his popularity among the Lombards grew to exceed the kings and his sister and her husband planned to have him assassinated. In 616 Gundoald was killed by an arrow while he was relieving himself.

Born in 540, Prince Garibald I (Garivald, Agolfing, Geribaldo) of Bavaria was the founder of the Bavarian Dynasty which ruled the kingdom of Lombard. As mentioned before, in 556 he was married too Princess Wuletrada (Waldrade) who bore him 4 children: Gertrude, mother of Pepin I the Elder, Tassillon I, father of Garibald II and Grimoald II, Gertrude, mother of Willibald II, and Romilde, mother of Geila, Acca, and Grimoald I. His second wife, Theodelinda gave birth to Saint Theodelinda and Grundoald whom we discussed before. Waldrada was the wife of King Theudebald of Austrasia, a member of the Merovingian Dynasty. When he died after a long illness in 555, his granduncle Chlothar I (Clotaire) was next in line for the throne since he was the son of Clovis I, 1st King of the Franks, whom we discussed in previous chapters. Chlothar decided to take Waldrada as his own wife, since she was the daughter of a king and because of the alliance made with her late husband, his nephew, there was peace between the Lombards and Franks.

Unfortunately, the bishops who control kings decided this was not good and forbade him from marrying her. Thus, Waldrada was given as property to cousin Garibald to marry in 556. This enabled the Bavarii to enjoy alliances with the Lombards of Pannonia and Bohemia which wasn't a positive thing once the Lombards moved into Italy. Around 585, the Merovingian court arranged the marriage of Garibald's daughter Theodelinda and King Childebert II while marrying Childebert's sister to King Authari, King of Lombard. Both arrangements failed as Authari was engaged to Theodelinda. Because of this and the already present enmity between the Franks and Lombards, Childebert sent his army to Bavaria (the man in the middle) and ran Garibald out of his kingdom. This is when the marriage of King Authari and Garibald's daughter Theodelinda took place at Verona in May 589 and Gundoald was made Duke of Asti. After suffering defeat against the Lombards, Childebert decided to make peace with the Lombards and Bavarii.

When King Authari died in 590, the Lombards asked Theodelinda to marry again and as discussed, she chose Authari's cousin Agilulf who was made the next king. Peace with Childebert lasted for decades and he named Garibald's son Tassilo to be the next King of the Bavarians. The line of Garibald was named Agilofings, meaning descendants of Agilof, the grandfather of Garibald and Prince of Suebi. For many generations they ruled Bavaria and parts of Italy and were members of the Austrasian (Frankish) court.

Grandfather Agilulf was born in the early 480s, son of Chilperic II, King of the Burgundies who was murdered by his brother Gondebad. Agilulf grew to become the King of the Suebi (Suevi), which is the land of today's Germany and Czeck Republic. The name Swabia comes from this. After migrating north of the Alps to the Right Bank of the Rhine a large portion of the tribe joined up with the Vandals at the end of 406. A couple decades later, the Suavi founded what became known as Spain, the Kingdom of Galicia. Agilulf's sister Theodoria was married to the King of Visigoths, Alaric II. Sister Clotilde, who was sainted, was married to King Clovis I of the Franks and another sister, Theodelinde was married to the King of Cambria, Ragnhard. Thus, the family were the kings of the Franks, Visigoths, and Cambrii as well and the blood of the Aldobrandini's spread throughout the rulers of Europe from this point on.

Chilperic II became King of Burgundy in 473 after co-ruling with his father, Gondioc, for a decade. Gondioc (Gonderic) inherited the title of King of Burgundy in 436. His father, Gundaharius (Gundahar) had crossed the Rhine with the majority of Burgundians and numerous other Germanic tribes. Together with King Goar, of the Alans, Gundaharius proclaimed Jovinus as a new emperor in Rome's Germania Inferior on the lower Rhine and was involved in Jovinus's campaigns in southern Gaul. In 413, Jovis was defeated and Constantius was sent to replace him. In the

430s, the Burgundians increasingly became enemies of the Huns and were also defeated by the General Flavius Aetius. In 436 Flavius was accompanied by Hunnish mercenaries and again attacked and destroyed the Burgundian kingdom, killing Gundaharius.

Upon his death, the kingdom was split between the sons which caused problems due to greed. In the 470's Chilperic was forced to submit to Roman rule, which only made matters worse. Soon brother Gundobad went on a land-grabbing rampage, removing brother Godomar from his rule. Soon he came after Chilperic. After drowning Chilperic's wife he exiled two of his daughters. Daughter Chroma became a nun while Clotilde fled to uncle Godegisel for protection until she was given to King Clovis to marry. With this alliance, Clovis assisted the family in a war against Gunobad but not before he assassinated his brother Chilperic. In his youth Gunobad had become a Patrician of Rome after his uncle Ricimer died. He had been taught by Ricimer who ordered him to execute Emperor Anthemius and followed in his footsteps. Initially serving under the magister militum Flavius Aetius, Ricimer reached the centers of political power. The Vandals' sack of Rome in 455 prompted the Visigothic King Theodoric II to proclaim Avitus as Emperor. Avitus, with Theodoric II's support, agreed to Visigothic entry into Hispania. Avitus, in turn, appointed Ricimer to a significant military position, forcing Ricimer to reluctantly support him. However, Ricimer achieved victory against the Vandals in 456 which gave Ricimer and Majorian the boost they needed to rebel against Avitus.

The Battle of Placentia in October 456 is where Ricimer and Majorian were able to defeat Avitus who they captured, deposed, and starved to death. As magister militum, Ricimer held sway over the Germanic tribes in Gaul, Hispania, and Northern Africa. Collaborating with Majorian, the two orchestrated a bid for power: Majorian would take the imperial throne, while Ricimer took command of the military as Ricimer's Germanic background rendered him ineligible for the imperial throne. Majorian's ascent took place in April 457 and was backed by Ricimer and recognized by Constantinople. Majorian's rule brought military successes against the Vandals and Visigoths, along with diplomatic and economic reforms. However, Ricimer soon turned the senate against him, leading to his arrest. Deposed in August 461, Majorian was then tortured and beheaded by his long-time friend Ricimer. Ricimer was immediately appointed by the Eastern Emperor Leo I and assumed control of Italy as vice-regent in the West. His life is an endless trail of murder for promotion, until his death in 472, after deposing Anthemius. Upon taking his uncle's position as Supreme Commander, Gunobad placed Glycerius in the position of Emperor of Western Rome just before his father died. Hearing of the death of his father, he returned to Burgundy to claim his portion. After he left Glycerius was deposed and Gunobad lost control over the Roman Empire which his murderous uncle had worked hard to obtain.

Following the line back through grandfather Pharamond (Faramond), who was one of the 7 children of Marcomir, King of Ripuarian Franks of Cologne in the mid-300s and founder of the Merovingian Dynasty. Marcomer, along with Sunno and Genobaud (other Frankish tribes' leaders), led an invasion of the Roman provinces Germania Inferior and Gallia Belgica in Gaul, breaking through the limes (Roman defensive structures), causing destruction, and creating panic in Cologne. After the raid, most Franks returned across the Rhine, while some remained in the Belgian wood. Roman generals attacked the remaining Franks, leading to an engagement in which General Quintinus's army was surrounded and beaten. Following this defeat, Quintinus crossed the Rhine in an attempt to punish the Franks in their own territory, but his army faced further struggles against these "barbarians" and some of his soldiers drowned in marshes while others were killed by the Franks. Only a few managed to make it back to the Roman Empire.

After the fall of Magnus Maximus in 388 Arbogastes was now in power and crossed the Rhine with a Roman army into Germania. However, Marcomer, now leading with Chatti and Ampsivarii, did not engage. Arbogastes instead held a meeting with Marcomer and Sunno who delivered hostages to him. The Liber Historiae Francorum states that Marcomer was a descendant of the Trojans, as we have already discussed in our first chapters of Part I. He proposed uniting the Franks under one king, suggesting his son Pharamond who is attributed as the author of the Salic Law, but this didn't take place until King Clovis arrived on the scene. Until then, the Frank and German tribes remained separated, ruled by cousin and brother kings.

Following the family back through the Salian Franks we come to King Anfortas Boaz who ruled the lands of Belgium and Netherlands called Troxandrie. He inherited the position of Grandmaster of the Order of the Grail and ruled a portion of Wales until 288. His father was the 8th Grandmaster of the Order while his brother King Childeric of the Sicambiran Franks ruled until the mid-200s. Their father Sunno Manuel (Emmanuel) was the King of Sicambres and Troxandrie.

Sunno's grandfather, King Clodomir IV ruled for 17 years during which time he expelled Nero's legions from Metz and Trier. His sons Roricus, Nicanor and Farabert ruled their own regions upon his death at the age of 61. The line goes back through Odemar, Righemer, Antenor, and several Clodomirs and Marcomirs, who were all the ruling dynasties of the tribes of the regions we have discussed thus far which spread throughout Europe. The genealogy leads us directly to King Francio of Lorraine, who is the namesake of the Franks and ruler of the Sicambrii tribe, also known as Sugumbrians and Sicambrians depending on the language. The tribe's name is a different spelling of the Cimmerians who they descended from, and their kings were called Priest Kings given their deeply religious rituals and practices in sorcery and paganism. The tribe occupied the Netherlands and Germany and were in constant conflict with the ever-invading Roman Empire. From 39 BC until 11 BC

Francio (Francus) ruled the people he named Franks. His army grew to 300,000 men who were among the few tribes powerful enough to defeat the Romans time and time again. Francio is a descendant of the King of Troy, Priam who was documented by the Greek historian Homer.

Coming back several generations we find the 1st Chlodius (Clorius) around 220 BC. He ruled the Sicambri like his father before him and defended the land of Gaul to Germany against the Romans. His father, Marcomir II, had defeated the Romans, Gauls, as well as the Goths. He had the tribe write their history down in poetic verses, as many at that time did to remember their heritage more easily. He named his son after his grandfather, Clodomir, son of Bazanus Magnus (Basarus), Priest King of Lilum, Cinmeria, and Sicambrai. Bazanus had been born in the Midi-Pyrenees and built the city of Bassanburg, in Germany, now called Aachen and was married to a Norwegian Princess, the daughter of Orcades. He died in 250 BC at the age of 70. His father, King Diocles Ilium, had been born in Pontus, Kymi, Finland and had 2 documented sons who both became kings. Diocles was an ally of the Saxons and fought against the Goths. His grandfather was King of Troy, Priam (Perenus, Priamos). Priam was the first to use the language called Saxon, derived from Sax which was a type of knife used by the people in that day.

Priam was the grandson of King Marcomir and Queen Cambra of Troy and Cimmeria. Following this line back through several generations of Priam's, Helenus', and Marcomir's who were all Kings of Troy, brings us to Priamos III, King of Troy and the Cimmerians, son of Alexandre (Alexandros) born around 700 BC in Troy, Turkey. Priamos was the father of Gentilanor, Teushapa, and Helena whose beauty began a war. In 900 BC Plaserius II was born to King Gaberiano of Troy and inherited the throne of his father. His grandfather, Eliacor "Of Troy", was the King of Cimmerians and Scythian's who made up the tribes of Troy. Going back 4 generations brings us to King Laomedon and his wife Queen Strymo Placia who ruled until 1235 BC.

> "There were twelve kingdoms with one over-king, and each kingdom contained many peoples. In the citadel were twelve chieftains and these excelled other men then living in every human fashion." – Prose Edda

Laomedon (Lacmedon, Loomedonte) was king during a time of extended war. For 10 years the Mycenean Greeks invaded his kingdom, named after his grandfather Tros. During his reign the kingdom of Troy became one of the world's wealthiest nations, as it was a city on the sea with access to trade routes leading to every region of the world. After being overrun in the Trojan War, the Romans moved in, followed by Byzantines and in 1998 UNESCO added the city to the World Cultural Heritage List. Among the remnants of Troy are the temple of Athena, sewer and plumbing systems, the city walls and gates, citadels, and the Odeon (theater). A marketplace and council house have also been uncovered. The city's fortifications were the most elaborate of their time. The houses were made of stone and mudbrick and connected in rows. Some were larger, with a megaron layout, likely depicting the status of the inhabitants.

King Laomedon had dozens of children with his concubines and wives, as many did during this era. One of his wives was Princess of Phrygia, Hecuba, who was the daughter of King Dymus. Among their sons was Helenus, who became King of Troy and founded Buthronum. He married the Princess of Thebes, Andromache, the widow of his brother, followed by Princes of Scyros, Deidamia. Helenus was the brother-in-law of Helen of Troy who had married his brother Hector, among others. After surviving the Trojan War, he became King of Epirus (the Scythians) and Troy. He was considered the cleverest amongst the Trojans as he was a "seer" like his twin sister, Cassandra. Laomedon's daughter Aigesta was married to cousin Assaracus, who was King of the Dardanians and son of King Tros. Son Tithonis was the father of Emathion and Memnon. Emathion ruled Aethiopia which is present-day Ethiopia and Sudan but was killed by Heracles. After his death his brother Memnon was made King of the region. The capital of Troy was named Illiona, after Laomedon's father Ilus who is also described in the Illiad and listed in the genealogies of Scandinavian kings who detail the line back to Adam. Let's get into this.

Tros was the founder and 1st King of Troy. Tros was the son of King Erichthonius who had inherited the position of King of Dardania, named after his father Dardanus, King of Arcadia. Erichthonius had inherited not only the kingdom and wealth of his father but also of his grandfather King Teucer of Teucria who had founded the Troad (also called Troas, the northwestern region of Turkey, on the coast). His father, Dardanus (Darah Judah), had been born in Goshen, Egypt around 1519 BC and was the great grandson of Zarah and Electra. When Dardanus was young, he left the enslavement of Egypt behind, like many others, and travelled to the Tracian region of Greece, which is considered the Sanctuary of the Great Gods. There, he was welcomed by King Teucer and married to his daughter. After being given land by the king he founded Dardania. One of his sons, Idaeus, named Mount Ida after himself and built a temple to Cybele there. He implemented rituals and "mysteries" to her there which were observed and recorded during Dionysius' reign in the 300's BC. Dardanus then travelled to the straits that separated Europe and Asia and named them Dardanelles. Soon thereafter he founded a fort in the land which became known as Troy. It is documented that King Solomon was wiser than all men, specifically wiser than the wisest man, Darda (Dardanus) son of Mahol, who was the son of Ethan who was the son of Zara.

Dardanus' great grandfather Zara (Zerah, Zarah) was the firstborn twin of Judah and Tamar. King Judah was one of the sons of Jacob, who was renamed Israel, and had 3 known sons: Er, Onan, and Shelah. He had arranged for his eldest son, Er, to marry a woman named Tamar but Er was killed for his wickedness. During that time, it was law that a man was obligated to marry his deceased brother's wife in order to continue the lineage and care for the widow. So, Onan was set to marry Tamar. After refusing to fulfil his duty he was also put to death and Judah hesitated to marry his youngest son to her. Tamar had the natural desire to secure her future by bearing children and in an attempt to uphold the law and her duty, she disguised herself as a prostitute and seduced Judah. Due to this success, she gave birth to twins Zara and Pharez in Canaan, Palestine, where the family lived. She is recorded in the genealogical documents of Genesis, because of the unusual actions she took to ensure her right to have children, and the fact that the genealogy of her sons leads to King David and ultimately to Jesus Christ.

"Thomas was not remembered for his bravery...his claim to fame came later, when he refused to acknowledge the resurrection. He just couldn't wrap his mind around it. The story goes that he needed to touch Jesus' wounds to be convinced."

"So, was he?"

"Of course he was! We are all convinced sooner or later." - Ben Linus, Lost

Like many during this time, Zara and his wife lived in Palestine, part of the original Israel (Canaan) which the country called Israel today, continues to invade and attempts to claim in a sad attempt to destroy all Biblically historical regions. It was also in this region that King Nebuchadnezzar of Babylon built his 90-foot-tall golden statue of himself in Dura. In 2014 the Nebuchadnezzar Cylinder, one of the cuneiform cylinders detailing the history of that time, was sold for $605,000. This cylinder detailed how he had to rebuild the city of Sippar, home of the temple of the sun god Shamash, several times as it kept being destroyed. This city was revered as a sacred center of Semiramis. Following the line of Zara back brings us through Abram, son of Thara and Maria. Thara was the son of King Nahor, born in 2122 BC in Ur, Chaldea (Iraq). Nahor was the King of Ur and Agade. He had at least 14 sons with his wife Iyaseka of the Chaldeans. Nahor was the great grandson of King Peleg of Babylon who was from a long line of Babylonian kings. Peleg was the 4th King of Babylon and had at least 19 sons, as documented. He was the son of King Eber and Azurad, daughter of King Nimrod and Queen Semiramis of Assyria.

Eber's father was King Selah, and his great grandfather was King Arpachshad. The Babylonians worshipped many gods including Marduk (Bel, Calf of the Sun) who was the patron god of Babylon and believed to live within the Statue of Marduk. Knowing the Fallen Ones as I do and as you should, this is more than possible. Those who warred against Babylon were forced to pay respects to him, and every ceremony of the government and religion was passed through him including the crowning of the kings. Marduk was associated with the planet Jupiter and represented by the symbol of the spade. He is often seen with a snake-dragon, called Mushussu, at his side, as depicted on the Ishtar Gate of Babylon. He is mentioned by the prophet Jeremiah who stated:

"Declare among the nations, and publish, and set up a standard; publish, and conceal not: say, Babylon is taken, Bel is confounded, Merodach is broken in pieces; her idols are confounded, her images are broken in pieces."

Much later, King Cyrus of Persia praised Marduk as the one he daily worships and credited him as the one behind the king's decision to allow the Jews to return to Jerusalem. Arpachshad (Arfakhsyadz, Arphaxad,) was born in Chaldea, Turkey, near the location of the ark's landing, around 2300 BC, 2 years after the flood, as documented. He ruled the land of Arapachtis, which includes Lake Van, the largest lake in Turkey. Arpachshad also founded the city of Ur on the west bank of the Euphrates where the Chaldees lived. He married Rasu'eya, the daughter of Elam son of Shem and Egyptus daughter of Ham and they had many children. Like most of his family he was buried in Jerusalem, Palestine. His brother Elam ruled the Elamites (Iran), Asshur ruled Assyria, on the Tigris River which became a powerful empire, Lud went on to rule Lydia and Arpachshad's other brother, Aram, became the leader of Aramea which was located in parts of Syria, Iraq and Turkey. They were the sons of King Shem, who was the son of Noah, born in 2448 BC and lived for 600 years. This brings us full circle, connecting the Aldobrandini's back to Noah as all families, including yours, are.

"The further a society drifts from the truth, the more it will hate those that speak it...In a world of Universal Deceit, telling the truth is a revolutionary act." – George Orwell

Remember, dear reader, there are 3 stages of Truth. First comes ridicule, the ignorant minds who joke or mock that which they refuse to understand. Next comes violent opposition, anger, and rage by those who have realized the lies they have believed for so long and are not only angry at themselves but all who have perpetrated those lies. Lastly is the fresh breeze of acceptance, the surrender of the mind of the wise who know that above all, they know nothing. I hope you are on your way to stage 3, dear reader, as the Truth is the ONLY thing that will set you free in this world. Now that I have once again linked the genealogy back to its beginning post-flood, proving a multitude of facts, let's go back to the family members who used the name Aldobrandini and continue their history!

Remember they changed the family name from Aldobrandeschi when the family moved from Germany? Brunetto Aldobrandeschi whose sons used the names Aldobrandeschi as well as Aldobrandini had several sons, including Nero. Nero's son Andrea became a Prior of Liberty in 1324, and in 1331 he joined the family's club

Dodici Buonomini. In 1329 he was made Gonfaliere of Company. He married Bella Davanzati, followed by Nicolosa Ceretani, and became the father of our Aldobrandino Aldobrandini who is attributed as the founder of the Aldobrandini dynasty. His siblings included Caroccio, Brunetto, Constanza, Giovanni, Neri, Jacopo, Lena and Bartolomea who became nuns at San Francesco monastery, Bongia, Bella, Benci, a Cannon of Siena, and Niccolo. Brunetto became a Doctor of Laws in 1339 and in 1347 he became a novice at the San Girolamo monastery. Caroccio held the family position as Prior of Liberty in 1370, followed by Gonfaloniere of Company. He was a member of the Dodici Buonomini and with his wife Angela Peraglia he had 6 children. Aldobrandino, as discussed before, became the Chamberlain of the castle. Aldobrandino worked as an accountant to enforce the Gabelle (tax) in 1357. As a member of the Papal Court, (the Royal Court of Pope Innocent VI, Etienne Aubert) which contained family members and other aristocrats, he served the castle as Camerlengo (chamberlain). He was married to Lisa da Vinci, followed by Selvaggia Ginori, and had several children. This, among other things, is why Leonardo da Vinci is so celebrated by the elite because he was an Aldobrandini and a humanist.

Son Giorgio Aldobrandini, was the first we discussed in this segment, born in 1360 and died in 1411. During this time, a cousin, Giovanni Benci Carrucci Aldobrandini had become Bishop of Gubbio in 1370. His custom-made crosier holds the family's coat of arms and can be seen at the Victoria and Albert Museum. He married Margherita Berlinghieri and had 3 children. In 1363 he was made Ambassador of Florence to the Pope and a member of the Dodici Buonomini. By 1390 he was a Prior of Liberty. In 1400 he became the Coin Officer and soon received the position of Gonfaloniere of Justice of the Republic of Florence. Before he died, he was made Podestà of Pistoia. As you will see, most of these positions were traditionally held by the family. Giorgio soon became the Ambassador of Florence among other things by 1400. Between his wives he had 7 known children.

Daughter Bartolomea was married to Nello de Nelli, Ambassador for the Pope and the Emperor. Bartolomea's son Stefano became the grandfather of the notorious Niccolo Machiavelli, a historian, diplomat, playwright, comedian, and philosopher, raised and educated in the humanist elite philosophy of the time. Political Science of today is derived from his work. His philosophy "The End Justifies the Means", was described in many of his works including The Prince and is still prominent today because it satisfies the elite. Several decades after his death he became known as "Old Nick", a term used to describe the devil which Niccolo had become equated with.

Giorgio's son, Jacopo became Prior of Liberty, Gonfaloniere of Company, member of the same clubs and Commissioner of Montepulciano. Jacopo's son Giorgio became Gonfaloniere in 1410, followed by Podesta of Pistoia and by 1440 he was a prior. Jacopo's second son Cosimo became a member of Docici Buonomini in 1466 and Podesta of Vicchio in 1478. The list of Giorgio's and Jacopo's in this family keeps growing, making it difficult to follow.

Biagio Aldobrandini was sent from his position as head of the company in Paris, to manage the London branch for the Frescobaldi brothers, Pepo and Bettino. The company focused on the trade of jewels and rings which were just beginning to be marketed by the elite families because of their use in sorcery/mysticism. On October 5, 1305, Biagio wrote a letter of exchange (a form of pension) to Humprey de Cloville and in the same year, he wrote a record of surety to Archbishop Piero of Savoy who was the Dean of Salisbury. From 1308-1309 many Italian merchants and bankers who had established international companies, pulled their businesses back to Italy, mostly due to bankruptcy. Because of his detailed reports and notes, the exchange rate between the currencies of the time can be calculated with ease. It seems that it was Biagio's lifestyle that caused him to hand his position to Nicoluccio di Cante in 1308. Aside from charging the company's account for his extravagance, he was accused of raping the wife of Guilicocco, the Cienturiere of London. He returned home to become a Gonfaloniere of Justice while his son Aldobrandino continued the family's trade business.

In the mass of medieval messages saved by historical societies, one can find that in 1404 Alberto Aldobrandini was working in Paris when he was contacted by Andrea de'Bardi to defend the honor of his friend Michele. Another Aldobrandini is documented through his letters sent from his office at the Gallerani, the Frescobaldi Bank. Ambassador Giorgio's son Aldobrandino, born in 1388, became Priori of Liberty in 1417, followed by Gonfaloniere of the Company as well as a member of the Dodici Buonomini. By 1428 he had also been made Commissioner of Montepulciano and 6 years later was given the post of Gonfaloniere of Justice for the Republic of Florence. He married Margherita Orlandini but in 1418 she died, before having any children. So Aldobrandino married again, to Antonia de'Bardi. In 1423 Brunetto was born, and his brothers and sisters soon followed. Like many in their family they were members of the Dodici Buonomini. In 1448 Brunetto was enrolled in the Wool Guild whose members included the Borghese family and began working with the Medici who ran the government of Florence. The family was very close with the Medici's for generations, as one would expect.

Brunetto was made Gonfaloniere of the Company by the age of 30 and was soon made Captain of Livorno in Porto Pisano, followed by Captain of Arezzo. He married Nicolosa Alberti who died in 1450. The following year he married Laudomia Rinuccini and had 7 children before becoming the Vicar of San Miniatro. Meanwhile his brother Salvestro married Nicolosa Nari. Together they had 2 children, Alessandro and Nicolosa. As an Aldobrandini, he was a member of the Dodici Buonomini and made Gonfalonieri of Company, followed by Prior of the Arts. After Nicolosa died,

Salvestro married Monna Alberti and had another son named Pietro. Salvestro was made Podesta of Modigliana which he held until his death. Brother Giorgio was a monk at San Giusto and a member of the Order of the Jesuits while Bernardo became a Franciscan friar of San Marco. Giovanni and Salvestro carried on the family's typical occupations. Giovanni was Podesta of Pisa, Dodici Buonomini, Prior of Art, Captain of Pistoia and more. Salvestro was also a Dodici Buonomini member, Gonfalonieri of Company, Prior of Art, and Podesta of Madigliana. He had 8 children.

During this time Cosimo Medici had brought the Medici family into total power over Florence. While previous generations of the Aldobrandini family had been happy to ally themselves with the Medici, Salvestro's sons were on the opposing team. Salvestro's son Giorgio became the Canon of San Lorenzo and Prior of San Martino and San Romolo. Giambattista was banned from Florence by the Medici family in the late 1520's. Born in 1457, son Alessandro was another Dodici Buonomini member. He married Maddalena Ridolfi and had 5 children, Raffaele, Podesta of Monte San Savino and Modigliana, Alessandra, Salvestro, Girolamo, and Bernardo. Salvestro was a Captain in the militia against the Medici's and was exiled to Tolentino. Girolamo married Bartolomea Pucci and had 6 children including Benedictine monk Cosimo and Bernardo who had 3 children including Aldobrandino, Podesta of Modigliana.

Alessandro's brother Pietro was a professor of law at the University of Pisa in 1489. He was then made Gonfalonieri of Company, Prior of the Arts, Commissioner of Montepulciano, and member of the Dodici Buonomini. Only one of his sons survived until adulthood. His name was Salvestro, also Sylvester II Aldobrandini. He was educated as a financial lawyer and was a humanist like all of his ancestors. Salvestro became the first Chancellor of Reformers in 1427, after serving as Procurator and consistorial and fiscal lawyer. Unfortunately, in 1530 he was exiled for opposing Alessandro Medici who had taken control of Florence. Alessandro demanded praise and ordered that his face be placed on the coins, besides the florin, and took away all weapons owned by the population in his elevation of humanistic tyranny. He was soon assassinated by his cousin Lorenzo and Salvestro Aldobrandini returned home. In 1535 he was rewarded with the post of Podesta of Fano, and soon Judge and Vice Regent of Torrone. He married Lisa Donati (also spelled Luisa Dati), the daughter of Guido Donati and Alamanno Medici. The Donati and Medici family had long been intermarrying. Together they had 8 children. In 1544 Salvestro was made Auditor General for the Duke of Urbino, Guidobaldo II della Rovere. His portrait hangs in the Santa Maria Maggiore in Rome. His son Bernardo became a Conservator of Rome and although Ormanozzo survived to adulthood, he was killed in battle in 1554. Daughter Giulia was married to Aurelio Passeri and had son Cinzio, whom we will discuss later.

Giovanni went to the University of Ferrarra and was a Doctor of Law. He was a Consistorial Coadjutor until 1556 when he became Auditor of the Sacra Rota. Soon he became the Governor and Bishop of Imola. He spent a long career in service to the Papal States and was a Chaplain of His Holiness, meaning he was addressed as "my lord". In 1570 he was given the titles of Santa Eufemia and San Simeone and was made a cardinal priest by Antonio Ghislieri who was Pope Pius V at that time. His final elevation was to Grand Penitentiary in the Roman Curia. This position meant that he was administrator of the Sacrament of Penance: overseeing matters related to the sacrament of reconciliation or confession. This includes handling cases of what the Roman Catholic Church deemed were "more serious sins", since everything of the elite is contained within a hierarchy. These "serious sins" require special permission from the Holy See for absolution.

Giovanni's position also gave him the responsibility of granting indulgences, which one can pay money to obtain. This is an ancient tradition in the elite's pagan religions dating back to the Cult of Semiramis and beyond, wherein someone can pay for forgiveness and escape any punishment attributed to the crime or sin they committed. As Grand Penitentiary he was also the supervisor of the Apostolic Penitentiary, a Roman tribunal within the Roman Curia (Senate) that deals with matters of conscience and grants absolutions and dispensations. Lastly, his position allowed him to be the one to provide moral and canonical advice to the Pope and other members of the Roman Curia on matters related to penance and the forgiveness of sins. When he died in 1573, he was buried in the family's chapel, in Santa Maria sopra Minerva which was dedicated to Giovanni's parents.

Meanwhile brother Tomasso had become the Pontifical Secretary of Latin Letters and Pietro, also a Consistorial Coadjutor and Podesta of Fano, was made Auditor of the Sacra Rota and Conservator of Rome. Elijah Menahem de Nola born about 1570 was an Italian Hebrew teacher who became a rabbi. He instructed Tomasso in Hebrew and was the reason he was baptized in 1568. As you can see, by this time confusion was rampant and already Jews and Catholics were considered the same to the elite who mixed their rituals and doctrines at will. In 1568 he was compelled to become a Catholic and was given the position of writer of the Vatican Library. Under the guidance and urging of the Pope, he authored several works including "Sacro Settenario" which is a compilation of extracts from the Bible, among other things which merged the Catholic paganism with Christianity, as one would expect. His works are commentaries on a variety of Biblical texts including Lamentations and Ruth. Just another elite writing more Talmudic documents. He eagerly dissected gematria in his writings and used this to discredit Jewish texts. With his wife, Flaminia Ferracci, Tomasso had 2 children, Pietro the son and heir and Olimpia who was married off to cousin Gianfrancesco Aldobrandini. Another of Salvestro's sons was Ippolito. It is this son and his nephew Cinzio (son of Salvestro's daughter Giulia) who made the biggest mark in Aldobrandini history at this point. Since this section is heavy with activity, let's discuss some of the family before we get into Ippolito and Cinzio.

Gianfrancesco, son of Jacopo and grandson of Giorgio Aldobrandini and Benedetta Bindi, had married Olimpia Aldobrandini, princess of Rossano Calabro and daughter of Pietro Aldobrandini and Flaminia Ferracci. They had 6 children including daughter Margherita, who married Ranuccio I Farnese, Duke of Parma, and Piacenza. The Farnese family worked with the Aldobrandini's at this time to form the Jesuit Order. Margherita Aldobrandini gave birth to at least 5 Farnese children, several who became part of the d'Este elite family. One of Gianfrancesco's sons, Silvestro Aldobrandini, became a cardinal, and his sister Lucrezia Aldobrandini married Marino II Caracciolo, the 3rd Prince of Avellino. Daughter Elena married Antonio Carafa Gonzaga Colona, Duke of Sabbioneta. Giorgio Aldobrandini, Prince of Rossano and Sarsina married Ippolita Lodovisi. In 1545 Gianfrancesco died from wounds sustained in battle, leaving son and heir Pietro to carry on the name and positions.

Cousin Ippolito Aldobrandini was born in 1592, a member of the 9th generation of Brunetto Aldobrandino/Aldobrandeschi. As the son of a prominent Jurist, he learned the family trade well and was soon climbing the ranks of the Church as Rota and the Datary. In 1585 he was made Cardinal Priest of the Title of St. Pancratius followed by the family position of Grand Penitentiary. He worked to gain the release of imprisoned Archduke Maximilian, among other political conquests and in the conclave of 1592, he was made Pope Clement VIII. Since he was a child, his handler had been Philip Neri. When he became Pope, Neri replaced himself with Baronius. Baronius was reluctantly made a cardinal and Ippolito "confessed" to him daily. He implemented the Forty Hours' Devotion (a written prayer lasting 40 hours). Ippolito's cousin, who is called his brother, became Cardinal Giovanni Aldobrandini. Nephews Pietro, Gian Francesco, and Cinzio Passeri Aldobrandini, were among the family members made into cardinals by their uncle Clement VIII, a common practice of the elite who were placed on the throne.

Pope Clement founded the Collegio Clementino in Rome as well as the Collegio Scozzese and revised many documents. He was a very busy pope. He ended wars by deploying the church's army and replacing a few kings and queens who were disagreeable with him. Some of the people he murdered include around 900 witches (female heretics) who he burned at the stake. Scientist-philosopher Giordano Bruno was also burned at stake in Rome along with philosopher Menocchio, both were accused of being "heretics". 600 people, including young children, were burned at the stake and many more were brutally tortured. Pope Clement Ippilito Aldobrandini issued the Congregatio de Auxiliis as a peace agreement between the Jesuits and Dominicans. Pope Clement expanded the Vatican's Index of Forbidden Books. Some Papal laws he passed included:
- The Cum Saepe Accidere on February 28, 1592 which forbid the long-

established Jewish community of Avignon to sell new goods, which forced them to make less income by only being allowed to have thrift shops.
- The Caeca et Obdurata, passed into law on February 25, 1593, confirmed the bull of Pope Paul III, from the 1540's, which established a ghetto for the community of Jews in Rome.
- Hebraeorum Gens, February 26, 1569, banned Jews from dwelling outside of the ghettos of Rome, Ancona, and Avignon, thus ensuring that they remained city-dwellers.
- Cum Haebraeorum malitia created a ban on Jews altogether. A few days later he forbade the reading of the Talmud, referring to the Jews as caeca, which means 'blind obstinace'.

These laws and methods were used for many centuries before and after Pope Clement, and made popular during World War II, which was just another Catholic Jihad. In 1573 Count Giovanni Aldobrandini of Ravenna, had joined a party of Dutch Protestants and accompanied them in a coup, to give the port of Ancona to the Sultan Selim II "the blond". During this time, the Jesuit order formed the Vereenigde Oostindische Compagnie or VOC, which is the Dutch East India Company. The purpose of which was to establish trade monopolies for the exploitation of goods and materials identified by Jesuits disguised as missionaries throughout Asia. Today we call it the TPP. The funds gained by such trade were used to further the Jesuit order and the Roman Catholic Church. The VOC was the first international corporation with shares. It expanded their international drug cartel by shutting down anything outside the agreement. It created the commercialization of poppy harvesting for opium trade to China and Europe. But I digress.

"All the world suffers from the usury of the Jews, their monopolies and deceit. They have brought many unfortunate people into a state of poverty, especially the farmers, working class people and the very poor. Then as now Jews have to be reminded intermittently anew that they were enjoying rights in any country since they left Palestine and the Arabian desert, and subsequently their ethical and moral doctrines as well as their deeds rightly deserve to be exposed to criticism in whatever country they happen to live." — Pope Clement VIII

During this time one Count, Francesco Cenci, because of his family's station and wealth, had become notorious for his violence. Francesco was born in 1549 to the Apostolic Camera of the Roman Curia, Cristoforo. He was first married to Ersilia Santacroce at the age of 14, after his father died and he had inherited the titles and estates. They had 12 children, only 7 who made it to adulthood, before Ersilia died. Francesco placed his 2 daughters in a monastery until 1592. A year later he married Lucrezia Petroni but had no children with her. The family endured his cruelty for years, but the situation reached a breaking point when rumors circulated about Francesco's rape of his daughter Beatrice. Francesco was especially violent to the females in his family, a trait often learned from the father and passed down through generations. He was arrested numerous times and convicted of sodomy, which was punishable by death.

Daughter Antonia pleaded with Pope Clement to free the family from his viciousness and the pope consented, marrying her off to Carlo Gabrielli. After this, Francesco placed his remaining daughter Beatrice and his wife Lucrezia in their castle at Salto Valley to ensure they would not turn on him. Soon he had become encumbered by legal proceedings and debts he owed that he joined them there. By this time, he was sick with mange and gout, making his violence all the wilder. In 1598, the remaining family members, including Beatrice, decided to murder Francesco, which is often the only remedy for a rabid dog. On September 9, 1598, the family forced him to drink an opium mixture. When he passed out 2 of the family's servants hit him in the head with a hammer, repeatedly, until he died. The servants and family then attempted to make it look like an accidental fall and threw him off the balcony. The family almost got away with it, but after he was buried, rumors grew about murder and Francesco's body was exhumed and autopsied.

Francesco's family members were arrested and tortured. After they confessed, under torture, his wife and daughter were beheaded. Giacomo was quartered with a mallet; his limbs were hung on display. The youngest, 17-year-old son Bernardo was found guilty of not denouncing his family and although he took no part in the murder or conspiracy, he was sent to row in the Papal Galleys for the rest of his life, after he witnessed the execution of his family on September 11, 1599. A few years later, he paid a large sum of money and gained his freedom. Pope Clement gave the properties of the Cenci to the Aldobrandini family.

Now, Cinzio's parents had died leaving him to be adopted by Pope Clement who groomed him to be Second in Command which caused discontentment between Cinzio and Pietro who expected to have that position. While Pietro was the Pope's brother's son, he was too young to become Cardinal before his elder cousin Cinzio, a position reserved for those over the age of 30, by law. However, laws are made by the elite to control and limit you, not them, and by the age of 22 he had been given the position. After graduating from the University of Perugia and Padua with a doctorate in law, Cinzio was made Papal secretary and soon became the secretary of state. Soon he was of age to be made Cardinal and documented as "the most pompous and munificent of the cardinals of his time". He made the ceremonies of the court mandatory, which remained that way until the French Revolution when unnecessary and irrational rituals were done away with (for the most part) in the Papal Court.

As the male heir, Pietro had more status and power by blood than Cinzio, a point which Cinzio complained about frequently to the Pope. Nevertheless, Pietro's authority and natural talent for diplomacy was noted by many historians and visitors of the Papal Court. He was prudent, zealous, and smart and called Pope Peter in England. Pietro's aptitude for the position was recognized and exploited by his uncle who treated him differently from Cinzio, whose lifestyle showed his spoiled nature. Pietro was involved in establishing peace in France, blessing the marriage of King Henry IV to Marie Medici. For this he was made Camerlengo (in charge of the Papal States' revenue and property) by Uncle Pope Clement followed by archbishop of Ravenna. As an Aldobrandini, he patroned many and expanded the Villa Aldobrandini at Frascati which had been owned by the Ruffini family. Pietro hired Carlo Maderno and Giovanni Fontana to design and build magnificent gardens and fountains while Domenichino Zampieri was hired to paint frescoes in the pavilion. One of Domenichino's paintings, called The Hunting of Diana, a Roman goddess, was confiscated by Cardinal Scipione Borghese who imprisoned the artists for several days. Pietro collected many things including art, much of which stands in the Gallery Doria-Pamphili. His entire material possessions were recorded and saved by the Church, which is sure to maintain that which has true value to the elite. Meanwhile, Cinzio's inferior position compared to his cousin is evident in the writings of Torquato Tasso, close friend, and confidant of Cinzio who was taken in by him upon his elevation to Cardinal.

During this time, Pope Clement worked to expand the Church's control over England, sparking The Archpriest Controversy which continued from 1598 to 1603. It was ignited with the appointment of Archpriest George Blackwell to oversee the English mission. For the last 20 years the Popes of Rome had been working on the Counter-Reformation of England through the Jesuit Order. One such instrument for this agenda was Jesuit Robert Persons whose efforts in England involved educational leadership, apologetic writings, and political activities. George was to act as the superior of secular priests and coordinate the Catholic mission in England. However, the Jesuits opposed his appointment which led to a division within the English Catholic community. On one side were the secular clergy led by George, and on the other were the Jesuits and their supporters who rejected his authority. Both sides sent representatives to Rome to present their cases to Pope Clement. The Jesuits naturally argued for the appointment of a Jesuit superior, while the secular clergy defended the legitimacy of George. In 1602, Pope Clement VIII appointed a new superior, Henry Garnet, who was a Jesuit. This created a temporary enraging of the secular clergy who knew full well who and what the Jesuits were.

It was described in reports how the Jesuit General had substitutes called Provincials in various parts of the world, overseeing Jesuits in their respective provinces. The Provincials, in turn, had authority over the Rectors of Jesuit colleges. These colleges housed three types of Jesuits: Statesmen or Politicians, Readers who taught, and Writers who produced scholarly works. As we have seen in the Jesuit chapter, nothing has changed. The report known as Swift's Declaration goes on to detail that the Jesuits aimed to expand their influence in both private and public spheres, attracting talented individuals through education, gaining fame through writing, and seeking to benefit their order. The report notes their efforts to control English Catholics abroad, influencing seminaries and establishing St. Omers. The Jesuits also used their influence to control appointments and placements, particularly in England, through individuals like Jesuits Father Baldwin and Father Parsons. The methods used include appointing a Jesuit-friendly presidents including Dr. Woorthington, and enforcing various orders, including oaths of allegiance to Jesuit authorities in colleges of England.

Nevertheless, the death of Queen Elizabeth I in 1603 marked the end of the Elizabethan era and had significant implications for the Pope. The new monarch, James I, was perceived by some as more tolerant, leading to a somewhat improved situation for the Popes ventures in England. The Jesuits were tolerated, and the Pope maintained control of the wayward region. Earlier, another tool of the Pope, Sir Anthony Standen, had arrived at the English court, working for including Cardinals Aldobrandino, Marcello, and Borghese and faced accusations of openly displaying Catholic sympathies despite representing a Protestant prince and having served Catholic Queen Mary Stuart whose life he saved. He attended Mass and participated in religious functions, leading to his imprisonment and accusations of negotiating with Cardinals for a cardinal's hat. After having papal gifts in his possession, he was taken to the Tower of London 1604. As you can see, when the Eternal City decides to invade, they do so thoroughly with a mass of puppets and spies set to do the work.

Meanwhile Cardinal nephew Cinzio had become a patron of the arts and culture, including publisher Giovanni Raimondo, Professor Francesco Patrizi, and homosexual poet Torquato Tasso. His Villa in Frascati was always kept stocked with rare fruits and flowers. His extravagant dinners were recorded in detail. As Cardinal he was always seated at the head of the table, with guests on either side. He had 3 valets, one who managed his cup, another who helped him wash his hands and wear a bib for eating, and another to serve him food. The same was done for each guest. Needless to say, there was an extraordinary number of servants in the Cardinal's Court, as in the Papal Court and daily life was all about the rituals included to make one feel superior and be seen as superior to others.

"Love is when he gives you a piece of your soul, that you never knew was missing." — Torquato Tasso

Due to his homosexual practices, rumors began to spread about Torquato which caused his mental illness to increase. Members of the court took it upon themselves to mistreat him as well and he was given a pension from the Pope. Only a few days before he was to be crowned by Pope Clement as King of Poets, he died.

Another nephew of Pope Clements was Gian Francesco. He wasn't brought into the Church offices but preferred a life in the military, serving as General of the Papal Army. He died while at war in Hungary. His eldest son Salvestro was educated like the rest of the family in Latin and Greek and at the age of 16 he was made Cardinal by Clement. He served as a Knight of Malta and soon he was made Prior of the Order of St. John of Jerusalem followed by Captain General of the Pontifical Guard and Governor of Borgo. Gian Francesco's other son, Ippolito "the Younger" became cardinal later on, and it is Gian Francesco's granddaughter Olympia who was given the rights to carry the family name and was married to Paolo Borghese forming the Aldobrandini line of the Borghese family. She had been named heir by her cousin Pietro and acquired all of his material possessions including the Emperor Tazze (also called Silver Caesars), which was a collection of 12 large tazze (which look like dessert serving dishes), depicting a series of historical scenes with the Emperor of the time standing in the middle of each. This set was made for Pietro in the 1590's and adorned his dining table. Each was signed with the number 52 and together the silver collection weighed 109 pounds.

Being an ambigram, the "power" mystics give to the number 52 is increased. There are 52 weeks in the solar year, as established by the elite, and 52 white keys on the piano. In the ritual of the elite's rosary of the seven pains of Mary, the Ave Maria is told 52 times. In numerology the 5 can be tuned upside down making the 2, and vice versa. Both can be inverted at will, giving more "power" to the numbers. 5 is typically associated with freedom, adventure, change and linked to challenges and restlessness. 2 is equated with harmony, balance, partnership, and duality. Together they represent dynamic energy, harmony, or cooperation. While this is interesting to those who believe that numbers have power, the number 52 being included on every piece of the collection could simply have been put there to mark its position in the larger collection of the family which is most likely, as numerology is used in events and for agendas, not for pottery. In 2013 one of the Tazze was sold at auction for over $1.4 million. Flaminio Allegrini was commissioned to supply paintings to the Palazzo Aldobrandini in 1625 and sculptor, architect, painter, scenographer Gian Lorenzo Bernini was hired by the Aldobrandini, Barberini, Borghese and other elite families.

Among the constructions that Pope Clement began was the chapel in Santa Maria sopra Minerva, which was finished by Pietro and became the primary burial spot for the family. Cinzio's elaborate tomb which is guarded by a large statue of the angel of death, complete with scythe, is in San Pietro in Vincoli (Saint Peter in Chains), his last church, decorated with the family's coat of arms. Pope Clement VIII, Ippolito Aldobrandini, died in 1638 to everyone's relief. During this time many Aldobrandini offspring had come into their own as Cardinals, Generals, Lawyers and more. The wealth and power of the family in the Papal States had been solidified, while their bloodline had been sacrificed.

Giorgio Aldobrandini and Ippolita Ludovisi had one daughter, Olimpia Aldobrandini in 1623. She was princess of Rossano and married Paolo Borghese, son of Camilla Orsini. They had 5 children, one of whom, Giovanni Battista Borghese, was the 2nd prince of Sulmona after Paolo's father. In 1647, Olimpia remarried Camillo Pamfili, prince of San Martino al Cimino and Valmontone, duke of Carpineto and Montelano, and marquess of Montecalvello. Following Olimpia's line is not difficult as it takes us from the 1st prince, her husband, down to Francesco Paolo Borghese, the 7th prince of Sulmona, who was born in 1776. He married countess Adèle of La Rochefoucauld and they had four children, the 8th prince, Marcantonio Borghese, Scipione Maria Giovanni Battista Borghese, who was duke of Salviati and marquess of Montieri and Boccheggiano, daughter Luisa Anna Maria Borghese-Aldobrandini, and Camillo Aldobrandini, who became the first Prince of Aldobrandini. Born in 1816, he had three children with wife Marie Flore Pauline, princess of Arenberg and two with his second wife, Maria Kethelyi, countess of Hunyady. But let's not get too far ahead of ourselves.

At this time, Olimpia's cousins were all females. Since the men had gone into service of the Church as Cardinals and Popes, only the women were left to carry on the family blood. Uncle Pietro had married Carlotta Savelli but had 2 daughters, both named Anna. Anna Caterina was married to her mother's nephew Prince of Albano, Giulio Peretti while Anna Maria was married to Duke Francesco Cesi, followed by Marquis Francesco Santinelli. Francesco Cesi was a family friend of Galileo and among the extremely wealthy men of the time. At the time he was married to Anna Maria Aldobrandini, he was 43 and she was merely 13. Being only a child, and very beautiful, she was hounded by many men. One such romancer was Count Francesco Maria Santinelli, who wrote her poems. Francesco Santinelli, who was an alchemist and Rosicrucian, who connected to Anna Maria's social circle which included the notorious Spara's gang. Her meetings with Priest Girolamo did not go unnoticed, as the young woman soon sought out a classic Jesuit poison called Aqua Tofana to end the suffering of her husband. Girolamo who gave her a bottle disguised as "Manna of St Nicholas" which was supplied by a renowned poisoner Giovanna de Grandis. The poison did its work and Anna Maria was about to be free. Unfortunately, Giovanna de Grandis saw the body of Duke Francesco in the basilica of Santa Maria supra Minerva and recognized the signs of poisoning. Believing this information may make her own troubles lessen, she exposed Anna Maria, her lover Francesco Santinelli, and the priest Girolamo in the assassination. While the Spara gang were rounded up and jailed, Anna Maria was never charged, and her name was forbidden from being used in court by order of Pope Alexander VII, Fabio Chigi.

Aunt Caterina Lesa was married to Prince Marino II Caracciolo, Aunt Elena was married to Duke Anontio Carafa and had 3 children. As discussed, Aunt Margherita married into the Farnese family, merging the two elite bloodlines and Aunt Maria became the wife of Marquis Giovanni Paolo II Sforza, another elite family. The blood of the Aldobrandeschi's had died out, after merging with the Sforza's, by 1438 and by the 1620's the Aldobrandini's followed suit. Interesting how certain bloodlines are weeded out, leaving only the females who pass on the blood, unnoticed.

Thanks to Olimpia, the Aldobrandini wealth, collections of art and sculptures, properties and businesses were absorbed into the Borghese family, whose symbol is the eagle. The Borghese family's ancestor Tiezzo da Monticiano was the first family member to settle in Siena, Italy, around the same time as the Aldobrandeschi's. A wealthy wool merchant, he bought the town of Monticiano and expanded his business into silk. Tiezzo had 2 sons, Bencivenne and Benincasa. Benincasa became the ancestor of the famous mystic Caterina Benincasa, Saint Catherine of Siena. Tiezzo's nephew was named Borghese and founded the dynasty of the Borghese of Siena, Florence, and the Borghese of Rome. Several generations brought politician and philosopher Niccolo Borghese, father of Pietro and Aurelia. Aurelia was married to Pandolfo Petrucci while son and heir Pietro became a Senator of Rome, appointed by Pope Leo X, Giovanni di Lorenzo de' Medici. Pietro was killed during the Sack of Rome.

In 1552 the first Borghese pope was born, Camillo Borghese. Camillo was the son of Count Marcantonio who was Ambassador of Siena to the Holy See and eventually a legal official of the papal government. A strong supporter of Galileo Galilei, Camillo who was now Pope Paul V, assured him that while he couldn't teach the theory of Copernicus, he would be safe from any persecution. Unfortunately, Camillo died in 1621 and Galileo was taken to trial and placed under house arrest for the rest of his life. Camillo finished the construction of the St. Peter's Basilica among other things and published a decree, regarding the immaculate conception, in Peru. He canonized several people, meaning they were acknowledged by the Pope as being worthy of public worship and idolization, including mystic Francesca Bussa. Among his elaborate constructions was the Pauline Chapel in the Basilica of Santa Maria Maggiore which became the family's crypt. As pope he gave land grants and positions and titles to his family members, increasing the Borghese wealth and status. In 1605 he founded the Bank of the Holy Spirit, the first national bank of Europe. In 1615 the Japanese samurai Hasekura Tsunenaga was welcomed by him in Rome. Hasekura sent the Pope a letter requesting that he send Catholic missionaries to Japan, which were immediately dispatched. Upon becoming Pope, Camillo made his brother Duke Francesco the General of the Papal Army.

> "The Rosary is the compendium of the entire Gospel." — Pope Paul V

Camillo's other brother Giovanni Battista became Prince of Vivaro, Governor of Borgo and Castellano and Conservator of Rome. His son Marcantonio II became the 1st Prince of Sulmona and married Camilla Orsini. He became the heir to both the Borghese and Orsini fortunes. Their son Paolo became the husband of Olimpia Aldobrandini, joining the Aldobrandini blood into the elite mix. Soon thereafter the Farnese and Chigi elite bloodlines were married into the family as well. To his nephew, Scipione, Camillo gave a cardinalship and the title of Prince of Vivero. During his reign the Borghese became one of the largest land-owning families in the kingdom.

Grandson of Olimpia and Paolo, Marcantonio III, became the 3rd Prince of Sulmona. As a young heir he made an impression on Pope Innocent XII, Antonio Spinazzola, by building an elaborate wooden palace on his estate, wherein to welcome the Pope and his guests as they travelled to Anzio. When he was 31 years old, he married Livia Spinola and soon had children. In 1721 Emperor Charles VI made Marcantonio the Viceroy of Naples. Son Camillo was the heir to his estates and titles and married Agnese Colonna. Together they had 10 children. Other grandchildren of Olimpia Aldobrandini included Cardinals Camillo Cybo Malaspina, Giorgio Doria Pamphili, and Francesco Borghese.

The great grandson of Marcantonio III, Camillo, was born in 1775 and married to Duchess Paulina Bonaparte. She was sister to Emperor Napoleone and along with being duchess, was Princess of France, Princess consort of Sulmona and Rossano and had only one child in her first marriage, to Charles Leclerc. Because of his marriage, due to the Borghese loyalty to France, Camillo was made Prince of France in 1804. Soon he became a commander in the Imperial Guard and Duke of Gaustalla. While he had once been in love with his wife, her unfaithfulness soon deprived him of romance. Paulina soon exhibited the traditional aristocratic eccentricities and madness. It is recorded that she would insist on being carried to her bath by large African slaves, and that she had many lovers. The couple decided to live separate lives and Camillo was made Governor of Piedmont. Napoleon also gave him charge over prisoner Pope Pius VII, Barnaba Niccolo Chiaramonti however, he was forced to sell hundreds of items from the Borghese family's estate. His brother Francesco inherited his wealth and estates, as Camillo had no children.

> "I am living in the Villa Borghese. There is not a crumb of dirt anywhere, nor a chair misplaced. We are all alone here and we are dead." — Henry Miller

Francesco Borghese, born in Rome in 1776, became the 7th Prince of Sulmona. During the French Revolution he supported Napoleon, like the rest of the family. In 1809, he married Duchess Adele de La Rochefoucauld and had 5 children. He distinguished himself in the French army, participating in the Battle of Austerlitz and earning promotions including the Grand Cross of the Ordre de la Reunion. When Napoleon's reign came to an end, Francesco, like the other Borghese, returned to Italy and to his estates and possessions there, without a hitch, receiving honors in both France and Italy. In 1832, after Camillo's death, Francesco inheriting vast fortunes and titles. He soon expanded the Gabii museum and supported other charitable works before his death in 1839. Naturally, his sons were granted titles, ensuring the continuation of parallel family lines through 3 of his sons: Marcantonio as Prince Borghese, Camillo as Prince Aldobrandini, and Scipione as Duke Salviati. Daughter Marie was married to Cousin Henri de Rochefoucauld and Marcantonio was married to Therese de Rochefoucauld.

Son Camillo Francesco Giovanni Battista Melchiorre Aldobrandini Borghese became the 1st Prince of Meldola and married Maria Hunyady, followed by sisters Princess Marie and Princess Louise d'Arenberg. He preferred a life in the military and served Pope Pius IX, Giovanni Matai Ferretti, in the First Italian War of Independence as Captain of the Papal Troops. Soon he was made Minister of Arms and organized a papal expeditionary corp. In 1848 he became a member of the High Council of State and declared his favor of continued war in the name of Unity.

Meanwhile his brother Marcantonio had become Prince of Nettuno, Vivaro, Rossano, Monte Compatri, Santangelo, and San Paolo, Duke of Palombara, Canemorto, Castelchiodato, and Bomarzo. He was Marquis of Noma, Mentana, Civitella Vicovaro, Patica and many more. He was the largest landowner in Latium and became an eminent public figure. He was president of the Cassa di Risparmio (a bank) and member of the Council of Rome. Soon he was elected to be the deputy of the first college of Rome and Ronciglione. Due to his interests in archeology, he was made President of the Pontifical Roman Academy of Archaeology. While Pope Pius IX was in exile, Marcantonio joined him, returning with him in 1850. At this time, he became president of the Chamber of Commerce and Roman Railways and retained his previous positions. In 1886 Prince Marcantonio died, leaving his remaining children, many which died during a plague in Rome, to maintain the wealth.

Marcantonio's son Paolo became the 9th Prince of Sulmona and married Countess Helena Appony and had several children including Scipione, 10th Prince who married Anna Maria, daughter of the Marquis of Ferrari. Scipione won the Peking to Paris race in 1907, though rumors claim that his chauffeur did most of the driving. He was an explorer, diplomat, racer, and mountain climber and journeyed from Beirut to the Pacific Ocean. He also traversed China, chronicling his adventures in books. As deputy of the Italian Parliament, after fighting in World War I, he implemented several projects in the Agro Romano (land surrounding Rome). He like his family supported the rise of fascism in Italy. His nephew, Prince Junio Valerio "the Black Prince" founded the Fronte Nazionale. During World War II, Junio played a pivotal role in commanding the Decima Flottiglia MAS, a special forces unit. The unit gained notoriety for employing manned torpedoes, known as "Maiali," in attacks against enemy ships in the Mediterranean. Following Italy's surrender in 1943, Junio eventually collaborated with the Germans and aligned himself with the Italian Social Republic led by Benito Mussolini. His relationship with Benito caused him to be accused of war crimes, after the dictatorship had dissolved. He was sentenced to 12 years in prison, which was later reduced, and he was released in 1949.

Upon gaining his freedom, Junio returned to public life and became involved once again in neofascist politics in Italy, founding the Partito Nazionale Monarchico (National Monarchic Party) and advocating for a return to monarchy. In 1970, a bored Junio orchestrated the infamous "Borghese Coup", a plan to overthrow the Italian government and reinstate a fascist regime. The coup failed, prompting him to flee to Spain to evade arrest, a typical move for a coward. Like the rest of the males in his family, he inherited memberships to the traditional chivalric orders.

Rodolfo, another son of Paolo's, became the 4th Prince of Neptune (Nettuno) and married Giulia, daughter of Count Giuseppe Frascara and Clarice Orsini. His children inherited the titles to Nettuno as well. He was also a member of the National Fascist Party and served as Deputy of the Kingdom of Italy, National Councilor of the Kingdom of Italy, and Senator of the Kingdom of Italy. He inherited the family's memberships and became an officer of the Order of St. Maurice and Lazarus, Knight and Officer of the Order of the Crown of Italy, Commander of the Order of the Crown of Italy, Frand Officer and Grand Cordon of the Order of the Crown of Italy, Knight of the Military Order of Savoy, and Commander of the Royal Order of St. Stephen of Hungary. He held the Cross of Merit of the German Order of the Eagle and the Littorio Scarf.

Rodolfo's sister Agnese became the mother of Prince Ugo Boncompagni-Ludovisi, Duke of Sora and Vice-Camerlengo of the Holy Roman Church. Brother Giolio Torlonia Borghese and his offspring were the Princes of Fucino while sister Ludovica produced the Princes of Scaletta. Brother Giuseppe had one son, Gian Giacomo Borghese. He became the Governor of Rome in 1939 and was a member of the National Fascist Party, Knight of the Order of Saints Maurice and Lazarus, Commander of the Order of the Crown of Italy, Commander of the Order of St. Sylvester Pope and Knight Grand Cross of the Order of St. Gregory the Great. Gian Giacomo was Prince of Leonforte and during World War I, he served as a lieutenant and captain in the Corps of Engineers. In 1922, he married Sofia Lanza Branciforte of the Princes of Trabia, a relative of famous musicologist Gioacchino Lanza Tomasi. He served as a councilor of the Opera Nazionale Combattants and worked on land reclamation consortia in Sicily. Between 1933 and 1936, he served as the prefect of Rieti, and soon became President of the Province of Rome before becoming Governor.

Great grandson of Marcantonio, Giuseppe Camillo Francesco Pietro Aldobrandini married the Duchess of Brindisi, Maria, and had 2 children. Clemente Aldobrandini inherited the title of Prince of Meldola and Duke of Carpineto and Sarsina, while Ferdinando became Duke of Brandisi. Clemente is the grandfather of Princess Olimpia Anna Liliana Aldobrandini, wife of Baron David Rothschild. This leads us into the next chapter, where I will discuss the infamous Rothschild family. Let's go!

~Rothschild~

The Rothschild line is so popular, even today, that I'm sure you know about them to some extent. Let's begin in 1528, the beginning of the mainstream narrative. Isak "zum Hahn" Bacharach (Isak Bauer, Isaac Elchanan Rothschild), lived in Frankfurt Am Main, Hessen-Nassau, Preussen and was married to Ester Katz. Together they had many children including Elchanan Isaac Bacharach Rotten Shield, Fogel Roten Schild, Naftali Hirsch Mosche Isak (Moses Isaac) Rothschild, and Raphael Rothschild. They used multiple variations of the family's many names and continued to live in Germany. Isak built the house named Rotes Schild around 1563 and the family identified themselves by this, like many other families in the Judengasse who took the description of their house as their name. Before we get into the next generation, let's keep looking back. So Isak's father who was born in the late 1400's, was Haune Elchanan (Eikan) Uri Bacharach and used the name Hirsch as well as Hahn (Han, Hon, Hane), a German line which the family are descended from. He married Fogele zur Roten Rose the daughter of the Rabbi of Worms, and began using the name Elchanan ben Uri, since his father was Uri Feibesch (Ouri, Fajsch) zu Bacharach, born 1430's, who lived in Burgau, Germany. Elchanan is noted as "A Jew from Worms with a Yellow Mark" who moved to the Judendasse of Frankfurt in 1530, which had been started by King Henry IV in 1074 who allowed Jews to live in the City of Franks, with certain privileges. Elchanan lived in the house called Roten Rose, to which he built a new house, adjoined to the old, called the House of Hahn and is from the Hahn family of Friedberg. Elchanan's brothers, Aser and Schmuel used the name Bacharach. Their offspring included several Rabbis of Germany. Meanwhile Elchanan became the father of many children including Isak, Moses, Uri-Feibesch, Abraham and David who used the names Bacharach zum Waage, Bauer, and others.

Throughout this family the males took on a random last name, every couple of generations. As one of the many Ashkenazim Rabbinic Dynasties of Frankfurt, the Bacharach's remained in the area of the Black Sea, Khazaria (Scythia). Uri, born in the 1430's, is the son of Lord Yoseph, (Feibesch, Bajfes, Beyfus) husband of Bella D'Ouri. Going back further still, we come to one of many mergings of the Bacharach and Oppenheim families through cousin and grandson of Shimon Bacharach-Oppenheim, Gottschalk Bacharach in 1391. He was a wealthy merchant who lived in Worms, Sobernheim and other places until 1398. As genetic studies have verified, the Bacharach's are among the many families who claim the bloodline of Levi, where no genetic markers of this lineage exist. The Germanic region the family comes from, was developed by the many tribes of the Huns which formed the Ashkenazi Jews. But let's keep going.

The line back through the Hahn family which they descend, through Isaac Hahn, were generational Barons and Knights of the Church. A branch of this family is Rotenhan, also Knights, Barons and Counts who had settled in Lower Franconia. So, having married into Ashkenazi Jewish bloodlines, it makes sense why the family would alter their name so drastically. They were likely disowned by the wealthy Hahn. The Uri branch of the family took the name Bacharach from the town in Germany of the same name, where they lived prior to migrating to Frankfurt several generations later. Bacharach means Altar of Bacchus and the town is still known for its wine making. The town existed long before the Romans moved into the region, as it lay on the Rhine, making it a key point of trade. First documented in 923, the Counts of Rome moved in by the early 1200's.

Following Isaac Hahn's lineage back through the Hahn family we come to the founder of the Hahn Dynasty in 1230, Eckard I (Eggardus) in Mecklenburg, Germany. He had many children with his wife Salburg von Ketelhodt. He was a Knight and Councilor to his cousin or uncle, Prince Johann of Mecklenburg who was married to Luitgart von Henneberg. The family motto was "Primus sum, qui deum Laudat", which means I was the first to praise God. The family holds estates in Holstein, Latvia, Hesse, and Mecklenburg where they originated. The family crest is a red rooster on a white background, as the name Hahn means rooster. The same is shared by the branch of the family who goes by the name Rothenhahn. The Hahn family held the positions of Counselors and Advisors to multiple Kings and Princes including the Kings of Denmark who were married into the family. The family leads through Eckard's father who is listed as a Nobleman of Wends. Wends was the term used for the Slavs who lived in Germany at that time, which was Veneti, Venethi to the Romans. The Wends include what are now known as Slovaks, Czechs, and Poles. In that region, for some time until the 700's, there were many tribes, all of whom paid tribute to the Huns who frequented the region, taking their women as wives. The tribes had been involved in the Gothic Wars of 536 and further back Ptolemy documented them in the 100s as Slovenes and even before this the term Wends was used. They were long described as being farmers for trade, sowing corn, barley, rye and more to sell, and were allies of the Kings of Denmark and the Carolingians. As the cousins of the Hahn were the Kings and Princes of the tribe, the Hahn family were of the House of Mecklenburg and held positions of Counselors and Knights, Dukes, and Lords, which at this time were only given to family members.

This line leads to Niklot who was born in 1090. He was a chief and prince of the Obotrite confederacy, and member of the House of Mecklenburg. Niklot was also Lord of Schwerin, Quetzin, and Malchow. For nearly three decades, Niklot resisted the influence of Saxon princes, most notably Henry the Lion, during the Wendish Crusade. His resistance began when German King (later Emperor) Lothar III granted the Obotrite realm to his Danish vassal Canute Lavard. Teaming up with Pribislav of

Wagria, Niklot opposed Lothar and Canute. After Canute's murder in 1131, Niklot and Pribislav divided the Obotrite territory. To weaken Pribislav, Niklot formed alliances with Saxon lords, particularly Count Adolf II of Holstein, enabling Slavic pirates to target the Danes. During the Wendish Crusade of 1147, Niklot's Saxon allies turned against him, forcing him to eventually pay tribute to the crusaders and negotiate peace with Adolf of Holstein, Duke Henry the Lion of Saxony, and Henry of Ratzeburg.

By 1158, tensions escalated as King Valdemar the Great of Denmark sought assistance in converting the Obotrites to Catholicism from Henry the Lion. In 1160, the Danish king and the Saxon duke formed an alliance, resulting in Niklot's demise. While the Danes distracted the Rani with coastal harassment, the Saxons killed Niklot at his stronghold of Burg Werle. The Christian partitioning of the Obotrite territory marked the end of Slavic control and brother Ludemar was made a governor of Werle while son Pribislav was left to reclaim his inheritance as Prince of Mecklenburg in 1167. Unfortunately, the time of tribal leaders was over, and he was forced to be a Saxon vassal while his brother Wertislaw became the grandfather of Nicholas I, Lord of Mecklenburg, leading us back to the House of Mecklenburg and the Hahn Dynasty.

Niklot's cousin Henry was King from 1093 to 1127 when the kingdom flourished, stretching from the Elbe to the Oder and from the Havelland to the Baltic Sea. The second son of Saint Gottschalk, who was killed in a pagan uprising in 1066, Henry was raised in Denmark and Lüneburg alongside his half-brother Budivoj while the kingdom was taken over by the pagan Kruto. It was Kruto who had killed his father and also killed Budivoj in 1075, leaving Henry as the only heir. In 1090, Henry, with Danish support, invaded Kruto's territory forcing him to cede a portion of the kingdom a few years later. Successfully eliminating Kruto with the help of Kruto's wife Slavina, Henry married her and emerged the victor and new king in the Battle of Schmilau. Henry maintained positive relations with Danish and Saxon neighbors, inviting foreign merchants, promoting agriculture, and expanding the trade business. His reign was not necessarily a peaceful one, as various tribes surrounding the Obotrites, including the Rani, Kissini, Circipani, Liutizi, and Western Pomeranians were constantly attempting to gain more territory. He defended against seaborne assaults, led expeditions, and suppressed revolts. In 1126, Vicelin sought permission to preach Christianity among the Slavs, receiving support from Henry, who allowed freedom of pagan practices until his death the following year. His surviving sons were young and unable to keep the divided inheritance and Niklot stepped in.

Henry's father, Saint Gottschalk, son of Udo had attempted to establish a Catholic confederation to unite the various Slavic clans of the region into one kingdom he formed on the Elbe River. The Church had set its eye on that region which had eluded their control for so long, and it was only a matter of time. Each generation for a hundred years had been whittled down by the Church until Udo weakened, allowing them to gain a foothold which continued through his son. After Saxons killed Udo of the Obotrites in 1028, Gottschalk was sent to be raised in the court of Canute the Great of Denmark. His uncle Ratibor led the Obotrite confederacy during Gottschalk's absence. Sven Estridson, Jarl of Denmark, made an alliance with the Obotrites, through Gottschalk. Sven wanted independence from King Magnus I of Norway and with his new allies, he went to war in 1042. Magnus was supported by his brother-in-law, Duke Bernard II of Saxony, and during battle, the following year, Ratibor was killed followed by his sons. Upon returning to his kingdom, Gottschalk founded monasteries in Oldenburg, Mecklenburg, and elsewhere and was naturally befriended by Archbishop Adalbert who had been sent by the Church to handle the situation. Unfortunately, his push on the nobles to become Catholics went unheard and most of the region remained in their traditional worship of nature and self. Gottschalk renounced Catholicism, in order to make war on those who killed his father, only to reconvert before his death in 1066.

Ratibor's sister Princess Tove (Tofa) of Wendland was married to King Harald "Bluetooth" Gormsson of Denmark. King Harald reconstructed the Jelling runic stones and other projects such as fortifying the fortress of Aros (Aarhus) in 979. He became known for his strategic construction of circular ring forts in five key locations which helped to consolidate economic and military control over his kingdom. Norse sagas portray Harald in a negative light, detailing instances where he submitted to the Swedish prince Styrbjörn the Strong. He faced challenges from Otto II, losing control of Norway after the Battle of Danevirke in 974. In 985 or 986 he was killed during a rebellion led by his son Sweyn.

A few generations back, Prince Aribert I, son of Visan, the 1st King of the Obotrites, and a daughter of the King of the Lombards. He was born in the late 600's and married a Sarmatian Princess. Grandfather King Wislaw (Wisislaus) of the Obotrites was born in Sweden. He was the son of Radegast II and Euphemia Brannsson of Norway. Radegast (Radigast) was the 23rd King of the Herulii and the Wenden and leads through a well-documented dynasty of Kings of Germanic tribes of the Wended and the Heruli, who were skilled warriors, often serving as mercenaries in various military campaigns. They, like many tribes of the region, had an on again/off again relationship with the Roman Empire. They participated in battles against the Huns and later turned against the Romans. The line of Kings of Heruli and Wenden contains many Alaric's. Alaric (Alaricus) I and II were the 20th and 21st Kings. Alaric II was married to Theodora, the daughter of King Chilperic II of Burgundy. Remember this was the bloodline of the Aldobrandini's. Chilperic was one of the sons of Gondioc. His brothers were Gundobad, Godomar and Godegisel. Chilperic was assassinated by his brother Gundobad who drowned his wife and exiled his daughters.

Great grandfather was Gaiserich (Godigisel), King of the Vandals. His elder brother Corsicus was the King of the Heruli. Married to Licinia Eudoxia, the daughter of Emperor Theodosius II of the Roman Empire, Gaiserich's rule was short lived as he was killed in a battle in 406. The kingdom was left to his sons who led the Vandals to victory against Gaul. During this time the tribes attempted to distance themselves from the Huns who were constantly attacking. Coming further back to the 16th King of the Heruli, Fredebaldus' kingdom was part of the Hun Confederation under High King Attila. When Atilla died the Heruli reverted to their own rule. After establishing themselves, and turning all surrounding tribes into vassals, the tribe assisted Orestes along with the Goths and Rugii in deposing Emperor Julius Nepos.

The infamous Radagaisus "the Vandal", a Horde military leader and King of the Heruli, reigned during the time of Emperor Honorius. Drawing from Germanic tribes including the Suevians, Burgundians, Vandals, and Celtic tribes, his army grew to an estimated 200,000 to 400,000 men. Sometimes referred to as a Scythian and occasionally as a King of the Goths, Radagaisus launched an invasion into Italy, laying siege to cities and notably besieging Florence. Coins buried in western Pannonia show how residents, knowing of the army's invasion, hid their material possessions but were unable to return for them. Unfortunately for him, he met his match when Stilicho turned against him. Radagaisus was surrounded by the army of Stilicho and starved into submission. Under the condition that the lives of his men would be spared, Radagaisus surrendered. Naturally this agreement was betrayed, and Stilicho executed him and enslaved his army.

Further back Alberic, King of the Herulii was born in 225, the son of King Teneric (Asdingi) and great grandson of another Alaric, the 8th King of the Heruli who was married to Bella of Cologne in Swabia, Germany. He, like the members of the next several generations, was buried in Italy. His mother was a princess of Norway, as the family continued to marry into the aristocracy of Scandinavia. His grandmother and great grandmother were both from Jutland, Denmark. The Heruli at this time were labelled as pirates by the Romans. They inhabited the Meotic swamps and frequented the shores of Greece and Asia Minor. A hundred years later, the tribe became a vassal of the Ostrogoths.

At the turn of BC to AD times Hutterus Visilaus I was born to King Anthyrius and Marina (of Jutland). He married Judith of Jutland and became King of the Heruli. During his father's lifetime, Octavian, who became Augustus, defeated Mark Antony and Cleopatra. King Anthyrius was named after his ancestors, particularly Anthyrius Curllus who became the 1st King of Heruli around 150 BC. It's at this time the land was called Eorle as H wasn't used in that part of the world yet. Also referred to as Erils, Erul, Aeruli, Ailouroi and more, the term means "Belonging to Marauders". Runes depict that they called themselves Erils. The main location of the Erils (meaning wild warriors) at this time was Odense, Gottland (Sweden), Auland, and Zealand (Denmark) and included in the culmination of tribes labeled as Cimbri. Soon hereafter historians note that they were either kicked out of the land or had simply migrated to the Baltic Sea region. Either way, the group began raiding the Black Sea region they inhabited, as well as Greece and Rome.

"Archaeologists in Denmark in 2012 reveal the bones of an entire army whose warriors have been thrown into the bogs near the Alken Enge wetlands in East Jutland after losing a major engagement. The river valley of Illerup Ådal is a well-known archaeological location which has produced several important finds, especially in the large wetland area where the River Illerup runs into Lake Mossø. Many of the bones bear the marks of cutting and scraping, and many skulls are crushed. After the bodies of the defeated warriors have lain on the battlefield for about six months. The remains of the fallen are gathered together and all of the flesh is cleaned from the bones, which are then sorted and desecrated before being cast into the lake. The warriors' bones are mixed with the remains of slaughtered animals and clay pots that probably contained food sacrifices." — The History Files

The tribe was known as stealers of temple gold and pig worshippers, having many pig statues and intricate golden religious jewelry, too heavy and extravagant to wear daily. Today the main meat in Denmark is still pig. They are documented as having fought naked, only covering their genitals. In several previous chapters I have detailed the lineage of the founders and aristocratic classes of this region as they came from Troy, forming the kingdom of Denmark under the rule of 1st King Dan, who was called Old Dan and Wodan, soon to be deified as the god Odin, as well as Brutus who founded Briton. I have previously detailed the genealogy of the Kings of Saxony, Scandinavia and elsewhere through Old Dan through Joktan, son of King Eber, through King Arphashad leading to Noah in the first few chapters of this book, as well as in the Aldobrandini lineage who are and have been intertwined with the Rothschilds. So, let's move on!

A century before Isak Hahn, our first noted Rothschild, arrived on the scene, the Ashkenazi religion created by descendent of Attila, King Joseph, had grown and strengthened, causing many problems throughout Europe as evidenced in the numerous inquisitions. Russia had established itself under Vladimir III, in the 1430's, who did all he could to take over the pagan Yiddish regions of Khazaria. Several hundred years after Vlad, the final Khagan King, Tzul took his 25 wives and 60 concubines and moved to Spain, uniting with the Talmudic Jews his family had befriended, with the Hunnic Ashkenazi's. This is how the maternal lineage of the Rothschilds (which they detail, hiding their paternal line) ended up in Spain. During this time, the Roman Empire, which had split in two prior to this time, had now become controlled by the Roman Catholic Church. The Roman Church implemented the Inquisitions (followed by the Crusades) to expand the empire beyond its former glory, conquering kingdoms through conversion, controlling who would be crowned ruler and more. The Inquisitions, as discussed before, were created by the Roman Catholic Church to "eliminate all heretics".

Since Heretic is such a vague term, like most they use, this allowed for anyone to be persecuted. The Khazars, and other Talmudic Jews, did not integrate and were racist and totalitarian minded. The Jews, sadly as a whole, had been exiled and run out of countries time and time again, because of extremist Talmudists and because of mysterious murders and missing children which occurred in areas surrounding Jewish neighborhoods. Rumors were spun and whether true or not, the elite, playing both sides, were able to keep the Jews on the move and the Yellow Badge was implemented through the next 400 years in this region, first by the Caliphate, then by the Spanish, German, Roman, and more. Remember the Yellow Badge which was the Yellow 6-pointed Star of Babylon used to identify the Ashkenazi's, the star the Rothschild family took as their own symbol.

By 1252, Pope Innocent IV issued a global governing bull which authorized the use of torture to extract confessions from heretics. Inquisitors were given absolution, just as they are today. By 1284, the Roman elite, becoming greedier, issued another bull (universal law) through Pope Lucius III, the chief aim of which was complete elimination of Christian heresy. By the 1400's, the only countries left without the Secret Police (Inquisitors) of the Roman Church were England and Castile. In the 1470's, Ferdinand and Isabella of Spain needed to strengthen their relationships with Rome. The Ashkenazi Jews had become a problem to Spain, just the way they had become a problem for other cultures, so they were removed. By evicting and persecuting Jews and Muslims, they were able to secure their allegiances. Because the Muslims maintained their stronghold in the Straits of Gibraltar, Spain was invaded repeatedly. Ferdinand II pressured Pope Sixtus IV to bring in the inquisition to assist and in 1478, the Pope's latest bull allowed monarchs power to create their own Inquisitions and appoint their own Inquisitors.

This brings us up to date on what was taking place at the time when the Hahn family member married a daughter of a Rabbi and moved into the Judengasse of Frankfurt. Since then, the Rothschild family has not only used the maternal names but have detailed their genealogy through that of Esther Rothschild of the HaCohen Katz family to maintain the illusion that they are Hebrew descendants and not Luciferian Talmudists. As you already know, there are many big differences between Talmud Ashkenazi Jews who invaded Spain in the 1200's and Torah Jews who inhabited Spain long before. One was that the Ashkenaz would eat a kind of fat called "five fingers" which was forbidden to the Sephardim. Rabbi Baruch Angel, who died in 1660, detailed that, in addition to this, in matters of returning the dowry, the Ashkenazi community would return the entire dowry to the wife's family, if she died with no sons within the first year of her marriage, in contrast to the Sephardic custom to divide it evenly between the husband's and the wife's family, even if she died after the first year of her marriage. Another difference between Shemite Jews and Ashkenazi Jews is that Ashkenazi name their children after the dead, Shemite Jews name their children after the living. He continues to state that regrettably, by this time, the Sephardim had already accepted the corrupted customs and would also eat the inflated meat.

"And thus to the matter of Passover," wrote Rashda'm, "the Ashkenazim are accustomed to several strictures that the Sephardim do not follow... and the hold tight to strange customs... on the seventh day of Passover they would read the Song of Songs and say the blessing over the scroll."

Esther Rothschild descended from HaCohen Katz, born in Spain. He became the head of the rabbinic court, in Galata and Pera, of Constantinople, the capital of the Byzantine (Roman) Empire, before it was taken over by the Ottoman sultan in the 1450's. The rabbinic court, Sanhedrin, had been in place for centuries, ever since the Romans took rulership over the Jews. This was the way the Romans were able to keep peace, by keeping the Jewish communities segregated, judged by their own leaders who were under control of the Roman's enforcers. For example, in the 500's, when Emperor Justinian passed the law that Jews could no longer own Christians as slaves, it was the rabbinic court who enforced it, handing out fines of 30 pounds of gold for the violation. During this time there grew a number of Jews who believed in the unaltered word of the Torah. This contradicted the elite's Ashkenazi-controlled Rabbinical Jews who believed in the Talmud, passed down by the Babylonian priests. If any of you are wondering who a "real" Jew is, know this: You are a Jew, by your genealogy which leads straight back to Noah like the rest of the world.

What used to identify those from the tribe of the bloodline of Judah has become a status anyone can claim today. If you come from the bloodline of the tribe of Judah, then you are a Jew (Juden) by genealogy. If you can trace yourself back to the sons of Noah and you are of the bloodline of his son Shem, then you are a Shemite: Semite. But considering the fact that Shem is the son of Noah as is Ham and Japheth, the fact is still unavoidable that we are all brothers. There is only one race. When Jesus rose from the dead, as is historically documented fact, this act dissolved ALL bloodline power which had before then been valid. Since then, there is no such thing as a Jew, no such thing as a Hamite, and no power in any bloodline on earth since that time. None of it has any meaning any longer and hasn't for thousands of years. Blood only holds the illusion of power in the minds of the racist elite, nothing more. Maintaining the ancient bloodline power, the elite are simply denying Jesus once again.

Following the line back from Chaim, we come to Rabbi Yitzak HaCohen Katz II whose father was a Talmudic rabbi, like his father before him. Like the Du Pont and many other families, their roots are from Slavic region, and before that from Rome/Egypt. Yitzak became a rabbi and a Kabbalist. He inherited his father's position as Rabbi of Stephen, before accepting posts as rabbi in Ostrow, Posen, and Frankfurt on the Main. After a severe fire destroyed the entire Jewish quarter of Frankfurt, Yitzak was imprisoned. He had not put the fire out, because he was "testing his amulets". Luciferians are the ones who believe in alchemy and witchcraft. Testing stones while people burned to death. After losing his popularity, he went to live with his friend David Oppenheim and wrote a few books on Kabbalah and out of his Occult/Mystic doctrine was born Hasidism. Both doctrines run in the family to this day. While unable to return home, he journeyed to Erez Israel, a state in Palestine. Before he made it there, he died in Constantinople.

Father Naftali Hirsch Katz was born in Prague around 1588 and became Av Beit Din (head of the rabbinical court) in Prussia, Lublin, and Ba'al Peirot Genosar and Kahal Kadosh (leader of the Holy Congregation) of Lublin and Pinsk. Like his father before him, he was married multiple times and had many children. His father Yitzak wrote many acrostic introductions to his own and other works such as a supplement to "Hatan Damim," a commentary on the Pentateuch, the Kabbalist "Pa'neah Raza" by Isaac ben Judah ha-Levi, a commentary on the Pentateuch, in German, notes on Midrash Tehillim, and another commentary called "Kizzur Mizrahi". Talmudic leaders have always written commentaries on the Torah, which then are used as doctrine and used instead of the Torah itself. Continuing back, we come to Rabbi Akiva Hakohen Katz who was born in Spain and in the mid 1300's moved to Greece where he was called the Elder of Salonika (Greece). He used the name Katz, a German derivation of the title Kagan, Kohen Tzedek, an Ashkenazi not Hebrew term. Khagan came from the title Khan, from Qaghan... Akiva immigrated to Greece from Spain and founded Talmudic schools and synagogues in the Macedonian region where many Ashkenazi Jews were established by this time. Remember Ashkenazim, like the Talmud used by them, come from Babylon, after that was used by the Order of the Pharisees, after that was used by the Khazars (implemented by the Huns) who continue the religion today. We can see now that it was several generations after this that the Jews were persecuted in Spain, which the Rothschild's claim to have been victims of. One must beware of the victim philosophy as it has permeated history without alteration and only leads to deception.

"International finance and banking are NOT primarily 'Jewish'. Many of the most powerful banking interests in the world are run by 'Gentiles'. One of the most powerful forces in international banking is the Knights of Malta, a Roman Catholic military order controlled by the Jesuit Superior General. Sadly, even a certain segment of the 'alternative media' helps to propagate the LIE that 'the

Jews' run international banking.

Interestingly, one of the titles of the Rothschild banking dynasty is 'Guardians of the Vatican Treasury'. 'The Jews', as a people, have been used for centuries as a 'scapegoat' by these international banksters and their secret societies, such as the Jesuit-controlled Knights of Malta. To label 'the Jews' as running banking, Hollywood, etc, is to throw out the proverbial 'red herring' designed to throw us off the scent of the 'real controllers'." — Darryl Eberhart

So, let's get back to the bloodline of the Rothschilds. Elchanan Bacharach, whose wife was Fogel Roten Rose and whose father was Rabbi Uri Feibesch of Worms, was born in 1475 in Burgau. Son Isaac used the name Bauer, Bacharach, Hahn, and Roten Schild, which his children used, as detailed in the beginning, He had many brothers and sisters including Moses (Mosche) Bacharach sum Han and Uri-Feibesch Bacharach zum Waage. Isaac married Esther Katz and fathered many children including Raphael and Moses, who both became Masons "of the Yellow Ring", Elchanan and Fogel. Elchanan was also a documented Mason, but whether he had a yellow ring is not specified.

Isaac's brother Moses had one documented son, Feibesch Joseph Uri Moses Bacharach zum Bisemknopf. Uri had several children including Elchanan Bacharach Waage whose daughter Fogel married Cousin Moses Herz Rothschild, the great grandson of Isaac. Meanwhile, son Elchanaan had married Chava Ammerscheiler and had children Raphael, Salomon, Isak, Elchanan, Moses, and Hirsch. Son Moses went on to Father Herz Moses zur Pfanne, Feibesch who also went by Uri, and Itsek Hase who married Fraidlen Hase the granddaughter of Isaac's brother Elchanan. The family, still living in Frankfurt, were merchants and lacked influence during this time, which is what kept them in the lower ranks of the elite until they reached elite status in the mid 1600's. Until then, as we can see, they intermarried and populated Frankfurt. However, during the lives of Isaac's grandchildren, the Hinterhaus Pfan in the Judengasse was used by the Rothschilds as not only a residential home but a commercial building as well. One of the many houses of the Rothschilds, up to 30 people lived there at a time. The ground floor contained an office and storage for many of their trade goods. This system enabled the family to not only hide their wealth but keep all work-related ideas and dealings within the family, as it remains today.

Isak Elchanan, born around 1614, married Kele Oppenheim and had several children including sons David Alcan and Raphael who became the first and only Rabbis of the family. Daughter Reizchen (Roschen) married Moses Metz with whom she had 4 children, followed by cousin Todres Oppenheim. For the past several generations the family had worked in trade, coming from a long line of merchants, but during this time several events took place in England which altered the family's thinking and solidified their focus for the coming generations. In 1571 the Royal Exchange had been formed in London, financed, and founded by Sir Thomas Gresham and opened by Queen Elizabeth I. Thomas was from a line of merchants, a tightly connected group of people. Thomas and the Bauer/Hahn/Rothschild families worked together closely, as international merchant families and members of the same guilds. Thomas worked with the King to negotiate favorable loans, among other things, which showed other select merchant families that control over governments took place through banking. While acting as an agent for the King, Thomas left England, working in the Netherlands, Germany, and France. By now Frankfurt, neighbor of Mainz where the printing press had just been invented, had become a center of economic importance in Europe due to trade, banks, and more which had been established by the Rothschild and Oppenheim families, among others.

So, the grandchildren and great grandchildren of Isaac Hahn, Bauer, Rothschild continued to sprout, and several more were married to their Oppenheim cousins. Several of David's offspring relocated to France, establishing the family there under the name Alcan. In Frankfurt change was a way of life. The guilds of the merchants (clubs of those days) regulated trade practices and maintained standards. Religion was severely impacted due to the Reformation and there were increasing tensions between the Catholics and Protestants. Meanwhile, the Frankfurt Stock Exchange was being formed through financial transactions which developed the necessary environment. During this time the family had solidified their trade to exotic and sought after silk, as they transitioned into the money exchange business. Silk was imported in its raw form and made into textiles and finished products, offering a range of products for silk merchants to maintain. Unfortunately like their past history, the present history is well shrouded aside from genealogical names and dates. This is why the Rothschilds would have been placed among the lower elite families, had it not been for their rise to power in these coming generations.

"Finance is the circulatory system of any country, as well as of the global economy. A smoothly functioning system is central to national growth and prosperity, to international trade, international economic growth, and development, and to fewer global crashes than otherwise would take place. But few financial systems can operate in a vacuum; given porous borders, they are always linked to, and influenced by, other national systems. Thus, they are truly borderless. They are therefore the very definition of globalization. The global financial system allows the world to grow faster because it channels savings - excess money - into places where the money is needed, to facilitate trade, for example, or to build roads, ports, bridges, or new companies. Global finance is also precarious because problems in one part of the world can spread like a contagious disease. Mayer Amschel Rothschild was one of the great pioneers of figuring out how to expand the possibilities of global finance and also how to deal with the consequences of the periodic crises that it spawns." – Jeffrey Garten, From Silk to Silicon

So, we have come to the 1700's, when the Rothschild family of Frankfurt had become well-known money exchangers! Because of Ashkenazi extremism, the Jews in many countries of Europe were kept in their own communities, such as the Frankfurt Judengasse. Conditions were as one would expect of a ghetto: overcrowded due to lack of emigration. As with any confined space, potential for advancement and change was low in part due to governmental restrictions. Like most Jewish ghettos the city was locked at night, and inhabitants were caged in like animals.

In 1710 the son of Moses Kalmann Rothschild (Hertz or Hirsch Bauer) was born. Amschel Moses married Schonche Lechenich and continued the family business. Together they had many children including the famous Mayer Amschel Rothschild, who expanded the family's wealth and status into the ranks of the lower elite. Amschel Moses died in 1755, followed by his wife the next year, leaving 12-year-old Mayer to take over the family business. Directly, he went to Hanover to learn from Uncle Wolf Jakob Oppenheim. During his teenage years he learned business and politics and was involved with other agents of the Royal Court who were experts in the financial industry. Mayer had also begun dealing in rare coins, and smuggled various items, which gained him notoriety throughout the courts of Europe. The following year he married 16-year-old Gutle, whose father was the Court Agent to Prince Charles William Frederick. This strategic marriage became the blueprint for all the generations to come. During these early years Gulte's many children slept together in a small room roughly 3 meters square. It was she who stated:
"If my sons did not want wars, there would be none."

Thanks to his father's wealth, the reputation of the family was well known, and his banking enterprises expanded quickly. Now that he was among the royals of Europe, he was able to make larger loans which were secured by taxes. This time was vital to Rothschild's expansion as Mayer was made the official Court Agent of Prince Wilhelm IX of Hesse (among the richest men in Europe) in 1769. His father Frederick rented out his army of Hessians to Great Britain under the advisement of Mayer, to aide in the North American Revolution. England especially had been involved in many wars and by the time the American colonies rebelled, the country was in debt to the amount of $140 million. This enabled bankers to invest and loan to a greater degree than they had been able to previously. It should be noted that the reason the family preyed on Jews was because they were the main group who would pay interest on loans. Christians and Muslims would not deal in loans at this time, therefore the Rothschilds couldn't gain a foothold there, but profited greatly by using Jews. Due to Frederick's sudden death, his son Prince Wilhelm had inherited a fortune which is estimated to have been $40 million and was a more eager friend of Mayer Amschel.

"No one does more to further the revolution than the Rothschilds themselves...and, though it may sound even more strange, these Rothschilds, the bankers of kings, these princely pursestring-holders, whose existence might be placed in the gravest danger by a collapse of the European state system, nevertheless carry in their minds a consciousness of their revolutionary mission. I see in Rothschild one of the greatest revolutionaries who have founded modern democracy." — Niall Ferguson

Being a member of several Orders already, including the Eternal Conspiracy (a group of wealthy men) whose goal was world domination, in 1773 Mayer joined with friend, Jesuit, and Ashkenazi Adam Weishaupt to create the Illuminati Order based on the Talmud. Also involved in its establishment was Jacob Frank, of the Sabbatean Cult. You see, in the 1600's mystic rabbi Sabbatai Zevi, born in Smyrna, Turkey, had become the latest Talmudic cult leader of the Kabbalah. He implemented wife swapping and other perverted rituals, further infiltrating and corrupting the Torah Jews. Sabbatai himself took up to 30 baths a day and practiced the Shiite Muslim and Catholic ritual of self-flagellation. He convinced his followers to abandon their previous religious ceremonies. In February of 1666 he was placed in prison by the Grand Vizier Köprülüzade Fazıl Ahmed Pasha in Constantinople where he was given the choice of execution or conversion to the national religion of Islam. After quickly converting to Islam and beginning to wear a turban to show his religious affiliation, he was given a large pension. Around 300 families followed the conversion and on June 18, 1666 (many 6's in that numerological display, in accordance with Kabbalist belief) he declared that he was the messiah of the Jews. After his death Jacob Frank was born to a wealthy family of Sabbateans. Being a megalomaniac like all cult leaders, he established himself as the reincarnation of Sabbatai and formed his own cult based on his philosophy. He expanded it to include ritual orgies to purify the soul, a Luciferian ritual. For some time he lived with Adam Weishaupt and/or Mayer Rothschild in Frankfurt and assisted in planning the new Order of Illuminati. His cult grew so perverse that the government banned them from being circumcised, buried, and limited their movements and rights. Jacob burned Jewish books and brought his followers to the Catholic Church.

"The Jesuits, now formally suppressed by the Pope, were allied with Frederick the Great of Prussia and Catherine II of Russia. The Jesuit General was in control of Scottish Rite Freemasonry and now sought an alliance with the Masonic Baron of the House of Rothschild. To accomplish this he chose a Jesuit who was a German Gentile (not a Jew) by race and a Freemason by association" - Adam Weishaupt

To form this Bavarian Order, Mayer had to convince the members of the Eternal

Conspiracy to pool their money together to make more profit. The detailed plan addressed issues that are still discussed today through the elite's various orders, including the use of terrorism, liberalism, classism, deception, mind control and indoctrination, pushing drug and alcohol use to further corrupt societies, propaganda, economic panic, subversion, and more. The Order was established several years later and followed the same principles the Jesuit Order did, as we have previously discussed. The Order was then used by the Jesuits, who co-founded it with the Rothschild's to implement numerous revolutions and wars across Europe and Russia. By this time the Rothschilds controlled not only the Central Banks they were establishing in major cities of Europe, but the printing press as well and all news outlets in Europe. The family had officially become members of the elite, and not only that but the controllers of the lower elite families altogether.

In the same year (1773) Amschel Mayer was born. At 12 he was also brought into the family business. Since children learn so much faster and so much more than adults, those who began any sort of business or education surrounded by experts and masters naturally knew more than they by the time they came of age. This is another huge difference between elite families and the families you know and have been a part of. While you are kept locked in a school which teaches you nothing of value or importance, until you are at least 18, the children of elite families learn and do and by that age they have accomplished more than you can for the remainder of your life.

"Give me control over a nations currency, and I care not who makes its laws." — Mayer Amschel

The formation of the Illuminati by the Rothschilds and friends allowed the Jesuits who had recently been disbanded by the Pope, to cut off the income to the Vatican, working through the new Order which immediately began propaganda and infiltrators to spark the French Revolution. Simultaneously, Mayer had his eye on the colonies of America who had recently fought against English rule, leaving the country bankrupt and in need of a benefactor. The Rothschild's were more than willing to help. Always playing both sides, the family noticed that North America was the new place to be if you wanted to create a monopoly from the ground up. In 1781 they established the First Bank of North America through friend Alexander Hamilton who was a cabinet member of President George Washington. During this time many documents were being published, exposing the Illuminati and Jesuits alike, forcing the group to go dark and work even more secretly.

While the French Revolution was going well, as planned, and the public was on board with the scam, Napoléon Bonaparte, the brother of the King of Naples and Spain had become Emperor of France and King of Italy (until 1814). The past few decades had been filled with propaganda put out from the Jesuits and sub-orders, attacking the Jews, the traditional scapegoat of the elite, and blaming them for all the problems faced by Europe. Napoleon worked diligently to eliminate the Jews in France, Germany, and Austria and even put a ten-year ban on all Jewish money-lending activity which left the Rothschilds in total control, as designed. In 1806 Napoleon stated that he was focused on removing Prince Wilhelm from rule and Wilhelm fled, with many other royals, and went to Denmark leaving around $3 million for Mayer to keep safe. Son Nathan had taken this and formed an intricate network of riders, ships, and carrier pigeons, which gave him news from all directions, keeping him up to date on Napoleon's moves. Nathan, having heard the outcome of the war before anyone else, sold off chunks of stocks, to convince other investors that Britain had lost. As prices fell, Nathan had his agents buy up the stock at rock-bottom prices. Same game as today. While Nathan was funding Britain's Duke Wellington, during the war, his brother Jacob was in Paris backing Napoleon. The Rothschild network utilized secret routes and couriers, allowing Nathan to receive news of the war over 24 hours before the British government.

In 1809, Nathan and his wife Hannah moved to New Court, St Swithin's Lane in London. By 1810 Nathan had become the arbiter of the Royal Exchange and Mayer founded Mayer Amschel Rothschild and Son in Frankfurt. He had previously (in 1805) established a Merchant Bank in London. After Mayer Amschel died eldest son Amschel Mayer was placed in control of the Frankfurt House, heading the family banking business. His brother travelled throughout Europe's courts, improving their networks, and making contracts. By the end of 1813, Nathan and his brothers were involved in collecting, minting, and supplying coins for Duke Arthur Wellesley's army and investing 800 million pounds of gold from the East India Company which we will discuss in a moment. Nathan's overseas bullion operations and alliances with associates such as Moses Montefiore were key for the family's development in the American States. In 1816 Nathan moved his family to a villa at Stamford Hill before establishing their townhome at 107 Piccadilly. Preferring the country, the family's estate called Gunnersbury, where Hannah died decades later, became a showcase for his impressive art collection. Much was happening during this time as the large family was expanding and infiltrating, so I will attempt to keep it from being too confusing.

The family coat of arms which now depicted an eagle holding 5 arrows was used by the Rothschilds in this generation. The 5 arrows represented the sons of Mayer who survived to adulthood. Son Amschel stayed in the family business in Frankfurt, Salomon was put in charge of Vienna, Nathan was established in London, Karl was given control of Naples, and Jakob, also called James, set up in Paris. In 1812 Mayer, Knight of the Sacred Constantinian Order of Saint George, and Crown Agent, died of smallpox, which plagued the Judengasse during this time, the cause of which should be easy enough to figure out. He left his sons an estimated 1 billion francs. In his will, Mayer made specific, and very detailed stipulations. The eldest brother would be head of the family. All marriages of the family were to be made within the family. Wealth would remain undivided. All public inventories were to be avoided, and inheritance suits were forbidden. Mayer left his wife a set amount of money to live on and commanded that his daughters and their offspring would have no part in the family business. That same year the charter of the first Bank of the US had ended, to which Nathan remarked:

"Either the application for renewal of the charter is granted, or the United States will find itself involved in a most disastrous war."

Thus began the American War of 1812. Son Amschel Mayer Rothschild had been involved in the family business since he was 12, traveling throughout Germany, and establishing a business center outside of Frankfurt. In 1814 he spent several months working with British allies' subsidy payments during the Napoleonic wars which profited the family greatly. However, Amschel had no children of his own and his hard work was inherited by his nephews. Regardless, he worked diligently to strengthen the family's empire and became Royal Prussian Pricy Councilor, Royal Bavarian Consul and more. He acquired many houses for the family and began the Amschel von Rothschild Foundation. Like his brothers, Amschel was also a Knight of the Sacred Constantinian Order of Saint George, a member of the family Order of Illuminati, as well as Commander of the Order of Leopold.

Nathan Rothschild's wife Hannah was the daughter of wealthy Levi Barent Cohen of Amsterdam who made his fortune dealing in diamonds. Together they had many children. Levi's brother Salomon was the ancestor of Chaim Hirschel Mordechai, also called Karl Marx, who became important to the Rothschild's in years to come. In 1815 Nathan gave a mere $10 million to Britain to aid in the Napoleonic War, an amount which would be around $900 million in today's money. In 1817, the Rothschild family received an Austrian noble title, 'von,' recommended by Count Stadion and the following year Nathan orchestrated a $5 million loan to the Prussian government. In 1819, Nathan, Alexander Baring, and others provided evidence to the Parliamentary 'Committee of Secrecy' on the Bank of England resuming cash payments. Nathan became the Austrian Consul General in London and the Rothschilds extended their influence further still, arranging loans to foreign governments, and establishing banks in major financial centers.

"The first occasion in which Nathan assisted the English government was in 1819, when he undertook the loan of $60 million; from 1818-1832 Nathan issued eight other loans totalling $105,400,000; he subsequently issued eighteen Government loans totalling $700 million. To the Rothschilds, nothing could have occurred more propitiously than the outbreak of the American revolt and the French Revolution, as the two enabled them to lay the foundation of the immense wealth they have since acquired." – John Reeves

During the past decade, the family had been profiting from the mint they made out of the gold shipped to them from their friends in South America. The family had been trading within Portugal for some time, through their web of relationships and international trade within the Jewish community's wealthy. Judith Cohen, newly married to Moses Montefiore, noted encounters with her sister Hannah Rothschild and Samuel Moses (Moshe ben Zanvil Pulvermacher) in her diary in 1812. Samuel, along with his brothers, had established trade connections with Portugal and Brazil (the first and main producer of gold since 1700s), at this time, leading to the formation of the firm Samuel & Phillips. The firm grew as Brazil opened its ports to trade in 1808 and soon their close friends, the Rothschilds, benefitted from the venture as well. The documented transactions between Samuel & Phillips and Nathan range from supplying wines and goods to providing financial support.

Nathan Rothschild's wife was the daughter of wealthy Levi Barent Cohen of Amsterdam. Together they had many children. Levi's brother Salomon was the ancestor of Chaim Hirschel Mordechai, also called Karl Marx. In 1817, the Rothschild family received an Austrian noble title, 'von,' recommended by Count Stadion and the following year Nathan orchestrated a $5 million loan to the Prussian government. In 1819, Nathan, Alexander Baring, and others provided evidence to the Parliamentary 'Committee of Secrecy' on the Bank of England resuming cash payments. Nathan became the Austrian Consul General in London and the Rothschilds extended their influence further still, arranging loans to foreign governments, and establishing banks in major financial centers. In 1821, the five Rothschild brothers were made Barons and soon dipped their fingers into Russia, becoming key in financial affairs, including the Russian Loan. Napoleon accomplished his duty by placing Pope Pius VII in jail until the Jesuit Order was reestablished, and the war on the Vatican was ended upon the signing of a treaty in 1822, one year after Napoleon was poisoned with arsenic.

By 1823, Nathan had been a member of the Bank of England's Committee of Treasury. In 1824 busy Nathan established the Sun Alliance life insurance company, and Alliance Assurance Co, with several friends including Moses Montefiore, Samuel Gurney, Francis Baring, and MP John Irving. Soon he gave 2 million pounds to Brazil, paying for their freedom from Portugal and the Samuel Brothers maintained control of the new government. The panic was triggered by a combination of factors, including speculative investments, overextension of credit, and economic downturns in various countries. After crashing London's stock market in 1825, Nathan bought up government securities and assets at depressed prices. As the panic subsided, the family's reputation for financial prowess became notorious, with their expanding wealth. By 1826 Nathan's firm injected more gold to save the Bank of England, solidifying his position as a leading City Merchant Banker.

"The few who could understand the system (cheque, money, credits) will either be so interested in its profits, or so dependent on its favours, that there will be no opposition from that class, while on the other hand, the great body of people, mentally incapable of comprehending the tremendous advantage that capital derives from the system, will bear its burdens without complaint, and perhaps without even suspecting the system is inimical to their interests." - Nathaniel Meyer Rothschild

In 1833, Greece sought to secure a loan to help rebuild the country after gaining independence from the Ottoman Empire. Nathan took it upon himself to serve as a financial intermediary and underwrote the Greek loan, guaranteeing the sale of a certain number of bonds. In 1836 Nathan died, leaving son Lionel to continue the business. Widow Hannah purchased land in Mentmore for her sons that same year and soon Mayer acquired the Manor of Mentmore. By the 1840s, the Rothschilds had begun acquiring large estates in Buckinghamshire. Now, let's stop here for a moment, as the activities are so numerous, and take a look at what other Rothschilds were up to during this time!

James/Jacob Mayer Rothschild was the youngest son of Mayer Amschel. At the age of 19, he moved to Paris to coordinate the purchases of bullion for Nathan and was stationed there to expand the family business in France, establishing the Rothschild firm of Rothschild Frères in 1812. Previously he had assisted Nathan in London, and helped the family's smuggling businesses develop and expand. James' French branch of the Rothschild's banking empire began with his deposit of £55,000 which grew by 1852 to £3,541,700 (equivalent to $550 million). The following year Salomon, a shareholder of James' branch who had already received a knighthood, was sent to Austria to establish the branch there and finance the Austrian government. There he founded SM von Rothschild in Vienna. As the family began building and buying the railways of Europe, Salomon financed the Nordbahn rail transport network. Among his elite friends and clients were Prince Klemens von Metternich. It is due to his relationship with the Emperor Francis I of Austria that the brothers were given the titles of Baron and Salomon was given honorary citizenship. During his time in Vienna, some of his deals included extensive state loans to establish and build up the government of Austria. These loans were given in 1823, 1829, and 1842.

Having a passion for art, James fit right into the royal circles and soon became a trusted adviser to ministers and kings. Among his royal clients was Leopold I, King of Belgium whose rule was financed by James. He was known for his dynamic authority, quick wit, and heavy German accent. In 1817 James bought the Château Rothschild, Boulogne-Billancourt, which lies vacant and abandoned today. The palatial residence, with its vast, sweeping staircase lies covered in graffiti and falling apart. In 1818 James purchased Greuze's painting, La Laitière, which expanded his ever-growing collection which also included Vermeer's The

Astronomer. Soon James expanded his investments, buying vineyards in North and South America, South Africa, and Australia. Following the French Revolution, in 1822, James was made Consul-General of the Austria-Hungary Empire. He saw to the French loans of 1830 and 1834 and was made Grand Officer of the Legion of Honor by King Louis-Philippe. Brother Salomon was also a collector of many things, including paintings by Carlo Dolci. His properties in Oderberg, Hultschin, and Schillersdorf were furnished with art from the French and Italian renaissance periods. During his short time in Austria, he bought the coalmines of Witkowitz; and the asphalt lake of Dalmatia, adding to the family's prosperity. Unfortunately, his fame and wealth in Austria brought him nothing but trouble and the public grew increasingly opposed to his presence in the country. Soon he was forced to leave the SM Rothschild branch to be controlled by his son, and Salomon moved back to Paris where he remained until his death.

In 1821 brother Karl had been sent to establish the business in Italy and had become the banker of the Papal States as well as the Kingdoms of Naples, Sardinia, Sicily and more. Among his clients was Luigi Medici and King Leopold of Belgium. Karl held influence over many kings in the region and was initiated into the Sacred Military Constantinian Order of St George by Pope Gregory XVI (Bartolomeo Alberto Cappellari) who let him kiss his hand, rather than his foot as was custom. In 1824, James married his 13-year-old niece, Betty, the daughter of his brother Salomon, and together they lived an extravagant life in their château de Boulogne, and at Ferrières. Among the artists patroned by James were Gioacchino Rossini, Frédéric Chopin who dedicated his Valse Op. 64, to James' daughter Charlotte, Honoré de Balzac, Eugène Delacroix, and Heinrich Heine.

By 1828 Andrew Jackson had run for President of the US and spoke out against the Rothschild's reinstated Bank of the United States. The exposure of the banking system and the country's debt won him the election and by 1836 the charter for the bank expired and was not renewed. This caused the country to have zero debt, for the first time in history, and an assassination attempt was carried out. Eventually the bank-driven Depression of 1842 had been enacted by Nicholas Biddle on behalf of the Jacob Rothschild bank owners. Soon the Civil War and Mexican War had been implemented and the country once again saw itself in debt, to the amount of $100 million by 1861. Meanwhile, in the 1830's James built the Saint-Germain Railroad, one of the most important in France. The family bought the Almaden quicksilver mines in Spain giving the family open access to the component needed to refine their gold from South America, and Africa. James and Karl worked closely with the Papal Treasurer, Alessandro Torlonia, and Pope Gregory XVI. While James had stabilized the French government, Salomon the Austrian, and Karl the Kingdom of the two Sicily's, the Vatican was obliged to be assisted by them as well and requested a loan of £400,000 (which is equivalent to $4 billion). Naturally there was much criticism because of this, as the public attacked the Rothschild's for being Jews, when in reality they had been, for several generations, the servants of the Vatican and Jesuits. In their contract the Rothschilds were given priority over all future loans.

> "Early in the 19th century the Pope approached the Rothschilds to borrow money. The Rothschilds were very friendly with the Pope, causing one journalist to sarcastically say "Rothschild has kissed the hand of the Pope. . . Order has at last been re-established." — Derek Wilson

In the same decade, Karl had become the Consul General of Sicily and built the Villa Gunthersburg outside of Frankfurt before buying the Villa Pignatelli in Naples, which views Vesuvio. In 1834, Karl enlisted Illuminati member and Freemason Giuseppe Mazzini to lead another of their revolutions, which he carried out successfully for decades. Karl helped establish several secret societies including Alta Vendita, as did his brothers, to continue his father's teachings of kabbalah and mysticism. Meanwhile Pope Pius IX and Pope Leo XIII both tried to have Karls Carbonarist documents published, once it had been exposed that they contained detailed plans to overthrow the Catholic Church. The group was quite distressed when a copy of this was lost and offered rewards to anyone who could return it. Originally written in Italian, the title translates as "Permanent Instructions, or Practical Code of Rules; Guide for the Heads of the Highest Grades of Masonry". Having since been published, an excerpt states:

> "Our ultimate end is that of Voltaire and of the French Revolution — the final destruction of Catholicism, and **even of the Christian idea**."

By reading this document, you will see that it is the same doctrine written in the Jesuit oath and many others. The same script passed down and repeated through all of time, and all secret societies are copies of themselves, under the philosophy and goals of the Jesuit Order. In the document, members are commanded:

> "You will contrive for yourselves, at little cost, a reputation as good Catholics and pure Patriots."

You should already know that the term patriot is an elite term of acknowledgment of totalitarian submission. In 1844 Salomon had bought the United Coal Mines in Vitkovice as well as the Autro-Hungarian Blast Furnace Company. In 1852, James built a hospital in the Rue Piepus, Paris, with the condition that it be used for elderly Jews. His wife, Betty, founded the Hospital for Incurables which contained 70 beds, and left 600,000 francs to charities upon her death. This was a sad time for Karl as his wife and son both died. After this, unable to recover, he left Naples to his sons and retired. In 1854 James built a castle outside of Paris called Château de Ferrières, which included botanical gardens and enormous rooms. In 1975 the family gave it to the University of Paris. Working with NM Rothschild & Sons, James's bank expanded and bought the Chem de Fer du Nord railway system, and joined with other investors to buy the Rio Tinto copper mines from the Spanish government. Before he died, James founded the Society for Jewish (meaning Ashkenazi) Studies in Paris.

While there is even more that these brothers did, let's continue onto the next generation. In 1808 Lionel Nathan Rothschild was born to Nathan Rothschild and Hannah Cohen. He was the brother of Charlotte Nathan Rothschild who was married to cousin Anselm Salomon Rothschild, Sir Anthony de Rothschild who became the 1st Baronet of Tring Park, Nathaniel de Rothschild who married Cousin Charlotte (daughter of James), Hannah who married Baron FitzRoy, Mayer Amschel de Rothschild who was married to Cousin Juliana Cohen, Louise de Rothschild who married Cousin Mayer Carl Rothschild, and Julia who was married to Andrew Maines. So, let's continue with the children of Nathan and see where it takes us.

Daughter Louise married Cousin Mayer Carl and produced only females. Their daughter, Clementine, died at the age of 20, and Louise founded a hospital in her honor. There are only two sentences to be found anywhere regarding Clementine, even on the family archives website, the cause of her death nor her brief life, are not expanded on in any way. The Jewish Women's Archive, obviously written by a sexist, adds this statement to her mention:
> "As females of the species, a subordinate position was accepted without question and considered as natural and as inevitable as sunrise."

Lionel inherited the Barony of the Habsburg Empire and eventually Prime Minister Gladstone proposed that Queen Victoria make him a peer. By 1836 he was married to the daughter of Uncle Carl Mayer Rothschild, Charlotte, and they had several children. Charlotte was the only one of Carl's children to produce offspring. The following year Lionel worked with Aaron Palmer of Wall Street, keeping the family apprised of the American situation. At this time, the US was a secondary focus for the Rothschilds, but their many friends whom they had placed there maintained correspondence which provided them a detailed view of affairs, including political challenges and economic prospects. August Belmont, the Rothschilds' intended Cuban correspondent had refused to leave New York, altering plans. Meanwhile Lionel's brother Anthony had married his cousin Louis Montefiore and together they had 2 daughters. Anthony worked with his father (Nathan) in London until his death, and from then continued working with Lionel. Lionel had a desire for politics, while Nathaniel cultivated his passion for wine. Anthony found himself the only one of his brothers who could focus on the family business but was unable to leave it to his children as they were girls. Nevertheless, he funded railways in Brazil and invested in ironworks in Mexico to support it.

In 1847, Lionel was brought into the British House of Commons as a member of Parliament. At this time, Jews were still barred from sitting in the chamber as a requirement was to swear a "Christian" oath (which is an oxymoron). However, close friend Prime Minister Lord John Russell of the elite Russell family, implemented the Jewish Disabilities Bill to make the swearing of the oath void. While the law was passed by the Commons, the Lords denied it and Lionel resigned his seat. This only strengthened his following and he was allowed to swear on the Old Testament rather than the Bible.

Brother Mayer, known as Muffy, had attended several London universities and joined the bank with disinterest. In 1847 he was made High Sherrif of Buckinghamshire, a region where his mother, Hannah Cohen, had bought up the land, leaving each brother a large estate in Aylebury. Here he built the monstrous Mentmore Towers, another Rothschild castle, and soon served as Liberal MP for Hythe. In that same year, Lionel had decided to donate money to assist the victims of the Irish Potato Famine, which we are told was caused by a water mold which killed off half of the crops in Ireland for many years. The first meeting of Lionel's British Relief Association was held on January 1, 1847, at his London home. Among the members, each of whom donated £1,000 to the club, were Mayer Amschel de Rothschild, John Abel Smith, George Robert Smith, and Honorable Stephen Spring Rice. During this time, millions of Irish died, and even more were sent to Bermuda to serve lengthy and harsh sentences because they stole food or committed other crimes during the famine. As usual, the real story of genocide is hardly revealed unless one digs into National Archives and works to unravel this web, like Woodham Smith, British Historian, did in her time, exposing a dozen British regiments who were sent to Ireland to withdraw food sources from the land by force.

"The truth is startling, 67 out of 130 regiments of Britain's Empire army were in Ireland in this period (100,000 at any one time). The troops were not on a humanitarian mission. Their job was to remove food by force." - Richard Merriman

"A million and a half men, women and children were carefully, prudently, and peacefully slain by the English Government. They died of hunger in the midst of abundance which their own hands created; and it is quite immaterial to distinguish those who perished in the agonies of famine itself from those who died of typhus fever, which in Ireland is always caused by famine...The Almighty, indeed, sent the potato blight, but the English created the Famine." - John Mitchel

200,000 British constables, militia, and troops seized millions of livestock, tons of flour, grains, and poultry, shipping them off to the mainland. Meanwhile London enforced propaganda against funding those who were starving and hid the now noticeable exportation of food under the label of famine. The purpose of this was to push Catholic and Protestant Irish out of the region by forcing them to emigrate to the US where they formed gangs and mafias in New York and more. Some of the comments made by leaders during this time were as follows.

"The land in Ireland is infinitely more peopled than in England; and to give full effect to the natural resources of the country, a great part of the population should be swept from the soil." — Thomas Malthus

"The only way to prevent the people from becoming habitually dependent on Government is to bring the food depots to a close. The uncertainty about the new crop only makes it more necessary." - Charles Trevelyan

"The Famine? No, the Starvation. When a country is full of food and exporting it, there can be no Famine." - George Bernard Shaw

"[existing policies] will not kill more than one million Irish in 1848 and that will scarcely be enough to do much good." - Nassau Senior, economist to Queen Victoria

"There is such a tendency to exaggeration and inaccuracy in Irish reports that delay in acting on them is always desirable." - Sir Robert Peel, Prime Minister

"We copy the evidence of Thomas Burroughs, M.D.: Examined the body of Thomas McManus; both of the legs, as far as the buttocks, appeared to have been eaten off by a pig; is of the opinion that his death was caused by hunger and cold. There was not a particle of food found in the deceased stomach or intestines. Those who saw the body were of opinion, from the agonized expression of McManus's countenance, that he was alive when the pig attacked him." - The Sligo Champion

The Fenian Brotherhood, founded in 1858, aimed to overthrow British rule in Ireland through armed insurrection and grew with the help of the Irish People newspaper, established in 1863 by James Stephens. A significant revelation came with the discovery of a bank draft at Kingstown Station in July 1865, payable to George Hopper, James Stephens's brother-in-law. The draft was given by the August Belmont Bank in New York and payable at the Rothschild Bank in London. August Belmont was a Rothschild man, in charge of Rothschild interested in American politics since Nathan established him there to assist with Tammany Hall (US Democratic Party discussed in the Astor chapter). The Fenians were, naturally, accused of socialism, money laundering, and more, as their notoriety spread through the US as well. An investigation, involving Superintendent Daniel Ryan, uncovered financial transactions totaling £5,807 (over $1.1 million today) between August

Belmont bank drafts and John O'Leary. The Rothschild Bank facilitated the Fenian finances from America to Ireland.

The National Archives of Ireland also provide insights into this False Flag conspiracy. Meanwhile, the Irish who had swarmed the US had been funneled to New York where they were assisted by the Rothschild's Tammany Hall. Jobs and support were given to the Irish immigrants, over all others, causing the Irish to support the Democratic Party of the US which grew and strengthened, destroying the Republic from within. Nevertheless history, written and published by the elite, is sure to praise Lionel for raising $600,000 ($20 million today) for the Irish, becoming the savior of the region.

While all of this was taking place, Lionel and his brothers had been working to bring about another war. Now that Europe and the US were thoroughly secured, they focused on Russia who had denied them entry thus far. Nathan Mayer Rothschild had promised in 1815 to execute the Tsar's entire family should they not surrender to the Rothschild banks. Since then, the Romanov family had suffered a series of "accidents". Using close friend, Benjamin Disraeli to author certain documents, brother Barons Anthony and Lionel Rothschild funded British and French governments, manipulating them through money and media, into war. The Rothschild brothers wrote loans to the Ottoman government as well as the French. As in every war, the Rothschild's manipulated the stock markets of Europe by using their vast spy networks to stay ahead of everyone in regard to the goings on in the Black Sea.

By 1853 the governments stormed across the Black Sea to stop the Russians from protecting the Orthodox Christians of the Ottoman Empire, particularly those undergoing persecution in the Holy Land (Palestine). Russia evacuated its Danube provinces, as the French and British governments declared war rather than assistance while Pope Pius IX creeped in the background. In 1848 Pope Pius IX had sought safety from the revolutionaries and requested yet another loan from the Rothschilds. They refused unless he took down the Jewish ghetto walls of Rome and more. The Pope refused for a couple of years, and finally surrendered to the terms in order to accept 33 million francs. For the next few generations, Rothschilds were married to leading Italian families, ensuring their position as Papal Treasurers. Looking through the Foreign Ministry Archives of the Russian Empire, it is revealed how Pope Pius IX and Napoleon III of France had been working to secure Catholic interests with Sultan Abdul Mejid. An agreement was formed, allowing the Sultan to exterminate Christian subjects, as long as favor was shown to Catholics. Emperor Nicholas I and the Orthodox leaders worked to protect the persecuted, and maintain Jerusalem, Bethlehem, and other Christian cities from the clutches of Rome.

"It was that inter-clerical strife concerning the Holy places in Jerusalem and Bethlehem, that flared up in the year 1850 had triggered the Crimean war." - Mikhail Yakushev

In February of 1856, Russia was forced to surrender, giving up the Danube River which had served to keep Rusia protected for so long. The Russian Empire suffered an estimated 200,000 casualties, the Ottoman, around 130,000, France lost 95,000 military men and Britain 21,000.

Several years before, Lionel took over his father's estate, Gunnersbury, enlarging the park, adding a pleasure lake, and installing gas lighting. He and his wife were known for hosting grand events, including their daughter Leonora's marriage to her French cousin Alphonse in 1857. Brother Anthony had negotiated the lease for the Royal Mint Refinery in London, allowing the Rothschild's to continue being the owners of the mint. In the 1850's he purchased the Aston Clinton House, to add to his collections of homes. His wife and cousin, Louisa, worked to keep the family involved in Jewish affairs, forming conventions and associations. The family now owned numerous estates throughout Europe, patroned artists, writers, horse racers, governments and more. After being reelected to the House of Commons, in 1852, Lionel refused to take the oath until 1858. By this time the House of Lords had decided to allow each House (Commons and Lords) to make up their own oath. During these years, Cousin Mayer Carl Rothschild worked with his brother Wilhelm Carl in the family's Frankfurt branch. By the mid 1850's he had become the Banker to the Court of Prussia, the Duchy of Parma, Consul of Bavaria, and Consul-General. By the end of his career, Mayer had been made a member of the House of Lords in Prussia. Because he only produced females, and his brother Wilhelm produced no children at all, upon his death, the Frankfurt branch was closed.

During the war in Crimea, Lionel focused on the importance of certain trade routes and decided the British government should control the Suez Canal. Meanwhile, brother Anthony was financing railroads, like his uncles before. Understanding that transportation is the gateway of trade, just as waterways are, he funded the Chemins de fer de Paris a Lyon, known as the PLM, in 1857. This railroad went from Paris to Lyon to the Mediterranean coast. Soon thereafter, the Imperial Lombardo Venetian Railway and the Central Italian Railway Company, which connected regions of Italy, caught his eye.

By 1875 the Khedive of Egypt was facing financial difficulties. He soon decided to sell his shares in the Suez Canal. One of Lord Derbys journalists informed him of this, and he relayed the information on to Prime Minister Benjamin Disraeli. Borrowing £4 million from Lionel, British control over the Suez Canal was secured and the Rothschilds profited once again. Afterward, Lionel's son Nathan, who was a Member of Parliament for Aylesbury, faced questions regarding potential violations of Act 22 which prohibited MPs from holding profitable offices under the Crown. Nathan responded that the Act didn't apply to him as he was not a partner in his father's firm. During his life, MP Lionel drafted loans to the British government which added up to £16 million. While she disliked the idea, in 1885, The Queen made Lionel a member of the House of Lords.

"Baron Lionel N. de Rothschild, head of the world-famous banking house of Messrs. Rothschild & Co. died at the age of 71. He was son of the late Baron N.M. Rothschild who founded the house in London in 1808 and died in 1836. His father came to the conclusion that in order to perpetuate the fame and power of the Rothschilds, which had already become worldwide, it was necessary that the family be kept together, and devoted to the common cause. In order to do this, he proposed that they should intermarry, and form no marital unions outside the family. A council of the heads of the houses was called at Frankfurt in 1826, and the views of Baron Nathan were approved." — New York Times, June 1879

Lionel's brother, Nathaniel, had attended Strasbourg University with brother Anthony before travelling to Paris, to work for Uncle James. Due to a fall as a child, he was left half-paralyzed and relied on a secretary to read letters and papers aloud to him and dictate letters to London almost daily. Despite his disabilities, he worked diligently. By 1847 Anthony was knighted and in 1850 he married James' daughter Charlotte and had several children. By 1853, he purchased the Château Brane Mouton estate in Bordeaux, renaming it Château Mouton Rothschild. While he had a passion for winemaking, his vineyard took several generations before becoming one of the world's renowned wines. Nathaniel was a friend and supporter of Giuseppe Mazzini, being "sympathetic" to Italian nationalist cause for national independence and unity. Giuseppe had expanded Rothschild's ideals and doctrines throughout his territory and established gangs throughout New York to enforce control while establishing the movement Young Italy in 1831 to implement Unity. Soon thereafter another branch of the political movement was implemented in Germany. Karl Schapper was a member of this German group and, with others, joined the communist revolutionary order called League of Outlaws. By 1836 he founded his own order called League of the Just.

During the 1830's the Rothschild's various Orders produced communism and spread it throughout Europe. This was done in preparation of the Rothschild's takeover of Russia. In 1839 the Jacobin-based League initiated a rebellion in Paris to form a Socialist government. However, upon failing, the order relocated to London, joining up with more communist leaders such as Karl Marx.

As a fellow Illuminati member and freemason, Karl Marx's father, Hirschel Mordechai Levy, had become a member of the Loge L'Ètoile anséatique (The

Hanseatic Star) during the Napoleonic War in 1813. While his father assumed the life of a Lutheran, in order to infiltrate Prussian society through order memberships, Karl's grandparent, Nanette Salomon Barent-Cohen, was a member of the Amsterdam elite. Karl Marx was raised to carry out the orders of the Rothschild's Order, Eternal Conspiracy. The Hassidic system had already been implemented, by the Eternal Conspiracy, through what was named the Socialist Movement, in Germany, France, Britain and beyond. Karl had been educated in the Talmud and infused with his bloodline's violent racism. He was only too eager to expand the elite's communistic beliefs, but mainly wanted to destroy those he considered to be sub-human barbarians. In 1841 Karl began working at the newspaper called Rheinische Zeitung, founded by Moses Hess who had also founded the German Social Democratic Party. Moses was used as a handler of sorts to Karl and was ever present in his progressions and deeply involved in his social circles as well.

In 1846 the Communist League was founded by Cousin Chaim Hirschel Mordechai, now called Karl Marx, and his friend Friedrich Engels. Using Friedrich and Adam Weishaupt's documents, Karl composed the Communist Manifesto while Karl Rothschild, Lionel's uncle, and father-in-law, was establishing his secret societies. 20 years after publication, Karl Marx's name was added to the Manifesto. Revolutionary communism (communism by force) had been established throughout London, Paris, Italy, and Germany and Karl Schapper joined Marx's league. As needed, Karl spent time in London to write, using Rothschild-owned media to incite Russophobia, which continues to this day. Little by little, Russian freedom was stripped away. Sometime later, the Rothschild's solidified the Communist Order under Vladimir Lenin. But let's not get ahead of ourselves. To facilitate the Marx movement, Nathan (Lionel's brother) gave Karl 2 checks for thousands of pounds. Karl Marx, nicknamed Destroy because of his frequent use of the word, joined the movement of fellow Luciferian and mystic, Joana Southcott who had a following of over 100,000 before her death in 1814. She had been in contact with the demon named Shiloh and for some time stated that she was pregnant with the messiah. Joining the movement, he altered his appearance to that of members of the cult.

"This world is now, at least for the most part, at the disposal of Marx on the one hand, and of Rothschild on the other. This may seem strange. What can there be in common between socialism and a leading bank? The point is that authoritarian socialism, Marxist communism, demands a strong centralization of the state. And where there is centralization of the state, there must necessarily be a central bank, and where such a bank exists, speculating with the Labour of the people, will be found." - Mikhail Bakunin

"I wish to avenge myself against the One who rules above." — Karl Marx

Karl had been writing many dramas and poems regarding his hatred of religion and especially the Living God. In letters to his father, he notes that his soul has been given to demons and soon he writes a poem called Oulanem, which is an inversion of Emmanuel (Jesus). This term is used by Luciferians, especially during the Black Mass ritual, as one of the many names of Satan. In another poem he writes:

"The hellish vapours rise and fill the brain, Till I go mad and my heart is utterly changed.
See this sword? The Prince of Darkness [name of Lucifer] Sold it to me. For me he beats the time and gives the signs. Ever more boldly I play the dance of death."

Fellow Luciferians Friedrich Engels, Pierre-Joseph Proudhon, and Mikhail Bakunin had become well known radicals and helped Karl form the First International which soon had 5 million members worldwide. The group's goal was to cultivate Satanic revolutions, as Mikhail Bakunin stated:

"In this revolution we will have to awaken the Devil in the people, to stir up the basest passions. Our mission is to destroy, not to edify. The passion of destruction is a creative passion."

"Come, Satan, slandered by the small and by kings. God is stupidity and cowardice; God is hypocrisy and falsehood; God is tyranny and poverty; God is evil. Where humanity bows before an altar, humanity, the slave of kings and priests, will be condemned." - Pierre-Joseph Proudhon, the father of anarchism

Upon his death in 1888, only 6 people attended Karl Marx's funeral. Of his 6 children, 3 had died of starvation and 2 had committed suicide.

Meanwhile, in 1856, Nathaniel and his wife had acquired the property at 33 rue du Faubourg Saint-Honoré in Paris, transforming it into their residence after extensive renovations. In 1868, his uncle and father-in-law, James, bought the neighboring Château Lafite vineyard, creating a family rivalry. While Muffy was busy racing his horses in the Epsom Derby, Nathaniel did his best to be the top winemaker in France, but in the Bordeaux Wine Official Classification of 1855, Château Mouton was ranked second. Among his artwork, saved by the Musée d'Orsay, are photographs of a mosque entrance, sail boats, and pastorals. In 1861 brother Anthony was made High Sheriff of Buckinghamshire, a position he added to his Barony. Daughter Annie was married to Honorable Elliot Constantine Yorke, son of the 4th Earl of Hardwicke and daughter Constance married Baron Cyril Flower.

In the 1870's, Muffy purchased 90 acres of land at Ascott, near his Mentmore Towers. His daughter Hannah was married to the PM and 5th Earl of Rosebery, Archibald Primrose. Hannah was known as the richest woman in Britain and had 4 children with Archibald, despite his homosexuality, and more Earls and members of Parliament were added to the Rothschild's family tree. Mentmore Towers remained Hannah's inheritance, and the inheritance of her children. Hannah died at the age of 39, another woman ignored by the males in her life who generously described her as having a well-balanced mind and common sense, but whom they made certain to ignore. After the 6th Earl of Rosebery died the estate was sold along with its contents in public auction. Simon Halabi bought the palace and converted it into a hotel, but seeming to always have some issue, the project was delayed time and time again, and eventually abandoned. This over-extravagant aberration lies rotting today, forgotten by those who took time and money to build it, once more, a Rothschild proof of squander. Throughout history the family proves they worship money, as they have stated. This idolization produces nothing good, nothing that lasts, and nothing that grows. They care nothing for those they kill along the way nor those they abuse; everything is rot under the Rotten Shield.

The remaining children of Carl Mayer Rothschild, brother of Nathan, James, and Salomon, included Charlotte. Charlotte was the only child to produce any heirs, with her cousin Lionel. Her children who were married to their cousins include Leonora, Evelina, and Nathan. We will discuss the next generation in a moment. Another Charlotte, daughter of James and wife of Cousin Nathaniel, son of Nathan produced Nathan James who married his cousin, Mayer Albert, and Arthur. Charlotte was a distinguished painter and is listed in the Benezit Encyclopedia of Artists. The daughter of Nathan was naturally named Charlotte too and she married Cousin Anselm Salomon, the son of Salomon. Of her 8 children Caroline, Albert, Ferdinand, and Hannah were married to their cousins. The males carried on the titles of Baron and inheritances of lands and positions.

Let's take a quick look at the rest of the children of James and Salomon, as we've discussed the other brothers' children thus far. Salomon's daughter Betty had married James, and brought forth Charlotte, who married Cousin Nathaniel, and sons Edmond, Mayer, Gustav, and Salomon James. Salomon James married the daughter of Mayer Carl Rothschild, Adele and had one daughter. After losing £1 million he was banished to Frankfurt. After some time, he was sent to travel the US, Canada, and Cuba, keeping an eye on the American Civil War for the family. Uncle Nathan had long since profited from slave trading in Manchester, and funded the government's bail-out of British slave owners when slavery was abolished there in the 1830's. After this, slavery existed in the US until after the war. The Rothschilds, being Talmudists, believe in their own superiority as do all Talmudic followers. All others are worthy of death, as the Talmud states. The same belief system is called Luciferianism, and all superiority and ego disorders stem from it. This makes slavery easy for the family, and funding and preserving it was necessary.

The grandsons of Nathaniel Mayer Rothschild, Arthur, and Nathan James, continued the family businesses. Arthur pursued his love of stamps while Nathan became the director of the family's Nord and Est railway companies. After marrying his cousin, the daughter of Mayer Carl, they had 2 children. Having always been interested in manuscripts he founded the Society of Ancient French Texts and the Society of Jewish Studies. Among the things he found was a hospital at Berck-sur-Mer. Nathan died three days before his 37th birthday. His son, Baron Henri James Nathaniel Charles became a French playwright under the pen names André Pascal, Charles des Fontaines, and P.L. Naveau. He was also a physician who never practiced medicine, man of letters and Commander of the Legion of Honor. Like the rest of his family, he was involved in many masonic orders.

Since the family had already developed the banking system in the New World, they had been exposed by every US president. The history and Constitution of the US is what make the American society, even today, well aware of the elite and their actions. Also, unlike every other country in the world, American's have been given a right, written in their constitution, to arm themselves against the elite, which they hold to today. Salomon James had more love for the south, as did the rest of the family and the Rothschild's supplied their French, British and Spanish armies to the south while financing support for the north as well. Since President Lincoln refused to pay the interest on the loans they offered, he turned to Russia. Because of his actions during the war and the way he handled the Rothschilds, Abraham Lincoln was murdered by their puppet John Booth. Unfortunately, Salomon James didn't live to witness the success of the north and the end of slavery, as he died in 1864, having produced one female who hadn't turned one year old yet.

While the family was involved in this, they also acted on their long-time grudge against Russia, forcing communism into the country, leading them to wars, and much more. Alfonse James de Rothschild's investments in Russian oil in the 1860s and the Rothschilds' presence in Baku, Russia's oil-rich region, played a crucial role in the family gaining its foothold in the country. Alexander II was the Emperor of Russia, King of Poland, and Grand Duke of Finland. Using Sergey Nechayev, friend of Mikhail Bakunin and others in the Marx group, he founded a communist revolutionary group called Narodnaya Volya and worked to overthrow the Tsar. The gang orchestrated several assassination attempts on the Tsar. Members who failed in their mission were executed. In 1881, after several bombing attempts, the Tsar was surrounded in his carriage, while four people threw crude bombs at him until he was killed. This didn't stop the Romanov dynasty and violence continued. Alexander III blamed Jews for the assassination, leading to increased anti-Semitic policies. By 1883 Baron Alphonse Rothschild, son of James, Grand Cross of the Legion of Honor, had founded the Caspian and Black Sea Oil Company. The company did so well, that in 1895 the Rothschild's made an agreement with Rockefeller's Standard Oil to divide world markets, rather than continue in competition, and the families prospered, monopolizing the world's oil since.

Alphonse had married the daughter of Uncle Lionel, Leonora, and had a daughter who was married to Cousin Albert Salomon. Alphonse and his brother Gustave had inherited an estate and vineyard from their father, along with their titles and business ventures including the Chemin de Fer du Nord company. Gustave carried on the banking business and married outside of the family, to the dismay of his relatives. None of his children married cousins either but married into the Beer and Sassoon families, among others.

"There is no one today who better represents the **triumph of equality** and work in the nineteenth century than M. le Baron de Rothschild." — The Globe, 1891

Having been in charge of gold bullion and coming from a family who owned gold mines and produced gold bullion for Europe, Alphonse encouraged France to adopt the gold standard. In 1873, he succeeded, saving the Rothschild's ability to use and exploit gold. Let's take a moment to discuss the family's gold operations.

Remember that in the 1700's the Rothschild's had become involved in manufacturing silver and gold bullion. This required quicksilver which the Rothschild family quickly bought into. The quickest, cheapest, and easiest way to manufacture gold is to crush the ore with mercury. Then it's heated so the mercury vaporizes. Thousands upon thousands of people have died from mercury poisoning, being forced to make the Rothschild gold. Since this method requires skill and strength women have been most often used for this. When the vapor of mercury is released, it stays, blown in the air, infecting water, and soil, causing a multitude of diseases and health problems in humans as well as animals. So, the Rothschilds, persuading governments that gold was valuable and necessary, were contracted in 1830 to handle the production of the Almaden mercury mine in Spain. Nathan Mayer had already bought quicksilver mines including those in Huancavelica, Peru, Almaden, Spain, Idria, Austria, Monte Ammiano in Italy, as well as Kweichow in South China. In 1848 the Rothschild's, who had previously established a banking center in California, alongside their mines, profited from the California Gold Rush, followed by the Australian Gold Rush two years later.

In 1850 California quicksilver mines boomed so significantly that it surpassed the value of Californian gold. The following year gold was discovered in New South Wales. Working with their cousins, the Montefiore's, the Rothschild's immediately took control of the region. Like California, Victoria surged in population as people flooded to dig gold and the Rothschild provided provisions and supplies. Cousin Joseph Barrow Montefiore, a seasoned colonist and businessman, sent detailed reports to NM Rothschild & Sons in London, describing the impact of the gold rush on the local economy, the scarcity of labor, and the enormous field for labor from the Mother Country. Making large purchases of gold, he forwarded everything to London, like so many friends and coworkers of the Rothschilds. NM Rothschild & Sons secured the lease on the Royal Mint Refinery in London in 1852, and closely monitored transactions.

Friend of the family, Cecil Rhodes, was a member of the Illuminati sub-groups such as the Round Table and other Freemason orders which eventually became the CFR, Bilderberg, and other groups we know today. In 1888 he founded the De Beers Consolidated Mines in South Africa. While he focused on diamonds, like the Oppenheimer family (relatives of the Rothschilds), he also branched out into gold. His ventures were financed by the Rothschild's who used the gold to finance Europe. Lionel Rothschild financed not only Cecil but his own mining ventures which included copper, mercury, nickel, lead, and nitrate mines, apart from purchasing the Suez Canal and involving himself in the oil of South America. In 1840, Nathaniel "Natty" Rothschild was born, son of Lionel and grandson of Nathan Rothschild. Though Natty tried to be political and involved in the Jewish protests of the day, he simply didn't have the skill nor mind for it. So, he also supported his good friend, Cecil, financing the buying out and consolidating of diamond mines in Africa. Natty funded the Rhodes Scholarship Program which was headed by Fabian Socialists who dominated the staff at Oxford during that time. Today the DeBeers Corporation is run by Sir Harry Oppenheimer who controls the South African gold producers and the Hong Kong diamond market.

Later, in 1919, the gold traders, including the Rothschilds, founded gold fixing in London. At first gold fixing was decided by the team over the phone, which the Rothschilds funded and brought to Britain. Soon the NM Rothschild & Sons offices were used, and the US was given a higher cost for gold than Britain. In 1933 US President Roosevelt required citizens to surrender their gold, after which the price was fixed even higher than it had been. Nothing changes.

> "The story of the gold-fixing has often been told. How every weekday at 11 a.m. the representatives of five firms of bullion brokers and one firm of refiners meet at the office of Messrs. Rothschild (except on Saturday) and there fix the sterling price of gold. There is, however, a great deal of activity which lies behind his final act -- this centralization of the demand for, and the supply of gold in one office and the fixing of the price of gold on that basis. A price of gold is first suggested, probably by the representative of Messrs. Rothschild, who also acts for the Bank of England and the Exchange Equalization Account." — News Chronicle, 1938

Alphonse's brother Edmond had become the director of Belgium's Banque Lambert as well as director of DeBeers Consolidated Mines in South Africa. Long since this time, the elite had their eyes on Africa. The region is not only a focus because the continent was the first empires after the flood and a hotspot for Fallen activity. United States Africa Command (AFRICOM) on the African continent was established in 2007 as the first overseas regional military command. Initially under the US European Command, AFRICOM became an independent entity in 2008, covering 53 African nations except Egypt and Western Sahara, dividing Africa into 5 military districts, each with a multinational African Standby Force trained by the US, NATO, and the European Union. "Integration teams" were deployed to northern, eastern, southern, central, and western Africa. The 5 districts of Africa today are called Arab Maghreb Union, East African Community, Economic Community of West African States (ECOWAS), Economic Community of Central African States (ECCAS), and Southern Africa Development Community.

The US has a multitude of bases in Africa including Djibouti, Gabon, Kenya, Mali, Morocco, Namibia, Senegal, Tunisia, Uganda, and Zambia. In 1975, South Africa revealed that Israel had agreed to sell it nuclear weapons, supported by an arms agreement signed by Israel's current President, Shimon Peres. This disclosure challenges Israel's previous denials and raises legal and ethical concerns. If Israel, a nuclear state, violated international treaties, the US is obligated to demand inspections and disarmament, making any aid to Israel illegal. Since both are owned by the Rothschild's, no one cared. During this time, Israel was also importing tons of uranium from South Africa and China invested significantly in African countries, not only for mineral exploitation but also financing industries, construction, and services. Africa's economic vulnerabilities, dependence on commodity prices, and the need for job creation amid demographic growth have made it an easy target for the elite throughout all of its history.

In 2011 Japan built a military base called Japan Self Defense Force in Djibouti, Africa. The base costed $40 million and claimed to be built to protect Japan's maritime interests. Japan's constitution, Article 9, renounces war, and the deployment violates its proscription on overseas military presence. The base in Djibouti underscores Japan's shift and alliance with the US and NATO. Djibouti, strategically located at the Red Sea and Gulf of Aden, is already hosting major military bases for the US, France, and NATO, making it a focal point for international military operations in the Horn of Africa. NATO has also been supporting the AU Mission in Sudan and Somalia, contributing to the operationalization of the African Force. The military arm of the elite (the US) has transformed the armed forces of Liberia, Rwanda, Uganda, and Ethiopia into military surrogates, as it has done throughout the Middle East.

Among the "security forces" in Africa, who protect elite agendas, is G4S, a Danish-founded British owned second-largest private contractor of the world, with forces in over 125 countries; Unity Resources Group, an Australian-owned security service in the Middle East, Africa, the Americas, and Asia; Erinys, guardian of Iraq's vital oil assets also operating in Africa; DynCorp, one of eight private military firms used by the US State Department globally; Triple Canopy, Aegis Defense Services, Defion and Academi (formerly Blackwater and Xe Services) are among the numerous mercenary companies owned by the elite, used by the US and others to take care of less savory missions which must be kept from public knowledge. I shouldn't have to mention the activities of the United Nations and Red Cross in this region, as their actions are well known.

The elite use Africa as not only a testing ground for biowarfare, chemical warfare, depopulation, trafficking, and more, but also focuses on draining the land of Africa of its rich minerals. These are then used against everyone in the world. The region continued to be a hotspot for Fallen activities still today. The Island of the Fallen, called Atlantis, ruled by Atlas who is depicted holding the world on his shoulders, stood just off the coast and now lies at the bottom of the sea as detailed in historical texts and archeological finds. Credo Mutwa, one of Africa's Shamans, details their activity in the continent, evident in the acts which are commonplace there: pedophilia, genocide, slavery, and all manner of corruption. He states in one interview:

"Because genocide, worse than anything that Hitler ever committed upon the Jewish people, is taking place in Africa NOW, and the people of America don't seem to care a damn. There are diamonds and coal in Angola, and I have learned from reliable people that there is more oil under Angola, in certain places, than there is in certain parts of the Middle East. You don't kill the goose that gives you the golden egg, so why would the bankers want to destroy Africa?

There is another force behind these people, a terrible, alien force, which does things behind the scenes which - and the sooner we recognize this, the better - it is very common for human beings who are in trouble to blame forces other than those inside themselves. But, I have studied the situation in Africa since the end of the Second World War, and before, and I have evidence that points to an alien force at work in Africa. There are over 24 other alien creatures, sir, that we Africans know about."

Just as every country has experienced UFO sightings and alien abductions, so too have the African nations. Their traditions and ways of life commonly relate to the lessons they have learned from dealing closely with the Fallen, similar to Asian cultures who have had close contact with them throughout history.

"Upon that part of the African continent nearest to the site of Atlantis we find a chain of mountains, known from the most ancient times as the Atlas Mountains. Whence this name Atlas, if it be not from the name of the great king of Atlantis? And if this be not its origin, how comes it that we find it in the most north-western corner of Africa? And how does it happen that in the time of Herodotus there dwelt near this mountain-chain a people called the 'Atlantes', probably a remnant of a colony from Solon's island? How comes it that the people of the Barbary States were known to the Greeks, Romans, and Carthaginians as the 'Atlantes,' this name being especially applied to the inhabitants of Fezzan and Bilma? Where did they get the name from? There is no etymology for it east of the Atlantic Ocean." -Francios Lenormant

Knowing that the elite are the servants of the Fallen, as they themselves state and as is evidenced in their actions, let's continue out of Africa and look at what Edmond Rothschild was in the midst of constructing.

In 1864, Zevi Hirsch Kalischer, a German rabbi and friend of the Rothschild family, established the Central Committee for Settlement of the land of Israel in Berlin. Many groups were created, and books written to indoctrinate people in the newly created philosophy of Zionism along with another Rothschild friend, Rabbi Alkalai, and James and Edmond. Zevi then proposed that Edmond's father James Rothschild should buy the land known as Israel, which is a portion of Palestine and at that time was part of the Ottoman Empire. James had founded the James Mayer Rothschild Hospital in Jerusalem during the Crimean War and Edmond was raised with his ancestors view of the Jews and the need to control and profit from them. In the 1880's the Tsar had worked to expel the Jews from Russia, as we have seen, in response to the Rothschild's attempted assassinations, bombings, and warmongering. Problem, Reaction, Rothschild Solution. Things went according to plan and the Jews fled to Palestine, forming colonies there. James then went to work building the place up and Edmond followed suit.

In 1891 close friend Charles Russell wrote a letter to Edmond Rothschild, detailing how to establish their Jews in Palestine, stating:
> "What is needed here, therefore, next to water and cleanliness, is a good government which will protect the poor from the ravenous and the wealthy. Banking institutions on sound bases, and doing business honorably, are also greatly needed... May the God of Jacob direct you, my dear Sir, and all interested with you in the deliverance and prosperity of Israel, and blessed will they be who, to any extent, yield themselves as his servants in fulfilling his will as predicted."

Since the Jewish community had been divided between original Judaism and elite Judaism, for so long, a new order needed to be formed in the name of Unity. In the late 1880's Baron Edmond bought the section of land, making it appropriate that the nation carries their Star as the state logo. Theodor Herzl, an Austrian journalist, was put in charge of the Zionist Congress in Switzerland, in 1897, one year following the publication of his book. Meanwhile the Rothschilds dictated which crops were allowed to be planted, and established glass works and wine cellars, among other ventures. Edmond pooled the Ashkenazi Jews of Europe together in one location, running out the Hebrew bloodlines from the region of Canaan. After being told to leave the colony alone, as the settlement of Yishuv had faced increasing problems, Edmond claimed that no one had a right to interfere since he alone created Yishuv. Soon Theodor was replaced by David Wolffsohn, followed by Otto Warburg of the lower elite Warburg family. In 1914 Edmond, now President of the Jewish Colonization Association, went to Palestine to see his city of Tel Aviv, now thriving. This led to Edmond, and his sons, formulating the plans for the Third Temple, which they would build in reality, in their land of Israel. This never came to fruition, however today all details down to the carpets are in place and stored, waiting for the green light.

By this time many of the Rothschild's were involved in the new development of Israel and many more of their friends were facilitating the formation. In 1904 Israel was defined by Theodore Herzl as being the land between the Red Sea and the Euphrates. However, by 1947 Rabbi Fischmann had defined it as extending through parts of Syria and Lebanon. Today, as conflict continues due to their continuing expansion, the state of Israel has taken over much of the Palestine country, as the state desires the death of those surrounding it, hoping to divide and dissolve Iraq. Lord Arthur James Balfour, Alfred Milner, and Baron Edmond Rothschild were still actively upholding the Order of the Round Table (much the same as the Eternal Conspiracy) after the death of Cecil Rhodes and authored the Balfour Declaration which had been previously discussed and supported by President Wilson, Lloyd George, and Winston Churchill. This political and legal act was only ever written in letter form, never established formally. However, it proves the British governments compliance to forming illegal colonies in Palestine, supporting Zionism, and much more under the control of the Rothschilds.

"Dear Lord Rothschild,
I have much pleasure in conveying to you, on behalf of His Majesty's Government, the following <u>declaration of sympathy with Jewish **Zionist aspirations**</u> which has been submitted to, and approved by, the Cabinet. His Majesty's Government view with favour the <u>establishment in Palestine of a national home for the Jewish people and</u> will use their best endeavours to facilitate the achievement of this object, it being clearly understood that nothing shall be done which may prejudice the civil and religious rights of existing non-Jewish communities in Palestine, or the rights and political status enjoyed by Jews in any other country. I should be grateful if you would bring this declaration to the knowledge of the Zionist Federation.
Yours sincerely, Arthur James Balfour"

This declaration was written on November 2, 1917. On November 7, Tsar Nicholas II, and family (all but two of his children) were murdered, and the Rothschild's finally had a victory over Russia. The Romanov family had originated with Prince Prus, brother of Emperor August of Rome, who founded Prussia. After poisoning numerous family members, further assassinations led to two Rothschild-funded revolutions as communism was forced upon the empire. On the night of Nov. 6, 1917, when a dozen Red Guards, led by Joseph Stalin and funded by the Rothschilds, drove a truck up to the Imperial Bank Building in Moscow. The trucks were filled with the contents of the bank including $700 million gold, Romanov Jewels and more. The Bolshevik Politburo and War Revolutionary Center had been formed following the October Revolution of 1917 and Vladimir Ilyich Ulyanov, now called Lenin, was made head of the Russian Soviet Federative Socialist Republic. But how did this happen? Let's take a closer look.

As an active communist, Lenin had been previously exiled for sedition. When he was a teenager, he became involved with Michail Bakunin and joined the Marx movements. He became a disciple of Adam Weishaupt and a Satanist. By the time he went to college he was a member of the French lodge Art et Travail and held the 31st degree (Grand Inspecteur Inquisiteur Commandeur) in Freemasonry. By the 1900's he was adamant about mobilizing workers and peasants into revolution, which is the philosophy of Socialism and Communism which more specifically desires the destruction of religious values. Financed by Dr. Fritz Warburg, financial attaché of the German legation, Lenin founded the Bolsheviks, meaning majority, Party. Apart from Fritz and Paul Warburg's contributions, other Rothschild financiers involved in the destruction of the Russian Monarchy was Jacob Schiff (who had grown up with the Rothschilds in their Frankfurt home), John Rockefeller, Averell Harriman, and Fabian Joseph Fels who donated $15,000 to the cause. Lenin was praised as the "greatest Fabian of them all" by fellow Luciferian, Mason, Fabian, et al. George Bernard Shaw. Christian Rakovsky, a Bolshevik politician and collaborator of Leon Trotsky wrote a detailed testimony of the events of Lenin and Stalin, so let's take a look at an excerpt of his first-hand knowledge.

> "At the same time remember the moderation of Marx and his bourgeois orthodoxy when studying the question of money. In the problem of money there do not appear with him his famous contradictions. Finances do not exist for him as a thing of importance in itself; trade and the circulation of moneys are the results of the cursed system of Capitalistic production, which subjects them to itself and fully determines them. In the question of money Marx is a reactionary; to one's immense surprise he was one; bear in mind the "five-pointed star" like the Soviet one, which shines all over Europe, the star composed of the five Rothschild brothers with their banks, who possess colossal accumulations of wealth, the greatest ever known...
>
> The Rothschilds were not the treasurers, but the chiefs of that first secret Communism... Marx and the highest chiefs of the First International... were controlled by Baron Lionel Rothschild... You know that according to the unwritten history known only to us, the founder of the First Communist

International is indicated, of course secretly, as being Weishaupt. You remember his name? He was the head of the masonry which is known by the name of the Illuminati; this name he borrowed from the second anti-Christian conspiracy of that era: Gnosticism. This important revolutionary, Semite and former Jesuit, foreseeing the triumph of the French revolution decided, or perhaps he was ordered (some mention as his chief the important philosopher Mendelssohn) to found a secret organization which was to provoke and push the French revolution to go further than its political objectives, with the aim of transforming it into a social revolution for the establishment of Communism. In those heroic times it was colossally dangerous to mention Communism as an aim; from this derive the various precautions and secrets, which had to surround the Illuminati.

What is not known are the relations between Weishaupt and his followers with the first of the Rothschilds. The secret of the acquisition of wealth of the best-known bankers could have been explained by the fact that they were the treasurers of this first Comintern. There is evidence that when the five brothers spread out to the five provinces of the financial empire of Europe, they had some secret help for the accumulation of these enormous sums: it is possible that they were those first Communists from the Bavarian catacombs who were already spread all over Europe. But others say, and I think with better reason, that the Rothschilds were not the treasurers, but the chiefs of that first secret Communism. This opinion is based on that well-known fact that Marx and the highest chiefs of the First International - already the open one - and among them Herzen and Heine, were controlled by Baron Lionel Rothschild, whose revolutionary portrait was done by Disraeli, the English Premier, who was his creature, and has been left to us.

"They" [Lionel Rothschild and his son Nathaniel] isolated the Tsar diplomatically for the Russo-Japanese War, and the United States financed Japan; speaking precisely, this was done by Jacob Schiff, the head of the bank of Kuhn, Loeb & Co., which is the successor of the House of Rothschild, whence Schiff originated. He had such power that he achieved that States which had colonial possessions in Asia supported the creation of the Japanese Empire which was inclined towards xenophobia; and Europe already feels the effects of this xenophobia. From the prisoner-of-war camps there came to Petrograd the best fighters, trained as revolutionary agents; they were sent there from America with the permission of Japan, obtained through the persons who had financed it. The Russo-Japanese War, thanks to the organized defeat of the Tsar's army, called forth the revolution of 1905, which, though it was premature, but was very nearly successful; even if it did not win, it still created the required political conditions for the victory of 1917. I shall say even more.

Have you read the biography of Trotsky? Recall its first revolutionary period. He is still quite a young man; after his flight from Siberia he lived some time among the émigrés in London, Paris, and Switzerland; Lenin, Plekhanov, Martov and other chiefs look on him only as a promising newcomer. But he already dares during the first split to behave independently, trying to become the arbiter of the reunion. In 1905 he is 25 years old and he returns to Russia alone, without a party and without his own organization. Read the reports of the revolution of 1905 which have not been "pruned" by Stalin; for example that of Lunatcharsky, who was not a Trotskyite. Trotsky is the chief figure during the revolution in Petrograd. This is how it really was. Only he emerges from it with increased popularity and influence. Neither Lenin, nor Martov, nor Plekhanov acquire popularity. They only keep it and even lose a little. How and why there rises the unknown Trotsky, gaining power by one move greater than that which the oldest and most influential revolutionaries had? Very simple: he marries. Together with him there arrives in Russia his wife Sedova. Do you know who she is? She is associated with Zhivotovsky, linked with the bankers Warburg, partners, and relatives of Jacob Schiff, i.e. of that financial group which, as I had said, had also financed the revolution of 1905. Here is the reason why Trotsky, in one move, moves to the top of the revolutionary list. And here, too, you have the key to his real personality.

Let us jump to 1914. Behind the back of the people who made the attempt on the Archduke there stands Trotsky, and that attempt provoked the European War. Do you really believe that the murder and the war are simple coincidences? As had been said at one of the Zionist congresses by Lord Melchett. Analyze in the light of "non-coincidence" the development of the military actions in Russia. "Defeatism" is an exemplary word. The help of the Allies for the Tsar was regulated and controlled with such skill that it gave the Allied ambassadors the right to make an argument of this and to get from Nicholas thanks to his stupidity, suicidal advances, one after another. The Bolsheviks took that which "They" gave them."

After Lenin's revolutionaries succeeded in assassinating Alexander II, they worked to overthrow the government further, forming various uprisings until 1905 when the Russo-Jap War broke out. After this, Nicholas began depositing money in foreign banks, foreseeing his future, and hoping to ensure his children's rights. He deposited more than $900 million in Chase, National City Bank, Guaranty Trust, J.P. Morgan, Hanover, and Manufacturers Trust. In 1914 these six New York banks, all owned and operated by the Rothschilds, bought the controlling stock in the Federal Reserve Bank which they have controlled since. Tsar Nicholas had $115 million in English banks and $100 million in Banque de France, $80 million in the Rothschild Bank of Paris, and $132 million in the Mendelsohn Bank. As one would expect, this didn't happen without the Rothschild's knowing about it and they soon planned the Russian Revolution along with Alfred Milner, Jacob Schiff, Sir George Buchanan, Olaf Aschberg, and others. By March of 1917 the Tsar had been forced to abdicate from the violence of the militarized people. This was not enough, as the Rothschilds demanded his death, and he was hunted down and murdered beside his wife and children in the middle of the night.

Since the October Revolution, Leon Trotsky (Lev Davidovich Bronstein) had been a member of the communist party, serving as the Commissar for War during the Russian Civil War. Unfortunately, he disagreed too much with Lenin's philosophy and was booted from the organization as Joseph Stalin, who had worked for the Rothschilds Baku oil refinery until he burned it down, had become Lenin's right-hand man. After burning down the refinery in Baku, in his early 20's, Joseph Stalin convinced the workers to strike and attempted to assassinate the director. The Rothschilds paid him to end the strike. By 1907 he had formed a gang of bank robbers, kidnappers, blackmailers, and assassins and used his outfit to help fellow revolutionary Lenin and the friendship bloomed. Coming back to the timeline, now Lenin was the leader and had become an "ism". By the end of 1917, the Jews of Russia had been given a special segregated section in the government called Yevsektsiya, which promoted Communism and worked to eliminate religious affiliations among the Jews. By the time the Russian Civil War was implemented, anti-Jewish pogroms had been reinstated. By the 1920's with Stalin in charge, harsh restrictions were placed over Jews and by the 1930's the Great Purge was enacted, to remove Jews and others from the land. This was implemented at the same time in Germany as well.

The Rothschilds won a grand victory over enemy Russia who had until that point been a protector of Christians, and soon they were able to establish the Russian Central Bank under the security of their newly formed Soviet government. While this region of the world was now being placed under control of a Rothschild "ism", across the ocean the Rothschild's had been working on another cult, Mormonism, which they funded through their bank Kohn Loeb Co. Since we already discussed the formation of this order and the grooming of the puppet leader, let's continue.

By now the children of Charlotte and Lionel had grown, and their daughters were married off to their cousins. Sons Nathaniel "Natty" Mayer, Alfred Charles and Leopold continued the business. As we have discussed Natty, let's move on. Alfred schooled with Edward VII, who later became king, but left without a degree. He immediately went into the family bank in London and by the time he was 26 he was made director of the Bank of England. When his father died, Alfred inherited several estates and was eventually made the High Sheriff of London. He was the Commander of the Royal Victorian Order, a member of the Legion of Honor, Order of the Crown, and Grand Cross of the Order of Franz Joseph. Brother Leopold was also a Commander of the Royal Victorian Order, as well as President of the British order of Mercy and member of various Jewish organizations. His son Lionel was a member of the Most Excellent Order of the British Empire and created the gardens at the family's estate Exbury. Lionel remained at home during World War I but was a Major of the Royal Buckinghamshire Yeomanry, nevertheless. In 1917 he co-founded the Anti-Zionist League of British Jews and soon became a Member of Parliament. Brother Evelyn was killed in the war while Anthony was wounded but survived. Upon his return, he took control of the family bank in London, allowing Lionel to tend to his gardens.

"Though they control scores of industrial, commercial, mining and tourist corporations, not one bears the name Rothschild. Being private partnerships, the family houses never need to, and never do, publish a single public balance sheet, or any other report of their financial condition." — Frederic Morton

In another region of the world, another puppet had been born. In 1888, Mohandas Karamchand Gandhi was still studying in England, where he was brought into the Rothschild's circles. Several members of the Indian National Congress were also devotees of the ever-growing Theosophical Society. Since the 1600's the East India Trading Company of London had been spreading control throughout India until it was recognized in 1757 as the ruling power and by 1799 Nathan Rothschild was deeply involved. Remember in 1708, Moses Montefiore and Cousin Nathan Mayer Rothschild had loaned the British Treasury several thousand pounds in return for an exclusive trading right to the region which gave them control over the British East India Company. The gold of India was taken to London and by 1715 opium flowed through the country, followed by China and the US shortly after. While the Astors and Russells had been given permission by the Rothschilds to trade in opium, Rothschild relatives, the Sassoon family, had made their name carrying out the smuggling trade of opium in China. Around 1.3 million Indian peasants were used to cultivate poppies for the East India Company which smuggled it into China.

By the 1800's the Rothschild's began forming banks in India and China under the Bank Charter Act which allowed them to profit further, being unrestricted by Britain. Soon the British had more Indian military personnel than British who then rose up against the occupiers. To appease the Indian people who did not want British control, Britain informed them that they were no longer under the rule of the East India Company but the Crown (meaning the Corporation of London which by that time was the Rothschilds). The British created and governed an Indian National Congress and a Muslim League and brought in trains and communications technologies. Needless to say, the people of India were frustrated and in 1919 British soldiers were brought in to murder 350 unarmed people who had dared to form a rally.

Meanwhile Mohandas was working in London during WWI and was made a Sergeant Major by 1916 after begging to be put in war against the Zulu whom he stated were one degree removed from animals. Groomed by Rothschild relative, the Russian Helena von Hahn, now called Helena Petrovna Blavatsky, who had come to India in 1879, the Rothschilds had been aware of Mohandas before he entered London. The family had given a headquarters to Helena in India and placed their star at the entrance. She introduced Mohandas to many Luciferian friends including Leon Tolstoy and soon Helena bestowed the title Mahatma on him, which he used from that day forth. When WWI hit 111,000 Indian soldiers were killed fighting for England and the Rothschilds profited. Mohandas was used by the elite as many have been, to be a puppet messiah and push the people into elite control under the illusion of freedom and independence.

"In 9 years flat, Madame Blavatsky would bamboozle this planet with occult and spirituality, and lay the foundation for Nazi Aryan Pride, from which the Jewish state of Israel would be born." — Ajit Vadakayil

In 1920 the elite's Indian lawyer launched a campaign against the British, leading a march in 1930 protesting Britain's monopoly of salt production. Many arrests and protests were made in Gandhi's name which helped subdue the population with the illusion that peace can be a weapon against those who do not want it. Among those secretly murdered by Mohandas' following was American William Francis Doherty. By 1940 the Indian people demanded a separate Muslim state which was met by the imprisonment of the National Congress leaders by the British. In 1946 unprecedented violence between Hindus and Muslims in Calcutta ensued resulting with Viceroy Mountbatten agreeing to the formation of Pakistan and Bangladesh. China and Russia remained the last places the Rothschild's had not yet taken over but while Communism was being formulated to create revolutions to overrun Russia, China was overrun by drugs. The monopoly of Indian opium continued until 1947.

Manuben Gandhi had come to look after Mohandas' dying wife and in 1946 at the age of 77 faithful servant Mohandas Gandhi received his 17-year-old grandniece as his mistress. According to her diaries he (referred to as mother) experimented on her sexually. He supervised her education, diet, dress, sleep, and every aspect of her life. For closer supervision and guidance, he made her sleep in the same bed as him, naked. She was his personal attendant massaging and bathing him and cooking for him. India and Pakistan became "independent", as dominions under Britain on 15th August 1947. Almost half a million people died in the violence that followed between Hindus and Muslims and one year later Mohandas was shot three times and killed by a militant Hindu RSS member named Nathuram Godse. Since the partition of British India in 1947, India and Pakistan have followed a path of mutual animosity. Today India with the population of around 1.5 billion people is 14% Muslim and 79%

Hindu.

The Rothschild controlled Gandhi family has been in power ever since, as nothing has truly changed. In the 1990's PM Rajiv Gandhi reversed his mother's policy of nuclear development, which PM Narasimha Rao resumed in 1991 and in December 1995 Narasimha was ready to authorize a nuclear test but was instantly discovered by a CIA satellite and discouraged by President Bill Clinton. In 1998 Prime Minister Atal Vajpayee ordered Indian scientists to proceed with plans for testing which caused an uproar in Pakistan. The US has treaties providing a nuclear umbrella to NATO nations and provided aid to the Pakistani military from 1954 to the 1980's. China has been the major military supplier to Pakistan and continues to occupy areas inside of India's borders as a result of the war of 1962. In 2006, when President George Bush visited South Asia, he remarked:

"[we] are now united by opportunities that can lift **our** people... The United States and India, separated by half the globe, are closer than ever before, and the partnership between our free nations has the power to transform the world."

As we have previously discussed, Helena brought India's ancient religion of Fallen worship to the Western world, including the ancient Luciferian rituals of mantras, yoga, chakras, and much more. Racists and Luciferians worldwide have embraced her plagiarized philosophies which have become so commonplace in most societies today that few understand the implications of it anymore. The Hindu symbol of the swastika is so well known and has been so deeply exposed I won't discuss it apart from noting that it was Helena's Thule society which Adolf Hitler followed, that passed on the philosophy and symbol for him to use for the Aryan Nazi Order. This was also the foundation for the Zionist philosophy which was formulated long before this order. Let's continue.

Unfortunately, not all of the world shared the Rothschild's view of Zionism, and they decided to enforce it with war, uniting the policies of Britain, France, Russia, Italy and the US. Without the support of France and the US, Zionism would die. Numerous Zionist leaders were used to persuade unconvinced governments, and soon the Declaration was incorporated into the League of Nations (the UN). Not everyone who promised support followed through and the pledges made by Sharif Hussein of Mecca failed. For a long time, Torah believing Jews protested the corrupt Zionism, and citizens of Israel would not serve in the Israeli army because they knew who created the abomination called Israel. In 2018 members of the Israeli army were arrested because of their involvement in a large Colombian pedophile ring. They raped and tattooed all the 14—17-year-olds they kidnapped to sell in other countries. But I digress... Due to force, Israel survives but Jerusalem remains in the hands of Palestine which is controlled by the Vatican. While Mohandas was being groomed, Adolph Hitler was as well.

Alois Schicklgruber, the illegitimate son of Maria Anna Schicklgruber had fathered Adolf Hitler in 1889. Maria was working in Vienna at the Rothschild's Vienna estate when she became pregnant with Alois. She was kicked out and went to the police. Thanks to her police report, discovered by Chancellor Engelbert Dollfuss, Maria claimed seduction by Baron Salomon Mayer Rothschild. Salomon was notorious for his sexual activities with young girls and being able to silence the police. In 1907 grandson Adolf travelled to Vienna where he lived for 10 months. Soon, he was brought into the Thule Society and studied Zoroastrianism. As previously discussed, the Thule Order was just like all elite orders, centered around black magic and Luciferianism. Over the past few decades, the media, owned by the Rothschilds, in Austria, Germany, and other European countries had begun spinning anti-Jewish propaganda. This had happened many times in the past and the forced migration of Jews from Russia helped facilitate the indoctrination. Making Jews a problem to many countries is an obvious and solid way to ensure the formation of the state of Israel. Adolf Hitler repeated Napoleon's attempt to destroy the Jewish population in the Empire as the Rothschilds merely funneled them from the top of Europe down to the Red Sea.

"The Rothschilds can start or prevent wars. Their word could make or break empires." - Chicago Evening American, 1923

After decades of propaganda the people were convinced, because regardless of intelligence, people will always listen to news and governments and believe everything they say. Among the many supporters of Adolf Hitler was William Averell Harriman who owned German chemical company IG Farben, a division of the Rockefeller's Standard Oil. The Rothschild's Royal Dutch Shell company provided fuel for Adolf's military while their banks provided funds.

"The Kaiser had to consult Rothschild to find out whether he could declare war. Another Rothschild carried out the whole burden of the conflict which overthrew Napoleon." — New York Evening Post, 1924

In order to make it seem as though Adolf was against the Rothschilds, he had Cousin Louis Nathaniel arrested in 1938 and according to the Daily Herald the ransom was set at £2 million which would be $10 million today. When you consider that Louis' bank account totaled $10 billion at this time, it was a small sum. He was soon released after donating $21 million to the cause. The war went well and accomplished many agendas which have been mentioned throughout this book, most especially instilling the Luciferian ritual word of Holocaust (meaning human sacrifice) into every mind on earth. The repetition of which has only further strengthened the Rothschild's agenda against the Jews in promotion of Israel, while absorbing Germany's accumulated gold.

"I soon realized that this displaced person camp was actually a trading post. Every one of the inmates had large sums of dollars. As I discovered, with the help of certain American Jews, they had used the money to buy up large quantities of cigarettes and coffee, which they sold on the black market. I knew millions of people were starving, but in Bergen Belson, the main dish was filet mignon." — Rabbi Joachim Prinz

Not all camps were in such good condition as Bergen Belson, and when thugs are in charge of imprisoned people corruption thrives. As previously detailed, millions were killed through starvation and disease, most of whom were Christians.

"And how we burned in the lamps later thinking: What would things have been like if every security operative, when he went out at night to make an arrest, had been uncertain whether he would return alive and had to say goodbye to his family? Or, if during periods of mass arrests...people had not simply sat in their lairs, paling with terror at every bang of the downstairs door and at every step on the staircase, but had <u>understood they had nothing left to lose</u> and had boldly set up in the downstairs hall an ambush of half a dozen people with axes, hammers, pokers, or whatever else was at hand? The organs would very quickly have suffered shortage of personnel...The cursed machine would have ground to a halt! If...if...we didn't love freedom enough. And even more — we had no awareness of the real situation. We purely and simply deserved everything that happened afterward." — Aleksander Solzhenitsyn

It was around this time that Rothschild employee, Paul Warburg, created the privately-owned bank in the US called the Federal Reserve, while William Harriman, Fritz Thyssen, Friedrich Flick, and others were used to create entities to help finance World War II. Robert Rothschild spent the war in America, retiring from polo while his sister married into the Sassoon family. His sons Élie and James served as officers in a cavalry during the war but were captured by the Nazis and sent to detention camps. Élie was released in early 1944. While suffering in a POW camp, he found the time to marry his childhood sweetheart, Baroness Liliane Fould-Springer. After the war, he took charge of Château Lafite-Rothschild and helped rebuild the Rothschild Frères bank and established many secret accounts in the Cook Islands. Brother James also worked at Rothschild Freres which he owned a percentage of. While sister Cecile maintained a dedicated hold on actress Greta Garbo, James became Chairman of numerous family businesses including the Society of Petroleum Investors, the Company of the North, and the Discount Bank of France. Soon he became the President of the Conservatoire de Paris followed by the French Consistory. Like most members of the family, he was an Officer of the Legion of Honor and was given the Croix de Guerre.

"The Rothschild family is the head of the organization I entered in Colorado. Supposedly the Rothschilds have personal dealings with the Devil. I have personally been in his villa and have experienced it and know it's true." — John Todd

While there are many other Cousin Rothschilds, their histories have been kept out of public record and even their gravestones leave little information regarding their lives, marriages, or children. Meanwhile the main line of the 5 sons of Amschel have trickled down and, as usual, have ended with most of the Rothschild men suddenly producing nothing but women. Nevertheless, the son of Nathan Mayer, Lionel Walter Rothschild, 2nd Baron Rothschild, born in 1868, served in Parliament and was made a Fellow of the Royal Society due to his zoological research and collections, including over 300,000 bird specimens, which can be viewed at the Natural History Museum at Tring. In 1910 he decided the Liberal Party wasn't for him and switched to the Conservatives. Soon he was given the Order of the British Empire, and the Gold Medal of the Royal Society. Apart from breeding exotic animals, and having a team of zebras pull his carriage, the Giraffa Camelopardalis Rothschildi was named in his honor. He had only daughters.

Brother Nathaniel Charles also worked in the family businesses while establishing nature reserves in the UK. In 1912, he founded the Society for the Promotion of Nature Reserves, which later became the Royal Society for Nature Conservation and was most interested in fleas, which he wrote many scientific papers about. His grandson is the Jacob Rothschild most have heard of today. We will discuss him soon.

In 1957, Baroness Marie-Hélène Naila Stephanie Josina van Zuylen van Nyevelt van de Haar married her third cousin, Baron Guy Edouard Alphonse Paul de Rothschild. Their home was Chateau de Ferrières, which was occupied during the Franco-Prussian War and later in WWII. For his service he was awarded the Croix de Guerre and after joining the French Forces in 1943 his ship was sunk by a torpedo. After the war Guy returned to the family business and was placed on the cover of Time magazine. In 1950 he became the first president of the Fonds Social Juif Unifie, which is a conglomeration of 200 Jewish associations. In 1959, Marie decided to reopen the family estate which is now known for being a den of Hollywood stars, Dukes, and Duchesses. Later, Guy became a partner of the Rothschild branch in London and established France's largest uranium mining company. Among his mining operations were Societe le Nickel, which took over Penorroya and La Compagnie de Mokta, gaining mines od lead, zinc, copper, manganese, sand, and gravel. He had one son with each wife, David Rene, and Edouard Etienne.

Cousins Leopold "Eddy" David and Edmund Leopold had been born to Lionel Nathan de Rothschild and Marie Louise Eugénie Beer. Leopold was a passionate musician, excelling as a pianist and violinist and sang with The Bach Choir of London for many years. He held leadership roles in various organizations, including the Music Advisory Committee of the British Council, English Chamber Orchestra, and Glyndebourne Arts Trust and became a trustee of the Jewish Music Institute, Royal College of Music, and the National Museum of Science and Industry. Brother Edmund became a Major in the British Army during World War II, after which he worked with various prospects including the British Newfoundland Development Corporation and the Churchill Falls hydro-electric dam. Leopold was given the Victoria Medal of Honor and made a Commander of the Order of the British Empire along with Edmund who also received the Territorial Decoration.

In the US the Rothschilds had been establishing radical Rabbis. One, Rabbi David Marx, made Jacob Mortimer Rothschild a Rabbi of The Temple in Georgia. During WWII, Jacob was a chaplain on Guadalcanal where he contracted malaria and returned home. He was abundantly involved in Civil Rights at the time and was a member of the Atlanta Council on Human Relations, the Georgia Council of Human Relations, the Southern Regional Council, the Urban League, and the National Conference of Christians and Jews. In 1958, fifty sticks of dynamite blew up his church, called The Temple. Jacob's wife, Janice, who became an author, and former president of the Southern Jewish Historical Society, labeled the crime as "the Bomb that Healed". False Flag Operations are speckled with terminology and sayings such as this. The Rockefeller's financed the restoration of the church. Jacob was a "close personal friend" of Reverend Martin Luther King Jr. and delivered the eulogy at his funeral.

Sir Evelyn Rothschild, a Knight Bachelor, ran the Paris-based branch in 1968 while Guy went to London. In 1982 he became chairman of Rothschilds Continuation Holdings AG, United Racecourses, The Economist (among other news outlets), and more, while also serving as co-chairman of Rothschild Bank A.G., and director of IBM UK Holdings Ltd. and De Beers Consolidated Mines. He founded EL Rothschild, to help manage Rothschild interests in India. Aside from all of this he was the advisor to Queen Elizabeth II and Governor of London School of Economics and Political Science. He and his wife bought controlling shares of Weather Central in 2011. Weather Central has more than 400 broadcast television clients in 21 countries worldwide. Evelyn stated this, after the purchase:

"As weather becomes more extreme around the planet, with greater human and financial ramifications, we believe that Weather Central will play a major role in mitigating damage and improving lives."

He wasn't talking about your life, but the elite's lives being improved, profiting from nature, and keeping you in the dark. Evelyn died in 2022, leaving sons Anthony and

David to continue the empire. The sons of Guy, David (who married Olimpia Aldobrandini) and Edouard, continue the French side of things. David was involved in the Peñarroya mining company before setting up shop at the bank. In 1967, the bank underwent changes due to French banking regulations, becoming a limited-liability company. After a shift in government, David obtained a new license in 1987, and founded the Rothschild and Cie Banque where Emmanuel Macron worked for some time before being made the Rothschild's President of France. His son Alexandre succeeded him as Chairman of Rothschild and Co, leading the next generation. Meanwhile brother Edouard joined David and cousin Éric to relaunch Rothschild and Cie Banque. In 2005 he invested €20 million in the newspaper Libération, founded by Maoist militant Serge July. In 2010, Edouard moved to Israel and is a member of Le Siecle (a "think tank").

Nathaniel Charles Jacob Rothschild, commonly known as Jacob, is the 4th Baron, member of the Most Excellent Order of the British Empire, Royal Victorian Order, Order of Merit, and numerous societies owned by the family. He owns several oil refineries, mines, and more. His sister Emma is a member of the Most Distinguished Order of Saint Michael and Saint George, has worked as a professor at MIT and is a Fellow of Kings College. Brother Amschel works on his farm and collects cars, leaving Jacob and his children (all Honorables) to keep the family businesses under control. Sir Jacob founded J. Rothschild Capital Management and assisted in merging the French and British branches of the banks, forming the Group Rothschild. In 2017, a plane **and** helicopter collided above Jacob's estate, four people were killed. News was silent on the rest of the story but shortly thereafter **another** plane crashed near the Rothschild residence.

In 2018 Steven Rothschild stabbed his wife to death, resulting in a mere 6-year prison sentence. In the same year, Jacob's son Nathaniel was not charged when his ex-wife, who he met on a beach in India, was found hanging from a doorknob in her bathroom. This is apparently not suspicious. Recently, Pope Francis has formed the Council for Inclusive Capitalism with the Vatican with Lady Lynn Forester de Rothschild. The Council claims to work towards a more "inclusive, sustainable, and trusted economic system", aligned with the UN Sustainable Development Goals, of course. Lynn, wife of Evelyn, includes in her circle of friends such notables as Henry Kissinger and Ghislaine Maxwell. The "guardians" of the Council, a group of influential individuals and foundations, include members of the Rockefeller Foundation, Ford Foundation, DuPont, various vaccine, and drug companies most of which are owned by Bill Gates, and former Bank of England head Mark Carney, among others. This Council is something to watch closely as time continues, though little — if anything — will ever reach public view. To no one's surprise the Rothschild family whose lawyer was supplied to Julian Assange, is also closely involved with the Greta Thunberg scheme, orchestrating the climate change propaganda, and supplying the lawyers and handlers of the child-led movement. As I have already discussed this laughable scam, let's finish with this family.

Another puppet of the family, carrying out the same agendas as before is George Soros. While the Rothschild's put out propaganda through their controlled medias praising the incorruptibility of Ukraine's Ashkenazi transvestite puppet President Volodymyr Zelenskyy, the world should already know by now that it's another repeat of what they did from 1917-1920. In the aftermath of the elite's created Bolshevik Revolution, they engaged bio-warfare in the form of the influenza pandemic, just as we have recently experienced the biowarfare attack called Covid. Rothschild controlled George has done well to activate the racist mentality, forming the Black Lives Matter movement, and taking it worldwide (which doesn't even make sense given the "reason" for the movement) solely to create racism, globally. By 2018, the central banks had begun working towards one, global, digital currency and George was used to spread the word. The Rothschilds own most of the digital currencies and those they didn't create themselves were quickly bought up. The smart grid the UN has installed throughout the world, makes it easy to log, track, locate, and control you entirely, as well as control your finances which are digitalized! As previously mentioned, the UN's smart grid can use frequency to map your entire being, thanks to your bio-acoustic resonance. There is no such thing as safe or secure if it is connected to the internet.

Let's take a peek at this man, George Soros. Born György Schwartz in 1930, he lived through Nazi occupation in, Hungary. His father was a lawyer and made false documents for George, so that the family could survive by claiming to be Christian. His time during the war was spent betraying Jews he had grown up with for money and food. As a Talmudist who hates Jews and Germans alike, he believes only in his own superiority. George has made countless hedge funds including Quantum Fund, Open Society Foundation, Soros Fund Management and more. Before he came to America, he stopped in England to get an education and work for Rothschild banks. By 1992, the British currency had low interest rates and high inflation which George played, eliminating the strength of the currency by short selling. In the same year, he did the same thing to the Italian lira. He has financed climate propaganda, including puppets Greta and Al Gore who have been used to indoctrinate the mindless. George is also co-partners with Rothschild in the London investment group St. James' Place Capital.

After he married healthcare consultant Tamiko Bolton, George increased his interest in health and began working through the Clinton Global Initiative, with the UN, to enable "certain health requirements and mandates world-wide". Another Rothschild relative, Sir James Goldsmith, is also a close friend of CFR member George. While George spread propaganda about Vladimir Putin being a racist, he infiltrated Ukraine and took over the government with the help of Hillary Clinton, establishing their new President. Let's remember in 1994, Menachem Mendel

Schneerson (self-proclaimed messiah) published the agenda which states:

"Our special tactics to combat Slavs is a secret knowledge, because of its exclusivity limited to the god's chosen people. The main weapon of struggle we will direct against the Slavs, except for renegades, "married" with the Jews by common interests. True, all these "married to us" will be withdrawn from our society once we use them for our own purposes. Slavs, and among them Russians - are the most unbending people in the world. Slavs are unbending as a result of their psychological and intellectual abilities, created by many generations of ancestors. It is <u>impossible to alter these genes</u>. Slav, Russian, can be destroyed, but never conquered. That is why this seed is **subject to liquidation**, and, at first, a sharp reduction in their numbers.

Our methods of conquest will not at all be military, but **<u>ideological and economic</u>**, with the use of power structures, armed with the most modern types of armament for the physical suppression of revolt with even greater ferocity than it was done in October 1993 with gunning of the Supreme Council of Soviet Russia. First of all, we will divide the Slavic nations (of 300 million, half of them Russians) into the small countries with weak and severed connections... We will try to pit these countries against each other and suck them into <u>civil wars for the sake of **mutual destruction**</u>. The Ukrainians would think that they are fighting against the expansionist Russia and struggling for their independence. They will think that they have finally gained their freedom, while they become fully subdued by us. The same will be thought by Russians, as though they defend their national interests to return their lands, "illegally" taken away from them, and so on.

We will do all of this under the guise of <u>different sovereignties</u>, the struggle for their national ideals... In this **war of fools**, the Slavic moronic herd will be weakening itself and strengthening us, the main controllers of the chaos, pretending to stand aside, not only without participating in the bloody events, but also without involvement... In the consciousness of the Slavic fools [uninitiated], we will lay such stereotypes of thinking in which the world "anti-Semite" would become the most terrible word. The word "Jew" would be pronounced in a whisper.

We will **scare** the cattle with several court cases [such as the trial of an anti-Semite Ostashvili] and other methods [radio, television, movies]. We will **frighten** the cattle so bad that not a single hair will fall from the head of a Jew, while the Slavs will be shot in packs, destroyed by thousands - on the borders, where the Jews do not serve in peacekeeping forces, via terrorist acts, and via criminal and professional killings [such as the false flags of the Beslan school, the

Moscow subway, and so on].

> Dumb Slavic people do not realize that the worst fascists are those who never and in no place proclaim fascism aloud, but, instead, organize it all supposedly according to the <u>most democratic standards</u>. On the contrary, we will make the very word "fascist" a dirty word. Everyone will be **scared** that we will stick this label to him. We know very well that nationalism strengthens the nation, making it strong. The slogan of "internationalism" is outdated and no longer works as before. We will replace it with "universal human values", which is the same thing. We will not allow any nationalism to evolve. And we will destroy by fire and sword all those nationalist movements that seek to lead people out of our dictate, as it is done in Georgia, Armenia, and Serbia. Instead, we will ensure the full prosperity of <u>**our**</u> nationalism - Zionism, and, more precisely: **Jewish fascism**, which, in its secrecy and power, is super-fascism.
>
> It is not for nothing that in 1975, the UN General Assembly adopted a resolution which defined **Zionism as the most blatant "form of racism and racial discrimination"**, but repealed this resolution in 1992, because of our triumphant march **<u>across</u> the <u>planet</u>**. We have made UN a weapon for our goals of <u>seizing power over 'all kingdoms and nations'</u>."

The obvious scam taking place in Ukraine today is another blaring sign of the ignorance and complacency of the people. The first era to have access to information is the first era where mindlessness abounds. This proves the fact that Information is not Knowledge just as Knowledge is not Wisdom.

In closing this chapter, one must remember the words of William Shakespeare:
> "All the **world**'s a stage, and all the men and women merely players."

~Li~

The Li (Lee) family is much like the others; books have been written about them, exposing their deeds; governments have been created and destroyed at their whim; many have been killed and controlled by the hundreds of lower elites. Today's Asian elite still include the Li aristocrats who have existed as an elite bloodline since the beginning of the population of that region. Having followed the descendants of Noah's son Ham to the area thousands of years ago, the Li lineage has grown through the dynasties and are hereditary members of the Knight Orders of KMT, the Illuminati sect of China, and much more. As seen in all other bloodlines, the family members, for generations, have worked in similar positions and have held hereditary titles and roles. Being a member of one of the elite Li families means selling opium, organizing gambling, taxing prostitution, running the White Dragon Society, dealing in organ and human trafficking (especially children), and printing their own money on duplicating machines. Just as the Rothschilds own the America's and Europe, the Li's own Asia. Typically, I begin with either a prominent or current member of the family to get us into the mood. However, this time, I'd like to save that for last, as the current Li's have been instrumental in the Covid Plan and that topic will lead us seamlessly into our next chapter! So, let's go back to the beginning and work our way up.

As we explored in early chapters, Hams descendants called Sinites inhabited the Asian region, after the flood. Just as the Romans and Egyptians described the giants whom they worshipped as gods and detailed their genealogy back to Noah, we see the similarities in Asia's documentation as well. In Ancient Chinese texts, such as the Shu Jing, an ark housed 8 people who began to repopulate the earth after the flood. Asian genealogy details their ancestors' lines back to Noah in their histories. Genetic studies verify history once again, showing that today 97.4% of China's genetic make-up is from Africa. Aren't we all... The tribe of Shinar was noted as being wicked for building a city and tower in the land of Shinar (Sinar) which was the Tower of Nimrod. After the curse at Nimrod's tower the peoples had dispersed, and I detailed several lines that migrated further east in Part I. They, like the Babylonians and Egyptians, worshipped their ancestors, practiced magic and witchcraft, and wore colorful clothing and jewels. Those who decided to forego the nomadic life settled in the region of the Yellow and Yangtze Rivers. The Li family grew in number until they were divided into tribes under separate leaders, known as the Nine Li, or Jiuli. They implemented a penal law code and were governed by shamans (sorcerers). They fought with the Yellow and Red Emperors of the Yellow River plains. They continued causing trouble amongst themselves and outside tribes and kingdoms until they splintered into the Zhou Dynasty and various tribes of the

Central Plain.

From roughly 2070 BC to 1600 BC the Xia dynasty ruled, according to archaeological finds and texts. Before then was the time entitled 3 Sovereigns and 5 Emperors, in Chinese texts. Like all other cultures the Sovereigns are deified hybrids, giants - what the Romans and Egyptians called Demigods. Similarly, the humans who ruled were deified and assigned attributes and skills they did not possess, so they could be worshipped by those in their clans. Today the Chinese culture, and several other Asian countries consider their ruler to be a god, and worship and blindly follow them according to their very long and unchanged traditions. This is why many regions have hundreds of gods and goddesses in their historical or current day rituals. After the hybrids died, the remaining line was founded by Si Yu the Great. Yu, like Nimrod, had been active in defending against floods. While Nimrod had built his tower to reach heaven and wage war, Yu went with the ideas of building canals and systems to control and route the water, should the world be flooded again. In this time there were many local floods and because of his success in controlling the waters, the region prospered, and Yu was named the next ruler. After establishing the first Dynastic rule through his son and heir, he died of an illness on Mount Kuaiji, where he had lived all his life. This was not yet the Li line we know today, rather they were the rulers, while the Li family were the aristocracy and military leaders. Over the generations of the Xia Dynasty much blood was shed, building up to the reign of the final Emperor of the Xia Dynasty, Jie. Jie reigned from 1728 until 1675 BC. He was well known as a tyrant and a violent womanizer. His many slaves were treated cruelly while Jie lived a life of excessive luxury. This is another "tradition" that hadn't been eradicated in that region yet. After years of beheading anyone who displeased him, his enemies grew. Finally, Zi Lu, known as Cheng Tang, had built an army in Shang that was growing in number. City after city was taken by the Shang. Jie fled but was apprehended quickly and exiled in Nanchao where he died of an illness. Thus began the Shang Dynasty.

This Dynasty lasted until 1050 BC and focused on the education and advancement of Astronomy and Math. The Shang also began keeping written historical records and logs which were etched into animal bones and kept by the oracles (the true rulers). The Li family members continued to thrive as officers, warriors, and upper political positions throughout this dynasty and the next. Archeological finds throughout China dating back to this time period include gold masks and scepters, bronze statues and molds of peoples' faces, elephant tusks, oracle bones, weapons for giants as well as giant burial grounds. Among other large finds was a bronze tree statue which was discovered that stood 4 meters tall.

In 1046 BC the Zhou dynasty had come into power and formed the Mandate of Heaven. The concept of the Mandate of Heaven has been a fundamental part of the

Chinese system which had now, thanks to the Zhou, become the same political-religious system as existed in Rome, Persia, and Egypt before. It was used to "legitimize" the succession of the emperors holding the idea that heaven would provide signs of its support for a particular ruler, such as good harvests, peace, and prosperity, while the lack of these signs would indicate that the ruler had lost the Mandate of Heaven. This concept also emphasized the idea that the ruler was responsible for the welfare of the people and was expected to govern with compassion and justice. While the grand majority of leaders have been corrupted and violent, as is typical of anyone given power, the values of the Chinese culture which survived to this time period were respect for ancestors and each other, honesty, and loyalty to the state. Archaeological sites confirm the religious importance of this day and large mountaintop religious sites have been excavated. Daily life involved ritual religious practices, as Roman, Persian, and Egyptian cultures had implemented. The political system developed during the Zhou Dynasty is held in China today. Music was also developed and considered a highly important subject to learn. During the Zhou Dynasty all of the famous philosophers were born including Confucius, Mo Ti, Lao-Tzu and Sun-Tzu. The skills and techniques developed during this time-period were used in all Dynasties from that time forward. This was the renaissance of Asia.

After the Zhou kingdom splintered and the states became independent, they began fighting amongst themselves forming what is called the Warring States Period. This era is reminiscent of Britain's Robber Barons time, when titles were thrown around and everyone was grasping for power. The States were Chu, Han, Qi, Qin, Wei, Yan, and Zhao. Around 600 BC, the Longxi branch of the Li line produced a famous member the Taoist sage Li Er also known as Li Dan or Laozi (Lao Tsu et al). Er became the royal archivist for the Zhou court which included the membership of Confucius, one of the aristocrats, as one would expect. Confucius was impressed by Li Er's philosophy of Tao and soon Er wrote it down in the Tao Te Ching. After years of passing around his ideas, he retired to the western mountains and lived as a hermit until he died. Lao Tsu's son, Li Zong, became a general of the Wei State and was granted Duangan as his fiefdom.

Over the next generations, the elite families began to formulate a story of the 8 Immortals. 8 people were given the title of Immortal over several hundred years. Coincidentally those people were bloodline elite, used in the same way the other families have used certain members to control an agenda. As in most other situations, the agenda was immortality and worship of men. Li Xuan was sainted, immortalized, deified, and consequently named Li Tieguai. The others were named He Xiangu, Cao Guojiu, Lan Caihe, Lu Dongbin, Han Xiangzi, Zhang Guolao, and Zhongli Quan, as they came about. The title was given to them due to their advanced abilities in sorcery through Taoism. Each of them was then assigned skills and deified. Li Xuan was a pupil of his relative Li Er (Lao Tsu) and was described as being mentally unstable, often depicted with a dirty face and messy hair and beard. Li Xuan lived in a cave for many months in the early stages as a sage of Er. It is said that Er tempted his pupil by carving the female figure out of a piece of wood. Apparently, Xuan was not deceived or tempted by this… Passing the test with victory, Er then revealed his trickery and congratulated Xuan on his self-control. There were **many** other "deceptions" that Er put Xuan through, and each time Xuan succeeded, he was given a "magic" pill.

In elite history, regardless of the family line, you will find endless evidence of ritual abuse and drugs that are regularly used by the family during the upbringing of their children in order to split their minds and control them. This is why few elites ever stop the things set in place for them to accomplish, they are totally under control. As the story goes, these pills gave Li Xuan the ability to never be hungry or ill and gave him the added gift of flight. As a god in the Taoist pantheon, Xuan is associated with medicine, because he was always popping pills… The Li family are involved in pharmacology to this day. Vases, paintings, carvings and more depict the 8 Immortals that were alive and died between the time of Li Er and the Tang Dynasty. None of them lived for that entire time period, and all have died, not to return. Nevertheless, let's continue following the genealogy here and see what else we can find in this very long line of military men, opium addicts, and politicians.

During this time literature and art expanded and another Li family philosopher, Li Kui, was born.
Around the late 400's BC, Kui was born in the state of Wei. He grew up studying famous legalist philosophers such as Han Fei and Shen Buhai. Unsurprisingly, he went into the same line of work. He was a strong believer in the power of the law to regulate human behavior and to prevent crime, and he believed that rulers should be absolute in their power and use fear and punishment to maintain control. Sound familiar? The book he wrote, Li Kui's Book of Law, was widely read and respected during his time. In his book, Kui argued that rulers should establish strict laws that would be enforced without exception, and that punishments should be severe and swift in order to deter crime. He believed that the people would be naturally inclined to obey the law if they feared the consequences of breaking it. The typical elite mentality: <u>Control through Fear.</u> His philosophy was embraced by those in power for generations.

In 280 BC the Li family tree produced Li Si, another legalist philosopher. Born in the Li hometown of Wei, he grew up a disciple of his grandfather Li Kui. Si worked as the Prime Minister of the Qin dynasty. In 221 BC, Qin Shi Huang had risen in power and conquered the independent states, forming another Dynastic Empire he named after himself. Si was instrumental in the formation of the central government and was responsible for the creation of the legal code of the Qin dynasty as well as forming the bureaucracy that would support the Emperor from that time on. Today it is called the Politburo. Eager to implement the policies of the First Emperor, he burned a multitude of books and slaughtered scholars he didn't agree with. Under Si's guidance, the Qin dynasty created a unified legal code that was violently enforced throughout the empire.

Si became notorious for his controversial views on censorship and intellectual freedom and advocated for the suppression of dissent. After the Emperor Qin had died, Li Si and his chief eunuch Zhao Gao decided to place who they wished on the throne, instead of the rightful heir, Fusu. Li Si was able to manipulate Fusu into committing suicide (so the story goes) and placed Qin Er Shi on the throne of the Qin Empire. It is interesting to note that throughout China's history thousands have been forced to commit suicide, or at least their histories are written to convince us of that, just like the histories of the Papal States and Egypt.

Overcome with ambition, Zhao Gao betrayed Si and charged him with treason. In 208 BC, Si's sentence of Five Punishments was carried out, according to the centuries old law. The Five Punishments were Mo - face or forehead tattooing; Yi – removal of the nose; Yue – amputation of one or both feet; Gong – castration; Da Pi – execution by quartering, boiling alive, beheading, strangulation or other. Sadly, Li Si was given "other" for this final punishment and was murdered by being severed in half at the waist in the public market. His family to the 3rd degree were also slaughtered. His son, Li Yu, was able to escape and continued his legacy. Such was the occupation and lifestyle of the Li family through to the Han Dynasty.

By now Vietnam was inhabited by the Dongson tribe whose artifacts have been discovered throughout Indonesia and the Philippines as well. A few dynasties had come and gone, and 5 tribes had joined together under the leader of the Qin, to unite China as an Empire. At this time, the Qin military was led by General Li Xin. Xins father was Li Yao, the governor of Nanjun. Xin was instrumental in the fall of the Zhao, as the military leader who took Handan in 228 BC. He was quite famous in many battles and wars ordered by the Qin rulers.

Unfortunately, Li Xin had a habit of taking too few men into battle and having his armies massacred. Regardless of his many failures as a military man, he was given the title of Marquis of Longxi upon his retirement. Xin was the great-great grandfather of Li Guang, whom I will discuss momentarily. As the family had always been the elite of the region you will find many things holding the name of Li. Archeological finds have uncovered the Li Village, outside of Kao-yi and just south of West Fengssu. Fengsuu was used as the Li family burial ground for generations because they had founded the territory of East and West Fengsuu. One of the names of the Li tribes, Longxi, was given to the Longxi County in Gansu, China. In 214 BC, the Li River became home to the Lingqu Canal, which joins the Xiang and Li River's opening passage from Xian, Guangzhou, and Shanghai. In the same year the

Great Wall of China began to be built, using forced labor and violence, to keep out the war-loving Huns. At this time, 460 scholars and philosophers were killed, and many were forced to work on the Great Wall. During the Sui Dynasty the Li's began to call themselves the Han. Let's take a look at the formation of the Han Dynasty!

In 268 BC Li Yiji, was born in Gaoyang, Chenliu and grew to become a well-known general. When he was old enough, he joined Liu Bang, the Duke of Pei, to rebel against the Qin dynasty. Liu Bang and Yiji became good friends and since Yiji had been born and raised in Chenliu, Liu Bang extracted all the information he could about the province in order to conquer it. Yiji suggested a diplomatic act and attempted to persuade the magistrate of Chenliu to surrender. Upon his refusal, the magistrate was killed, and the Qin fled. After the retreat of the Qin, 10,000 men from the province joined Liu Bang. Over the next decades, aside from being a trusted advisor to the Duke, Yiji had many military successes against the Xiongnu, which made him quite famous in the region. The Xiongnu were a confederation of nomadic tribes, of Mongolian and Chinese, known as the Modu Shanyu. In 209 BC they became so powerful that the Xiongnu Empire was founded. While Li Yiji was growing up, the Xiongnu were in constant battles against the Dynasties. On the other hand, the Dynastic kingdoms themselves were full of internal wars and attempted rebellions from those of the previous ruling bloodlines who felt they had a right to rule.

In 204 BC the Chu and the Han were at war. Yiji worked diligently to talk Liu Bang into forming the independent states, as it was before. This would ensure Liu Bang his rightful throne and kingdom. However, Liu Bang decided against it. Yiji then volunteered to negotiate surrender from the Qi kingdom and travelled there to discuss the matter. King Tian Guang of the Qi agreed to serve Liu Bang, and all was well. Unfortunately, Li Yiji's military leader, Han Xin, had grown jealous of Yiji's fame over the years. If there was not a victorious battle in Qi, Han Xin would once again be standing behind Yiji who would get the praise for his diplomacy. Han Xin decided that he deserved recognition and blood. He ordered the army to invade. They crossed the Yellow River and destroyed their startled new allies. Because of this betrayal, King Tian had Yiji boiled alive. A couple of years later Liu Bang was made Emperor of the newly formed Han Dynasty. He gave Yiji's son Li Jie the title of Marquis of Gaoliang, with all properties and powers included. Finally, the Li family had risen from the leading military ranks to the titled upper class. Yiji's brother, Li Shang, who had also been a military general, was given the titles and powers of Marquis of Quzhou.

The Li family was part of the royal court during the reign of Emperor Ching (Jing) as well, in the 180's BC. His wife was a Taoist and religious rituals were increased. Both the Emperor and the Empress performed rituals to communicate with spirits. Enter Li Shao-Chiin (also Chun). One of the classic alchemist Li's, he implored the

Emperor to worship his fireplace and instructed him how to achieve immortality through diet. Shao-Chiin was an expert in magical arts and was immediately brought into the Emperors inner circle. His popularity grew and because he never divulged personal details about himself, the cult of Shao spread like wildfire. People far and wide knew of him, sent him clothes, food, money and more. People believed that he was able to control spirits and keep himself from aging, simply because he said he could. His friends included marquis and other higher aristocracy, as all Li members. To solidify his claims, he told the Emperor that one of his bronze vessels was from 676 BC and belonged to Duke Huan. When the Emperor deciphered the engraved writings on the vessel, he found this to be true and believed that it proved Li Shao was an ancient spirit. The Records of the Grand Historian, by Shiji, details:

> "Li Shao-chiin then advised the emperor, 'If you sacrifice to the fireplace, you can call the spirits to you, and if the spirits come you can transform cinnabar into gold. Using this gold, you may make drinking and eating vessels which will prolong the years of your life. With prolonged life you may visit the immortals who live on the island of P'eng-lai in the middle of the sea. If you visit them and perform the Feng and Shan sacrifices, you will never die. This is what the Yellow Emperor did. Once I wandered by the sea and visited Master An-ch'i, and he fed me jujubes as big as melons.' 'Master An-ch'i is an immortal who roams about P'cng-lai. If he takes a liking to someone, he will come to meet him, but if not, he will hide.'"

The Emperor did as Shao instructed and soon thereafter Shao became ill and died. This did not stop the people, including the Emperor himself, from continuing his rituals and believing in his immortality.

Li Shang's son, Li Guang was born in the 180's BC. A son of the Marquis, and grandson of Li Xin, he grew up in the center of the military and political leaders of the region, surrounded by the entitled. He joined the army as soon as he could and fought against the Huns. 9 years later he was promoted to General of the Calvary and ordered to protect Emperor Jing. He excelled in tactics and archery and became known as The Flying General by his enemies. He was in constant war with the Xiongnu tribe of the north. His defense abilities were known far and wide, which caused many to think twice before attacking his territories. Even the opposing Emperor Wen respected him and stated that he would have given lands and money to Guang, had he not been born on the "other" side. Although he was a caring and highly esteemed general in his lifetime, he had one major problem which resulted in his untimely death. He had no sense of direction! In the battle at Yanmen, in 129 BC, he narrowly escaped capture while his army was annihilated. He was stripped of official titles and demoted.

9 years later Guang and one of his 3 sons, Li Gan, were surrounded again and had to be rescued. Emperor Wu, having secretly ordered Commander Wei Qing not to

assign important missions to Guang, was enraged. One day 3 Hun riders snuck into town and killed some guards. Guang took 100 of his soldiers and in all haste rode after them. After killing 2 Huns, he tied the last one to his horse. Suddenly, thousands of Huns appeared! Guang was too far from the city to expect help. He told his frightened soldiers to remain calm and pretend to be decoys. They slowly began to ride towards the Hun. When they were within one kilometer of the Huns, they all dismounted and made it seem as though they were setting up camp. The confused Huns decided they must be waiting to ambush during the night and went home.

In 119 BC, Guang and his army were on their way through the desert to the Battle of Mobei. Once again, he got lost in the desert and arrived late to the fight. Because the battle had been planned down to the minute, his tardiness caused a gap in the encirclement, which allowed the Yizhixie Chanyu to escape. Because of his epic blunder at Mobei, Guang was going to be court martialed and humiliated. Instead, he committed suicide. Enraged by the death of his father, Gan barged into Wei's tent and beat him up. Shortly thereafter, Li Gan was shot in the back by Wei's cousin General Huo. Emperor Wu was with Huo at this time, but no consequences came from the assassination since Wu, Huo, and Wei were all related. If I had written more chapters about the Asian elite bloodlines, you would see them intertwine just as the European bloodlines do! For instance, during this time, genealogy records detail that the rulers of the Yu bloodline in China married with the women of the Li bloodline. At one time they were even more closely related. It's **all** in the family.

Other Li members during this time include Li Zhong, a general who served the Han dynasty and was appointed as the governor of the Sichuan province, and Li Ling, the grandson of Guang. Ling was born in Longxi. Like his grandfather, he was an avid archer and from a young age he had the eye of Emperor Wu. The Emperor made Ling the new Imperial Servant, a very public position. He was then assigned to the military and placed on the Xiongnu border. The young officer led 800 men and went on reconnaissance missions. His leadership skills impressed Wu, who then promoted him to Calvary Commander. Now young Ling was in command over 5,000 elite soldiers as well as the local reserve forces in Jiuquan and Zhangye. Soon Ling was made an escort for higher-level generals, including his cousin Li Guangli who was Emperor Wu's uncle. Emperor Wu had many wives and concubines, like his father before him. Wu's mother was Lady Li Fu-jen. Lady Li's brother, Li Yannian was a famous musician, composer, and singer for the Princess. He became a minister to the Emperor and impressed the court with his musical knowledge and skill. Because of his abilities to persuade, he was able to influence the Emperor to enact ancient ritual worship once again.

Finally, Ling was gaining real military roles and was sent to conquer the Chanyu's army which he had boasted he could do. The Chanyu was the Khagan/King of the Xiongnu. On one fateful mission, Ling found himself and his 5,000 men surrounded by 30,000 horsemen. Since he had not sent for reinforcements, Ling was trapped and ordered his men to circle the wagons and take cover. The Han arrows flew and the Xiongnu were massacred. The Xiongnu were able to call for reinforcements, unlike Ling, and 80,000 more soldiers came to the battle. Ling retreated and upon seeing his soldiers so defeated in spirit and body, he killed the women (called camp followers) who served as cooks and cleaners for the army. Apparently seeing the slaughter of the women who cared for them was enough to give the little soldiers back their fighting spirit. The next day his men killed 3,000 Xiongnu warriors. The next week was spent retreating and attacking, through the swamp and fires and forest. Believing that Ling was leading them back to the border, the Xiongnu continued to pursue. One of Ling's men defected to the Chanyu and told them that Ling had no reinforcements or supplies and the Chanyu was humiliated to not have been able to defeat him yet. Days of bloodshed followed as the enraged Xiongnu chased the Han soldiers, crushing them with boulders when they were trapped in the valley. In one day, Ling and his men fired 500,000 arrows at their enemy. Ling and his men were equipped with crossbows that could fire multiple arrows at a time. Ling's men had been whittled down to 400 when he decided they were defeated. He gave each man some food and they broke the wagons into weapons and scattered in the night. Ling surrendered to the Xiongnu. Upon hearing this news, the Emperor was incensed, and Li Ling was condemned as a traitor, and his family was executed. Li Ling was accepted into the Xiongnu and given a position as military trainer and a new name: Li Shaoqing. The Chanyu gave his daughter Tuoba to Li and granted him the title Lord Youxiao, a high position in their governmental structure.

In 90 BC the Xiongnu invaded Han territory. Li Ling's cousin, Li Guangli, led 70,000 men in the army against the Xiongnu. Ling was sent to attack a regiment of 30,000 with the same number of men. The battle went on for 9 days before Ling had to retreat due to heavy casualties. Li Guangli defected to the Xiongnu, causing more of the family to be executed. Lady Li would have been killed as well, but she had died a few years before from a long illness. Several more members of the Li family defected to the Xiongnu over the years, and more of the Han military officers had also defected. After Emperor Wu had died, Ling was contacted by several of his high-office Han friends, attempting to bring him back to the empire. He refused each time, not wanting to be shamed. He died of an illness in 74 BC and his descendants went on to become the Khagan bloodline of the Yenisei Kirghiz as well as the tribe of Tuoba.

The Qin Dynasty had accomplished the building of the bloody Great Wall of China to keep its many enemies at bay. Now, the Han Dynasty was forming the Silk Road trade route from Asia to the Mediterranean and Eastern Africa and Confucianism became the religion of the empire. The Li family had risen in the ranks, holding fast to the upper crust in the Han Dynasty.

Li Jue (also known as Zhiran) died in 198 AD. At first, he was the military leader under Han ruler Dong Zhuo. He was one of the earliest recruits for Dong Zhuo's army and tasked with containing the warlords of the east and protecting the Liang Province. In March of 184 Jue helped to suppress what was called the Yellow Turban Rebellion. This began because the peasants were angry about the greed of the eunuchs, who manipulated the Emperor to become more wealthy and powerful themselves. As their greed grew, the peasants paid the price with plagues, famines, and floods. Taoist master, faith healer, sorcerer and sect leader, Zhang Jue, became the leader of the rebellion, sending his disciples through the empire to gain supporters. When news of the plan to revolt in April reached the Han government, hundreds of supporters were arrested and executed. Zhang Jue had no choice but to begin his revolution earlier than planned with his 360,000 followers. They were called to put on their yellow turbans and march on their government. Villages and their government offices were plundered and within a few days the rebellion had engulfed China. By the next year most of the rebels had been slaughtered and the rest were forced to scatter. The Yellow Turbans rose again, sporadically, but never achieved victory.

By winter of 184, Li Jue had continued on to serve in squashing another rebellion, in Liang Province. Two groups of Qiang people took the opportunity the Yellow Turbans created to revolt as well. The Han leaders had been taken by surprise at how large and powerful the Yellow Turbans were, and how quickly they had been able to take over. With the army being so spread out across the empire, the Qiang jumped at the chance to mutiny. Many Qiang were in the military, which enabled them to kill the commanding officers and take over several towns. Li Wenhou and Beigong Boyu were appointed their leaders. In the spring, they marched on the Han capital of Chang'an (Xi'an). The people demanded their own territory, not under the control of the central government. Naturally, they were denied. They did manage to keep the region they had conquered on the upper Yellow River. Over the next year many died and were killed off, including Li Wenhou and Beigong Boyu. In 187 the inspector of Liang Province, Geng Bi, reclaimed the Longxi commandery which was lost when Grand Administrator Li Can defected. Mutiny broke out again and Geng Bi was killed.

Meanwhile, Dong Zhuo had been assassinated by Lu Bu and Li Su under the orders of Wang Yun. Wang Yun was the typical politician and had been working on the assassination plan for some time. He worked in shadows, under the noses of 3 Han Emperors and carried out many conspiracies against certain people so that he could maintain his position. Li Jue along with the other 3 advisors to Dong Zhuo, begged Wang Yun for mercy. Because they were the closest people to Dong Zhuo they were planning to flee when Jue decided to attack the crumbling city of Chang'an.

After the coup and Dong Zhuo's assassination, they were in the best position to take over. They formed an army of several thousand men and attacked the district of Chang'an. Wang Yun sent two of his military leaders to the Liang Province but on the way one of them was killed and the other decided he and his troops would join Jue's army. The residents of Liang Province also joined the army against Wang Yun which raised their numbers to well over 100,000 by the time the capital was surrounded. After 8 days Lu Bu's army rebelled and opened the gates for Jue's followers, and the siege was over.

The people of Liang were so exuberant that during their looting of the capital that more than 10,000 people were killed. Wang Yun was forced to surrender and was killed, and Emperor Xian was taken hostage. The men became greedy and ordered the Emperor to give them many titles. In 194 a local warlord named Ma Teng began a rebellion in Mei County. After this had built up and several leaders had attempted to reason with Ma Teng, Jue sent his nephew Li Li, as well as Guo Si and Fan Chou to dissolve the situation. Unfortunately, the Li's were defeated with over 10,000 dead. Jue knew the rebels would soon be out of food and ordered Fan Chou to eliminate them now. Fan Chou was friends with one of the rebel leaders and refused to carry out his orders to attack. In March 195, after learning of this, Jue threw a party for his officers. During the feast Fan Chou was openly executed. After this evening meal the Emperor and closest friends of Jue were afraid of him. By the end of his blood-soaked legacy, Li Jue was betrayed by his right-hand man and butchered along with his entire family in the summer of 198 AD.

Other military leaders who appeared during this time, as the Han Dynasty crumbled, include Li Dian, Li Meng, Li Kan, and Li Tong. Li Dian's uncle was Li Qian. Qian had an empire in business and was a powerful man of the Chengshi region. Both Dian and Qian assisted in suppressing the Yellow Turbans and after their victory, continued in the military field. Qian was sent to gain more support for the warlord Cao Cao from his hometown of Chengshi but while there, Lu Bu attempted to convince him to defect. Unfortunately, Qian refused and was killed by Lu Bu. Qians son, Li Zheng, took command of his father's soldiers and slaughtered Lu Bu and his followers. While Zheng and Dian had active military lives, so did Dian's cousin Tong, who became a military general for Cao Cao. After defeating Guan Cheng, Li Dian was promoted to General Who Captures Barbarians and received the title Marquis of a Chief Village. As Marquis he had 300 households under his authority. In addition, 3,000 of his family and supporters were then relocated from Chengshi to Ye. After Zheng died, Dian was appointed Prefect of Yingyin and General of the Household. Dian died suddenly at the age of 36, but his titles, wealth, and positions were now hereditary. His eldest son Li Zhen became the Marquis with all houses and lands included. His cousin, Tong had also been given titles for his loyal work, including Administrator of Runan, Marquis of the Chief Village, Marquis who Acquires Merit and General of the Household who Inspires Might.

This brings us up to the time known as the Three Kingdoms. The Han Dynasty had crumbled and many warlords (the equivalent to Dukes or Princes at that time, through blood) had begun to rise in power and go to war with each other, resulting in the formation of three states: Cao Wei, Shu Han, and Wu. The state of Wei formed in 220 AD and after a couple of short decades, the states' constant attacks on one another allowed the other powers to take them over one by one. Millions were killed during these 50 or so years. The Li family were members of the Shu Han state. Li Yan served Liu Bei as Administrator of Jianwei and General of Initiating Career by 222 AD. Yan was involved in multiple revolts and rebellions. For his bravery and tact during these times he was given the title General Who Assists Han. Liu Bei appointed Yan to be the Central Commandant, in charge of all the military in Shu. Zhuge Liang became the next ruler of Shu and did not listen to Yan as much as Liu Bei had. Much of Yan's advice over the years that followed fell on deaf ears. To compensate for this, Zhuge Liang named Li Feng (Yan's son) as the next eastern commander, after Yan. After being thrown around the region on tasks he didn't want or approve of, Li Yan was unable to provide supplies to a military camp of Zhuge's and tried to cover it up. Unfortunately, the misleading letters Yan had sent were saved by Zhuge who exposed him publicly. Li Yan was immediately stripped of all titles and exiled to Zitong. After hearing of Zhuge Liang's death in 234, Yan became ill and died. His son Li Feng went on to become a general with a long military career. Other Li's of the Shu State include General Li Sheng, General Li Miao and Li Hui. Hui's titles include the Inspector in Jianning Commandery, Assistant Office of Merit and Registrar, Assisting Officer to Liu Bei and Marquis of Hanxing, among others. Hui had seen the inevitable defeat of Liu Zhang and defected to Liu Bei. Liu Bei and Zhuge Liang were respected by Li Hui, and he accepted important positions during their administrations. Because of his military valor, Hui was appointed Governor of a new region and his nephew, Li Qiu, became the Right Commander of Imperial Bodyguard for Liu Shan.

Lady Li, also called Lishi, was born in Jiangyou in the Shu Han state. She married the Governor Ma Miao and is most known for her actions during the Conquest of Shu by Wei. Ma Miao had a more laid-back view on war and when the Wei began to attack his city he didn't take it seriously. Lady Li took matters into her own hands, as women must, and raised the morale of the troops, leading them to defend the city. As soon as the Wei army had broken the lines and entered the city, Miao ran to their leader, Deng Ai, and threw himself on the ground, begging for mercy and claiming surrender. Lady Li hung herself for shame of living with a coward and a traitor, proving her loyalty to the Shu Han state. Deng stopped the attacks to honor her and wrote a poem which states:

"When the Ruler of Shu had wandered from the way, and the House of Han fell lower, Heaven sent Deng Ai to smite the land. Then did a woman show herself most noble, so noble in conduct that no leader equaled her."

Thus, the State of Shu Han fell.

The Li Yan mentioned earlier had several sons who continued the line for a few generations until 351 AD, where we find the son of Li Chang: Li Gao, called Li Hao, also called Prince Wuzhao, after his death. Li Gao is a direct descendant of the Hans famous military leader General Li Guang. The Hans, who had at first agreed to the rule of their cousins, the Qin, overthrew them and took control of China. Gao studied the military teachings of Sun Tzu (Sunzi) and was quite the intellectual and expert in military tactics. When Prince Duan Ye decided to break from the kingdom of Later Liang, forming Northern Liang, Gao became one of his county magistrates. Because of his popularity, Gao took over as governor when his predecessor died in 400. As a higher-ranking official in the Northern Liang kingdom, his desire to have his own dominion to rule grew. Hearing of his ambition, Duan Ye replaced him with snitch Suo Si. Suo Si, one of Li Gao's friends, had told Duan Ye of a prophecy which told that Gao would become ruler of his own kingdom. Using his military skills Gao sent messengers to pay respects to Suo and, once he had let down his guard, to attack.

Suo Si fled back to the capital. Gao's anger over the betrayal of a friend grew into a rage and he demanded that the Prince allow Suo to be executed. Unfortunately, Suo was not well liked, and many urged Duan to have him executed, so he was. Soon after, Li Gao was given the title of Duke of Liang, and established Western Liang. He formed Dunhuang into his capital. In 401, Later Liang went to war with Later Qin. Prince Duan Ye was killed, and the Northern Liang city called Jiuquan was absorbed into Gao's Western Liang. Gao became a vassal to the Later Qin kingdom. In 404 Gao's heir, Li Tan died, making his younger brother Li Xin the new heir. In the next year Gao gave himself additional honorific titles and sent messengers to the Jin Empire to request becoming a vassal to them. Soon Gao had entered into a peace treaty with Southern Liang's prince Tufa Rutan. After 3 years, he had received no response from the Jin Empire, so more messengers were sent! In 410, Gao's heir was captured in battle. Gao ransomed him with silver and gold, but surprise attacks continued throughout the region. As soon as they would agree on peace, one side or the other would exit the meeting and declare war on a capital. Gao was able to enjoy many battles and wars, in which to hone his military tactics. In 417 he became ill, and entrusted the young heir, Li Xin, to his brother Song Yao. After his death, Gao was given the title of Prince. His 8 surviving children included the Marquess Mu of Xinxiang, Li Rang. The kingdom of Western Liang lasted 21 short years, but the bloodline continued on, growing to become the Tang Dynasty.

In 618 the Li family, under the Tang dynasty, seized power creating the decline and collapse of the Sui Empire. The Emperor and founder of the Tang dynasty was Li Yuan, born in 566, the 7th generation descendant of Li Gao. Growing up in the Sui

Dynasty, as a member of the upper class, he had inherited the title Duke of Tang, and was made Governor of Shanxi. In 617 the Sui Dynasty began to fall apart, and Yuan was urged by his son, Li Shimin, to join the rebellion. By the following year, Yuan had titled himself Great Chancellor followed promptly by Emperor. His wives were Lady Dou and Princess Xiangyang. Altogether, Yuan had 19 wives in his harem and a multitude of children. His son, Li Shimin, was now Prince of Qin and when his father died, Shimin gave him the title of Emperor Gaozu (founder). Son Li Jiancheng was named crown prince and Li Yuanji became Prince of Qi. When Yuan took power, several others rose against him as one would imagine. One of his rivals was Li Gui, a warlord of Liang. Gui had a short and ambitious rule. In 617 he gathered the chiefs of his region and together they attacked the crumbling Sui. He gave himself the title of Great Prince of Liang West of the River. Reading through all of these histories and seeing how meaningless titles truly are, I think I will give myself one too, at some point. What would your titles be?

Moving right along...

Gui was warring with various entities on the river and Yuan was making himself Emperor, so in the spring of 618 they attempted an alliance. Gui sent his brother Li Mao to meet with Yuan. Yuan decided to name Gui the Prince of Liang but before he could, Gui took the title of Emperor of Liang and crowned his son Li Boyu as Prince. Gui's brazenness allowed the other chiefs of his region to get more powerful and cocky themselves. Soon his son, Li Zhongyan accused one of them of being a traitor, because Zhongyan was offended by him. When Zhongyan told his father of the treasonous chief, Gui had the man poisoned to death. Gui was naturally involved with sorcerers, as rulers were then and are to this day. One of his sorcerers told him that a goddess would come to him soon. Gui built a tower for her, while his citizens starved because of famine. His decision not to waste food on the weak made him quite unpopular as did his extravagance. The very next year Gui was executed along with his sons and brothers for refusing to submit to Emperor Gaozu (Yuan). Gui wasn't the only chief that Yuan had to face in a battle. Ever since he took the throne for himself, everyone who had an army attempted to take a piece of the cake.

Around 620 Prince of Xia, Dou Jiande, attacked Hebei and Henan, two major cities who had just submitted to Yuan. He kidnapped Yuan's cousin Prince Li Shentong, the Princess Tong'an, and Uncle Li Gai (Li Mi's father). Li Mi surrendered his army when he heard about his father's capture. General Li Shanghu surrendered as well, and the pair plotted against Dou. Regrettably, their plan was discovered and Shuanghu was killed. Mi was able to escape back to Tang. Back and forth it went. When Dou had had his fill of battle Li Zitong stepped in and began taking over territories in Tang. Emperor Yuan killed Dou, resulting in Dou's general retaliating. Ambush after ambush and one more assassination attempt after that, Li Shinim was successful in executing his rivals and their sons. Once the region was reasonably secure, Yuan passed the throne to his son and Shinim became the next Emperor Taizong of Tang. Yuan died in the spring of 635.

Yuan's daughter, Princess Pingyang, was Shinim's elder sister. Pingyang was said to be equally as skillful as her father and became the first female General of the Tang Dynasty. She married Duke Chai Shao. In 617, her father sent her a letter warning her to escape the city she was in, as he would be overthrowing it soon. Chai Shao and Pingyang separated to escape more easily, and Chai met up with her brothers while she was trapped in the city. Proving once again that women are never helpless, she gave away her wealth and bought the loyalty of many men. Rebel leaders joined her in what became known as the Army of the Lady. She went on to have 2 sons and died in March of 623. She had the funeral of a military General, fitting her legacy, complete with a band.

Her brother, Emperor Taizong (Li Shinim) was now on the throne. He had already assassinated two of his brothers who would have contended the title. The first thing he did was to send the concubines home and made his wife, Zhangsun, the Empress and their son, Chengqian, the Crown Prince. The Eastern Turks were still invading and attempting to build up rebellions but in 626 he was able to appease them with titles and land. As Emperor he was unafraid of change and paid close attention to the rumors and writings of his subjects, implementing changes whenever necessary. He demoted many of his trusted advisors while advancing those who would have been his enemies. He rewarded criticism and was open to new ideas. In his book Emperor's Preface to the Sacred Teachings, he dissected Taoist and Buddhist religions. Monasteries were built, as well as monuments. He forced those who plotted behind his back to commit suicide. After the death of his father, Li Chenqian was placed in charge, while Li Shinim took 2 months off for mourning.

Thereafter, Chenqian oversaw minor matters. After the death of his wife things changed for Shinim. In 637 he attempted to recreate the system of feudalism he had worked hard thus far to eliminate. The next year he decided the clans of Cui, Lu, Li, and Zheng were abusing their power over the people. Shinim called on several politicians to gather data and compose the Records of Clans. The record would document the past actions of each clan and divided them into 9 classes. Tensions rose and a Tibetan clan rebelled against Shinim. He was able to diffuse the situation by giving titles to the chief's sons and marrying one to his daughter. Then there was an issue with the Turks! After an assassination attempt on the Emperor, many wanted the Turks pushed out of the main city. Soon they were forced to evacuate to the land north of the Great Wall. Hostilities continued between the Turks and the Tang for several years. In the early 640's Shinim's two sons, Tai and Chengqian had begun to divide support between them, creating a disunified population. Shinim spent the next year marrying off more of his daughters in the name of peace. In 643 Shinim expanded trade to Byzantine. Gifts were sent from Emperor Constans II to Shinim. The Sasanian King, Yazdegerd III was also paying tribute to Shinim in hopes of gaining an ally for war. Persia was lost, however, and the Islamic Caliphate began. The Sasanian Prince Peroz III fled to Tang China and the Tang Dynasty became known throughout the world.

In 643 Prince Li You decided to declare rebellion against his father the Emperor. You was soon betrayed and captured by his own men and Shinim ordered he and 44 of his associates to commit suicide. Unfortunately, Shinim's worries were not yet over. His son and heir, Chengqian had been growing increasingly paranoid that he would be passed over for his brother Tai. So, he decided to act first and gathered General Hou Junji, Uncle Prince Li Yuanchang, Zhao Jie, Du He, and General Li to plan a takeover. In the investigation of You's rebellion, one of Chengqian's guards spilled the beans to Shinim about what Chengqian had been planning. Immediately an investigation was carried out as Shinim continued to wonder what in the world went wrong with his offspring. Shinim's advisor talked him into leniency, so Shinim deposed Chengqian but allowed him to live, while the others involved were killed. Shinim chose to have his son Li Zhi become the new heir because he upheld the Han culture, beliefs, and traditions. Many long years of assassination attempts, and exposed conspiracies left Shinim seriously ill. After taking pills from his alchemist, he died. Gentle Li Zhi, the 9th son of Shinim, was named Emperor Gaozong.

The Tang Dynasty is called the Golden Age and is known for its poetry, art, music, and extravagance. Much of the ancient Chinese art seen today is from this time period, and as you see, the palaces are intricate and beautiful as are the women, dancing with fans or holding flowers, draped in silk and lace. The Tang at this point had a population of 80 million. Thanks to Shinim and his father before him, many clans now paid tribute to the Li Emperors. The Code of Law, which is 500 Articles, was written in 653. The punishments for crimes were based on rank. Private palaces had been built throughout China in the major cities where the Emperor would visit which stand today. The Tang capital, Chang'an (Xian), became the largest and most modern city in the world. Because the religious practices were not part of the state governance, the people had freedom and lived in peace amongst each other, enjoying trade and prosperity without racism, judgement, fear, and hate. The Tang Dynasty is such a popular and desired governmental time in history because of the cultural diversity. Living as we are made to, together and free, separate, and equal. During this dynasty Li Bai arose and became one of China's most famous poets along with Wang Wei and Du Fu. Li Bai, also known as Li Bo, grew up to compose around 1000 poems which were famous in his time. He had 4 wives and lived for chivalry and romance. Writing poetry and killing men in swordfights are the ways Li Bai spent his time. Most of the Li's of this time became musicians, painters, poets, and entertainers.

Another cultural advancement made by the Tang was the acceptance and acknowledgement of equality between the sexes. Women were now allowed to ride horses, become members of the military or other official positions, play polo and become famous poets. Li Zhi, if you remember, was now named Emperor Gaozong. Zhi's wife became the first and only female Emperor of the Tang Dynasty. Let's take a closer look at the happy couple.

Wu Zhao, known as Zetian, was brought to the palace when she was 14 years old to be one of many concubines to Emperor Taizong (Shinim). After the Emperor died, she was sent to Ganye Temple to become a nun. Such places have always been used for keeping certain people away from public knowledge. After some time, Empress Wang wished to please Emperor Zhi and brought Zetian back to the palace. The Emperor liked her, and she knew how to manipulate him. One day her child was killed, and the death was blamed on Empress Wang. Because of this, Zetian convinced Zhi to depose her and get rid of several concubines. Zetian's motivation in life was greed and jealousy, but there is not conclusive evidence to state whether she killed her own child or if Wang did. Soon Wu Zetian was crowned Empress. Zhi had been very ill his whole life and there was much drama in the harem when Zetian had been a concubine. Once she gained power, she had Zhi make Luoyang the second capital of Tang. She overturned the government and removed all the officials she didn't like (or who didn't like her) through false accusations of treason and demotions. She was a Tao sorceress and had an explosive temper. When Zhi had a son with one of his concubines, she had the child exiled and put under house arrest. Many of the children born to Zhi's concubines were targeted by her rage and bloodlust. The ghosts of Empress Wang and the others she had killed haunted her in her dreams and is the reason why the palace was remodeled. As historians note, this didn't stop the hauntings as she had hoped. Her relatives also wanted to prosper from her good fortune, and many were moved to the palace. When Zetian heard that Zhi was considering one of her nieces to be a concubine, she had her poisoned, blaming another niece. Many of her family members died suddenly during 666 AD and many more were executed on her whim.

Zhi's health had declined to the point where he finally decided to leave his Empress to handle the affairs of state, which didn't bother her. She had many of his relatives imprisoned where they starved to death, or exiled, or poisoned. In 683 Zhi died and Zetian named Prince Li Xian as Emperor. He was dethroned very quickly on grounds of treason, exiled, and replaced with another of Zetian's sons, Li Dan. In 690 she also dethroned him and changed the state title to Zhou with herself as Emperor, founding the Wu Zhou Dynasty. She ruled for the next 50 years, enlisting her nephews Wu Sansi and Wu Chengci to oversee important government positions. During this time, she continued to redistribute aristocratic titles and wealth, taking from those who she thought weren't loyal and ensuring the loyalty of others with grander titles and more wealth than they were accustomed to. In 705, The palace guards, Li Chen, and Li Duozuo, along with the Prime Minister, conspired to carry out a coup. Two of Zetian's most trusted and favorite men were killed. That year was her last as Empress. She had gained many titles by this time including Holy Golden Goddess Emperor, Heavenly Empress, and many variations of these. She was remembered as a ruthless ruler, who killed her own children for power.

After the coup was carried out, Li Xian, the 6th son of Li Zhi, claimed Emperorship and the Li's were back in power, but for a short time only. Zetian had him arrested and forced him to commit suicide. In 706, Li Xian's brother, Li Xiǎn, was Emperor for a time and gave Xian a proper burial. Coup after coup took place in rapid succession as the Li brothers and uncles attempted to take the title. Li Dan, who had previously been Emperor but was dethroned by the Empress, became Emperor again in 710. His reign was again short lived, and he abdicated to his son, Prince Li Longji who was then crowned Emperor Xuanzong. Longji killed everyone who even thought of opposing his position and ruled a "stable" China for 44 years. His 16 wives gave birth to over 50 children. Unfortunately, the power also went to his head, and he spent most of his time drinking with his concubines. He made Li Linfu his Prime Minister but thanks to total incompetence the royal court was destroyed along with the stability of the nation. After Li Linfu died one of Longji's concubines was put in his position. Longji then began to involve himself more in his duties and restructured the military. This allowed for a revolt to take place in 755, which resulted in Prince Li Xiang being placed in power over Lingwu as Emperor Suzong. It took 8 years of war before Longji was able to regain his taken lands.

Following the Tang Dynasty through the generations we come to the last Emperor of Tang, Li Zuo, now called Emperor Ai. Born in 892, Zuo was the 9th son of the Emperor. He and his brothers were named Imperial Princes and Zuo was given the additional position of Deputy General. He was 11 years old. The following year, Zuo's father was assassinated by Zhu Wen, a greedy official, and an edict was passed which named Zuo as the new young Emperor. His name was changed to Li Chu and then Emperor Ai. Zhu Wen was a tyrant and massacred dozens of senior elite who were forced to commit suicide. While he was killing off the government of Tang, he passed laws and edicts in the child Emperor's name. Zhu Wen also had Zuo's brother killed and passed accusations against the Dowager Empress who was quickly killed as well. Li Keyong, Li Maozhen, Yang Wo, and Wang Jian became independent warlords and Zhu Wen took the throne, titling himself Emperor of Later Liang. The Tang Dynasty had come to an end and in 908 Zhu Wen had Zuo poisoned.

Moving right along we find Li Qiu, who was the commander of the Baisheng Army. In 911 he assassinated his prefect, Lu Yanchang, and took over all of Qian. Zhu Wen, now called Emperor Taizu, rewarded his initiative, and made Qiu the Defender of Qian. When he died officer Li Yantu took his place for 2 years then died as well.

This decade was another time of division and warring, bringing us to Li Yuanhao who was born in 1003.

Li Yuanhao grew up in a time of struggle, especially in the northwestern regions of China where multiple tribes had been forced to pay tribute to the Song Dynasty after the fall of Tang. Yuanhao became the leader of the Tangut when his father died. Yuanhao was eager to establish independence and ended the tribute to the Song. He ordered men to shave their heads, or they would be executed. He drastically changed every area of life that the Tanguts had known. He altered the writing script, implemented education in writing, and had Chinese books translated into the language of the Tanguts. He had an army of 500,000 men and only one target: the Song. In 1034 he began to attack territories and claimed large portions of land. In 1038, after his great expansion, he named himself Emperor Jingzong of Western Xia, also called Xia and Daxia. In 1044 a treaty was signed between the Song and Xia empires and Song agreed to pay tribute to them. Yuanhao's constant attacks on the region left it vulnerable to the Mongols who later conquered China, destroying the Western Xia Dynasty in the process. In 1048 Yuanhao died, after a botched assassination attempt. Instead of being killed with a sword, only his nose was chopped off, which apparently got infected and killed him several agonizing days later. His son, Li Liangzuo became Emperor Yizong of Western Xia.

Li Bingchang was the 3rd Emperor of Western Xia at the age of 6. Known as Emperor Huizong, his mother ruled in his stead, until he turned 16. In 1076, when he came of age, his mother worked her influence to fight for the throne. She had him put under house arrest, but the Song army came to free him. Young Bingchang was forced to marry his mother's niece who became the 2nd Empress Dowager Liang. After many years of deep depression, Bingchang died at the age of 26. His son, Qianshun was crowned Emperor Chongzong at age 3 and Empress Liang, also called Zhaojian, was in control of the empire until she was poisoned in 1099. Qianshun held the longest reign of all the Xia Emperors and had many children. His children were brought up in Confucianism and went on to build many temples to worship Confucius in.

The 7th Emperor was Li Anquan, born in 1170 and named Emperor Xiangzong. He attacked the Jin Dynasty who had been peaceful allies and attempted to become allies with the Mongol Empire. Genghis Khan considered Western Xia nothing more than a bump in the road to China and Anquan was forced to surrender to him. His daughter, Chaka, was given to marry Genghis and tributes were paid. One month before he died, Anquan's nephew, Li Zunxu, overthrew him. This taking of the crown through coup d'état is the common theme. The 9th Emperor, Li Dewang, didn't have to coup to be named Emperor because his father decided to abdicate. The empire was weak from years of reckless leaders and senseless wars. Dewang attempted to repair the relationship with the Jin and detach from the Mongols, but his armies were too weak to fend off the attacks. Before he died, his nephew Li Xian was named Emperor Mo the last of Western Xia. While attempting to defend the empire from the constant barrage of Mongols, an earthquake hit causing disease and food shortages. Matters could not get any worse for this Li line and in 1227 Xian surrendered to Genghis Khan. He and his entire family were killed. The Jin Dynasty collapsed in 1234 and in 1253 the Mongols had taken the Kingdom of Dali. The Song Dynasty was the last to go and surrendered in 1279. So, the Mongols continued to Vietnam and many battles and wars ensued before it was all over and done.

The next century was spent working to get the Mongols out of China, which was achieved with the creation of the Ming Dynasty by Zhu Yuanzhang in 1368. The Li family tried to maintain their status as military professionals during this time, which was increasingly more difficult. The Emperor created surnames for the Jewish population to choose from including An, Zuo, Bo, Nie, Ai, Shi, Gao, Jin, Li, Zhang, and Zhao. In 1489 it was recorded that there were 14 clans in the Kaifeng Jewish community. Kaifeng was the city given to them long ago by the emperor in the mid 1100's. They had come from India and before that, Babylon. As we already know, by the time Jews left Babylon, Babylonians had married Hebrews or decided to practice the Jewish religion, calling themselves Jews. They followed the Talmud like good Babylonians, were only allowed to intermarry with the Han bloodline, and practiced foot binding and polygamy.

Li Shizhen was born in 1518 to a family of doctors. He grew up in his father's medical practice while his grandfather, who was also a doctor, wandered the country. Although he never passed the Imperial Exam, Li Shizhen was brought into the Chu royal court after healing the prince's son. After becoming an official at the Imperial Medical Institute, he began studying the documents he was now allowed access to. Realizing the inconsistencies in recent medical documents compared to ancient ones, he devoted his time and energy to organizing, researching, and compiling the most accurate and correct natural medical text in history. He travelled extensively, to gather more information and speak to various local healers, and because of his focus and ambition for accuracy, his book was very large. Shizhen's book, Bencao Ganmu, was divided into volumes but the court refused to print or publish it for many years. Finally in 1644 it was published, followed by the Manchu invasion. To this day the Bencao Ganmu is considered the authority on medicine.

Li Sancai was a Minister of Revenue for the Ming Dynasty when his political ambitions came to light. In the 1600's Sancai had become angry at how the eunuchs' taxes and mines had begun to destroy the Confucian culture. Once again, the eunuchs' greed started the fires of rebellion. Sancai wrote many letters to the Emperor, informing him of the actions of the eunuchs and how crimes had been committed in his name. He spent his adult life attempting to change the tax policies, through diplomacy. Others didn't agree and the Donglin movement grew. During this time the Jesuits had infected the courts, just as they had in Europe and thanks to their puppet Columbus, the Americas as well.

In 1606 the rebel leader who overthrew the Ming Dynasty was born. His name was Li Hongji, also known as Li Zicheng. In 1633 he inherited a rebel army of 30,000 men as well as the nickname Dashing King. In 1642 a flood wiped out Kaifeng and 300,000 residents. This was a devastating blow to an already crumbling Ming Empire and the rebellion couldn't be controlled. In 1644 Hongji stood in the capital of Beijing and declared himself Emperor of the Shun Dynasty. Because he was of Han blood, he was given the Mandate of Heaven. Unfortunately, by June 1644, the Ming had recaptured Beijing and Zicheng fled. Now the Ming (Han Chinese who were the original settlers) and Qing (Manchu Chinese who came from elsewhere) Dynasties ruled China.

The Rothschilds had grown to own Europe and the Americas by this time and moved their gaze to China. Ever since 1540, the Jesuits (upper elite) had been focused on gaining control of Asia, the last region of the world not under their total control, as we have previously discussed. This is why the Rothschild's were sent there to start a war and destroy the country in a genocide by opium, chemical warfare. The events that have happened throughout history have been orchestrated and directed by the elite. While you see them creating banks and starting wars or opening universities and hospitals, they are merely carrying out the agendas given them.

In 1760 Li Zibiao was born in Liangzhou. His parents were devout Catholics, thanks to the Jesuit missions that had taken place for centuries, and he was sent to Italy to become a priest when he was just 11. Zibiao attended the College of the Holy Family of Jesus Christ, also called Chinese College…and excelled in Latin. He became an interpreter for the Macartney Embassy. Having grown up in Europe, he became vital to the negotiations between Britain and China during the 1st war. While he understood both cultures well, and was able to communicate with each, the separate parties attempted to gain control of the situation. In September of 1793, Macartney and Zibiao went to meet with the Emperor Qianlong. Qianlong expected Macartney to kneel 3 times, touching his head to the ground, as was Chinese tradition. Macartney refused and formal diplomatic relations and trade were discontinued by the Emperor. Zibiao returned to China but was now considered foreign because he had lived outside of the country. He spent the rest of his life in hiding.

In 1839 Britain declared war on China and opium began to flood the streets, as you likely remember from the Rothschild and Astor chapters. Since I went into detail there, I will summarize some relevant information to keep the timeline together. In 1433 Britain had desired trade and expansion in China, but China had refused.

During these next years, the Rothschilds had flooded China with opium, causing nationwide disease and death. Because opium was used for medicinal purposes throughout China for centuries, it had always been there. However, the Rothschilds forced more into the general population, taking China's typical import of opium from 200 chests, as it had been for known time, to 40,000 chests. More than enough to annihilate an entire population, which it practically did. Many things like opium are acceptable for medical purposes, but like everything, when it's abused and misused it does nothing but destroy. Britain sent the Navy to China by way of Hong Kong, filled with Rothschild opium grown in India. In 1841 they attacked Guangzou and were given $6 million for ransom. The soldiers of the Chinese armies were no match for the well-established and modern military of Britain, which the British Empire knew and had previously ensured with opium. One Imperial Commissioner threw 2.6 million pounds of opium into the ocean but no matter what the Qing Empire did to get the opium out of their country, the Rothschilds' might overpowered it.

China was effectively crippled for generations to come. By 1842 China had given Hong Kong to Britain and the Rothschilds had established ports all around. For many centuries the Chinese had strived to keep foreigners out, so their culture could remain pure. Thanks to Britain, their distrust and dislike of foreigners was only validated and heightened. This led to the persecution of those who were Chinese but had lived abroad, and anyone involved with the Catholic Church, thanks to the Jesuits. In round 1 of the Opium wars 350 British invaders had been killed and thousands of Chinese had been slaughtered. After the 2nd Opium War over 30 million Chinese had been massacred. The numbers climbed over the generations as more and more have been killed by opium. But the elite don't want you to focus on the multitude of horrific genocides they have personally carried out, so they only focus on one: the Holocaust of Germany, which is one of the smallest ones they have ever imposed. This is only for one reason: to further the Rothschild agenda. But I digress...

In addition to the overload of opium, the Rothschilds assisted in creating a mass migration of Jews, not Hebrews, to China over the next decades. This is why Asia and most of the world hates Westerners. The elite have destroyed them repeatedly. Thankfully, China came up with a genius plot to conquer the materialistic west with materials! 80% of everything bought and used in the western world is made and sold from China. Today China controls most of the world through its technology as well as its diseases and vaccines!

Li Hung Chang, born 1823, was the Viceroy of Zhili, Huguang and Lianguang. In 1899 he sent over 4,000 pounds to Hongkong Bank, to be used by the Rothschilds to buy shares in the Pekin Syndicate. A photograph of him, with a personal inscription, was given to the Rothschilds and has been immortalized in their archives. By now the Rothschild family had gained control over Hong Kong finance, the Great Wall to

China had been breached. At this time, China was becoming known for its "superior" coal and iron deposits. Remember that in the 1700's the Rockefellers had published a report on the effects of mining which detailed how this destruction of the earth would cause exponential warming which would not stop and could not be corrected while mining took place anywhere in the world. The Rothschild's Pekin Syndicate secured rights to the coal and iron and were backed by the government. As one would expect, it was the government that they already controlled. Yes, dear reader, the Li family is under the control of the Rothschilds, like almost every lower elite family is. While they seem powerful and important, they are merely chained dogs. The Rockefellers' coal industry reports had shown that mining coal would directly affect climate, exponentially increasing the heat, at an alarming rate, even if mining (stealing the life-forces from the earth we live on) had been ended when the report came out in the early 1700's. But that is exactly why the families continued in the industry. China was one of the last places in the world that had been untapped. Until now.

Let's continue with Li Hung Chang. Having grown up in upper society it goes without saying they had connections to not only the Rothschild family but many in the social circle. Hung's father was an official in the imperial capital. Hung enjoyed writing and composing poetry. He became an adviser and assistant to Lu Xianji during the Taiping Rebellion. Soon he was given command over the province, to keep the rebels subdued. In 1853 Lu Xianji committed suicide, after the rebels defeated an imperial army and Hung was given command over the rebels of other regions. When the rebellions had ended, in 1864, Hung was given the title First Class Count Suyi, giving him the right to wear a peacock feather in his hat. After this he was promoted to Viceroy of several provinces and founded the Tianjin Military Academy in 1885. As a general in the 1st Sino-Japanese War, he found himself disgraced. The armies who were supposed to join him did not show up, and they were too short on ammunition. He was a modern military man, with a seriously limited military and even more limited allies. He removed his feather, in despair. In 1895, an assassination attempt on Hung was carried out by Koyama Toyotaro, who shot him in the left cheek. Due to this, a treaty was signed, and the war was ended.

In 1896 Hung visited the US and EU and attended the coronation of Czar Nicholas II. During his time in Britain, he became a Knight Grand Cross of the Royal Victorian Order. When he returned to China, he took control of the telegraph system and became the negotiator for the foreign takeover of Beijing. He became a member of the Imperial Order of the Double Dragon as well as a Grand Cross of the Order of the Red Eagle in Germany. After his death, he was given the hereditary title of Marquis Suyi of the First Class.

During this time when China was in upheaval and death, 4 Chinese aristocratic families moved to Hong Kong. They were the Li, Ho, Lo, and Hui. In 1822 Li Leong was born in Guangdong Province and moved to Hong Kong to become a merchant. In 1854 Li Sing fled his hometown of Xinhui, China, because rebels had taken over. He joined his cousin Li Leong in Hong Kong and together they founded Wo Hang, an international shipping company. In 1856 they worked with the British and supplied them with Chinese soldiers and funding to continue the Rothschild's 2nd Opium War. Already the entire region had been crippled with the lingering horrors of the 1st war but those who worship wealth, don't care how they do it. The cousins were repaid by the British with gifts of artifacts and relics from China.

In 1864 Leong died and Sing took over the business, which soon grew into a monopoly in opium and gambling. The streets in the city were named after Li Sing's sons, Ko Sing, Li Po Lung, Wo Fung, and Kom U. His real estate empire had grown significantly as well, so much so that when his American Trading Company collapsed, it mattered little. In 1889 he founded Hong Kong Land Investment and Agency Company. Opium king Pang Wah-ping, Rothschild worker Sir Catchick Paul Chater, and James Johnstone Keswick of the Scottish Keswick Dynasty (which came about through international trading companies who smuggled opium to China) were the other founding members. The Hong Kong Land company created the beginnings of the city we know today. In 1877, Sing founded the On Tai Marine Insurance Company which made him the first Chinese-owned insurer. As his real estate and trade businesses grew, and the Insurance gig was up and running, Sing founded the Wa Hop Telegraph Company and laid the first telegraph line in Guangdong. His estate was estimated to be worth over $6 million, more than 3 times the yearly income of the Hong Government. After he died, Li Po-kwong, his firstborn son and heir, inherited the wealth.

Li Sing had many sons. Chi-tang had a revolutionary heart and became the treasurer of the Revive China Society and later financed the publication of their newspaper. He helped fund rebellions and believed he would become Emperor. Almost all of his inheritance was spent on rebellions and uprisings. This gained him a position in the revolutionary government which had a foothold in Guandong Province. By this time Li Po-kwong's first born son and heir, Lee Sai-wah, was living an extravagant life. He owned a bit of an island as well as the first Rolls Royce in Hong Kong. It is during this time period that last names' spellings were interchanged, Li named his son Lee. Another son of Sing, Li Po-chun founded the Li Po-chun Estates and began developing more properties. He made many charitable donations like all the wealthy do. To get around tax laws, it's vital to have many businesses, funds, trusts, and charities. Meanwhile, Li Sing's brother Li Chit and his son Po-kwai helped supply food during the 1920's when there were large strikes taking place. Chit founded the University of Hong Kong, Chinese Chamber of Commerce, Confucius Hall, and more. Other members of the family became members of parliament for the Chinese Republic and founders of estates and organizations.

Meanwhile, over in China, the Li families continued. In 1875, Li Chun from Nanjing, Jiangsu, China, was the military and civil governor of Jiangxi and military governor of Jiangsu. He and 3 others remained neutral in the civil war of 1910's but "suddenly" died in 1920. Li Tsung-jen attended the Guangxi Military Elementary School and went on to defeat the warlords who had controlled Guangxi Province, in 1925. Yet another Li born in 1875 was Li Jizhun, who became a General of the Republican Army. In 1912, the Republic of China was being formed, by the Rockefellers and Rothschilds. While the "Republic" continued to expand, many individual kingdoms/states became upset. Not everyone wanted to become a republic when they could be King or Emperor instead. So, in 1933, when the Rockefellers invested $37 million in China, mainly through their China Medical Board and Union Medical School, the Japanese invaded Manchuria. This is how things work. This is why people say, "follow the money" in order to see the true agenda. Unfortunately, most of it (child, drug and other trafficking organizations and rituals) is kept hidden, once again allowing you to only see the nonessentials or more minor orchestrations. Jizhun was now the leader of the National Salvation Army, consisting of 10,000 men. Jizhun hoped that by allying himself with the Japanese, his people would be granted independence and their own territory. Unfortunately, Jizhun and his army didn't matter to the Japanese and once they had fought and won victories, his army was disbanded by the new leaders from Japan and Jizhun disappeared, never to be heard from again.

In 1903, the Rothschild's founded Yale Divinity School within schools and hospitals throughout China. These became collectively known as Yale in China, whose top graduate Mao Zedong was groomed and financed by the Rockefellers and Rothschilds. This group was an intelligence network used by the elite to carry out their agendas in the region. By 1949 the People's Republic of China had been formed and secured, one year before the central bank was established in China. Can you see by now how countries are taken over in reality? Not with bullets or armies. Politics is a game designed to keep you oblivious, nothing more.

Lee Kuan Yew, who graduated from Cambridge with elite connections and memberships to various clubs, became the Prime Minister of Singapore. Singapore had received its so-called independence in the 1960's and Lee Kuan Yew was put in power. His reign left Singapore as one of the smallest but most developed economies in the world. It was a time of great development, industrially and financially for the country. In 1976, Lee Kuan Yew met with Yale graduate and friend of the family Mao Tse-tung (Zedong). Tse-tung was the leader of Rothschild's Communist China and member of Skull and Bones, like those he was closest to. Every US Ambassador to Beijing has been a member of Skull and Bones, just as every US president has been while every leader of every country has been a member of a similar order, whichever is the prominent club of their respective regions. They have all gone to school together, they have all gone to the same club meetings, together. Do you get it, dear reader? Or are you still indoctrinated into ignorance? Tse-tung grew up close to the Li family. Even his bodyguard was a Li, Li Yinqiao, and for a time Tse-tung used the name Li Desheng. Li Ta-chao, head of the communist party in Northern China, was Tse-tung's mentor. Both were affiliated with the Red Spears Secret Society and Ko-Ino Hui Society, who assisted him in the revolution.

Tse-tung was put in the position of Chairman of Communist China by the Rothschild's who not only worked with and established the Li's of Hong Kong and the Li's and Lee's of opium trade, but started the Yale in China college, which Tse-tung graduated from as planned and predetermined. In 1949 Tse-tung was made Chairman of the Chinese Communist Party. The Rothschild's handled Tse-tung, who had been brought into the family at a pliable age and indoctrinated accordingly. Working with Henry Kissinger and David Rockefeller, Tse-tung was able to solidify the elites' control over the region. Thanks to this, China became the world's largest opium producer and every single leader put in place since this time has been solidly controlled by the elite of the west, rather than by their own elite blood. Chairman Mao was praised and welcomed by US and Soviet leaders alike. Why not? It's a worldwide web. They are all on the same page, regardless of what their media outlets say, regardless of what they say publicly, they are professional liars, and they are all playing the same game: control over **YOU**. Tse-tung used excessive violence to subdue the citizens of China, and the citizens of China and the population of the world allowed it all to happen. Over 70 **million** citizens were murdered through starvation, execution, and torture. 70 million human beings. From **1958 to 1962** the world watched in silence as the population of China was culled by the elite. People. Mothers, fathers, sons, cousins, grandchildren, aunts, sisters, and the count increases significantly more when you include the forced murder and trafficking of infants due to the one-child policy. In 1973, when President Bush visited Tse-tung, almighty god of China, David Rockefeller stated:

"The **social experiment** in China under Chairman Mao's leadership is one of the most important and **successful** in human history."

If only people would listen when the elite speak. They always tell and show you very plainly what is really going on. Rights must be exercised and protected, or you lose the right to have them. There are no rights without the responsibility needed (by everyone) to uphold them. All through history, even in this very small summary of a book, one can clearly see the endless trail of humanity's epic failures to be what humans are. Every person alive spends their entire life attempting to be something they never were, never even comprehending their purpose or ability. The Rothschild's had succeeded in their task of gathering all world powers under their rule. Like the Rothschild's Stalin and Hitler, Tse-tung was ruthless and extremely manipulative. His followers viewed him as their god, and the masses were brainwashed into servitude. Ever since their first Emperor demanded to be worshipped and acknowledged as god, the Chinese have been happy to submit to false leaders, idols, and be slaves in every way. Quotes from his cult following include this one from Jiang Qing, who said:

"Everything I did, Mao told me to do. I was his dog; what he said to bite, I bit."

Yet another proof of the sad fact that people are eager to give up their own free will and lies are always sugar-coated. This is seen in cults, small and large, throughout history. Puppet kings of the Elite used to puppet others. Tse-tung's life is a direct mirror of Adolf Hitlers life and sooo many other pawns before him. Chairman Mao's people were abused and oppressed, propaganda was rampant and outrageous, and, as in all communist countries, the population was killed in large amounts painting China Red. As we can see from Asia's history, the culture has been used to slavery and death and has barely known anything else. Tse-tung had many wives and children, several of them have used the Li name including Li Na and Li Min. In 1976, after years of well-deserved illnesses and disease, Chairman Mao died. His personal doctor and confidant, Li Zhisui had escaped China after being accused of attempting to poison Tse-tung's wife, Jiang Qing. Zhisui, wrote a book called The Private Life of Chairman Mao which exposed quite a lot. In 1995 he died of a heart attack. One of the statements made by Tse-tung, which is in the book is:

"We have so many people, we can afford to lose a few. What Difference Does It Make?"

Do you remember, dear reader, when Hillary Clinton said the same thing in her court scam about Libya? They all get the same script...which is why they always tell us that history repeats itself. It does indeed because they are the only ones running it. No one else cares because Facebook and Instagram and TikTok are more important than being a real human. If people ever looked up from their screens, they would feel the need to DO something...and that's something we can't have. The Chairman's personal secretary, Li Rui, became his biggest critic and was outspoken against the Communist era (after the fact) until he died at the age of 101. In 2018 he was quoted by Hong Kong newspaper Ming Pao:

"A country like China produced people like Mao Zedong. Now it gives birth to Xi Jinping."

Li Xiannian was involved in the power struggle after Mao's death and was President of China. For a number of years Li Xiannian was considered one of the four top leaders of Red China. For many years Li Xiannian did lots of travelling to places like Africa where he held high level meetings with other leaders. Asian rulers have been worshipped, deified, and consume the mind and attentions of the entire population. Now China has been working to expand the empire through technology, which is the new warfront of the day. It will be interesting to see how that goes over the next 5-10 years. While we're on the topic of mind control, let's look into some other Asian cults.

The White Lotus Sect was created in the 330's. Over time it became known as the Hung Society, which was changed to the Triad Society, also known as Three United Society in the 1700's. Like every elite cult, it is not new or original and includes ritualistic initiation, oaths, secret handshakes (because that's so important), blood sacrifices, and sorcery. The Triads use a culmination of concepts taken from Confucius, Buddha, and Tao. Because religions are all the same, at their core, and created by the elite, they always use them interchangeably and intertwined. This is why Catholics today outrageously call themselves Christians and believers of the same god as Muslims and Buddhists and everyone: ALL Luciferian (also known as elite) Religions ARE the same. But more on that in Part II. Leaders of the cult include Li Chi-tang, who handles overseas affairs, Li Kai-chen and Li Ping-ching, lead Triad groups of Shanghai, Li Lap Ting, leader of the Kwangsi, Li Chol Fat is the leader of the Hong Kong cult, Li Jarfar Mah is leader in Britain, Li Shih-chin, Li Wen-mao, Li Yuan-fa, and a great many more Li's run the Triad cults located throughout the world. By 1854 the California Triad sect called Five Companies had 35,000 members. Like all cults, they have only grown.

In 1945, aside from the Wo Shing Wo and the Sun Yee On, another society of that time was the 14K Society. Chiang Kai-shek and his mentor Big-Eared Tu were likely responsible for setting up a league through Kot Siu Wong, which oversees all the various Triad groups called Five Continents Overseas Chinese Hung League. Like the others, they handle human trafficking, drugs, extortion, robberies, and all the usual gang stuff. Like cults, gangs offer identity, an illusion of belonging and worth, and use the same mind control tactics, baiting the weak and easily manipulated, as well as initiations. The 14k is the largest of the Triad Orders and target schools and children from poor neighborhoods to both sell and initiate. The gang has an estimated 20,000 members, not including their dozens of subgroups, worldwide. The 14K in South Africa are called the 14K-Hau and 14K-Ngai. They have worked with the Yakuza, the Sinaloa Cartel, as well as Abu Sayyaf. The group is present in the Netherlands, Belgium, France, Ireland, Spain, Australia, and the UK as well as the US, Canada, and Mexico.

1954 brought the self-named "Reverend" Sun Myung Moon to the foreground. He founded The Family Federation for World Peace, also called The Unification Church, another elite Order (cult), which quickly spread throughout the US. Like all cult leaders he gave himself the Christian title of Reverend. This is done simply to corrupt, to show indignance and disgust, to invert. This is something even KKK leaders do, as noted before. It's just like calling yourself a Doctor, never having gone to college for anything medically related (which many cult leaders do as well). Moon forced his followers to work as peddlers and manufacture trinkets to sell in the street, refusing them food, drink, or bathrooms. His many slaves (members) were tortured when they disobeyed or complained when they became sick. Sickness was seen by the Moons as proof of demon possession. Sun Myung claimed, like hundreds before him, that he was the new Messiah, and that Korea was God's chosen nation. He viewed and taught that Christian churches were furthering Lucifer's power, stating:

"When Jesus grew up, he failed as a leader because he was unable to love his disciples enough to motivate them to kill for him or die in his place."

In 2012 Sun Myung died of pneumonia and his son took over the cult. After forming his own branch called the Sanctuary Church, his mother Hak Ja Han is now the leader of the order.

The 1990's brought us the philosophy of Li Hongzhi, called Falun Gong. Hongzhi believes he is an alien who is here to help mankind. Although he hasn't helped anyone yet, he has made a lot of money off of the ignorance and gullibility of "people" and has had a wonderful time! He claims that he grew up in a school for Buddhist magic and mastered many things including invisibility and levitation under his teacher Quan Jue, the Tenth Heir to the Great Law of the Buddha School. By the age of 8 he was a noted expert and by 12, he had graduated to Taoist instruction in martial arts. He continues, claiming that during the Cultural Revolution he was taught by Master Zhendaozi of the Great Way School. Unfortunately, Hongzhi, born Li Lai, was an ordinary child of the times. His parents were divorced, and he grew up in the state-controlled school system. He didn't go to high school after the Cultural Revolution interrupted his commonplace education. His classmates claim he was undistinguished and unnoticed in school and his coworkers agree. He married and began a family before starting to formulate his qigong system in the Falun Dafa. In 1989 he began training students. The government, his friends, and classmates, all worked hard to expose the lies he was spreading about himself and insisted repeatedly that he was unremarkable in every way. His so-called teachers are not to be found. His claims of having the same birth date as Buddha have been proven false as well. His motto is Truthfulness, Compassion and Forbearance.

In 1995 Hongzhi expanded his schooling abroad, starting in Paris. For some strange reason, he wasn't accepted in China, surrounded by people who knew the truth about him. So, he traveled the world giving lectures and Falun Gong organizations began popping up all over the place, especially on University campuses. Universities are owned and controlled by the Jesuit upper elite, through their lower elite pawns. This is why so many elite agendas are created in them and why everyone who is educated by them, is corrupted by elite indoctrination. The following year he was given honorary citizenship by the city of Houston, Texas. Toronto, Canada, was next on the list to give him honors, followed by Chicago, Illinois, and **more**. In 1996 he became a citizen of the US and moved his family to New York. Meanwhile the tension in Beijing against the Falun Gong school grew. In 1999 it was banned in China and charges were brought against Hongzhi. That same year a multitude of Fulan Gongians were arrested and tortured to death. One victim, Fu Guihua, was sentenced in February 2021 to 7.5 years in Jilin Women's Prison for practicing Fulan Gong. She died 2 months later because of the severe conditions. Many more are being tortured to death today, right now.

In 2001 the Freedom House awarded Hongzhi with the International Religious Freedom Award, and he was nominated for the Nobel Peace Prize and the Sakharov Prize. Although his teachings include abstinence, self-control, and civility, if the teachings were truly good and deserving of note, they wouldn't be covered in lies. He continues his work through Epoch Times, which he founded in 2000, under his umbrella companies of Epoch Media Group and New Tang Dynasty Television. Epoch Times had an increasing revenue of $15.5 million as of 2019. $900,000 has been donated to them by Robert Mercer. The revenue of the Epoch Media Group is between $15-25 million and New Tang Dynasty TV's revenue went from $7.4 million in 2016 to $18 million in 2017. Yes, Li Hongzhi is a typical elite. He sleeps well at night while his countrymen suffer to death for his idea, based on lies. While hundreds are tortured to death through starvation, gang beatings, sleep deprivation and more, he's welcomed by politicians and aristocrats in numerous countries and worshipped by his world-wide following who throw all of their money at him. A worthy man.

General Li Mi was born during the Communist takeover of China. Troubled times indeed. The Chinese Communist Party controlled all aspects of life. He grew up to become a powerful and high-ranking military officer and used his army to fight Communism. During the Chinese Civil War of the late 1940's, he was pushed back to Thailand and Burma. He set up bases there and continued to fight through guerilla warfare. While in Burma he began working with the CIA. The CIA called their relationship Operation Paper and Mi's army used the CIA's airline, Civilian Air Transport, to take weapons, supplies, and massive amounts of opium through Thailand. Mi had a plan to take over the Thai opium business and his men began to marry the local women. Soon Mi controlled the poppy fields, monopolizing the opium industry. In 1960 General of the KMT 3rd Army, Li Wen-huan, took over the empire when Mi died. Other Li's include Florence Li Tim-Oi, a Catholic priestess, and multiple Li's who are directors of American Express and many other banking systems.

Li Baodong graduated from Johns Hopkins University and Beijing Foreign Studies University. After some time working for the Ministry of Foreign Affairs, he became the ambassador to Zambia, and permanent representative to the United Nations and other organizations in Switzerland. In 1978 Li Qiang became the Minister of

Foreign Trade for the Central Committee of the Communist Party. Li Changchun joined the Communist Party in 1965. When he was 39 years old, Changchun became the youngest Party Secretary of Shenyang. He was a member of the Central Committee of the Chinese Communist Party and pushed for less state involvement. Changchun became the Chief of Propaganda from 2002-2012 and was vital to China's censorship. He was finally made a member of the Politburo Standing Committee in 2022. The Politburo runs the government of China, as stated before, it is simply a renaming of the eunuchs of old. Li Peng, Premier of China, was the head of the inner circle of this group along with Li Ruihuan, head of Communist Propaganda until 2003. The other members of the inner circle are Zhu Rongji, Hu Jintao, Jiang Zemin, Liu Huaqing, and Qiao Shi.

Let's look at Li Peng more closely. Peng's father, Li Shuoxun was a leading communist writer, which got him killed in 1931, when Peng was just 3 years old. Peng was raised by a family friend, Zhou Enlai, who became the Prime Minister of the Peoples Republic of China (PRC). His life was decided for him, if not before his birth than absolutely by the time he was sent to school. His university years were split between China and Moscow, and he ended up specializing in hydroelectricity. In 1945 he joined the Chinese Communist Party, following in his father's footsteps and was a strong advocate and enforcer of the Soviet style of economics. As one of the elites, he was born into certain social circles, inheriting memberships to clubs as well, making it no surprise that he was very intimate with the Rockefeller, Rothschild, and Bush families, to name a few. In 1982 Peng joined the Central Committee and was soon made a Secretary of the Politburo. He quickly grew to be a permanent committee member, as one would expect.

In 1987 Peng was also made the Premier of the PRC by Deng Xiaoping. Zhao Ziyang was put in office as his successor and Secretary General. Ziyang decided to implement price reforms in 1988 which increased inflation. The economic atmosphere was already stifling, and the people began to riot, as expected. Students began protesting the government because reforms were too slow in being put into effect. As more students became aware of their enslavement by the government, their numbers grew and their fight against corruption became a force to be reckoned with. In April protesters gathered in Tiananmen Square. Although President Zhao Ziyang publicly claimed he wanted a peaceful solution, the President wasn't in control, as no president or king ever is. The man behind the curtain was Deng Xiaoping, who had the strictest loyalty from Li Peng. Ever since he was brought into politics, Xiaoping had been Li Peng's handler, ordering him to do the things he did. Like everyone in leadership positions, Peng was merely the puppet — the face. This doesn't excuse his surrender of free will, as that is never excusable, but with his background and upbringing it is to be expected. It's the same mentality of those who join military forces and many other clubs: they don't want to think for themselves, they can't handle the responsibility that is freedom, they just want to feel like they are part of something and blindly follow orders. In May 1989 Martial Law was enforced and Peng told the students:

"The situation will not develop as you wish and expect."

June 4, 1989, a massacre was caused by a power struggle between Li Peng and Zhao Ziyang. Peaceful protesters took to the streets, on hunger strikes, in order to create a communist party "without corruption" that would allow freedom of press and freedom of speech. Sadly, this isn't possible, and neither concept means what people assume they do. The strikes went on in 400 cities and the military was sent out. Tanks filled the streets, and 300,000 troops were sent to one city alone, under Li Peng's orders. The people were told they had 1 hour to disband, but after 5 minutes the multitude of troops with assault rifles opened fire on *unarmed* civilians who were trying to block the military advance. Armored vehicles ran over the civilians at 40 miles per hour, according to the media. Wounded girls and boys were bayoneted and those who attempted to aid infants and mothers were shot. Snipers had free reign from the tops of buildings, and other places cowards hide. Bulldozers were brought in to scrape the piles of bodies out of the square which were then burned and hosed down street drains. A classic False Flag event (an event planned and orchestrated by the government which may or may not include the deaths of civilians, to generate excessive propaganda in order to control the population). The propaganda is always the same, as is the objective. Fear. Not to worry dear reader, like most of the False Flags, what you read about in the news and see on TV is a program, a show. Entertainment. So, you may as well enjoy it!

Let's take a look at the **real** story. In 1986 the CIA decided that was the time to infiltrate for their next mission: the massacre. The CIA formed an anti-government movement within the student body, and protests began. As you know by now, False Flag events and Organized movements, are financed by the same groups, and crisis actors and paid protesters do this for a living. George Soros gave over $1 million to the task. Leaders were picked, and handled, and a couple of years later, protests began. One good massacre, real or not, and the Euro-elite would have full control of China. Pictures of the square after the 4th show the burned tanks and military vehicles (buses), which were burned by protesters' Molotov cocktails. Also rarely seen is the picture of a young soldier who was brutalized, stripped naked and tied to a bus, and burned to death by the elite's peaceful protesters on the 3rd. The Chinese government stated that there were 300 fatalities during that time period, but not at the Square, and not from one incident. These are the things exposed by the 1st wave of news: the stories that have the most truth. After the fact, once the stage has been set and pictures taken and videos made, those stories are wiped away, censored, and rewritten to include the elements needed for indoctrination. Those who try to go against the new narrative are silent one way or another. This is exactly the same as September 11, the Malaysian flights...and more as discussed previously. As always, I go by what verified eyewitnesses state, immediately after an event. A compromised eyewitness would be Soros-controlled student leader Wu'er Kaixi who was used in the spotlight, claiming that 200 students were mowed down by gunfire. In reality, he wasn't even at the Square and no shots were fired. That's who mainstream media, propaganda machines, use and quote. That's how it works. It's just a game.

Like every good False Flag, the pictures are key. A tiny man, dressed in a suit, standing in front of a line of tanks was used and expanded upon. He was simply waiting for the tank to stop, and then he climbed onto it, and they drove off in the direction the tanks were headed in the picture, which was **away** from the empty Square. Reporters Richard Roth and James Miles were in Tiananmen Square during the time of the massacre and testified there was no massacre. Graham Earnshaw of Reuters stated that the military came, negotiated, and left, killing no one. The American mainstream media, which controls most of the world's media, has always had it out for China and Russia, mainly due to their lack of police and military violence. The US has to point fingers at everyone else and be the world police to hide the extremist military state that it is today, which has developed into decades of endless bloodshed. US policies and tactics wouldn't be tolerated in other countries, like China, Russia, many African countries. But Americans love it that way and do nothing at all to slow their downfall.

> "They were able to enter and leave the [Tiananmen] square several times and were not harassed by troops. Remaining with students ... until the final withdrawal, the diplomat said there were no mass shootings in the square or the monument." - Wikileaks cable US Embassy in Beijing.

This senseless and outrageous propaganda earned Peng the nickname the Butcher of Beijing.

After the faux massacre, Peng was elected to the Politburo for his 3rd term, remaining Premier until 1998. In 2000 Peng was accused of his part in the incident at Tiananmen Square by 4 academic leaders who filed documents in the Manhattan Federal Court. The accusation was dismissed on the basis that Peng had not been summoned to court in a timely manner. That wasn't the end now that Peng was in the spotlight. In 2005 the Tibetan Support Committee filed charges against several men, including Peng, for genocide, terrorism, and crimes against humanity in the Spanish National Court. Peng's involvement in the very real oppression of Tibet came to light as well. Torture methods used on Tibetans were exposed. People had regularly been beaten with chains and metal bars and sticks with nails, shocked with cattle prods and more. Women were raped, mutilated, and electrocuted. Population control was implemented and families who didn't conform to the policy, and limit the number of children, suffered the consequences. 87,000 Tibetans were murdered and 80,000 more were exiled to India, Nepal, and Bhutan.

Although Peng wasn't directly involved in Tibet, as one of the leaders of the country he is responsible. The Spanish court accepted the accusations against Peng and the other leaders on the basis of universal jurisdiction and the trial began in 2006. In 2008 the charges were broadened to include more cases of genocide and torture, and after several years war crimes were added to the ever-growing list. In 2013 arrest warrants were issued for Li Peng, Deng Delyun, Chen Kuyian, Jiang Zemin, and Qiao Shi. As one who knows the elite would expect, before the warrants were put into action, new laws were put in place in Spain regarding universal jurisdiction. Spain dropped the warrants, and the case was put on a shelf and forgotten. Those who commit genocide are always allowed to live freely. Always.

"I think this would be the time because you really need to bring China into the creation of a new world order, financial world order." — George Soros

It's about the deeds you do. Those who empower the Fallen with their deeds are rewarded in this realm because this one is run by them. Those who are not of this realm, not under the rulership of the Fallen or their puppets, are merely waiting to go home like me, therefore have never had cause to do the deeds detailed in this book. But I digress, now that his political life was over, he dedicated himself to the Three Gorges Dam, which is what he had gone to school for in the first place. Naturally, energy is owned and controlled by the government of China, so positions are only given to the chosen ones. He died of an illness in 2019 and was given a funeral fit for the Emperor he was. Everyone who's anyone was there, and flags were held at half-mast as the country mourned the Butcher. His obituary stated:

"He made an important contribution in this fundamental struggle, which was critical to the future and fate of the Communist Party and the state."

Li Peng's daughter "China's Power Queen" Li Xiaolin became Vice-President of the China Datang Power Corporation. She funneled over $2 million into her overseas accounts. Peng's son, Li Xiaopeng, became the chairman of the China Huaneng Power Corporation before becoming the Governor of Shanxi. In 2017 he became a member of the Chinese Communist Party's Central Committee. The elite of China had never changed and the children of the leaders of the Communist Party are treated like royalty, same as their parents before them, and are dubbed "princelings". In 2014 the CCP princelings were exposed, thanks to the Swiss Leaks (called Panama Papers by media), for running shell companies in tax havens across the world to hide and collect their financial resources from the state. The state-owned energy sector held the most corruption and wealth. Peng's children were exposed in this leak along with a great many others. The timing couldn't have been better, as with most orchestrated leaks. President Xi Jinping had been waging a war on corruption in order to get rid of his rivals. Sadly, for him, his corruption came to light too. It seems the President and his family are worth $376 million with stakes and holdings for far more on top of that. Another Li named in the Panama Papers (Swiss Leaks) was Jasmine Li. Jasmine graduated from Stanford University and is one of the debutants of the current time. Her debut was in 2009, when she first attended the most exclusive global elites' Le Bal Des Debutantes, in Paris. Her father is a member of the Politburo.

Li Li became the Communist Party Chief and was soon established in the Shanghai branch of the Exim Bank (handling export and import) of China. Considered the godmother of the shipping industry, she was promoted to head of the Beijing branch in 2019. The Exim Bank has surpassed the World Bank in the amount of loans it has signed to supply "foreign aid" in its task to develop and establish control over other countries by financially supporting foreign governments and corporations. Most recently the bank poured $100 million into a lithium mine in Chile. As most of you should know by now, Lithium is obtained through the trafficking of children. Children are used in mines because of their small hands. However, due to the harsh and inhuman conditions of mining (which no one should be doing...ever) most of the children die before they become teens. But people love those battery-operated devices the elite have made for you to use every moment in front of. Unfortunately, Li Li was kicked out of the Communist Party in 2022, due to an investigation into corruption. Only time will tell if she was disappeared like fellow bankers, party members and so many billionaires who have been selected for "investigation of corruption". Speaking of Chinese banks, in 2008 the Bank of China (Exim Bank) bought 20% stakes, for $336.5 million, in the La Compagnie Financière Edmond de Rothschild!

Li Ka-shing has a vast empire in Hong Kong, the gateway of opium trade. The mainstream story is that Li Ka-shing had no formal schooling and was an overnight money maker. When he was 12 the family moved to Hong Kong, where he lived and worked with his uncle as a watchmaker. His interest in real estate grew and in 1950 he started his first company. While the real estate side was taking off, Ka-shing had begun manufacturing plastic flowers and other items, which exploded his revenue. In the 1970's Ka-shing was ready to go toe-to-toe with the largest property developer, Hong Kong Land, owned by Jardine Matheson (the empire of the elite Keswick Dynasty of Scotland). Simon Murray is one of Ka-shing's most trusted managers and was in the French Foreign Legion and worked at Jardine Matheson. During his time haggling with the elite of Europe, he became intimately involved with international banking. Sadly, his wife, Zhuang Yueming, died after "taking the wrong medicine". She was taken to the hospital but there was nothing to be done. Although Ka-shing couldn't respect his wife enough to not cheat on her while they were married, he never married again and worships her grave every New Year. His leap into media included investing around $50 million in Spotify, $15.5 million in Siri Inc, and acquiring joint ventures with MTV, AT&T, Motorola, Warner Media and more. His oil business, Husky Oil, is valued at $1.3 billion and his Canadian Imperial

Bank of Commerce in Toronto has a market value of $4.3 billion. That's not all dear reader.

Ka-shing donated an estimated $85 million to create a University in Shantou in South China. In 1998 he sold his 1 million square foot tower on 60 Broad Street in Manhattan, for $62 million. Among his real estate enterprises is Vancouver's $2 billion Pacific Place, another is Singapore's $1 billion Suntec City. He has invested interest in Canada and thanks to his real estate empire there, and his promotion of the city, 39.3% of Vancouver's citizens are of Asian descent. In 2000 he was knighted by Queen Elizabeth and by 2010, his eye was fixed on Britain. He invested $9.1 billion into the country's power grid operators and in 2019 he bought the Greene King Brewery for $5.5 billion. Over the course of his life, Ka-shing has donated billions to charity. He has been awarded the Grand Bauhinia Medal and been made Knight Commander of the Order of the British Empire. Along the way he has rubbed elbows with Hong Kong's mafia bosses and become a Godfather of Banking, himself. His empire was successfully split between his sons who are Canadian citizens and devout Buddhists.

Li Ka-shing's sons graduated Stanford University as members of the elite they were born into. Victor and Richard have been well prepared to take over the empire. As the eldest son and heir, Victor Li Tzar-kuoi received degrees in engineering, and an honorary degree in Law from Stanford. If only we could all be worthy of an honorary degree... When he was in his 30's Victor was kidnapped by one of his father's business partners, Cheung Tze-keung, whose badass gangster name is Big Spender. He had kidnapped before, murdered, and robbed too. Victor's father, who was also kidnapped until the ransom was paid, gave $132 million for his safe return. Big Spender spent his life like most criminals, running and hiding, until he was executed by firing squad in 1998. After such grand publicity, Victor went on to become a member of the Standing Committee of the 13th National Committee of the Chinese People's Political Consultative Conference. He is also a member of the Chief Executive's Council of Advisers on Innovation and Strategic Development of the Hong Kong Special Administrative Region. He is Vice Chairman of the Hong Kong General Chamber of Commerce, Chairman of CK Hutchison Holdings Limited, Husky Energy, HK Electric Investments Limited, CK Asset Holdings Limited, CK Infrastructure Holdings Limited, CK Life Sciences International, and many more. Victor is also the director of the Hongkong and Shanghai Banking Corporation. He is Grand Officer of the Order of the Star of Italy, following his father who had been made Grand Officer of the Order of Merit of the Italian Republic in 2005.

His brother, Richard Li, is the Chairman of the largest telecom company in Hong Kong, PCCW. After dropping out of Stanford, Richard went to Canada and worked in investment banking. After some time, he began his own company called Star TV in Hong Kong. Star TV was sold to Rupert Murdoch in 1995 for $950.5 million. In

2017 the Walt Disney Company bought it for $52.4 billion. Richard then founded the Pacific Century Group, an investment company, and was also an executive director at Hongkong Electric Holdings until 2000. A very busy man, like his father, he founded Pacific Century CyberWorks in 1996 and acquired Cable & Wireless HKT. In 2001 he became a member of the board of the Bank of East Asia. By 2011 he was the chairman and CEO of many companies and grew to have a net worth of $4.7 billion. That the same year he was given the Lifetime Achievement Award as well as the Queen Elizabeth II Diamond Jubilee medal. When a dancer for Mirror named Li Kai-yin was injured after a large LED screen fell on him during a concert, Richard donated $1.2 million dollars to the family. Soon he became the Governor for the World Economic Forum for Information Technologies and Telecommunications. As one would expect, he is a member of the Global Information Infrastructure Commission, the United Nations, and the Center for Strategic and International Studies' International Councilors Group.

The Grandson of Li Guan-chun, who founded the Bank of East Asia, is Sir David Li. He and his sons Adrian and Brian Li are currently running the family's bank. The sons are CEOs with David as Chairman. David was schooled in Britain and graduated from the Imperial College, London and Selwyn College, Cambridge. Naturally, he was given an honorary degree in law as well as social sciences. He became a member of the Legislative Council of Hong Kong and climbed the ranks to the Executive Council. He is a director and board member of many companies in Hong Kong. In 1991 he was made an Officer of the Order of the British Empire and soon he received the Gold Bauhinia Star from the Hong Kong Government. By 2005 David had been knighted and was given more honorary doctorates from Cambridge, Imperial College, University of Hong Kong, and the Chinese University. Just a few years later he was given the Grand Bauhinia Medal. Unfortunately, what goes up must come down.

In 2008 he was charged by the Securities and Exchange Commission of the US with insider trading, resulting in a mere $24 million settlement. However, his time as the board member for Dow Jones was over. In 2017 David was taken to court again after being investigated for corruption. David gave money to Hong Kong Chief executive, Sir Donald Tsang Yam, to use to buy a broadcasting license for Wave Media. Both men had shares in the radio company. Over several years, David funneled money to Donald which paid for the refurbishment of Donald's penthouse and other properties. Donald had not been given permission by the government to upgrade his domiciles, which brought him under the microscope. While Donald was approving many changes, he was being paid by the Li family. The Bankers own governments. Always have. Always will.

David's brother, Arthur Li went to Cambridge as well and was interested in medicine. Soon he became a patron of the Royal College of Surgeons of Great

Britain and Ireland and a regent of the Royal College of Surgeons in Edinburgh. Like his father and brother, he has been given the Grand Bauhinia Medal and the Gold Bauhinia Star and is on the Executive Council of Hong Kong, in addition to being Deputy Chairman of the Bank of East Asia. He earned the nickname King Arthur early in life, due to his notorious dictatorial nature. He owns a multitude of properties and is a member of the Hong Kong Medical Council, Hospital Authority, Education Commission, and numerous other hospital governances. He holds honorary fellowships with 4 surgeon college associations. Arthur held fast to his interests in the education system but because of his well-known hatred for freedom, academics grew concerned and distanced themselves. His greed is matched by his crappy attitude and disposition, like so many other elite, and his legacy will be left to his children so that they can continue living self-absorbed menial lives set up for them before they were born.

Li Li (not to be confused with the previous Li Li) is President, Chairman, and co-founder of Shenzhen Techdow Pharmaceutical. Li is also Chairman and Director of Shenzhen Hepalink Pharmaceutical, supplying the world with heparin sodium, a blood thinner. In 2010, Li's Hepalink shares rose to $7.8 billion, and the company value was estimated to be $10.5 billion. The startup became successful in 2000 when Goldman and others invested. As of 2023, Shenzhen Hepalink expects its profits to triple. He is also the Executive Director of Shenzhen Luckykind Technology Co., Ltd and Flystone Technology as well as Urumqi Feilaishi Equity Investment Co. Ltd. He manages to find time to be the Director of Shenzhen Topsun Biotechnology, Cytovance Biologice Inc. This amazing transformation happened to Li Li, who started out working in a meat processing plant, thanks to his chemistry degree from Sichuan University.

Today the Li's in the Politburo include Li Keqiang, Li Qiang and Li Xi, confidants of Xi Jinping. Li Kenqiang was born in 1955. He graduated high school in the midst of the Cultural Revolution and joined the Chinese Communist Party. After graduating Peking University Law School, in 1982, Kenqiang was made the secretary for the Communist Youth League at the University. In 1998 he became the youngest provincial governor and pursued his interest in economics. His province was struggling to fight HIV/AIDS, waves of crime, and fires.

In 2007 Kenqiang became a member of the Politburo. In 2010 he spoke at the World Economic Forum and after a series of predictable events he was elected Premier in 2013. Soon he had an arrangement with Britain, that China would design, own, and operate their new nuclear power plants. Like a good Chinaman, he is firmly against freedom of Tibet, holding fast to the traditional racial hatred of them. Li Qiang is expected to become the next Premier of China after Li Keqiang. Qiang became a member of the Chinese Communist Party in 1983 as the secretary for the Communist Youth League. While in Shanghai, after hopping around to different jobs in the party, he opened the Shanghai Stock Exchange. Over the years he has grown into his position as the 2nd most powerful man in China. Qiang has become famous for his recent involvement in lockdown etiquette in Shanghai during the Covid event. 26 million people in Shanghai were locked in the city, doctors and nurses were forced to test them all without food or drink. As anyone who understands how diseases work will tell you...one of the main things needed to heal is hydration, FRESH air, and sunlight. Of course, simply keeping your body alkaline, as it should be, eliminates the possibility of being able to contract a disease so.... there's that... The more you know about diseases and reality, the more ridiculous the Planned Biowarfare Attack called Covid becomes. While I will get into the False Flag event named Covid in another chapter, this was the event that brought Qiang into the spotlight. After forcing millions to be locked in their homes, many starved to death. The South China Morning Post stated in 2022:

"This is a farce of political struggle. The stage is Shanghai, and the props are 26 million people in Shanghai."

'Nuff said. As Premier, Qiang now struggles with the task of "fixing" the economy of China, as protests carry on. No doubt he will play his part well and remember all his lines.

In today's world, even with all of the information we are able to access and the numerous leaks that people have risked their lives to get out to you, the majority of the population of the world is satisfied living in denial and complacency. Today we deny the proven fact that government rulers are puppets and the mainstream media companies (including many alternative news) are fronts, nothing but propaganda mills. Most people in the US are well aware of this fact, which is exposed by the constitution itself, but the rest of the world is asleep while those who are awake remain obsequious. Over the past few decades, China has been stockpiling weapons and ammunition of various kinds for quite some time, buying them from Russia. In 1997 China leased a vacant US Navy Pier, in California, to help speed their enormous imports into the US. By 2014 China had become the dominant buyer of American investment green cards and land purchases. Small towns like Thomas, Alabama, are giving land away to China for free. The land this town gave away was worth $1.5 million. One large company, Smithfield Foods, which holds 460 farms and contracts 2,100 others, has facilities in 26 states and was bought by China for $4.7 billion. The balance of US payments with China shows a growing deficit of 50 billion dollars, which is expected to reach 100 billion in no time. China is also attempting to gain the Panama Canal area, through long-term leases at each end. This would easily lead to the US having to divide its military, assuming the US is still a country by that time.

North Korea, Serbia, Russia, Turkey, and Iran and several other countries have been forming an Alliance to bring back the empires which existed thousands of years ago.

They have already created the necessary currency changes, trade agreements, military alliances, and more with the other countries around the world. While we're on the topic, let's discuss money. Since 2008, the Rothschild's European Central Banks and Italian Banks have bought over 88% of Italian Government debt. Germany wants the money printing to stop as it lost Europe's largest Central Bank, Deutsche Bank several years ago. Brexit helped to create more currency issues within the EU, which will enable the continent to accept the Single Global Currency, as planned. This is the reason many non-European countries are being funded and added into the conglomeration. Qatar supplies gas and more to Europe, Russia, and US but recently all countries have begun to turn away from it, unless Qatar cut all ties with militant Islam. This is impossible as the country is used by the elite specifically to funnel money to these groups. Analyst Giorgio Cafiero of Gulf State Analytics stated:

"If these countries fail to resolve their issues and such tensions reaches new heights, we have to be very open to the possibility of these six Arab countries no longer being able to unite under the banner of one council." (Meaning the Gulf Cooperation Council, which works with the World Bank branch in Washington DC.)

In 2013 23 countries, constituting 60% of the world's GDP, began establishing new swap lines to bypass the US dollar, SWIFT, and the BIS. The countries involved in setting up these lines include Brazil, China, India, Japan, Russia, France, Germany, Iceland, Italy, Luxembourg, Switzerland, the United Kingdom, Australia, New Zealand, Singapore, Turkey, Argentina, Canada, Chile, Iran, South Africa, South Korea, and the United Arab Emirates. The establishment of the BRICs bank, initiated by China along with Brazil, Russia, India, and South Africa, plays a crucial role in facilitating this transition, serving as a bank of international settlement and a lender of last resort. Even Saudi Arabia, a key player in the petrodollar system, is open to renegotiating its ties with the US. China has anticipated becoming a financial superpower and has been diligently working to replace the Dollar with a Chinese-denominated "super-sovereign" international currency.

Africa is naturally a focal point in this global currency war, with South Africa endorsing the Chinese currency in a pilot program to make it the standard for international trade in emerging markets. This initiative challenges the current global financial regime dominated by the World Bank and the International Monetary Fund. Meanwhile, in 2016, Russia became the top global buyer of gold, having $386.9 billion stored in the Ural Mountain Complex. Russia has in the recent decade spent billions to keep Venezuela afloat under US sanctions and has paid off all of its own national debt. Meanwhile the US is in debt over $34 trillion and counting, which will never be paid off, combined with the debt of Europe, it is well over $39 trillion. Karen Hudes stated:

"There is 170, 500 metric tons of gold deposited in a vault in the Bank of

Hawaii. 130,500 metric tons in AMEX Hong Kong. Plus 150,000 metric tons in the Bank of Singapore, for a total of 451,000 metric TONS. There is an additional amount exceeding 100,000 metric tons in other American banks."

Russia has created another research city, called Era. Fedor Dedus, the director of the 'technopolis' has stated that the secret military city:

"will concentrate on the following initiatives: information and telecommunication systems, artificial intelligence, robotic complexes, supercomputers, technical vision and pattern recognition, information security, nanotechnology and nanomaterials, energy tech and technology life support cycle, as well as bioengineering, biosynthetic and biosensor technologies."

The Li family has led us from Opium to Vaccines and Politics. Today they have also conquered the technology industry with the help of Russia and the US, through the work of Robin Li, who hopes to play a game-changing role in what he's sure will be Beijing's dominance in AI. With the help of Google's vice president of wireless services, Milo Medin, a member of China's Military Defense Advisory Board, China's tech industry will grow exponentially, as we have already seen. In Google's Project Dragonfly China's search engine was born. China's nanotechnology companies have also teamed up with the US' Veeco Instruments.

"Google employees have carried out their own investigation into the company's plan to launch a censored search engine for China and say they are concerned that development of the project remains ongoing." - The Intercept.

Let's continue with the last upper elite, world-impacting family before we move onto the latest False Flag Event: Coronavirus and expose some others too.

~Du Pont~

In 1737, the Du Ponts come into the spotlight of the US. The lineage is one of the easiest to trace back as it quickly becomes the Le Riche line of Viscounts in France. The bloodline moving forward includes the blood of the Rockefeller, Roosevelt, Natoli, and the Vanderbilt families.

Remember our KIA Bishop, Pierre di Nemours, mentioned in Part I? His son Éleuthère Irénée du Pont was the founder of EI du Pont de Nemours & Company. Following the genealogy of Pierre di Nemours back we come directly to Arnould Éveillechien le Riche, who was born in 894. His parents were Roger III du Maine and Carolingian Princess Rothilde Rothnaililde du Bourges (born 'du France'), Countess of Bourges and Maine. Roger founded the second House of Maine. Though he was driven out of Le Mans by his cousin, King Odo in 893, he was given back Count-ship before he died. During Roger's childhood, France, was engulfed in battles from the Normans (northern France's Norse inhabitants) and the Britons. Odo was the eldest of Robert the Strong's two sons. There had been a family squabble during the course of his teen years which had grown after his father was killed in a battle against the Normans. Odo and his brother were not given the land their father ruled. During the Danish siege of Paris in 885, Odo proved his worth and by 886 he had regained the counties and monasteries that his father had ruled before. He became very rich and popular due to his monasteries and soon the king had been deposed and the French kingdom was quite divided. But the nobles of Paris decided to crown the simple Count Odo as the new King of Paris and called him Eudes I. Thus, the Du Pont bloodline of kings and nobles continued.

Roger's line leads back to the very first Maine, Gozelin I du Maine, son of Herve du Mans and member of the court of Charlemagne. Counts all. When Goslin was born in 745, France, his father, Gozlin Rogon was 35 and his mother, Altrude Champagne of the Bourges family, was 16. Her father was Cunibert I (Umberto), who was appointed by Pepin the Short in 761. Following the line back, the last names were changed in each generation, as we have seen before. At this time the last name was typically the name of the place the person was from or ruled. Herve du Mans father was Erlebert Therouanne. Erlebert inherited the positions of Duke of Neustie, Count Palatin du Baviere and Chancelier du Rio. His brother Robert was also known as Chrodebert I and became the Bishop of Tours. Robert served King Dagobert I, the last king of the Merovingian Dynasty, and his son Clovis II. Daughter Angadrisma always wanted to be nun, and almost managed to escape a planned marriage by contracting leprosy. She was deified and married to a monk, Saint Ansbert of

Chaussy. These couple of generations in the family are littered with saints. Erlebert's son was deified as Saint Lambertus. Erlebert's other brother was made Saint Hermeland Indre and yet another relative at this time was made Saint Erembert! Erlebert and Rober's father was Charibert de Haspengau, son of Merovingian Chlotar who was made the King of France. When Chlotar became king, France was divided between him and his three brothers. Even though Chlotar had been given immunity by the Holy Roman Church, full-out war was avoided by the brothers. However, they pillaged and plundered each other's lands whenever noble overlords of an area died. Chlotar exiled bishops who wouldn't bend to his will and raised taxes on churches.

Brother King Chlodomer had died leaving his widow, Guntheuc, to be assigned to another king. Unfortunately, her new fiancé killed all of her children, so she fled to her brother-in-law, King Chlotar and married him, becoming one of two of Chlotars wives to be deified. King Chlotar had numerous children with his 5 wives and eventually there was tension in the family. His ex-wife and her son were discontent and in 556, his two eldest sons Charibert and Guntram were sent to do battle against their stepmother and brother Chramn. While negotiations were going on Charibert received a forged letter from Chramn, saying that their father had died. The two sons went home, to find this was not true, which successfully dissolved the potential battle. Chlotar had spent his entire life involved in war in order to take back the lands of his father's empire. Once he obtained it and before his death, according to Du Pont tradition established by his father Clovis, it was divided between his 4 sons. Charibert obtained Neustria, Aquitaine, and Novempopulana, keeping Paris as the capital. He lived much like his father, taking on many wives, including two sisters, for which he was excommunicated from Rome. Guntram received Burgundy and part of the Kingdom of Orléans. Sigebert received the Kingdom of Metz, and last son, Chilperic, ruled the territories north of the Kingdom of Soissons. This is the split that led to the subsequent family squabble that Roger III had been caught up in later. Each sector became ruled by its own new dynasty, all of the same bloodline. As this is such an interesting time, let's dig deeper into King Clovis I, the first King of the Franks.

In 481, Clovis I, also known as Hlodowik (which is Louis), succeeded his father as King of the Franks at age 15. During this time, there were numerous tribes in the northern European area, on the outskirts of the Roman Empire. By 486, Clovis decided to expand his kingdom, taking power from Rome. Remember that during the time of the tribes, many had been taken over by Rome but left with their own rulers in place, who would then pay Rome to be in leadership. Clovis joined forces with his cousins, Ragnachar and Chalaric and marched against the Roman state called Soissons (Northern France). Chalaric betrayed his cousins, refusing to fight. After Clovis and Ragnachar defeated the region of Soissons, they invaded Chalarics land and imprisoned him and his son. Clovis proposed to Princess Clotilde after she had been exiled by her uncle and they went on to have 5 children. They were a legendary love story in the region and many tales were told of them. Clotilde's father had been forced to convert to Roman Catholicism during his rule and held his authority over his land under the leadership of the Roman Empire. Clotilde insisted her children be baptized as the Holy Church decreed. Their first born died following baptism, and the second grew very ill afterwards, but recovered.

In the 490's, Clovis continued across Germany, destroying (uniting) the various tribes. It is recorded that Clovis became a believer of the Living God during the extreme devastation that was happening to his army at the battle of Tolbiac. When all was going to be lost, Clovis prayed:

"O Jesus Christ, you who as Clotilde tells me are the son of the Living God, you who give succor to those who are in danger, and victory to those accorded who hope in Thee, I seek the glory of devotion with your assistance: If you give me victory over these enemies, and if I experience the miracles that the people committed to your name say they have had, I believe in you, and I will be baptized in your name. Indeed, I invoked my gods, and, as I am experiencing, they failed to help me, which makes me believe that they are endowed with no powers, that they do not come to the aid of those who serve. It's to you I cry now, I want to believe in you if only I may be saved from my opponents."

Immediately, the leader of the enemy tribes was killed with an axe and the army began to flee. Having said before battle that should he win, he would convert to his wife's religion, Clovis was baptized on December 25, by Bishop Remigius of Reims and later he and his wife were Sainted (deified). A statue of his baptism can still be seen in the Abbey of St. Remi. Other Shrines and altars and statues to Clovis are still present in Abbeys in Paris. His battlefield conversion is a mirror account of Constantine the Great. This is how politics works. Clovis' conversion allowed him to enter into crusades with the approval and support of the Holy Roman Church. This enabled his nearly defeated army to prosper and for bloodshed to continue. Clovis had quite an exciting blood-filled life as expansion and control were his objectives. He received word that his imprisoned cousin, Chalaric, planned to escape, so Clovis had him killed. As Clovis continued defeating tribe after tribe he was also able to take over control of them through other means. He manipulated Prince Chlodoric to murder his own father and pay tribute to him. When the Prince brought the payment to Clovis, he was betrayed and murdered. Clovis went on to slaughter his other cousins and their families and finally his last relative King Ragnachar and his brothers were killed.

After all of this, now that his entire family were killed, Clovis set up an order of 33 Gallic Bishops, in Orléans, to "reform" the Church. They constructed 31 decrees on the **duties and obligations** of individuals. Clovis' newly united kingdom, which included France and much of Germany, had no standard money system or government. Therefore, the Salic Law which uses money as payment of crimes was written and the

Roman Law was rewritten to include the Salic traditions. When Clovis died, he was buried in Paris, which made that city the family's' center from that time on. Though he tried to unite the tribes he had conquered, when he died the kingdom was split between his 4 sons, Theuderic, Chlodomer, Childebert and Clotaire. This created nothing but division in the family, who, like their father, wanted a united kingdom, not a broken one. Clovis continued to be worshipped throughout the whole of France, for many hundreds of years, having his own feast days and rituals which were enforced by the Cult of Clovis. Remember that the lines of the Rockefellers, Medici, and Aldobrandini all join here, which is why Clovis is mentioned in all of their chapters. Since we have detailed the line from here back, let's continue with a summary of the line so as not to repeat ourselves.

In 412 BC the King of the Scythian (Cimmerian) tribe, Marcomir (Markomir) was in power. Remember, back in the Germanic region, many tribes including the Scythians had inhabited the area on the Danube, before the Goths drove them over to the German Sea, where they then became known as Franks. Well, King Marcomir conquered Gaul, what we call Holland, today, and relocated his people there. As we already dissected in the Aldobrandini chapter, his grandfather, and ancestors for generations before, were the Kings (Ilium) of the Cimmerian tribe, also known as Scythians, leading back to King Helenus IV and Scythia. The Cimmerian Dynasty leads us back to its founder Priam III, King of Cimmerians. Following Priam back we discovered Francus in the late 1100's BC, and his great grandfather, Priam who was the High King of Troy around 1230 BC. Priam was a direct descendant of Tros, the founder of Troy. Priam's son Helenus (also called Scamandrius) was the twin brother of Cassandra and given the name Helenus by a Trojan soothsayer. He was described as a brave warrior. One story states that while he and his sister slept in the temple of Apollo Thymbraeus, which has been uncovered by archaeologists as discussed before, snakes came to them giving them the gift of prophecy and ability to understand the language of birds. After Paris died, Helenus and his brother both focused on gaining Helen of Troy's hand in marriage. When Helen refused Helenus' offer, he stormed off to Mount Ida, and was captured by the Greeks. He then advised them to build the wooden horse and carry off the Palladium. After the Trojan war, he settled in Epirus. Helenus married his friend's widow, Andromache, and became king. This line leads straight to Noah as we already know, so let's move on!

Continuing on, the King of Sicambri, Merovachus lived in 95 BC. After battling Goths and other tribes, he led his army of 22,000 men, across the Rhine and against the mighty Roman Empire and succeeded in overthrowing Bohemia. From Chlodio to Merovachus and throughout this line, you will continue to see kings in every generation. This family was one of many who fought back against the Roman Empire's expansion, continuously, and from his bloodline the name of Merov continues to pop up, in various forms. Merovech, also known as Meroveus, Merwich, or Merowig, is considered the founder of the Merovingian Dynasty, the Kings of the Salic Franks.

His father, Clodion le Chevelu V, was born around 390. Also called Chlodio, Clodius, and Le Chevelu (Long Haired/Hairy), he was a king of the Salian Franks and resided in Dispargum. His relatives and sons were all known as The Long Haired, as long hair was a staple quality of the family. Born in the Rhine, Chlodio invaded the Roman Empire. In 428 he settled in Northern Gaul (France) before expanding his territory down to the Somme River, after dealing with numerous counter attacks by the Roman Empire.

Following the line we come to King Odo, whose great grandson was King Philip, the son of Anne of Kiev. Philip was made king when he was 7 years old, making his mother the ruler of France until he came of age. He was called "the Amorous", a reputation he earned. In 1007, he married Bertha to form peace with the Count of Flanders (Holland). He soon fell in love with the wife of Anjou Count, Bertrade and claimed his wife was too fat to love so he could leave her. His lies worked and he married Bertrade. He was excommunicated by Bishop Hugh of Die, and again by Pope Urban II. A French Abbot Suger recorded:

> "King Philip daily grew feebler. For after he had abducted the Countess of Anjou, he could achieve nothing worthy of the royal dignity; consumed by desire for the lady he had seized, he gave himself up entirely to the satisfaction of his passion. So, he lost interest in the affairs of state and, relaxing too much, took no care for his body, well-made and handsome though it was."

During his reign his kingdom was filled with battles and blood-feuds between the Counts and other landholders, however, he was able to accomplish peace between France and England, which was ruled by Rollo's descendant, William the Conqueror. When the first crusade was launched, he was hesitant to join in due to his disagreements with the Pope, so his brother was sent in his stead. He left behind 6 children, including the next king, Louis VI "the Fat" who founded the House of Capet. Louis had several wives, including Adelaide, niece of Pope Callixtus II and had many children. He was advised by Abbot Suger, even before his reign. He began to form a centralized government in France, as there was no control or order in the various Counts who battled endlessly. He eventually died of dysentery, after a lifetime at war. His descendants were a continuing line of Kings of France, mostly consisting of the names Philip or Louis. The royal court was notorious for the rampant debauchery and pagan rituals. The same as it is today in ruling circles.

The House of Capet continued as Louis IX (Ludovico, Hlodowik) was born in 1214. The House of Capet came to an end in 1328, because the sons of Philip IV didn't have any more males. Such happens in most lines as we have seen...the reason for which is up to speculation although given their actions through generations, it makes sense. When the House of Capet died out, Philips brother who had formed the House of Valois took the throne until it was passed to another relative, the son of Louis IX, who founded the House of Bourbon. After this it passed to the House of Orleans (another descendent of the Capets) and the French kingdom was only out of the hands of this family during the short reign of Napoleon. When Louis was 9 years old, his father was made king. By then, he had been learning Latin, public speaking, writing, military arts, and government by special, private tutors, in preparation of his own rule. Unfortunately, his father lived only three more years and when Louis was 12, he was made king. His mother ruled in his stead, until he came of age. Like a devout Roman she is quoted as stating to her son:

"I love you, my dear son, as much as a mother can love her child; but I would rather see you dead at my feet than that you should ever commit a mortal sin."

To a young child, this is quite violent and shows her passion for the elite's paganism that doesn't believe in the Living God of forgiveness and love. Louis grew up under her vigorous, religious tutelage and when he was 20 years old, he became King of France with his mother as his advisor. He immediately named his brother, Charles, as Count of Anjou. When he was 20, he married 13-year-old Margaret (Marguerite) of the House of Barcelona. Her sisters were Queen Eleanor of England, Queen Sanchia of Germany, and Queen Beatrice of Sicily. It was only natural that she be Queen of France. Louis and Margaret got along well together and enjoyed the same things, which caused much jealousy in mother. Mother did her best to keep them apart as much as she could. In 1239, Louis paid off his friend, Emperor Baldwin II's exorbitant debts. Louis became well known for his excessive religious fanaticism, as well as his peace-making skills when it came to treaties, allies, and friends. In 1242, Pope Gregory IX decreed that the Talmud be destroyed. King Louis obeyed, burning 12,000 Talmuds and a multitude of other Jewish documents on June 12, 1242. The numbering here should satisfy all Talmudists and Kabbalists. He went on, in his religious purification of the country by enacting punishment to anyone who blasphemed. The punishment for this was mutilation of the tongue and lips. As southern France was home of the pagan Cathars, who still practiced the original religions of the region, unaltered, the number of punishments were higher in this region. Property was confiscated from the Cathars and others in increasing amounts, until Louis went off on his crusade.

In 1249, Louis set off on his first Crusade, called the Seventh which took him to Egypt. For many decades now the Roman Empire had been trying to regain territory lost when the empire collapsed and was reborn as the Papal States. Since they lost control of Jerusalem, they wanted to take it back, but the Egyptians wanted it too and had become the heart of the Muslim Empire. Thus, it was disguised as a Holy Quest to save the Holy City. Decade after decade, more and more people were killed in the name of Holy War. Louis' father was involved in a Crusade, during his short reign, like his father before him and so forth. Brothers Charles and Robert accompanied Louis and as they came to the Nile, the sultan had died. His widow took the opportunity to take control of the army and when Louis and his crusaders landed in Damietta, the town had evacuated due to the death of the king. The soldiers were able to cross the Nile uninterrupted. The peace didn't last long for Louis, as the queen sent her army down and ordered the citizens from all around to move back to Damietta. The population proceeded to use guerrilla warfare on the invaders and the crusade came to a standstill.

Luckily, Louis' other brother heard about the sultan's death and hurried his army over to help out. The plan was to take Cairo. Robert took the Knights Templar and went by way of the canals through several towns, in a boat-ride bloodbath until he came to the royal palace in Al-Mansurah. The queen took the advice of her military leaders and opened the gates of the palace. Robert and his Knights ran in, only to be locked inside by the Egyptians. The crusaders were hit from all sides, as the population and the military attacked relentlessly. Only 5 Knights made it out of the city alive. Robert was killed, after attempting to hide in a house. The crusaders retreated to camp only to be attacked by the queen's forces, who used Greek Fire (flame throwers). The only reason the French saw this mass slaughter as a victory was because the Egyptians had taken more losses in battle.

Shortly thereafter, the crusaders were all hit with a plague. Louis attempted to talk the Egyptians into giving up Jerusalem in exchange for surrender. This was rejected. The crusaders hobbled out of Cairo, followed closely by the Mansurah Army who attacked and took captives back to Cairo. In their panic, the crusaders forgot to blow up the bridges they crossed, as was customary, and the Egyptians stayed close behind. The Egyptians were able to destroy the bridges and trap the crusaders at Fariskur. Thousands were killed and taken prisoner. Louis and his remaining brothers were all taken captive and chained underground in Al-Mansurah. Upon hearing of this, France exploded in an uproar and a crusade to rescue King Louis was created by his wife, Margaret. Because she was with Louis, during the entire crusade, she managed to win the hearts of France and ransomed Louis for 400,000 dinars ($273). Louis, his brothers and 12,000 other crusaders were released by the Egyptians. While recovering in Damietta, before setting out for home, Louis and Margaret had a son, Jean Tristan. Louis was banned from entering Egypt again, and it was the last time crusaders ever dared.

Louis built many houses and facilities, hospitals and more during his time back in France. His wife and him had a total of 11 children, only 8 of whom survived. Louis' brother, Charles, called Charles du Anjou, became the founder of the second House of Anjou, within the Capetian Dynasty. In 1246, when Charlie was about 20 years old, he became the Count of Provence, and Maine as well as Count of Forcalquier (a district of the Holy Roman Empire). As one would guess, given his appointment by Rome, he was quite intimately acquainted with the Papal lines. By 1266 he had become King of Sicily, proclaimed King of Albania, and Prince of Achaea. After the crusade, he purchased a claim to the Kingdom of Jerusalem. Louis stayed in

Jerusalem for several years, after Egypt. In 1267, he got the itch to join the Eighth Crusade and took his sons, Philip III, and Jean Tristan. He landed in Tunis, followed by his brother Charles. Only a few years later most of the knights died of dysentery, which claimed the life of Louis and son, Jean Tristan, as well.

After Louis' death, his brother took his intestines and heart and preserved them in an ancient funeral ritual. The process, called Mos Teutonicus, starts with the body being dismembered. Then, the pieces are put into a giant pot and boiled in water, wine, milk, or vinegar, until the flesh melts away from the bones. The flesh and internal organs were typically buried or preserved with salt. The clean bones are then sprinkled with perfumes or fragrances. Louis' bones were sent, in procession, across many countries from Sicily to Paris. In 1297, thanks to the promotion of his brothers, after his death, Louis became the only King of France to be sainted by the Holy Roman Church.

Following the line, we come to Philip III's grandson, Philip IV, who was called the Iron King, and Philip the Fair. Born in 1268, he had seen his share of death by the time he was 3 years of age. His grandfather was killed in the crusades, his mother, who was pregnant with her fifth child, died when she fell off her horse, and then his younger brother died. A few years later his brother, Louis, died, leaving him as the heir. In 1284, Philip married 11-year-old Queen Joan of Navarre, who had grown up with him, under the protection of King Philip III. Philip became emotionally dependent on Joan, which meant she was never able to visit her own kingdom of Navarre. While Philip didn't trust her with authority over much of France, she was allowed to stay Queen of Navarre and Countess of Champagne. They had a total of seven children. After a victorious battle against a Count who tried to invade Champagne, Joan founded a college in Navarre, in 1305. That same year she died. Bishop Guichard of Troyes was arrested in 1308 for "killing her with witchcraft" but was released five years later.

After many wars and crusades, Philip had incurred a great deal of debt, in many things, but particularly to the Knights Templar. Due to the crusades losing their popularity with the public, at long last, the Knights were able to be pushed out of France. On Friday, 13 in 1307, a massive sting operation was conducted leading to the arrests of hundreds of Templars in France. They were taken and tortured into admitting heresy within the Order. Those who confessed were burned at the stake, without trial. After 7 years imprisoned and tortured, in 1314, Jacques de Molay, the last Grand Master of the Temple, was slowly burned at the stake, in the palace garden. Eight months later, Philip died a few weeks after suffering a cerebral stroke during a hunting excursion. His sons took their turn as ruler, but all of them died very young, leaving no heirs behind. Philip's only daughter became queen of England and the House of Capet ended, in France. Philip's brother, Charles of the House of Valois, took over French rule.

In 1396, Philip III, also called Philip "the Good" was born. His father, John the Fearless was the Duke of Burgundy, a placement Philip was given as well. When Philip turned 8, he was made the Count of Charolais and engaged to his second cousin, 9-year-old Michelle de Valois, Duchess of Bourgogne. In June of the following year, they were married. After his father was assassinated, Philip attacked those he thought were culpable and civil war ensued. Michelle died in 1422 and a couple of years later, Philip married Bonne de Artois, who died the following year. Philip strengthened bonds with England and captured Joan of Arc in 1430. He sold her to England, who then orchestrated a trial that would condemn her, regardless, and burned her at the stake. In the same year, Philip founded the Order of the Knights of the Golden Fleece. The Order was sold to the public as a Catholic Order, but was shrouded in pagan symbolism, including the Golden Fleece itself! Knights of the Order were forbidden from joining other Orders. Today members include: King Felipe VI of Spain, Constantine II of Greece, Carl XVI Gustaf of Sweden, Emperor Akihito of Japan, Princess Beatrix of the Netherlands, Queen Margrethe II of Denmark, Queen Elizabeth II of the United Kingdom, Albert II of Belgium, Harald V of Norway, and Enrique Iglesias, to name a few.

Philip became well known for his extravagance and excessiveness and now called himself the "Grand Duke of the West". He married Isabela de Portugal, who was an avid fan and patron of art, and educated in several languages. She was responsible for arranging many marriages, within the court. After many battles and wars against England, peace no longer satisfied Philip and he sided with the French Nobles to battle some more. Isabela distanced herself from Philip and court life, creating her own separate court, out of the victims of Philips decrees. Philip carried out his excess in sexual promiscuity, having numerous lovers, including (but in no way limited to): Katherine de Bourgogne, Isabelle de La Vigne, Catharina Schaers, Jeanne Céline de Presle de Liezele Countess de La Roche, Jacqueline van Steenberghe, Nicoletta (Casteleyn) de Bosquiel. He had over 20 children, in all, though very few of them survived infancy. Philip died in 1467.

Moving right along, in 1519, King Francis I and Claude had a son Henry II. By this time the French royals had become notorious for their extravagance and Henry was to be raised in the magnanimous Château de Saint Germain en Laye, now a national museum. In 1525, his father was taken prisoner in Spain where he made a plea to Charles V, Emperor of Rome, whom he had gone to war against, to set him free in exchange for his two sons. At 7 years of age, Henry and his older brother, Francis, were sent to be imprisoned in Spain for the next 4 years. When he was 14, he married Catherine de Medici of Florence. Catherine's parents died just after her birth and she was raised by her paternal grandmother, Alfonsina Orsini.

In 1520, Alfonsina died, and Catherine went to live with her aunt, Clarice de' Medici. Pope Clement VII, her uncle, housed Catherine at the Palazzo Medici Riccardi for some time. As previously discussed, at this time a revolution against the Medici's took place because the family had become so notorious for sodomy and paganism. Catherine was forced into hiding and for several years she went from convent to convent to keep safe. When she was 14, she was brought back to her uncle in Rome and her marriage was arranged. Unfortunately for Catherine, her uncle died without having paid her extensive dowry. After this blow, she was disregarded. Henry's mistress, Diane de Poitiers (who was several decades older than he), was given authority over state affairs, while Catherine had no authority or title other than that of marriage. Throughout the rest of Henrys life, Diane was involved in every decision he made, and even wrote his letters for him. Henry gave Diane a castle called Château de Chenonceau, known to be Catherine's favorite.

In 1536, Henry's brother Francis, died very suddenly, leaving Henry an abrupt ruler of the kingdom and in need of an heir. Catherine, being a Medici, one of the top Luciferian families, turned to the occult to get herself pregnant. She performed rituals using incantations which required consuming cow feces, mule urine and more. Henry had numerous mistresses and once he had a child with Philippa Duci, the pressure was on Catherine to produce an heir. Henry and Catherine were seen by their royal doctor, and it was discovered that Henry's penis was not formed in a way that would allow for proper impregnation. After a bit of adjustment, Catherine finally became pregnant, and 10 children were born to her, in total. 7 survived infancy. However, Henry's sexual encounters were not hidden, in public or private. He is noted for laying in Diane's lap in public and fondling her breasts. His extravagance and perversions became as well-known as those of his ancestors. Henry created the use of patents, requiring inventors to disclose the details of their inventions for publication, in exchange for monopoly rights. He decided to raise Mary of Scotland as his own, because she would be the next queen of Scotland and arranged that she would marry his son, uniting the two kingdoms. While Mary was living there her handmaid, Janet Stewart, became another mistress of Henry's before being recalled to Scotland. She had Henry's son, named Henri de Valois, Duke d'Angoulême. During this time Henry implemented punishment to all Christians, then called Protestants — anyone against the Roman Church. Those caught being Christ believers and anti-Catholics had their tongues cut out and many were burned at the stake.

In 1559, Henry signed the Peace of Cateau-Cambrésis, ending a long period of Italian Wars. The treaty was sealed by the betrothal of Catherine's 13-year-old daughter Elisabeth to Philip II of Spain. During the celebration, King Henry decided to have a go at jousting. After being knocked off his saddle, he insisted on riding against the same man. This time, the opposers lance shattered in Henry's face. The thick splinters went into his eyes and face and the gory scene caused many to faint. Henry was taken to the Château de Tournelles, and five large splinters of wood were removed from his head. One had pierced his eye and brain. Over the next ten days the king lost his sight, speech, and reason, and died at the age of 40. Suddenly, all eyes were on Catherine to lead the kingdom she had been restricted from. King Francis II was only 15, and very frail and died the following year. Next up was 10-year-old King Charles IX. Catherine became regent and was granted sweeping powers. Charles died in 1574, and his younger brother Henry III took over. During this time, the kingdom was in constant civil war. Henry III died only 6 months after his mother.

Following the line and the name changes as they move through history, you will notice the last name, Pont. A pont is a bridge and, interestingly, there was a very popular and huge bridge in ancient Rome crossing to France called the Pont du Gard. The dynasty de Nanteuil (of Natoli), House of Châtillon, de Nemours Du Pont, Pont d'Arc and de Villebéon are all branches of the same family. Often the translations of their names seem to tell a story of their own. Now, in 1538, we find the Du Pont name coming into use. Jehan ou Jean Dupont was a painter and a knight in Bretagne, France. He married Lady Guillemine Brière in 1556 and they began having little Du Ponts. They had 10 children together, before Guillemine died in 1581. Jehan then decided to get another wife and married Loyse des Hommets the same year. They had a total of 3 children. Jehan died at the age of 70, in Normandy. Today, the Normandy Du Ponts are still alive and well, keeping up the family estate La Vigannerie.

In the 1600's Maria Xaintes Du Pont Cloutier, the 24th great-granddaughter of Charlemagne, landed in Canada. Her husband, Zacharie was a master carpenter and Ship Wright. Zacharie married Xainte Dupont in 1616, and together they had 6 children. In 1634 the family embarked on a two-month journey from Dieppe, France, arriving in Quebec on June 4, 1634, on the ship Saint-Jehan. Initially contracted to work under Robert Giffard, Zacharie contributed to the construction of the Giffard manor, the Quebec church, and Fort St. Louis. However, disagreements with Robert led Zacharie to part ways and engage in construction projects, including Fort Saint-Denis. He was granted the fief de la Clouterie and later sold it in 1670. Zacharie and Jean Guyon took possession of the fiefs promised to them by Robert, named "du Buisson" and "La Clouterie" despite disputes and boundary issues. Zacharie became a bourgeois seigneur and master carpenter. By 1668, he had sold his fief to Nicolas Du Pont de Neuville. The Du Ponts, through Zacharie, were vital in the formation of New France, now called Quebec. Xaintes father Paul Du Pont remained in France with her other siblings, while Uncle Benoit took his family to Belgium. In France her brother Guillaume passed on the positions and titles of Lord of Ponthaut to his son who changed the family name to Duval. Following this line for the next 2 generations we come to Francois DuPoleau Duval who had been born in Quebec with his brothers and sisters.

Meanwhile, in the late 1700's Samuel, son of Samuel Benel Nathanael Cahen married Keilche Catiche Du Pont and used the name Du Pont as well as d'Augny. Together they had many children who continued the family business of manufacturing in Paris.

Son Orly Du Pont became a jeweler and member of the Israelite Consistory while his brother Samuel became a forge master and married Rosalie Dreyfus. He had 4 children including Pierre Du Pont and Mayer Du Pont who grew to become an ironmaster, President of the Israelite Consistory of Moselle, and Knight of the Legion of Honor. The family had for several generations been involved with the elite families of France and Germany, mainly the Rothschilds, and had become invested in banking, manufacturing, and trade. In 1896 James Nathaniel Rothschild was born to Henri James. James married the great-granddaughter of Orly, Claude Andree Stephanie Marie DuPont. Claude and her 2 daughters are seen in their photograph taken in 1935 at the Joan of Arc Festival in Compiegne. Claude was a Captain of the Free French Forces and Knight of the Legion of Honour.

Speaking of the Rothschilds, the Rothschild Investment Corp's most recent portfolio value is calculated to be $1,185,327. Rothschild Investment Corp top holdings are Apple Inc., JPMorgan Chase Bank, National Association, NVIDIA Corporation, Alphabet Inc., Chevron Corporation, Kenvue Inc., Truist Financial Corporation, The Dow Chemical Company (which is the DuPont Chemical Company), Patterson-UTI Energy, Inc., and iShares Trust.

Let's wander into Ireland, where John Philpot Curran was born in 1750. Along with King George III, he formed the Most Illustrious Order of St. Patrick, also known as, The Monks of the Screw. The Order was much the same as the Order of Bath, an elite club used to gain control of the politics of Ireland now that it thought it was free. Priory Curran named his estate after his position. It is now called St. Comuba College. The Right Honorable Prior John Curran is best known for his writings, including the famous quote:
"Evil prospers when good men do nothing."

This appears to be true, not only in his personal life but throughout history and especially today. John was known for dueling, as well as being a captivating orator. After overcoming his stuttering, he made many famous friends, including Byron and Fitzgerald. John married his cousin Sarah, and they had eight children before she left him for another man, whom John later sued. His favorite daughter, Gertrude, was killed at age 12 by "falling" from her window. He disowned his other daughter, Sarah, for running off with a man he did not approve of. The man was later judged by him, jailed, and decapitated. He was a ruthless man, displaying all the qualities of the elite. Reference to his friendship with Du Pont can be found in his letter from Amsterdam, dated August 5, 1785.

Meanwhile Jehan Du Pont had sons Eustace, Jehan, Jonas, and Abraham I. Three generations later Pierre Samuel Du Pont was born in Nemours, France, 1753 and Cousin Abraham was taking his family from Europe to America. Samuel, Pierre's father, was a watchmaker. His mother, Anne de Montchanin, taught him mysticism and how to contact demons and the Fallen. Anne was from occult nobility and Pierre took after his mother far more than his father. Pierre became a watchmaker's apprentice by the time he was 14, even though he disliked it. His real passion lay in politics and writing. Pierre was a genius, able to translate Greek and Latin fluently by the age of 12. By 16, his mother had died, and his father had become increasingly abusive. They had never gotten along well as Pierre was more educated than his father. So, Pierre ran away and lived with his uncle, Pierre de Monchantin. In 1762 some of his treatises on economics were published and he was instantly noticed by the "right" people. Young Du Pont was initiated into the Rothschild's Illuminati group and obtained many influential friends. A few years later, his career began to take off. To this day, because of him, those among the inner circle of the Illuminati receive a custom stand-up clock from the group, upon marriage. The clock must always be kept in the family, set five minutes early, and kept in good order. The elite know that every event they plan and process they make is kept in a delicate balance of time. They waste none of it.

During the next decade, he became editor of the Public Library of Moral and Political Sciences (Les Éphémérides du Citoyen). By this time, he was well within the elite clubs and circles, as one would expect. After his document, Observations on the Slavery of the Negresins, was published, Pierre was invited by fellow King Stanisław II to help organize the Polish-Lituanian National Education System. In the early 1770's he became a member of the Commission of National Education. Pierre was a deist, like his friends and family, and believed that inbreeding was vital to both preserving the family fortune and ensuring "purity of blood". This mentality thrives, as we have seen, throughout elite bloodlines because of their Luciferian beliefs.

> "Pierre-Samuel du Pont, founder of an American dynasty that believed in inbreeding, hinted at these factors when he told his family: 'The marriages that I should prefer for our colony would be between the cousins. In that way we should be sure of honesty of soul and purity of blood.' He got his wish, with seven cousin marriages in the family during the 19th century." – Discovery Magazine

As a deist, Pierre believed that nature was god. Again, it's easy to see how people misinterpret the meanings of words used by the elite. Many people generally assume that those who mention 'god' mean the Living God or Jesus, His son. Nothing could be further from the truth. To the elite, christ and god are Lucifer. Pierre believed in his ancestor, Plato's, idea of government, which included a philosopher king. Plato also worked to combine his pagan mysticism with Christianity to destroy Truth, as many are doing today, calling it Christian Science. Pierre's time in politics was spent discussing the New World Order and he was instrumental in establishing a nationalized education system.

> "Those who are able to see beyond the shadows and lies of their culture will never be understood, let alone believed by the masses." – Plato

During this time, two of Pierre Du Pont's best friends and fellow Masons, Jaques Necker and the Marquis de Lafayette, "loaned" him exorbitant funds for his schemes in business and in forming a communist society. By 1776, Benjamin Franklin, another close friend of Pierre Du Pont and other elite families, had become a member of the Collin's Hell Fire Club. Though his name should be a big enough clue of his lineage, he is a FreeMan who were called Frank, Frankline. He is descended from Father Unk Franklin-Francline, from 1495 Ecton, Northamptonshire, England (also spelled Franklyn, Franclyne, and Fraunclein when they lived in France, etc). Benjamin Franklin and Thomas Jefferson, fellow members of the clubs were known for practicing satanic sexual occult rituals with the groups, were deists which is further exposed in their writings, and served elite interests in the New World. But I digress...

In 1784 Pierre Samuel du Pont de Nemours was made a noble, regaining his family's fortunes as well as titles, through "letters of noble patent" from King Louis. Sadly, Pierre's second wife, Nicole Charlotte Marie Louise Le Dée de Rencourt, died, having only 2 surviving children, Victor and Eleuthère. Pierre was given the position of Inspector General of Commerce by King Louis XVI and was instrumental in writing and negotiating many treaties during his time in office. In 1786, three years after writing the treaty, Pierre Samuel Du Pont planned to sit with Benjamin Franklin at the treaty table in Paris, and finally see it signed. Unfortunately, he was deceived by John Adams. It was he who got the Americans to sign a treaty with Britain but *without* France's involvement. Alexander Hamilton was not only an agent of Mayer Rothschild's American banking system, but also Pierre Du Pont's lawyer in the US and because of his absence, the United States remains a British Colony. It was **never** signed off as an independent nation which is why the taxes collected in the US are given to Britain. During his life, Pierre had travelled back and forth from France to the US as he not only had business there, but many friends. During this time of upheaval in Europe, a multitude of Freemasons and Jesuits (elite Luciferians) had emigrated to the US to create a New World. But let's not get too far ahead in our timeline.

In 1771, the Duc d'Orleans, Louis Philippe II became Grand Master of the Grand Orient of France was head of all the French masons. He was a believer in "enlightenment" (term of the elite for Illuminated meaning having the "Secret" knowledge). During the time of the French Revolution, there were 1250 Masonic Lodges in France. Louis, along with two other key Masons, Charles Talleyrand, whose last name became a slang term for cynical/crafty given his diabolical character, and Gabriel Riqueti, known for his violent nature, formed the Society of the Friends of the Constitution. Another year, another Order. The name of the original lodge of the Jacobins was changed to Club Breton and then Jacobin Club. The Jacobins were an

Illuminized type of Freemasonry, another sub-sect of the Jesuits. They practiced mystic rites including human sacrifice, as all Orders do.

"You've got to find some way of saying it without saying it." — Freemason Edward Ellington

The President of the Jacobin Club was Freemason Georges Jacques Danton. Danton was a member of the famous and powerful Nine Sisters Lodge. Nine being 3+3+3, as well as an inversion of 6, the master number for Luciferianism, and sisters or muses, as the Pleiades is called. It always leads to the Occult. Always. This IS the language of the Kabbal, of Lucifer. Some Jacobins include Lafayette, George Washington, Maximilien Robespierre, Adam Weishaupt, and Jean Jaques Rousseau. As we have already discovered, these men later produced the orders of Socialism and Communism which have their roots firmly in Luciferianism. Today it would be called "New Age" and other some such nonsensical terms to hide the facts from the ignorant.

Around this time, King Louis had become increasingly resentful of Parliament. They were to merely record the Kings laws and wishes and give advice, accordingly. However, they had begun to grow unruly as the reputation of the royals had fizzled out. The French court had not improved since Pierre's du Pont branch had been in place. The court had become known for only one thing: excess. Excess orgies, spending, drug and alcohol use, perversion, and corruption on every level. The royals had been so overly extravagant and pagan for so long and the public had been successfully agitated, with help from Rothschild and others' propaganda. Because of the king's increasing debts, many Acts and Taxes were passed and the struggle for power between Parliament and the king grew. He had an argument with Louis Philippe II who had given him some attitude, and Louis Philippe and a couple of his friends were placed under house arrest. The government was officially at a standstill.

In 1788 the King had called the military to Parliament to regain control. Riots broke out across France and the Estates General was convened once again, in an attempt to resolve the conflicts. The Estates General consisted of 3 Estates. The First represented the Catholic clergy, the Second the nobility and the commoners made up the Third. The First Estate was the parasite of the Third, owning much of the land and collecting taxes from the peasants. The Second Estate owned roughly 25% of the land, collecting dues and rent from the peasants as well. The Third Estate, those pesky commoners, were the lawyers, local officials, industry workers and some were landowners. The representatives for each group were elected and this year, half of the delegates were from the Third Estate. This would be a pleasant surprise, if it were truly the members of the Third Estate who were in charge of representing it. Those elected were nobles including Jean Joseph Mounier and Gabriel Riqueti, Count of Mirabeau. Many representatives of the Third Estate were executed in the following years. After the meeting of the Estates General, the issues brought up were the financial crisis and the abuse of power, as one would guess. To address the issues of the meeting, a convention was planned.

Director-General of Finance Jacques Necker was one of the speakers. All the speakers ignored the abuse of power problem and focused on the fiscal information, strictly. This only agitated the crowd further. A debate followed on what the roles and political power would be regarding the three Estates. Though the King resisted the reorganization of his government, one year later, the Third Estate finally had a voice and renamed the Estates General the National Constituent Assembly, of the people not the king. Pierre du Pont decided to stand with King Louis and Marie Antoinette, both notorious Luciferians. King Louis made Pierre president of the National Constituent Assembly in charge of managing the people and added the name Nemours to his name. He worked with Gabriel Riqueti, a Mason and friend of Jacques Necker, Maximilien Robespierre and many others. Maximilien was a speaker and addressed many issues during the protests that followed and spoke out against the requirements to be in office. In 1790 Maximilien was elected president of the Jacobin Order. Instantly he began the task of forming civilian militias, in every district and town. Several months later, he was made secretary of the National Assembly and called for a restructuring of the judicial branch of government, dividing France into sections. He called for salaries that exhibited a "fraternal equality" (occult keywords meaning Elite Control Over All), also known as socialism and communism. By 1791, he had established the Freedom for Defense, which allowed citizens to defend themselves and made the National Guard a service of the people.

"To be armed for personal defence is the right of every man, to be armed to defend freedom and the existence of the common fatherland is the right of every citizen." - Maximilien Robespierre

On June 25, 1971, King Louis XVI was officially suspended from duty. Pierre Du Pont and his son, Eleuthère, stood by the king, physically, as the mob sacked Paris. Robespierre announced that France was now a republic, with a monarch. Over the next year many of those mentioned here were living on the run, hiding wherever they could and giving speeches, when possible, as the country was tearing itself apart. Francoise Du Pont was a militant Jacobin during the Revolution. As a laundrywoman, she didn't make a name for herself, but she became infamous during the persecution of political dissidents. She reported suspected contra revolutionaries to the Committee of Public Safety. Those she would point her finger at would soon find themselves facing the guillotine. After posing as a patient, she targeted the nuns of the Maison de Hospitalieres. She led many protests and because of her spy work, killed dozens of people. In September of 1972, France was declared a Republic and King Louis and Queen Marie-Antoinette were put on trial. Conventions went on for months until finally, in January of 1793, the King was found guilty and, thanks to Maximilien Robespierre's enthusiastic speeches, sentenced to the guillotine. But not enough blood had been spilled to call off the constant violence across the nation.

In November 1793, the true colors of the Freemasons were seen in their campaigns against religion. Many priests in France were killed. The Illuminati posted one of its mottos in public 'Death is an eternal sleep". The translation of this being that Death is another name for Lucifer, and Sleep is a term equated with Freedom. Luciferians believe that Lucifer has a very precise plan which he entrusts only to his very select few at the top, those of elite blood. The Catholic Church is based on this, with its bishops, generals, princes, presidents and popes and rituals and chants. Much of what seems coincidence and unrelated is carried out according to a very controlled and detailed plan that has been carefully orchestrated and carried out for thousands of years, as you have now witnessed in this book. As Aristotle stated, "Nature does nothing in vain". Hopefully, by now, you understand what the elite mean when they say things like Nature, Chance, Fate, Pan...

While the French were revolting, the US saw its first "official" President, George Washington, member of the Knights of the Garter, and member of the Scottish Rite. The Order of the Garter is the secret inner elite club within the Order of St. John of Jerusalem which is the British branch of the Knights of Malta. George Washington performed the 'Rite of the Mystic Tie' in a cave-complex near Winchester Virginia during the French and Indian war. George then nominated 11 Supreme Court Justices, 6 of whom were confirmed Masons. There isn't one Senator, Governor, Congressman, Mayor, Vice President in any country who is not **fully** aware of the Elite control. It is impossible to achieve a high status without being in the club.

"The United States is in no manner founded on Christian principle." - John Adams, during the Treaty of Tripoli

No truer words were ever spoken and ignored. At this time Baron Von Steuben, Knight of the Order of Fidelity, was relieved of his post as General in the American military. While Banjamin Franklin and Silas Deane were visiting France, they heard about their friend's activities and wrote to George saying:

"Lieutenant General in the King of Prussia's service was obliged to leave due to Zeal for our cause."

Zeal, in this case, means rape. When reading the writings of these people one mut understand the language they speak. In 1794, Pierre married Francoise Robin de Livet and adopted her daughter. She was the widower of Pierre Poivre, a botanist. That same year, the Jay Treaty between the United States and Great Britain was signed. America agreed to pay 600,000 pounds sterling to King George III, as

reparations for the American Revolution. The treaty was ratified by the Senate in a secret session who ordered that it not be published. Benjamin's grandson published it, and Congress passed the Alien and Sedition Acts in 1798 so that Federal Judges could prosecute editors and publishers for reporting the truth about the government. Freedom of speech was lost at that time. Eleuthere Irenee Du Pont was already a major printer for the Jacobins since the Du Ponts owned all of the printing presses, aside from those owned by the Rothschilds. This is how the media was twisted and controlled by the Luciferian Elite. They have bought every invention and inventor ever since. Realize this, dear one, by the year 1800 ALL printing and ALL media was controlled by the elite. You may be asking, Why did they agree to pay 600,000 pounds in silver, 11 years after the war ended?

Subversion, dear reader. America was made complete once given the French monstrosity of the pagan statue called Liberty holding the light high up over the citizens to better see their every move. Frederic Aguste Bartholdi, the Freemason sculptor of the Statue of Liberty referred to Liberty as "Libertas", the representation of occult freedom and liberty. Freedom and liberty in the Luciferian context in which it is given, mean sexual liberation, perversion, lust, and gluttony. Libertas was a goddess of victory and war, fighting for immorality. Libertas has lit the way in America for the elite's LGBTXYZ agenda, which will help complete the New World Order. Libertas is depicted wearing a wreath, carrying a spear or sword or scales. There are many sculptures and paintings of her/him with fine robes on, or nude. Libertas was used on coins in ancient Rome.

A word on Mithras, Ishtar, Liberty: The "Mystery of Mithras" also called the "Mystery of the Persians" was active for several centuries in early AD times. Unique underground temples called Mithraea have been excavated in Syria, England, Rome, and other locations. Mithras fought and killed a bull, which then became the ground of life for humans. Mithras' birth was celebrated on **December 25**, along with winter solstice, Nimrod's birthday as I'm sure you remember. Rituals include dining on the hide of a freshly killed bull and eating bull meat and...parts. There are murals in which Mithras is surrounded by the **12 signs of the zodiac**. The early Christian writer, Tertullian, wrote about Mithraic cultists re-enacting resurrection scenes which had been newly implemented long after Christ's time. This is how Luciferians are, they work to twist all things related to Jesus Christ, so you are left confused and blind. There were 7 levels of initiation into the cult. Initiates were welcomed into the community through a handshake, as they do today. One of their initiating rituals is: Mithraic priests place initiates into a pit, suspend a bull over the pit, and slit the bull's stomach, covering the initiates in blood and gore. Zoroastrian cultures used the deity of Mithras as well since it is the original Persian/Arab religion. There are many gods in the Mithraic cult. Caelus is sometimes depicted as an eagle, bending over a **sphere** of heaven, marked with symbols of the zodiac. Another god, whose figure is called Leontocephaline, was a naked lion-headed man, found in Mithraic temples. Entwined by a **serpent**, with the snake's head resting **on** the lion's head, he is represented having 4 wings, 2 keys and a scepter in his hand.

In September of 1797, Pierre's estate was demolished by the mobs. Madame Germalne de Stall, daughter of Swiss financier, Mason and friend, Jacques Necker, protected the Du Ponts during their hardships. She was an astrologer and medium mistress of St. Simon. A couple of years later, the public called for his execution as people were slaughtered daily. He took his family to America, reuniting with long-time friend Thomas Jefferson.

"In 1799 he (Pierre Du Pont) emigrated to the U.S. with his family, and at Jefferson's request, started on a plan for national education in this country. He returned to France in 1802 and was instrumental in promoting the treaty of 1803, by which Louisiana was sold to the U.S." - 10,000 Famous Freemasons by the Missouri Lodge of Research

In 1800, Henri de St. Simon wrote The Globe and The Reorganization of the European Community, which laid out ideas and plans for European Unity. St. Simon suggested, in the early 1800's, that the year 2000 be the target date for the agenda to be in effect. In order to rearrange the world into the New Order, several items and stages needed to occur:

1. Two canals, one through the Suez and one through Panama, were needed to create "**Interdependence**" between the nations. They also suggested a high dam on the Nile.

2. The **technological** transformation of the earth, and the biological creation of a new, **androgynous** humanoid. Progress would be brought about by a series of revolutions. We see this war rages full force to this day and the current generation has already become androgynous thanks to stunted education, hormonal imbalances, and total corruption of the young.

3. St. Simon would have a child with Madame de Stall which would become the anti-Christ. Although this clearly didn't take place, the rest of it has, which is enough.

Upon relocating to the US, the Du Ponts instantly planted themselves in Delaware. Victor and Eleuthère were both Freemasons and members of other elite groups as well. Victor was an aide-de-camp to Lafayette from 1789 to 1792. After the family relocated in 1800, he helped found the Freemason lodge in Angelica, New York and was a member of the Washington Lodge No. 1 of Delaware as well as Knights Templars of Delaware. Meanwhile, Pierre travelled back and forth from the

US to France, helping Napoleon and establishing a few treaties. In 1817, Pierre Du Pont died. By 1819 Victor had become the Grand Marshall of the Grand Lodge of Delaware and a few years later was Grand Treasurer. Lafayette visited the Du Pont's in Delaware in the summer of 1825. The Du Pont's helped build the American capital Washington DC, which was laid out and constructed with numerous occult patterns just like the rest of the elite's landmarks. The third city-state was complete, and the trinity of power the elite hold on this earth was for the first time since Noah, **fully operational** as of 1825.

Eleuthere, having grown up studying chemistry in France, founded the El Du Pont de Nemours and Company in 1802. He used French funds and gunpowder machinery to set up his first company in the US. Over the next decade the company exploded in growth, as the US was far behind Europe in the way of factories and weapons. When the family started in gunpowder, they dominated the industry and by the end of the century they had a monopoly on it. Today, it is an international industry with corporations in Singapore, Taiwan, Brazil, Australia, UK, Korea, Belgium, Luxembourg and more. The Du Ponts implemented a contract with the Coopal Companyin Belgium for smokeless powder. When the formula was received, it was found to be inferior to what the Americans were already producing. The ordeal concluded with the Du Ponts going with their own formula and setting up a new plant at Carney's Point, New Jersey.

In 1810, Eleuthere had a daughter named Sophia. She went on to become a popular artist and writer, creating hundreds of journals and drawings. One article describes two of her drawings stating:

"The first is a drawing by Sophie du Pont of one of the duPonts dressed up like Satan with long paper horns and a tail. Interestingly, according to a 12/12/1829 letter by Sophie to one of her relatives Sophie comments that the costume of Satan was mistaken "for Old Nick". The next drawing is a drawing that went with a letter from Sophie to Clementina Smith, 21 July 1837 which is a self-portrait of what Sophie calls "blackies" (black servants) who "toted" her to her bath in a special chair." – The Event Chronicle

This should sound a bit familiar to you, dear reader, as it mirrors several elite women whom we have discussed. The Du Pont children were noted by nannies and tutors to be spoiled, self-indulgent and self-consumed. Just as one would expect...these poor children are raised completely separated from everyone else, in a world that few can comprehend. They have no love in their lives and no true friends. Growing up this way, of course they are completely out of touch with reality, the whole lot of them!

A letter dated February 24, 1832, and addressed to El du Pont de Nemours and Co. details. In this letter Robert Taylor, the company's agent in Philadelphia, arranged passage for Bernard and Biddy McIlheaney from Londonderry, Ireland, to Philadelphia, Pennsylvania. DuPont was billed $77 to cover the passage costs, and Patrick McIlhenny, who worked at DuPont's gunpowder works, was reunited with his family. The DuPont Company, through its agents, actively assisted emigrants from this region of Ireland, facilitating pre-paid passages for emigrants. In the 1830's, the Du Pont brothers organized a local militia called the Brandywine Rangers. Their flag was a beehive on white silk. Remember the bee was transformed into the fleur d'lys by the Salics (this same bloodline). The bee is also the male aspect of this occult symbol, the flower being the female, as the bee is often depicted on a lotus or other flower. The beehive represents the elite quite well, as they are those who work towards the Hive Mind, a denial of free will. Like bees they protect their queen and attack, sting, torture, poison, murder any who come too close. The hive symbolism also links to the pentagram symbols, as well as the cube symbols.

The same year he died, 1834, Eleuthere Irenee Du Pont had been made director of the second United States Bank. His friend, Nicholas Biddle was the third and last president for the bank and like Eleuthere, worked for the Rothschilds. The Du Ponts' gunpowder company supplied 1/3rd of the gunpowder used in the American Civil War. The family continued expanding, producing smokeless powder, dynamite and more. Some of those who took over various Du Pont gunpowder manufacturing affairs included Alfred Du Pont, Pierre Samuel Du Pont II, Thomas Coleman Du Pont. By the end of the American Civil War, 1865, the Du Pont family owned all of Delaware and, though they were publicly known as Episcopalians, they are and have always been deists.

Another son of Eleuthere, Alfred Victor Philadelphe DuPont, came to the US in 1800 with his brothers and studied chemistry at Dickinson College. He took over the family business in 1818, after an explosion killed 33 people. He married occultist Margaretta Elizabeth Lamott. Their children included Eleuthere's namesake, Lammot, Mary, Antoine and 3 others. Margaretta was a Swedenborgian, Swedish mystical Freemason. Alfred V. P. and his wife organized Swedenborg church. After many years around Du Pont poisonous chemicals and gun powders, which the Du Ponts have placed into water sources, air, and more across the entire world, Alfred retired in 1950, sick and tired. He died 6 years later.

Son Alfred Victor founded the secret society of Phi Kappa Sigma, in 1850. Another son, Lammot, graduated the University of Pennsylvania in 1849. By 1857 he had patented a blasting powder and a few years later he enlisted in the army and was stationed as Captain, at a Fort in Delaware. He became a member of the American Philosophical Society and in the 1880's he advised the family to go into dynamite, before founding his company called Repauno Chemical. He had 11 children with his wife, Mary Belin before being killed in an explosion in 1884. The University of Delaware named their Laboratory complex after Lammot. Their daughter, Louisa d'Andelot du Pont, married into the illustrious Copeland Dynasty and had one child, Lammot Du Pont Copeland, with Charles Copeland. The Copeland family is very large in religious in America, and consequently the world. Like the Collins', they are one of the top lower elite families of the religion agenda.

For example, Kenneth Copeland, a televangelist cult leader, has an estimated net worth of $760 million. That's money he takes from the desperate and alone, who are glued to their screens all day looking for hope, typically the elderly who can't afford it and who are easy to manipulate. 33rd degree Freemason Kenneth Copeland is joined by his fellow Luciferians who include Bishop Eddie Long, Pat Robertson, Robert Schuller, Oral Roberts, Louis Farrakhan, and Billy Graham.

After graduating Harvard, Lammot travelled to Paris, where he met his soon-to-be wife, Pamela Cunningham. They built a castle on 250 acres of land and called it Mount Cuba. Lammot was on the cover of Time Magazine with the title "Modern Alchemist". He then became the Chairman and Chief Executive Officer of his great-great grandfathers' company E.I. Du Pont de Nemours. The New York Times described him as:
    "A heavyset, bespectacled man with a forthright manner."

Lammot Copeland not only doubled the family's oversees businesses but expanded the business' oodles of chemicals and plastics. He branched the company interests out to electronics, instrumentation, pharmaceuticals and more. He was the Director of General Motors for almost 15 years and then, together with Hugh Moore and William Henry Draper Jr., founded the Population Crisis Committee now known as the Population Action International. This advances the interests of depopulation. You can see from its website it is another United Nations Agenda 2030 pusher, making profit off your donations so they can spread more patented Du Pont diseases worldwide. Lammont Copeland also established the Andelot Fellowship at the University of Delaware, which is listed as one of Harvard's financial aid funds. In 1978 he, like his father, was elected to the American Philosophical Society. He died in 1983, but not before having three children and, consequently, 10 grandchildren.

In 1836, Eleuthere's son, Alexis, married Joanna Maria Smith. They had 5 children together, their daughter married into the Coleman line. One son, Eleuthere's namesake, became the senior partner at the company, over his uncle Henry. In 1857, Alexis was killed in an explosion at the factory that also killed Antony Dougherty, Edward Hurst, and Louis Vache. Such things happen with alchemy.

Uncle Henry Algernon Du Pont applied for election as senator of Delaware in 1895, but the following year he was rejected due to proof of voter fraud. He resided on the family's Winterthur Estate with wife, Mary Pauline Foster and children Henry and Louisa. Henry graduated from West Point in 1861 and soon became 2nd

Lieutenant of Engineers. After being promoted to 1st Lieutenant in the 5th Regiment, US Artillery he served in the American Civil War. After he had served the military for over a decade, he became President and General Manager of the Wilmington & Northern Railroad Company until 1899. He was then made a member of the Military Order of the Loyal Legion of the United States and of the District of Columbia Commandery. Following his debacle in 1895, Henry was finally elected to the US Senate in 1906, and again in 1911. During his time in office, he was Chairman of the Committee on Expenditures in the Military Affairs Department and then became Chairman of the Committee on Expenditures in the War Department.

The Du Ponts had also become deeply involved in Silver, as it was the main currency of the time. Rothschild puppet Henry was opposed to the free and unlimited coinage of Silver and while he was able to wield his powers in politics, Henry voted for the Federal Reserve Act of 1913. Henry was also the main participant in the Anglo-French Loan of 1916, to finance World War I. It was the Pilgrims Society of which he was a member, that built the Federal Reserve building, as well as buildings that hold the US Supreme Court, Department of Justice, Department of the Interior, the Du Pont building, 26 war manufacturing plants, and the United Nations building to mention a few. Henry died at home, in 1926. His son, Henry Francis, went on to reconstruct their estate into a museum, expanding the mansion to 175 rooms, filling them with imported furniture and furnishings including hand painted wallpaper from China and the Montmorenci spiral staircase. Who doesn't want to show off the things they can afford and grew up with, and charge an outrageous amount of money for it? He was asked by Jackie Kennedy to oversee the White House renovations from 1961 to 1963.

Henry Francis Du Pont went to Groton School, an Ivy League Episcopalian boarding school in Massachusetts, founded by the son of Samuel Peabody, a partner of the London banking firm JP Morgan & Company, which funds the school. After moving to the US, son Endicott graduated from Jesuit controlled Trinity College, Cambridge, and married his cousin Fannie. Soon they opened the boarding school and implemented the Spartan educational system, cold showers and cubicles included. In 1999, three students came out about sexual abuse in the school's dormitories and as usual, it was silenced even as others came forward.

By 1902, Eleuthere's 24-year-old grandson Louis Cazenove Du Pont committed suicide by shooting himself in the library of a Club followed by the death of Alexis' son, Eugene. The company was passed to three of his grandsons. By 1912 the company had bought up several chemical companies and became influential in law-making. After a bit of tampering the Du Ponts were called out as a monopoly, which they denied and split the company into smaller ones. The same practice is done today to escape the entanglements of law. It's about this time that DuPont was splitting its companies and giving them strict and narrow purposes, that they focused more on chemicals than weapons. El du Pont de Nemours & Company was renamed Central Research Department. Located at DuPont Experimental Station and Chestnut Run, in Delaware, it has since expanded to include laboratories in Geneva, Switzerland, Seoul, South Korea, Shanghai, China, and India. Don't make the mistake of thinking that these people have nothing to do with you.

By 1915, the DuPont family had grown so large that it moved from controlling gun powder and chemical industries to automobiles as well. For $25 million, General Motors was bought, and Pierre DuPont became president. GM became the number one automotive company in the world at that time. Alfred P. Sloan Jr. was the founder of the Sloan Foundation, and the Hyatt Roller Bearing Company. He made a fortune through Oldsmobile and bought up several companies, forming the General Motors Corporation. The Corporation was soon bought up by Pierre, noticing the business's success and monopoly potential. Once Pierre took over, the company exploded. When WWII took place, Alfred Sloan, along with the Rockefellers, Du Ponts and others, worked to advance the German army. Sloan was a long-time friend of Adolf Hitler and GM sent factory machinery and more to Germany along with airplanes and trucks. The equipment that Alfred provided helped Adolf successfully invade Russia and defeat Poland. The Sloan Foundation funded the MIT School of Industrial Management, which was later renamed Alfred P. Sloan School of Management. He went on to fund and build Sloan Institute of Hospital Administration at Cornell University, a Sloan Fellows Program at Stanford Graduate School of Business as well as London Business School, and the Sloan-Kettering Institute and Cancer Center.

In 1951, Alfred received the Hundred Year Association of New York's Gold Medal Award and maintained an office at the Rockefeller Center. He was not only involved in machinery and cars, but funded movies for Warner Bros. and MGM. He became intimately involved in producing propaganda films, as did his friends, to instill the Master Race mentality of the elite into the public and promote mass production and slow death through vaccines, pesticides, and other Du Pont-made chemicals. Today's Sloan propaganda film companies include Sundance Film Festival, Tribeca Film Festival, San Francisco Film Society, Black List, and film schools of Columbia, Carnegie Mellon, NYU and UCLA. They are all used to promote elite philosophy which is: Eugenics and Ethnic Cleansing.

The Sloan Foundation was involved with the Rockefellers' eugenics movement called Human Genome Project. Working with WHO, they set up the plan to depopulate through a series of vaccines, as seen in the UN's Agenda 21. This is one of the current agendas of today, commonly known as CoVid. The point is only to get you to be vaccinated so you can die in the next few years. You should be thrilled with this, as the entire world accepted this elite solution so eagerly, and it was only their first run. Needless to say, the Sloan Foundation works hand in hand with the Gates

Foundation, which has the same objective. In 1927, the US Supreme Court Justice Oliver Wendell Holmes stated:

"It is better for all the world, if instead of waiting to execute degenerate offspring for crime, or to let them starve for their imbecility, society can prevent those who are manifestly unfit from continuing their kind . . . <u>Three generations of imbeciles are enough</u>."

Yes, dear reader, they are not talking about themselves. Getting back to the Du Ponts, in 1930 the company created Freon, making mass-market refrigerators and air conditioners possible for the first time. Do you have a refrigerator? The Du Ponts are in your home in more ways than one, no matter what country you live in. They manufacture Vespel, Neoprene, Nylon, Corian, Teflon, Mylar, Kapton, Kevlar, Zemdrain, M5 fiber, Nomex, Tyvek, Sorona, Corfam, and Lycra and many agricultural "aides" such as those Monsanto provides to over 120 countries. Cellophane and Rayon are household names to this day.

In 1935, a DuPont scientist invented Nylon, a synthetic fiber that proved invaluable during World War II. During the wars I and II, DuPont made a killing selling tires, parachute bags, and more to the military. WWI enabled the Du Pont's fortune to rise from $74 million pre-war to $329,121,608 post-war. When you die, they profit. The faster and in greater numbers you die, the better. They had made a nitrate plant, paid for by the Allied parties of WWI, before absorbing US Rubber Co. and General Motors. After the American government seized the German Dye Trust, their patents were given to the Du Ponts who then began to build a great chemical empire of synthetics: shatterproof glass, paints, rayon, nylon, dyes, photographic film, rubber, chemicals, drugs, etc. They were involved in the Manhattan Project and founded a couple of facilities to research and create the hydrogen bomb.

In 1937, a lead chemist for Du Pont, Wallace Carothers, was found dead from poison after he made amonumental discovery in polymer research, in the Du Pont experimental station. We see this often happen to those who "get too close". Frank Plummer, a Canadian Scientist and The Head of Winnipeg lab, was involved in the Coronavirus Investigation. For this he was assassinated in Kenya. In 1938, DuPont chemist Roy Plunkett, while experimenting with refrigerants, discovered a white, waxy, slippery, material. The material turned out to be inert fluorocarbon called Polytetrafluoroethylene (PTFE). By 1945 DuPont had patented it as Teflon. By 1948, 2 million pounds of it was being made each year. Though it goes a bit further into the future timeline, let's take a look at this one Du Pont company a little deeper.

In 1951, DuPont began using another laboratory-formed chemical known as Perfluorooctanoic (PFOA) acid, also known as C8 or GenX or others, depending on the region of the world you are in. By 2004 a billion dollars were made each year from Teflon. Teflon is found in fast food wrappers, waterproof clothing, electrical cables, and pizza boxes, pots, pans and much more. Unfortunately, it becomes airborne and doesn't degrade with time. Rather, it builds up in the bloodstream more and more with every bottled water and Big Mac you consume. Documents show that signs of C8's toxicity emerged quickly as DuPont scaled up its Teflon production in the 1950's. Naturally, the company funds its own safety-testing laboratory, the Haskell Laboratory of Industrial Toxicology and are regulated by no one but themselves.

"We have been proud to publicize the fact that more than 60 percent of our sales in 1950 resulted from products that were unknown, or at least were only laboratory curiosities, as recently as 1930." - DuPont representative, 1955

In 1961, company lab tests linked C8 exposure to enlarged livers in rats and rabbits. DuPont scientists then conducted tests on humans, asking a group of volunteers to smoke cigarettes laced with C8. Researchers stated:
"Nine out of ten people in the highest-dosed group were noticeably ill for an average of nine hours with flu-like symptoms that included chills, backache, fever, and coughing."

As you can guess, nothing was done to resolve the problem, but everything was done to cover it up. In 1981, after the company's own researchers had labelled the substance extremely harmful (in 1960's) women began to have children with extreme birth defects caused by the poison. DuPont laid off many female workers. Just as the Mercury poisoning in Asian countries was passed off as birth defects from "radiation" (after being bombed), the coverup for Du Ponts poisoning was equally extreme. In 1984 DuPont began telling workers to bring samples of their water into work to be tested. They also tested public water outside the factory since, of course, they had known about the problem for decades now but had gotten away with burying the waste in rivers and landfills, destroying the water table. Having grown up surrounded by Du Ponts, I know all too well of their pollution cover-up. Even in school I had friends who did projects about water contamination, tested water outside of Du Pont plants and in our own neighborhoods to find the devastating results. Water Kills. But what can kids do? The work my friends did was taken by officials and never heard of again. Over the decades, many people complained about Du Pont pollution to no avail. Nothing happened when animals and people began dropping like flies. No one really cares enough.

In 1998 a farmer sued Du Pont for killing his cattle who had drunk the water from the river. The Du Ponts bought the farm and used it to dispose of waste. It wasn't long before the toxic substance built up in the water table and the rivers turned black and foamy. The farmers in the surrounding area experienced massive cow die-offs and autopsies revealed their internal organs glowed neon green. Many farmers died of cancer and other unusual unnatural illnesses. The population, even those not living next to the river, encountered various cancers, and breathing problems. Many lawsuits were filed. Such is the abomination of damaging water...it seeps through everything, into plants that you grow to eat and feed your children, the water from your pipes which you drink and bathe in and wash your clothes and dishes with. Since Du Pont chemicals build up in the body and do not leave, one sip is enough to corrupt the body. You, dear reader, are contaminated. Understand the beliefs of the elite and what they have already done to you. This is called the Slow Kill, a preferred method of depopulation because no one does anything about it. Tomorrow you will forget and the next day you will die.

C8 is so pervasive it can be found in almost every Americans blood. What about in your country? Does your country even know or care to tell you? Not likely. The poison remains, even in umbilical cord blood and breast milk. It gets passed on. It's found in the blood of seals, eagles, and dolphins around the world, including in animals living in remote wildlife refuges including those in the middle of the North Pacific.

There is no mandatory safety testing for most of the tens of thousands of chemicals used. Just like everywhere else, doctors and public health officials have little information given to them about substances used, even if they attempt to identify potential health hazards. Researchers concluded that <u>C8 posed health threats at just 0.05 parts per billion</u> in drinking water, for people who drank that water for a single year. It's almost as though they discovered that people with natural bodies shouldn't consume poison! Today the toxicity of people has become such that this actually has to be explained... They found that the average C8 level in blood samples from the mid-Ohio Valley was 83 parts per billion. The average C8 level for those living closest to Du Pont plants was more than 224 parts per billion. How close do you live to a Du Pont plant?

Once this got out thousands of Ohio residents sued Du Pont. A class action lawsuit was raised against Du Pont for poisoning 80,000 Ohioans and six districts' water supply. Like all elite court cases, it ended with Du Pont settling for over $100 million, a drop in the bucket. Du Pont stated it would pay another $235 million if research, funded by the settlement, turned up evidence of wrongdoing on their part. The Du Ponts worked to create the laws, or rather, alter them to fit their needs and helped draft the Toxic Substances Control Act, which is still the regulatory law for chemicals in the US. This was sold to the public as "look how responsible the Du Ponts are, surely they wouldn't do anything damaging" and the public swallowed it as easily as poisoned water. <u>The law ensures that industrial chemicals don't have to be tested before they are sold.</u> The law also enables companies to claim everything, even the name of the product as trade secrets. The number of chemicals that EPA has banned or widely restricted under TSCA is asbestos, PCBs, dioxin, CFCs, and hexavalent chromium. That's it.

In 2003, Du Pont received the National Medal of Technology, the highest US honor for technological innovation. The company led global research, developing non-ozone-depleting hydrochlorofluorocarbons (HFCs), such as Suva refrigerants, launched in 1991. This and other chemicals were designed for existing air conditioning and refrigeration equipment, avoiding significant societal disruption and expenses associated with new technology. The company received previous National Medal of Technology Awards for advancements in high-performance polymers, herbicides, and aramid fiber. The company, like all elite companies today, has made a commitment to the UN's Sustainability and Climate Change Agenda and participates in the Chicago Climate Exchange initiative for this. This same year DuPont won an arbitration dispute against Unifi Inc., which was accused of not meeting the terms of their polyester manufacturing alliance. Naturally, the arbiter ruled in favor of DuPont, awarding $16 million in damages. DuPont had initially sought $85 million since Unifi wasn't fulfilling their obligations to buy enough product from DuPont.

In their mission to conquer Asia, DuPont established itself in Shanghai, China, in 2003. The DuPont Shanghai Innovation Center is located in the Pudong District's Zhangjiang Hi-Tech Park along with the DuPont China Research & Development Center. Here the empire focuses on enhancing various markets, including automotive, energy, computers, communications, and consumer electronics (3C), as well as food and food packaging. It cost $15 million to build but has recently doubled its size and is now equipped with a 5G network, advanced digital tools, and a virtual tour through the HoloLens mixed reality tool. In 2018 DuPont invested over $80 million to construct a new manufacturing facility in Zhangjiagang, Jiangsu Province, East China. The facility produces compounded high-end engineering plastics and adhesives for applications in transportation, electronics, industrial, and consumer products markets. The facility focuses on DuPont's Zytel nylon engineering plastics, Delrin acetal resins, Hytrel thermoplastic polyesters, Multibase thermoplastic elastomers, lubricants, and specialty silicone materials.

In 2004 DuPont was charged with concealing information, even after millions of internal documents exposing their decades long coverups had come forward in previous court cases. Du Pont paid $16.5 million in settlement to the EPA. Du Ponts counsel Bernard Reilly, showed that company officials planned to push regulators to allow the public to be exposed to higher levels of the chemical than DuPont itself had recommended. By 2015 Du Pont began renaming its companies. The newly named Chemours now operates the Washington Works plant. Chemours' net worth stood at just $695 million as of December 2019. Another major company was renamed Corteva Inc., in 2019 while DowDuPont was renamed DuPont. The more companies one has, the further **removed** they are from legal obligations.

"Spinning off your legacy liabilities into a separate corporation and to some other responsible party appears to be part of the standard playbook in these industries." - Clark Williams-Derry, an analyst with the Institute for Energy Economics and Financial Analysis

A 2019 study done by the Social Science Environmental Health Research Institute at Northeastern University and the Environmental Working Group, identified at least 610 locations in 43 states that are known to be contaminated by PFAS, including drinking water systems serving an estimated 19 million people. Thanks to the Du Ponts, none of these matters, because it's **not regulated** by the Environmental Protection Agency under the Safe Drinking Water Act.

In 2011 DuPont was awarded $920 million in damages from South Korean company Kolon Industries. The court ruled that Kolon stole trade secrets related to a fiber used in DuPont's Kevlar body armor which is used in various applications, including body armor, tires, and fiber-optic cables. The chemical, like most of DuPont's poisons, has been found to produce cancer. Remember, things that touch your skin are absorbed into your body. Plastic, which destroys hormones — especially testosterone. Teflon, which covers your food from all fast-food restaurants, is ingested and absorbed through the skin, causing birth defects, cancers and more. Nylon, which damages the thyroid and liver, causes cancer, skin rashes, headaches, spine pain and more as the natural body attempts to warn of damage and death.

By 2016, more than 3,500 personal injury and wrongful death suits were filed against DuPont in West Virginia and Ohio. The company will see 40 trials per year due to C8. In one case Du Pont was charged $5 million for malice. The DuPont Forever Chemical, called C8, has been allowed to pollute drinking water throughout the world and their other favorite, Teflon, coats cookware and more. In 2020 the Sixth Circuit Court of Appeals affirmed $40 million and $10 million jury verdicts against DuPont in a case related to personal injuries caused by "forever chemicals".

C8 is called GenX in Europe. The European Union eventually created several regulatory standards including REACH (Registration, Evaluation, Authorization, and Restriction of Chemicals) in 2003, which wasn't implemented until 2006 and enforced the following year. However, Persistent Organic Pollutants (POPs) regulation had been adopted in 2001 and implemented in 2004. Due to this, labs were created for testing. These labs are Eurofins, Intertek, UL Solutions, and TÜV Rheinland offer PFAS testing services and make billions in revenue. In 2022 Denmark realized the extreme toxicity of the water but has yet to realize it's because of the Du Pont factories in the highest polluted area. Though the government isn't concerned about the people living now, they do understand this is a generational and global issue. Over the past decade, Du Pont has paid over $1 billion in legal fees and settlements, yet nothing has been done to resolve the issue of poisoning the water table, which is life for everything on earth. $1 billion matters little when one company makes more than $35 billion in one year. That's just a peek into one of Du Ponts companies. Just one.

In Africa PFAS levels are higher in urban and industrialized areas compared to rural areas, with perfluorooctane sulfonic acid (PFOS) and perfluorooctanoic acid (PFOA) being dominant in human samples. Levels of these poisons in drinking water exceed EPA guidelines. Birds' eggs in South Africa show higher PFAS levels, while other environmental media in Africa exhibit levels comparable to industrialized countries.

In 2021 DuPont was awarded a $1.3 million grant from Singapore's National Water Agency to increase Sustainability for clean water. If you see the irony in this, dear reader, you finally understand the DuPont family. DuPont will now research Closed Circuit Reverse Osmosis (CCRO) technology in desalination processes in Singapore. In 2022 the Du Ponts were sued again, for the toxic firefighting foam they produce.

"During its 123 years on the site, DuPont released some 107 million pounds of hazardous waste into the soil, air, and water, according to an environmental analysis completed in 2016. After six months of reviewing hundreds of thousands of documents and using a computer program widely employed by regulators and the military to estimate cleanup costs, Jeffrey Andrilenas, the consultant Carneys Point hired to assess the environmental contamination, calculated it would cost more than $1 billion to remediate the site." — The Intercept

Like every elite family, the Du Ponts have numerous cemeteries and institutions, mental facilities, and hospitals. They are known for having buildings surrounded by tall thick concrete walls with broken glass embedded across the tops, so none may look in, such as at the Nemours Estate. They would house their children there since many of them were so badly dysfunctional from birth. Knowing what we do about the experiments these families are involved in, one can imagine the horrors that have taken place behind their closed doors. The Du Pont facilities today are leading in pediatrics and genetics studies.

Son of Eleuthere Irenee Du Pont II, Alfred Du Pont had a typical Du Pont life. By the age of 13, his mother had been admitted to a mental institution where she died a week later. One month later, Eleuthere II died of tuberculosis. In college at MIT, Alfred roomed with his cousin, Coleman Du Pont with whom he bought out the families' explosives business in Delaware. In 1910, Coleman Du Pont, went in business with President Taft's brother Charles P. Taft of Skull and Bones, to build

McAlpin Hotel in New York City. The Taft family helped start the Skull and Bones Order. Coleman bought New York Equitable Life Assurance Society, which was America's largest insurance company and became Director of Union National Bank, President of Central Coal, and Iron Company and much more. Around 1910 the Round Table orders begin to appear, re-configuring themselves from the branches of Freemason groups, today called Think Tanks.

Coleman Du Pont went on to buy up numerous hotels and gained control of Morgan's Equitable Life Assurance Society. Alfred Du Pont had married Bessie Gardner and had four children as Coleman married his younger cousin and had one. Alfred was shot in the face while out hunting, and eventually his eye had to be removed. He divorced his wife and married the wife of his secretary and had a child before the divorce was finalized. Once Alfred and Coleman had their share of philanthropy, they went into politics, against each other. Alfred won control of Delaware's politics and, in 1911, bought the top paper, the Wilmington Morning News. In 1920 his second wife died. Eyeless and deaf, Alfred decided to marry Jessie Ball whom he had been in contact with since she was 14, when he was 34. Alfred bought up all the newspapers he could and soon controlled 9 of Delawares newspapers and the censorship grew and grew. He was involved in Egyptian occult and after traveling there, returned with a dog named Mummy who he claimed was his reincarnated familiar spirit. He wrote many letters about his magical dog which in one he stated:

> "I have one or two more jobs for Mummy and then I will give her a vacation before I put her to work again."

The public was given the narrative that Alfred Du Pont died of apoplexy, however, those close to him at that time have recorded that he was killed by his long-time mistress, Maggie Payne, who owned the most expensive brothel in the area. Alfred frequented often and Maggie had become pregnant with a Du Pont. When Alfred refused any support, she shot him in the heart. Alfred died instantly and was taken to a friend's house, before the coroner was informed, in 1935. Alfred Victor Du Pont, Alfred's son, served as a private in the marines during WWI, and in WWII as a consultant to the Joint Chiefs of Staff from 1943 to 1945.

The DuPont facility in Waynesboro was found to have leaked mercury into the South River between the 1930's and 1940's, causing long-term contamination. In 2016 the US and state governments proposed a $50 million settlement to address the environmental damage, considered to be the largest in Virginia's history. This will supposedly fund projects for wildlife habitat restoration, water quality enhancement, and recreational area improvements. Over 100 miles of river in the South River and South Fork Shenandoah River watershed remain contaminated by mercury from the Du Ponts. DuPont Corporate Remediation Group issued an official statement which said:

"Since 2003, DuPont has worked cooperatively with U.S. and state governments to assess portions of the South River and South Fork Shenandoah River for impacts from past mercury contamination. The team conducting the NRDA was made up of <u>technical experts from DuPont</u> and a group of trustees from the U.S. Fish & Wildlife Service, the Virginia Department of Environmental Quality, and the Virginia Department of Game and Inland Fisheries...In keeping with its long history of cooperation with, and participation in, government initiatives, and its ongoing support of the local community, DuPont's is committed to a long-term presence in the Waynesboro area and to maintaining transparency with its citizens...The company funds the South River Science Team which is run by the Virginia Department of Environmental Quality and conducts testing and evaluation of the river's water quality...Soil containing the highest concentrations of mercury is being excavated and hauled away and replaced by clean topsoil."

One would wonder where the heavily contaminated soil is going. In this year Du Pont heiress Lisa Moseley passed away, nearly 18 years after her 3rd husband orchestrated the murder of her son's drug-addicted girlfriend. Lisa was recently involved in loaning a politician millions of dollars in exchange for a building permit at her golf resort. Her life, which had been entangled in the typical Du Pont scandals and controversies including her leaving her 1st husband to marry her gynecologist and then her gardener. She gained notoriety once more when her husband Christopher Moseley hired assassins to murder Pati Margello in 1998. Her son Dean was also a drug addict whose brother Peter died from a heroin overdose. Drugs like alcohol are tools used by the unhappy and empty. Rather than turn to Truth and freedom, the lost wallow in their misery until they die. Lisa had been questioned about the murder of her sons girlfriend but never accused or jailed and later she was involved in a federal corruption scandal related to a $2.3 million loan, but the case was dropped in 2007.

Several of the Du Ponts have graduated from Yale, as well as Harvard, like Emile Francis Du Pont and Robert Du Pont, Jr., a research psychiatrist. Robert was the delegate for the US at United Nations Commission on Narcotic drugs from 1973 to 1978. He is especially knowledgeable about what drugs will do to a person. Francis Marguerite Du Pont is deep into genetics research. In 1977, Governor Pierre S. Du Pont, IV and his wife Elise, heir to the Wawa chain.

Lammot Du Pont Copeland's son Gerret van Sweringen Copeland is the proud owner of Bouchaine Vineyards winery. Lammot Du Pont Copeland, Jr. nicknamed Motsey, is Chief Executive Officer of Associates Graphic Services which he founded. He is also a Trustee of Christiana Care Health Services, Brooks School, The Mount Cuba Center for Piedmont Flora, Red Clay Reservation, and the University of Delaware Library Associates. Roger Linscott summed up Lammot best when he stated:

"There are **35 Duponts** on the *Forbes* list of the 400 richest Americans. Interestingly, one of the few members of the clan who even tried to become a big entrepreneur on his own was Lammot du Pont Copeland Jr. who flopped so dismally in 1970 that he was obliged to file the biggest personal bankruptcy action in U.S. history, listing liabilities of $59 million. But all's well that ends well. By 1985 the timely arrival of some new inheritances had restored his fortunes and put him back on the *Forbes* 400 list with a net worth of $150 million."

His sister is Louisa Du Pont Copeland Duemling who graduated from Cornell University in 1958 and became the director of E.I. DuPont de Nemours & Company. She married James Biddle, who were the first family of Philadelphia, and bankers under the guidance of Rothschilds. James was a Princeton graduate and curator of the Metropolitan Museum of Art's American Wing before becoming President of the National Trust for Historic Preservation. Louisa Du Pont Copeland Biddles' children are Letitia Copeland Biddle, Pamela Copeland Biddle, and James Copeland Biddle. Louisa became President of the board at Miss Porter's School and trustee of Corcoran Gallery Art, Winterthur Museum, and the Maryland chapter of Nature Conservancy. She was on the board directors for the National Parks Foundation as well. Cornell University has a bench dedicated to her. James Biddle died in 2005, and though it's not clear if they were ever divorced officially, Louisa had married Yale graduate and distinguished Foreign Officer, Robert Werner Duemling, in 1982.

Before Robert died, from leukemia in 2012, he had been given an Honorary Doctor of Laws degree, Superior and Meritorious Awards from the Department of State, Honorable Order of the Palm of the Republic of Suriname and more. He was a member of the Metropolitan and Alibi Clubs in Washington, DC as well as the Century Association and the Confrerie des Chevaliers du Tastevin. The couple moved into what is now called the most expensive home in Kent. Daughter Letitia was married to Seth Matthew Blitzer by Rabbi Emily Korzenik. Yes, married by a Rabbi because it was now time for the family to relabel itself once again. The shift happened in this generation who went from Episcopalian to Judaism. Letitia graduated from Miss Porter's School and the University of Vermont, an Ivy League school. Ivy League simply means entirely created and controlled by the Jesuit elite. Pamela was married to Joel E. Fishman by Rabbi Bruce Goldman as well as Episcopalian Reverend Gregory Straub. Finally, James Copeland Biddle was married to Kristin Anne Cater by an Episcopalian. He was president of BDC Entertainment.

One family member decided to turn whistle-blower and exposed the Du Ponts and others in the international drug trafficking rings. Lewis Du Pont Smith wrote a book called Dope Inc. which I highly recommend you read as the book details much of the elites' agendas and procedures. His family had a judge rule that Lewis was incompetent after the scandal and the court declared that Lewis could only have

$15,000 of his fortune. The Du Ponts also tried to stop his wedding. In 1992, a federal informant saved Lewis from getting captured, and taken 60 miles into the Atlantic on his father's yacht to be tortured and "re-educated". His family had hired a motorcycle gang with black hoods and some CIA mercenaries to kidnap Lewis. Lewis was able to escape, but as the elite families own the justice system, no charges were placed against them.

Another proud member of the family was John Eleuthère du Pont, who murdered Olympic gold medal winning wrestler Dave Schultz in 1996. As a Du Pont with all the mental instability and excessive wealth that comes with it, John was a self-proclaimed wrestling coach. The Hollywood version of his life canbe seen in the amusing movie Foxcatcher. As is typical of any movie, most of the truth was left out. John Du Pont was described as a "cocaine-snorting, gun-toting, homosexual, psychopath" and like most in his family, was delusional to say the least. He built the Delaware Museum of Natural History to house his personal collection of seashells and birds' eggs as well as his 100,000 stuffed birds. He spent much of his time having the local police over to shoot his various weapons. After buying a medal from an Australian competition, he still wanted more. Unfortunately, he wasn't smart or influential but a laughingstock because of his insanity. Thinking of himself as more than he was, he'd regularly try to impose control over others and gain a version of dictatorship to ease his ego. In 1983, 45-year-old John married Gale Wenk. Shortly thereafter, his paranoia and mental illness started to show, again. He started drinking heavily and the violent altercations between him and his wife became news stories. The Times wrote:

"On a February night in 1984, she said, her husband of five months entered the bedroom and turned the television to a channel featuring patriotic music. When asked to turn down the volume, Mr. du Pont pulled a pistol from a dresser drawer, placed it to his wife's temple and, according to her, said, 'You know what they do with Russian spies? They shoot them.'"

His wife took him to court, and they were divorced, settling outside of court as rich families always do. Unable to get notoriety anywhere, he started a wrestling team in partnership with local Villanova University. He built a state-of-the-art facility on his family's Foxcatcher Farms. He then worked on gathering desperate and impoverished persons, like Dave's brother, Mark, to join his "Olympic team". Dave had won the gold in 1984, and his brother was naively eager to rise to the top of stardom as well. Mark Schultz described Du Pont in an interview stating:

"When I first met du Pont, I thought he was the biggest loser on Earth. His head was caked with dandruff. His teeth were caked with food. He had these little twig arms. It looked like he had swallowed a basketball... I knew I couldn't be around this guy."

Unfortunately, Neither Mark nor Dave listened to their instincts... Dave was invited to move his family to the estate so he could better train his brother but declined for a time. During this time, John had recruited some major wrestling champions, solely based on money and his name. Soon, these turned into sexual relationships for John, and things got weird. In December 1988, former Villanova wrestling coach Andre Metzger, took John to court for being fired after refusing John's homosexual advances. That same year, Villanova dissolved the team because Du Pont's donations and recruiting tactics violated the NCAA regulations. After this, John joined the Team USA Wrestling and continued training his team for the Olympics and donated $400,000 a year. Meanwhile, his drinking and drug addictions became worse, and he rampaged through the county, without consequence thanks to his police buddies. The Times related how Team Foxcatcher participants then started to notice things with John were getting even more bizarre:

"They said he placed infrared 'ghost-finding' cameras in his house, believed the walls were moving and grew afraid that clocks on the treadmills were taking him back in time."

By 1996 John had become dangerously psychotic, pointing machines guns at people, and staying locked in his giant estate for months on end. At the end of January, John drove over to David Schultz's guesthouse, as he now lived with his family on the estate. John's bodyguard was in the car with him when he hopped out of the car and shot Dave, who was working on a car, in his driveway. John shot Dave 3 times, killing him, and then drove home. A two-day standoff ensued between gun-hoarding John and 75 local police and SWAT team members. The police shut off the heat to the house and caught John when he came out to check on it. In 1997, John was found to be an active psychotic, and charged with 13-30 years in prison. During the 75-minute videotaped interview, John referred to himself as the Dalai Lama, the last Czar of Russia, successor to the Third Reich and that the CIA had dispatched a clone of himself to Foxcatcher Farm to kill David. He stated that David was his protector. He died in prison, of natural causes, in 2010.

Emily "Pemmy" Du Pont Frick can be seen in the tabloids and gossip columns helping to keep the family public front going. After all, the papers you own, and control must be filled with something. What could be more sympathy raising than stories of how her dear old mother was living in squalor, "somehow". The Du Ponts today have their hands in the New Age religious movement sweeping the world, as well as genetics, and manufacturing, the perfect example of how the elite profit whatever way the pendulum swings. Like most of the elite families, the Du Ponts are involved in railroads, horse breeding and racing, and other such hobbies of the rich.

The great-grandson and heir of Alfred Irénée Du Pont, Stephen Dent, was married in 1986 to Valerie Johnson. In 2009, this Harvard graduate was extorted and blackmailed **three times** by his prostitutes, to whom he paid tens of thousands of dollars. Stephen Dent enjoyed visiting SeekingArrangement.com and setting up extravagant hotels and sex parties costing more than $200,000. He is reported to call those he pays for "sex slaves" and does "vile and vulgar acts".

Around this time, a study was published in Integrated Environmental Assessment and Management and discussed the exposure of PFAS through munitions in Russia-Ukraine conflict. Due to their thermally resistant chemical properties, PFAS are used as binders in plastic/polymer-bonded explosives (PBX) and in various components of munitions as well as cosmetics, textiles, roofing materials, and more. However, when munitions are detonated, PFAS are released into the air, spreading throughout, contaminating soil, surface water, or biota. PFAS are a class of toxic, manufactured chemicals (not natural ones) found in commercial and consumer products such as nonstick cookware, food packaging, and firefighting foams. Because of its persistent nature, PFAS remains in an environment long after armed conflict, indirectly impacting ecosystems, food sources, and human health.

In 2009, Robert H. Richards, son of Mariana Du Pont Stillman, was charged and convicted of raping his 3-year-old daughter. He was sentenced to 8 years in prison, but the sentence was suspended because, well...he is a Du Pont and therefore immune. He paid a measly $4,395 fine and promised to attend high-end treatment. In 2014, wife Tracy Richards filed a civil suit against Robert, leading to public outrage and media scrutiny. Despite being a self-admitted rapist and child abuser, Robert still did not serve jail time, drawing attention from then-Attorney General Beau Biden. Naturally, elite puppet Beau Biden defended the plea deal.

Among the family's properties is one estate called the Cult House. Cossart Road, known as "Devil's Road," has gained a reputation because of the mysterious occurrences tied to its mansion hidden in the woods. Cult House was originally owned by the Du Pont's who practiced numerous Luciferian rituals. The mansion's history includes associations with Satanists and KKK members. The fact that it is also a hotspot for natural phenomena, including trees that inexplicably bend away from the road, helps facilitate the rumors. Stories of encounters with guards and unexplained lights, symbols, and sounds are among the tales circulating the local area.

From a long line of Du Pont Counts, in the region of Ligonnès, France, one can easily find Xavier Pierre Marie Dupont de Ligonnes, son of Count Hubert du Pont. His life was that of most Du Ponts, surrounded by old money and titles. He was a philanthropist like just about everyone in the book, meaning he had too much money to know what to do with. Rough and tumble, Xavier spent much time travelling. Upon returning home, one year, he noticed his old girlfriend was pregnant and decided to help her. When Agnes' son was 2, and she was pregnant with their first child, she married Xavier. A couple of years later, a daughter arrived. Agnes was a deeply devout Catholic and instilled her beliefs into her children. In 1997 their last child was born. Suddenly, Xavier seemed to hit a low point in his life. All at once he closed the lease on the family home, as well as all bank accounts. He bought a rifle, a silencer and bullets and obtained his gun license in 2011.

Xavier bought many bags of concrete, quicklime, a shovel and hoe and other suspicious items and a couple of months later, in April, his entire family disappeared. By the 6th of April, all signs of life were gone from the house including their dogs. A few days later the younger children's school received a letter that they would no longer be attending the school because the family moved to the US under Witness Protection. The same typed letter, which rambled on about the super-secret work the family had been involved in was sent to Agnes' workplace as well as family members. While Xavier had taken off, travelling through France alone, neighbors and friends kept wondering what had happened. Finally, over a week later, a super concerned friend had the police go through the house...what a help.

After all of that time, by the time the police had gotten there, the house looked normal, just empty. By the 15th of April, Xavier had disappeared completely. By the end of the month the police had begun the search for bodies, too late as usual. The family was found wrapped in plastic bags and buried under the porch. The children had been drugged and shot, wrapped in their blankets, and thrown under the porch with candles and religious paraphernalia. No blood was found in the house. A manhunt for Xavier commenced. For years, nothing turned up. Monks of a monastery of Neris-les-Bains told police they hid him for some time. However, he remains to be found.

Daniel DuPont was made a member of Northleaf's Private Equity Investment Committee in 2011. He is the Senior Advisor to Northleaf's European private equity team and is active in the family business in Europe and Canada. Before he was put on the committee, he had been a senior at Caisse de Dépôt et Placement du Québec and the International and Treasury Divisions at the National Bank of Canada. In 2023 Northleaf Capital Partners finished collecting its 8th fund, having collected $675 million which is will dedicate to exploiting opportunities. Before I move on and get into a couple more of the elite's final agendas to create their Global Government, let's see what they have been up to in recent years.

"We must move as quickly as possible to a one-world government; a one-world religion; under a one-world leader." — Robert Muller, UN

In 2022 DuPont became a Founding Member of the Semiconductor Climate Consortium (SCC), an initiative under the SEMI Sustainability Initiative as ordered by the UN. The SCC was officially launched during COP27 in Sharm El Sheik, Egypt. The following year DuPont successfully concluded its $3.25 billion accelerated share repurchase (ASR) transaction initiated in November of 2022. The company retired a total of 46.8 million shares at an average price of $69.44 per share in connection with this transaction. In September, DuPont paid $2.0 billion and received 21.2 million shares. This was a busy and profitable year for Du Ponts.

DuPont was also awarded not one, not two, but three 2023 Edison Awards, recognizing excellence. DuPont received two Silver awards and one Bronze for its innovative material technologies which included Kevlar, FilmTec Fortilife, and **BETASEAL APEX**. DuPont pleaded guilty to negligent release of the extremely hazardous substance methyl mercaptan, resulting in a poisonous gas leak that killed four Texas plant workers in 2014. In 2023 a US District Judge ordered DuPont to pay $16 million and serve two years of probation, with full access to all operating locations. Additionally, DuPont was ordered to pay a $12 million penalty and make a $4 million community service donation. Corteva, a branch of DuPont, expressed deep regret and commitment to safety.

Members of the US House Oversight and Reform Committee interviewed representatives from 3M, DuPont, and Chemours which are all owned by the same people and are the same company, about their roles in manufacturing per- and polyfluoroalkyl substances (PFAS) and their failure to prevent contamination in source and drinking water in 49 American States. While companies expressed support for certain proposals, they did not accept responsibility for the contamination, despite evidence suggesting their knowledge of potential harm.

"Denise Rutherford, senior vice-president of corporate affairs for 3M, argued the **chemicals pose no human health threats at current levels and have no victims**, conflicting with a large body of research and 3M's own internal documents." - The Guardian

3M has agreed to pay $10.3 billion to at least 300 plaintiff communities as part of a settlement related to the PFAS, also known as "forever chemicals" contamination. On September 19, 2023, Joseph Du Pont, former vice president at Alexion Pharmaceuticals, and Slava Kaplan pleaded guilty to securities fraud in connection with an insider trading related to Alexion's acquisition of Portola Pharmaceuticals. Joseph and Slava each pleaded guilty to one count of securities fraud, with a maximum sentence of 20 years in prison. Assistant US Attorneys Margaret Graham, Sarah Mortazavi, and Samuel P. Rothschild are handling the prosecution. We must wait and see how the sentence is carried out, or not carried out...when the time comes.

Today DuPont is everywhere, in every home, in every water source, and in every living organism including you! DuPont Plants are located in Canada: Kingston, Mississauga, Thetford Mines, and Varennes. In Mexico operations are held in Mexico City and Reynosa while Holland, Denmark and most every European country enjoys their toxins. In the US almost every state contains a DuPont Plant, but those that don't are still contaminated by their poisons (like everywhere else). Some states include California, Delaware, District of Columbia, Georgia, Idaho, Illinois, Kentucky, Iowa, Louisiana, Massachusetts, Michigan, Minnesota, Missouri, New Jersey, Texas, Ohio, and Virginia. Meanwhile DuPont has oozed into Australia and China, Hong Kong, and India. The poison company has infiltrated Indonesia, Japan, Korea, Malaysia, Philippines, Singapore, Taiwan, and South Africa.

~Designer Diseases~

As we have now finished the family genealogies I will discuss in this book, let's finish by discussing a couple more of the elite's agendas to form their global government. Many families have been involved in this one, as well as every country's leader. These agendas have been under way for many years now and are all but finished. All of those reading this have lived through the Covid event, the latest worldwide false flag of biowarfare. For those who have followed previous false flags and understand how it works, you may have been shocked to watch the entire population of Earth surrender so willingly and quickly to the elite. No hesitation, no independent thought. Let's get into it.

"Coronavirus have not previously been known to cause severe disease in humans but have been identified as a major cause of upper respiratory tract illness, including the common cold. Repeat infections in humans are common suggesting that immune response to CoronaVirus infection in humans is either incomplete or short lived." - CoronaVirus Patent US7220852B1

The Antonine Plague was spread from 165-180 AD, killing 5 million people. In 249 AD another plague hit Rome, causing blindness, deafness, and death at an average of 5,000 per day. By 541 the Justinian plague began infecting the world for the next 200 years. In 1155 Emperor Barbarossa poisoned wells in Italy with dead bodies. The Bubonic plague was created and dispersed in 541 AD. It, and several other diseases, were dispersed throughout the centuries until once again the Bubonic plague was set loose in China, in 1331. Known commonly as the black plague, it was one of the elite's finest and most used depopulation tools. They have waited a long time to expand on that project, and luckily for you, dear reader, you were allowed to be a part of it this time! You remember in the Li chapter when the Mongols took over China? In 1335 Mongol King Abu Said died of the plague. This caused the Mongol empire to crumble which meant that the Chinese elite finally had China back, after a long occupation.

In 1346 the Mongols catapulted the bodies of plague victims over the walls of Caffa. Wine was mixed with the blood of lepers and sold to the Italy in the late 1400's. In 1650 Poles shot the saliva of rabid dogs at their enemies. In the 1700's smallpox ravaged Europe killing 400,000. In 1763 the British distributed blankets of smallpox patients to native Americans, a century later the Confederates do the same to Union troops during the Civil War. In 1797 Napoleon flooded Mantua to spread malaria. In 1855 the black plague was set loose again, killing over 10 million in

China, and in 1921 it depopulated Bombay, India by 15 million. By 1918 the Rockefeller created Spanish Flu had been perfected and set loose on the world, killing more than WWI. Today there's no need for a true virus, as fear rules the minds of people alive today. All that's needed to implement the solution is mild propaganda. Biowarfare has been going on for all of time and should be well understood by all living today.

"Everything has two purposes. One is the ostensible purpose, (public) which will make it acceptable to people; and second, is the real purpose, (secret, private) which would further the goals of establishing the new system and having it." — Dr. Richard Day on March 20, 1969

"Leprosy arose with vaccination." - Sir Ronald Martin, 1868

As mentioned before, the Rockefellers in conjunction with the UN funded and created the Aids disease. If you aren't fully aware by now, dear reader, the diseases you know today as commonplace do not exist in nature and never existed before this current era: Cancer, Dementia, ADD, Autism, Diabetes, you name it. These and more have been created by the elite to depopulate using the Slow Kill method. In 1969, the Department of Defense's Dr. Robert MacMahan requested $10 million to develop a synthetic biological agent for which no natural immunity exists. Dr. Robert Strecker's published work regarding AIDS described how there are NO genetic markers in the virus typical of the primate, as mainstream propaganda first claimed it was transferred by monkeys. He proved that it simply cannot thrive in monkeys. He also relayed that AIDS was non-existent in Africa before 1975. Even today when visiting Gibraltar tourists are warned to keep distance from the monkeys as they are "infected with Aids"!

In 1969 the US Department of Defense received $10 million to study immune-system-destroying agents. Soon the World Health Organization (WHO) began experimenting with Bovine Lymphotropic Virus (BLV) which they found was like HIV and able to be passed to humans. Once the disease was released on the elite's main target: Africa, it was then used for other agendas, primarily the final agenda of Luciferianism: homosexuality (in all of its forms). Dr. Len Horowitz exposed:

"I investigated the Department of Defense's germ warfare appropriations request and learned that the option to develop synthetic biological agents - bioweapons as alternatives to nuclear weapons - came from Dr. Henry Kissinger, who was gradually placed in his position of authority as National Security Advisor under Richard Nixon by Nelson Rockefeller and his affiliates at the Council on Foreign Relations. Moreover, I traced where the money went. It went, in fact, to a firm called Litton Bionetics, a subsidiary of the mega-military contractor Litton Industries, whose President, Roy Ash, was being considered as an alternate to Henry Kissinger for the National Security Advisor post. Instead, Roy Ash became Richard Nixon's chairman of the President's Advisory Council on Executive Organizations, and Assistant to the President of the United States. And Litton Industries was given over $5 billion in military contracts during the first term of the Nixon administration, $10 million of which went towards the development of AIDS-like viruses... The World Health Organization started to inject AIDS-laced smallpox vaccine into over 100 million Africans in 1977. And over 2000 young white male homosexuals in 1978 with the hepatitis B vaccine through the Centers for Disease Control/New York Blood Center."

A study funded by the Fogarty International Center at the US National Institutes of Health revealed that almost half of the malaria vaccines used in Southeast Asia and sub-Saharan Africa are substandard or entirely fake. Non-profit organizations distribute these vaccines along with Medicines for Malaria Venture and the Bill and Melinda Gates Foundation. The Gates Foundation has been a prominent advocate for malaria vaccines, among others which they have forced on the world with the stated goal of depopulation: medical murder. Insulin-dependent diabetes (which is a virus) is the result of vaccines, just like Multiple Sclerosis, Parkinson Disease, Tourette's syndrome, Autism, and other neuropsychiatric disorders.

"According to the 1993 Annual Report of the Council on Foreign Relations, the Rockefeller Group, Sullivan & Cromwell, and the Chase Manhattan Bank are all listed on the Corporate Member Roster of the Jesuits' Council on Foreign Relations. Along with these are the drug giants, Dow Chemical, Bristol-Myers Squibb, Johnson and Johnson, Pfizer, and Procter & Gamble." — TabuBlog.com

Meanwhile, in Nicaragua, Mexico, Philippines and other regions, the Sloan and Rockefeller Foundations worked with the World Health Organization, on Agenda 21. If you remember, one of the main goals is depopulation which they have detailed to be taken care of through vaccines and wars. These regions which never experienced tetanus, were forcibly vaccinated for it. Most vaccine initiatives target children whose rights are to be protected by their parents. Most of these initiatives are brought to you by the Rockefeller Foundation and the Rockefeller Institute for Medical Research. Remember the Rockefellers also own the UN, along with several other families. The UN creates an initiative for the public to abide by, and the foundations and other organizations finance the propaganda, and push regulation, vaccination and more on you. Today parents take no responsibility for their own rights, let alone the rights of the innocent and every child on earth today has been violated and corrupted, causing the mass of child illnesses we know today. But I digress...

The tetanus vaccines given to the children of these nations and distributed by WHO contained hCG, which when combined with tetanus toxoid carrier, stimulates the formation of antibodies against human chorionic gonadotropin, causing involuntary abortion. The Sloan Foundation funded the Community Blood Council of Greater New York, Inc., which injected more than 10,000 hemophiliacs and others with HIV/Aids. As previously discussed, Alfred Sloan of the Sloan Foundation assisted the elite in WWII through his companies and holds around 53,000 shares of Merck and Co. The company was formed by Karl Merck, a member of the Nazi party, who was made the leader of manufacturing biocides and chemicals. It is George Merck who directs the biological weapons industry and has created Hepatitis C and Polio vaccines to assist in spreading Aids and other designer diseases.

Remember, Polio is simply heavy metal poisoning which is resolved with a good detox and proper diet. However, by ensuring the heavy metal toxicity in children the US and other countries were able to feed the propaganda to vaccinate their developing children against it. This agenda was pushed in the Middle East in 2014 as Bill Gates' Foundation along with its Global Alliance for Vaccines and Immunizations forced the vaccine on Pakistan, killing 10,000 children. After this became known, 500 Pakistanis were arrested for refusing to vaccinate and the initiative was pushed on Syria. As documented in their reports, the US DOD funded Ebola research and awarded a contract of $140 million to Tekmira to research injecting and infusing humans with Ebola in 2014. While propaganda states this is a deadly disease, no disease is deadly if proper care is taken to maintain a healthy human body. However, due to the propaganda and lack of independence hundreds of thousands of people in Africa were rounded up and taken to quarantine. This is another word for Concentration Camps and serves the same purpose. Needless to say, hundreds of thousands were killed through starvation, dehydration, and vaccination. Numerous organizations continue the work of the Red Cross and other medieval Knight Orders which continue to be eugenics through vaccination under the direction of the Jesuits, according to their oath.

"I have seen leprosy and syphilis communicated by vaccination. Leprosy is becoming very common in Trinidad; its increase being coincident with vaccination." - Dr. Hall Bakewell, 1868

"Cancer is reported to be increasing not only in England and the Continent, but in all parts of the world where vaccination is practised." - Dr. William S. Tebb, 1892

Zika and Ebola were designed diseases made just for you. The Rockefeller Foundation owns the patent for Zika. The Republic of Congo was used for the first Ebola test in 1976. Every time it was upgraded the name was changed. Now there are 5 types: Bundibugyo, Cote d'Ivoire, Reston, Sudan, and Zaire. The last 2 have a mortality rate of 80-90% for humans and are favored by the elite. US Navy epidemiologists traced Ebola back to 430 BC, the plague of Athens. The Soviet Union began creating Ebola smallpox in the 1990's.

"As a weapon, the Ebolapox would give the hemorrhages and high mortality rate of Ebola virus, which would give you a blackpox, plus the very high contagiousness of smallpox." — Kanatzhan Alibekov, Chief Scientist and 1st Deputy Director of the former Soviet's Biopreparat

In 1992 Japan acquired Ebola cultures in a "medical mission" to Zaire. Neuroscientist Aafia Siddiqui was arrested in Afghanistan, in 1998. He had copies of a detailed plan for an Ebola dirty bomb attack which would take place in the US. Today, since the end of Covid, Ebola has come into the spotlight again and has been predicted to become the next biowarfare plandemic. The CDC owns the patents for Ebola, all viral strains, as well as the Ebola vaccine patent: No. CA2741523A1.

"Based on US hospital experiences to date, one Ebola patient will likely generate **eight 55-gallon barrels of medical waste per day**, making storage, transportation, and disposal of the waste a major challenge for hospitals..." - Hospitals Face Ebola Waste Challenges by Environmental and Energy Management News 2014

That's the mainstream narrative... In 2019 George Soros' media created a Hoax (not real but completely staged for news only) showing an extraction of "Ebola-infected" people from Africa to Texas. The people shown in video footage were paid actors, as were many who were interviewed in Africa as "proof". All controlled opposition (alternate news) outlets jumped on the story to create more fear in the public, as well as racism which is what old George is in charge of! As anyone can see in the videos called news footage, the actors are wearing specific colors according to the Hegelian dialect and everything is quite staged, like the numerous videos from the UN Peacekeepers in Syria and other false flags we have discussed. The color used for Ebola was Green. Green is the color of fertility, sexual and Satanic allusion, as well as immortality, resentment, disorder, illness, and greed. Watch the many videos of naked African children who were paid to walk a few steps and gently lay down, demonstrating their illness while promoting pedophilic entertainment. This recent "outbreak" allowed for the US to send 3,000 soldiers to various countries in Africa...you know, for "safety". In 2020 the CDC and FDA assured the public that the new Ebola vaccine was 100% effective. They were also considerate enough to warn that tests <u>could turn out to be false positives</u>.

Like every false flag event, there are a dozen other agendas taking place at the same time, working together to fulfill the true purpose. The elite create a Problem: A fake or man-made disease. They then use their media, movies, and the internet to **Program** your Reaction: Fear and Panic leading to your total obedience to whatever they say. These 2 steps ensure that you will accept the elite's Solution (which was the point anyway): blindly allowing "authorities" and corporations strip you of your rights and forcibly penetrate your body with foreign objects. As stated before, Vaccines have always been used for death. Let me show you yet another example.

"In 1993, WHO announced a "birth-control vaccine" for "family planning". Published research shows that by 1976 WHO researchers had conjugated tetanus toxoid (TT) with human chorionic gonadotropin (hCG) producing a "birth-control" vaccine. Conjugating TT with hCG causes pregnancy hormones to be attacked by the immune system. Expected results are abortions in females already pregnant and/or infertility in recipients not yet impregnated. Repeated inoculations prolong infertility. Currently WHO researchers are working on more potent anti-fertility vaccines using recombinant DNA. <u>WHO publications show a long-range purpose to reduce population growth in unstable "less developed countries"</u>. By November 1993 Catholic publications appeared saying an abortifacient vaccine was being used as a tetanus prophylactic.

In November 2014, the **Catholic Church** asserted that such a program was underway in Kenya. Three independent Nairobi accredited biochemistry laboratories tested samples from vials of the WHO tetanus vaccine being used in March 2014 and found hCG where none should be present. In October 2014, 6 additional vials were obtained by Catholic doctors and were tested in 6 accredited laboratories. Again, hCG was found in half the samples. Subsequently, Nairobi's AgriQ Quest laboratory, in two sets of analyses, again found hCG in the same vaccine vials that tested positive earlier but found no hCG in 52 samples alleged by the WHO to be vials of the vaccine used in the Kenya campaign 40 with the same identifying batch numbers as the vials that tested positive for hCG. Given that hCG was found in at least half the WHO vaccine samples known by the doctors involved in administering the vaccines to have been used in Kenya, our opinion is that the Kenya "anti-tetanus" campaign was reasonably called into question by the Kenya Catholic Doctors Association as **<u>a front for population growth reduction</u>**." - HCG Found in WHO Tetanus Vaccine in Kenya Raises Concern in the Developing World by John W. Oller, Christopher A. Shaw, Lucija Tomljenovic, Stephen K. Karanja, Wahome Ngare, Felicia M. Clement, and Jamie Ryan Pillette

In 2000 Dr. Joseph Kim, a member of the Global Agenda Council of the World Economic Forum, and Dr. David Weiner, the pioneer of DNA Vaccinations, began a company called InOvio, funded by DARPA, to provide the Zika and Ebola Vaccines. They were given tens of millions of dollars in grants to produce poisons for profit. These and other designer diseases were put out to test and lead us to Covid. Ebola, named after the original outbreak region on the Ebola River, attacks the immune system. Like every immune disease, the symptoms include headache, sore throat, cough, fever, muscle pain and weakness before progressing. The classic "flu" symptoms are used in most designer diseases to ensure that you ignore it as something minor. Naturally, if you are healthy to begin with then your body will fight off anything and clean it from your system before it becomes an issue. This should give you an idea of how healthy you have maintained your body...do you get the flu? Don't worry, I will detail some health tips that will enable you to cure yourself and be whole again.

As these viruses are pushed into you, selected authors write books and producers make movies to further the indoctrination regarding plandemics, promoting fear and uncertainty in the weak.

"Vaccines manufactured using human fetal cells contain residual DNA fragments. It is possible that these contaminating fragments could be incorporated into a child's genome and disrupt normal gene function, leading to autistic phenotypes...Not only damaged human cells, but also healthy human cells can take up foreign DNA spontaneously. Foreign human DNA taken up by human cells will be transported into nuclei and be integrated into host genome, which will cause phenotype change. Hence, residual human fetal DNA fragments in vaccines can be one of the causes of autism spectrum disorder in children through vaccination. Vaccines must be safe without any human DNA contaminations or reactivated viruses and must be produced in ethically approved manufacturing processes." – Dr. Theresa Deisher

By 2001, President Bush rejected the 1972 Biological Weapons Convention citing 38 problems with it. The Bioweapons Convention allowed for appropriate types and amounts of biological agents to be used for defensive purposes but while it permitted research, it denied the ability to develop. Since then, the US Government has invested $44 Billion in biological warfare research. Several years before the president's rejection, 700,000 people had been targeted with depleted uranium and other toxic substances used in vaccines. Their effects were called Gulf War Syndrome. Over 12,000 died from this small-scale human experiment. Canada, the home of D-Wave, was the largest Uranium producer in the world until 2009 when Kazakhstan took the lead. In 2013, Canada produced 9,331.5 tons of uranium from mines in northern Saskatchewan and in the same year delivered Uranium to India for the first time.

"Genetic engineering can do far more damage than nuclear bombs." - Michael Crichton MD

Let's continue the timeline. In 2002, cases of a "life-threatening respiratory disease" were reported from Guangdong Province, China, followed by reports from

Vietnam, Canada, and Hong Kong. The syndrome was designated Severe Acute Respiratory Syndrome" (SARS) in February 2003 by the CDC. In 2004, the CDC filed a patent for a newly isolated human virus called SARS, which expired on January 24, 2020. Also in 2004, a SARS virus 'leaked' from a lab in Beijing. CoronaVirus was identified as the causative agent of SARS. Basically, they tore apart SARS and tested the individual strands of viruses on us all.

Understand this, dear reader, **most diseases are given through vaccines**! Those that aren't are given to you through your contaminated food products and frequency-altering devices.

"Vaccinations are now carried out for purely commercial reasons because they fetch huge profits for the pharmaceutical industry. There is no scientific evidence that vaccinations are of any benefit." - Dr. Gerhard Buchwald

In 2006 Drs. Weiner and Kim were providing HIV Vaccines for the planned epidemic in Africa. March 11th, 2009, Japan Times said their Yamaguchi strain of bird flu could be contracted by humans. Tens of thousands of animals were slaughtered to prevent the spread. The culling of millions of animals has happened with more frequency as biowarfare has waged on, as the populations don't think that this will have negative repercussions on our entire ecosystem. In 2016 the name of the Avian (bird) flu was changed to Philippine flu. This and Swine Flu are fairly common now and help ensure the continuation of genocide. In 2009 the company Baxter distributed vaccines throughout the Czech Republic, Germany, and Slovenia which contained the H5N1 avian flu and had a 60% "success rate" (kill rate). Like all of these epidemics the elderly and young are more affected, as their immune systems are already weaker and the elderly especially have other medical conditions which cause complications, as intended. 24,000 birds were culled in Kelantan. 300,000 chickens were culled in Miyagi and Chiba. 34 million were killed and wasted in the US and 776,000 in Germany. South Korea and other countries are importing eggs after culling 33 million. Hundreds of thousands more have been murdered in UK, Ireland, and many countries worldwide. Food in grocery stores gets limited, prices rise, and people die. The point is to do so. You must be forced to eat the food the elite provide, not free range or organic, but Genetically Modified and Processed. This keeps you enslaved.

"The vaccination myth is the most widespread superstition modern medicine has managed to impose, but, being by the same token the most profitable, it will prove to be also one of the most enduring, though there was never the slightest of scientific evidence upholding it." - Hans Ruesch

Keep in mind, it doesn't matter what country or region of the world you are in, you eat genetically modified food. One small example is that since 1950 the wheat you use has been corrupted. As mentioned before, you must understand everything that contains this poison wheat. Original Einkorn Wheat contains the minerals and vitamins the human body needs to survive and is very healthy in its 14 chromosomes, compared to the 42 that modern wheat contains. This was taken out of wheat and in its place another strand of gluten was added. This gluten strand is what many people are allergic to. It causes diabetes, celiac disease and more as it is unable to be processed by the body. This wheat is used worldwide while real wheat has become all but extinct. Natural wheat also contains drastically higher amounts of zinc, iron, fiber, manganese, and more which most people are deficient in because vitamins and minerals have been purposely taken out of GMO products. The same is true of salt — another vital product for human health. Today salt contains all sorts of chemicals which cause diseases whereas true salt, Celtic or Himalayan, contains the hundreds of minerals your body needs to function properly. This is why you have so many deficiencies, like everyone else in the world. Your bones degrade and chip and fill with holes…your body doesn't function as it should…and you don't notice because you are used to feeling sick! Do you have a belly? Are you tired, even when you've only just woken up? These symptoms which almost everyone in EU and US suffer from daily is caused by hormonal imbalances and/or gluten!

Everyone should be gluten-free, using Almond or Rice or other such flours which still contain nutrients. A great many diseases and health problems are from what you put in your body: wheat or dairy mainly, as both are obscenely altered today. All food used to be organic which is why people were not sick and incompetent in past generations. Speaking of real food, natural oils help lubricate your body from the inside out so everything can function properly: Olive Oil, Coconut Oil, Sesame Oil. Your body needs various nutrients which is why there are so many natural nutrient sources for our bodies: fish, beef, fowl, fruits, vegetables, roots, herbs, flowers, nuts, and the list goes on. Do your own research and discover what your unique body needs. You are what you eat. This is why the health issues seen today have not existed before the past 70 years…this is what you should already know…

Apply this understanding to everything you buy in a store as your ability to produce your own food has been diminished. It should make you angry that these people are all dying painfully and slowly **ON PURPOSE**. It should make you angry that your air and water and food have all been infected and modified **TO DAMAGE YOU!** It should make you angry that the **NATURAL CURES** for these elite genetically modified diseases are kept from you! But people today are so generationally polluted your brains cannot function.

As previously discussed, aside from diseases and GMO's, Chemtrails and frequency-altering devices such as TV's, Phones, Computers, have been pushed into everything, turning you into programmable unnatural matter. As already mentioned in previous chapters, cancers, heart diseases, diabetes, Alzheimer's, Dementia and numerous other diseases and symptoms **ARE** due to unnatural frequencies: microwave radiation, EMF, and RF waves. Just imagine what the flicker of a TV, Phone or Computer Screen does to your brain, knowing what we discussed in earlier chapters.

"It goes back to the 50s the 60s and the 70s, when microwaves were found to be such a perfect weapon, and so dangerous to the military that the United States Defense Intelligence Agency told the western governments to keep this quiet. And they did. Everything was known by 1976, we needed no more proof, no more research. Nothing was needed then." - Whistleblower Dr. Barrie Trower, MI5

All of your thoughts, sensations and actions arise from bioelectricity generated by neurons and transmitted through complex neural circuits inside your skull. Transcranial Magnetic Stimulation can selectively control your brain function. This technique uses powerful pulses of electromagnetic radiation beamed into a person's brain to jam or excite particular brain circuits. Our natural bodies are made to be Alkaline, which is an environment where no disease can grow. **NO DISEASE CAN GROW.** However today most things are bleached before you pay money to consume them: flour is bleached, rice is processed, salt is processed, so natural minerals and vitamins our bodies need are no longer present. Natural cures include a variety of herbs that help clear viruses from your body, high doses of D (which everyone is deficient in), oregano oil, zinc, omega oils, among other things.

Practice good hygiene, sanitize, hydrate and be intelligent. Everyone's body is different, and unique. This means that each person's body needs certain nutrients that someone else doesn't. There is no way any vaccine is ok for everyone, because of this basic fact. When correcting your own health, learn what **YOUR** body needs. Walk barefoot in the grass, as you are supposed to, so your body can produce serotonin. Take in the sun, so your body can heal and be well. If your hormones are imbalanced, like everyone's today, then you will be sick, mentally, and physically. There's no getting around that. 90% of the health problems you experience on a daily basis, even those you no longer recognize as illnesses, are due to an irregularity in your body's chemistry: hormones! The rampant imbalance is why we have experienced a rise in unnatural disorders such as Bipolar, Schizophrenia, PTSD, ADHD, and the like. Parents wrap their children's food in plastic, which destroys hormones, and wonder why children can't figure out what's between their legs. Parents give their children fried, sugared, and fake processed foods and wonder why their children have horrible and unnatural health problems FOR LIFE. Educate yourself on what your body needs. Get the amount of real oxygen and water your body needs every day to function. Without the appropriate amount of hydration, brain cells wither, meaning if you are not hydrated enough, you **cannot** think properly. Sugar calcifies around the brain, forming a hard shell which is programmable through frequencies...which surround you. Give your body the fuel it needs to be healthy. Whatever the elite throw at us, we live on a natural earth, which IS self-sustaining. Be intelligent, not SMART.

Let's continue with GMO's for a moment. First published in Le Monde Diplomatique in 1997, the African National Congress was exposed for promoting a new policy for land expropriation in Mozambique which established indentured servitude on farms. One of the elite's puppets, President Nelson Mandela, supported the project. For a thousand years, if not longer, the elite have controlled the leaders of South America, Africa, and the middle east. These regions are not free or independent but propaganda mills and experimentation platforms. The policy was led by General Constand Viljoen and soon another mandate was implemented: Food Corridor. This was aimed to extend agricultural businesses into neighboring countries and forcing GMOs on all farms, as they are forced on all farms worldwide. As one would expect, those who funded this project were major banks, the World Bank, and the EU. Donors, including the Bill and Melinda Gates Foundation, have invested millions in researching, developing, and promoting genetically modified technologies and diseases in partnership with local NGOs and government bodies. The Kenya Agricultural Research Institute announced at this time that GMO drought-resistant corn would be available to Kenyan farmers within 5 years. Meanwhile the Zulu nation has joined the white African farmers in their fight against government takeover.

"The possibilities of an attack on the food supplies of S-E Asia and Indonesia using B.W. agents should be considered by a small study group." - New Weapons and Equipment Development Committee, 1947

Bill Gates funded the Alliance for a Green Revolution in Africa with $120 million which has been used to promote GMO seeds. Bill Gates' Foundation and Monsanto Company, along with the Rockefeller Foundation, push GMO seeds which have known negative consequences for humans and animals alike. All they do has led to increased debt and environmental degradation worldwide. In the US and other countries, farmers who refuse to accept GMO crops are forced to sell, persecuted when they don't, jailed and killed. Farm death crops or die. This is the same mentality the elite have regarding vaccines: you must be penetrated and infected or you will be silenced. Even though the Bill and Melinda Gates Foundation has been charged with crimes against humanity, citing the numerous cases their vaccines have poisoned people in India, Chad, Kenya and more, their work continues unhindered.

"When you engineer a plant, you put a gene in the plant. That gene is going to make a protein, and that gene can go anywhere in the plant because you have no control. It goes anywhere in the genome, anywhere in the chromosome. Biotech companies and government agencies are ignoring the science that refutes GMO arguments. It is about the money. It becomes very important for the biotech companies to push aside the studies that are not confirming the corporate line or questioning safety. But it's simpler. Most investors in the biotech companies just want to make money. It is the bottom line. They may think if they can get away with selling it then why not?" - Dr. Thierry Vrain

"For the first time the researchers have been able to mutate the H5N1 strain of avian influenza so that it can be transmitted easily through the air in coughs and sneezes. Until now, it was thought that H5N1 bird flu could only be transmitted between humans via very close physical contact. Dutch scientist and researcher Ron Fouchier, carried out the controversial research." — Bill Brenner

In 2009, the Swine Flu epidemic was set loose again, funded by NIH. Dr. Kim of InOvio not only worked on a Vaccine for Swine Flu but also created PCV1 and 2, (Porcine Circovirus) which uses Pig DNA. He is funded by Merck and Company as well. Bill Gates stated that the Swine Flu helped them see how and where they were lacking in response tactics and tracking abilities. Once again, the elite have perfected the ability of injecting animal or bird DNA into human chromosomes, altering your DNA and causing things like fever, cancers, hemorrhaging, and death. In early 2013, some 16,000 dead pigs (including corpses infected by Porcine Circovirus) floated to Shanghai along the Huangpu river, contaminating the water supply along the way. The same year the movie titled Coronavirus was released. Regarding the Ebola event in 2014 Bill Gates stated:

"Again, the world was much too slow to respond."

Over the past few decades "global pandemic" has been the topic of interest at Bilderberg, UN, and other elite club meetings. In 2004 academic research about Covid was <u>altered</u> and edited by Arild Underdal of Norway. In 2010 the Rockefeller Foundation created the simulation called Scenarios for the Future of Technology and International Development which described the Covid scenario as the trigger for police-state controls. This was a success, as it was planned to be.

"At first, the notion of a more controlled world gained wide acceptance and approval. Citizens willingly gave up some of their sovereignty - and their privacy - to more paternalistic states in exchange for greater safety and stability. Citizens were more tolerant, and even eager, for top-down direction and oversight, and national leaders had more latitude to impose order in the ways they saw fit. In developed countries, this heightened oversight took many forms: biometric IDs for all citizens, for example, and tighter regulation of key industries whose stability was deemed vital to national interests." - Scenarios for the Future of Technology and International Development pg. 19

Before Covid, the hysteria being spread around was about a toxic chemical known as Hydrazine. Hydrazine is an inorganic chemical compound, colorless, volatile liquid with powerful reductive properties, used in chemical synthesis and in certain kinds of rocket fuels. Hydrazine is highly toxic and dangerously unstable unless handled in a solution. Toxic is derived from the Greek Toxon meaning "arrow" which is how biowarfare was carried out in ancient times. This was a concern in mainstream news because the Tiangong-1 Chinese space station, was said to be "erratically flying through space toward the Earth carrying large amounts of Hydrazine". As usual they had no idea where it would hit or when, but the propaganda spun during this caused enough fear for the moment. Bio warfare has always been in play. Perhaps you can remember some that you have heard of taking place in your own country, such as anthrax attacks, which Americans have experienced to a mind-numbing degree. The fact that one cannot transport anthrax in paper envelopes through the mail never once enters discussion because it's not about facts, it's about fear!

In 2014 another false flag event (occult ritual of human sacrifice) happened to a Malaysian Airlines Passenger Plane, flight MH370. Two planes were taken down in all. The passengers on this flight included the scientists who were carrying the physical patents for semi-conductors. All of the owners of the patent were passengers on the same plane. The plane disappeared out of the sky. Immediately after, the Rothschilds "obtained" the patent for Freescale Semiconductor's ARM microcontroller 'KL-03'. THIS is why 239 innocent people were slaughtered. These people were engineers and experts working to make chip facilities in Tianjin, China, and Kuala Lumpur. There are NO accidents. NO Coincidences. The company works with Aerospace and Defence, HF Radar Band L- and S-, Electronic Warfare, and Identification, Friend, or Foe, among other things. While we're on this topic let's take a moment to dissect the backstory. Why is this flight of kidnapped or murdered people important to Covid? Let's find out.

The transition to 5G had been going on for several years by this time, as mobile operators rushed to upgrade their networks with 5G gear made by companies like Huawei, Nokia, and the like, in order to implement the UN Smart City Agenda to enable a smooth transition into the Global Government. The Telecom Industry is a game of "Whoever has the most patents, wins"! A Telecom company strives to get its patents adopted as "standards". These "standards" are set by a "global body" to ensure that all phones work across different mobile networks. Therefore, whoever's patents end up making it into the standard will reap huge royalty licensing revenue streams. Qualcomm is the dominant company in the entire market. It holds itself as the standard and sells the chip designs that work with those standards. Qualcomm makes HALF of all core baseband radio chips in smartphones. The 3rd largest company, Huawei, develops their own chips through subsidiary HiSilicon. Huawei's HiSilicon chip unit also designs semiconductors manufactured by industry-leading plants owned by Taiwan Semiconductor Manufacturing Co. Huawei was a major purchaser of Qualcomm's Snapdragon processors. Qualcomm began heavily redacting product information, as Huawei grew, even though they were still a customer. Qualcomm sells to everyone, but only Huawei uses HiSilicon chipsets.

In 2018, President Donald Trump blocked microchip maker Broadcom Ltd.'s $117 billion takeover of rival Qualcomm as the Huawei heiress Meng Wanzhou was arrested in Canada and illegally held for months before the US called for her extradition. The allegations brought against her were for breaking trade sanctions against Iran. Naturally, sometime later, documents were "discovered" to support something that was too sensitive to disclose. Huawei was making its own chips, not America's. In July 2019, Huawei's senior vice-president Catherine Chen announced that the company had secured 50 commercial contracts for 5G, 28 of which are with European contractors which are fundamental to the establishment of SMART cities on the continent. 5G roll out was October 31, 2019, in Wuhan. Wuhan is the center for semiconductors and high-speed tech. For those who are totally unaware, there is a heavy 5G and Semiconductor rivalry war between US and China. This is why Wuhan was targeted to be used as the center of the Covid "outbreak" when in reality it was not. In 2019 Huawei was blacklisted by President Trump, which has since been regretted as the company spent $10 billion a year on US products, but the rest of the world continued to expand their Smart and Secure networks, using them! The US until that point had the monopoly on much technology used and built, especially semiconductors and nano-chips.

Let's remember what we've discussed regarding the truth about technology and the reason it has been forced on you at an increasing rate. Studies have proven what healthy people witness: your cellphone, which is smooshed against your face most of the time, increases alpha wave activity. A study done by the Brain Science Institute, Swinburne University of Technology in Melbourne, Australia showed that the greatest effect was in brain tissue directly beneath the location of cellphones. These brainwaves reflect a person's state of arousal and attention. Another study done by the Loughborough University Sleep Research Centre in England concluded that not only could the cellphone signals <u>alter a person's behavior</u> during the call, the effects of the <u>disrupted brain-wave patterns continued</u> long after the phone was switched off. The damage to the human brain's sleeping abilities is astonishing. Remember who is targeted most: children.

"Millions of children and adults in schools around the world spend significant amounts of time around wireless devices and Wi-Fi. Many schools are introducing Bring Your Own Device (BYOD) policies and installing industrial wireless routers for tablets. However, wireless devices expose students and staff to <u>microwave radiation that can impede learning and overall health</u>. Studies have shown that microwave radiation can **damage reproductive systems, impact the immune system, alter brain functioning, and increase cancer risk**. Tablets have up to 5 antennae that are constantly emitting short intense bursts of radiation even when not connected to the Internet. Wireless devices in classrooms thus result in multiple sources of wireless radiation exposure." - Environmental Health Trust

"Many computer monitors and TV tubes, emit pulsed electromagnetic fields of sufficient amplitudes to cause such excitation (of DNA) that it is possible to manipulate the nervous system of a subject by pulsing images displayed on a nearby computer monitor or TV set. The image pulsing may be imbedded in the program material, or overlaid by modulating a video stream, either as an RF signal or as a video signal. The image displayed on a computer monitor may be pulsed effectively by a simple computer program. For certain monitors, pulsed electromagnetic fields capable of exciting sensory resonances in nearby subjects may be generated even as the displayed images are pulsed with subliminal intensity." — Patent #6506148 B2, named "Nervous System Manipulation"

As intended 5G networks generate radio frequency radiation that damages DNA (causing disease and death), causes oxidative damage (causing premature aging), disrupts cell metabolism; and leads to other diseases through the generation of stress proteins. Our bodies have a natural frequency, you mess up the natural frequency and guess what? The body is negatively affected.

Professor Hecht evaluated nearly 900 studies from Russian sources, which demonstrated the harmful effects of this technology. His research took place between 1960 and 1996, LONG before the 3G and 4G cellular systems were built. More than 240 scientists published an appeal to the UN to reduce public exposure, calling for a moratorium on 5G citing "established" adverse biological effects of RF radiation. Naturally, they were ignored and those who continued to speak out were targeted. Scientific data on the biological effects of radiofrequency indicate the immediate need for a cautionary approach to protect the public. The research has accumulated enough to provide strong evidence that EVEN LOW LEVELS ARE NOT SAFE.

"It turns out there is a biological interaction at many different levels with different waveforms...So I investigated further, and this EEG Cloning used to be called in both Russia and the US; "Psychic Warfare". The Pentagon had a unit back in the 70s, and it's been rolled into psychological operations and informational warfare. Traditionally it's a mystical energy of how people can remote view and perform other tasks, well there's an actual technology behind it. We can go into more detail, but this is real. This has been around for a while; it is a type of mind reading... This gets much more complicated in depth when you talk about these individuals that are very directly targeted with this weaponry, and they can control their lives, break them down, turn them into Manchurian candidates...[Mind Control] operates at many levels, from the individual (understanding the individual mind). The brain has been deciphered (behavior modification). You are correct in saying this has been explored at least since [the] 1950s if not much earlier..." - Whistleblower Dr. Robert Duncan, CIA

The highly dangerous biological effects of EMFs have been documented by thousands of studies since 1932. To refresh your failing memory, here are some of the **common** symptoms linked to microwave exposure: Fatigue, Chronic headaches, Heart palpitations, High pitched ringing in the ears, Dizziness, Disturbed sleep at night, Sleepiness in daytime, Moodiness, Unsociability, **Feelings of Fear**, Anxiety, Nervous tension, Mental depression, Memory impairment, Pain in muscles and joints, Pain in the region of the heart, Breathing difficulties, Allergies, Yeast infections, Blood sugar swings, Heartburn, Bowel problems, Thyroid dysfunction, Weight abnormalities, Rashes, Immune system weakness, Behavioral aberrations, Inflammation (caused by excess histamine in the blood), Oxidative stress, Autoimmune responses, Reduced blood flow to the region of the thalamus, Pathologic leakage of the blood-brain barrier, Myelin damage to the central nervous system, Hormone imbalance, Deficit in melatonin metabolic availability, DNA damage, Metabolic dysregulation, Cancer, Heart disease, Neurological dysfunction, Diabetes, Immune system suppression, Cataracts of the eyes, Sperm malformation, Hearing loss, Vision loss, Cognitive impairment, Alzheimer's, Depressive mental illness, Fetal abnormalities.

ALL LIFE is devastatingly affected by this. Flocks of birds have dropped from the sky and/or lost senses vital to their survival when hit with blasts of radio frequencies. Thanks to MIT, the Translational Acoustic-RF communication (TARF), has been created which provides communication from air through water (from plane to submarine) by applying telecom's new favorite bandwidth for IoT and 5G networks: millimeter wave, sometimes known as mmWave. Whales, Dolphins and more have been severely depopulated by sonar frequencies destroying the specific tissue of their biological, natural, sonar systems.

In 2017, while Pharma companies were developing and manufacturing deadly viruses, Russian Aerospace Defence Forces discovered that United Airlines 857 had become infected with a virus they recorded as "not from Earth and not recorded in any database". That same year, Dr. Tedros Adhanom Ghebreyesus (health minister of Ethiopia) was accused of covering up 3 cholera epidemics. Having served as the Executive and Central Committee member of the Tigray People Liberation Front, his beliefs were clear. The Tigray Liberation Front is a worldwide blacklisted terrorist organization. He has been strongly supported by Chinas elite and supports the One China Agenda. This was the man the World Health Organization couldn't wait to make Director General. Immediately after becoming the Director, he went to China for 3 days. While there he met Premier Li Keqiang, privately, and Vice Premier Liu Yandong, Vice Chairman Han Qide of the Chinese People's Political Consultative Conference (CPPCC), and National Health and Family Planning Commission Minister Li Bin. WHO then received $20 million from China to **improve health** in the 60 countries engaged in the Belt and Road Initiative in 2017. By now you know what this means. It all ties together and now the appropriate propaganda leader was in place.

"More than 80% of patients have mild disease and will recover. In 2% of reported cases, the virus is fatal, and the risk of death increases the older you are. We see relatively few cases among children. More research is needed to understand why." - Tedros Adhanom Ghebreyesus

"Imagine that somewhere in the world a new weapon exists or could emerge that is capable of killing millions of people, bringing economies to a standstill, and casting nations into chaos. This should concern everyone because history has taught us THERE <u>WILL</u> BE ANOTHER deadly global pandemic." — Bill Gates at the Munich Security Conference, 2017

On October 18, 2019, Event 201, a high-level pandemic exercise, was hosted by the Johns Hopkins Center for Health Security in partnership with the World Economic Forum and the Bill and Melinda Gates Foundation. By December 23, 2020, Corona Virus came to Wuhan China. A simulation had been finished at Johns Hopkins Medical Center, just two weeks before, which showed that 65 million people would be killed during Covid-19. After receiving a $9 million grant, InOvio made the vaccine within 2 hours, so it reports. Huawei installed its 5G network in all of the emergency hospitals which were set up in Wuhan. These hospitals and all of the equipment for them were already prepared and ready to be set up beforehand. Wuhan was indeed ground zero, but not for the outbreak...for the Planned Event. When something is done on such a large scale, it must be orchestrated properly, so that all various media have the same story, and everyone follows the same script.

In 2019 a worldwide, all consuming, synchronized event took place. A strain of SARS virus, designed by Canada, was set loose in Europe where it spread quickly. Mainstream media began claiming that it had originated in China, the current enemy of the US. China is where you are supposed to be looking, which means something more important is happening somewhere else. However, China has collected the DNA of 70 million men and boys... But this is old news, in April of 2008, "for the reason of National Security", US President Bush ordered a law to gather the DNA of **all** citizens. Records are kept in government genomic biobanks and considered governmental property. The DNA taken at birth from every citizen is essentially owned by the government, and every citizen becomes a potential subject of government-sponsored genetic research. For many generations now all birth certificates, bank accounts, and the like from every person in every country, have been logged by their respective governments and copied to be sent to the Vatican as well.

In England they decided doctors should look at problem children and have those children reported and their DNA taken in case they would become criminals in the future. Senior police forensics experts believe genetic samples should be studied, because it may be possible to identify potential criminals as young as age 5!

"We should be collecting it from everybody. The only ones who have anything to worry about from DNA testing are criminals." - New York City Police Commissioner Howard Safir

As usual we see the UN has misused DNA. Francis Gurry (Director General of WIPO) ordered security officers to steal DNA samples from his staff members so that he could identify anonymous letter writers he **suspected** of criticizing him. This is one example of how your DNA is used in reality, by anyone and for any ridiculous reason. There is a worldwide database filing DNA and medical information of a large percentage of the world. FBI agent Murphy relayed:

"It began in the 1960's in America and slowly more doctors were bought off. It would be fair to say at least 92% of doctors worldwide have been paid for this information. Then they started paying off other medical professionals as well. It started off as an easier way to solve crimes like murder, but it has gotten out of hand. If you have had a blood test your DNA is put into this file as well as the results of all the blood tests you have had. Key people in police agencies around the world can access the database for whatever they deem fit. No warrant needed. It is simple."

The "first" DNA bank was opened in London, as far as the public is concerned. In 2015 Michael Farzan, an immunologist at Scripps, started the first human trial called immunoprophylaxis by gene transfer, or IGT. IGT is being sold as a new and different type of vaccination. Scientists isolate the genes that produce antibodies against certain diseases, then synthesize artificial versions. The genes are placed into viruses and injected into human tissue, usually muscle. The viruses invade human cells with their DNA payloads. They cure you by giving you a disease that attacks and alters your DNA FOREVER.

In 2016, 150 scientists from all over the world gathered behind locked doors in a secret meeting. They discussed gathering DNA from newborns without parental knowledge. In order to use it to create DNA that did not consist of any natural DNA. This practice is called Crisper. Bill and Melinda Gates have provided significant funding to the University of North Carolina to develop ultrasound infertility technology that could render human sperm unviable for up to six months as they march towards perfecting their depopulation techniques. Ancestry websites offer DNA testing so they can save and own your DNA.

Because DNA can alter itself through our emotions and frequencies, there is no such thing as predisposition without hope of change. You are in control of your own body and mind through your DNA. The world allowed the simultaneous lockdown of every country during Covid-19, as implemented by elite order members who had coordinated the agenda years in advance. Violators were fined and jailed, depending on the country. As soon as anyone spoke out against vaccines they were labelled and treated by their communities and governments as though they were extremists or terrorists. As usual, Christians were primarily targeted as the enemy in this attack. Austria, Germany, Australia, France, Italy, and dozens more became dictatorial empires overnight. They finally had the chance, and people gave it to them.

People were forced to wear paper masks, sick or not, and stand 2 meters apart. The mask alone proved the ridiculousness of the event, and its fallacy. Only a sick person needs to take precautions such as covering their mouth when they cough (as anyone with a brain would do) and washing their hands frequently. Hygiene is something we all learn as children and have known about for centuries so spreading a disease is not common unless those who are sick are also ignorant and abusive towards others, violating everyone's rights wherever they go. Spit guards/masks which were implemented worldwide and mandatory, do not keep out disease and should only be worn for a few minutes at a time. However, the reason for this implementation was to finish perfecting technology for the elite. For some time, they had been attempting to perfect their tool of facial recognition, but without being able to also identify those who cover their faces, the technology is pointless. Now they can easily identify everyone, regardless of facial coverings. No one noticed that suddenly it was forced for you to wear a mask in a bank, store, or government building. Only months before it had been illegal for hundreds of years to conceal your identity within these institutions. Surgeons and nurses came out immediately exposing this farce, but no one listened...no one ever does.

"Although surgeons do wear masks to prevent their respiratory droplets from contaminating the surgical field and the exposed internal tissues of our surgical patients, that is about as far as the analogy extends...We should all realize by now that face masks have never been shown to prevent or protect against viral transmission. Which is exactly why they have never been recommended for use during the seasonal flu outbreak, epidemics, or previous pandemics.

Unlike the public wearing masks in the community, surgeons work in sterile surgical suites equipped with heavy duty air exchange systems that maintain positive pressures, exchange, and filter the room air at a very high level, and increase the oxygen content of the room air. These conditions limit the negative effects of masks on the surgeon and operating room staff. And yet despite these extreme climate control conditions, clinical studies demonstrate the negative effects (lowering arterial oxygen and carbon dioxide re-breathing) of surgical masks on surgeon physiology and performance.

Surgeons and operating room personnel are well trained, experienced, and meticulous about maintaining sterility. We only wear fresh sterile masks. We don the mask in a sterile fashion. We wear the mask for short periods of time and change it out at the first signs of the excessive moisture build up that we know degrades mask effectiveness and increases their negative effects. Surgeons NEVER re-use surgical masks, nor do we ever wear cloth masks. **The public is being told to wear masks for which they have not been trained in the proper techniques.** As a result, they are mishandling, frequently touching, and constantly reusing masks in a way that increase contamination and are more likely than not to increase transmission of disease." – Dr. Jim Meehan, Surgeon, ignored entirely by the ignorant public

Viruses and bacteria can easily pass through masks and cloth and get into the air! It is not a preventative measure but an elite propaganda game to see how far you will let them go! You let them go all the way! Congratulations. You allowed them to violate not only your own rights, but the rights of others, allowing the elite to take control over our bodies. These facts are as true as the fact that locking yourself in your house, being away from fresh air and sunlight, spending hours on end in front of a screen is devastating to one's health – even if you're perfectly healthy! Sunlight reduces disease and quickly heals the body, which is why you have always been placed outside or in front of an open window when sick, to get not only much needed fresh air but sun! A study done by Baylor University took 2 groups of animals and fed one group the standard American diet, which is known to cause serious illnesses. That group was then exposed to sunlight and got cancer. The group which ate proper food did not get cancer. You are what you eat. This is common sense, but because of the poisoning done to so many people generationally, people are barely able to function as human beings today. Parents for the past couple of generations have been unaware or uncaring about the food given to their children and as a result, we see the confusion and sickness created by this. While on the topic of cancer, Chernobyl, Nagasaki, and the rest in that group of false flags taught us was that no one gets sick from radiation poisoning or anthrax or any such toxin, if they have the proper nutrients.

In the case of Chernobyl, a handful of scientists including Dr. Lawrence Royce were sent there by the CIA to study one town where the people were healthy and lived longer than 100 years, thanks to their probiotic diet given to them by the Russian governments Enzymes Ltd.

"We used a lactobacillus cell fragments after Chernobyl, conducting experimental work on animals exposed to radiation, then later on humans. We found the cell fragments provided protection from radiation cell damage, and also anti-mutagenic activity, which meant the genetic material was protected from radiation. The main damage of radiation is destruction of the bone marrow cells and genetic damage that causes cellular mutation."- Dr. Luba Shynkarenko, former dean of the Institute of Biotechnology at the National Technical University in Kiev

"The probiotics researched in this study are as follows:
- Lactobacillus acidophilus: This strain is known for its ability to produce lactase, an enzyme that breaks down lactose in milk. It may help improve digestion of lactose in individuals with lactose intolerance.
- Bifidobacterium bifidum: This strain is found naturally in the human gut and is associated with promoting healthy digestion and supporting immune function.
- Lactobacillus rhamnosus GG: This strain has been extensively studied and is one of the most well-documented probiotics. It has been shown to have potential benefits in preventing and treating gastrointestinal infections, reducing the risk of antibiotic-associated diarrhea, and improving symptoms of certain gastrointestinal disorders.
- Saccharomyces boulardii: This yeast strain has been researched for its potential to prevent and treat diarrhea, particularly that caused by antibiotics or infections such as Clostridium difficile." - Teslatelegraph.com

Contrary-wise in the US, Canada, Australia, Europe, and other regions, even toothpaste is designed to poison the body and especially the brain. One such neurotoxin is fluoride. This causes docile and submissive behavior and decimates IQ. In 1955 Crest became the first toothpaste to use fluoride which calcifies the pineal gland and is considered hazardous waste by the EPA. Used in concentration camps to sedate detainees, fluoride is the ingredient in rat poison and Prozac. It has since been added to city water filtration centers and used by dentists who help enforce the propaganda. Since your mouth absorbs instantly, it's the best place to insert toxins regularly! How often do you brush with fluoride and drink city water? Like all natural minerals, probiotics, and vitamins, they are too cheap to be produced and sold to you by the government. Instead, they make poisons and give them to you through their middlemen: doctors. This is the reason the very simple cures for all these fake diseases are hidden from you. Cancer can be cured in many ways, none of which involves barbaric butchery. High doses of Vitamin C, since nothing unnatural can survive in alkaline environments, using Caster Oil properly can draw tumors and anything else unnatural out of your body, etc. etc. etc. It's all too cheap, free, and used to be known as food, not cures. Because people 200 years ago ate real food, because people 2000 years ago ate even better food, they lived much longer and were much healthier. This is why the elite tend to live much longer than the average blue-collar family who don't exercise their bodies or minds, nor do they nourish themselves.

As stated by the CDC, clean water eliminates diseases, not vaccines. A CDC report states:

"The occurrence of diseases such as cholera and typhoid dropped dramatically. In 1900, the occurrence of typhoid fever in the United States was approximately 100 cases per 100,000 people. By 1920, it had decreased to 33.8 cases per 100,000 people. In 2006, it had decreased to 0.1 cases per 100,000 people (only 353 cases) with approximately 75% occurring among international travelers. Typhoid fever decreased rapidly in cities from Baltimore to Chicago as water disinfection and treatment was instituted. This decrease in illness is credited to the implementation of drinking water disinfection and treatment, improving the quality of source water, and improvements in sanitation and hygiene.
It is because of these successes that we can celebrate over a century of public drinking water disinfection and treatment - one of the greatest public health achievements of the 20th century."

Someone else everyone ignored was Professor Jihad Bishara, lead virologist in Israel who stated:

"The virus is not airborne, most people who are infected will recover without even knowing they were sick. The global panic is unnecessary and exaggerated."

Denmark's new laws enforced double penalties for a Corona-related crime which other EU countries had enforced as well. Any non-citizen to commit a Corona-crime during this time, was immediately thrown from the country. This law was implemented in addition to legal home invasions based on **suspicion** alone and without need of warrants, forced vaccination and more. Scandinavia and the EU have cultivated a culture of suspicion-based crimes for many decades as they sit on the edge of communism. The elite used their multitude of puppets to push vaccines and get rid of all other options. In most countries one was no longer allowed to work without being injected. This caused many to be forced out of work, out of homes, and out of food.

"I think we are looking into a realistic scenario where we need to

vaccinate and maybe revaccinate the populations over and over and over again."
- Mette Frederiksen Danish Prime Minister

Bayer CEO Werner Baumann announced a plan to create a Chloroquine (malaria medication) facility in Europe. This company then immediately partnered with Curevac to create the Covid vaccine CVnCoV. The Health Minister of Germany, Jens Spahn was one of hundreds who promoted vaccines, preaching that they were the only way out! Fellow Bilderberg member Audrey Azoulay (UNESCO Director General) was also used to heavily and forcefully promote the vaccines and the elite agenda. Naturally, there was Bill Gates who is present in all things dealing with your extermination. In 2017 he stated:

"Whether it occurs by a quirk of nature or at the hand of a terrorist, epidemiologists say a fast-moving airborne pathogen could kill more than 30 million people in less than a year. And they say there is a reasonable probability the world will experience such an outbreak in the next 10 to 15 years."

Meanwhile, Pharma Co.'s license was suspended after its vaccination sterilized 500,000 women and children in Kenya. In Uganda, one of many countries with no reported deaths or recoveries from CoronaVirus, the President announced a forced Martial Law lockdown, beginning March 31, 2020. No driving was permitted; No opening of shopping malls or stores, including grocery stores were closed which led to people starving to death. China required citizens to use their cell phones to generate "health codes" so their movements could be tracked and controlled. The system assigned users a green, yellow, or red "health code" in the style of a traffic light, dictating what they could or could not do. Police worldwide have, naturally, taken advantage of their unlimited power. French President Emmanuel Macron not only put 100,000 police on the streets to enforce the lockdown, but also called in the military reinforcements. The US is used to living under Martial Law, as it has been a police state under legal Martial Law since 9/11 and the population have lived in constant fear ever since, thanks to the amount of propaganda the US is responsible for putting out. Even after knowing the truth about the elite for generations, since it is explained and exposed in the American Constitution, the people are enslaved and eager to bend as the elite dictate.

"This is what a police state is like, it is a state in which a government can issue orders or express preferences with no legal authority and the police will enforce ministers' wishes." -Former Supreme Court Justice Lord Sumption

Vice President of the European Central Bank, Luis de Guindos, dedicatedly worked to indoctrinate the public into the belief in the economic benefits of fast vaccine rollouts. Beijing authorities announced on March 19, 2020, the number of Chinese cellphone users "dropped" by 21 million in three months. 21 million people disappeared out of a technocracy wherein none can survive without being connected. People do not just disappear. But they often get slaughtered by their governments and NO ONE DOES ANYTHING ABOUT IT.

"Impossible for a person to cancel his cellphone. Dealing with the government for pensions and social security, buying train tickets, shopping ... no matter what people want to do, they are required to use cell phones." - Tang Jiangyuan

Meanwhile the world was told by the UN and WHO that millions were dying from Covid. No one listened to the truth. Anyone admitted into a hospital with even a cold was labelled as having covid, and those who died of other illnesses during the following years of the plandemic were labelled as having died from covid. One person, Ashley Ferrell, commented to a US news outlet who wrote an article stating that her grandmother was among those who died from covid stating:

"My grandmother did NOT pass away at SAMMC. She passed away at a local inpatient hospice facility. She did NOT pass away from Covid-19. She passed away from Alzheimer's that she had suffered with the past 12 years, and a case of aspiration pneumonia that worsened her ailing state."

Another news report which stated that a police lieutenant (important detail) died from covid received a comment from a family member who stated:

"My papa never died from this virus! And the media and the lying ass government is fraud! He had health issues way before this even happened! They did not confirm with our family that he had that shit, and the media want to clout off his name!"

Former WHO employee, Astrid Stuckelberger stated in an interview:

"[the vaccines are] a biotechnological, synthetic experiment... In the vaccines they see graphene, parasites, metals. Therefore, we should stop the vaccination, and ban all injections. Those who continue should be prosecuted...Organizations such as GAVI - the Global Alliance for Vaccine Immunization led by Bill Gates - they came to WHO in 2006 with funding. Since then, the WHO has developed into a new type of international organization. GAVI gained more and more influence, and total immunity, more than the diplomats in the UN. GAVI can do exactly what they want, the police can do nothing...GAVI presented a global action plan for vaccination 2012-2020. Bill Gates handled the vaccination, he took over...GAVI, the World Bank and the WHO entered into a contract called IFFM: International Facility Finance for Immunization. Our countries, our people, pay to the WHO, the World Bank and GAVI to carry out their immunization programs. Which means vaccinating the entire population. When you see the plan from GAVI, you see that from 2012 to 2020 they have had this as a goal. But then it did not work, they had to create a pandemic."

In her interview she cited the research done by Professor John Ioannidis at Stanford University which proved that the mortality rate in 2020 was not higher than other years, which many other scientists and doctors came forward to expose from the beginning of this plandemic.

"It's a lie, and no pandemic." - Astrid Stuckelberger

Because of her words, Astrid's courses at the universities of Geneva and Lausanne were put to an end, along with her medical license. As one would expect, the numbers you are given by elite organizations are not the reality and while European EudraVigilance showed 29,000 dead by the end of 2020, the numbers are much closer to 300,000. While everyone today understands that doctors are paid to "practice medicine" not to cure, they are also paid to promote certain medications, vaccines, among other things such as claiming cause of death without proof.

Former UK prime minister Gordon Brown immediately called for a global government to be established in the wake of the CoronaVirus. France's President Emmanuel Macron implemented forced vaccines in order to access common facilities in 2021 (which was more than a year after all of this had been exposed for what it was). Naturally, Germany's Angela Merkel, a relative of Adolf Hitler, has pushed fiercely to develop the society her ancestors had formed and related that the EU Summit of 2021 was a success, stating:

"<u>Everyone agreed</u> that we need a digital vaccination certificate."

"Eventually we will have some digital certificates to show who has recovered [from Covid] or been tested recently or who has received the vaccine." — Bill Gates

Soon Covid passports were implemented worldwide, and the circus continued. People were unable to travel into certain countries and even stores, without being vaccinated. Bill Gates immediately had MIT Develop a '**Tattoo ID**'. Those who came forward to expose the elite during this time were shot to death, like so many before them and no one paid attention. John Maguguli of Tanzania, Hamed Bakayoko of the Ivory Coast, Swaziland's Ambrose Dlamini and many more all died suddenly after refusing to enforce the Covid vaccines in their countries. They were replaced by better puppets. One was CDC Whistleblower Dr. Tim Cunningham who worked tirelessly to expose the deadliness and truth of vaccines:

"Some of the patients I've administered the flu shot to this year have died, I don't care who you are, this scares the crap out of me. We have seen people dying across the country of the flu, and one thing nearly all of them have in common is they got the flu shot."

President of the EU Commission Ursula von der Leyen is another corrupt politician who has taken it upon herself to personally persecute the elderly by violating their health care rights. Her husband Heiko von der Leyen is the Medical Director of Orgenesis Inc which is a genetic telecom company (whose revenue was $7.7 million in 2020 and $35.5 million in 2021). Orgenesis developed the vaccine for Pfizer. Their rule of Europe ignited during Covid and Ursula has promoted her husband's work throughout the event, making them millions and is now attempting to make vaccines mandatory for the EU. The same is going on in every country. This dynamic duo believes strongly in their own racial supremacy, considering all who are not German or Belgian through blood as inferior. Their genealogies lead straight back to Nazi volunteers, slave traders, and more which is why Ursula, John Biden, and Angela Merkel are such close friends. As part of the elite and specifically Pfizers' inner circle, Ursula has become business partners with Minister Frank Vandenbroucke, notorious for bribery schemes. While he controls the population by militarizing the police and using them like hunting dogs, he ensures that Ursula has had free reign to force vaccines, take health care rights away from those who don't agree, and more. When Covid began, Ursula had already been discussing deals with vaccine companies on her phone. She has received a slap on the wrist for her "disappearing messages" with Pfizer's CEO Albert Bourla. A total of 3 contracts have been made, under the table, with the company, adding up to 1.8 Billion doses and 36 Billion Euros. All while lining her husband's pockets with your money and your blood.

Pfizer gave a significant grant to Ruobing Li in 2023, to research why people are hesitant about vaccines and how to get them to not hesitate in the future. You see, you did not inject yourselves thoroughly enough this time. The elite are always improving, adapting, and expanding. Their goal is to eliminate YOU.

"Among the large number of factors that may contribute to an individual's vaccine **hesitancy**, we will be able to tell other researchers what the most influential ones for each population or subpopulation are, and we can also **identify important moderating variables** that could tell us how different factors predict vaccine hesitancy differently to resolve some of the conflicting findings that exist in the vaccine hesitancy literature." — Ruobing Li

Do you understand what she just exposed?

The reason intelligent people are against vaccines is because they understand them and the rights that we are all born with, regardless of what paper government officials have signed. The population of every country have now been divided by their willingness or lack thereof to violate themselves with vaccines. The CDC called everyone in the US to perform a survey regarding willingness to vaccinate. Those of us who didn't get vaccinated and don't live in fear, got the Covid flu and had the flu symptoms associated with SARS and...HEALED! Just like when we got the bird flu, swine flu, and other designer diseases. We took ginger to rejuvenate and reactivate our livers, so they could fight off the disease as our bodies are made to do; we took extra C and D and did heavy metal detoxes to assist our natural bodies. The natural human body is healed and self-sustaining when it's given the correct natural nutrients. Honey is another natural healer, so use it in excess (on cuts, burns, in teas etc.). Don't be deceived. There is ALWAYS an agenda which is given to you under the lie that it is good for YOU. If you have a natural human body, then take care of it naturally.

If you don't want to continue pumping your body full of medications and foods that have horrible effects, your body will be capable of functioning properly. The food you eat, the drugs you take and the air you breathe are filled with toxins, depending on where you live it is worse or better, but everyone in every country is experiencing this type of warfare. So, dear reader, heal yourself with one of the multitudes of Natural Cures for these Man-Made Diseases!

You see, joint shareholders of Orgenesis and Pfizer include Orgenesi Vanguard Group, Inc. at 3.77%, Pfizer The Vanguard Group, Inc. 7.78%, and SSgA Funds Management, Inc. 4.97%. In 2020 the Vanguard Group bought the largest number of shares of GlaxoSmithKline, essentially taking it over. Official stock exchange sources reveal that some of the owners of the Vanguard Group shares include Rothschild Investment Corp., Edmond De Rothschild Holding, Orsini and other upper elite family holding companies. As you know by now, these investment funds own over 90% of the media institutions. In March 2020, Pfizer along with Orgenesis patented the mRNA project together with the Germans of BioNTech. The politicians bought them and forced them into you.

Thankfully her misconduct has been taken to anti-corruption court along with Didier Reynders and other EU staff members. Many atrocities against the elderly have taken place under the fog of Covid. Now they are called Economically Inactive by Ursula's new laws and illegally cut off from their health care benefits, pensions and more. Under the direction of Ursula von der Leyen, Tina Nilsson and Monika Mosshammer were glad to help with bribery-extortion schemes. Dr. Leszek Sachs, a lawyer and whistleblower, has received many threats on his life from Ursula, but continued fighting the EU Commission on behalf of the elderly. He states:

"This scheme is in fact worse than Qatargate, the bribery sums involved much larger, and also Von der Leyen sponsoring what is in effect a threat of murder of EU citizens who decline to pay bribes to the friends of Didier Reynders, with many victims to be hurt in the future if this scheme is not stopped. Von der Leyen has ordered that Commission offices be used to help operate and extend a Belgian scheme extorting bribes from EU citizens for their Freedom of Movement / Health Care Access rights in Belgium, and in particular that EU staff join her and Reynders in direct violations of EU Court Order C-535/19."

Over 17,000 physicians and scientists called for Pfizer, Moderna, BioNTech, Jassen and AstraZeneca to be indicted for fraud, declaring that these corporations had purposely withheld safety and effectiveness information. They were ignored. While the Covid event has been going on, Ursula began visiting her buddies in the elite circles: President Biden, Prime Minister Justin Trudeau, King Charles, and many more enacting the "Green Alliance" — a mineral trade agreement. This agreement is part of the Ukraine War False Flag event.

Cathy Berx, Governor of Antwerp, Bill Morneau, Canadas Finance Minister, and Norwegian Prime Minister Erna Solberg are just a few of the rulers who directed billions of dollars into vaccines, while simultaneously ensuring the enforcement of them in their own countries. These politicians worked in tandem with their paid puppets like Dr. Alan Fischer of the Edmond de Rothschild Foundation, journalist Stefano Feltri, Media King Juan Luis Cebrian, Canadian journalist Andrew Coyne, Mathias Dopfner, Francois Lenget of France, Regina Dugan (DARPA, FB, Google, and Wellcome Trust), and all mainstream media outlets, which are controlled by George Soros, ensuring the steady flow of propaganda to subdue the populations. As we covered in previous chapters, everyone you see on TV, even if they are said to be experts, are paid puppets. Mere actors just like those we see today taking the floor of the UN meetings: Leonardo DiCaprio, Angelina Jolie etc. Just as every president and king is a mere actor, nothing more. Understanding the herd mentality and the mentality of mass paranoia and panic (fear), billions of people still believe the things they read in news and see on TV or on the internet, which is appalling. By this day and age almost every person has access to the internet and movies and news, meaning they are all aware of the causes and reality of Mass Panic, propaganda, and everything in this book! People alive today are well aware of how the herd mentality enables those who feed it to create the same symptoms and events that are feared like hypochondriasis and dozens of other mental **disorders caused by fear**. These people, the mentally impaired, guaranteed that **all** of us would be forced into solitary confinement for months on end and develop a wide range of mental and physical health problems and more. Immediately commissions were set up worldwide to poll the population regarding various aspects of the inhumanity they were accepting.

"People act like they have a choice. You don't have a choice. Normalcy only returns when we've **largely vaccinated the entire global population**." — Bill Gates

Thus was the propaganda forced on the world at the time. Fools. From the beginning **thousands** of whistleblowers including doctors and scientists and geneticists came out to proclaim the truth only to be ignored like the rest of us. Thousands were murdered and the public remained silent.

"Sergei Kolesnikov, of the Russian Academy of Medical Sciences, said the propagation of the SARS virus might well have been caused by leaking a combat virus grown in bacteriological weapons labs. He claimed that the virus of atypical pneumonia (SARS) was a synthesis of two viruses (of measles and infectious parotiditis or mumps), the natural compound of which was impossible, that this mix could never appear in nature, stating, 'This can be done only in a laboratory.'" - Global Research

Norwegian and British vaccine scientists published unequivocal evidence that SARS-CoV-2, the coronavirus responsible for the COVID-19 pandemic, was man-made. It was ignored. The authors state two conclusions:
1. The mutations that would normally be seen in the course of animal to human transmission do not occur in SARS-CoV-2, indicating that it was fully "pre-adapted" for human infection.
2. SARS-CoV-2 has insertions in its protein sequence that have never been detected in nature and contribute to its infectivity and pathogenicity. SARS-CoV-2 has a receptor binding domain specifically designed for the human angiotensin converting enzyme-2 receptor (ACE2) found in lungs, kidneys, intestines, and blood vessels.

In addition, SARS-CoV-2 has a furin polybasic cleavage site not found in any closely related coronaviruses and contains other artificially inserted charged amino acids that enhance the virus' ability to bind to and enter human cells by forming "salt bridges" between the virus and the cell surface. As the authors correctly note, the development of an effective vaccine cannot be accomplished without an objective analysis of the structure of SARS-CoV-2, its mode of action and its origin. Creating a vaccine takes a lot of time, but as you already know, the Covid vaccine was ready in days. Those modifications are key to understanding the unique transmissibility and potency of SARS-CoV-2. The COVID-19 event reveals neurological, hematological, and immunological pathogenicity, which cannot be explained by infectivity via the ACE2 receptor alone. The wide-spread systemic release of the virus, due to its co-receptor enhancement, explains the multiple clinical findings on the cardiovascular system, immunological T-cells, cells associated with neuropathological conditions and, finally, the severe hypoxia seen in advanced cases.

No less than the Office of the Director of National Intelligence in the United States has blindly accepted the scientific "conventional wisdom" promoted by the

Chinese Communist Party, issuing the following April 30, 2020, statement:
"The Intelligence Community also concurs with the wide scientific consensus that the COVID-19 virus was not manmade or genetically modified."

Operation A Spreading Plague was implemented by Sam Nunn (who was also instrumental in Operation Dark Winter) in 2019, followed by the Preventing Global Catastrophic Biological Risks Exercise the following year. These exercises (like military exercises) are very telling. If only people would pay attention. Event 201 and Preventing Global Catastrophic Biological Risks Exercises were implemented by the ex-Deputy Director of the CIA and Director of National Intelligence, Avril Haines, and Sam Nunn. Bilderberg member, Sylvia Burwell, is also the Co-Chair of the Council on Foreign Relations' Independent Task Force on Improving Pandemic Preparedness. Why would a "think tank" have an independent task force, one might wonder? Philip Zelikow, who did such a good job drafting the 9/11 Commission Report, was put in charge of the University of Virginia's Covid Commission Planning Group.

In March 2020, G20 leaders agreed during a virtual summit to do "whatever it takes" to "minimize the social and economic damage of the COVID-19 pandemic". G20 members have taken upon themselves, independently as vigilantes do, to create a $5 trillion stimulus through targeted fiscal policy and insurance schemes.

What was the reason for Covid, you may be asking? Like all other False Flag Events the purpose of was to <u>pass laws</u>. This is always the main agenda apart from depopulation, which was achieved through enforcing new vaccines on the population of the world. These new vaccines which were instantly available and ready for human testing before the virus was set loose are merely another gigantic red flag that was ignored. This event succeeded in solidifying the elite's control over the entire population, finalizing their goals at long last. Abbott Laboratories, BASF Plant Science, Bristol-Myers Squibb, DuPont Central Research and Development, Eli Lilly Corp., Embrex, GlaxoSmithKline, Hoffman-LaRoche, Merck & Co., Monsanto, Pfizer Inc., Schering-Plough Research Institute, and Syngenta Corp. of Switzerland are a few of the dominating vaccine companies of your new government.

Numerous vague laws were established in each country which state they expire but are easily extended. As history has shown us, the useful ones are NEVER rescinded. The Minister of Health and the Elderly in Denmark (and other countries) is now allowed, at the recommendation of the National Board of Health, to make amendments and create new lists in this law. This law is a Martial Law giving full control over the land as well as the physical person of every citizen in Denmark. Air Transportation was shut down worldwide, leading to stock market crashes, economic downfall, bankruptcy. Shipping, Trade, Railroads, Public Transportation were shut down or severely restricted! All countries who have allowed Public Transportation to be forced on them by their governments and rely on that to function, realized for one moment that the elite successfully control how and where one can travel even within their own city. Businesses and schools shut down, forcing even more gullible minds to stampede onto the internet. Grocery stores raised the prices of goods, no gatherings were allowed. Doctors were arrested for treating CoronaVirus patients because they were sharing information (between themselves, privately) online. People were barricaded in their homes where they died and decomposed.

"Every single Chinese person, every member of the Chinese nation, should feel proud to live in this great era. Our progress will not be halted by any storms and tempests." - President Xi Jinping in Wuhan, China February 2020, when making a statement about the hundreds who had dropped dead.

Surveillance in South Korea reached a new height, like most countries, using CoronaVirus as a reason to ignore human rights. A live GPS map shows EVERY infected citizen, age, where they have been, time, sex, how long the person has had the disease, as well as who that person has contacted and/or infected. This is called Smart Security.

Once people allowed their governments, doctors, nurses, and friends to label them as having Covid, forced vaccinations were immediately implemented in almost every country. A multitude of people who died were labelled as having died from Covid, despite family and friends protests that the deceased had never had the virus. Truth doesn't matter when it comes to news. Thousands on Social Media **posted** about the deaths of their loved ones who had taken the government promoted vaccine. Others took to the streets to protest and got arrested and fined. Naturally, it was far too late for any of it to make a difference once so many had surrendered to the elite for so long.

The statistics are proven time and time again to be totally false. Another example is that WHO claims vaccines are 95% successful and you believe they mean that to be 95% success in eliminating the virus. This is not the purpose. The vaccines ARE 95% successful in destroying you, which is their purpose. Those who are vaccinated are then able to **infect** unvaccinated persons because it is passed from person to person, violating their rights and raping their bodies. Those who are vaccinated are **guaranteed** a debilitating disease or death within the next 10 years. So yes. WHO is correct when they say it's a success, you just don't understand what they mean.

Pfizer put out a report stating that in order to save 1 person from Covid, 22,000 had to be vaccinated and that for every 1 person unaffected by the vaccine 2 will die from it. People all over the world died in hoards, **from the vaccine** after standing outside for hours in long lines to be penetrated by their Doctor. This was suppressed and censored by the media and the internet, like everything else is. 90% of hospitalizations were force-vaccinated, in order to spread the agenda. According to mainstream, no one dies of vaccines. According to them, only the non-life-threatening CoronaVirus kills. The Covid Tracker (another massive violation that everyone was happy to accept) recorded that over 12.7 billion vaccines were given during the 2-year period. 12.7 Billion. 12.7 Billion people injected themselves with experimental, unknown, alien, foreign objects, which they knew would then be spread to their families and anyone in contact with them, out of **fear** developed by propaganda. Fear is one of the most powerful tools the elites have at their disposal. They purposefully inject fear into the public to manipulate and control.

"He who has overcome his fears will truly be free." - Aristotle

People have shown that the instant the media tells them to live a life scared in their homes, they will comply in order to stay safe. Whether the virus was ever real or not, is not the point. Unafraid and compassionate people are impossible to control therefore you must be made to fear. Propaganda placed into developing minds through schools and media eliminates critical thinking and logic. This makes it next to impossible for you to use your own mind because though you don't realize it, your thoughts are not your own — neither are your opinions and beliefs. Fear is the best weapon of all great manipulators. It can move people to do **anything**, no matter how nonsensical it is. Turn on the news, open a newspaper, watch the latest movie, and you'll see this, or shut it all off and begin to have a real life. Your current life is not all there is, nor all that you are, but it is everything you've been taught to believe. It is all negative.

Our emotions are energy, and they all have a frequency. Just as negative emotions cause diseases, positive ones cause healing and resistance to them. Just as the frequencies of music, Wi-Fi, and curse-words cause damage able to be seen on a cellular level, True Love Conquers All. As studies have proven, saying the words 'Love', 'Peace', and 'Thank You' cause cells to form beautiful formations just as prayer and classical music do. Likewise, negative words like 'I will kill you', or curse words and various genres of music, cause chaos and disrupt all formations. As detailed before, music affects various parts of your brain as well and is used in Mind Control Techniques. When listening to music your corpus callosum is activated, your sensory cortex gives tactile feedback while your motor cortex and cerebellum causes you to move. As your Auditory cortex listens to the sounds and analyzes the tones your prefrontal cortex is anticipating and creating expectations as the hippocampus is memorizing everything. Meanwhile, your nucleus accumbens and amygdala are producing emotional reactions to what you hear!! This is why it's vital to know what you listen to, and what you allow into your life as it affects your DNA. This is why parents of generations past have protected their children against certain music, movies, and other influences. Love is our natural frequency. Peace. Whether Kahuna of Hawaii, Catholic, Christian, Native American, African, Aborigine, Peruvian, faith healers, Hindu, or shaman's the world over — all the real effective healers regardless of faith, were found to release a frequency of 8 cycles per second or 8 Hz, from the brains, and to entrain the brain waves of those being healed, inducing a form of "self-healing". DNA molecules duplicate themselves at a frequency of 8Hz. The frequency of love heals DNA, relieves pain, and rejuvenates. YOU are able to control these processes, but that knowledge is kept from you. But I digress.

Louis Arbour and Dido Harding are two other Bilderberg members who were instrumental in the tracking system. Louis was made Honorary president of Covi Canada while Dido was given the task of producing the NHSX app. Emmanuelle Charpentier, founder of the genetic manipulation tool CRISPER which is used to develop diseases, received the Nobel Prize for her success in 2020. Jared Cohen of Jigsaw, Reid Hoffman of Linkedin, Robert Kimmitt of Facebook, Eric Schmidt of Google, Jens Stoltenberg of NATO, and Patrick Pichette of Twitter are only a handful of the Bilderberg and other elite club operatives involved in the worldwide censorship scheme which was agreed upon in March of 2020 and continues in many countries through 2024.

"I urge world leaders to fully support the Global Vaccination Strategy I launched with the World Health Organization last month. We need to get vaccines into the arms of 40 per cent of people in all countries by the end of this year - and 70 per cent by mid-2022." — Antonio Guterres, UN Secretary General, Bilderberg, and World Economic Forum member

The World Health Organization began as the International Health Division, founded by the Rockefellers. Their vaccine companies exploded during this time, making them a fortune at the expense of YOUR lives. These vaccines were proven to cause deadly effects on the body in a short time, without knowing the long-term consequences at all because they alter RNA... Given the fact that RNA is a newly "discovered" thing according to science, it is a wonder that anyone would allow this to be done to them, but thanks to technology everyone has become desensitized to the point that the elite can have unquestioned and unchecked authority.

"Indian researchers are baffled by segments of the virus's RNA that have no relation to other coronaviruses like SARS, and instead appear to be closer to HIV. The virus even responds to treatment by HIV medications." - Zerohedge

As nurses exposed, there were 3 coded Covid vaccines. One is a placebo for "select people", another is the mRNA slow-release toxin, and the third is known to cause fast-acting cancer. The numbered identification is part of the Unique Service Identifier code. Another easy way to tell is that some companies, like Pfizer, have a yellow-colored vaccine and a white-colored vaccine. EU Parliament President, David Sassoli, died slowly over several days from lethal injection of the Covid vaccine. One of the elders of the Wakkawakka tribe died immediately after his 2nd injection which was part of the public propaganda to enforce vaccines. Dan Kaminsky, one of the creators of the internet, died 10 days after his 2nd shot. A multitude of movie stars and musicians as well as entire sports teams were disabled by the vaccines. 2 of Pope Francis' Jesuit friends were also killed by the Covid vaccine. This is in no way a complete list, as millions were culled by these toxins. This agenda allowed the elite to wipe out anyone who was a threat, oh so easily and on camera! When victims of the vaccine began to immediately emerge with various ailments such as Bell's Palsy, heart failure, and much more, the FDA wrote a report to state that these are not serious conditions and those permanently damaged by their doctors were ignored. Not to worry dear reader, not many gave one thought or moment to consider the many very well-known risks and even less acted on it.

Most leaders were given a saline solution, rather than a real vaccine, in order to be seen through pictures and gain attention for the cause, California's Governor Gavin Newsom was given the Moderna COVID vaccine, known to cause hallucinations, suicidal urges and permanent disability. Unlike Angela Merkel and others, he was not given the placebo. He had an <u>immediate</u> adverse reaction, similar to Guillain–Barré syndrome (a neurological disorder), a known side effect of many vaccines. Robert Kennedy Jr., chairman of Children's Health Defense, said:

"If it's true the governor has suffered debilitating neurological injuries following vaccination, it raises grave ethical questions about his seemingly dishonest efforts to conceal his injuries while implementing aggressive policies to force the children and working people of California to endure similar risks."

You should pay attention to the elite, to the "stars" of the world. They do not allow their children to eat fast food, have cellphones or laptops, and they above all NEVER vaccinate their children. According to US data, in the first 11 months of Covid vaccinations contained 68% of recorded vaccination deaths of the last 30 years. 60% of all life-threatening issues over the last 30 years occurred after covid vaccines were implemented. 55% of all recorded hospitalizations in the past 30 years followed the covid vaccines over an 11-month span. While these numbers don't need to be known by anyone, to understand that injecting foreign objects into a human body is not good, ignorant people respond to them. Try to find the numbers in your country if your country allows them to be known.

Effects of the vaccines can be slow and, according to scientists, can take up to 10 years to grow, however, already people are dying off in droves. Immediately, death and sterility rates went up **20%** in vaccinated persons. The target group was the elderly, which is now considered anyone older than 40. Those who are most likely to go against the deadliest agenda of the elite: the Gender-Neutral Society. Within a year the death rate in the US alone rose by 50 times. So, today the EU has seen death rates rise 11%, not as much as they had hoped, but birthrates are down 14% thanks to the sterilization caused by the vaccine. The elite are happy enough to simply eliminate procreation through sterilization, abortion, or any means. Other sterilizing factors pushed on the public is plastic, as mentioned, gold and silver which kill testosterone, and especially heavy metals which have been floating through our air, permeating our soil, and flowing through our water thanks to Chemtrails. Australia has seen a devastating decrease in births with a ratio of 21 births per 2.9 million people (post-vax). As the inevitable truth has become more and more well-known, businesses who originally forced people to leave their jobs because they would not take the vaccine, have refused to employ those who have been vaccinated because they are sick and make others around them sick. Over a 4-week period in 2021, 80% of deaths in the UK were directly linked to the vaccine.

"I happen to be in the morbidity business; I'm the CEO of a large insurance group... Based on what it is we are seeing; the rates right now are excess mortality of 84% and excess of every kind of disease at 1100%. We are expecting a 5000 or so percent increase in excess mortality for this year (2022). An enormous number. I don't think that it's by coincidence, by the way, that Moderna has now just received licensure of their emergency use authorization HIV vaccine. So, they gave everybody AIDS, and here's your salvation, which is **this new vaccine**." — Todd Callender

On February 7, 2020, Li Wenliang died. He was a 34-year-old doctor-turned-whistleblower who warned his colleagues of a very contagious virus. The group of 7 doctors were arrested and threatened to silence before they began to turn up dead. Wenliang had spoken out on WeChat about the way the virus was handled, in Wuhan, and created a large awakening in China. Because of the awakening brought out by Dr. Li, Fang Bin, a local clothing salesman, went on to become a citizen journalist on YouTube and exposed many horrendous events happening inside Wuhan. Chen Qiushi was another unfiltered independent YouTube live-streamer, who posted dozens of videos exposing what was really going on, inside China. Both of them were disappeared. Chen on February 6th, and Fang on February 9th. The last video Fang posted to his YouTube channel came on February 9. In it, he repeated again and again:
"All citizens resist, hand power back to the people!"

Li Zehua, another citizen journalist, truth speaker, freedom fighter, quit his job and went to Wuhan to independently report. He went, in hopes of following in the footsteps of disappeared journalist Chen Qiushi. In his last video he stated:
"I don't want to remain silent or shut my eyes and ears. It's not that I can't have a nice life, with a wife and kids. I can. I'm doing this because I hope

more young people can, like me, stand up."

The live stream, posted on YouTube, shows two men in plain clothes entering the apartment and then cuts out. He has not been heard from since. Know that this is a **very** small list. Without informative and truthful speech, we are blind. Let's continue.

The number of patents put out by the elite during the Covid event would take an entire chapter to cover, but let's look at one. John Bell of the Gates Foundation was also on the UK Vaccine Task Force and proudly stated to the public that the vaccine gives each person a 60-70% chance of total sterility. In 2015, the Pirbright Institute (funded by the Gates Foundation and owned by the Rothschilds) filed a patent for a live attenuated CoronaVirus "to be used in the production of vaccines". Before this, in 2015, the Rothschild's had patented their covid-19 test kits which were distributed in 2017. The Pirbright Institute was used to patent the Virus and Vaccine (US Patent Number US 10,130,701 B2), which was also patented in Europe (WO 2016/012793) states:

"The present invention provides a live, attenuated coronavirus comprising a variant replicase gene encoding polyproteins comprising a mutation in one or more non-structural proteins."

SERC-O is a UK owned company that runs the US Patent Office. SERC-O formed The Pirbright Institute that submitted their Coronavirus invention to the US Patent. They received funding from Bill and Melinda Gates Foundation (Microsoft), Wellcome Trust (publicly "sold" to GlaxoSmithKline), the European Commission, World Health Organization, Defra, and DARPA. The World Health Organization is under the Vatican's United Nations umbrella.

Other Patents include Microsoft's patent for Crypto Mining Systems using Body Activity Data. This is what Vaccines will be used for. Vaccines, for the past decades, have been using technology instead of medicine. It **will** be used for the next worldwide currency. This was planned and put in motion in the 1960's while everyone was distracted by the Vietnam War, another Rothschild created war which was used to hide the genocide and communist takeover of Cambodia and other countries in the region which immediately implemented revolutions to place militant children in charge. Bill Gates and his wife have been working towards perfecting their vaccines throughout the world, in order to achieve technological vaccines. The Covid experimentation allowed it to be finalized.

The Covid Vaccines are made with Luciferin, the name given to a bioluminescent compound that reacts to oxygen by fragmenting and releasing energy. Luciferin is mixed with a 66.6 ml phosphate solution and then must be frozen and shielded from the light before administration as it reacts violently to light. Thanks to Bill Gates' dedication, he created a micro implant which uses Luciferin to mesh technology and biology together in order to create the elite's much needed link to control your finances completely. Living tech.

"The chip may be remotely charged with all your personal data, including bank accounts - digital money. Yes, digital money that's what "they" are aiming at, so you really have no control any more over your health and other intimate data, but also over your earnings and spending. Your money could be blocked or taken away - as a 'sanction' for misbehavior, for swimming against the stream. You may become a mere slave of the masters. Comparatively, feudalism may appear like a walk in the park...It's not for nothing that Dr. Tedros, DG of WHO, said a few days ago, we must move towards digital money, because physical paper and coin money can spread diseases, especially endemic diseases, like the coronavirus." — Peter Koenig of Global Research

Already the world has jumped onboard with cashless and biometric banking, as we have discussed before. This will allow us all to become golems of the elite. Luciferin communicates with apps and the like, successfully turning you into nothing more than data. The purpose of all of this is to generalize and normalize vaccinations, in order to further the true agenda: Technology. Jim Thomas of ETC Group has stated that genetically modified mosquitoes and more may be used as potential biological weapons, just like they have been used in the past. This is nothing new in the field of technology but it's something to keep in mind. Tech is in the air we breathe and the food we eat, and you can rest assured that it has also been disguised as bugs.

"My only concern is whether [countries] have the courage of conviction to do it now (push for a responsible regulation of killer robots), or whether we will have to wait for people to die first." — Toby Walsh

Lately, Cornell engineers have constructed a DNA material which is capable of metabolizing, in addition to self-assembly and organization by using DASH (DNA-based Assembly and Synthesis of Hierarchical). These capabilities are essential in life, meaning now technology is living. This is something NASA has also been using and working to perfect as it would ease contact with non-human entities, just as technology does.

"Even from a simple design, we were able to create sophisticated behaviors like racing. Artificial metabolism could open a new frontier in robotics. Everything from its ability to move and compete, all those processes are self-contained. There's no external interference. Ultimately, the system may lead to lifelike self-reproducing machines." - Shogo Hamada of the Luo lab

This technology is already being used, injected into the body, under the guise that it will automatically release medicine and cure diseases.

"Over 1,200 emails released under open records requests reveal that the US military is now the top funder and influencer behind a controversial <u>genetic extinction technology</u> known as "gene drives" pumping $100 million into the field. The trove of emails, obtained through open records requests, also shed light on a $1.6 million dollar <u>UN gene drive advocacy operation paid for by the Bill and Melinda Gates Foundation</u>." – Friends of the Earth NGO 2017

"The Bill and Melinda Gates Foundation invested more than $21 million to perfect a "microneedle technology" – Robert Kennedy Jr.

Covid was implemented in order for Bill Gates to perfect the crypto-bio tech before worldwide forced vaccinations are enacted, as he stated himself. This will come next. All you have to do is what you have done your entire life: wait for it. For those interested in the Hegelian Dialect, the code language used by the elites, Bill Gates' patent number for ID2020 was WO.2020.060606. The number used by the media repeatedly for the Covid Event was 33 which can be found everywhere. As in all planned events the elite carry out, gematria is present. Many countries have already begun the legal processes to implement the ID as standard in their country. Now all they need is the next event!

This, dear reader, is why those indoctrinated and/or controlled by the elite (Controlled Opposition and Conspiracy Theorists) corrupt the truth and spread fear by preaching that technology is the Beast System. Every aspect of technology is covered in Fallen Angel symbolism and purpose, yes. Do not fear, dear reader, it is not the system or Mark of the Beast, it is just another Luciferian system. There are many things that must happen before the Mark of the Beast is implemented, like the dozens of prophecies that **precede** the New World Order. However, time is passing quickly and as soon as these things begin, the rest will follow with incredible speed. This is why we must use our minds and be vigilant but also, we must, in using our minds, use wisdom and fact. This means you have a lot to learn for yourself, as you should have done in your childhood... Truth is simple and direct. Confusion creates Fear. Fear is Control, the opposite of Truth.

"Human body activity associated with a task provided to a user may be used in a mining process of a cryptocurrency system. A server may provide a task to a device of a user which is communicatively coupled to the server. A sensor communicatively coupled to or comprised in the device of the user may sense body activity of the user. Body activity data may be generated based on the sensed body activity of the user. The cryptocurrency system communicatively coupled to the device of the user may verify if the body activity data satisfies one or more conditions set by the cryptocurrency system, and award cryptocurrency to the user whose body activity data is verified." — Cryptocurrency System Using Body Activity Data Patent Abstract

Bill Gates has worked diligently to finish his goal of tagging humans for over a decade. This has always been his purpose. Because the Living God is all knowing and all seeing, Lucifer desires the same but must use other means as he is not a true god and contains no real power. In 2011 he began funding the tracker implant through TransDerm Inc, quickly expanding to give grants to Vaxxas Pty Ltd and Vaxxas Technology, Micron Biomedical Inc, and more. From 2016 to 2019 Pfizer made a total of $13 Billion. In 2021 Pfizer's revenue increased to $81.288 Billion because of you in one year. 2022 has given them a 23.4% increase meaning they have made $100.33 Billion off of you even after numerous facts have come forward about the Fact that They are Trying To Kill You! Moderna has seen a 1,238.33% increase since 2019. Johnson and Johnson went from $82.6 Billion in 2019 to $93.8 Billion in 2020. On and on it goes, but it's so easy to follow the money that I will leave that to you.

In 2022 Danish Newspaper, Ekstra Bladet, apologized for jumping onto the fear porn bandwagon without knowing or looking for any facts. Many other media outlets followed suit. These are the people you believe. You honestly think that any of them are there to "write the truth"?

<u>It's easy to apologize after the fact, after exterminating the population with whims and lies.</u>

Let me touch on another one of the designer diseases that has been forced into children ensuring an entire generation of addicts. After propaganda related to overactivity in children and lack of focus (which is a developing mind, also called childhood) the pharmaceutical companies created a new disorder ADD/ADHD. These companies, who run the US and many other countries began their intensive indoctrination programs for the drugs children needed to be on in order to be non-childlike, mainly Adderall. Adderall was well known for causing emotional and cognitive effects including euphoria, disruption of libido, increased wakefulness, and other hormonal disturbances at minimum dosage. Larger doses of Adderall impair cognitive control, causes rapid muscle breakdown, and can induce a psychosis (delusions and paranoia) which would then be labeled as schizophrenia or another disorder by the Medical Industry causing one to be forced to take many other medications.

Today millions of children have grown up on daily doses of amphetamines. This is why so many horrendous false flags have been allowed to be carried out at an escalating rate: children who are now adults were developed on drugs and have no ability to be independent because they are totally dependent on drugs. Again, if you are healthy, and you protect and have responsibility for your children by ensuring their health and natural development through high activity, correct diet, and various other things, they will develop into the Future. The future you and your parents and their parents have been responsible in developing and have failed.

Drug tolerance develops rapidly in amphetamine abuse so over time each child who has been drugged from a young age, or any age, will have to raise the dosage repeatedly as time goes on. Adderall and generic brands of the same are available in over 100 countries. You can pick any drug and discover the same patterns, propaganda, profiteering, and persons involved and silenced. By 2018, over 70 million US children aged 2 to 17 had been prescribed ADHD medication, the majority of whom were children aged 2 to 5, taking daily doses of addictive drugs. Parents have been exploiting their children in this way since the 1960's. Their generation was raised on drugs too...

"We now know from history that those vaccines have been used for more than 40 years and the diseases, all of them, are still here. Meanwhile, autism, diabetes, and all kinds of autoimmune diseases have increased." – Dr. Shiv Chopra

"Vaccination is a monstrosity, a misbegotten offspring of error and ignorance; and, being such, it should have no place in either hygiene or medicine...Believe not in vaccination, it is a worldwide delusion, an unscientific practice, a fatal superstition with consequences measured today by tears and sorrow without end." - Dr. Carlo Ruta

Another drug forced on the public through indoctrination is Obetrol. This is amphetamine mixed with salts which includes methamphetamine. Obetrol was approved by the US Food and Drug Administration on January 19, 1960. Instead of promoting healthy, natural diets, Americans are marketed to by drug companies and forced to have a constant diet of gluten and dairy, which is why it is the fattest and most unhealthy country in the world. In the 1980's Aspartame, a synthetic sugar, was developed and pushed as a replacement for sugar. Unlike natural raw sugar which is filled with nutrients from molasses and other natural substances that your body can digest and use, processed and fake sugars including Aspartame are addictive! It was instantly put into all diet drinks. You know, the drinks that diabetics consume. On and on it goes and we didn't even cover the horrendous MMR vaccines, as they are so well exposed everyone knows about their "side effects" already. A good number of people in their 30's today have suffered from the effects of this. Speaking of addiction, we cannot ignore the addiction to technology, which has caused numerous health issues.

"Facebook Reels activate the same neurons and chemicals in the brain as coke addiction. When I scroll through the Reels I have the same reaction I had when hunting for cocaine, I'm looking for the best one. When I find the right video, this craving in my body and mind that is activated by the Reels, is satisfied just as if it were a hard drug. As an addict of 27 years, having explored many different drugs, this reaction is interesting. Makes me think about the fact that this is given to children today, and children spend an average of 3 hours a day on these platforms." — Anonymous

Most of you have grown up with the elites' education and medication, which is ever useful in creating new disorders, diseases, vaccines, and pills. Pumping you full of psychology and drugs help them to further cement the illusion that this is all normal — that the level of education and the number of diseases we see today is normal. They know all they need do is to tell a lie often enough and you will believe it is the truth. They keep repeating this reality is normal life. It is a lie. The most basic form of mind control is repetition. It has stolen your humanity.

Know the agenda of reality. Anyone who is a fully functioning human is shunned by those who have been indoctrinated by the elite. Free will and knowledge are crimes in this world. They are working on how they can adapt their propaganda so that YOU will buy it again next time. So, know this, dear reader, Love knows no Fear. Perfect love eliminates fear! Fear involves punishment, so, understanding this and perhaps next time you will love yourself and those around you enough to be human. Live life, for real: Outside! Breathe in fresh air, wash yourself well, and drink clean water!

What is worthy of living for, is worth dying for.

~Land of Confusion~

Here we are at last, dear reader. You've almost made it to the end. This is the final agenda I will discuss in this book and unfortunately, it is one that is well underway now: the death of innocence and future. Since the Roman Empire split and the Papal States formed, societies of the world have become more biblically inclined. No longer is slavery, murder, and ritual sex a part of our daily lives as it was before. The old ways must be implemented again in order to form the Global Government, as previously discussed. The agenda has increased since the 1900's as the two world wars achieved the broken family and opened the door to the Luciferian rituals of murder, called either war or abortion, and divorce. It is now common for both parents to work instead of parenting their children. Responsibility has been lost along with respect and honesty and commitment. Money is the object of the day, and we are all slaves to it. Upon the completion of these agendas the rest has been easy. The damage done to the mind when a family breaks, splits the mind of the children, even when those children are all adult in age. It destroys all trust and commitment and respect. Because of this the gateway is open to a multitude of elite agendas which they have thus far fulfilled. When I began this book several years ago this agenda had only begun to be noticed in a handful of societies. However, today it is everywhere like a plague, proving the speed and damage the elite have caused for the past few generations.

I have previously explained many of the tools the elite have used to affect natural development of not only the mind, but the body as well, many of which are focused on sexualizing children. Children are now sent to facilities to be educated by the elite's totally controlled and censored system. Many countries implement an 8-hour day in the system while in other countries, young children leave their parents homes entirely to be put in government organized boarding schools. Children are bored as they have no knowledge-building stimulation or structure in their lives and irresponsible parents who forced this life on them use their boredom to drug and further indoctrinate them into complacency and silence. Humanity's natural structure was also affected by mass production. This allowed the elite to push consumerism: extorting lust and greed. You work to earn an elite-dictated value, to spend it in order to obtain what you are allowed to afford, getting nothing of true value in return. The solution to these elite-created problems and reactions is Technology!

Tech has facilitated world-wide systematic control. First radios were forced on the public as a must-have in every home. Then TV had to be in every home and was given to the public to ensure they would have them. Next came the handheld devices we can carry in our pockets, use all day in school, at work, and now we use them at all ages, even set above the crib so infants can get an early dosing. As everyone should already know, children are cognitively and psychologically defenseless against advertising. Anyone can observe the effects of the culmination of agendas we have discussed throughout this book: bored, self-consumed societies given nothing to strive for in life, no focus on the bigger picture or true purpose, but the narrow, closed-off focus of the self because critical thinking, character building, logic and reasoning skills have all gone out the window. Mind control. Programming is caused through repetition and trauma. Without further ado, let's dive right into the culture of the Global Government in our New World.

"The folks who know the truth aren't talking... The ones who don't have a clue, you can't shut them up!" — Tom Waits

One example of mind control specifically designed to target children to hypersexualize them is the internationally known Disney. For generations Luciferianism has been animated into subliminal messages for the developing mind to take in as parents use TV to raise their children. Disney is seen by every country, culture, society, grouping the future generations into one mindset. Disney has been one of the most effective tools to destroy the mind, as it normalizes inappropriate relationships with children and animals, while instilling Luciferian doctrines and philosophies including sorcery and witchcraft into each story. These ideals are cemented in the developing mind through the repetition of songs and subliminal messages. The entertainment industry is well known as being run by pedophiles since the only reason for the existence of this industry, like fashion, is to control the mind to destroy the innocent: children. Finn Wolfhard of Stranger Things and cast-mate Millie Bobby Brown have exposed the sexualization forced on them by pedophiles in their productions just as Macaulay Culkin, Elijah Wood, Judy Garland, Shirley Temple, and thousands of others have experienced and come forward to expose, only to be ignored. Numerous musicians have exposed the same, such as Michael Jackson, Kesha Sebert, Britney Spears, Justin Timberlake, and the list goes on, since the formation of the industry.

In the past generations it wasn't uncommon for parents to monitor what their children watched and listened to, to keep the delicate child's mind away from the trauma of violence and sexual influences which distort the mind. Because of the agendas of the elite, sex has been lowered to basic perversion, leaving those who experience it in its unnatural sense to feel degraded and disrespected, a natural response. Much effort goes into how one looks and is labelled since attractiveness and only what is on the outside matters. The reality is that only what is on the inside has value. Our worth is not based on what we were born looking like, which changes throughout our entire lives. Human sexuality is not merely a matter of biological reproduction (as in the case of animals) but about intimacy. It is a sacred act, regardless of what Luciferians have indoctrinated you to believe. Today most people feel the need for intimacy and security but are only fed sex, thereby loneliness and emptiness from the lack of respect from others and for ourselves is created instead.

Mega-corporations such as Disney make billions marketing sexy products to children. French Vogue, like any child-model fashion agency, sexualizes children as young as 6 in their magazines. Like the music industry and Hollywood, the fashion industry has long been a pit of trafficking, sex exploitation, drugs, and abuse. Shocking, disturbing, and traumatizing content found in countless videos aimed at children, featuring children wearing inappropriate clothes and doing inappropriate things, are easily accessible and monetized, thanks to internet platform promotions. Several years ago, toy-maker Mattel introduced a version of Barbie called "Lingerie Barbie", stating the doll was for ages 14+. The average market for Barbie is ages 8 to 12. The product description shows how children are forced to confront sexuality issues:

"Barbie exudes a flirtatious attitude in her heavenly merry widow bustier ensemble accented with intricate lace and matching peekaboo peignoir."

Another sexualizing tool are Bratz dolls, ranging from infants wearing makeup to preteen dolls wearing fishnets, miniskirts, heavy makeup, and outrageous outfits. The name says it all. A generation of young boys aspire to be like what they see on TV, movies, and music videos: aggressive and uncontrolled, without respect or honor. Their dress reflects their backward role models as well as their actions. Movie-maker Roman Polanski was arrested in 1977, after drugging and raping a 13-year-old girl. Hollywood awarded him an Oscar for best director. In pedophile-backed movies, shows, events, we often see the typical symbolism: the blue spiraling triangle framed by another triangle, is a symbol for a pedophile who targets boys; the blue triangle spiral drawn in a child-like scrawl, is the pedo symbol for those who target very young boys; the heart inside a heart, is for young girls; the butterfly made up of love hearts is for the pedo with no preference. Commonly seen is the teddy bear, used in commercials and news articles. These symbols are used on social media accounts, by clothing, food, toy brands, and more. Researchers in Washington, DC wanted to start a program to prevent sexual activity in youth, but after offering the program to seventh graders it was **ineffective** because **too many seventh graders were already having sex**! In generations past one had to steal a neighbor's Playboy to get a glimpse of a naked body, which was elegantly, tastefully, and respectfully displayed. Today children have full access to millions of sex-sites with graphical or interactive video and live-feed of the most perverted and debasing sexual acts thanks to Technology.

Everything that a child sees, experiences, hears, senses, work to develop and strengthen, or weakening the mind as a whole; feelings and emotions change frequently, during development, and because of this, humans learn to control our emotions and govern out minds, as children and teenagers so we can become adults. Growing and regulating chemistry, learning right from wrong, self-control, self-respect and other techniques are learned during this time and are much needed to use the mind over emotion (unlike today's society: emotion over all things). Let's dig deeper into this movement and the effects of it witnessed today on children — our future.

"People are hard-wired to notice sexually relevant information, so ads with sexual content get noticed. Some young men actually **think** Axe body spray will drive women crazy, but brand impressions are shaped by images in advertising, too. Our findings show that **the increase in visual sexual imagery over the three decades** of analysis is attributable to products already featuring sexual content in ads, not necessarily widespread adoption by other product categories, specifically, alcohol, entertainment and beauty ads are responsible for much of the increase." - Tom Reichert head of the department of advertising in the UGA Grady College of Journalism and Mass Communication

In 2002 the AJPH published a report by Harriet Washington which stated:
"A number of studies have determined that children are 3 times as susceptible to tobacco advertising than adults and that such **advertising is a more powerful inducement than peer pressure**. Peer pressure can be seen in every area of a child's life, thanks to technology and the ability to have 24/7 access to all the disgusting people of the world."

Let's jump back a ways to get a better perspective of the progression. In the late 1970s, the Federal Trade Commission held hearings, reviewed the existing research, and came to the obvious conclusion that it was deceptive to advertise to children younger than 6 years. Sweden and Norway forbid all advertising directed at children younger than 12 years, Greece banned toy advertising until after 10 pm, and Denmark and Belgium severely restricted advertising aimed at children. Research of 3,232 full-page ads published in 1983, 1993 and 2003 in the popular magazines Cosmopolitan, Redbook, Esquire, Playboy, Newsweek, and Time, revealed sexual imagery in 20% of the ads. Using sex to sell everything from alcohol to banking services to filters for TikTok, has increased over the years: 15% of ads studied used sex as a selling point in 1983. That percentage grew to 27% in 2003. Out of 18 product categories, those most often using sexual imagery in advertising were health and hygiene at 38%; beauty, 36%; drugs and medicine, 29%; clothing, 27%; travel, 23%; and entertainment, 21%.

"In many ways, the concern that investigators like I have is that we're sort of in the midst of a natural kind of uncontrolled experiment on the next generation of children." - Dr. Dimitri Christakis

By 1980, after the rise of technology, the fall of education, and the crumbling of the family structure, the elite had caused the world to become so stressed (fearful) that the anxiety disorders were reclassified, and panic disorder (the minds inability to cope with unnatural abuses) was incorporated as a new diagnostic entity. Definitions and terms were **changed** to accommodate various versions of the same to create more labels to divide us into, and more drugs to conquer us with. The same process has been used, as we have discussed, in all agendas. A 2000 FTC investigation found that violent movies, music, and video games have been intentionally marketed to children and adolescents. The average young person views more than 3000 ads per day on TV, Internet, billboards, and in magazines. Increasingly, advertisers targeted younger and younger children and today they target infants and the unborn. Back in 2002, teenagers accounted for **more than $1 billion in e-commerce dollars**, and the industry spent $21.6 million on Internet banner ads in that year alone.

A study done by Psychologists at Knox College in Galesburg shows that most girls as young as 6 already think of themselves as sex objects. MOST. Their research showed that it is either the media or the parent which sexualizes and predisposes their children toward objectifying themselves, as the remaining influence reinforces the messages, amplifying the effect. However, mothers who used TV and movies as teaching moments (which is parenting time) to inform their children about bad behaviors and unrealistic scenarios were less likely to have unrealistically sexualized daughters. The power of maternal instruction. An American Psychological Association task force report found that children exposed to sexual messages are more likely to have low self-esteem and depression and suffer from eating disorders. It doesn't take a genius to figure these things out…just common sense.

A study from the National Citizen Service found that, rather than talking to their parents, children today seek comfort on social media, making them more likely to experience frequent pressure and stress. Females are more emotional by default as they are wired to become mothers, nurturers, and when they feel insecure and unsafe and unprotected, stress and anxiety and other products of fear are the natural response. This causes numerous physical and mental health problems through hormonal imbalances. While males are not as emotional, their hormonal imbalances have been ensured in other ways and have been targeted for much longer. The elite's societies are geared to strip the female of femininity, the males of their masculinity, and **invert** the entire natural structure according to Luciferianism. Divide and Conquer. This used to be understood through basic common sense but today must be explained and even then, no one cares. Insecurity and confusion cause people to be easily manipulated and controlled as they will turn to whoever appears to have a Solution. The United Nations has already told you what you are being pooled into and conformed for: the formation of the Global Government and One World Under Lucifer. All innocence must be destroyed.

"The Prince's Trust has been gauging youth opinion for 10 years and found that just under half of young people who use social media now feel more **anxious** about their future when they compare themselves to others on sites and apps such as Instagram, Twitter, and Facebook. A similar amount agrees that social media makes them feel **inadequate**. More than half (57%) think social media creates **overwhelming pressure** to succeed. **Suicides** now occur at more than 5 in 100,000 teenagers (in England), which contrasts with a figure of just over 3 in 100,000 in 2010." — The Guardian

Emotions (if properly established and developed) can be good informants, which is what they are for. But emotions will always be bad advisers because they are **constantly changing**, which is why we have **minds**. Exercising courage in the face of an emotion such as fear builds self-esteem, just as succumbing to flight in the face of fear reduces self-respect. We are not made to be cowards, it is unnatural. The number of young people in the UK who say they do not believe that life is worth living has **doubled** in the last decade. More than a quarter believe that that their life has **NO** sense of purpose. Anxiety and depression and subsequent suicide continue to rise as the family structure has been replaced by technology. Adolescence is a crucial period for developing and maintaining social and emotional habits that are vital for mental well-being. These include healthy sleep patterns, regular exercise, coping, problem-solving, interpersonal skills, and managing emotions. Supportive environments in the family are obviously important. Research has shown that teenagers need 9.5 hours of sleep each night but on average only get 7.5 hours. A lack of sleep can make teenagers tired, irritable, depressed and more likely to catch colds, flu, and gastroenteritis, not to mention the mental disorders that develop from lack of sleep.

"It is alarming that the teen stress experience is so similar to that of adults. It is even more concerning that they seem to underestimate the potential impact that stress has on their physical and mental health. In order to break this cycle of stress and unhealthy behaviors as a nation, we need to provide teens with better support and health education at school and home, at the community level and in their interactions with health care professionals." - **APA CEO and Executive Vice President Norman B. Anderson**

This should not be alarming, because adults know that children are deeply influenced by everything they hear and see and experience. Today children are raised by internet "influencers" and social media, which is filled with pedophiles and other under-educated, emotionally stunted children. All it takes to permanently damage a child is for the parent to be stressed. This causes the child to grow up stressed but parents have allowed even more to be forced on their children as music, movies, friends, texts, images flood the developing mind with competition, rating and approval which is overwhelming. This trauma enforces the mind control used in these systems, as designed. The parents of past generations are the ones relied on to safeguard the future. The parent, who procreated by choice, has the responsibility, upon implementing that act, of caring for most aspects of the young life, ensuring the protected and mature product. If a person is not mature enough or responsible enough to fulfill their duty, they have no right to perform the act. Period. Unfortunately, human beings have free will. Like any superpower, it takes responsibility and wisdom to wield it properly.

"A man who cannot command himself will always be a slave." — Johan Wolfgang

To be an adult is to know yourself and your purpose. Childhood, real childhood, instills in the developing mind the tools needed to be a productive adult and discover your purpose. This is only accomplished with love: protection, teaching, and care.

"Some of the mightiest works of parenting is emotional self-awareness so you can teach emotional self-regulation. When kids understand that their parents can handle tough emotions and yet be resilient, it gives them permission to do the same thing." - John Duffy

In Denmark, one of the first countries to legalize prostitution and pornography, leading to a complete societal inversion, about 70,000 Danes between the ages of 15 and 29 are without education, work, or a bright horizon, because a growing number of young people are facing several serious mental health problems. Even in this small and very controlled society built around the dedication to self-comfort, 3 times as many **children** and adolescents are diagnosed with anxiety or depression as they were 10 years ago! The American College Health Association's 2016 survey showed that 62% of the undergraduate students reported "overwhelming anxiety," which is a significant increase from 50% in 2011. In 1985, when the institute began surveying students, 18% said they felt overwhelmed. By 2010, 29% and in 2016, the number jumped to 41%. More recent studies show that 5.6 million US children had been diagnosed with anxiety as 9 million European children are known to be diagnosed with the same. Thanks to Covid these numbers have increased further as children were not only forced to remain inside but also forced to spend even more time on the elite's technology!

In 2014, the American Psychological Association's Stress in America survey found that Millennials, aged 18-33, were the country's **most-stressed generation**. Now, the honor belongs to an even younger demographic: Generation Z: teenagers. Z being the final letter in the English alphabet and an ambigram! As we already know, one all-consuming stress trigger is frequency, specifically frequencies emitted from all electronic internet capable devices. Stress creates a multitude of issues mentally, physically, and outwardly. One study showed **changes in brain structure** among children who use smartphones and other screen devices. According to the study, kids who spent 2 hours per day on screens scored **lower on language and thinking** tests. Also, kids who spent 7 hours per day on electronic devices showed **premature thinning of the cortex**, which happens later in development. Since the iPhone came out in 2007, kids born after 1995 entered adolescence with the internet in hand. Since then, children have developed entirely around these devices.

"Social media has become **omnipresent** in the lives of young people and this research suggests it is exacerbating what is already an uncertain and emotionally turbulent time. Young people are critical to the future success of this country, but they'll only realize their full potential if they believe in themselves and define success in their own terms. It is therefore a moral and economic imperative that employers, government, charities, and wider communities put the needs of young people centre stage." - Nick Stace UK chief executive of The Prince's Trust

The children of today are seriously lacking in communication skills, social skills, decisiveness. They are not goal oriented but are increasingly unmotivated, unambitious, and all of this leads to even more stress, anxiety, and depression, causing them to hunger for the dopamine fix of whatever feels good for even a brief moment which is satisfied by the pulses of the screen! All the while the elite's propaganda of Tolerance is pounded into the minds of all alive today. Tolerance creates perfect slaves.

According to the UK's National Society for the Prevention of Cruelty to Children, cases of child-on-child sexual abuse have **risen** to a third of all children sexual abuse cases in the UK. Internet-initiated sexual assaults among US adolescents have also **risen** and teenagers, who have watched sexually explicit materials and are ill-equipped with a definition or ability for consent, have no idea how to draw the line between values, let alone consequences, and find themselves behind bars and printed in sex-offender registers for clicking "send" on pornographic photographs. For the victims, there are long-term consequences of trauma and guilt over the liability of the perpetrator's actions, which are increased with the knowledge that nothing will be done about it. As sexualization increases, children become increasingly confused, pedophiles rejoice as the elite's battle is all but won. One primary school teacher reported a series of disturbing incidents in the classroom involving pupils as young as 10 being sent explicit photos via social media and sexual assault between two 7-year-old boys. One teacher with 20 years' experience, said she believed unrestricted access to the internet was partly responsible for the sexualization of children. She stated:

"As a primary teacher, I have been appalled by the rise in **sexual language and behaviour** in children as young as 5. Unfiltered access to the internet and age-inappropriate computer games is exposing more and more young children to things they are not able to cope with or understand. Many **parents haven't got a clue** what is happening."

They don't have a clue because they are not parents. Even with the added hormones in our food today, 5 is still 5 years away from being naturally curious about sex and 8 years away from being mentally mature enough to comprehend the impact and meaning of sex, and over 15 years away from the mind being developed enough to be able to handle it or be close to understanding it in such a way that a decision can be made about it. A secondary school teacher, in London, reported "several sexual assaults and a possible rape" over seven years of teaching. A BBC investigation in 2018, based on freedom of information requests to police, revealed that 5,500 sexual offenses were recorded in UK schools over a 3-year period, including rapes. In the 1980's UK's Margaret Thatcher covered up numerous pedophiles among her group of friends including BBC's Jimmy Savile. Under her administration the guesthouse of Margaret was used for child rape rituals. Jimmy Savile raped over 450 children, most of whom were boys. Operation Yewtree arrested 18 TV personalities including BBC's Rolf Harris, for pedophilic acts. Previously, a 2014 survey by Girlguiding UK found that 59% of young women aged 13-21 had faced some form of sexual harassment at school or college in the past year. One secondary head of PHSE, based in Lincolnshire, told the Guardian that 95% of a class of 7-year-old boys told her they had accessed pornography online. In many countries, children (aged 4-14) are raised in primary boarding schools, cutting parents entirely out of the developmental picture, and replacing them with pedophiles who are known to rape students. Children become pregnant and abandoned by the men who forced it on them, just like their mothers before them.

"Girls who do not have a father will hit puberty, on average, at least a year early. This is substantially earlier, indicating a real biological impact of the lack of a masculine figure in the household. Boys who have lack of father at the age of 12 have telomeres, a genetic difference, that makes them approximately 15% shorter." — Jordan Peterson

The "Drag Queen Story Hour" is another program that the trans movement has forced on children through schools and libraries in North America, EU, and beyond. As it indicates, a drag queen reads homosexual literature to children. As one can easily find, most of the readers have been exposed as pedophiles who have already been convicted of numerous sex crimes. This job gives them unrestricted access to your children. Drag queens are men, typically homosexual, who dress flamboyantly and behave with exaggerated and offensive feminine mannerisms. Some, but not all, receive sex change surgery. Onyx a Canadian drag queen describes his disillusionment with transgenderism and with the drag queen lifestyle, stating:

"I wanted to follow my own **egoistic** path and...my thirst for glitter and shows led me into a superficial world. I have been a Drag Queen entertainer named Onyx for about 4 years around Quebec and Montreal. I discovered...corrupted ideas of gender and sexual freedom that are becoming harmful to our society. Many things woke me up. I couldn't accept seeing last year's Montreal Pride's leading light Drag Queen 'Lactatia' who was only **8 years old**. As I have been working in gay bars, I became aware of the pedophilia that was creeping in there. I've decided to quit the Drag scene because **I couldn't live this illusion anymore**. Everything was getting fake to my eyes, and I didn't like to be called 'she'."

This mind control disorder is usually outgrown as people mature and become disillusioned. Even those who don't understand any of the facts of the movement still have a human conscience which is used by the Holy Spirit and guides us all towards Truth once we listen to it. Other forms of self-hatred can be seen in body-altering surgeries such as one man who spent hundreds of thousands of dollars to transform himself into a tiger, only to commit suicide. Another man used surgery to become a plastic-looking Ken doll, while another man used implants and facial mutilation to make himself into an "alien'. Plastic surgery has helped to facilitate the self-hate Luciferian agenda of destruction.

"Because mental illness as well as gender non-conformity is stigmatized in our society, many transgender individuals with depression are in the position of having to contend with two stigmas, which in turn can exacerbate **their mental health problems**. When a people who identifies as trans has internalized society's negative view of them, it is often the case that they do not seek out the treatment they need." — Medical Daily

From 2001-2006, Yale University's LGBT program was greatly helped by the Larry Kramer Initiative for Lesbian and Gay Studies. Larry was a **NAMBLA** supporter, and in a 2004 speech in New York City, he reminisced on how a "sweet young boy who didn't know anything and was in awe of me. I was the first man who had sex with him. I think I murdered him." He is correct as he infected the child with **AIDS**, which doesn't matter to Larry who would rather view the child "in awe of him", as if this were true. In reality children who are molested and raped by adults are torn apart mentally, the awe he speaks of is the child's terror and trauma. The Brea Olinda School District in California has included in their "comprehensive sexual education" curriculum, the positive portrayal and teaching of pederasty, the act of adult sex with boys. Karen England, executive director for the Capitol Resource Institute, which discovered the school hiding their curriculum, stated:

"Under the guise of providing so-called 'appropriate sex education' to children, many school districts are beginning to incorporate some of the most offensive, absurd, graphic, and inappropriate sex acts to some of the youngest students."

Since boys feed pornography the most, their further abuse against women focuses on sexual and emotional abuse, degradation, and more along these lines. In a 2002 drive, non-governmental organizations advocated for both abstinence and the use of condoms when self-control cannot be maintained. They tried in 2004 to openly distribute condoms to children but society still didn't accept it since they often break and do not protect against sexual diseases. It was brought up again in 2018 and 2019, as the elite always do until something they want is pushed through. The goal is to push easy access of all things debasing to children, so that during the time when one naturally learns self-control, integrity, respect for others, and responsibility, the child's mind develops under attack. Michael Mulwana, a father of three, told his story:

"The other day I was shocked when I lifted my eldest son's pillow from the bed and found condoms lined up. I stood in shock staring at the condoms and my son. Because I was so shocked, I could neither beat him nor shout at him. So, I asked him where he got the condoms from. 'They gave them to us at school,' he answered. What do you use them for? I asked. 'To enjoy life.' he said walking away."

Michael then sat down asking himself what he had not done and what he was going to do while condoms are freely given, encouraging promiscuous lifestyles, abuse, and death. Catherine Watson, the director communication at Straight Talk Foundation stated:

"It is wrong for condoms to be given away in a disorganized and haphazard way in schools. Because this gives **false confidence** to the students and **creates pressure** on them to start sex even when they are not ready. Sex should be **systematically thought through** before being indulged in."

As schools work to indoctrinate the elite agenda into children, and parents are forced from their responsibilities, companies spend millions per year in advertising sexual products including Viagra, Levitra, and Cialis. The human brain no longer reacts to natural human dopamine and other natural chemical changes which should naturally occur during natural sexual circumstances. Sexual information we put into our minds triggers a cascade of neurological, chemical, and hormonal events, because that is biology. When the brain views sexual images, there is a rush of sensation because of the human body's natural chemical releases of dopamine and oxytocin and vasopressin. They make one feel excited and aroused as well as help one recall long-term memories. Another hormone released in sex is serotonin, which bring us feelings of tranquility and relaxation but like anything else, if the brain associates these feelings with an artificial experience (like porn), it will subsequently direct a person back to porn, rather than a true relationship which will fulfill human needs. By abusing these natural products of the brain, the brain becomes overworked, needing more and more dopamine to give the same reaction, wearing out the brain. Sex during adolescence has lasting **negative** effects on the body and mood well into adulthood, most likely because the activity occurs when the nervous system is still developing. Any adult who was sexually active as a child can tell you the negative impact it has had on their life and their ability to maintain adult relationships. When we do not control what we put into our minds, when we do not protect ourselves, we become corrupt. A Cambridge University study found that pornography triggers brain activity in sex addicts in the same way drugs trigger drug addicts.

"All morning I had become more and more desensitized to the squalor, the stench of poverty, mothers fetching water to wash clothes, chickens cooking in pots under homes roofed by tarps or any other available material from the nearby trash pile. There were feces running through the streets, children playing and running barefoot through the myriad dirt alleys without regard for the impoverished life into which they had been born. Such was the scene in the squatter camp in Diepsloot Extension 13, a 4.6 square mile township outside Johannesburg, South Africa.

It was in this camp that morning where we walked the streets and alleyways handing out flyers to let mothers know of a new pregnancy crisis center (Impact Baby Rescue - part of Impact Africa, a local NGO) which is now available to them in their own community where mothers and fathers could receive vital help for their unborn child, their family, and even a place to take their newborn instead of dumping the newborn into the nearby stream, which is, sadly, a frequent occurrence in that area. As we turned the corner, I was hit in the face with the unexpected - a small vehicle sitting off to the side with the label "USAID."

The female driver asked what we were doing in the neighborhood which I explained. Imagine my confusion and abhorrence when asking her in return what USAID was doing in a community like this when she replied: 'We're providing vital transgender services to the residents of Diepsloot.' I simply commented: 'Wow, I'm surprised with all the people here who suffer from food insecurity and deprivation of basic needs that my federal government (USAID) would be focused on transgender services. Seems like there are much bigger needs on which to focus.'

At this, the USAID representative driving the car replied: 'Oh yes, there are many here who are trying to transition and need our help.'" — Clint Thomas

Japan is another country that exemplifies child sexualization as the national commercialization of the "Lolita complex" has earned its own abbreviation: Rorikon. On the streets of Tokyo, plastic models of prepubescent girls hang open-bloused from price-tagged windows, while their uniform-clad real-life counterparts sell their time to men in "JK," or "schoolgirl" cafes. Although child pornography was banned in 2014, soft porn known as "Chaku Ero" featuring children is permitted as long as the children in question do not display naked genitals, chest, or buttocks. Children and teenagers are the biggest consumers of online media. This is not limited to Japan.

"Pornography? It's a new **synaptic pathway**. You wake up in the morning, open a thumbnail page, and it leads to Pandora's Box of visuals. There have probably been days when I saw 300 [women] before I got out of bed.... Internet pornography has absolutely changed my generation's **expectations**. Twenty seconds ago, you thought that photo was the hottest thing you ever saw, but you **throw it back**...How does that not affect the psychology of having a relationship with somebody? It's got to." - John Mayer

This doesn't take a genius to figure out. Pornography destroys human sexuality by ripping it out of its intended purpose and inverting true intimacy between two consenting adults. Human beings are objects of consumption rather than individuals deserving dignity and respect. The extreme trauma done is not only sociological and psychological, but spiritual. Porn is a counterfeit, a lie, an abuse on yourself and others, causing you to abuse others throughout your life. The brain integrates what it is being fed into memories, making sense of the world, and developing our sense of self. Brains cannot decide what influences to keep and which to discard, which is why it is so important to protect our minds and control our thoughts, teaching the future to do the same. If the brain is being fed images of violent sexuality, which all porn is, objectification of sex and an unstable, insecure familial structure, it should not come as any surprise that that brain will see the world through a filter of insecurity, anxiety, depravity, and corrupted sensuality, as witnessed in societies worldwide today.

"Compulsive behaviours, including watching porn to excess, over-eating and gambling, are increasingly common." - Dr John Williams, Head of Neuroscience and Mental Health at the Wellcome Trust

A report in 2014 found a link between watching unprotected sex on screen and going on to have unprotected sex in real life. For instance, the number of women who underwent a 'labiaplasty' rose by almost 40% in 2016 in the US alone. In 2016 the analytics report of just one website, Pornhub, revealed that its videos were watched 92 billion times last year, by 64 million daily visitors.

"Having a sexual experience during this time point, early in life, is not without consequence, affecting males' susceptibility to symptoms of depression, and could also expose males to some increase in inflammation [in their brain tissue and structures in key signaling areas of the brain] in adulthood. There is a possibility that environmental experiences and signals could have amplified effects if they occur before the nervous system has settled down into adulthood." - John Morris

The "barely legal" study conducted by researchers Bryant Paul and Daniel Linz presented images to 154 undergraduates. Some images depicted adult women at least 21 years old, and other images depicted female minors. Afterward presenting these images, the researchers administered a classic test of unconscious association. The study results prove that ordinary people have no trouble learning to associate 12-year-old girls with sexuality. That was after only a **brief exposure** to simulated images of teen sexuality in the laboratory. Corruption is always easy, being moral and pure is not. Pedophilia is taught, just as all sexual perversions are.

Whether physical or mental, rape is rape, because no child can consent to it. All sexual imaging and acts are rape to a child because no child has the mental capacity to understand the repercussions of such a decision therefore, it is not their own. Children are not capable of making adult decisions, which is why they are children and expected to be protected by their Parents. "Consent" is the term pedos and homosexuals love to use to excuse their perverse actions. Using this, or any excuse to exploit children, proves that they know in their minds that what they are doing is wrong, that it goes against the fabric of nature. But Consent only applies to **fully developed brains** that can consent. Being able to consent means that one understands all avenues and outcomes and consequences of the given situation and can make a true decision on it. Since our brains are not fully developed until age 25, the depravity of our culture today is unbelievable and unacceptable. Twenty-five years is the minimum age the brain becomes developed enough to consent. Naturally, for the males this is more like 30, as females must mature faster, be wiser, and take on more in their lives. But it's not the point, because it's not about sex or love or moral, or even legal, it's about splitting another human's soul, mind, and body.

>"Research conducted over the past decade indicates that a wide range of **psychological and interpersonal problems are more prevalent among those who have been sexually abused** than among individuals with no such experiences." - APSAC Handbook on Child Maltreatment

Not even "stranger danger" is taught any longer, as the internet demands interactions with strangers to function. If it were, it would not be normal for 1 out of 3 children **under the age of 8** to be physically raped in what we call civilized societies. Unfortunately, it is normal and the confusion evident in children and adults today is the proof. There was a time it was NOT acceptable, and NOT encouraged. But today Tolerance is the mantra and Do What Thou Wilt is the way. Today parents themselves share pictures and videos of their children and all of their details, online for all to see and use, permanently violating the rights of their children before they can even understand them.

Pope Francis spoke at his summit for the Sexual Abuse Crisis, claiming, as every

pedophile does, that:
"there are more important issues than sexual abuse of children."

The elite have most of the world believing that humans are nothing but animals and therefore sex and violence is all you are allowed to know. Humans are spiritual and mental beings, this is what makes us not animals but human: To be led by the mind, not the body, the ability to change ourselves completely, through the power of our minds. Free Will proves that emotions are not our ruler. Our souls and minds require nourishment just as our bodies do. We are much more powerful than the elite believe and far more than you allow yourself to believe. The loss of education, the loss of health, the loss of mental capacity, the loss of stability and security, the loss of communication abilities, respect, self-control, wisdom, the censorship of information, financial censorship, perversion, and corruption and more all directly lead to the end of natural humanity.

Private lives used to be just that because **your** preferences and lifestyle choices are **no one else's business**. In the world of today, thanks to technology, mainly social media, your thoughts are no longer your own. Every aspect of your life, personal and public, must be known by anyone who desires it because you have been programmed for years on this. This confusion and control combined with the lack of physical and mental health in the world, has allowed the elite to implement their final societal agenda before their Global Government is enacted. The purpose of all of this has been, from the beginning, to create homosexual, nonreproductive cultures which will help to legalize pedophilia as it used to be and ensure that selected countries will die out due to lack of reproduction. Until the past decade, transgender people had to wait until adulthood for surgery and/or hormone therapy to physically damage their bodies for life. Before, people knew the importance of puberty and the deeper importance of leaving the body to its natural chemical workings during that **VITAL** time. The agenders took off, a few decades ago, and have now grown to the point where so-called 1st world societies are producing an entire generation that believes it is uncool and wrong to be a natural heterosexual. The programming began through small and constant messages received every minute through social media, ads, popups, fashion, music, movies and more. This agender began in movies and TV shows, which were forced to depict this dangerous lifestyle regularly. It is difficult to find an American movie made in the last few years that does not refer to or promote pedophilia as being normal. Childrens cartoons, music and more also advance the agender and parents using these outlets to occupy their children are criminally negligent.

Thanks to the introduction of "comprehensive sex education" and the sexualization of the entire educational system, the developing mind, still unable to undertake the complex reasoning necessary to process sexual messages, will be required to abandon biological reality. Women and children are again being driven into compromising positions and put at risk of harm from the new "sexuality" that will once again relegate them into the position of second-class citizens, exposing them to even more harassment and rape to fit the newest pansexual ideology. The stress and lack of emotional control that we see in children today is the result of their environment.

Now heterosexuality is censored and flagged as hate speech, homophobia, and bigotry while Pride has become the religion. Less than a decade ago, after many decades of gay rights riots, violence from the homosexual community, false flags and movements, gender "fluidity" came marching in. A National Citizen Service (NCS) poll of 1,000 teenagers found that only 63% of them aged 16 and 17 defined themselves as 100% straight. 78% of young men identified as 100% male, and 80% of young women identified as 100% female, according to the same poll. Back when I was in school, within one year, suddenly, everyone in my class started advertising that they were bisexual. Every single one. They acted like this **only** because it was **cool**. Teenagers. That's how it goes, and you know how many grew out of the PHASE? All of them... Today those whims and confusions are forced on children just as it is forced that whatever they feel at that influential and ever-changing moment in time, will be the way they are for life. Life is full of phases, and most are emotional and end as quickly as they began.

"The Idea that "identity" is subjectively defined and that each of us is only what we feel we are, whatever that means. Especially the notion that that can change in a moment, as a consequence of subjective whim, is so psychologically preposterous that **it's a miracle of stupidity that it's ever been accepted at all**. This is the mentality of an **impulsive, immature, narcissistic tyrant** who wants to bend every interaction to their narrow whim." - Jordan Peterson

This is not natural, it is epidemic, systematic, and planned. The forced homosexuality we see in society today discredits those who truly suffer from this disorder, as it is listed in the 4th version of the Diagnostic and Statistical Manual of Mental Disorders. As you know by now, renaming and redefining are classic techniques used in disinformation just like rewriting of laws and public education. Using the keyword: TRANSition and Affirming helps promote the ridiculousness. Because immature, undeveloped children need Affirmation (emotionally). Because everything immature, undeveloped children WANT to do (emotionally) at any age is **right**. Because there is no moral or ethical code (as they are not dictated by emotions), there is no responsibility or maturity or concept of reality anymore! Expanding and developing delusions until they become accepted as Truth is accomplished by Affirming and Tolerating the whims of those targeted who have always been the easily manipulated and unintelligent. Dysphoria is now transgender, gender is now personal (not physical/biological/natural) sexual identity, definitions altered to fit the narrative.

"First you destroy those who create values. Then you destroy those who know what the values are and who also know that those destroyed before were in fact the creators of values. Bur real barbarism begins when no one can any longer judge or know that what he does is barbaric." — Ryszard Kapuscinski

When someone has a neurological disorder such as alien hand syndrome, or mirror-touch synaesthesia, body dysmorphia, boanthropy, they are given the proper treatment. They are not encouraged to chop off parts of their bodies, or to continue believing their hand is not their own, or continuing to believe they are a cow or a penguin. By definition a mental disorder is a mental or behavioral pattern that causes suffering or poor ability to function in life, because it affects **the way one thinks**, thereby affecting every aspect of that person's life, not reality but personal perception and emotion and mentality. That is why non-elite psychologists, true healers of the mind, are able to assist in identifying the root causes so one may heal the true **underlying issue**, instead of being controlled by the effects. This takes free will and honesty, which few have developed today. It is ok to have irregularities and issues because **everyone does**, and everyone needs help sometimes, but everyone must do the work and put in the effort to heal. People under the age of 21 have less capacity to assess risks, which is why they are targeted the most, by the elite, especially in regard to the latest movement.

"What doctors once treated as a **mental illness**, the medical community now largely affirms and even promotes as normal. Gender identity disorder was **renamed** "gender dysphoria" in 2013. In 2014, there were 24 of these gender clinics, clustered chiefly along the east coast and in California. One year later, there were 40 across the nation." - Michelle Cretella

Two leading pediatric associations, the American Academy of Pediatrics, and the Pediatric Endocrine Society, have endorsed the "transition affirmation approach" even though the latter organization concedes within its own guidelines that the transition-affirming protocol is not based on evidence. These elite-run entities admit that the only strong evidence regarding this approach is its **health risks to children**. Like all elite henchmen, pediatricians were trained in 2015, in a transition-affirming protocol. GID, also called Gender Dysphoria, by definition causes "impairment" and "distress", making it a **psychological** issue. The unusual character of "sex reassignment surgery" as a psychiatric treatment merely feeds the disorder, which is why it has been warned against and not encouraged in the past. But now it serves the agenda.

These surgeries do nothing but cause even more damage to the patient. These humans with mentally and emotionally devastating challenges are now pushed to be physically mutilated and sterilized and thrown back into society. According to elite propaganda we must tolerate mental illness and the **systematic abuse** of those with it. Japan's government has been an ardent supporter of "LGBT" as all countries under the United Nations must be today. The difference is, even the leading transgender rights activists in Japan want their doctors to stay in control of the diagnosis and procedures they allow rather than allowing children and the sick to have free reign over society. Labeling and mutilation are only the beginning of an even bigger problem of this agenda. Those who suffer from mental illness and disorders, must learn how to live with them, how to heal them, not relabel them and pretend false reality is sane. Effort and love are killed by tolerance because both are needed to heal.

99.8% of lesbian, gay, and bisexual teens change their sexual orientation within years, returning to the natural human state. The American Psychological Association's Handbook of Sexuality and Psychology admits that prior to widespread propaganda that 75 to 95% of pre-pubertal children who were distressed by their biological sex **outgrew that distress**. That's PUBERTY! As programming continues to increase, those who would wish to be free of the community will find it more difficult to leave than it already is. **It is a cult.** Regardless of what one **Feels**, it is a **mental decision**. Today doctors (servants of the elite) offer hormone blockers to families who chose to interrupt puberty for their children permanently destroying their health. A study published in the Journal of Neuroscience shows: During early development, exposure of the brain to testosterone and estradiol leads to irreversible changes in the **nervous system**. Fetal exposure to sex steroids has a major impact on the sexual differentiation of the brain. In male rodents, testosterone treatment before and during adolescence, but not after adolescence, caused reorganization in parts of the amygdala and hypothalamus. The drugs, called gonadotropin-releasing hormone analogs, freeze development before a child begins showing signs of natural, biological, human puberty, such as voice changes, genital enlargement, hair growth and breasts.

The Kinsey Institute tracked the sexual development of 34 Danes (men and women in their mid-20's) whose mothers were treated with a hormone to prevent miscarriage. When compared with a control group of mothers without hormone medication, the children whose mothers were treated with progesterone were significantly less likely to describe themselves as heterosexual since they were overwhelmed by added progesterone and estrogen during fetal development. Medications and any toxins are harmful to the development of a baby and giving hormones to a child before it's even born is, of course, devastating to the system.

"Progesterone exposure was found to be related to increased attraction to males." - June Reinisch

"Reproductive hormones have effects on all of these stages of brain growth and development. For these and other reasons, the study of sex differences in the brain is both complicated and fascinating. Understanding the impact of hormones on sex differences in the brain is important for understanding human health and disease." - University of Michigan biopsychologist Jill Becker

In one study performed by the University of British Columbia, Liisa Galea details how a form of estrogen called estradiol effects memory. She states:
"We found that low levels of estradiol improved the animals' working memory, but high levels impaired both their working and their reference memory."

In normal life, and in psychiatry, anyone who "consistently and persistently insists" on anything contrary to **physical reality** is considered either **confused or delusional** and is conveniently ignored. Unfortunately, today, they are no longer ignored or locked away, but still they are not helped! As in all elite movements those involved believe themselves to be superior to all others, and demand special treatment and rights. In the real world, we all have different problems, **equally**, that we each must overcome and grow from. As equals no one is above another, and none deserves special rights or worship. Human rights are enough rights for everyone and include everyone already. Those who violate those rights for others are the ones who call for rights for just themselves.

Successful indoctrination cannot take place without the proper terminology. Some of the terms and placement of GIV-related categories in the DSM that have undergone recent changes include: DSM-I (American Psychiatric Association, 1952) and DSM-II (American Psychiatric Association, 1968) had not included specific terms for persons with GIV; some such individuals were subsumed under Sexual Deviations (e.g., Homosexuality or Transvestism). (Hamburger et al., 1953). In DSM-III (American Psychiatric Association, 1980), the new category of GID, with the subcategories Transsexualism, GID of Childhood, and Atypical GID, was placed in the group of Psychosexual Disorders. In DSM-III-R (American Psychiatric Association, 1987), GID, now subdivided into "Transsexualism", "GID of Childhood", "GID of Adolescence and Adulthood, Nontranssexual Type" (GIDAANT), and "GID NOS", was separated from Psychosexual Disorders and placed under Disorders Usually First Evident in Infancy, Childhood, or Adolescence. DSM-IV (American Psychiatric Association, 1994) and DSM-IV-TR (American Psychiatric Association, 2000) created the **supraordinate category** "Sexual and Gender Identity Disorders," which included GID (with separately formulated criteria for children and for adolescents/adults) and GID NOS. The DSM-IV text also introduced the term "autogynephilia" as a fetishistic feature "usually reported in the history of **adult males** who are sexually attracted to females, to both males and females, or to neither sex." Today pedophilia is being labeled a Sexual Orientation, so it can be covered by the same rights and laws and medical treatments as the homosexual community. The APA has altered the terminology from 'pedophilia' to 'pedophilic disorder'. Bestiality will follow unnoticed. A pedophile group formed called Minor-Attracted Persons, a term now added to the list of Sexual Orientations. The American Psychiatric Association removed pedophilia from its list of sexual perversions in 1994 and shortly thereafter released a report in the Psychological Bulletin claiming that sex with a child is not harmful. It was instantly rejected, as there are mountains of evidence to the contrary. Dr. Laura Schlessinger commented on the report stating:

"This study is the first step on the road to normalizing pedophilia — just as homosexuality has been mainstreamed to the point where **tolerance is no longer sufficient**: we have to "embrace" it."

"The more corrupt the state, the more numerous the laws." — Tacitus

Everything about human beings is influenced by DNA, but very FEW traits are hardwired from birth. All human behavior is a composite of varying degrees for nature and nurture. Identical twins contain 100% of the same DNA from conception and are exposed to the same prenatal hormones. So, if genes and/or prenatal hormones contributed to transgenderism, BOTH twins would identify as transgender close to 100% of the time. But the largest study of twin transgender adults, published by Dr. Milton Diamond in 2013, concludes that your genes do not make you homosexual or trans. Born This Way is just another elite lie to force the weak into a permanent and dangerous lifestyle. Transgenderism is a mental choice, or more correctly a perversion, and will not manifest itself without outside nonbiological factors: mind control, brainwashing, subliminal messaging, programming.

"Scientists never speak of genes causing behaviour except as a kind of laboratory shorthand and they **never mean it literally**." - Sociobiologist Edward Wilson

A 2014 Spanish study showed no specific chromosome aberration associated with MtF (male to female) transsexualism. A 2013 study done by the Sapienza University of Rome was looking for molecular mutations in the genes involved in sexual differentiation but found none. Your child was not born in the wrong body but a perfect one that has been corrupted by external influences: food, media, etc. Like everything it is learned. A few of the television programs which have all used transgender female-to-male 'actors' and male-to-female 'actresses': Eastenders (BBC), Coronation Street (ITV), That Seventies Show (Fox), Are You Being Served (BBC), The Golden Girls (NBC), Will and Grace (NBC), Gilligan's Island (CBS), Lost in Space (CBS), The Avengers (ITV), Sex and the City (HBO), Friends (NBC), The Lucy Show (CBS), How I Met Your Mother (CBS), M.A.S.H. (CBS), Cagney and Lacey (CBS), and Dawson's Creek (Sony) and the list goes on and on. The 2018

Oscars praised Call Me By Your Name, even though it was a financial flop. The movie normalizes and glorifies pedophilia. All of these rituals: Grammy's, Oscars, etc. are only there to promote the Luciferian agenda. Today there isn't a movie produced that doesn't promote this agenda. Music, which has the ability for subliminal programming, is even more lurid today. It is next to impossible to find one TV show, one song on the radio that is not perverse, over-sexed, and pushing perversion.

One commercial for Celine Dion's new clothing line, geared towards infants, shows her as the mother goddess "savior" of babies in a hospital ward. Police are depicted trying to stop her from telling babies to be gender neutral and finally, she casts a spell on them all. Suddenly the children are all gender neutral and wearing her clothing line. Notice how children no longer smile in photos. We are supposed to get used to seeing unhappy as normal. Children look up to the stars: actors who have been raising their children as transgender or as the opposite gender, and musicians whose lyrics and images promote their activism for the trans-agenda and tv shows which promote homosexual behavior and parenting as the ideal lifestyle. Keeping in mind, these "stars" have always been trans or homosexuals, today they are simply not hiding any more.

In 2013, the propaganda to normalize pedophilia continued as Los Angeles Times ran an article which stated:

"Many researchers taking a different view of pedophilia: Pedophilia once was thought to stem from psychological influences early in life. Now, many experts view it as a deep-rooted predisposition that does not change."

Thanks to today's promotion of this cult, the Gender Identity Development Service in the United Kingdom has seen a **2,000%** increase in referrals. Kristina Olson, a University of Washington Assistant Professor of Psychology, authored a study done on a group of transkids and a group of normal kids. The study can NOT be used in any factual way or as any valid data because of its impartiality, as it states:

"The forms were **completed by parents**, who may have been inclined to show the best portrait of their child's mental health."

This study has left clinicians with no added scientific evidence with which to make recommendations on how to provide care. Puberty blockers have been studied and found safe for the treatment of a medical disorder called precocious puberty. This **Disorder** is caused by the abnormal and unhealthy early secretion of a child's pubertal hormones. However, The New Atlantis points out, these studies do not prove whether or not these blockers are safe in physiologically normal children. The authors note that there is evidence for decreased bone mineralization so young adults can worry about bones breaking, instead of being allowed to age and grow naturally so their bodies function properly, increased risk of obesity and testicular cancer in boys. They also note that this chemical corruption has an **unknown** impact on psychological and cognitive development. In Adults, the risks of cross-sex hormones include, but are not limited to cardiac disease, high blood pressure, blood clots, strokes, diabetes, and cancers.

In 2006 and 2007, the journal Psychoneuroendocrinology reported brain abnormalities in the area of memory and executive functioning among adult women who received blockers for gynecologic reasons. Many studies of men treated for prostate cancer with blockers also suggest **significant cognitive decline**. Without the correct chemical balances in your natural human body, that body will not function correctly! There are **no** extensive, long-term studies of children placed on blockers for gender dysphoria however, studies conducted on adults over the past decade give cause for concern.

"There is an obvious self-fulfilling effect in helping children impersonate the opposite sex both biologically and socially. This is far from benign, since taking puberty blockers at age 12 or younger, followed by cross-sex hormones, sterilizes a child. [The reason why Homosexuality was recommended for black communities in 1974 by Henry Kissinger and so on.] The only study to have followed pre-pubertal children who were socially affirmed and placed on blockers at a young age found that 100% of them claimed a transgender identity and chose cross-sex hormones... These harms constitute nothing less than institutionalized child abuse. Sound ethics demand an immediate end to the use of pubertal suppression, cross-sex hormones, and sex reassignment surgeries in children and adolescents, as well as an end to promoting gender ideology via school curricula and legislative policies." — Michelle Cretella

The 1972 Gay Rights Platform worked, and continues to work, to remove the legal age of consent in order to normalize pedophilia, in many countries.

"Pedophilia, or more commonly, pederasty, is a form of human sacrifice. Anyone who assaults a child sexually knows they are not only killing that child's soul, but some would say, from a psychotherapeutic perspective, they are turning that child into a dysfunctional, self-destructive individual, and they know the child-victim will also act out on other children, perhaps hundreds, for the rest of his life, and so the human destruction is perpetuated." — Dr. Judith Reisman

In order to normalize something, language must be created. Since terms were forcibly altered, the trans-community has been running full speed to ensure **laws are changed** so that natural men, women and especially children are no longer free. As immaturity and brain damage collide, violence towards homosexuals has increased thanks to the George Soros-driven Rothschilds Value Trans Lives Movement marches on. Dr. Paul McHugh, former psychiatrist in chief at Johns Hopkins, and its current Distinguished Service Professor of Psychiatry, exclaimed that:

"Transgenderism is a mental disorder that merits treatment. Sex change is biologically impossible. **People who promote sexual reassignment surgery are collaborating with and promoting a mental disorder."**

He referenced studies that the suicide rate among transgendered surgical patients is **20 times higher** than normal people. Out of the children who express transgendered feelings 70% to 80% spontaneously lost those feelings before adulthood where 99% more revert to the natural state. **Feelings change.** Paul writes that transgender surgery is not the solution for people who suffer a "disorder of assumption", the notion that their maleness or femaleness is different than what nature assigned to them biologically.

"This intensely **felt** sense of being transgendered <u>**constitutes a mental disorder in two respects**</u>. The first is that the idea of sex misalignment is simply mistaken - it does not correspond with physical reality. The second is that it can lead to grim psychological outcomes. Policy makers and the media are doing no favors either to the public or the transgendered by treating their confusions as a right in need of defending rather than as a mental disorder that deserves understanding, treatment, and prevention. It is a disorder similar to an anorexic person who looks in the mirror and thinks they are overweight."

Like most who understand the mind and health, Paul warns against enabling or encouraging those afflicted by transgenderism since they are extremely "susceptible to suggestion" and that schools' "diversity counselors" who like cult leaders, "encourage these young people to distance themselves from their families and offer advice on rebutting arguments against having transgender surgery".

"'Sex change' is biologically impossible. People who undergo sex-reassignment surgery do not change from men to women or vice versa. Rather, they become feminized men or masculinized women. Claiming that this is civil-rights matter and encouraging surgical intervention is in reality to collaborate with and **promote a mental disorder**." - Dr. Paul McHugh

A study done in Sweden of all 324 sex-reassigned persons (191 male-to-females, 133 female-to-males) in Sweden from 1973-2003, concluded that:

"Persons with transsexualism, after sex reassignment, have considerably higher risks for mortality, suicidal behaviour, and psychiatric morbidity than the general population."

"I started my transgender journey as a 4-year-old boy when my grandmother repeatedly, over several years, cross-dressed me in a full-length purple dress she made especially for me and told me how pretty I was as a girl. This planted the seed of gender confusion and led to my transitioning at age 42 to transgender female. Hormones, surgery, regret: I was a transgender woman for 8 years. Time I can't get back..." - Walt Heyer

Whether you have fallen for the elite's mind control on this agenda or your own, what feels nice or good doesn't automatically mean it is truth or what is right. Deception is deception and most corrupt things are purposely clothes in whatever will lure you to it. That's how it works.

Young boys involved in Boy Scouts orders are now seen involved in public humiliation rituals by being forced to wear a dress under their boy scouts' uniform jacket, in public. It was appalling to see one such small child trying to hold back his tears of embarrassment and shame as he stood in a flowered, above the knee, sundress in a public mall in Denmark. Because Boy Scouts has been exposed numerous times for its pedophilia, it's a wonder that the order still exists. Parents are just that irresponsible.

"The people who encourage very young kids to act out, switch genders, and live a life of pretend need to understand that children could be suffering from a dissociative disorder just as happened with me. My feelings of not wanting to be a boy started in early childhood as a result of cross-dressing at the hands of my grandma. Caregivers all too often **collaborate with a mental disorder instead of treating it**. My gender counselor approved me for gender reassignment surgery, a surgery that, **if I had been provided proper psychotherapy, would never have been necessary or appropriate**. Thankfully, like me, many transgender persons return to the gender they once shed. Slowly they restore the life that was lost." — Walt Heyer

Medical Daily attempts to dance around the truth in their ultra politically correct article but states:
"One study of LGBT adults showed nearly **six times as likely to have high levels of depression; More than eight times as likely to have attempted suicide; More than three times as likely to use illegal drugs**; and **More than three times as likely to engage in unprotected sexual behaviors** that put them at increased risk for HIV and other sexually transmitted infections."

This is what parents want for their child's future? A life of emptiness and despair? Another study shows that even when men are born with a micropenis (underdeveloped penis occurring in the womb), they are happier when raised as **men**. It is not a physical issue, but a mental one. The top three disorders evidenced in transgenders are depression (33%), specific phobias (20%) and adjustment disorder (15%). Dr. Apu Chakraborty of University College in London was involved in the first time the mental health and well-being of gay, lesbian, and bisexual people has been examined in a random sample of the population. The team writes:

"Our study **confirms earlier work** carried out in the UK, USA and Holland which suggests that **non-heterosexual people are at higher risk of mental disorder, suicidal ideation, substance misuse and self-harm** than heterosexual people."

Journalist Ryan Sorba went to a gay bar where he recorded candid answers to his questions about homosexuality being a choice. The trans community, from the beginning, have attempted to manipulate the masses into the lie that they are born this way in order to justify their conditions. Ryan Sorba found many men who identify as gay were molested as children. This goes without saying. It is the same for the majority of mental disorders as the mind is split through trauma during childhood. In a traumatized mind that is constantly trying to regain control, the victim's mind: control must be taken by any means necessary as healing has not taken place. A survivor does not give power back to the abuser, a survivor has healed and become stronger because of it.

"Parents be on guard. If you know and child or teenager who has developed same-sex attraction, let this footage be a warning to you. It is a **red flag** that the child has been molested, by an adult, a teenager, or another child." - Ryan Sorba

"Fears, posttraumatic stress disorder, behavior problems, sexualized behaviors, and poor self-esteem occurred most frequently among a long list of symptoms noted." - Kathleen A. Kendall-Tackett, Linda Myer Williams, and David Finkelhor

The long list of debilitating effects suffered by the survivors of child sexual abuse, includes what David Finkelhor described as "a legacy of childhood abuse that permeates all of the important domains of its victims' lives". Their analysis of 54 studies identified prominent affects and affective states of anger, fear, helplessness, loss, guilt, and shame, and salient cognitive sequelae which includes the inability to legitimize the experience as abuse. It is such a devastating shock to the undeveloped system, it cannot be understood, it cannot be comprehended. Even when sexual abuse happens to adults, the mind can no longer function as it has been torn apart. The act goes against all-natural being. The study goes on to detail what every survivor of sexual abuse already knows because they live with it every day: negative schemas about the self and about people and self-blame, pervasive issues around gender and sexuality, and interpersonal difficulties dealing with feelings of betrayal, isolation and alienation, and negative childhood peer relations.

"When you complain, you make yourself a victim. Leave the situation, change the situation, or accept it. All else is madness." — Eckhart Tolle

Contrary to the opinions of those who would minimize the multitude of negative consequences of adult-child sex, the effects are immediate and often severe. One effect is the development of homosexual tendencies. Secondly, male victims of sexual abuse often turn their rage outward and attempt to reassert their masculinity in inappropriate ways. Another effect is that some boy victims try to recapitulate, or re-enact, their victimization. This is the brain's attempt to understand what happened as well as to gain a feeling of control. If children had natural human families that were the embodiment of security and love, as intended, then at least children would be able to heal from the damage and go on to have productive lives.

"Child abuse, and sexual abuse in particular, has come to be regarded by many clinicians as making a powerful contribution to adult pathology." - P. E. Mullen

In British public schools, today, children are being recruited through manipulation, bullying, and sexual assault by the transgender community. The primary targets in schools are children with Autism: the easily manipulated. Meanwhile college campuses are now enforcing punishments for "microaggressions" towards people who suffer from this disorder as they must, at that age, be enforced to remain broken. Data from the National Health Service (NHS) revealing that AT LEAST one-third of all young people who go in for transition surgery show signs of what the health authority describes as "moderate to severe autistic traits". Not only are parents not told of what is truly going on, but teachers are afraid of losing their jobs, should they slip-up in speech. One schoolteacher stated:

"I'm now so alarmed by the **force** of the transgender agenda that I'm not sure how much longer I can go on for, as I can no longer be honest with the students."

12 New Jersey Junior High schools (ages 11-14) have implemented programs for "LGBTQ-focused" curriculum. One parent exclaimed:

"They are pushing a political agenda."

In the UK, at least 40 secondary schools have banned girls from wearing skirts. Children are forced into "gender neutral" clothing to help warp the mind. Meanwhile boys are encouraged to wear skirts, as males are indoctrinated to further disrespect and abuse women with this movement. Homosexuality is not only an offense against women but an afront to the Living God, which is the purpose. For those who have managed to make it this far into the book and have still not understood the elite: The reason the elite have always been against your ability to produce children is twofold. The angels, including the Fallen, do not have that ability and the Living God urged humans several times to produce children! Everything the elite do is to corrupt the Living God's desires and commands as is the will of

Lucifer, depicted as the man-goat surrounded by children.

"I am not a dress to be worn on a whim. A man in a dress is nonetheless a him. Women are not simply what we wear. If this offends you, I do not care. I am not an idea, in any man's mind. And my purpose in life is not to be kind. So, while my rights are trampled every day of the week, I will not stand by being docile and meek. We are women. We are warriors of steel. Woman is something no man will ever feel. Woman is not a skill that any man can hone. **Woman is our word and it is ours alone.**" — Megyn Kelly

Going beyond DNA which dictates sex, women must pay in blood...lots of blood, sweat and many tears to be women. Not to mention they are the only ones with the ability to produce life, as well as the ability to feed and maintain that life. Anyone **born** without a vagina can never be a woman regardless of the self-hatred and mutilation and drugging the poor fool forces on himself. Likewise, a woman cannot be a man, because to be a man requires not only appendages dangling between the legs but a certain strength both physically and mentally, which men need to be providers and leaders, as well as the ability to be decisive and ambitious with a lack of emotional display. Men and women are vastly different in every single way possible, down to the DNA.

The modern transgender movement began as the brainchild of 3 elite puppets who shared a common bond: all three were pedophiles. Dr. Alfred Kinsey, a biologist and sexologist, Dr. Harry Benjamin, an endocrinologist, and Dr. John Money, a disciple of them both, worked to form the trans-movement through human experimentation, pedophilia, and satanic ritual abuse of children. It was Harry who created the term "transsexualism", based on their experiments on transvestites. John Money is the reason we use the term "gender" to refer to sexuality today when gender isn't something that exists. The first transgender surgeries were conducted by these men, in university-based clinics, starting in the 1950's. Results proved this butchery was only harmful and never successful.

In 1825 Germany lived one Karl Heinrich Ulrichs who has become known as the "grandfather of the 'gay' rights movement". As we already know the Rothschilds and friend (Oppenheimers, Weishaupts, and other Jesuits) were in control of Germany and all movements that stemmed from that country throughout history. This is no different than all of the movements and puppet revolutionaries we have discussed thus far. Karl was a lawyer, political activist, and known pedophile. During his life, sodomy (now called homosexuality) was illegal according to the German Penal Code. In 1860, Ulrichs began broadcasting his **theory of a third sex**, those with same-sex attraction. Though he didn't get the law abolished, his theories are forced on society today. During his time a writer, Karoly Maria Benkert, coined the term homosexual. Until this point Sodomites were called sodomites. Ducks were called ducks.

Pedophilia was a crime of the most depraved mind. The gay community of Germany during this time called themselves Uranians, instead of sodomites. Their militant rallies rang with the chant: "Uranians of the World, Unite!"

This was soon changed to homosexuals once the term was given to them. What used to be a physical act was now becoming an identification. As propaganda continued, the militant group expanded, <u>terms changed</u>, <u>definitions changed</u>, because the mind must be changed to accept what is unnatural. Today, the pedophile organization B4U Act, is lobbying for changes to the Diagnostic and Statistical Manual of Mental Disorders, or DSM, the guideline of standards on mental health. The pedo-promoting organization states on their website:

"Stigmatizing and stereotyping minor-attracted people inflames the fears of minor-attracted people, mental health professionals and the public, without contributing to an understanding of minor-attracted people or the issue of child sexual abuse."

"Each formulation raises the stakes: One can object to and even criminalize an act; one is obligated to be sympathetic toward a condition; but once it's a full-fledged 24/7 identity, like being Hispanic or Inuit, **anything less than whole-hearted acceptance gets you marked down as a bigot**." - Mark Steyn

As we skip ahead through history, we find one of the gay sects, The Community of the Special, helped change the terminology once again, to "special". An older version of NAMBLA, their founder wrote that he wished for Germany to have a:

"thirst for a revival of Greek times and Hellenic standards of beauty after centuries of Christian Barbarism. The positive goal...is the revival of **Hellenic chivalry** and its recognition by society. By chivalric love we mean in particular close friendships between youths and even more particularly the **bonds between men of unequal ages**."

Fraternity!

As you will find, if you know your own history, the leaders of these movements merge terminologies and historical timelines that never existed, similar to what Helena Blavatsky did in her writings. Nonsense. Chivalry didn't exist until 1292 and is defined as: a knight whose essential character is devotion to Woman and to Honour. Chivalry was not even a concept in the Greek and Hellenistic times... In Hellenistic Greece, the power was shifting as was money, it was a time of turmoil and change. Consequently, many groups arose with agnostic philosophies, which caused another power shift from their poly gods to themselves. Plato argued that love between males is the highest form of love and that sex with women is lustful and only for means of reproduction. Throughout ancient Greece and Roman histories, as we have discussed, homosexual pedophilia was accepted and encouraged, much like it is in middle eastern countries today and the elite have been working to bring it back to their empires ever since the Roman Empire fell. During the 1900's the Pornography Industry began to fight for the spotlight. Backed by the sodomite elite, pornography depicts perverted, and typically sodomitic sexual acts which is a Luciferian ritual. The porn industry uses children, who are trafficked and raped, in these videos and images, thus programming viewers for pedophilia. In combination with the breakdown of the family, through the elites' various movements and wars, and the rise of pedophilia, children have been conditioned to believe that sex is love. This warping of the mind has brought us to where we are today.

All through history, pedo's have been taking control over others. Jim Kepner, former curator of the International Gay and Lesbian Archives in Los Angeles states:

"If we reject the boylovers in our midst today we'd better stop waving the banner of the Ancient Greeks, of Michelangelo, Leonardo da Vinci, Oscar Wilde, Walt Whitman, and others. We'd better stop claiming them as part of our heritage unless we are **broadening** our concept of **what it means to be gay** today."

In the 1950's, member of the Communist party, Henry Hay, became known as the founder of the modern 'gay' rights movement. He defined himself as a neo-pagan and participated in the occultic rituals at the "Los Angeles lodge of the Order of the Eastern Temple, Aleister Crowley's notorious Luciferian cult. Remember, dear reader, that every elite order requires rituals which include pedophilia and sodomy. Henry openly endorsed **NAMBLA** and founded a New Age group called Radical Faeries. He was a close friend of the "founders" Alfred Kinsey and Harry Benjamin, as well as Margaret Sanger who was deeply involved in this group. Henry's other group, Mattachine Society, followed the gay community's philosophy and increased public militant demonstrations. As the notoriety of Alfred and Harry grew, sex surgeries were done on American transvestites, in Germany. Margaret Sanger's work to bring about legal murder of children and normalize depopulation was vital to the homosexual agenda. She was the Bill Gates of her time: a eugenicist, racist, and Luciferian (as are all of the people mentioned here). As discussed before, she is the reason we have sex education in schools. Not to teach children what "bad touch" is, nor to discuss the changes happening to them and how to control themselves without destroying their lives...but to have adult strangers expose children to sex. If you can't support having a child, then you shouldn't be having sex. She explicitly approved of mothers who exposed their infants in ancient Sparta and Rome, as well as the drowning their girl-infants in contemporary China. She regarded the right to kill their infants as evidence of women's high status in antiquity. Meanwhile not even animals murder their own. This is called Choice. In reality the choice was made before the act of sex took place. This is labeled as Women's Rights but in reality, it is the denial of rights of the innocent who were chosen to be created upon the act of sex. Since 2017 the Sanger International

Planned Parenthood Federation has been working to change laws to accept child prostitution and pedophilia.

"The "evolution" of killing the unborn became a methodological advancement achieved by simply moving the practice farther up the birth canal. Invisibility encouraged Acceptability." – Bob Perry

On June 27, 1969, the pro-sodomy movement officially adopted terrorism as a means to achieve power when a mob of "drag queens, dykes, street people, and bar boys" physically attacked police officers conducting a raid across the street at a mafia owned bar in New York. **The gay mob trapped the police inside the bar and set it on fire.** This day is celebrated as Gay Pride Day. After this, the "Gay Liberation Front" was formed, so named after the National Liberation Front, a Viet Cong alliance. Gay Lib sects began nationwide in US and the member used intimidation and coercion to achieve political gains. The US has been the main focus of this agenda, as the US must be dissolved before the New World Order of the Global Government can be implemented. While the rest of the world will easily accept the takeover, Americans have been generationally conditioned to be independent and to not be controlled by any government or order. These beliefs still remain, which is why the attack against them today is so strong. It must be destroyed.

Soon the group started using the Biblical symbol of Living God's promise of peace, the rainbow, as their own in yet another blatant perversion of a Torah believers and Christians who are the only groups of people opposed to sodomy.

"If you know an asteroid's trajectory, you can predict not only where it was years ago, but where it will be in the future. And so it is with cultural trajectory." – Selwyn Duke

In 1973, gay activists began attacking the meetings of the American Psychiatric Association and the American Psychological Association because these are the people who change definitions of disorders. The attacks continued until committee members, three of whom were homosexual, relented and removed homosexuality from the list of mental disorders. The decision was based on fear and intimidation. A poll taken a few years later showed that the majority of the members disagreed with the decision but were ignored. Very soon after, the elite's media which has always been controlled by homosexual pedophiles, was under the instruction of the Gay Manifesto, written by Marshall Kirk and Hunter Madsen. Their book details the agenda and how they will manipulate culture so that it becomes pro-gay and pro-trans. After this was implemented, anyone who spoke about homosexuals on TV, Radio and Movies was attacked, fired, and censored, if the LGBT community didn't approve of it. As is detailed in the manifesto, the attack was most focused on destroying Christians. As exposed previously, Catholics were not included in this as that system is and always has been completely upholding of the elite ways. The manifesto states:

"Use talk to muddy the moral waters...undermine the moral authority of [conservatives] by portraying them as antiquated backwaters, badly out of step with the times......**set science and public opinion against institutional religion.**"

In 1999, the American Psychological Association published a report, A Meta-Analytic Examination of Assumed Properties of Child Sexual Abuse Using College Samples, which surmises that:

"child sexual abuse could be harmless and beneficial."

It could be if it weren't for the fact that it is. So how did this all begin? As with every movement, there are key puppets used by the elite to enhance and develop the doctrine for the cult. Let's talk about them before we come further along in the timeline.

Dr. Harry Benjamin was born in Germany on January 12, 1885. He joined the Prussian Guard before he met his friend Magnus Hirschfeld who pointed him in the direction of medicine.

"I do remember going, as a young person, to a lecture by Auguste Forel, whose book The Sexual Question was a sensation at the time, and which impressed me greatly. I also met Magnus Hirschfeld very early on through a girlfriend, who knew the police official Kopp, who was in charge investigating sexual offenses. He, in turn, was a friend of Hirschfeld's, and so I met both men. That was around 1907. They repeatedly took me along on their rounds through the homosexual bars in Berlin. I especially remember the 'Eldorado' with its drag shows, where also many of the customers appeared in the clothing of the other sex. The word "transvestite" had not yet been invented. Hirschfeld coined it only in 1910 in his well-known study." — Harry Benjamin

The police officer, Kopp, was used frequently by Benjamin to help transport patients to and from Germany for sex operations. Magnus Hirschfeld was a doctor who studied hermaphroditism, transvestism and particularly, homosexualism. In 1897, Magnus established the Scientific-Humanitarian Committee which was the world's first gay rights organization. Its main goal was to fight for the abolishment of Paragraph 175 of the German Imperial Penal Code, which punished sexual contact between men. The earliest sex reassignment surgeries were performed at his institute in Berlin. Harry was an avid disciple of his and graduated from Tübingen University with a degree in medicine; his thesis was on tuberculosis. During his graduate work with other doctors, one had found a cure for TB of the joints. A wealthy man in New York heard of the cure, as newspapers exaggerated the results, and paid for Harry to come treat his son.

In 1913, he went to the US but was unable to cure the man's son and the man refused to pay him. Stranded in the US, he eventually obtained passage back to Germany but was turned back as war broke out. He ended up opening his own practice out of his apartment in New York for many years. In New York, Harry got married to a woman and became interested in the work of Dr. Eugene Steinach, traveling to Vienna to see his research on vasectomy. His obsession with his theory that sterilization would extend life led him further in his experiments. By 1922, Harry had performed 22 vasectomies. He also sterilized women with radiation to their ovaries which he sold as "rejuvenation" - a cure for aging. He did not address any complications or results but only noted how the patient felt afterwards. After the death of Harry's father, his mother moved from Germany to live with Harry and his wife, soon followed by Magnus Hirschfeld. Soon Harry was contacted by Alfred Kinsey to study a boy who wanted to be changed into a girl.

As his popularity grew, especially given his association to Alfred Kinsey and other German sex doctors, many of his patients were referred by doctors including David Cauldwell, Robert Stoller, as well as doctors in Denmark. The Erickson Educational Foundation, which published educational booklets, funded medical conferences, counselling services, also funded Harry Benjamin. Reed Erickson was a millionaire who had been married 4 times and was involved in the New Age and trans movements which go hand in...hand. In the 1950's, Harry founded the Society for the Scientific Study of Sexuality and created the "Sex Orientation Scale" whereby he classified various forms and subtypes of transvestitism and transsexualism in males. By the 1970's, Benjamin had formed what later became the Harry Benjamin International **Gender Dysphoria** Association, which devised a set of "standards of care" that sanctioned the criteria and diagnostic procedure for transsexuality. In 2007, HBIGDA became the World Professional Association for Transgender Health. His work opened the doors for societal acceptance and normalization.

"Using the same tactics used by 'gay' rights activists, pedophiles have begun to seek similar status arguing their desire for children is a sexual orientation no different than heterosexual or homosexuals." - Jack Minor

Dr. Alfred Kinsey, known today as the "Father of the Sexual Revolution", was born June 23, 1894, in New Jersey. Alfred graduated Bowdoin College with degrees in biology and psychology and went on to teach biology and zoology at Harvard working autonomously under William Morton Wheeler. After his thesis on Wasps, he graduated from Harvard, a zoologist. He married his student, and they had 4 children. Most Luciferians carry on traditional marriages and families as a front, which has worked well for centuries. As his wife once stated: "The (bedroom) door was always open". In 1947, Alfred received funding from the Rockefeller Foundation and founded the Institute for Sex Research at Indiana University now called Kinsey Institute. This was the American copy of Magnus Hirschfield's Berlin Institute for Sex Research.

Alfred would not permit persons of color, Jews, or Christians on his staff. Alfred believed that all sex acts were legitimate including pedophilia, bestiality, sadomasochism, incest, adultery, prostitution, and group sex. He experimented on infants and toddlers to justify his view that children of any age "enjoy having sex". Alfred lobbied against laws that protected innocent children and punished sexual predators. Today pedophiles in the US are no longer sentenced but set free. Alfred wrote about pre-adolescent orgasms using data gathered from his own observations of over 300 infants and children. At least 188 children were timed with a stopwatch. Infants were raped for up to 24 hours straight. Alfred's definition of Orgasm was given to him by correspondent and pedophile Dr. Green.

The Pedophilic Definition is as follows: Extreme tension with violent convulsions, sudden heaving and jerking of the whole body, gasping, hands grasping, mouth distorted, sometimes with tongue protruding; whole body or parts of it spasmodically twitching, violent jerking of the penis, groaning, sobbing, or more violent cries, sometimes with an abundance of tears (especially among younger children), hysterical laughing, talking, sadistic or masochistic reactions, extreme trembling, collapse, loss of color, and sometimes fainting of subject. Some suffer **excruciating pain and may scream** if the penis is even touched. Some, before the arrival of orgasm, **will fight away from the partner and may make violent attempts to avoid climax** although they derive definite pleasure from the situation. This is rape.

"One person could not do this to so many children - <u>**these children had to be held down or subject to strapping down, otherwise they would not respond willingly**</u>." - Lester Caplan of the American Board of Pediatrics

Staff member and co-author Paul Gebhard admitted that they were relying on information being sent to them by a man named Rex King, a serial rapist who was guilty of raping more than 800 children. A 1998 British television documentary, Kinsey's Paedophiles, recounted how German newspapers uncovered Alfred's connection to notorious Nazi pedophile Dr. Fritz Von Balluseck (Dr. Green) when the former Gestapo director was on trial for the sex-related murder of a little girl in 1956. The German papers found letters from Alfred thanking the pedophile for his ongoing child-rape which continued until 1954. Alfred, who "kept up a regular and lively correspondence," wrote:

"I <u>rejoice</u> at everything you send, for I am then assured that that much more of your material is saved for scientific publication. Watch out, or you might be caught."

In the name of science or medicine, the elite are able to do anything they wish since those terms are accepted today, by the masses. Alfred also corresponded with Nazi

MkUltra technician Ewen Cameron. He tried hard to obtain Aleister Crowley's sex-magic diaries after he died and traveled to Thelema Abbey, where Aleister conducted pedophilic rituals.

"Kinsey vigorously promoted, juggling his figures to do so, a hedonistic, animalistic conception of sexual behavior, while at the same time he consistently denounced all biblical and conventional conceptions of sexual behavior." - Dr. Albert Hobbs

The only people he could get to participate in his experiments were prostitutes, prisoners, or pedophiles. Serious scientists know that they can't rely on volunteers for sexual studies because it attracts a disproportionate number of "unconventional" men and women. Alfred and his staff engaging in all kinds of sex acts, in the attic of his home, that were filmed by professional cinematographers.

"This **contraceptive mentality was born in the kind of sexual license that Kinsey endorsed**. He believed pornography was harmless, that adultery can enhance a marriage and that children are sexual from birth. Keeping these and other Kinsey myths alive is why the porn industry is thriving and why abortion and contraception providers rake in millions of dollars every year. He was a pederast who developed such an extreme sadomasochistic form of autoeroticism that some believe it caused his untimely death." — Zenit.org

After his second sex book came out and flopped, he was accused of being a communist which resulted in the Rockefeller Foundation pulling his funding. In the 1950's the US was under an extreme propaganda attack regarding Russia and suddenly everyone was a Communist. Alfred suffered from congestive heart failure, until he got pneumonia and died in 1956. After his death, his work lived on and expanded at the Kinsey Institute, with funding by the Federal government to carry out many experiments. Indiana State Rep. Woody Burton recalls:

"It was 1998, and I was concerned about a $666,000 appropriation for the Kinsey Institute. They were doing a lot of things that I thought were improper ... the **manipulation of children**, sexual stimulation. So, I was trying to cut off the funding."

Thankfully, in 2004, a group of 2400 lawmakers from 50 states concluded that Alfred's work was a fraud and contained "manufactured statistics". His theories have been used to push sexual deviance, which is proven to not only cause **irreversible mental damage** but **physical diseases** and damage as well as to the **soul**. This is what Hugh Hefner a disciple of Alfred Kinsey, has helped to expand his work to force sodomy and pedophilia on the world.

The last of our "founders", as the movement claims, is John Money. Born on June 8,

1921, in New Zealand, he had a brother Donald Frank Light Money and sister Joy Hopkins. John's parents were deeply involved in a cult called the Plymouth Brethren. In this fraternal cult you can easily see the typical MK programming every order contains. The community is well known for its treatment of women as merely child producers, and men as having the power and authority. A study showed that 18 of 44 participants of the New Zealand Brethren, had been sexually abused as children. John was no exception and learned to compartmentalize and manipulate. John Darby started the cult after he produced his own translation of the Bible. Like all cultists, John Darby enforced a separation from the modern world. If one of the members of the community were considered no longer pure enough, they would be cut off and thrown out. The Brethren in New Zealand are involved in politics and education, outside of the cult communities. Former teachers at Brethren-run schools claimed the schools heavily censored reading material, ripping out chapters on reproduction from science texts, and dictated every aspect of the children's lives.

John Money graduated from Victoria University before moving to the US and attending Harvard. Under the leadership of Lawson Wilkins, he studied Hermaphroditism and became the Professor Emeritus of Pediatrics and of Medical Psychology at John Hopkins School of Medicine where he founded the Johns Hopkins Gender Identity Clinic with Claude Jean Migeon and Howard Wilbur Jones, Jr. who immediately started experimenting on children. While he married for a short time, John never had children of his own. Being a homosexual pedophile, he and Howard Jones removed an infant boy's (David Reimer) penis and told his parents to raise him as a girl, convincing them it wouldn't make a difference. John personally oversaw the infant's "treatment" and "monitored" him regularly. During the next 10 years, he did various pointless experiments to satisfy his perverted mind. In one case of many, he forced David to mimic sexual acts with his twin brother as they grew. John would force the baby to lay down and spread his legs while his brother was forced to climb on top of him. He would make the twins take off their clothes and inspect each other's genitals; he photographed them naked; he showed them graphic photographs of a 7-year-old girl giving birth. John took numerous photos of the naked children. According to John a boy who picked up a doll was not just being curious, expressing interest in the human body, or merely picking up a toy but was "expressing his feminine side". As we always see in these scenarios, medical relevance has nothing to do with anything.

The Reimer twins grew up in terror and rage. David was forced to wear dresses and play with dolls and pretend he was a girl. The boy had to pee through a small hole surgeon had created in his abdomen and was forced to take female hormones which only caused physical changes and did not make him feel female. Finally at age 14, David was told the truth, that he was a male and not a female! He was left to live his short life with these horrendous physical and mental scars. His mother tried to commit suicide while his father and brother turned to alcohol and drugs to try to wash away the shame they had caused and allowed. David had to have breasts removed, and hormone treatments to correct the total chaos created by going against his biological makeup. The extreme stress from his wretched treatment and past and physical problems caused by not having a natural human body grew until he one day committed suicide. The result of John Money's experimentation caused both twins and their parents to commit suicide. John Money never suffered for his crimes but was applauded and his experiments were carried out worldwide.

During his career, John was supported by numerous organizations including the Josiah Macy, Jr. Foundation and the National Institute of Child Health and Human Development. He was an outspoken advocate for pedophilia and debated the topic often. As so many Luciferians had done before him, John made up words and terms to force pedophilia on others.

"[John] wrote lengthy perverse diatribes that gave rise to a whole range of Orwellian newspeak, sophistry, and gibberish that has been adopted by the transgender movement. To give only a sample, there was the "Adam Principle," the "exigency theory," "gynemimesis," "mindbrain," "neurocognitional," "normophilia," "phylism," "troopbondance" and a whole slew of paraphilias, such as "apotemnophilia," "autassassinophilia" and "autonepiophilia." — Russ Winter

John created the word "gender" and defined it as something alterable. He changed "sexual perversions" to "sexual paraphilias", and "sexual preference" to "sexual orientation". He is also responsible for claiming that there are different kinds of pedophilia, among other things. His writings on gender, his new vocabulary, and his theories have been celebrated and Accepted. He received national awards and honorary degrees, was featured in Time magazine, and included a chapter on the Reimer twins in one of his textbooks. His work enabled thousands of infant sexual mutilations to occur. In any other age he would be considered a monster. This goes to show how far the elite indoctrination had come by the time the world wars were implemented. **After many surgeries had been done**, Johns Hopkins Hospital decided to have a study conducted to verify John's claims that the surgery was beneficial and medically necessary. Dr. Jon Meyer, the chairman of the Hopkins gender clinic, selected 50 subjects from those treated at Hopkins who had undergone gender reassignment surgery and those who had not had surgery. On August 10, 1979, Jon Meyer announced his results:

"To say this type of surgery cures psychiatric disturbance is **incorrect**. We now have objective evidence that there is no real difference in the transsexual's adjustments to life in terms of job, educational attainment, marital adjustment, and social stability."

He later told The New York Times:

"My personal feeling is that the surgery is **not a proper treatment for a**

psychiatric disorder, and it's clear to me these patients have **severe psychological problems** that **don't go away following surgery.**"

Harry Benjamin's friend and fellow Endocrinologist, Charles Ihlenfeld, after 6 years of administering drugs to transsexuals publicly announced:

"There is too much unhappiness among people who have had the surgery...Too many end in suicide."

He promptly quit and changed his profession to psychiatry so he could offer patients the kind of help they really needed. Less than 6 months later, the Johns Hopkins gender clinic closed. Other university-affiliated gender clinics across the US followed suit. Immediately, a committee was formed by Harry Benjamin, John Money, and Paul Walker (a fellow homosexual and transgender activist) to draft standards of care for transgenders that furthered their agenda; by the end of the year, the "Harry Benjamin International Standards of Care" was published. John Money was taken to St. Joseph's Hospital in Baltimore with a fractured nose and left sinus bone and throughout the week he deteriorated until he was comatose. Soon after, he died on his birthday, which was also the 20th anniversary of the gay law reform bill in New Zealand.

Because of these men private surgeons have replaced hospital regulated clinics without any scrutiny or accountability for their results. As people believe the Standards of Care dictated to them by those who merely seek to profit from and fulfill their own perversions, they turn to these devastating surgeries, paying human mutilators to leave them with nothing but shame, regret, and death. Confusion runs rampant as the ability to think critically and logically has been dampened for generations. The is a 3-step agenda that should be obvious to you by now.

1. Gay rights and destruction of the biological human family, focusing on forcing Acceptance of sexual preference and rights pertaining to that. (Problem: goes against natural order and creates stress and agitation)

2. Sudden focus on permanently altering the biological human identities. (Reaction to the problem)

3. Legal and open pedophilia, and rights legalizing perversion. (Solution brought on through Tolerance)

Humans are no longer sympathetic or understanding, because tolerance eliminates that along with all love and honesty - successfully shutting off the individual's perceived ability to challenge, to change, to advance. Tolerance is Censorship.

With the help of Alice Bailey and other leaders of the movement to make Luciferianism mainstream, her company Lucis Trust published her work called Esoteric Healing: The Basis Causes of Disease. In this book she and co-author Djwhal Khul divided homosexuality into 3 parts. Again, the Luciferian agenda is wrapped in sodomy and pedophilia. It states:

"It might be pointed out here that homosexuality is of three kinds:
1. That which is the result of ancient evil habits. This is the major cause today and indicates:

> - Individualisation upon this planet susceptible to these dangerous characteristics.
> - A consequent study of sex magic, plus a constant insatiable physical and sexual urge.

2. Imitative homosexuality. A number of persons of all classes imitated their betters and so developed evil habits in sexual intercourse from which they might otherwise have remained free. This is one of the prevalent reasons today, among many men and women, and is based upon a too active imagination, plus a powerful physical or sex nature, and a prurient curiosity. This category accounts for many of our Sodomites and Lesbians.
3. A few rare, very rare, cases of hermaphroditism."

In 2009, Barrack Obama was made President of US and though he was not the first homosexual pedophile to be in the White House, as it is a requirement of the orders, he was the first to openly support the movement. His motto was change, and change he brought.

> "While increasingly visible in mainstream advertising, are often discursively constructed by television advertisements in ways that limit subject positions that family members can occupy if they are to be **seen as an ideal family unit**.... The branded narratives of corporations weighing in on same-sex family issues have a discursive effect on social understandings of same-sex families.... Recent years have seen a significant surge in normalization and legitimation of same-sex unions within Western nations. LGBT adoption rights have been extended to same-sex couples in most Western nations, with notable exceptions including in the Australian states of Queensland, the Northern Territory and South Australia; the state of Mississippi in the United States; and all districts of Italy...It is widely recognized within queer literature that gay and lesbian families have been commonly framed by mainstream gay rights activist organizations such as PFLAG (Parents, Families and Friends of Lesbians and Gays) and GetUp! as being no different from straight families in order to press the case for mainstream recognition of same-sex families. Rather than encouraging acceptance of difference, it positions homosexual parenting within a hetero-normative and traditionalist framework of family and marriage. It positions traditional family structures as the norm which homosexual families must emulate." — Wholesome Homosexuality

That is because it is not about being gay. It is about destroying the natural family. A study done in Texas on people ranging from 18-39 years of age, showed that those who had same-sex relationships before they were 18 were more likely to suffer from a broad range of emotional and social problems. The US National Health Interview Survey done in 2015, concluded that emotional problems were over twice as prevalent for children with same-sex parents than for children with opposite-sex parents. Attention-deficit hyperactivity disorder was more than twice as prevalent among children with same-sex parents than in the general population.

"This is a tragic day for America's children. The SCOTUS has just undermined the single greatest pro-child institution in the history of mankind: the natural family." - Dr. Michelle Cretella, president of the American College of Pediatricians

Marriage is the structure put in place to ensure stability in the family unit. It is what adults do when they are prepared to begin to reproduce. Since homosexuals cannot reproduce, they have no legal basis for this argument to begin with. Studies prove that 87.7% of children with same-sex parents exhibited symptoms of depression, compared to 47.2% of children with opposite-sex parents. 32.4% of children with same-sex parents reported feeling fearful or crying almost every day, compared to 3.1% of children from natural families. A 2013 Canadian study of data from a very large population-based sample, revealed that the children of gay and lesbian couples are only about 65% as likely to have graduated from high school as are the children of natural married couples. Daughters of lesbian "parents" displayed dramatically lower graduation rates. A study of 174 primary school children in Australia exposed that married heterosexual couples **offer the best environment for a child's social and educational development**.

"The deep roots of the gay movement were overtly anti-religious and anti-nuclear family, and pretty much reduced all human beings to nothing more than sexual objects. Gay Liberation was always about sexual liberation for all, no matter what age. It's ironic that now that gays — and especially married gay and lesbian couples — are part of the establishment, they express revulsion over the pedophiles' identification with gay rights." — Doug Mainwaring

In keeping with cultic rituals, the homosexual community has Adoption and Fostering Week, among others, urging those who live a homosexual lifestyle to adopt and be in care of young, fragile, and impressionable minds, not to mention the easy 24/7 access to children. The UK Department of Education published in 2015 that the country has seen a record number of homosexuals adopting children stating:
"We have invested £17 million to boost voluntary adoption agencies in **recruiting and supporting** adopters, including £400,000 to launch the **first adoption service exclusively for LGBT people** and £400,000 to Barnardo's to

recruit adopters for siblings, with a focus on LGBT adopters."

The agenda has attacked every area of society, to make it seem normal. Militaries have had to change their laws and regulations, which were put in place for good and obvious reasons, to accommodate the militant pedophiles. A multitude of people have been forced to advertise the movement including Bradley Manning who was suddenly female after months of solitary confinement and torture. The community is not about freedom, or equality. It is about Fascism. They do not want equality, or there would be no exclusivity. Governor Dannel Malloy has stated that Connecticut wants to be known as a state that welcomes and embraces the LGBT community. The state's Child Welfare Agency launched an initiative to **actively recruit members** of the state's homosexual community. Connecticut Department of Children and Families Commissioner Joette Katz said there are roughly 100 LGBT adoptive families already in the state's system. The state put many programs in place to pull the gay community into adoption and foster care as there are roughly 4,300 children in state care. The Kentler Project was initiated in the 1970's in Berlin by Helmut Kentler. He rounded up homeless children from West Berlin and placed them in the homes of pedophiles. The pedophile's (all males) were paid for the next 30 years to prove that sexual conduct between children and adults was good. After Helmut's death the experiment was exposed and several children, now adults, have come forward, exposing how the government, educational system, the senate, and youth welfare offices are all involved in promoting pedophilia.

Today homosexuals can be heard chanting "10% is not enough, RECRUIT, RECRUIT, RECRUIT!" in their parades of pride, as they now demand to be allowed to be parents even though they cannot reproduce nor be fit to influence a child. The 10% refers to Alfred Kinsey's false statement that 10% of the population was homosexual. This is not, and never was, true. The gay population in any given country has never been above 3%. Like every cult, they **must** recruit, or the movement would never grow. Guess who they are focused on recruiting, dear reader. Not consenting adults. Luciferian rituals have been occurring increasingly in Gay Pride Marches, such as children dancing, stripping and mimicking sex acts in public, in front of groups of grown men. 10-year-old Desmond is an MK victim of the LGBT community who says he was first exposed to dressing up in drag when he saw a Ru Paul (one of the main promoters of the movement) performance on TV. He is now exploited by the community.

"As a pediatrician, I will go one step farther and say that the parents of these children and others promoting this are guilty of **pedophilic grooming**." - Dr. Michelle Cretella

LGBT Campaigns like I AM: Trans People Speak continue using terminology of the Living God in inverted and corrupted form, just as they have corrupted His symbols.

Trans People Speak is a video-based storytelling campaign by the Massachusetts Transgender Political Coalition and GLAAD. TransRespect is one of many ad campaigns implemented worldwide by the District of Columbia Office of Human Rights. AIDS 2020 and HIV 2020 are two of the annual international conferences held by multiple organizations including GATE. GATE, like all LGBT organizations, holds many campaigns to indoctrinate. GLSEN, the Gay, Lesbian, and Straight, Education Network, has long used tools like "North American History Game Cards" in elementary schools, teaching children about famous pedophile Americans like NAMBLA member Allen Ginsberg and Walt Whitman to support the propaganda. As usual, they purposely leave out the Luciferian and pedophilic history and goal of homosexuality.

In 2012, Adweek reported that the LGBT community was estimated to represent a $743 billion market at that time. When Chevy Volt began advertising homosexuality, it did not do so alone. Companies including JC Penney, Target, Gap, (which all sell children's products) have had to alter their advertising to be queer-centered and push the agenda on the developing mind. This was done through violent, riotous protesting, picketing, and boycotting. If only natural humans were as dedicated to a healthy humanity to force their beliefs and power over others. Meanwhile, the Tobacco Industry has begun to advertise to LGBT youths specifically. That same year, the Miss Universe Canada pageant disqualified Jenna Talackova, for being transgender. Soon after he was given his own reality TV show called "Brave New Girls". The new keyword for the movement being Brave. America's Next Top Model TV show was the next to feature transgenders and overnight, they took over public television and the fashion industry worldwide.

In the US, which was behind EU in sexualizing children, California's AB 329 Health Education Framework 2019 aligned with the Healthy Youth Act 2016 requiring schools provide information and instruction on **performing** various types of sex acts with various types of partners, as well as gender fluidity. According to a Lompoc Unified School District administrator: Using information to "keep children safe", could not be taught in the traditional scientific method of biology, physiology, or microbiology to facilitate a deeper knowledge and understanding of the natural processes, because it "would not meet the tenets of the law".

In 2016, the US started passing gender laws regarding bathrooms in public places. The laws passed and boys and men were allowed to use girls' bathrooms and vice versa. Once public outrage began, trans bathrooms were installed in schools and public places. A trio of Republicans, Brad Klippert, Tom Dent and Dan Griffey introduced a bill that required that a person's DNA be used to determine what facilities they are and aren't allowed to use. In 2017, a boy who claimed to be a girl, won the Connecticut girls' state titles for sprinting. The next year he was joined by another boy, who called himself a girl. Fear keeps everyone silent when it has never been fair or okay for a biological male to compete in girls' sports, due to the differences in the physical bodies of males versus females. Tolerance. Men and women walk, run and sprint differently. Opposite sex hormones and surgery don't change these genetic and biological differences.

"You never hear about biological women that are transitioning into men and their desire to use the men's room. Interesting, huh?" — Chad Prather

In 2016 the United Nations appointed a human rights expert to head the **protection of LGBT**. United Nations Office of the High Commissioner for Human Rights sanctioned a sexual revolution that will legalize and whole-hearted support of transgenderism but will also support the legalization of pedophilia. Micah Grzywnowicz, of the Swedish Federation for LGBTQ Rights (RFSL) remarked:

"This is truly momentous. This is our opportunity to bring international attention to specific violations and challenges faced by transgender and gender non-conforming persons in all regions."

"Today, the UN took a historic step forward. By creating a UN expert, the Human Rights Council has given official voice to those facing violations because of their sexual orientation or gender identity the world over. The new UN-LGBT **Enforcer** will come with the might and muscle of the United Nations, the European Union, and the United States and with the power to **enforce this radical new belief**." - John Fisher, Geneva director at Human Rights Watch

That year the US federal government stated that the Department of Health and Human Services found the risks were often too high, and the benefits too unclear to allow body mutilations. Naturally, the World Professional Association for Transgender Health pressed ahead, claiming without any evidence that these procedures were "safe". By 2019, the state of Minnesota helped a child get sex-change surgery without the consent of her parents. Local governments, medical providers and school districts can legally end parental control over their minor children, "without a judicial order of emancipation, without parental waiver, and without parental notice". Again, this doesn't change the fact that your individual biology remains the same. Your genetic structure and DNA are the same for life, no matter what you do to pretend otherwise.

"If more people were aware of the dark and troubled history of sex-reassignment surgery, perhaps we wouldn't be so quick to push people toward it." — Walt Heyer

Ambiguity is an old form of mind control. In the last 10 years advertisements have been used aggressively by companies in places where children will see them.

Companies including Expedia, Amazon, American Airlines, Anheuser-Busch InBev, Bloomingdale's, Crate & Barrel, Gap, General Mills, Google, Hyatt, JetBlue Airways, Kraft Foods, Johnson & Johnson, MasterCard, Microsoft, J. C. Penney, Facebook, X, and Redhook Ale Brewery are just a few of the major corporations funding and promoting LGBT in their public ads. The keyword "acceptance" is the focus of a campaign from MasterCard Worldwide, which offers a hashtag, AcceptanceMatters. Never before have people expected to be accepted, since that's not how the world works. However, this group must be uplifted and praised, all others must be censored and abused. Facebook is just one social media platform which offers its users 58 different ways to describe a person's gender, including "neither" and "intersex". General Mills homosexually pedophilic campaign "Lucky to be" was blasted out through Lucky Charms Cereal, a common breakfast food for children in US. Doritos, a common snack food brand, even made rainbow-colored chips. The title of this article says it all: Ads Change the Way We Think About Gays and Lesbians.

"LGBT individuals have often consolidated their identity through the acquisition of market commodities that embody this identity; because **group identity** has been **central to building political power** among disenfranchised groups, identity-based movements gain visibility through capitalism. Using **cause-related marketing helps to brand the organization**, while reinforcing the status of the LGBT citizen as a consumer and the social validation that is to be earned through consumption.... While other movements have used upscale images to get away from negative stereotypes about their communities, this practice arguably has greater impact among LGBT individuals because of the Queer sexual practices and lifestyles. Interestingly enough, this taboo has, to a great extent, been pushed to the side and **misconceptions about LGBT wealth have become the new stereotype**." - Erica Nelson

One pharmaceutical executive rose to infamy after raising the price of a drug used for AIDS-related conditions by more than 5,000% and promoted "clover gender". This gender identification was attacked as a hoax by the LGBT community because they didn't come up with it themselves. Still, Big Pharma makes Big Bucks off of Big Gays. A recent study by Harris Interactive and Witeck Combs Communications found that 74% of gay, lesbian, bisexual and transgender consumers polled said they would be less likely to buy a product from a company if they advertised on a program that expressed negative views of gays and lesbians, while only 42% of heterosexuals shared that view. That is because the gay community is ruled by hyper-emotional programming and a militaristic mindset. It has always been a violent movement since its inception.

Germany's Kim Petras became the world's youngest and most famous transsexual when he completed gender reassignment surgery at age 16. The child was allowed to start hormone therapy at age 12, so that he never went through a natural chemical change/regulation/development, permanently damaging his brain. Due to a music career that was started at a young age, in gay bars, as well as continued extensive media attention, this child's life mirrors that of every elite-owned star. Promoting the same agenda, using the exact same descriptions and sentences, this boy is young enough for your children to pay attention to everything he does. Just like pedophile promoting Sia and other elite pawns, Kim Petras was made an international star, praised by celebrities everywhere.

"Transgender should be a normal thing. I feel like a big part of normalizing it is a transgender person being known for being good at something." — Kim Petras

By 2018, a Toronto man named Paul in his 50's decided to live as a 6-year-old girl. After abandoning his wife and 7 children, he now has adoptive parents who enable his weak-minded illness. Paul stated:
"I've moved **forward** now, and I've **gone back** to being a child. I don't want to be an adult right now. I don't mind going to six. So, I've been six ever since."

He doesn't know if he's going forward or backwards anymore but his actions will have a lasting effect on his many children and the **choice** was made by him. In a study called Wholesome Homosexuality, author Christopher Drew states:
"Sexual deviance, bi-sexuality and flamboyant homosexuality are frequently rendered absent [from advertisements]. Ambiguity has the effect of allowing consumers to 'choose whether or not to see' the people in advertisements as friends or romantic couples, enabling advertisers to net a larger target audience."

In 2018, Thomas O'Carroll, a convicted British pedophile, published an essay in a peer-reviewed academic quarterly arguing for legalized pedophilia. Journalist Justin Lee described him stating:
"He's a testament to the degraded standards of interdisciplinary scholarship. He argues that in an ideal world, virtue would be understood in such a way as to include such practices and even celebrate them."

The homosexual Human Rights Campaign receives nearly $49 million in contributions annually and influences law makers and the media in the US. HRC pays out more than $11 million in salaries and spends more than a quarter of a million dollars every year on lobbying Congress. The organization embraces pedophilia and attacks and slanders all who oppose the Agender in any way. A 2019 report stated:
"1,028 of the nation's largest businesses demonstrate their commitment to LGBTQ equality and inclusion."

One of the criteria which the HRC uses is whether the businesses "**affirm coverage for transition-related care.**" In other words, these companies are forced to provide health insurance plans which cover body mutilations and cosmetic surgeries. Meanwhile as long as women have been allowed to work in the US, they are rarely allowed the amount of time off of work that they need to have a child, and for dad's it's next to impossible. In Europe both parents commonly have several months off when they have produced a new life. The HRC is focused on reducing the age of consent for sex acts with minors and changing the language of "child abuse" to "man-boy love", as homosexuality and pedophilia are pushed on the public.

In 2019 the United Nations' health agency released a revised version of the International Classification of Diseases (ICD) that reclassifies "gender identity disorder" as "gender incongruence" which is now featured under the sexual health chapter rather than the mental disorders chapter. Calling a tomato, a squash doesn't make it one. A rose by any other name, is still a rose and a mental disorder still needs to be healed and not abused further. To be labeled with a mental disorder tends to cause stress, anger, resentment, and numerous other emotions to surface in anyone suffering from it. What has changed is that now the problems are being cultivated, expanded on, encouraged, and praised rather than healed. In the same year a Chicago man was accused of sexually assaulting two 6-year-olds and an 8-year-old on repeated occasions. He told police officers that he's really "a 9-year-old trapped in an adult's body".

Don't you think serial killers also want murder to be legal so they will never be punished? Don't you think child traffickers want to be able to traffic freely and openly? All Pedophiles are serial offenders. Just as gays are serial in their partnerships. But humans are still in control of their own minds and actions if they choose to be.

Dr. Fred Berlin, a Johns Hopkins Psychologist who worked under John Money, has been instrumental in the fight to bring pedophilia into normalcy by advocating that it's a neurobiological condition. Remember, just as with homosexuality, and other pride (emotion) related problems, once the public can label it, especially as a disorder, it must be accepted and tolerated and covered by law.

> "Dr. Berlin protected the predators in his care while ignoring their acknowledged ongoing child victims." - Judith Reisman

Since children hold the internet in their hands today, apps are installing pro-LGBTP features. Snapchat implemented one in 2019 for Gay Pride MONTH containing a "love has no age" filter to help promote pedophilia. Snapchat, like Whatsapp, is still one of the most used apps of pedophiles. All one need do to see the extent of pedophilia practiced on these apps is to set up an account on any of them, with your age as low as possible and a picture of a child. It will only take a moment before you're flooded with messages from homosexuals/pedophiles. The Upz app was designed to connect **LGBTQ homeless youth**, or those at risk of becoming homeless, with emergency resources such as shelters, medical care, hotlines to prevent suicide and self-harm, and food. Pedophiles typically manipulate children into running away but now they don't have to; they just have to be there with open arms when the mob of confused and unprotected children come their way.

Anyone who has worked in child psychology or development knows how impressionable and fickle children's minds are and how easy it is for predators to talk them into doing anything. A Chinese gay dating app called Blued is forming another an app called Bluedbaby which will assist in the homosexual adoption and surrogacy. The company is trying to get into the pharmaceuticals market by applying for a license to market PrEP, an HIV-prevention drug regimen. In the gay community the constant change of partners makes dating apps for fast hookups a necessity for this lifestyle; due to the promiscuous lifestyle disease is rampant; the agenda must target children and get them into this destructive mentality. A report entitled Homosexuality and Child Sexual Abuse, shows that while homosexual men make up less than 3% of the adult male population, they commit a disproportionate number (one third or more) of child sexual molestations. This is because regardless of what they say, they are all pedophiles. They practice Luciferianism which includes the mandatory ritual of homosexuality and pedophilia which are one and the same thing. Based on a study of three large data sets, the General Social Survey, the National Health and Social Life Survey, and the U.S. Census:

"a recent study in demography estimates the number of exclusive male homosexuals in the general population at 2.5%, and the number of exclusive lesbians at 1.4%.... Pedophile themes can be found throughout "mainstream" gay literature, including fiction anthologies such as: The Penguin Book on International Gay Writing, The Gay Canon: What Every Gay Man Should Read, and A History of Gay Literature: The Male Tradition."

Apple has 2 Apple Watch designs to celebrate Pride 2020. In addition, Apple has approved a gay dating app that claims to be safe for children as young as 12, and aims to lead adults, teens and tweens to places that are "clean, social and fun". In the iTunes store, Distinc.tt is described as "an LGBT app that you can bring home to Mom!" Investors include PayPal cofounder Peter Thiel and Keith Rabois, a former executive at PayPal and LinkedIn. CEO Michael Belkin stated that he wants **"the good-taste part** of the gay stereotype to gain traction with advertisers and cross the mainstream divide".

"Youth who use these apps are, many times, also looking for partners on Facebook, Instagram, Tinder, etc. If you're using something like Grindr, the likelihood of you having a sexual relationship with this person is higher." - Dr.

Kathryn Macapagal

In 2019, 206 large corporations filed an amicus brief citing three cases where employees claimed to be fired because of their orientation, urging the US Supreme Court to ensure that gender identity, and sexual orientation are included in the prohibition of discrimination on the basis of 'sex'. At the time the discrimination law was enacted no one thought that sex meant 'sexual orientation' or 'gender identity'. As the Alliance Defending Freedom (ADF) attorneys pointed out to the Court:

"Both at the time of Title VII's enactment and today, the word 'sex' refers to a **person's status as male or female** as **objectively determined by anatomical and physiological factors**."

Soon these corporations urged the Supreme Court to redefine these terms which will continue to take place, along with forced law changes as the violent movement demands mental stunting called Tolerance. So, let's look at some more facts. Keep in mind, dear reader, this is the lifestyle you are encouraging and allowing your children and the children you know to emulate and become. Fair warning, personal protective equipment is needed beyond this point...

70% of gays estimated that they had had sex only once with over half of their partners, and gays average somewhere between 106 and 1,105 different partners per year. Homosexuals fellate almost all of their sexual contacts, ingesting semen from about half of these. Semen contains many of the germs carried in the blood, with all its medical risks. The body of a woman is designed to immediately produce an immunologic reaction when semen enters the vagina. This attacks and eliminates the foreign bacteria which is semen. This process, much like the immune systems attack against a cold or flu, normalizes with repetition as long as the woman maintains the same sexual partner for life. Each new partner activates the natural defense, weakening the entire structure of the immune system. Only with one partner can the immune system regulate, becoming used to the specific seminal fluid. This protective system is not in place in the anus, or any other part of the body used by pedophiles and homosexuals. Since the penis often has tiny lesions and most often has recently been in unsanitary places, such as a rectum, individuals become infected with hepatitis A or gonorrhea and even HIV and hepatitis B.

About 90% of gays have engaged in rectal intercourse, and about two-thirds do it regularly. Rectal sex is dangerous — for obvious reasons. It's unnatural. During rectal intercourse, the rectum becomes a mixing bowl for saliva and its germs, artificial lubricant, feces, semen, and any other germs, infections, or substances the penis has on it. Since sperm readily penetrates the rectal wall, which is only one cell thick, this causes immunologic damage, tearing and bruising of the anal wall allowing these dangerous substances to gain direct access to the blood stream. Rectal intercourse is the most efficient way to spread hepatitis B, HIV, syphilis, and a host of other blood-borne diseases which plague the pedophilic and sexually perverse communities. Tearing or ripping of the anal wall, causing hemorrhoids, fissures and more, is especially common when "toys" or "fisting" are employed. The rectum was not designed to accommodate the fist, or any objects, and those who do so can find themselves consigned to diapers for life. Very sexy.

About 80% of gays admit to licking and/or inserting their tongues into the anus of partners, and thus ingesting significant amounts of feces. In 1980, the annual incidence of hepatitis A in homosexual men was 22%, whereas no heterosexual men acquire hepatitis A. While the body has defenses against fecal germs, exposure to the amount of fecal discharge received from sodomy, from dozens of strangers each year, overwhelms the system. Ingestion of human waste is the major route of contracting hepatitis A and the enteric parasites collectively known as the Gay Bowel Syndrome. Consumption of feces has also been implicated in the transmission of typhoid fever, herpes, and cancer. In 1976, a rare airborne scarlet fever broke out among gays but missed sweeping through San Francisco. The CDC reported that 29% of the hepatitis A cases in Denver, 66% in New York, 50% in San Francisco, 56% in Toronto, 42% in Montreal and 26% in Melbourne in the first six months of 1991 were among gays.

A 1982 study suggested that "some transmission from the homosexual group to the general population may have occurred". These people do not use proper protection on themselves or you. As previously exposed, pedophiles use those who carry these diseases to recruit and infect children, deliberately. Is someone with HIV preparing your food? Sneezing in your face in a line at the store? About 10% of Alfred Kinsey's gays reported having engaged in "golden showers" (drinking or being splashed with urine). In the largest survey of gays ever conducted, 23% admitted to urine sex. In the largest random survey of gays, 29% reported urine sex. In a San Francisco study of 655 gays only 24% claimed to have been monogamous in the past year. Of these monogamous gays, 5% drank urine, 7% practiced "fisting," 33% ingested feces via anal/oral contact, 53% swallowed semen, and 59% received semen in their rectum during the previous month. Death and disease accompany promiscuous and unsanitary sexual activity.

A large percentage of gays engage in sexual torture since deviance only increases perversion. 25% of gays admitted to sex with boys 16 or younger, as adults. In a 9-state American study, 33% of the 181 males, and 22% of the 18 female teachers caught molesting students did so homosexually. 70% to 78% of gays reported having had a sexually transmitted disease. The proportion with intestinal parasites (worms, flukes, amoeba) ranged from 25% to 59%, depending on the study. Every year, a quarter or more of homosexuals visit another country. Fresh American germs get taken to Europe, Africa and Asia, and fresh pathogens from these continents travel back. Unfortunately, the danger of these exchanges does not affect only homosexuals. Travelers carried so many tropical diseases to New York City that it had to institute a tropical disease center, as gays carried HIV from New York City to the rest of the world. In 2013, the BMA (genitourinary medicine) called for the HPV immunization program to be widened to include gay men, stating:

> "The increasing incidence of HPV and development of anal lesions in gay men, particularly HIV positive gay men, is alarming... We believe that a vaccination programme with Gardasil which included this group would be of enormous benefit in reducing the increasing incidences of anal warts, anal pre-cancers, and cancers, as has been borne out in Australia."

We have already discussed vaccines...as well as the promotion of sodomy and pedophilia in religions such as Catholicism, Talmudism, Muhammadism, Buddhism, Hinduism and more, with only Christianity and Torah Judaism being the only ones who deny this perversion. Because of the number of drugs used in this promiscuous lifestyle, homosexuals have a significantly higher risk of other mental health problems as well. Suicide and HIV are the leading causes of death for those living in the homosexual/trans lifestyle. HIV is so rampant in the gay community that even WHO has "warned" all homosexuals to take Antiretroviral Drugs. As we have discussed, this drugging and vaccinating of certain communities is a tool used by the elite to control and expand the agenda. The plethora of health problems that come from these life choices result in homosexuals and trans persons having a lifespan that is shortened by 20 years, as studies show. This is your child's future. This is the future many of you reading this may already be on the path of. It is a dark, empty, and ravenous one which will consume you until the sickness in your mind and soul eeks out and kills you. This is the reason Christians are so against it because they **care** about you. Only the soulless would welcome this existence. It is unsurvivable, as individuals, and as a species.

> "Americans no longer know the difference between anger and hatred, criticism and harassment, moral condemnation, and gay bashing. They've become convinced that it's ALL intolerance." — Stephen Bransford, author of Gay Politics Vs. Colorado and America

On March 8th, 2023, UNAIDS in collaboration with the International Committee of Jurists (ICJ) and the Office of the High Commissioner for Human Rights (OHCHR), implemented a change of law enforcing a new:

> "approach to laws criminalizing conduct in relation to sex, drug use, HIV, sexual and reproductive health, homelessness and poverty."

Principle 11 of this law states that nations must adopt the following:

> "No one under the age of 18 may be held criminally liable for any conduct that does not constitute a criminal offence if committed by a person who is 18 or older."

Following Principles go on to further detail that an individual must not be charged for expressing their sexuality unless there is a lack of informed consent. Now no one may be held criminally liable for sexual acts between adults and minors.

"Consensual sexual conduct, irrespective of the type of sexual activity, the sex/ gender, sexual orientation, gender identity or gender expression of the people involved or their marital status, **may not be criminalized** in any circumstances. With respect to the enforcement of criminal law, any prescribed minimum age of consent to sex must be applied in a non-discriminatory manner. Moreover, sexual conduct involving persons below the domestically prescribed minimum age of consent to sex may be consensual in fact, if not in law." – UN Principle 16

"Kids are dying from causes of sexual activity. We aren't going to find a tombstone stating that Frankie died because he was a virgin." – A. C. Green

To those affected and suffering from homosexual programming: Do not despair. We have all fallen prey to one or more of the elite's agendas, some more strongly than others since everyone is different. People, individuals can change. It is a choice. Brainwashing takes much time and work to correct, but it is correctable. YOU can be free. Luciferian dogma, which is based on lies alone, tells you that resistance is futile, and you will be assimilated. But if you understand the prophesies of the Living God, then you can see through whatever lies the elite throw at you. If you are empty, denying your true Father, hating Truth, you will be blind and you will be fooled. No one can keep Truth from you, only yourself. When studied and understood by using free will to choose faith in Jesus and the Holy Spirit He gives to you upon that decision, the Bible as it is even today exposes all lies Satan and his followers, the elite, attempt to pull. Not only their lies but the reasons for them. The Living God gave John the knowledge of what Satan would attempt in the future and what he would accomplish and why, which he wrote in his book Apocalypsis, commonly known as Revelation, meaning Uncovering. Today the elite have made it out to be synonymous with The End of The World! Wonder why? Apocalypsis is the **exposing** of lies, **uncovering** the mystery, **taking away all confusion**. The Living God has always been the God of Truth, revealing it to whomever SEEKS. Amos 5 states:

"There are those who hate the one who upholds justice in court and detest the one who tells the truth. Therefore, the prudent keep quiet in such times, for the times are evil. Seek good, not evil, that you may live."

"I count him braver who overcomes his desires than him who conquers his enemies; for the hardest victory is over self." - Aristotle

~Dying for Truth~

Those who speak the truth and expose the corrupt elite are slaughtered in silence. True whistleblowers are killed without notice from media or the masses. The truth they died to bring you is forgotten and buried. Let's discuss some of the exceptional people who have died for you to be able to have bits of truth. While I have discussed several throughout the book, as their work was relevant to the timeline, they all deserve note.

Dan Muresan, the son of a former Romanian Minister of Agriculture who was imprisoned for embezzlement in 2012, was found dead in a Kenyan hotel room while working on President Uhuru Kenyatta's campaign in 2012. Dan had studied at the LSE in London and had coordinated election campaigns in Europe, Africa, and the US. He became the head of elections at SCL Group, Cambridge Analytica's parent company. The company used data collected from Facebook and the like, to control election outcomes. Fellow whistle-blower and friend, Chris Wylie, revealed to the New York Times and the Observer newspapers the illegal practices of Cambridge Analytica and the data harvesting that took place and speculated that his friend Dan was poisoned because of it. The police had been told not to enter his room for 24 hours. He was discovered with his laptop on his knees, the TV set on fire, and a glass of wine next to him.

> "When you work for senior politicians in a lot of these countries you don't actually make money in the electoral work, you make money in the influence brokering after the fact - and that a deal went sour." — Chris Wylie

Member of the Dominican Republic's Círculo de Locutores Dominicanos, director of the radio station, producer of the Milenio Caliente program, president of the Association of Graduates of the Universidad Central del Este and the official announcer for the Estrellas Orientales Baseball team, Luis Manuel Medina was quite popular for debating issues including corruption within law enforcement, politics, and businesses. On February 14, 2017, journalist and broadcaster, Luis, was murdered while he was broadcasting a live video at 103.5 HICC's broadcasting studio, in San Pedro de Macorís. He was shot several times, along with the station's manager, Leónidas Evangelista Martínez. Their secretary Dayana García de Hernández miraculously survived being shot in the head and in the stomach. Some reports claimed that the gunman was identified from CCTV footage as José Rodríguez, who was then believed to have murdered Luis and Leonidas. Some reports stated that two individuals entered the studio, while others stated three men were arrested, but not charged. Local media later reported that the gunman appeared to have acted alone, entering the radio station, located inside a shopping center, and opening fire without warning. Shots and shouting can be heard on the live feed, which was cut when Luis stood up to see what was happening.

Police were quick to state that they believed the shooting was a personal vendetta, and not an attack on journalism. When the event occurred, many media outlets and journalists reported their valid concerns that the case would not be investigated but rather covered up like so many before. Police have described their suspect, Jose Rodriguez, as a violent drug addict who had been deported from the US...claims his family have denied. He died under unclear circumstances. According to police who were chasing him, after they suspected him of murder, Jose killed himself. However, witnesses say he was killed during a gunfight with the police, which lasted several minutes, close to the city's fire station. Though all who knew him report that he was a gentle and polite man, his family later claimed that he went after the journalists due to their involvement in an allegedly fraudulent land scheme, resulting in a major loss of money for Jose.

10 of the 17 journalists murdered in 2016 in the region of Latin America worked for radio stations. In two of those cases, they were attacked live on air. In 2016, more than 200 people died at the hands of police in extrajudicial killings, according to the National Commission of Human Rights. Fausto Rosario, the editor of the Acento, told the Guardian:

"The extrajudicial murder of suspects is very common here. And when this happens, investigations are closed."

There was no investigation into the murder of Leonidas and Luis, but only into the land dispute.

In 2011 Tracy Lawrence had enough of her job. She had been a notary public and had uncovered the process of repossession carried out by major banks, which involved her notarizing forged documents that would force people out of their homes. Two of the title officers she named had been charged with 606 counts of falsification. They not only offered false instruments for recording and notarization but also false certifications. Tracy herself had attested that she signed tens of thousands of false documents in the fraud. After not appearing in court to be sentenced, she was found dead in her home. The death was ruled suicide and blamed on an overdose of medication.

Philip Haney exposed President Obama's terrorist group which ran America, slaughtering innocent people, during his administration. Philip studied Arabic culture and language while working as a scientist in the Middle East, before becoming a founding member of the Department of Homeland Security in 2002 as a Customs and Border Protection agriculture officer. Philip retired from DHS, also known as FEMA, in 2015. He could not continue working there after witnessing such corruption first-hand, in particular, the US Governments involvement with Islamic Terrorism due to the Obama administration's ties to the Muslim Brotherhood. Changes to national security policy were forced by the members of this group who were also placed into the highest chambers of influence. A policy known as Countering Violent Extremism emerged, downplaying the threat of supremacist Islam as unrelated to the religion and just one among many violent ideological movements. Philip had been ordered to delete hundreds of files about associates of Islamist terrorist groups. After coming forward with his concerns and attempting to tell the public about the corruption and genocide perpetrated by the government, he was brought under investigation and censored.

So, Philip decided to write a book: See Something, Say Nothing. His eyewitness accounts, supported by internal memos and documents, exposed the federal government's punishment of those who reject the elite's narrative. In a 2016 interview with Frank Gaffney, Philip explained:

"The mosque that [San Bernardino terrorist] Syed Farook attended was part of that Tablighi Jamaat network. The Obama administration deleted sixty-seven records out of the system that I had worked on as a component of the Tablighi case."

Today we are bombarded with the propaganda stating that Islam is a religion of peace, which is a direct contradiction to the Quran, as we have discussed in this book. Unfortunately, the ignorant of the world who know nothing about history or religions believe their indoctrination. On February 19, 2020, Philip Haney went missing. He was found two days later, shot in the chest, near his vehicle. His assassination occurred just weeks before he was planning to publish another book exposing the Obama administration. He and his fiancé were scheduled to be married in one month. According to the sheriff:

"Mr. Haney was located in a park-and-ride open area immediately adjacent to State Highway 16 near State Highway 124. Highway 16 is a busy state highway and used as a main travel route to and from Sacramento. The location is less than 3 miles from where he was living."

Reps. Louis Gohmert and Steve King, friends of Philip, said he carried a thumb drive containing sensitive documents, which was missing at the scene.

"He warned something could happen to him." - Jan Markell tweeted

Though it had already been officially recorded as Not a Suicide. The mainstream narrative claims that Philip is a 66-year-old suicide. Philip was murdered at 74 years of age, by cowards who are afraid of words.

"When you tear out a man's tongue, you are not proving him a liar; you're only telling the world that you fear what he might say." — George Martin

When President Obama passed the bill making it legal to assassinate anyone in the world without trial, with a drone, no one batted an eye. Following this there was a worldwide sweep, culling hundreds of reporters and journalists who were not under the control of the elite. In 2020 over 100 top medical researchers were murdered to keep them silent. Dozens of judges were killed not to mention scientists and others, in an attempt to keep the truth about the current agendas from reaching the public. You will not find out about it on the news.

Some of the British Petrolium (BP Oil) Company whistleblowers include Gregory Stone, a scientist for LSU, who died suddenly of an "unknown illness" in February 2011. The previous summer BP representatives met with him and asked him to keep his work confidential for the next 3 years. He refused and warned his colleagues against making a deal with the corrupt company which became notorious after covering up an extensive and ongoing oil spill which has contaminated and killed thousands of fish and birds and continues to destroy much of the ocean. This coverup was exposed by BP Marine Systems Engineer George, who then moved to Australia, knowing what the US does to those who speak. He spent his remaining days in the ocean, which he loved, fishing and scuba diving. One day as he was diving, his friends noticed a mass of bubbles followed by the body of George floating to the surface, dead. Although sharks kill fewer than one human per year, he was killed by a shark, making it the 3rd fatal attack in 2 months and the 4th of that year, in Australia.

George's superior, James Patrick Black was an incident commander for BP's Gulf of Mexico oil spill response team. In 2010 he was killed in a plane crash, along with two of his family members. Senator Ted Stevens had received communications from whistleblowers regarding the oil spill and published papers exposing it. After refusing a $1 million bribe from BP to stay silent, he was killed in a plane crash. Dr. Geoffrey Gardner disappeared after he began investigating the effects of the spill on birds which were dying in large amounts. He was never heard from again. Ex-Pentagon official, presidential aide, defense consultant and expert on chemical and biological weapons John Wheeler was beaten to death and thrown in the Wilmington Delaware landfill on December 31, 2010. He had begun investigating the spill.

Other BP workers who had blown the whistle on the companies' practices were jailed to keep them silent, like Mississippi Department of Marine Resources officer Anthony Nicholas Tremonte who was arrested on child porn charges, after exposing the extent of the BP Oil spill. Dr. Thomas Manton was the former President and CEO of International Oil Spill Control Corporation. He worked to expose the Gulf of Mexico's BP Oil spill. He was immediately imprisoned on false charges. While in jail he was murdered. Matthew Simmons, an executive of BP Oil and founder of Simmons & Company International, exposed the cover-up in 2010 and was found dead in his hot tub. Dr. Chintra Chaunhan was found dead from cyanide poisoning, which the news claimed was suicide. Scientist Joseph Morrissey was studying the effects of the spill on cells. He was tied up and shot to death before his house was set on fire. His wife was able to escape with their daughter, but the killers remain at large, and no leads have been followed. Some of these people were not official whistleblowers, but rather, refused to be controlled. However, like some others I will discuss, their occupations and deeds spoke to the effect that they were willing to die for the truth.

Barry Jennings was the Deputy Director of Emergency Services Department for the New York Housing Authority. On 9/11, Barry reported that he and Michael Hess, counsel to New York City Corp., had been blown back by a big explosion inside Building 7. He had been ordered to report to Mayor Rudy Giuliani on the 23rd floor which held the Office of Emergency Management. The two men were the only ones in the evacuated building. Their testimonies proved the planned demolition of the buildings and the involvement of not only the Mayor but NIST and other government organizations. The building was destroyed to cover up CIA operations and feed an insurance scam, as many have already detailed. Barry heard explosions in Building 7 before either World Trade Tower had collapsed and reported that he was stepping over bodies, contradicting the official government claim that no one died in the building.

"All this time I'm hearing all kinds of explosions. And I'm thinking maybe it's the uh, buses around me that were on fire, but, I don't see no [gesturing] you know, but I'm still hearing these explosions. When they [the rescuers] finally got to us, and they took us down, to what, what they, they, uh, called the lobby, because I asked them when we got down there I said, 'Where are we?' He said 'This was the lobby,' and I said, 'You gotta be kidding me.' Total ruins, total ruins. Now keep in mind when I came in there, the lobby had nice escalators. It was a huge lobby. And for me to see what I saw was unbelievable." — Barry Jennings

Those who were watching during this event know there were explosions and bodies dropping from the buildings, and lying all over the floors inside of them, as live footage showed. Within hours the footage was altered, obviously, and those who spoke out about it were murdered. Barry died two days before the release of the NIST Report's first draft. His family hired a private investigator to uncover the reason for his death, but after a brief search the PI refused the case, and the family immediately sold the home.

Some other 9/11 witnesses who were murdered include Beverly Eckert, who became one of the members of the 9/11 Family Steering Committee after her husband died in the attack. She became the co-chairperson for Voices of September 11, and was energetic in her activism up until her death. She was offered money by the US Government to keep silent but denied it, opting to take the corrupt to court. Because she did not comply, she was killed in an airplane crash a week before she was to meet with Obama to discuss the lawsuit.

"I never envisioned myself speaking to the public having to say anything other than about my own little life. I was just like everyone else, very complacent, very content. World events didn't seem to affect me, that's what I believed at the time. All that changed on Sept. 11th, and I guess I just found that I couldn't just sit back and be a victim." — Beverly Eckert

Kenneth Johanneman was a janitor at the World Trade Center. He witnessed and discussed the explosions that took place inside the buildings that day and rescued someone who had massive burns from the explosions at the base of the building. Because he was late to work, he was saved from the blast. A humble and real man, he was shot in the head. This was deemed suicide, like so many others.

"I was working in the basement, came down and all of the sudden the elevator blew up. I dragged a guy out, his skin was hanging off, and I dragged him out and helped him into the ambulance." — Kenneth Johanneman

Phillip Marshall worked as a pilot for the DEA and CIA. He worked with Barry Seal, who smuggled drugs for the CIA. After 9/11 Phillip wrote several books including: Lakefront Airport, False Flag 911, The Big Bamboozle:9/11 and the War on Terror., exposing the Bush administrations involvement with the Saudi Intelligence and more. A year after his last book was published, in February of 2013, Phillip and his two children and his shih tzu, Suki, were all shot to death in their California home. The children looked to be sleeping, meaning there was more than one shooter. Phillip was found lying on his back. None of the family who flew out there were allowed to attend the funeral. The public was told that Phillip went crazy and killed everyone and himself. NSA officer Wayne Madsen insisted that it was a black ops hit, which was further confirmed by neighbors and the fact that a professional cleaning crew secretly and thoroughly cleaned the scene.

Michael Doran was a good pilot and had just bought a Cirrus plane, which featured parachute technology. Shortly after take-off his plane crashed in Ohio, the parachute not being deployed, and Michael died. He had recently volunteered his services as a lawyer to 9/11 victims. Christopher Landis was a former Operations Manager for Safety Service Patrol for the Virginia Department of Transportation. He was within view of the Pentagon and witnessed the coverup. His pictures showed 9/11 "secret" agents in their government vehicles setting up the scene. About a week after he sent film makers his pictures as well as CITGO witnesses' testimony, Christopher was killed. No details were ever put out.

A commercial flight from Israel to Novosibirsk blew up over the Black Sea after being targeted by a Ukrainian surface-to-air missile, killing 5 Ukrainian microbiologists. Vladimir Psechnik was a microbiologist and top scientist in the Soviet Union's bioweapons program which used DNA sequencing. In 1989 he defected to the UK where he exposed the USSR's germ warfare program as well as a vast network of biological weapons labs. In November 2001 Vladimir was hospitalized after having a "stroke" shortly after expressing concerns that he was a targeted individual (TI). During the previous months, several of Vladimirs friends had already been targeted and killed by the KGB. The doctor, who exclaimed how unusual it was, exposed that his brain was covered in clots that happened simultaneously. Dr. Leonard Horowitz states:

"There are a number of nerve agents that can mimic a stroke and leave no traces."

Also on November 21st, 2001, Benito Que, a cell biologist, and expert in DNA sequencing that could provide a genetic marker based on genetic profiling/genome specific biological warfare, was beaten with a bat by four men when walking to his vehicle outside of his lab at Miami Medical School, after receiving a call which caused him to leave. After being taken to the hospital, in a comatose state, on November 12, 2001, he died on December 6. There was no sign of trauma to his head. During this time over 100 of the leading microbiologists and germ experts, across the world, were murdered, including Dr. Robert Schwartz. While Benito wasn't a known whistleblower, given the focus of his work it's possible that he discovered something that he intended to expose. Either way, his work placed him in the way.

Australian astrophysicist Dr. Rodney Marks worked for the Smithsonian Society at the Antarctic Submillimeter Telescope and Remote Observatory which was controlled by the US National Science Foundation. One year prior, Rodney had worked at the station and was excited to return, especially since he was able to work alongside his girlfriend. After spending the day working with his infrared telescope, used to improve vision in Antarctica, Rodney suddenly became ill, having trouble breathing and seeing. After attempting to sleep it off, his symptoms only worsened, and he began to vomit blood. He saw the station's doctor, Robert Thompson, and his symptoms increased in intensity and pain. He saw Robert 3 times in one day but the doctor with his "limited resources" couldn't find what was wrong. As the intensity grew Robert decided to give him an antipsychotic to help him calm down. This sent Rodney into cardiac arrest. After attempting for 45 minutes to revive him, Rodney was declared dead on May 12, 2000. Once planes were able to fly into the area again, Rodney's body was taken home where it was autopsied. It was discovered that he had been poisoned by 150 ml of Methanol, a toxic form of alcohol used for industrial purposes, such as on observatory equipment. Robert was questioned as to why he didn't use the blood analyzing equipment, which would have easily detected this, to which he replied that he didn't use it because it was too difficult to power up, a claim that was immediately disproven. Robert then became hard to locate and nothing more was done to bring justice to Rodney as those involved became suddenly silent.

Another scientist, Robert Leslie Burghoff, was an expert in gene mapping and had been studying a virus that had been attacking cruise ships and had also spread across Texas. While walking in the Texas Medical Center, Robert was run down by a van that intentionally drove onto the sidewalk to murder him, in 2003. John Mullen, a retired nuclear research scientist, renowned for his theories and discoveries, had been working for Boeing when he was poisoned with arsenic. His girlfriend was also found dead at their home. British microbiologist, Ian Langford, is noted as one of Europe's foremost experts on environmental risks. In 2002, he was found covered in wounds, half naked, and positioned under a chair, dead. His property was also splattered with blood. During this time, over 40 leading microbiologists and scientists were murdered, the number quickly grew to over 100 in the following years and included Russian microbiologist, Valdimir Korshunov, Alexi Brushlinski, and Eugene Mallove who were all beaten to death. In Russia, 2019, 5 scientists were killed in an explosion which caused radiation spikes 25 miles away. In 2011 another grouping of nuclear scientists of the Bushehr nuclear plant were all on a plane that had taken off from Russia when the plane crashed, killing everyone aboard. In the 1980's 25 of the workers of GEC-Maconi were killed upon finishing their secret projects or deciding to leave the company. Over 70 NASA scientists were culled over a 2-year span and as in all assassinations, the patterns of the deaths of leading scientists, doctors, reporters, and others are clear.

Milton William Cooper wrote a book called Behold the Pale Horse, exposing the elite. Labelled a Conspiracy Theorist, he became very well known as a troublemaker for the US government. During his time in the Navy, he witnessed sub-aquatic UFO's and was forbidden to speak of it. As we already know, "aliens" live underground and under the ocean, as well as on what the mainstreamers call planets. In 1989 he released an indictment against the US government for its role in culling humans for "Aliens" (the Fallen). After this, he published his book which was then called a manifesto by The Guardian. From this time on, he ran his own radio station discussing the topics of his book. Because of his militia mindset he was soon linked by mainstream media to violent militants in the US who labeled him in order to discredit and slander. This is the tactic they use on anyone who speaks out about the elite. Meanwhile, in his lectures, he urged people not to revolt but to become involved in their own governments, as they should be naturally. Nothing changes otherwise, which is why this book is only for educational purposes, as stated in the beginning. Nothing but your personal involvement in the proper way will alter anything. It's my hope that after reading this you will understand HOW to become involved in a proper and impactful way rather than become a reactionary child as you have been thus far. After years of harassment and abuse from the US government's organizations and agents, Milton was charged with tax evasion, a common cover. In 2000 the US government named him a Major Fugitive, obviously someone far more dangerous to the people of the world than a hitman or mass-murderer. People may have used their free will to read his book! So, the following year police were sent to his home to kidnap him. Milton refused and was shot on sight.

"I've got 'em right where I want 'em. If they touch me, everyone who's ever heard me talk is gonna be absolutely enraged and is gonna know that everything I've said is true. As long as they don't touch me there's gonna be some of you who are always gonna be wondering. But eventually we're gonna bring enough proof out, and if you're here during the workshop you're gonna see an awful lot of it that's gonna prove to you that it's true. It's real. And it's happening! Okay, I've tried to cover a lot of stuff, just briefly, because there's no time in 45 minutes to get into anything very much." — Milton William Cooper

Daphne Caruana Galizia was a journalist for The Sunday Times of Malta, and Malta Independent, where she repeatedly exposed the corruption in Malta, after investigating the Panama Papers. She exposed, from these documents, how the island's prime minister and his closest political allies, worked with the ruling family of Azerbaijan on organized crime, money laundering, and more. She stated:
"I don't know why we should be surprised that organized crime has insinuated its tentacles into the highest echelons of government in Malta, using democracy for the purpose while undermining it thoroughly. If it happened in Italy and eastern Europe, it can happen here, where the institutions of state are so much weaker."

After years of harassment and stalking, having had her house set on fire and her dogs killed, her house was set on fire once again in 2006, while everyone slept. After this a 3rd pet was murdered and in 2013, she was arrested. In 2016 the Panama Papers were leaked, confirming much of what Daphne had been writing about for over a decade. In October 2017, outside of her home, she was murdered when a car bomb which had been installed in her vehicle was set off. After this, all of her enemies were now sympathizers with her remaining family, as is often seen.

In May 2015, Survey Monkey's CEO, David Goldberg, was discovered lifeless. Along with a White House source, David had been warning about the government's involvement in major events, such as 9/11 and Israel's control of the US. David also discussed what he called Project Zyphr and Project Pogo, plans to disrupt the global economy, and eliminate targeted political dissidents from 2020-2021 under the guise of a worldwide viral outbreak. This, as we have already discussed, took place. David detailed another plan to eliminate 15 million Americans through disease, accidents, and outright murder. The projects he disclosed were further validated by documents leaked, which detail the elite's desire to collapse the economy in order to force people to call for a global government. These projects were also exposed and detailed during the Jade Helm drills of 2015 and confirmed by numerous whistleblowers including those from the FBI. David also stated that President Trump would title himself King of Israel, which Trump and Wayn Root, 3 months after David's death, both proclaimed. After David was found dead in his apartment, his friends gained access to his accounts and uncovered top-secret government documents and White House memos related to the planned Iran War as well as a note left by David which stated:

"595,000 sq. ft. 41 levels, 5000 kids, ages 2-12 prisoners."

Immediately all reports of David's death noted that he fell while running on his treadmill. He had blunt force trauma to his head and died of blood loss, according to the autopsy. His friends noted that many things were taken without explanation, but they were still able to retrieve certain items.

Journalist Sean Hoare was forced to live the life of a rockstar to fit into his job at News of the World. As his health deteriorated, so did his work. He exposed numerous counts of phone tapping and deliberate pinging to pinpoint locations of sources and others and in 2010 Scotland Yard got involved. In police interviews and interviews with various newspapers, he exposed the involvement of his bosses, including Andy Coulson, who ordered his staff to hack phones and voicemails to get stories.

"I know, we all know, that the hacking and other stuff is endemic. Because there is so much intimidation. In the newsroom, you have people being fired, breaking down in tears, hitting the bottle... I was paid to go out and take drugs with rock stars - get drunk with them, take pills with them, take cocaine with them. It was so competitive. You are going to go beyond the call of duty. You are going to do things that no sane man would do. You're in a machine." — Sean Hoare

Following his interview with the New York Times, The Guardian soon contacted him, to inquire about the injuries he had when talking to the Times. Over the following week he was not able to be reached and on the 18th of July 2011, police found him dead in his home, cause unknown. His interest in the phone hacking scandal was then attributed to his drinking problem and ignored.

Serena Shim was born in Michigan, to a Lebanese family. In 2007 she began working for Press TV and travelled to the Middle East to report on events in Syria, Turkey, Iraq, Lebanon, and elsewhere. In 2014 she was accused of being a spy for Turkish intelligence and reported that she had been threatened by Turkish authorities. Understanding that Turkey is one of many countries who ruthlessly persecutes reporters, she continued in her work. Meanwhile other journalists questioned her claims, minimizing her reality. While she was reporting on the Siege of Kobani, an ISIL attack, she was on her way to her hotel after a long day. Her cousin was driving and noticed a large truck behind them, speeding up. Continuing in the proper lane, Serena's cousin reported that soon the truck had begun to pass them when it suddenly veered, intentionally crashing into them. Serena's cousin walked away with minor injuries while Serena herself, being the target, was killed.

Serena's death came just days after she spoke on camera of her fears of being arrested, and how Turkish agents had accused her of spying after one of her reports suggested ISIS militants were being smuggled back and forth over the Syrian border in the back of aid vehicles. The truck driver was never named, and the Turkish government claimed it was the fault of the women, as one would expect. After the accident Selena's cousin was taken to a nearby hospital while Selena was taken to one more than 2 hours away. While numerous photos of the accident were produced, none included the car the women had rented and driven. Meanwhile, Selena's family wasn't informed of her death and when they viewed her body before burial, there were no marks to be found. Today, the US will not investigate the deaths of its citizens when they take place overseas, which made it convenient for them to ignore the Shim family.

Sergei Magnitsky was a Russian tax lawyer who, in 2009, investigated a massive $230 million fraud involving Russian tax officials. Sergei had previously worked as an auditor at the Moscow law firm Firestone Duncan, representing Hermitage Capital Management, an investment advisory firm co-founded by Bill Browder. Soon Hermitage faced accusations of tax evasion and fraud by the Russian Interior Ministry and in 2007 the Hermitage and Firestone Duncan offices were raided by Russian officers. The raids were irregular and materials unrelated to the allegations were seized. Sergei was then given the job of investigating one of the firms maintained by Hermitage which had been accused of an unpaid debt of hundreds of millions of dollars. This finger-pointing and accusations went back and forth but during his investigation, Sergei discovered the truth about how the world really works.

Sergei's investigation revealed that police, judiciary, tax officials, bankers, and the Russian mafia were all involved in the scheme. The documents taken by the police in 2007 had been used to forge a change in ownership of Hermitage. Forged contracts claimed that Hermitage owed $1 billion to shell companies and the owner was revealed to be convicted murderer Viktor Markelov. The fake debt made the companies look unprofitable, and they were given a substantial tax refund. The fraudulent tax refund of $230 million, the largest in Russian history, was uncovered by Sergei who then exposed the fraud. After pointing out how governments work, Sergei was then charged with crimes, arrested, and imprisoned in 2008 at Moscow's Butyrka Prison. Those involved in the tax fraud were never questioned. Why would they be when the government of Russia knew about hem all along?

In prison, being poorly treated and under a great deal of stress as those who are falsely accused and forced into confinement often are, Sergei developed a number of health problems, for which he was denied proper care. Sergei was tied to his bed and beaten to death by 8 guards. According to the official death certificate, Sergei died from a "closed cerebral cranial injury", in addition to the pre-existing conditions. Post-mortem examinations revealed numerous bruises and wounds on his legs and hands. The Moscow Public Oversight Commission, an independent investigatory body, reported in December 2009 that "psychological and physical pressure was exerted upon" Sergei. This is the main reason innocent people are imprisoned: to silence them without repercussion.

However, the circumstances of Sergei's death gained international attention, after the fact, and the US Congress passed the Magnitsky Act in 2012 which froze US assets of Russian investigators and prosecutors involved in illegal detention and death of Sergei. That year, President Putin claimed that he died of a heart attack. In 2016 the Global Magnitsky Act was written, authorizing the US government to sanction foreign government officials involved in human rights offenses. After his death, Sergei's family hired lawyer Nikolai Gorokhov to fight on their behalf and attempt to achieve some justice for Sergei's abuse and murder. In 2017, Nikolai was thrown off a 4th floor balcony, just before he was to give evidence in court. He survived this and 2 other attempts on his life while 8 others involved in this case were murdered. As the outrage continues, more activists in this cause have been poisoned and killed off.

Alexander Perepilichnyy was another employee who defected to the UK in 2009, as the Hermitage fraud had been exposed. In a Swiss inquiry, he provided extensive evidence against corrupt Russian officials involved in a money-laundering scheme. While out on his routine jog, Alexander became the 4th person linked to the Magnitsky case to have been killed after he was found dead on the side of the road by a neighbor, in 2012.

In 2003, Dr. David Kelly, formerly a United Nations weapons inspector and member of the Ministry of Defence in the UK, became one of over 50 top scientists in the world who were murdered in that decade. During the build-up to the Iraq War, the UK government, led by PM Tony Blair, released a dossier that claimed Iraq possessed weapons of mass destruction and posed an imminent threat. David was named as the source for a BBC report that challenged the accuracy of the PM's claim, stating that the government simply wanted to go to war and made up the excuse. On the 15th of July 2003, Dr. David Kelly appeared before a parliamentary committee where he was questioned about his contact with the media and the government's handling of intelligence. A few days later his body was "found near his home in Oxfordshire". According to the coverup story, this brilliant doctor walked into the woods near his home, ate a couple dozen opiates, slit his left wrist, and died. David planned to publish a book exposing the government's work to weaponize Ebola and other deadly pathogens which were modified to attack specific targets. Before he was murdered, he had told friend Martin Bengtsson of this and his plans to move to the US as people involved in the development of the weapon were being eliminated. After being given a ride by MI6 agents, and attacked by the media, David, not giving in to threats or intimidation, was murdered. His murder is forbidden to be investigated, by order of the UK government.

Surendra Kumar Shakya was the general manager at Madhya Pradesh Warehousing and Logistic Corporation in Shahpura. He exposed, in June 2014, how 2 lakh quintals of wheat, which equals 200,000 kilograms, went missing in one years' time. He also exposed how in Jabalpur 23,000 quintals (2,300,000 kilograms) had gone missing in the same time span. Having collected evidence, after exposing the company's multi-core wheat scam, he was harassed by the company. In July 2015 he was found dead in his home. In his possession were celphos tablets, wrapped in paper, and a liquid sample of pesticide as well. He likely intended to have these samples tested or used as proof of something he had been working on. His handwritten notes were also found, naming people involved and more. Police covered up the crime and labeled it a suicide.

Shehla Masood was an activist for wildlife preservation and the secretary of NGO Udai. Shehla led a life of relentless pursuit of justice and environmental activism in India. In 2005, utilizing the Right to Information Act as a tool to uncover corruption and misuse of state funds, she focused on environmental issues, particularly the nexus between politicians and officials. She co-founded RTI Anonymous, a service for whistle blowers filing anonymous Right to Information. In her research she uncovered financial irregularities and corruption at the highest levels of government, such as the $4.7 billion diamond mining project initiated by international mining giant Rio Tinto in the Chhatarpur district of Madhya Pradesh. She filed numerous RTI applications and engaged in direct action, including contesting a court case aimed at putting a stop to the mining.

Shehla's advocacy placed her in the spotlight of influential figures associated with the ruling Bharatiya Janata Party, who perceived her as a threat. Despite facing intimidation and threats to her life, Shehla was undeterred, expressing her fears publicly but continuing the fight for good governance and environmental conservation. On August 16, 2011, Shehla was about to join the anti-government protest to bring the Jan-Lokpal Bill when she was found shot to death in the driver's seat of her car outside her Bhopal home. Although there was no weapon at the scene, it was labelled a suicide. The family demanded an investigation, and the case was given to the Central Bureau of Investigation, revealing flaws right away. Four people were tried and convicted of the conspiracy of her murder.

In the ever-growing list of dead whistleblowers from India, Lalit Mehta is included. Lalit was an activist with the Right to Food and Right to Work and worked to expose the corruption in the National Rural Employment Guarantee Programme in Jharkhand. He was working on a social audit of NREGP works in the Palamau district when he was murdered in May 2008. No arrests were made and like most assassinations, the police acknowledge that he was targeted for revealing the truth. The Chief Minister of Jharkhand, Madhu Koda, offered reassurance in the form of a blatant and obvious lie, stating that those involved in exposing corruption will be protected.

In 2016, Sundar Singh Jadhav exposed kidney harvesting and trafficking carried out at Mumbai's renowned Hiranandani hospital. This is a common practice in hospitals as one can guess. He was not only a victim of India's illegal organ trafficking network but became a notable whistleblower of the case. The Hiranandani case quickly become notorious when around the same time in Delhi, another organ transplant racket was exposed at the Apollo hospital. The revelation that kidney trafficking occurred in major urban private hospitals was shocking and Sundar's story received extensive coverage from both Indian and international media. Sundar detailed to the media how he was manipulated into giving up his kidney in 2016, after being promised a sum of money by an agent. Unfortunately, this happens often in poverty-stricken regions. Remember, the elite love the poor. Determined to expose the scam, Sundar's information led to the arrest of 14 individuals in the Hiranandani case, including the hospital's CEO, doctors, and organ transplant coordinator. As his international fame grew, because of this exposure, so did the threats on his life. Soon his health deteriorated. No convictions were ever made in the case, and he was left abandoned. In October of 2019 Sundar's decomposed body was found hanging from a ceiling fan in his home. This was immediately labelled a suicide and ignored.

Aaron Swartz was a computer programmer who developed RSS format which most use today. Until 2007 he worked to make Reddit what it used to be, when it was free. In 2010 he was drawn into Harvard, where he became surrounded by those who control others. Being an avid activist, he strived to make information free to the public. One day he decided to release what should be public information and logged into his MIT account and began downloading large amounts of JSTOR documents, which he then made public. Immediately he was charged by the government disproportionately and given outrageous sentences, as the US often does with hackers. The US has consistently used the overkill technique to "make an example" rather than enact any sort of justice as the Justice System of the US is just as corrupt as that of every other country, if not more so. The university dropped all charges as it was not a huge problem, but the Federal government of the US insisted on persecuting the boy in their personal vendetta. As his family details, he was mercilessly stalked, bullied, and psychologically tortured before he was found hanging in his apartment in 2013.

"If this is the price to be paid for an idea, then let us pay. There is no need of being troubled about it, afraid or ashamed. This is the time to boldly say:
Yes, I believe in the displacement of this system of injustice by a just one. I believe in the end of starvation, exposure, and the crimes caused by them. I believe in the human soul regnant over all laws which man has made or will make. I believe there is no peace now, and there will never be peace, so long as one rules over another. I believe in the total disintegration and dissolution of the principle and practice of authority. I am an Anarchist and if, for this, you condemn me, I stand ready to receive your condemnation." — Voltairine de Cleyre

Dr. Udo Ulfkotte was the editor for Frankfurter Allgemeine Zeitung, one of the largest newspapers in Germany. Before this, he had lived in multiple countries in the middle east before returning to Germany where he joined an anti-Islamist movement and fought against the ever-increasing Islamization of the country. After being involved in and founding a few political groups which were aimed at stopping the Muslim takeover, he published his book, Bought Journalists. The book was subsequently suppressed because it exposed how the CIA pays journalists in Germany, France, Britain, Australia, and New Zealand to plant fake stories. This had been going on for many decades, and occurs in many more countries than this, but still Udo was persecuted for his words. Udo had survived several heart attacks, which we know are easily brought on by the CIA's weaponry. On January 3rd, 2017, he was found dead, only ten months after he exposed collusion between the CIA and German Intelligence, another common practice between the CIA and all sub-order SS which are the SS of every other country.

"When I told the Frankfurter Allgemeine Zeitung (Ulfkotte's newspaper) that I would publish the book, their lawyers sent me a letter threatening with all legal consequences if I would publish any names or secrets - but I don't mind. You see, I don't have children to take care of." — Udo Ulfkotte

On June 19, 2015, Dr. Jeff Bradstreet was shot in the chest and left in a river. His death was the beginning of a murder spree that eliminated over 85 holistic doctors, most of whom were Christians. It was ruled a suicide, easily ignored by the public. But why? He had found a way to cure autism after it had been created by vaccines. Being one of many who exposed the vaccine poisoning of children, Jeff treated over 2,000 autistic children with GcMAF, a modified vitamin D-binding protein. Because of his natural treatment, 85% of his patients improved and 15% were cured entirely of autism. As his successes grew, he had to be stopped. On June 6th, 2015, a search warrant was put out on his office which detailed the items to be confiscated were his cures and research. Jeff was outspoken about the fact that autistic homeschool children, who are traditionally Christian and therefore unvaccinated, are "nowhere to be found". Autism doesn't exist outside of toxins transmitted via vaccine, just like many cancers and other health problems.

On the day Jeff was murdered, 4 other doctors were murdered in Mexico, one week after several others had been found in much the same condition. Their families revealed that the bodies returned to them to be buried were not the bodies of their family members. As more and more bodies of Christian holistic doctors turned up dead, even more went missing. June 21, 2015, Dr. Barron Holt, and Dr. Bruce Hedendal, both chiropractors, with the same initials, were found dead. Barron is said to have died from a Molly overdose, while Bruce had been found dead in his car. The cause of his death was never mentioned. He wasn't even given a made-up story like the others, just silence. Bruce, Barron, Jeff, and several others worked together like many other natural doctors, to fight against the FDA. Their work proved that cancer enzymes were added to vaccines, among other things.

In 2018 Timothy Cunningham went missing after complaining to friends and family that he felt sick. After several weeks with no word, a $10,000 reward was offered by Atlanta Crimestoppers, in return for information regarding his whereabouts. Timothy had worked for the CDC for some time, as an epidemiologist. During his time there he had been sent to investigate Ebola and Zika. Just before he disappeared, he told his neighbor to delete his phone number. His wallet, car and dog had all been left behind. Two months later, Harvard graduate Timothy was found by a fisherman, who noticed his body in a hard-to-reach section of the river. His death was labeled as suicide by drowning. He was still wearing his jogging clothes. The CDC, like BP Oil, DynCorp and other elite-controlled companies is known for eliminating employees who know too much and who would speak out about the child-killing corporation. Other workers including Dr. William Thompson had previously come forward to expose the CDC's cover-up and media control regarding MMR vaccines that cause autism and death.

Dr. Sebi, born Alfredo Bowman, was a world-renowned vegetarian herbalist, healer, pathologist, and biochemist who exposed the cure for AIDS, HIV, Cancer, and other so-called terminal illnesses. Governments went after him for decades to try to find a way to silence him. After being charged with the crime of curing AIDS, in 1988, a judge asked Dr. Sebi to bring in one patient who could testify that he had cured him or her of these potentially fatal diseases. He provided 77 patients and won the case. In 2016, he was arrested by the Honduras' FBI for money laundering. He was kept in jail for months without trial. During his custody, he was rushed to a local hospital reportedly suffering from complications of pneumonia and died.

Dr. Dean Lorich was a recognized orthopedic trauma surgeon who worked on a medical team that was sent to Haiti following the 2010 earthquake. He worked with the Clinton Foundation, which raised $28 million for Haiti disaster relief, and exposed his findings that the Foundation was not helping much at all. During this time, many of the Clinton Foundation workers turned up dead, and DNC workers were soon murdered as well. It was uncovered by others how the Clinton Foundation was used to traffic children from Haiti during this time. However, years later, in 2014, Dean, who had continued his practice in Manhattan, was sued by a former New York Giants player, Michael Cox, who claimed that he messed up surgery on his fibula which cost him a $2.3 million contract. His contract with the team had been lost because during a game he broke his leg. Other doctors who saw him after his surgery noted that the bone in his leg couldn't be salvaged because it had deteriorated too much. Nevertheless, someone must be blamed and forced to pay whoever "feels" they are owed something. The well-known surgeon operated on many "stars", including Bono. On December 10, 2017, Dean was found dead in his apartment with a knife sticking out of his chest. A knife which missed his heart... This was ruled suicide, as most murders are and the details were never released, no investigation ensued. After Dean's death, Michael Cox was awarded $28.5 million.

In 2016 Bill Clinton was exposed as having met secretly on a tarmac with Attorney General Loretta Lynch. This meeting took place just days before Hillary Clinton was to testify before the FBI regarding her mishandling of confidential information, among other things, several years after she had been exposed for her child trafficking networks, cannibalism, and fraud scams in Libya and Ukraine. The list goes on and on regarding the activities the Clintons were involved in, like every other president. As the world watched, her court room charade went off without a hitch and no sentences or charges were ever carried out. Loretta's testimony to the House Judiciary Committee and the House Committee on Oversight and Government Reform was also scripted. She described the meeting as an awkward and forced encounter, directly contradicting her earlier statements that it was a casual and social interaction. At the time that their meeting was exposed, Bill claimed that he was golfing in Phoenix which was an obvious lie given the temperature that day was 110 F. The only reason the public was aware of this secret and illegal meeting was thanks to the work of Christopher Sign who exposed it. In 2020 Christopher published a book called Secret on the Tarmac, detailing the meeting. Since publishing, he and his family received death threats and other harassments including having his credit cards hacked. By mid-2021 Christopher was found dead in his home. Ruled a suicide it was not investigated further, and all details of his death have been kept out of the media, thanks to the control of the elites' puppets, the Clintons.

Anthony Boudain and Kate Spade had both spoken out against the Clintons child trafficking ring, and in 2018 both were found hanging from their doorknobs, dead. Both were ruled suicide, like so many other doorknob hangings, and occurred within one week of each other. Chris Cornell also claimed to have evidence exposing the cocaine and child trafficking of the Clintons and was soon found hanging from a doorknob in a hotel room. Soon after, his friend Chester Bennington was also found dead in his home, hanging from his doorknob. On and on it goes. Many of the people associated with the Clintons who turned up murdered included those in Hollywood who were going to expose the pedophile rings that encompass Hollywood and the Whitehouse, such as Robin Williams and more recently Matthew Perry. Robin Williams had been found in August of 2014 hanging from his doorknob, by his necktie. No drugs or alcohol were present in his system, and it was ruled a suicide to hide the truth.

In 2018 actor Isaac Kappy exposed Steven Spielberg and Seth and Claire Green of pedophilia. Isaac detailed how the Greens kept children in a hidden room on their estate. After spending the following months tweeting accusations and being interviewed by journalists, Isaac stated he was not suicidal. In May 2019 Isaac "jumped" off of a bridge, in the middle of nowhere, near a military base, at 7:30 in the morning. His death was ruled a suicide and not investigated further.

Anne Heche, homosexual partner of the elite's puppet of the LGBT movement, Ellen DeGeneres, had been working on a new movie about child sex trafficking. Despite warnings to stop working on the film, she persisted. In her 2001 memoir Call Me Crazy, Anne recounted her father's sexual abuse which caused her to become an advocate for children targeted by pedophiles. Now she was working on a true story film called "Girl in Room 13" which would expose the disturbing reality of elite pedophilia. Her popularity was growing, as were the threats against her. In August 2022 Ann's car drove into a home and ignited in an inferno, after she had purchased a wig from a nearby store. Videos showed her sitting up after being placed in a body bag and talking to firefighters during her rescue. No signs of burns or damage were to be seen in the footage. The person taking the video exclaimed that the person was trying to get away. The footage also shows the men who were pushing her back into the body bag, who were not wearing the correct uniforms. Following this botched scene, she was taken not to the nearest trauma center but one that was almost 24 miles away. Mainstream media claimed she was all but dead, due to her severe burns. She was put on life support, which was taken away after one week.

In October 2023, Matthew Perry, who was working on a tell-all book that delved into the pedophilic of the entertainment industry, was murdered. After becoming a Christian, and being banned from Hollywood a decade before, he received warnings and threats from Hollywood. Like all Hollywood employees, he used drugs and alcohol to handle the perverse environment he was caught in. When living the life of an actor, a professional liar, involved in Hollywood which is controlled by the elite, one who wishes to be in the good movies will be forced to participate in the rituals which enable this. Those who don't go along never get far, and usually end up dead. Matthew was determined to speak the truth and collaborated with producers, directors, and other actors, gathering testimonies to ensure the accuracy of his revelations.

Matthew's Instagram included a video he put out just days before his death, wherein he placed three cranberries on a table, which some interpret as a reference to the 3 remaining members of the band The Cranberries. One member of the band, Dolores O'Riordan, had been found drowned in her hotel hot tub in 2018. What is it the other 3 are hiding? Due to their involvement in the music industry, they have been involved with the pedophiles who run it, and participated in the rituals allowing them to become the stars they were. In October 2023, Matthew was found in his hot tub. His death was ruled suicide and ignored.

On February 6, 2020, Li Wenliang died. He was a 34-year-old doctor who turned whistleblower after he tried to warn his colleagues of a very contagious virus. The entire group of 7 doctors were arrested and threatened to silence. Li Wenliang had spoken out on WeChat about the way the virus was handled, in Wuhan, and created a large awakening in China. Because of this, Fang Bin, a local clothing salesman, went on to become a citizen journalist on YouTube and exposed many horrendous events happening in Wuhan. He can be seen in his video, peeking into a van, and counting 8 body bags. Several live streamers, who I previously discussed, went to report on Wuhan and ended up killed for what they exposed.

Two individuals were sentenced to death for abusing detainees at the Kahrizak detention center, south of Tehran, in 2009. The trial, which concluded on June 30, 2010, involved 12 people, reported to be 11 policemen and one detainee. The 12 unnamed men were tried for committing abuses at Kahrizak, where at least peaceful protesters who had been arrested, died in custody as a result of torture following the presidential election in June 2009. The deaths of the 3 detainees were claimed to have been caused by meningitis, until forensic reports revealed they had died from severe beatings. Dr. Ramin Pourandarjani had been a physician to those injured or killed in the protests of 2009 and uncovered his governments illegal torture of political prisoners. After he testified in court regarding the prisons' corruption, in July, Kahrizak was closed by order of Iran's Supreme Leader Ali Khamenei, and many prison officials were reportedly arrested.

After he had given his testimony, Ramin was arrested and interrogated by the police force's investigative unit, the martial court, and the Physician General's regulatory council. Upon his release, he was threatened to keep silent, or he would lose his medical license. 26-year-old Ramin received many threats after his release and feared for his safety. His father, Reza-Qoli, was called and told that Ramin had broken his leg. After racing to Tehran to see his son, he discovered that Ramin was dead. The official cause of death was said to be a heart attack. After this, Ramin was said to have been poisoned. Officials then told Reza that Ramin had committed suicide at the Tehran Police Headquarters, due to depression. In addition to this case, other unresolved incidents, such as the deaths of many individuals like Ramin Qahremani, who died shortly after being released from the prison. Amnesty International has since called on Iranian authorities to disclose the full facts surrounding the case of Ramin Pourandarjani to no avail.

Karen Silkwood was a chemical technician at the Kerr-McGee plutonium plant. In the early 1970's, she became concerned about the unsafe working conditions and the lack of proper safety measures at the plant, which exposed workers to hazardous materials. She joined the Oil, Chemical and Atomic Workers Union and worked to document and expose the violations. In 1974 Karen uncovered evidence of contamination, falsified records, and inadequate safety measures at the plant. With this evidence she decided to expose the company once and for all. Unfortunately, the company knew of her plans and on November 13, 1974, as she was on her way to meet a journalist and a union representative with the evidence she had gathered, her car went off the road. When she was found, there was evidence on the rear bumper that her car had been forcibly pushed off of the road. The documents she had with her were gone, and her body had been filled with Quaaludes. After this, the Atomic Energy Commission had her organs analyzed and found a large amount of plutonium in her lungs and digestive system. Her father and three children sued Kerr-McGee for negligence which ended with a guilty verdict on the company and a $10 million settlement for the family. Books and movies have been made, immortalizing her story.

In March 2005, an engineer for Vodafone, Costas Tsalikidis, exposed spyware which targeted the phones of top officials, military officers, activists, as well as phones within the US embassy. His discovery led to an 11-month investigation by the Greek government. The investigation uncovered that Vodafone's eavesdropping transmissions took place in real-time near the US embassy in Athens. Vodafone's CEO stated that the people who planted the spyware were from the embassy. The software in Vodafone's network enabled recording conversations of up to 5000-6000 mobile numbers. In the same month that he exposed the CIA spy network of using the telecom industry to wiretap everyone, Costas was found dead in his apartment. While his family disputes the suicide verdict, it remains unchanged.

In 2006, Adamo Bove exposed a CIA operation in Italy involving the kidnapping of cleric Abu Omar, leading to outrage from Italian prosecutors. The CIA's violation of Italian sovereignty included stays at luxurious hotels and the use of unsecure cell phones for coordination. CIA Milan Chief Robert Seldon Lady's sudden departure left behind a surveillance photo of Abu Omar in his apartment, among other things. While the operation was denied, at first, it was soon exposed how the Italian government had given permission to the CIA for it. Wiretapping, a common tactic in Italy, revealed a Sismi spy den with dossiers on enemies of the government. Italian telecommunications security expert Adamo had been assisting in the investigation after he had exposed the CIA's kidnapping of Abu Omar. He was an investigator and leading expert on electronic surveillance who was hired by Telecom Italia to manage their Radar software system. This is how he found a flaw that allowed anonymous access to the system. He used mobile phone records to trace over two dozen American agents, exposing not only the vulnerability of Telecom Italia but it's collusion with the CIA. In July of 2006, Adamo was thrown off of an overpass and labeled a suicide. For those who are still unaware, wiretapping of every phone worldwide has been uncovered as having taken place since the creation of the NSA. Everything you do involving technology is logged. This is why people who want things kept secure only communicate in person, with no devices present.

Michael Hastings was a well-known war correspondent and investigative journalist. Having worked for Newsweek, Buzzfeed, and Rolling Stone who had just published his article about NATO General Stanley McChrystal, top commander in Afghanistan, for which he received many threats. He had published several books detailing certain events in Afghanistan and Iraq. His friends and family were harassed as well but Michael continued his work to expose the CIA and Obama's increase of illegal surveillance and how they targeted whistleblowers and reporters.

"It appears that Mr. Hastings made multiple contacts with sources directly associated with the illegal NSA domestic spying program, and either recently acquired materials and/or information about the extent of, the targets of, and the recipients of the information of domestic spying program."   - Canada Free Press

In June 2013, he contacted Wikileaks with his concerns about the FBI and several hours later he was driving his Mercedes much faster than he ever would, according to friends. In a surveillance video, which turned up later, as they seem to do in many cases...the vehicle lost control and crashed, exploding on impact...which happens in movies but not often or without tampering, in real life. As revealed, the "new" technology forced on us in our vehicles today allows agents or hackers to control anyone's car and has been used in numerous assassinations. SMART. No investigation into the crash, and no autopsy was done. Shortly after Michael was murdered, Wikileaks put out their Vault 7 documents, confirming all that Michael had worked on.

"He had been told, 'If we don't like what you write, we will hunt you down and kill you. For him to say something like that - those are his own words - that's pretty intense." - Staff Sgt. Joe Biggs

"There is no impact damage to this car. The only damage there is BLOWN OUT in the back, not smashed in the front and it obviously missed the tree as it rolled to a stop." — Jim Stone

Let's take a moment to discuss the people who have for all of their history been the true enemies of the elite. They are those who have not been selectively noticed but who have been wiped off the face of the earth in silence, ignored and even hated by you, throughout history.

In the 50's AD Emperor Nero Claudius Caesar Augustus Germanicus put Christians to death while mocking them. He had their bodies covered with animal skins and confined them to areas where wild dogs would devour them. He nailed them to crosses and covered them with flammable materials, setting them on fire to light his garden by night. In 95 AD Emperor Domitian instituted a culling in which thousands of Christians were murdered in Rome and Italy. Under Emperor Trajan (98-117 AD), many Christians were murdered, among them Simeon (a son of Mary and Joseph), who was crucified in 107. Ignatius of Antioch was thrown to wild beasts in 110 AD. Pliny, the governor of Bithynia, reported the progress of his extermination of Christians in a letter to Trajan stating:

"The method I have observed towards those who have been denounced to me as Christians, is this; I interrogated them whether they were Christians; if they confessed I repeated the question twice again, adding a threat of capital punishment; if they still persevered, I ordered them to be executed....Those who denied that they were Christians, or had ever been so, who repeated after me an invocation to the gods, and offered religious rites with wine and frankincense to your statue (which I had ordered to be brought for the purpose, together with those of the gods), and finally cursed the name of Christ (none of which, it is said, those who are really Christians can be forced into performing), I thought proper to discharge.... The [pagan] temples, at least, which were once almost deserted, begin now to be frequented, and the sacred solemnities, after a long intermission, are again revived..."

Under Emperor Hadrian (117-138), Telephorus and many other Christians suffered martyrdom. Emperor Antonius Pius (138-161) and Emperor Marcus Aurelius (161-180) persecuted Christians with the enthusiasm of Nero. Under Marcus' rule, thousands were beheaded and thrown to the lions. The Games, called the Olympics, are celebrated today in honor of the elite's human sacrifice rituals. Emperor Septimius Severus (193-211) persecuted Christians in Egypt and North Africa, burning, crucifying, and beheading many. Emperor Decius (249-251) murdered untold numbers of Christians throughout Rome, North Africa, Egypt, and Asia Minor. Cyprian, Bishop of Carthage proclaimed before his execution:

"The whole world is devastated."

Emperor Diocletian (284-305) was known for the most severe persecution of Christians among the ancient Emperors.

"For ten years, Christians were hunted in cave and forest; they were burned, thrown to wild beasts, put to death by every torture cruelty could devise. It was a resolute, determined, systematic effort to abolish the Christian Name." - Henry Halley

Christian leaders killed during this time include Polycarp, John the apostle's pupil who was arrested, brought before the governor, and offered his freedom if he would curse Jesus. Polycarp was burned alive when he refused. Ignatius, also John's student, was sentenced to be thrown to wild beasts by the Emperor Trajan in Rome. Papias was martyred at Pergamum. Justin Martyr was martyred at Rome as was Iranaeus. Origen died in prison while being tortured under Emperor Decius. Millions of Christians were crucified by the Holy Roman Empire and millions more have been harvested since.

"In 312 AD, the Emperor Constantine decreed that Christianity was to be the official religion of Rome. But, of course, no one can decree that another person become a Christian. Christianity is a matter of the heart. Rome embraced Christianity, but the Romans themselves did not become Christians. People joined a religious system, but they never had a change on the inside. During the next 1,200 years, many unbiblical practices were taught by the institutional church. Church leaders did not clearly teach the biblical declaration that salvation is based on a personal relationship with Jesus Christ, and the necessity of salvation." -Richard Booker

For the first 2 centuries AD, in Rome, Christians lived in the catacombs to escape persecution. Today, an estimated 7 million Christian graves and 4 miles of inscriptions can be found in these tunnels.

In the early 1200's the Roman Catholic Crusades in southern France, slaughter approximately 20,000 citizens of Beziers, most of whom were Albigensian Christians. By the time the Roman Catholic armies finished almost the entire Christian population of southern France had been exterminated. The crusaders then went on to kill the Jews. In the 1500's, Roman Catholic armies murdered at least

900,000 Waldensian Christians of all ages. Then they went on to slaughter at least 250,000 Dutch Protestants by torture, hanging, and burning. During the reign of "Bloody Mary" Queen of England, an estimated 200 bishops, scholars, and protestants who protested the Catholic Cult, being both men and woman, were burned to death at the sake. The Anabaptists document states:

"Charles V, in 1522, established the Inquisition, and ordered all Lutheran writings to be burned. In 1525 prohibited meetings in which the Bible would be read. 1546 prohibited the printing or possession of the Bible. 1535 decreed 'death by fire' for Anabaptists. Philip II (1566-98), successor to Charles V, re-issued the edicts of his father, and with Jesuit help carried on the persecution with still greater fury. By one sentence of the Inquisition the whole population was condemned to death, and under Charles V and Philip II more than 100,000 were massacred with unbelievable brutality. Some were chained to a stake near the fire and slowly roasted to death; some were thrown into dungeons, scourged, tortured on the rack, before being burned. Women were buried alive, pressed into coffins too small, trampled down with the feet of the executioner. Protestants of Netherlands, after incredible suffering, in 1609, won their independence; Holland, on the North became Protestant; Belgium, on the South, Roman Catholic."

By 1559 there were about 400,000 Protestants in France. St. Bartholomew's Day Massacre, August 24, 1572, was the name given to the day that the French Roman Catholic knights began killing Protestants in Paris. They killed at least 10,000 Protestants in the first three days. At least 8,000 more Protestants were killed in the countryside as they fled for their lives. In the 1600's we see the Thirty Years' War. This crusade led by the Roman Catholic Jesuit Order was another attempt to exterminate all the Protestant Christians in Europe. After this there were 8 years of Jesuit orchestrated Roman Catholic murder of at least 100,000 Irish Protestants. And then in 1685, French Roman Catholic soldiers (called knights) killed approximately 500,000 French Protestants. Pope Urban VIII (1623-44), with the Jesuits, exterminated **all** the Protestant Christians in Bohemia.

"In Bohemia, by 1600, in a population of 4,000,000, 80% were Protestant. When the Hapsburgs and Jesuits had done their work, 800,000 were left, all Catholics. In Austria and Hungary half the population Protestant, but under the Hapsburgs and Jesuits they were slaughtered. In Poland, by the end of the 16th century, it seemed as if Romanism was about to be entirely swept away, but here, too, the Jesuits, by persecution, killed Reform. In Italy, the Pope's own country, the Reformation was getting a real hold; but the Inquisition got busy, and hardly a trace of Protestantism was left." - Henry Halley

From 1481 to 1808 there were at least 100,000 Christian martyrs and 1,500,000 Christians banished in Spain. During this time more and more persecuted Christians fled from Europe to the British North American colonies. Nonconformists could expect no freedom and were executed as heretics. From 606 AD until the middle of the 19th century the Roman Catholic Inquisition "Crusade" has killed an estimated 50 million "heretic" Christians in Europe.

Why this irrational hatred of Jesus? He eliminated the old rituals, bloodlines, and more, creating something that the elite could never control: Salvation Through Faith. No longer do bloodlines have significance or power. No longer do rituals cleanse us eternally. THAT is why Christians have been labeled, censored, and slaughtered.

An estimated 100,000 Christians are murdered for their faith every day, according to statistics from a Pew Research Survey and the International Society for Human Rights, a non-religious organization.

"The ethnic cleansing of Christians throughout the Middle East is one of the crimes against humanity of our time, and I am appalled that there has been little serious international protest." - Jonathan Sacks

"This is cultural and human genocide. Christians have for centuries been the bridge that connects Eastern and Western cultures. Destroying this bridge will leave an isolated, enculturated conflict zone emptied of cultural and religious diversity." - Diana Momeka

Turkey used to be 30% Christian until the Turkish government massacred 2 million Armenian Christians between 1905 and 1918. Many remaining Christians fled or faced torture, jail, and systematic discrimination and harassment. From 1941 to 1945, the Roman Catholic Ustashi in Croatia, butchered up to 1 million Serbian Orthodox Christians. Roman Catholic death squads are often led by Franciscan (Jesuit) priests, monks, and friars. This genocide was overseen by Jesuits Aloysius Stepinac and Ivan Saric. By 1979, when the reign of self-appointed President of Uganda Idi Amin had finally been toppled by Tanzanian troops, some 500,000 Ugandans had been murdered; 300,000 of them were Christians. During the past 30 years, 30,000 Chiapas Christians have been driven from their homes and hundreds have been murdered. In 1997, around 5,000 Christians fled, after 500 were killed. Now in "modern" civilization we have government organizations taking children from their Christian families in Germany, UK, America and elsewhere on behalf of the Jesuits.

Since the fall of the USSR, thousands of Christian prisoners have been released and are free to be Christian. During the 70 years of Soviet Communism, around 20 million Christians were murdered. In the past 20 years, during a 6-year span, more than 1.3 million Christians and other non-Muslim people were killed in Sudan. This is more than Bosnia, Chechnya and Haiti combined.

Before 2003 there were 2 million Christians in Iraq. Now there are maybe 180,000. In the 10 years before Mosul fell to the CIA's ISIS, an estimated 500,000 Christians fled Iraq, leaving possessions and homes behind. This is the agenda of ISIS. It is **always** about the elimination of the Followers of Christ. Christians were not allowed to sell their homes; they had to simply leave. Christians houses are marked with an N for "Nasrani", meaning Christian. Father Douglas Bazi, was captured and tortured by al-Qaeda in Iraq in 2006 and recalled:

"The Muslim guy, he went to the Christian's door (who had been his neighbor for 30 years) and knocked and said, 'did you hear about the decree, the announcement is to leave in 24 hours by Allah's name, and if I see you here tomorrow, I'm going to kill you because I have the right to take your home'."

In June 2014 ISIS gave Christians the option of leaving or staying and being killed. They had 24 hours to decide.

"ISIS said kill the Muslims, not just the infidels. They started with killing the Muslims that aren't according to Sharia, so imagine how they look at us. Overnight 100,000 Christians escaped from Mosul and escaped from ISIS. When they arrived and took over Mosul they told the people we have three conditions according to Sharia. Number one was convert. The second was to pay Jizya (Islamic taxes) and they asked for each person to pay 4,000 to 8,000 US dollars. (It is a US agency after all) Third, they said you have to leave or you will be beheaded...

Overnight 100,000 Christians escaped from Mosul and escaped from ISIS. When they arrived and took over Mosul they told the people we have three conditions according to Sharia. Number one was convert. The second was to pay Jizya (Islamic taxes) and they asked for each person to pay 4,000 to 8,000 US dollars. (It is a US agency after all) Third, they said you have to leave or you will be beheaded." — Douglas Bazi

In many cases, the Christians who get out of these severely violent countries alive, still have loved ones left behind. If they say anything outside, their family inside Iraq will be identified and pay for it. Muslim Brotherhood member, Barack Obama released a statement in 2015 accusing ISIS of committing genocide against religious minorities. One reporter, Raymond Ibrahim, revealed that one Christian is slaughtered **every 5 minutes**. In his article he relayed:

"Father Behnam Benoka, an Iraqi priest, explained in a detailed letter to Pope Francis the horrors Mideast Christians are experiencing. To his joy, the pope called the Middle Eastern priest and told him that "I will never leave you." As Benoka put it, "He called me. He told me certainly, sure I am with you, I will don't forget you... I will make all possible to help you."

However, later in September, when Pope Francis stood before the world at the United Nations, his energy was, once again, spent on defending the environment. In his entire speech, which lasted nearly 50 minutes, only once did Francis make reference to persecuted Christians - and even then they did not receive special attention but, in the same breath, their sufferings were merged in the same sentence with the supposedly equal sufferings of "members of the majority religion," that is, Sunni Muslims (the only group not to be attacked by ISIS, a Sunni organization).

Yet, as the following roundup from September shows, "members of the majority religion" - Sunnis -- are not being slaughtered, beheaded, and raped for their faith; are not having their mosques bombed and burned; are not being jailed or killed for apostasy, blasphemy, or proselytization."

In 2013 Reuters announced over 100 million Christians were persecuted worldwide.

It has always been illegal to be a Christian in China, but in 2019 China warned Christians not to speak up about persecution, in a call for silence. If authorities release someone after interrogation, they are then committed to silence. As always, snitches are rewarded. The Guangzhou Department of Ethnic and Religious Affairs is offering about 10,000 yuan (2 months wages) to anyone who has verified information about and can help hunt down Christians. During China's Cultural Revolution, which started in 1966, 30 million Chinese were slaughtered, the target group were Christians. Only 300,000 Christians were left when the Communist government decided to scatter them throughout China and restrict them to discourage their faith. This enabled the remaining Christians to spread their faith throughout China, causing even more to believe in the Living God. 3,000 Chinese Christians were killed between 2000 and 2007. In China today Christians are put in harsh labor camps and prisons, for speaking about Christ, or being involved in Bible distribution or 'underground' house churches. Meanwhile, North Korea views Christianity as a direct threat to the nation. There, Christians aren't simply killed for their faith in Christ, they are pulverized with steamrollers, used to test biological weapons, shipped off to death camps or shot in front of children, while newborn babies have their brains pithed with forceps in front of their mothers. This behavior began in 1910 under the rule of Japan after which, in 1950, the Soviet Communism took control and continues today. This systematic murder of Christians has picked up speed under President Xi Jinping. Lawyers and activists who attempt to defend or speak for Christians are arrested. In January 2018, the Chinese People's Armed Police used excavators and dynamite to destroy a Christian Church in the city of Linfen, Shanxi province.

"The person who exposes that information, (that they were interrogated) which is called revealing state secrets, can face between 7 to 15 years in prison simply for indicating that they were interrogated...if governments around the world recognize that the Chinese government is engaged in religious persecution, this creates real problems for the Chinese government." -Eric Foley of Voice of the Martyrs

"China is trying to cut off the growth of Christianity and other religions by cutting off the pipeline - stopping the religious education of children." - Thomas Farr, president of the Religious Freedom Institute

In Denmark and other European and Scandinavian countries, Christians are equally persecuted, as they are in the rest of the world. One pastor, Torben Sondergaard had to flee in the night with his family, to the US as Danish authorities were going to arrest him and his wife the following day for preaching the Bible. Their children were to be taken from them and placed under the care of the government. Like many countries, no one in Denmark can preach the Bible but must send the speech they intend to give to the government to be regulated and approved first. Like all European and Scandinavian countries, the government leaders are all Freemasons and Jesuit puppets working for the Vatican. Teachers also must "profess that their teachings are compatible with the philosophy of the Chinese government and support the Chinese Communist Party". As usual, this has been backed by the Vatican's provisional agreement, which church and Chinese officials signed in September 2018. Singaporean Prime Minister Lee Hsien Loong stated:

"There is no irreconcilable ideological divide between the US and China."

Let's remember why there are so many Christ Followers murdered each year, unnoticed and unmentioned. Christians are the ones who know what is coming next. They are the ones who expose the elite's plans without speaking a work, as it is written. They will forever be the ones proclaiming the truth and being culled in the elite's attempt to control the world and form the Global Government. Let's continue.

As a police detective Mark Minne became aware of corruption, particularly the child trafficking carried out by the Apartheid government of South Africa. He published a book called The Lost Boys of Bird Island, exposing this trafficking ring on August 5, 2018, exposing high-level government officials and elite involved in trafficking children though Bird Island. As previous authors had exposed, before they were murdered, many children in these rings are tortured and murdered. When children become sick or injured or when they simply don't listen to the commands of the adults who have stolen them, they are put down like rabid dogs. Because of his work, many people came to him to expose in greater detail the activities of the ring. His friends and family have stated that he was afraid for his life, knowing what these people do to those who expose them. Corrupt and weak people only work in the darkness, and once light is shined on them, they react like wild animals, all they know is attack as they cannot handle the truth. Mark planned to write another book, to include the new evidence. On August 14, Mark was found shot to death. Police who investigated the scene noted that the suicide note found there was like others they had seen, obviously fake.

Val Broeksmit, born Valentin Gregory Cherednichenko in Ukraine, had been adopted by William Broeksmit, a recently retired executive at Deutsche Bank AG. After the unexpected death of his father, who was found hanging in his home in 2014, Val gained access to his father's documents, through his email. The death was ruled a suicide and written off, like the handful of other Deutsche Bank employees who died in a 5-year span. William Broeksmit had worked at Merrill Lynch in the 1990's with Anshu Jain, Deutsche Bank's co-chief executive officer. His confidential files exposed Deutsche Bank's involvement in money laundering and dealings with Russia and the Trump Organization. Val decided to become an informer and for 5 years, naively teased the FBI, congressional investigators, and journalists with information implicating the bank. Val Broeksmit's life took a controversial turn when, as a certified informer, he gained access to embarrassing documents stolen from Sony Pictures Entertainment. This incident, along with sharing banking files with the Financial Times, caught the attention of the FBI and led to connections with notable figures such as Rep. Adam Schiff. Deutsche Bank agreed to pay $130 million to end the investigations. In April of 2022, Val's body was found on a High School campus in Los Angeles, a school and city he has no connection to, after missing for almost a month. This too was ruled a suicide and ignored.

Speaking of bank whistleblowers, Bradley Charles Birkenfeld gained international attention when he decided to expose the widespread tax evasion practices within Swiss banking. Bradley worked in finance, with the Union Bank of Switzerland in the early 2000's where he became aware of the bank's involvement in helping clients evade taxes by hiding assets in offshore accounts. In 2007, he provided detailed information to the US Department of Justice, Internal Revenue Service, and the Senate Permanent Subcommittee on Investigations about UBS's practices. His revelations led to a series of investigations and legal actions against the bank, resulting in billions of dollars in fines to UBS. In 2008, he was indicted by the US, for his involvement in the tax evasion scheme with UBS. In 2009, Bradley pleaded guilty to charges of conspiracy to defraud the US and was sentenced to over three years in prison but was given credit for time served. He remains alive, so far.

Gabriela Conteras worked for the Lewis Corrections Department in Arizona. After witnessing the extreme environment within the prison, she leaked surveillance tapes which detailed the lack of security and uncontrolled violence. One segment of the video recorded an officer who was ambushed and beaten by 15 inmates who had freely opened their own cells. This was something that had been going on for years. Prisoners unable to open their doors are subjected to attacks as are the guards. Gabriela's footage revealed the corruption on the side of the Arizona Department of Corrections which receives $5 million every year to maintain the prison. In March of 2020, after months of harassment by prison personnel and others, Gabriela was found dead in her home. No details were released about her death, but police were quick to assure the media that it would be treated as a suicide, no investigations, and no autopsy.

John McAfee, a man who everyone today knows, was a British-American entrepreneur, cybersecurity expert, and founder of the antivirus software company McAfee. After establishing McAfee, the first commercial antivirus program, his fortune had been sealed. He had been a long-time LSD addict, among other things but soon even that couldn't mask the environment he was a part of. Working too closely with people such as Bill Gates who then used his work to spy on people rather than protect them, he decided to leave in 1994 and cashed in his shares. As drugs took their toll and his eccentricities grew, John became more and more outspoken about government surveillance, corruption in the antivirus industry, and privacy-focused cryptocurrencies. His new businesses now included a cigar making company and a coffee distribution company and soon he decided to make his own antibiotics company. Needless to say, he was arrested many times in his life, sometimes for unlicensed firearms, sometimes for drugs. He was a wild and reckless man, but that doesn't take away from what he exposed over the years. After his arrest in Guatemala, he finally made his way back to the US.

Now an older man, with health problems that matched his lifestyle, John was soon charged with tax evasion, the classic charge given to those the elite cannot pin down. While in Spain, on his way to Turkey, he was arrested. As Spain was waiting to extradite him back to the US, he was found dead in his cell. His wife, knowing the forces he had fought against most of his life, also knew he was not suicidal. The last tweet John sent out was that he was content and had friends. He knew how the game is played and that once in jail, he would likely be picked off like so many before him. The last thing he told his wife was that he would call her in the evening. Before his call, he was labeled a suicide by the prison.

As people who attempt to speak out against US presidents continue dropping like flies, the list continues to grow. Dozens of people were killed during the Clinton administration, followed by many more under Obama and Trump and today Biden's administration has seen its share of whistleblower deaths as well including Ukrainian energy company's co-founder Mykola Linsin (who died in a "car crash" in 2011 when Joseph Biden was Vice-President) whose wife has been outspoken regarding the bribery Joe Robinette Biden Jr. has accepted over the years. Recently, an unnamed IRS whistleblower has come forward regarding this as well, focusing on Hunter

Biden. We will have to see what unfolds regarding this, and how long these whistleblowers are allowed to live. However, let us not forget that like Trump and Obama, and all the previous puppets of the US government, Joe also has the task of keeping the truth hidden. In the early 1980's, Philip Agee and others aimed to reveal the CIA's support for brutal dictatorships. In 1984, Joe supported the CIA's efforts to further criminalize leaking, addressing concerns about "graymailing" through his legislation, the Classified Information Procedures Act, he enabled the government to redact classified information in legal proceedings, hindering whistleblowers' ability to expose wrongdoing. CIA Director William Casey praised him for his anti-leak stance, and he went on to endorse a strict application of the Espionage Act.

"Leaked documents from the Ukrainian General Prosecutor's office indicate complex money transfers from foreign sources into the control of a 'slush fund' owned and operated by Devon Archer, John Kerry Senior, John Kerry Junior, Heinz Jr, and Hunter Biden." – Michael Coudrey

These leaked documents detail the millions of dollars and front-companies used to transfer money illegally to those named above. In November 2023 another trove of leaked documents came forth, revealing a multi-million-dollar trail linking Russian Roman Abramovich to two individuals, Sergei Roldugin and Alexander Plekhov, known friends of Vladimir Putin. The leaked documents, originating from Cyprus, show evidence of a $40 million deal in 2010 involving the transfer of shares in Video International, at a value lower than their worth. Finoto Holdings and Grosora Holdings bought a combined 25% stake in Video International in 2003. Both are owned by the Sara Trust Settlement of which Roman is a beneficiary, who then sold their stakes to Med Media Network and Namiral Trading. Meanwhile the rich get richer.

Dr. Eithan Haim anonymously exposed the illegal surgeries being performed on children in the Texas Childrens Hospital, the largest in the US, in May of 2023. The hospital has enforced the elite's agenda by implementing their aggressive transgender program. Performing permanent mutilations on children is banned in many US states, even though the agenda to form a completely homosexual country is still going strong. It is child abuse to the extreme. Eithan leaked redacted medical records of the children being abused by the corporation, editing out their names. The documents prove the hospital as well as Baylor College of Medicine were and are today pushing doctors to perform these operations on children which include but are not limited to implantable puberty blockers, cross-sex hormones, and genital surgeries. Such are the dreams of Nazi doctors. The profit margin for such deformities is quite high, as one would expect. This is all hospitals accomplish: reaping in money from their medieval butchery. Children as young as 11 have been permanently disfigured by "medical professionals". Naturally the DOJ immediately began investigating the source of the leak, not what the leak was proving. Federal agents of the Department of Health and Human Services immediately arrived at Eithan's house, finding his identity through a hospital server search. What is surprising is that he is still alive. For how long? Nothing Eithan did was illegal, as he had redacted all personal information according to the law. That matters little, as he suddenly discovered that the US is no different than the 3rd world countries discussed in US propaganda.

"I reached this unavoidable conclusion that Texas Children's Hospital is providing this outward appearance that they shut down the program, when in actuality, within the hospital, it's a very high priority... If you counter the dominant political ideology, they're going to come after you." - Eithan Haim

While he, like many others, has not been suicided yet, knowing the elite as we all do now it is only a matter of time. It's up to you to stand with him and protect him, or to continue living in ignorance of reality and watch him be murdered in front of you. You are an accomplice to all of the murders discussed here, and the thousands of others who remain unnamed. You are an accomplice, dear reader.

In 2023 Egyptian investigative journalist Mohammed Al-Alawi exposed the purchase of a luxury villa by Ukrainian President Volodymyr Zelenskyy, a drug addict and transvestite, who put the house in his mother-in-law's name. Al-Alawi reported on the purchase of the villa for $4.85 million in August, exposing the corruption and misappropriation of US financial aid to Ukraine by the elite-controlled Zelenskyy family. In December his body was discovered in Hurghada, showing fractures and bruises. His death was listed as a cerebral hemorrhage from a severe brain injury. Al-Alawi's brother stated that he received death threats after the investigation, and the police suspect an assassination by Ukrainian operatives who work to keep a lid on the US and Russian elite's control of Ukraine and the fake war.

Brandy Vaughan worked for Merck and Co. as a representative for many years until the company's drug Vioxx was exposed for causing an estimated 50,000 deaths. After leaving the company she travelled the world, speaking out against the Pharmacology Industry and founding Learn the Risk, a company promoting vaccine truth. After some time, she returned home to the US, only to discover that her property had been trespassed. This wasn't a new occurrence as her home security system showed and her harassment and threats on her life continued to increase. Investigators have revealed that high level intelligence technologies and methods were used. Planning to leave her home, she documented the abuse in a video which can still be found online. On December 8, 2019, her body was found inside her home by her 9-year-old son. No details of the cause were ever given, and no investigation was carried out. Rather, she's just another whistleblower written off while she was at the peak of health.

Another vaccine whistleblower was Italian pharmacologist and biochemical researcher Dr. Domenico Biscardi. In his research he had uncovered the use of nanotechnology, quantum dots, and Graphene in Pfizer vaccines and planned to expose his proofs to the European Parliament at the end of January 2022. After stating that he found nano-devices in Covid Vaccines, and warning that his exposure would cost big pharma billions, he was silenced. Less than 2 weeks before he was to testify before the European Parliament both he and EU Parliament President David Sassoli were found dead, one day apart. David's death was labelled a health complication while Domenico was found dead in his home and labeled a heart attack.

Babita Deokaran, exposed corruption in the Gauteng Department of Health in South Africa during the Covid event. As the chief director of financial accounting, Babita combated irregular payments and maintained the evidentiary paper trail for the Special Investigations Unit. She uncovered massive corruption at Tembisa hospital, attempting to stop $6.3 million in suspect payments she exposed potentially fraudulent transactions reaching $54.4 million. As she uncovered the corruption and exposed it, she blocked payments and initiated investigations into the many suspicious transactions at the hospital which had inflated prices for purchased medical supplies. In the days leading up to her murder, Babita warned a superior about the danger to their lives but to no avail. In August 2021, Babita was assassinated in a hit-style killing outside her home, involving 6 men who showed up and shot her 9 times. Investigative journalists, using documents found on Babita's laptop and phone, revealed the mafia's involved in procurement at the hospital and looting the budget. When the 7th man involved in the planning of Babita's murder was discovered, he was found dead. Because of the public nature of her death, she could not be ruled a suicide. Nevertheless, no justice has been done.

Janet Ossebaard was a Dutch documentary filmmaker, photographer, author, and cereologist, who worked as a freelance coach and trainer, and trained as a naturopathic therapist. In 1994 she encountered a crop circle near Witten which led to her beginning her research into them. She mapped circles, took soil samples, and produced documentaries on the subject, and was convinced of their extraterrestrial origin. In 2005, she became chairman of the Dutch Centre for Crop Circle Studies and continued publishing on crop circles. In March 2020, she suddenly appeared as a corona expert and spoke about attacking Prime Minister Mark Rutte on podcasts. In November of 2023, after missing for several weeks, Janet was found dead. Ruled a suicide, she will be remembered by the Conspiracy Theory community due to her work with MI6 agent Qanon.

Geologist Philip Schneider worked for various US government and private organizations. In the early 1990's he began revealing classified information about his involvement in the construction of deep underground military bases (DUMBs) which speckle every continent of the world and connect under the oceans. He worked on top-secret projects, including the development of advanced technologies. During his work there was a misunderstanding and consequential battle between US personnel and the greys, causing him to lose 2 fingers and his toenails, as well as leaving him with a burned foot and a large scar on his chest, from a beamed weapon, in 1979. In the 1990's, he was diagnosed with a terminal illness, due to the materials he had been exposed to. He decided that it was then time to expose his work and knowledge to the world and he began giving lectures. During his lectures, which can still be found online, he stated:

"I was involved in building an addition to the deep underground military base at Dulce, which is probably the deepest base. My job was to go down the holes and check the rock samples and recommend the explosive to deal with the particular rock...As I was headed down there, we found ourselves amidst a large cavern that was full of outer-space aliens, otherwise known as large Greys. I shot two of them. At that time, there were 30 people down there. About 40 more came down after this started, and all of them got killed. We had surprised a whole underground base of existing aliens."

Philip exposed the American collusion with aliens, since the 1950's, as we previously discussed, as well as the fact that technology as we know it today is reverse engineered alien tech. He also exposed that a vacuum was needed to create special metals, which is the reason for the International Space Station and others. Among the technologies that he exposed was the US' earthquake device which was responsible for several earthquakes. As mentioned before, other tech like this includes HAARP, DEWs, and more. On January 17, 1996, Philip was found in his apartment, strangled with a catheter tube which had been knotted, still wrapped around his neck. Prior to his murder he stated that over the last 22 years 11 of his friends had died, most of whom he believed were murders and not suicides as media claimed.

Mark McCandlish had offered to testify before the Senate Intelligence Committee and had contacted Senator Marco Rubio. His career was spent in defense and aerospace industry, particularly the Air Force, which is where he witnessed his first encounter with a UFO, as many Air Force personnel do. Remember the Air Force's purpose which we discussed before, dear reader. As the UFO research community will confirm, UFOs are often seen in close proximity to nuclear energy, one of numerous reasons why nuclear development is kept from many countries. Mark, an expert engineer, saw several reverse-engineered anti-gravity saucers which he detailed in his art. Naming them Alien Reproduction Vehicles, he spoke about them in great detail. Gordon Novel, Fred Bell, and James Allen are others who were killed for their knowledge about these vehicles. In April 2021, Mark was found shot to death with a shotgun in his home. It was claimed a suicide...

"The call to world unity is a prelude to disclosure of extraterrestrial life."
- Corey Goode

In 2023, Major David Grusch testified before a US House committee, revealing the existence of a long-standing US government program to retrieve unidentified flying objects. He restated what many have exposed regarding non-human biologics taken from crash sites along with their technology. While working in Air Force intelligence and the Pentagon UAP task force, David had investigated unidentified aerial phenomena until earlier in the year when he decided to disclose a multi-decade UAP crash retrieval and reverse-engineering program. The hearing featured testimonies from Ryan Graves, a former Navy pilot who almost collided with a UFO in 2014, and former Navy pilot Dave Fravor, who witnessed a "Tic Tac"-shaped object off the coast of California in 2004. David, the star witness at the hearing, stated that he had not seen the recovered alien vehicles or bodies himself. Mainstream media has immediately discredited him as mentally unstable. Meanwhile, David exposed that the US had retrieved a UFO from Benito Mussolini based on a tip from Pope Pius XII. The Vatican was involved in America's UFO retrieval program's first mission in 1933.

"1933 was the first recovery in Europe, in Magenta, Italy. They recovered a partially intact vehicle, and the Italian government moved it to a secure airbase in Italy until around 1944-1945...The Pope back-channeled that and told the Americans what the Italians had and we ended up scooping it." – David Grusch

Those who expose the Vatican's child sex rituals wind up dead as well. The Vatican has paid over $4 billion to the US alone, in settlements of these cases, so keep them hidden. Whistleblower Archbishop Carlo Maria Viganò challenged Pope Francis to address sexual misconduct and has been on the run, since August 2018 when Vatican Intelligent agents (Jesuits) began hunting him. Priest Joseph Moreno, who was found dead after collecting evidence of clergy sexual abuse. Denver priest David Nix reported cases of potential sexual misconduct involving priests to Archbishop Samuel Aquila. He remains homeless and hunted. As more and more people step forward to expose what is already known by those who live a life of awareness, we must wait and see how many more human beings end up dying for Truth.

As I stated at the beginning of this book, the information presented has been published by numerous sources preceding me. I've simply rephrased and compiled what has long been readily available to everyone and ignored. Every sentence of this book can be verified by at least 3 sources. The purpose of this book is not to accuse anyone of undisclosed matters. It's not intended to point fingers; rather, it aims to inform the ignorant and blind of historical facts. This said, I have not included my personal details here as they are not important to the book.

Nevertheless, if I were to face harm because of the written word, I would still emerge victorious. By publishing this book, I have triumphed, and my death would merely be another victory for me, as I would finally attain the peace and glory I've yearned for throughout my existence on this mind-numbing plane. The next life is the one I have been waiting for. All I have known in this world is manipulation and abuse, like most people alive today. For believers in the Living God, there is no loss and no death, only life. The individuals listed here met their fates right in front of your eyes, yet it evoked no outrage, no reaction, and no change. Consequently, my demise wouldn't make a difference. You, dear reader, would remain indifferent and inactive.

In bidding you farewell, my dearest of readers, remember that the journey doesn't end with these words but begins anew within you. I wrote this book with the hope that it lights your path. Be free, dear reader. Awaken your true potential. Fulfill your purpose, and may your story be as exciting as the ones you've just experienced. May the Living God use what we have started here and grow something inside your heart that will change the world. I leave you with this final question.

> "Are you willing to sacrifice yourself for the work of another, to pour out your life sacrificially for the ministry and faith of others?" — Oswald Chambers

For those who would like to research more, in the link is a small, unsorted list of sources, many of which are likely deleted by now: https://archive.org/details/sources-for-el Not even Pastebin or Hastebin would allow this list of sources to be posted. The Amazing fonts used are free for commercial use and provided by Font Space. Font styles include Rye, Playtime, and Freebooter.

"I'm a freak, they say I've lost my mind
But I know I've never seen so clearly
When I speak, they say I've gone too far this time
Which lets me know, I have not gone nearly." — O.C. Supertones

Made in the USA
Monee, IL
17 April 2025

789d16bb-e70a-4a17-8bb7-983e0866c264R01